Fairness and Freedom

FAIRNESS AND FREEDOM

A HISTORY OF TWO OPEN SOCIETIES,
NEW ZEALAND AND THE UNITED STATES

DAVID HACKETT FISCHER

OXFORD
UNIVERSITY PRESS

OXFORD
UNIVERSITY PRESS

Oxford University Press, Inc., publishes works that further
Oxford University's objective of excellence
in research, scholarship, and education.

Oxford   New York
Auckland   Cape Town   Dar es Salaam   Hong Kong   Karachi
Kuala Lumpur   Madrid   Melbourne   Mexico City   Nairobi
New Delhi   Shanghai   Taipei   Toronto

With offices in
Argentina   Austria   Brazil   Chile   Czech Republic   France   Greece
Guatemala   Hungary   Italy   Japan   Poland   Portugal   Singapore
South Korea   Switzerland   Thailand   Turkey   Ukraine   Vietnam

Copyright © 2012 by David Hackett Fischer

Published by Oxford University Press, Inc.
198 Madison Avenue, New York, NY 10016

www.oup.com

Oxford is a registered trademark of Oxford University Press

Library of Congress Cataloging-in-Publication Data
Fischer, David Hackett, 1935–
Fairness and freedom : a history of two open societies :
New Zealand and the United States / David Hackett Fischer.
p.   cm.
Includes bibliographical references and index.
ISBN 978-0-19-983270-5
1. United States—Politics and government—Philosophy.
2. Political culture—United States—History.
3. Democracy—United States—History.
4. Individualism—Political aspects—United States.
5. New Zealand—Politics and government—Philosophy.
6. Political culture—New Zealand—History.
7. Democracy—New Zealand—History.
8. Individualism—Political aspects—New Zealand.
9. Comparative government. I. Title.
E183.F55   2011
973—dc23   2011037520

1   3   5   7   9   8   6   4   2
Printed in the United States of America
on acid-free paper

For Friends and Colleagues in New Zealand
Tom Brooking
Raewyn Dalziel
Peter Gibbons
Jeanine Graham
Erik Olssen
Jock Phillips

And for the Memory of
Rollo Arnold

CONTENTS

PREFACE

Two Americans in New Zealand

> My greatest trouble is going to be to avoid getting a
> reputation of being a Munchausen by simply telling
> the truth about you.
>
> —American writer Henry Demarest Lloyd, on
> visiting New Zealand, 1899

FROM BOSTON TO DUNEDIN we were twenty-two hours in the air. The total distance, going and coming, exceeded the circumference of the earth. The change of time zones was seventeen hours—more than to any other nation. By every measure, it was a long trip.

It was also a great adventure. Our travels began in 1994, with an invitation from Raewyn Dalziel to talk in Auckland about my book *Albion's Seed.* Other invitations followed from universities in Dunedin, Christchurch, Wellington, and Hamilton. We had never been to New Zealand and leaped at the opportunity. Between events we rented cars, visited every region within reach (all but Southland and Nelson), and met many New Zealanders. The result was a journey of about a month, through much of the country.

The following year brought more extended appointments at Otago University on the South Island and Waikato University in the North. My wife is a biologist and botanist, and I am an historian. We botanized and historicized together on both islands. To explore a country for the first time is not only to discover a new place. It is also to see one's own country and the world itself in a new light. The result is this book.

Discovering the Regions of New Zealand

For many visitors, the strongest impression of New Zealand is the beauty of the place. To travel widely through the country is also to discover that it is beautiful in many ways. We were deeply interested in the diversity of its regions and the complexity of its history.

People think of New Zealand as a small nation. Its population of four million people compares with more than three hundred million in the United States. Its area seems very small by contrast with Australia, Canada, and the United States—all of continental dimensions. On a world map, New Zealand appears even smaller in the great Pacific spaces that surround it.

But travelers on the ground are quickly disabused of these distant impressions. From the tip of North Cape to the bottom of Stewart Island, New Zealand spans more than a thousand miles, or thirteen degrees of latitude. Its area is larger than Great Britain, and only a little smaller than Japan. In American terms, New Zealand is the same size as the entire eastern seaboard of the United States, from midcoast Maine to central Florida. It has a similar range of climates, but in reverse. New Zealand is said to have a North without a winter and a South without a summer. The region called Northland is subtropical. Citrus fruits grow there, and flowers bloom through the year. In the far South, winter days can be bitter cold. On our first July night in Otago, the southern mountains were colder than Antarctica.

Much of New Zealand is mountainous, and the rugged terrain is important to its history and culture. Hundreds of major peaks (223 by official count) rise above 7,500 feet. Many are striking in their appearance; most are within sight of the sea. They come in many varieties. In the northeast, the narrow peninsula of Coromandel has wooded sugarloaf mountains, with rounded tops and steep sides that rise from the water's edge. Much of this old mining region can be reached only by foot. We botanized there in deep ravines and found patches of old-growth kauri trees that the woodcutters had left.[1]

Across the waist of the North Island are mountains of another sort, in a broad belt of big volcanic cones. Some were active when we went there; others were sleeping restlessly beneath a mantle of snow. The most striking is Taranaki, a solitary peak of perfect symmetry, much like Fujiyama in Japan, or Mount Rainier in Washington. Taranaki soars high above the Tasman Sea, incongruously surrounded by dairy farms, domestic cottages, and English country

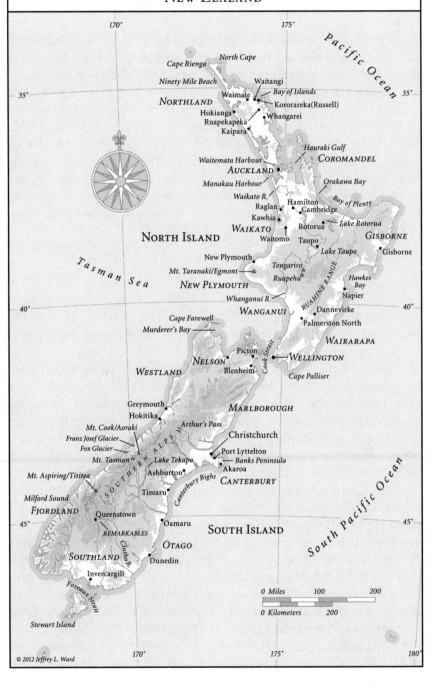

NEW ZEALAND

Pacific Ocean

170°   175°

North Cape
Cape Rienga
Ninety Mile Beach
Waitangi
Waimate   Bay of Islands
NORTHLAND   Kororareka(Russell)
Hokianga   Whangarei
Ruapekapeka
Kaipara

35°   35°

Hauraki Gulf
COROMANDEL
Waitemata Harbour
AUCKLAND
Manakau Harbour   Orakawa Bay
Waikato R.
Raglan   Hamilton   Bay of Plenty
Kawhia   Cambridge
WAIKATO   Rotorua   Lake Rotorua
Waitomo   Taupo   GISBORNE

NORTH ISLAND

New Plymouth   Lake Taupo   Gisborne
Mt. Taranaki/Egmont   Tongariro
NEW PLYMOUTH   Ruapehu   Hawkes
Whanganui R.   Bay
WANGANUI   Napier
Dannevirke
Palmerston North
WAIRARAPA

Tasman Sea

Cape Farewell
Murderer's Bay
Picton
NELSON   Cook Strait   WELLINGTON
Blenheim   Cape Palliser

40°   40°

Greymouth
Hokitika   MARLBOROUGH
Mt. Cook/Aoraki   Arthur's Pass
Franz Josef Glacier   Christchurch
Fox Glacier   Port Lyttelton
Mt. Tasman   Lake Tekapo   Banks Peninsula
Mt. Aspiring/Tititea   Ashburton   Akaroa
SOUTHERN ALPS   CANTERBURY
Milford Sound   Timaru   Canterbury Bight
FJORDLAND
Queenstown   Oamaru
REMARKABLES   SOUTH ISLAND
OTAGO
SOUTHLAND   Dunedin
Invercargill
Foveaux Strait

45°   45°

South Pacific Ocean

Stewart Island

0 Miles   100   200
0 Kilometers   200

170°   175°   180°

© 2012 Jeffrey L. Ward

gardens. They were planted in an early colony called New Plymouth, which flourished on this volcanic soil, and shaped the culture of a region.

On the South Island, the mountains have yet another character. Chief among them are the Southern Alps, a long chain of craggy peaks similar in appearance to the Swiss Matterhorn or the American Grand Tetons, but with a majesty all their own. From the air they make a stunning panorama as they stretch three hundred miles from northeast to southwest. Near the center of this range is Mount Cook, New Zealand's highest mountain at 12,315 feet. It is flanked by twenty massive peaks of more than 10,000 feet.[2] We went there by helicopter on a bright winter day when the air was very dry and the wind completely calm. Above each summit, a thin plume of white cloud rose straight into a cerulean sky—dozens of plumes altogether, as far as the eye could see.

Exploring the South Island

The Alps are the spine of the South Island, which they divide into many regions. The windward slopes of the great mountains receive as many as four hundred inches of rain a year—a dramatic contrast with the leeward approaches to the east, which get as little as twenty inches. Later in our travels, we decided to visit the west coast by an old road that crossed the Alps at Arthur's Pass, 150 miles north of Mount Cook. A wise friend in Dunedin, Tom Brooking, warned us not to attempt it in midwinter, but the road was open, and off we went from Christchurch in a big Australian Falcon that had been built for long journeys on rough terrain.

The eastern slopes were clear and dry, and we reached the top of Arthur's Pass without incident. Then we crossed the summit and suddenly found ourselves in a winter storm of extreme violence. The wind rose to a howling gale, and thick rods of rain blew horizontally in our faces. One side of the road became a waterfall. As we crept slowly around a hairpin curve, the other side of the road had vanished in an earthquake, and nothing remained but a narrow track of mud and water on the sheer edge of the mountain. The wreckage of shattered cars lay in the depths of Otira Gorge, two thousand feet below. At last we reached sea level and entered the quiet coastal town of Hokitika. Our hostess received us with that sovereign restorative of English speakers everywhere—a cup of tea. "Lucky you came today," she said. "Yesterday the road was not so good!"

Hokitika is the center of an old mining region where fortune hunters swarmed in the great gold rushes of 1865–67. The town has a different feel from other parts of New Zealand. Wide streets and wooden buildings with false fronts give it the air of a frontier settlement. The inhabitants call themselves Coasters. Their manners and speech have a strong Australian flavor in this region that looks to the west across the Tasman Sea, or "the Ditch" as they call it.[3]

From Hokitika we drove south into the region that New Zealanders call Westland. Here turquoise glaciers descend from high alpine peaks into deep green rain forests—three hundred glaciers altogether. An inspiration for this book was Lake Murchison. Its surface reflects New Zealand's two tallest peaks and largest glaciers in a double image of high complexity and surprising unity. It became a symbol of what we found in this inquiry.[4]

A clue to the scale of this complex terrain appeared in 2011, when Tasman Glacier calved in a major earthquake. The piece that broke off was smaller than two earlier calvings, but it held thirty million tons of ice that turned incredibly bright blue when exposed to the air. Altogether, 360 glaciers flow from the alps into Westland. The people we met in this thinly settled region had an air of autonomy and a bond with the environment that brought to mind the Olympic Peninsula in the American Pacific Northwest.

Further south below Westland is another region called Fjordland, after its dozens of deep blue inlets between spurs of the southern Alps. Much of this area is a huge national park where New Zealanders go tramping on rugged tracks around Milford Sound. Their tramping is to our hiking as marathons are to jogging.[5]

Near the bottom of New Zealand is a large region called Southland. We were not able to travel through it, but went part of the way from Dunedin on an old narrow-gauge railroad that climbed upward through rocky gorges to a landscape of high plateaus, emerald pastures, sapphire lakes, and snowy peaks. Here are deep-veined mountains of yet another character, which New Zealanders call the Remarkables. The regional capital at Queenstown is a busy center for sports. In winter its slopes are favored for helicopter skiing, with downhill runs of twenty miles through fields of pristine powder.[6]

Yet another distinctive region lies below Southland. In the mid-nineteenth century, people wrote about "the three islands of New Zealand." The third is Stewart Island, a favorite haunt of American whaling ships in the early nineteenth century. Today much of it is parkland, known for austere mountains, dense forests, and spectacular displays of *aurora australis*.

To the east of Southland is the large region of Otago. Its rocky coast and rigorous climate reminded us of Maine, with many differences. The hills above the Pacific are capped by stone-built farms of Scottish appearance, with open pastures and large flocks of hardy North British sheep. On a high headland we visited a farm that was worked by the family who had cleared the land 160 years before. Much of Otago was settled by a migration from the central counties of Scotland. The capital city of Dunedin bears the old Scots name for Edinburgh. Children wear the kilt to school, and elders sound their *r*'s with a strong North British burr. But this is not another Scotland. Along the coast are rookeries of rare yellow-eyed penguins and nesting sites of royal albatrosses, which orbited high above us. Antarctica is three hours away.

After our first visit in Otago, we drove north to the old province of Canterbury, where the terrain opens into a great plain with long views and a large Pacific sky. The eastern landscape is covered with a tough brown grass that New Zealanders call tussock. Here and there, the broad sweep of grassland is broken by lone cabbage trees and thick clumps of native flax. We saw flocks of sheep and large herds of captive deer grazing near braided rivers that Samuel Butler compared to "tangled skeins of silver ribbons." The channels of these gentle streams divide and unite again, sparkling in the strong southern light as they flow toward the sea.[7]

Canterbury was settled by Anglican Reformers who named its capital Christchurch after their Oxford college, and it still bears the stamp of its founders. Part of the city's center resembles an English university town, with grassy "backs" and a gentle stream lined with English willows.[8] Today Christchurch is a major modern city, second largest in New Zealand. After a series of severe earthquakes shattered the central business district in February 2011, with heavy loss of life, it is rapidly rebuilding. The epicenter of the largest earthquake was near the old port of Lyttelton. A New Zealand journalist reported that its buildings were broken, but "its spirit is intact."[9]

Beyond Lyttelton to the east is Banks Peninsula, with dramatic terrain and yet another history. It rises on the remains of two ancient volcanoes and collapsed caldera. Steep slopes offer spectacular views as they drop down to the sea. Its coastal waters and beaches are a marine reserve for blue- and yellow-eyed penguins and the unique Hector's Dolphin, with an abundance of fur seals, and whales offshore. At the end of Banks Peninsula we were amazed to find an old French village with the Maori name of Akaroa, settled in 1840. Its houses have a Gallic air, and its lanes are lined with yellow poplars from Normandy. The town bank is painted in pleasing Parisian shades of lavender and green. Peter Tremewan, a teacher of French history at Canterbury University, writes that "some of the families were very large and many New Zealanders can trace their family back to this failed French attempt to annex the South Island."[10]

North of Canterbury, at the top of the South Island, the Alps divide into great ridges that reach downward to the sea like the splayed fingers of an open hand. Between the fingers are yet other regions. They were colonized by military men and bear the names of British heroes and victories: Nelson, Collingwood, Picton, Havelock, Marlborough, Blenheim. This part of the country is known for its sunny coast, nature reserves, and some of the best scenery in New Zealand. In the late twentieth century it became a center for aquaculture, agriculture, and vineyards that show how Anglo-Saxon tastes have changed (green-lipped mussels, garlic, and chardonnay).

Scattered along the coast of the South Island are *marae* (meetinghouses) of eighteen Maori communities, of the Ngai Tahu tribe. We met and talked with one of their very able leaders, Sir Tipene O'Regan, about the success of the Ngai Tahu Holding Company and Development Corporation, a major presence in the country.

Visiting the North Island

New Zealand's North Island is also very diverse in geography and rich in history. At its upper end is the long peninsula called Northland, which extended nearly three hundred miles from Auckland to North Cape. On its west coast is a sweeping arc of sand called Ninety Mile Beach. To the east is the subtropical Bay of Islands with hundreds of secluded isles, inlets, and natural harbors where Maori and Europeans met and mixed before the great migrations. Other ethnic groups followed from Europe in great variety. Every settlement in the North has its own tale to tell.

Below Northland is the metropolis of Auckland, planted on an isthmus between two natural harbors that open eastward toward Hauraki Gulf and the Pacific, and westward to the Tasman Sea and Australia. From the start, the town and its region had a unique character that shaped this modern city. Auckland is big, busy, and very diverse, with a large flow of immigration from Asia, Australia, and the Pacific islands. It had always been a center of Maori settlement. Within the city are the remains of many small volcanic cones, which Maori builders carved into fortified villages and ancient terraces that are still visible today. Nearly a third of New Zealanders make their home in Auckland. By comparison, 2 percent of Americans live in New York City.

Below Auckland is the Waikato Country, a fertile region of flourishing farms, with a large Maori population. Its center is Hamilton, the only large inland city in New Zealand (Palmerston North is becoming another). The surrounding region is a web of prosperous country towns such as Cambridge. Its happy air of rural urbanity reminded us of Concord in Massachusetts, or Burford in Oxfordshire.

East of the Waikato Country is the Pacific coastline, which curves south to form the Bay of Plenty. Here our colleagues at Waikato University introduced us to Orakawa Bay, one of our favorite places in New Zealand. Its beach is a perfect curve of clean white sand. Behind the beach are grassy slopes and a majestic row of big pohutukawa trees that are brilliant with scarlet flowers in the Christmas season. Further down the east coast are Poverty Bay and Hawke's Bay and their cities of Gisborne and Napier, with spectacular art deco buildings in the central district. This farming region was called Eastland in earlier generations, when it was reached mainly by sea. It is shifting from sheep farms to other forms of agriculture.

On the opposite side of the North Island, the west coast has a distinct character. Its dark iron-sand beaches hold layers of historical debris. Near the sheltered harbors of Raglan and Kawhia are the wrecks of European vessels, and the legendary landing places of Polynesian voyagers nearly a millennium ago. We were fascinated by the remains of an old teak ship that some believe to have brought Tamil seamen from India to New Zealand before the Europeans. That story has been challenged, but in 1836 an ancient Tamil bell turned up in New Zealand. It was cast in 1450 and bears an inscription in ancient Tamil script, "Mohoyideen Buk's ship's bell." How it got there is a puzzle.[11]

At the bottom of the North Island is Wellington, New Zealand's capital city. Its colorful houses rise one above another on a ring of high hills that overlook a handsome harbor and the windswept waters of Cook Strait. The hinterland of Wellington has developed rapidly into a region of thriving high tech industry, like the flourishing exurbs of Washington and Baltimore.

The broad midsection of the North Island is a thinly settled region of volcanic mountains and crater lakes. We were fascinated by the geology of this region, and by the optics of Blue Lake and Green Lake, side by side yet of distinctly different colors. At every opportunity we went tramping with friends in wild woodlands that New Zealanders call bush. Its appearance is unlike other forests in the world, largely because of its giant tree ferns. A common species is the great black fern, which reaches a height of sixty or seventy feet. One of the most striking is the silver fern, with undersides so bright that Maori used it to mark their trails at night. The silver fern has become a national emblem. Altogether, hundreds of ferns and at least 2,300 native plants are found nowhere else in the world. We marveled at the metamorphosis of the lancewood tree, which completely changes its form as it grows older, and cursed the coils of supplejack vines that caught our feet, and laughed at the tangled plants that New Zealanders call bush lawyers.

Some of the most memorable places in New Zealand are not its great mountains and grand scenery. We remember the quiet places that abound in this country. In Northland we came upon groves of ancient Kauri trees with enormous trunks that rise in majestic silence, like the columns of a medieval cathedral but much older. In Waipoua one ancient tree is called Te Motua Ngahere, Father of the Forest. It has been growing there for two millennia.[12]

Other places of quiet beauty have been created by human cultivation. They have a deeper meaning when one studies their history and ecology together. We remember the long green lawn and great trees at Waitangi, the old-fashioned gardens of Pompallier House in Russell, the serenity of Bishop Selwyn's mission house at Waimate, and the grassy ruins of the great Maori Pa at Ruapekapeka high above the eastern sea. In the center of the South Island, among the high sheep runs of the Mackenzie Country, we sat quietly in the small stone Chapel of the Runholders near Tekapo. Behind its altar is a great window that looks across a glacial lake toward the Southern Alps. The lake was milky white when we were there.[13]

East of the Waikato Country we took off our shoes, entered a Maori meetinghouse, and listened in fascination as our Tainui hosts explained the language of complex carvings that tell the history of the people who made them. Near the center of the North Island one feels another sort of reverence on discovering hidden streams where shafts of golden light slant downward through a canopy of fern, and nothing is heard but a bellbird's song. The longer we stayed, the more we found of these quiet places. They are everywhere in New Zealand.[14]

Meeting New Zealanders

After the land itself, every intellectual traveler has written about the character of the people. Taken together, New Zealanders today are as mixed as any other collection of four million human beings.

They do not all climb mountains, play rugby, raise sheep, and consume large platters of Pavlova for dessert. By temperament and inclination, New Zealanders cherish their individuality, and they delight in eccentricity. They have formed dozens of political parties, and changed the electoral rules to give more of these groups a voice in Parliament. They disagree profoundly on public questions, but often have the same values in mind, which are not the same as American values. Ethnic groups are multiplying rapidly. Religious beliefs are more important than secular accounts suggest, and also increasingly diverse.[15]

Here is a paradox of modernity in the twenty-first century. Like other peoples in the modern world, New Zealanders are growing more conscious of their differences, but in some ways they are also growing more alike. They share a national identity and a national culture, however diverse they may be in other ways. During the 1980s, a generation of relativists and postmodernists (now passing from the post-postmodern scene) persuaded themselves that nations were merely "imagined communities." Events after 1989 have demonstrated that they were very much mistaken. Nations have a material existence that is independent of our thought about them. New Zealanders and Americans live under national laws, speak national languages, and share national cultures that make a daily difference in our lives. Americans in New Zealand—and New Zealanders who travel in the United States—meet the reality of national culture at every turn.[16]

We observed it in the way that New Zealanders receive visitors from abroad. Like many travelers before us, we were struck by their unstinting hospitality, warm generosity, unfailing decency, and high good humor. Wherever we traveled in New Zealand, we met the kindness of strangers. Whenever we stayed, strangers became friends. Other visitors have had similar experiences.

Through the years many waves of intellectual tourists came to New Zealand and wrote about their experiences. The early British settlements attracted novelists Anthony Trollope and Samuel Butler, historians Edward Freeman and James Anthony Froude, politicians Charles Dilke and James Bryce, poets Rudyard Kipling and Rupert Brooke, and the American humorist Mark Twain. All of these visitors recorded their impressions in vivid detail.[17]

Other groups came in the late nineteenth and early twentieth centuries to study New Zealand's legislative and social experiments. They included British socialists Beatrice Webb, Sidney Webb, and George Bernard Shaw. The American Progressive Henry Demarest

Lloyd wrote two of his best books about New Zealand. French scholars Albert Métin and André Siegfried published studies of New Zealand's institutions in the early twentieth century.[18]

A third wave of intellectual visitors arrived in the mid-twentieth century. Many were scientists and scholars who came to teach at New Zealand universities. Among them were the Austrian philosopher Karl Popper, Canadian geographer Andrew Hill Clark, Anglo-American political scientist Leslie Lipson, and Oxford scholar Margery Perham.[19] A fourth group has been coming since the 1990s to study New Zealand's latest round of institutional reforms.[20] Nearly all of these visitors remembered New Zealanders with affection and respect. As early as 1863, Samuel Butler wrote of the Canterbury settlements, "There is little conventionalism, little formality, and much liberality of sentiment; very little sectarianism, and, as a general rule, a healthy sensible tone in conversation, which I like very much." Butler's impressions were remarkably similar to those of later visitors, including ourselves.[21]

These intellectual tourists could be difficult people, who severely tried the patience of their hosts, but even some of the most difficult warmed to New Zealanders. A case in point was George Bernard Shaw, who curbed his cutting tongue (for half a sentence) and said of New Zealanders, "They are a pleasant people and better spoken than the people of England—but then we are such a miserable sort of advertisement." On his departure from New Zealand, Shaw amazed a reporter by confiding, "If I showed my true feelings I would cry; it's the best country I have been in."[22]

A few visitors were hostile. They tended to come from the fringes of British society, both far right and far left. An example from the right was a demented aristocrat named Diana Cooper who visited in 1941 and expressed complete amazement at the good humor of New Zealanders. "I suppose they are happy," she wrote in her contemptuous way. "I couldn't bear it." This British racist regarded the entire nation as a genetic experiment that had gone wrong. In one of the more bizarre writings on record she observed, "The blood of New Zealand is so stale that they are reverting to type—Maori type—growing longer torsos and weenie legs, and you can't get a bed in a loony bin."[23]

Examples of hostility from the left were Sidney and Beatrice Webb, an arrogant pair of Fabian Socialists (later outspoken Stalinists) who professed to love humanity in general but had less affection for human beings in particular. After a visit in 1898, Sidney Webb wrote, "The great reproach which can be made against the New

Zealand government is without doubt its complete vulgarity. It is a failing common to all New Zealanders." Beatrice Webb added, "New Zealanders are an easy-going race, moral but gay, lacking in Puritan pugnacity, with perhaps just a suspicion of the Polynesian." By Polynesian, she appears to have meant lazy. But by the end of her stay even Mrs. Webb was won over. In her parting entry she wrote, "New Zealand and its people have left on our mind an agreeable impression. . . . Taken all in all, if I had to bring up a family outside of Great Britain I would choose New Zealand."[24]

Another difficult visitor was Austrian philosopher Karl Popper, a refugee from fascism who had been forced to flee his beloved Vienna in 1937 and found a job at what is now the University of Canterbury until 1946. Popper missed the urban life of middle Europe, argued with college administrators over his teaching load, and battled colleagues around the world. But New Zealand was a productive environment for him, and he wrote two major works there: *The Poverty of Historicism* and *The Open Society and Its Enemies*. Like the Webbs, Karl Popper warmed to New Zealanders. After his cruel experiences in central Europe, he added with an air of surprise, "there was no harm in the people."[25]

At least one visitor from the United States formed a negative opinion of New Zealand. He was a psychiatrist named David Ausubel, who complained that New Zealanders were distant and hostile. We were amazed, until we read his book. Dr. Ausubel put the entire nation on his couch and diagnosed it as suffering from a personality disorder caused by excessive authoritarianism, which he traced to the unhappiness of its collective childhood. Forty years later, a few New Zealanders remember Dr. Ausubel, more with a laugh than a frown.[26]

Studying the Culture of New Zealand

When one compares these many accounts, one notices that the same language of description tends to occur. Karl Popper described New Zealanders as "decent, friendly and well-disposed."[27] His choice of words in the mid-twentieth century was very similar to Samuel Butler's in the mid-nineteenth century, and to the words that came to our minds in the early twenty-first century. But in this remarkably consistent testimony, a curious puzzle appears. Through many generations, travelers' accounts have tended to be similar in descriptions of New Zealand culture, but different in their explanations.

In much of this literature, three explanatory themes recurred. The first was that New Zealand is "more English than England." This idea received its classic expression from Anthony Trollope. On a visit in 1870, he wrote that "the New Zealander among John Bulls is the most John Bullish. . . . [H]e is more English than any Englishman at home."[28] For Trollope, these were praise words. Others made them pejoratives. In 1977, an Australian journalist wrote, "While we don't exactly hate New Zealanders, we're not exactly fond of each other. While they regard us as vulgar yobboes, almost Yank-like, we think of them as second-hand, recycled Poms."[29] There is an important measure of historical truth in this stress on British beginnings. In the census of 2001, more than 60 percent of New Zealanders reported that they were wholly or partly of English and Scottish descent. That proportion compares with about 40 percent in Australia and roughly 20 percent in the United States. Many families we visited in New Zealand were actively in touch with relatives in Britain.[30]

But in other ways, New Zealanders of British ancestry have distanced themselves from their "mother country," and they have learned to think of themselves as a people of the Pacific. Today they are secure in that identity, and strong in their pride of place.[31] At the same time, Britain moved apart from New Zealand. It became more European in its identity and unilaterally ended special trading relations with former colonies. After 1974, annual immigration from Great Britain fell from more than 90 percent of all arrivals to less than 10 percent, and other ethnic groups rapidly increased.[32] In short, the idea that New Zealand is "more English than England" may have seemed plausible in Trollope's time, and it still has a foundation in historical fact, but it is increasingly distant from New Zealand in the twenty-first century.[33]

Another explanation of New Zealand's culture has stressed physical factors of distance, remoteness, isolation, and insularity. Its nearest neighbor is 1,200 miles away—a geographic condition that is unique among nations. Many visitors from the late nineteenth to the mid-twentieth century described New Zealanders as an "insular people, isolated from the world," as one observed. A leading example was political scientist Leslie Lipson, who wrote in 1948, "The mental world of New Zealand has been, on the whole, as self-contained as its insular geography."[34] This observation may or may not have had a measure of truth during an earlier period of New Zealand's history (I think not), but it no longer applies today.[35]

Since 1960, New Zealand's place in the world has been transformed by a continuing revolution in global communications.

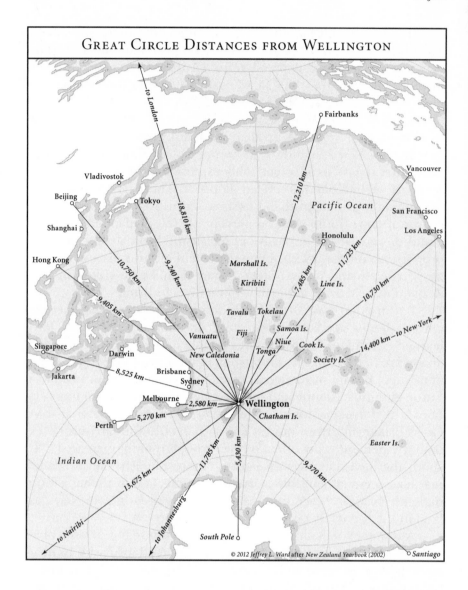

GREAT CIRCLE DISTANCES FROM WELLINGTON

Empirical studies show that New Zealanders are the most widely traveled people on the planet. The computer and the Internet have made a major difference. Insularity, distance, and isolation may have been important in an earlier period of New Zealand's history, but not today. The rapid progress of communications has wrought a revolution in the spatial condition of New Zealand, and yet its culture remains very distinctive. This fact suggests that distance itself is not the key.[36]

A third explanation of New Zealand, often repeated in academic literature during the mid-twentieth century, is that New Zealanders are driven by a "national obsession with security, both individual and collective." This idea referred to New Zealand's elaborate system of social welfare that began to develop in the 1890s. Writers such as Leslie Lipson, David Ausubel, and William Sutch made it into a general interpretation of New Zealand's culture.[37]

That idea seemed correct to many observers in the mid-twentieth century, but fifty years later it is clearly mistaken. Since 1984, New Zealanders have dismantled large parts of their welfare state with the same energy that they brought to its construction. While preserving a safety net, they led the world in privatizing public institutions and in a great wave of restructuring.

In more individuated terms, the oft-repeated idea of a "security obsession" does not describe people who have perfected bungee-jumping into gorges a thousand feet deep, jet-boating through class A rapids, black-water rafting on dark subterranean rivers, and a maniacal form of alpine racing in which men and dogs hurl themselves down frozen mountain precipices in the hope of hitting the bottom before anyone else. While we were there, the great-aunt of our New Zealand friends Jeanine and John Graham was asked what she wanted to do for her eightieth birthday. She answered that she wished to go body-sliding over underground waterfalls in the caves of Waitomo, and it was done. People who do these things for amusement can hardly be said to be consumed by an obsession with security.

The weakness of these explanations presents an interesting problem. Through two centuries, many visitors to New Zealand described a culture that still exists in our time. But leading theories that were offered to explain it are far off the mark.

Another Approach: Parallel Histories

Other patterns appear when one compares New Zealand with other open societies in general, and with the United States in particular. At first sight, much of New Zealand's history seems familiar to an American. Both nations were founded by English-speaking people in distant lands. Both began with a heritage of the English language, law, and customs. Both entered into complex relations with native populations, Indian and Maori. Both developed what Frederick Jackson Turner called frontier societies, received large numbers of immigrants, and became more diverse in ethnicity and religion. Both industrialized and urbanized, and had reform movements in the Progressive Era and the era of the Great Depression, and in the restructuring of the late twentieth century. Both were allies in the great wars of the twentieth century and underwent comparable processes of restructuring in the 1980s.

The people of these two nations are also similar in some of their most cherished beliefs. Erik Olssen, our colleague and friend at Otago, had some of his schooling in the United States and knows America well. He told us with a laugh of his discovery that both countries cherish exactly the same sense of national uniqueness. The classic example was one of New Zealand's great characters, Richard "King Dick" Seddon. On a voyage home in 1906, he sent a radiogram: "Just returning to God's Own Country." The next day King Dick died at sea, but his message traveled on. New Zealanders began to call their country "God's Own," or "godzone" as it would be written by another generation who stridently mock this idea even as they secretly believe it. Americans think the same way. The slums of New York were "God's Crucible." Even the desolate plains of West Texas are called "God's Country"—by West Texans.

Both people also share the attitude that H. G. Wells called optimistic fatalism. In the United States, this is the teleological idea that history in general—and American history in particular—is an inexorable march of progress that no mortal power can arrest, though many have tried. On another level, optimistic fatalism also appears in the "American Dream" of individual improvement. Even in eras of economic disaster, American strivers continue to be optimistic fatalists. It is a source of our striving.[38] New Zealanders share this optimistic attitude, and express it in another way. "Never mind!" they often say. "She'll be right!"

Most important for this inquiry, New Zealand and the United States are both what Henri Bergson and Karl Popper called open societies. They share democratic polities, mixed-enterprise economies, pluralist cultures, individuated societies, a respect for human rights, and a firm commitment to the rule of law. In all these ways, the United States and New Zealand are very much alike.[39]

And yet for every similarity we discovered many differences. Some appeared to be trivial details of language and custom, but we kept finding more of them. They were clearly linked in untrivial ways. New Zealand and the United States are open systems, in very different ways. This is a fact of growing importance in a world where many societies have been opening, but never twice in the same way. As we reflected on this large subject, another problem appeared. In open societies, more than closed ones, individual people make choices, and their choices make a difference in the world. Every open society is similar to all others in that way, and yet when we compare one open system with another, we find that people made fundamentally similar choices in profoundly different ways. New Zealand is a case in point.

We began to think that something of extraordinary importance happened in the history of New Zealand. But what was it, exactly? The more we pondered these questions, the more puzzling they became. Then suddenly a clue to an answer appeared. It came to us on a wintry August afternoon in Canterbury, as we were driving along a narrow country road from Akaroa to Christchurch. What we discovered there became a key to this inquiry.

Fairness and Freedom

INTRODUCTION

Fairness and Freedom: Ethical Choices in Open Systems

"A Fair Go for the Ordinary Bloke"

—Campaign slogan of New Zealand Prime
Minister Robert Muldoon

"Liberty, Freedom, Bush"

—Campaign button of American President
George W. Bush

I N 1994, a by-election took place in New Zealand. Only a single
seat was at stake in the South Island constituency of Selwyn, but
the conservative National Party held power by one vote in Parliament. Selwyn was a National seat; a change threatened to bring down
the government.

By chance we were there during the election. Much of it looked
very similar to American contests. Electoral placards along the roads
were indistinguishable from campaign posters in the United States.
Journalists were out in force, and their role was much the same as in
America. Newspapers and media screens showed images we had seen
at home, of telegenic candidates surrounded by the happy faces of
telegenic families. At the climax of the campaign, the National Party's champion added a herd of telegenic dairy cattle and won a
narrow victory, perhaps by the margin of New Zealand's nostalgic
"cow-cockie vote," which brought to mind country-western conservatives in the United States.[1]

When the ballots were counted, the National Party remained in
power. The media instantly lost interest in Selwyn, but we kept

thinking about it. Something was puzzling in what we saw and heard there. The election looked familiar to an American eye, but its sounds were strange to an American ear. At first we could not think how or why. Then suddenly it dawned on us that Selwyn's many candidates had little to say on the subject of liberty and freedom. In the United States, the rhetoric of a free society is heard everywhere. Liberty and freedom were the founding principles of the American republic. Through many generations, public discourse in the United States has been a continuing debate over contested meanings of those great ideas.[2]

Selwyn's candidates had more to say about another value, which is not so prominent in American politics. Most of them talked urgently about the idea of fairness. It was discussed by politicians of every major party and analyzed by journalists and scholars who were looking on. "Fairness may not be everything," Jonathan Boston wrote during the Selwyn campaign, "but it is an extremely important value—and one which has been in short supply for too long."[3]

The Selwyn election became a sustained debate on the subject of fairness, and in a very large-minded way. Candidates did not merely demand fair treatment in particular ways for themselves and their supporters. They discussed fairness as the organizing principle of an open society, which happens rarely in the United States.

The occasion for this debate was a sweeping change in social policy. From 1984 to 1994, New Zealand had privatized many of its public institutions. That great restructuring had a special relevance to the Selwyn election. The seat had been held by Ruth Richardson, former minister of finance in the National government and a born-again apostle of neoclassical economics. One of her goals was to change New Zealand's system of support for elderly people, which she pursued with such zeal that her policies were called "Ruthanasia" in the press. In 1994, Richardson lost her job as minister of finance and resigned from Parliament. The by-election of her successor in Selwyn became a referendum on the new reforms.

After the election, we wondered if Selwyn's debate on fairness was peculiar to that particular moment. To answer this question we explored earlier periods of New Zealand's history. We found an abiding concern for fairness, from the mid-nineteenth century to our time. Often it was combined with urgent complaints about the existence of unfairness, which was thought to be inevitable in other nations, but intolerable in New Zealand.

Two Ideas of Fairness:
Robert Muldoon and Roger Douglas, 1975–90

We kept reading and found something even more interesting. Even as most New Zealanders agree that fairness is "an extremely important value," they have understood that idea in many ways—even opposite ways. Examples appeared in the writings of Robert Muldoon and Roger Douglas. These men were political rivals. Muldoon was a former accountant who led the National Party and became prime minister of New Zealand from 1975 to 1984. He was a politician of a type rarely seen in the United States since the defeat of the old Federalists in 1800: a staunch conservative with a strong ideal of active government. Muldoon often remarked that "the whole concept of government is based on intervention." As prime minister he gave New Zealand the most costly welfare program in its history—a huge expansion of its "superannuation scheme," roughly comparable to American Social Security. Muldoon promised every householder over the age of fifty-nine a pension equal to 80 percent of the median wage, and supported not from contributions or trust funds but from current income and massive borrowing. This program was justified by an appeal to fairness. Robert Muldoon's favorite slogan was "A fair go for the ordinary bloke," or "A fair go for the decent bloke." Both expressions are foreign to American speech, but they had broad appeal in New Zealand and became the motto of Muldoon's enthusiastic supporters, who called themselves Rob's Mob.[4]

Another major figure in New Zealand's modern history was Roger Douglas. In many ways his principles were diametrically opposed to Robert Muldoon's. Where Muldoon was a politician from the right who favored active intervention by government, Douglas was a leader from the left who embraced free-market economics. He came from a trade-unionist family, began his career in the Labour Party, and was elected to Parliament from one of Auckland's poorest districts. In New Zealand's Fourth Labour Government (1984–90), Roger Douglas became minister of finance. To the horror of many in his own party, he led the movement for privatization. So prominent was his leadership that New Zealand's analogue to Thatcherism and Reaganomics was called Rogernomics. It was Rogernomics that opened the way for Ruthanasia.[5]

In 1993, Roger Douglas laid out his ideas in a book called *Unfinished Business.* He believed that Muldoon's superannuation scheme threatened to bankrupt the country, as truly it did. In its place, Douglas proposed a system of private pensions, supplemented by public spending where necessary for a "fair outcome." He titled a chapter on the subject "Security and Fairness," and summarized its argument in a sentence: "The only fair way to manage a universal scheme, in terms of cost and equity, is for everyone to provide for their own retirement to the extent that they are able."[6] Muldoon and Douglas were far apart on this subject, but both men appealed to a large idea of fairness, and used it to justify opposite policies, much as American leaders of the left, right, and center all claim to be the true friends of liberty and freedom.

Many Ideas of Fairness:
Party Manifestos in New Zealand, 1990–2000

Shortly after the Selwyn election, we left the country. When we returned in 1995, the debate had grown even more intense. A good place to study it is Waikato University Library's excellent New Zealand Collection. Its able librarians have assembled strong holdings of New Zealand imprints, and they added a large collection of "ephemera" that are invaluable to historians because they are so rarely preserved in a systematic way.[7]

There, in 1995, we found files of policy statements, manifestos, mimeographs, photocopies, e-mails, and faxes issued by New Zealand's many political parties during the 1980s and early 1990s. They disagreed profoundly on public policy, but most invoked a general idea of fairness and gave it a variety of special meanings.

In 1990, for example, the National Party issued a manifesto called *Economic and Social Initiative*. The leading name on the document was Jim Bolger, a progressive conservative soon to become prime minister. Bolger's manifesto announced that he would be guided by "four key principles" of "fairness, self-reliance, efficiency, and greater personal choice." Fairness led the list, and its meaning was summarized in a sentence. "It is essential," Bolger and his colleagues wrote, "that adequate access to government assistance be available to those in genuine need, but those who can make greater provision for their own needs should be encouraged to do so." Here was a moderate conservative idea of fairness—that people have a primary responsibility to provide for themselves, but those truly in need should get help from the government.[8]

To the left of Jim Bolger was New Zealand's Labour Party, which was in disarray during the mid-1990s, after a bruising fall from power. Its factions issued three manifestos in that period. Each centered on a different idea of fairness. Old-line Labour leaders produced several policy statements in 1994 that centered on the theme of "fair shares." They argued for an idea of fairness as distributive justice and a more nearly equal distribution of wealth, to be achieved by full employment, higher real incomes, sustainable development, and progressive taxation.[9]

Another manifesto from the moderate wing of the Labour Party was titled *A Fair Go for Youth*. It said less about the redistribution of income and wealth, and more about economic growth as an instrument of social justice. Most of all, it promised fairness in the form of opportunity for young people, through new policies for employment and education.[10]

In 1989, yet another party of the left took the name of New Labour. Its founder was Jim Anderton, a former Labour leader who was deeply unhappy with the policies of Roger Douglas, a feeling shared by many on the left, and by Anderton's working-class constituency of Sydenham in Christchurch. In 1991–92 Anderton organized a coalition called Alliance, of four small parties: New Labour, the Green Party, the Democratic Party, and the Maori Mana Motuhake. He published a manifesto titled *Fairness and Balance for New Zealand*. Once again the primary value was fairness, in yet another meaning. Anderton wrote: "Fairness means that everyone should have not only the opportunity but also the means to live their lives to the full. . . . There is no fairness if one group in the community gets rich whilst others become poorer."[11]

The key to Jim Anderton's idea of fairness was his second major principle. "Balance," he explained, "means that no region and no section of the present and future population should be allowed to flourish at the expense of another." Here was a middle way that combined the thinking of many groups. It was also a mediating solution that might be understood as a meta-ethic of fairness. Anderton used a larger understanding of fairness to reconcile different ideas of what was fair.[12]

Political leaders were not alone in addressing these questions. The heads of New Zealand's largest religious denominations also joined the great debate. In 1992, after deep cuts were made in social welfare, Methodist Keith Rowe and Roman Catholic Cardinal Tom Williams organized a Christian Coalition of ten major denominations and religious groups in New Zealand: Anglican, Apostolic, Associated Christian Churches, Baptist, Lutheran, Methodist, Presbyterian, Quaker, Roman Catholic, and the Salvation Army. These spiritual leaders jointly published several books and manifestos. "We recognise," they wrote, "that recent governments have sought to address the nation's serious economic difficulties, and we realise that any solution to our economic problems will cause pain. Our deep concern is that the pain has not been shared fairly."[13]

Once again fairness was a fundamental concern, and it was understood in yet another way. The ten Christian leaders all agreed that the "basic moral test of society is how its most vulnerable members are faring." This simple rule flowed directly from the words of Jesus that "whatever you do for the least of my brothers, you do for me." It did not appear in the manifestos of any political party. The most vulnerable members of open societies are the least likely to vote. But as an ethical principle, this test of fairness was true to the teachings of Christ. It united the heads of ten Christian groups in New Zealand.[14]

Also heard in New Zealand's great debate was a chorus of voices from the civil service and the universities. When scholars went to work, the result was a definition of fairness in five volumes, plus a thick summary volume called *Toward a Fair and Justice Society* [*sic*], published by New Zealand's Royal Commission on Social Policy. This idea of fairness derived in part from the work of American philosopher John Rawls. It rejected the utilitarian calculus of "the greatest good for the greatest number" and adopted the Rawlsian model of social justice as "fairness to the individual." The lead author, Maxine Barrett, argued that a fair society should do justice not to groups or classes of people, but to individuals according to their rights, needs, and just "deserts."[15]

That individuated calculus of fairness found its opposite in the collective thinking of the New Zealand First Party. Its leader was Winston Peters, a figure of high complexity in New Zealand politics. Part Maori and part Pakeha, part conservative and part populist, he appealed to New Zealand's pride of national identity. Where Maxine Barrett's thinking centered on fairness to individuals, Winston Peters developed a very different idea of fairness as the right and duty of full belonging to the nation. He spoke of a "sharing" of service, an equitable principle of collective participation, and a responsibility to serve something larger than the self: in a phrase, "New Zealand First." That idea was anathema to some of his opponents, who called it "Winston First," but many New Zealanders saw it as a genuine altruism. It attracted support from voters in the generation of World War II and had strong appeal to Maori voters. In 1996, all five Maori seats in Parliament were won by New Zealand First.[16]

Maori leaders also invented other ideas of fairness. One Maori activist wrote in the journal *Mana*, "Only crumbs off the Crown table are available for claims purposes, and even these are being shorn away as speedily as possible under the so-called Crown protection mechanism. Is this a Fair Go?" Another observed, "Pakeha officials should think about their own values: the concept of 'the Fair Go' would do more for policy delivery to Maori than all the Marae experience in the world."[17]

In these applications, Maori activists enlarged the idea of fairness and rooted it in Maori traditions. A leading example was Annette Sykes, an Arawa lawyer from Rotorua. She explained: "For me, it's a simple *kaupapa* [plan]—it's *te tino rangatiratanga*, Maori control over Maori things, with a Maori value base." This was her idea of a "fair go." At the same time she took the idea of fairness to another level. Like Jim Anderton, she made it into a meta-ethic for the coexistence of different ethical systems in an open society.[18]

Feminist groups joined the great debate by forming the Women's Coalition, a broad alliance of four hundred organizations including New Zealand's National Council of Women, its Federation of University Women, and many labor groups. Together they issued a lively manifesto entitled *A Matter of Fairness: Employment Equity* (1990). Once again fairness was the central idea, and feminists gave it yet another meaning. The Women's Coalition defined fairness as equity, and equity not as simple equality but as a more complex idea of "equal pay" for "equal value." To that end, they urged passage of a new "employment equity bill," against gender discrimination in private employment, much as it had already been prohibited in the public sector.[19]

The Women's Coalition met strong opposition from the New Zealand Business Roundtable, which issued its own manifesto, *In Pursuit of Fairness: A Critique of the Employment Equity Bill* (1990). The business leaders agreed that "equity should be a concern of governments," but they opposed "coercive egalitarianism" and argued that "attempts to manipulate outcomes in the name of equality only serve to erode freedom and human dignity and lead to impoverished economic performance." Their idea of "the pursuit of fairness" insisted that "a true concern about equity must emphasise individual freedom and opportunity."[20]

Other groups carried ideas of fairness in different directions. New Zealand's Green Party argued that environmental problems could be solved only if issues of fairness were addressed. A policy statement to that effect appeared in *Greenlink*, the party newsletter, in 1990. It asserted that "Industrial society is seen as patently unfair. . . . [T]he exploitation of the many by the few is integral to continued growth. Social justice is therefore seen as a prerequisite to a sustainable future."[21]

On the far right in the 1990s, a very small Fascist movement called itself the New Zealand NEO Party. Its mimeographed manifesto was embellished with conventional icons of fascism, complete with an art deco eagle. But one Fascist symbol was missing. In place of the swastika, New Zealand Fascists substituted an open circle. Party leader Raymond Mehlhopt explained that the circle represented national unity and racial equality. He promised that Maori would be fully and fairly included within the New Economic Order of National Socialism. In New Zealand, even Fascists appealed to an idea of fairness.[22]

Ideas of Fairness in Law, Business, and Sport

These competing ideas of fairness in political debate captured only a small part of its many meanings in New Zealand. A keyword search of *fairness* and *fair* in the digital catalogue of Waikato University's New Zealand Collection turned up a broad range of other uses. Political manifestos discussed fairness mainly as a substantive idea. Other writings discussed it primarily in procedural terms. Once again, they did so in many ways.

One of these procedural ideas centered on something similar to what Americans call "due process," after the United States Constitution's Fifth and Fourteenth Amendments, which guarantee that "no person shall be . . . deprived of life, liberty or property, without due process of law." New Zealanders think of similar legal issues in a different way: not as a formal written constitutional right of due process, but as a common law tradition of "free and fair trial." We found a large literature in New Zealand on fairness in this sense.[23]

Another procedural idea referred to fairness in commercial dealings, and specifically to a New Zealand statute called the Fair Trading Act (1986). It is very different from the American "fair-trade laws" in the mid-twentieth century, which were price-fixing statutes, enacted by corrupt legislators for predatory businessmen. American fair-trade laws were designed to prohibit efficient, low-margin, high-volume, price-cutting competition in a free market. Their purpose was to protect the profits of entrenched high-margin retailers, at heavy cost to everybody else. The intent of New Zealand's Fair Trading Act was the very opposite—to protect consumers and enterprising businessmen against "unfair trading practices" of the sort that American fair-trade laws had been designed to promote.[24]

A third procedural idea of fairness in New Zealand centered on sport. Many writings on that subject flowed from the Hillary Commission, founded by Parliament in 1987 and named for Sir Edmund Hillary, a national hero in New Zealand for his climb of Mount Everest, and still more the example of his integrity. The purpose of the Hillary Commission was to "promote fair play and good sporting behaviour while discouraging a win-at-all costs attitude among children." It concerned itself not only with conduct on the playing field, but more broadly with the extension of fair play to social relations in general. The Hillary Commission sponsored a "Fairplay Programme" called "Don't Get Ugly." Within a decade, it reached 120,000 teachers and a million students in 95 percent of New Zealand's schools. A generation later, the commission is still active in the country.[25]

Foreign observers have often remarked on the importance of fairness in New Zealand sports. An example appeared in the America's Cup races at San Diego in 1995, which were won by New Zealand's yacht *Black Magic*. The *New York Times* congratulated the New Zealanders on their victory, and even more on their spirit of fairness and good sportsmanship, which had not always been evident among American competitors. In earlier contests, American yachtsmen had sometimes ruled the waves by waiving the rules. In 1995, American officials rewrote the regulations in a way that allowed the United States to change boats but forbade challengers to do so. New Zealanders won anyway, and promised that next time the rules would be "fair for both groups." Captain Peter Blake formally pledged a "fair go" for all contestants when the race was run in New Zealand. The *New York Times* thanked him for introducing a principle of fair play to a competition that had lacked it in the recent past. It observed of Peter Blake that "his feeling for fairness is another good reason to hail the Kiwi victory."[26]

New Zealand's Highly Developed Language of Fairness

That "feeling for fairness" is prominent in the culture of New Zealand, and evident in its speechways. New Zealanders have a large vocabulary of colorful words for various forms of fairness and unfairness. Some of these terms exist in American and British English, but many do not. More than a few were old English folk-words that appear in the *English Dialect Dictionary* or are identified as archaic in the *Oxford English Dictionary*. They continue to pass current in New Zealand. Others were invented in New Zealand, where they have multiplied in an extraordinary way. Consider the following examples.[27]

Fair go means decent treatment. In the 1990s, one of New Zealand's most popular television shows was called *Fair Go*. It exposed outrageous acts of unfairness. The phrase is common in New Zealand and Australia; I have never heard it spoken in the United States.[28]

Fair do or *fair doo* is a New Zealand expression for straight dealing. It is obsolete in Britain and uncommon in American speech.

Fair buck is defined by the *New Zealand Dictionary* as "an appeal for fair play or fair hearing." It is not in American dictionaries.[29]

Fair spin means "honest or equitable treatment," and a fair chance in the lottery of life. We found it in twentieth-century works of New Zealand fiction.[30]

Fair burl comes from the game of two-up, in which two coins are tossed from a small board and players bet on heads or tails. It means an honest toss, and fair dealing in general.[31]

Fair shake or *fair shake of the dice* is a gambler's expression, broadened to mean decent treatment in general. It is one of New Zealand's few fairness words in this list that is also common in America.

Fair whack is a clean blow, or a fair chance in any conflict or competition. It is also used in America.

Fair suck of the sav or *fair suck of the sauce* is a feminine appeal for fair play: "All we want is a fair suck of the sav," one woman wrote in 1992. *Sav* is short for *saveloy*, a savory sausage much favored in New Zealand, and sometimes devoured by the men at the table before the women are able to sit down.[32]

Fair field and no favor means a society open to talent and effort. It was a common expression in Victorian England. British emigrants used it to explain what they hoped to find in New Zealand, and they introduced it to this country.

Fair dinkum or *square dinkum* or *straight dinkum* means an honest, fair-minded account, as in Frank Sargeson's short stories in the *Listener*. "Everybody always said the butcher was exaggerating. . . . The butcher would say no, it was the fair dinkum truth." *Fair dinkum* is very common in Australia and New Zealand, but rare in Britain and unknown in America.[33]

Dinkum or *dink* is a noun for any honest, straight, open, decent, good-hearted, fair-minded person. In World War I, *Dinkum* was originally a nickname for men in New Zealand's Rifle Brigade. British and Australian soldiers applied it to New Zealand troops in general—sometimes also to Australians, but mainly New Zealanders. The variant *Dink* became a common call name for New Zealanders in that war.[34]

Tika is a Maori word that literally means straight and direct. It is used by Maori and non-Maori alike as a synonym for fairness, and appears in both Maori and English dictionaries in New Zealand with that meaning.[35]

Kiwi Idioms for Unfairness

New Zealanders also have many words for unfairness. They share with all English-speaking people several common expressions such as *one-sided, partial, inequitable, biased, unethical,* and *dishonorable.* To those common terms, New Zealanders add their own folk-idioms. Some of these words refer to unfair practices, or to people who do them. Others describe unfair conditions or institutions, or an unfair conspiracy of circumstance.

Many imply that unfairness is more common in less fortunate nations that have weaker traditions of fair play. For example, one New Zealander will say ruefully to another who faces unfair competition or impossible odds, "Best of British luck to you, mate!" The phrase is so familiar that sometimes it is shortened to "Best of British!" In New Zealand, *British luck* is an oxymoron. It describes a condition so grossly unfair that one can hope for no luck at all—a memory of lives that ancestors lived in the United Kingdom.[36]

Another example is the New Zealand idiom *Yankee start,* which is defined as an unfair start in a race, or any unfair advantage. *Yankee grab* is a disreputable gambling game played with cards or dice, where players seize whatever unfair advantages they can obtain. A *Yankee tournament* is a pell-mell sporting event where contestants compete not in teams but individually, each against all, and anything goes. A *Yankee shout* is a party where the host refuses to pick up the tab and guests are forced to pay their own way. These expressions betray a belief on the part of some New Zealanders that Americans suffer from a chronic condition of ethical impairment. It is a prejudice that is reciprocated by some Americans toward New Zealanders in regard to liberty and freedom.[37]

On another subject, we also heard New Zealand businessmen complain of *Nip tricks,* by which they meant the burdens that Japanese leaders placed on others in their own country while demanding full access to other economies. *British luck, Yankee starts,* and *Nip tricks* all identify unfairness with foreigners and imply that New Zealanders are more fair-minded than other people.

Other New Zealand words for unfairness come from cricket. One of them is associated with Australians, whom Kiwis regard with a mix of affection, amusement, and wary attention. *Underarm delivery* is a cricket term that refers to an infamous match between New Zealand and Australia on the Melbourne Cricket Ground in 1981. Australian captain Greg Chappell told his brother Trevor to bowl the last ball underarm and on the ground, which made it difficult for the New Zealand batter to hit, and gave him little chance to win a close-fought game. Thereafter, *underarm delivery* entered common usage in New Zealand for any action that is allowed by the rules but is an unsporting attempt to take unfair advantage of another person. In this instance it was associated with bad behavior by Australians, who are thought to require eternal vigilance by their Kiwi cousins across the Tasman Sea. Thus, Australian *underarm deliveries* were added to *British luck, Yankee grab,* and *Nip tricks.* None of these words occur in American and British usage.[38]

Other cricket terms for unfairness include *left-hander, not on,* and of course *not cricket.* Yet more words, unknown to American English, are drawn from horse racing—as *stumer* or *stoomer,* which is to run an unfair race. Another large set of pejorative nouns refer to individual people who are habitually and even professionally unfair to others. A *slinter* or *slenter* is a chronically underhanded, deceitful, unfair, or dishonest person—perhaps an Afrikaans expression that New Zealand troops brought home from the Boer War. A *swiftie* is a piece of sharp practice, or any sort of unfair trick. People who do such a thing are said to *pull a swiftie.* And a *crookie* is someone who treats others unfairly. It derives from the adjective *crook,* which describes circumstances or outcomes that are unfair or undeserved— a different word from the American noun *crook* or the adjective *crooked,* which are synonyms for *criminal.*[39]

Origins of the Words Fairness *and* Fair

Where did this language of fairness come from? What is the origin of the word itself? To search for the semantic roots of *fair* and *fairness* is to make a surprising discovery. Among widely spoken languages in the modern world, cognates for *fairness* and *fair* appear to have been unique to English, Danish, Norwegian, and Frisian until the mid-twentieth century.[40] They remained so until after World War II, when other languages began to import these words as anglicisms.[41]

The ancestry of *fair* and *fairness* also sets them apart in another way. Unlike most value terms in the Western world, they do not derive from Greek or Latin roots. Their etymology is unlike that of *justice* and *equity,* which have cognates in many modern Western languages. *Justice* derives from the Latin *ius*, which meant a conformity to law or divine command, "without reference to one's own inclinations." *Equity* is from the Latin *aequitas* and its adjective *aequus*, which meant level, even, uniform, and reasonable.[42]

Fairness and *fair* have a different origin. They derive from the Gothic *fagrs*, which meant "pleasing to behold," and in turn from an Indo-European root that meant "to be content."[43] At an early date, these words migrated from Asia to middle Europe. There they disappeared in a maelstrom of many languages, but not before they migrated yet again to remote peninsulas and islands of northern and western Europe, where they persisted to our time.[44] In Saxon English, for example, the old Gothic *faeger* survived in the prose of the Venerable Bede as late as the year 888.[45] By the tenth century, it had become *faire* in English speech.[46]

In these early examples, *fagr*, *faeger*, *fair*, and *fairness* had multiple meanings. In one very old sense, *fair* meant blond or beautiful or both—*fair skin, fair hair*. As early as 870 a Viking king was called Harald Harfagri in Old Norse, or Harold Fairhair in English. In another usage, it meant favorable, helpful, and good—*fair wind, fair weather, fair tide*. In yet a third it meant spotless, unblemished, pleasing, and agreeable: *fair words, fair speech, fair manner*. All of these meanings were common in Old Norse, and Anglo-Saxon in the tenth and eleventh centuries. By 1450, it also meant right conduct in rivalries or competitions. *Fair play, fair game, fair race, and fair chance* appeared in English texts before 1490.[47]

The more abstract noun *fairness* was also in common use. The great English lexicographer (and father of the *Oxford English Dictionary*) Sir James Murray turned up many examples, some so early that they were still in the old Gothic form—such as *faegernyss* in Saxon England circa 1000, before the Norman Conquest. It became *fayreness* and *fairnesse* as an ethical abstraction by the mid-fifteenth century, as "it is best that he trete him with farenes" in 1460.[48]

As an ethical term, *fairness* described a process and a solution that could be accepted by most parties—*fair price, fair judgment, fair footing, fair and square*. Sometimes it also denoted a disposition to act fairly: *fair-minded, fair-natured, fair-handed*. All of these ethical meanings of *fair* and *fairness* were firmly established by the late sixteenth and early seventeenth centuries. *Fair play* appears in Shakespeare (1595); *fair and square* in Francis Bacon (1604); *fair dealing* in Lord Camden (before 1623).[49]

To study these early English uses of *fairness* and *fair* is to find a consistent core of meaning. Like most vernacular words, they were intended not for study but for practical use. In ethical applications, they described a way of resolving an issue that is contested in its very nature: a bargain or sale, a race or rivalry, a combat or conflict. Fundamentally, fairness meant a way of settling contests and conflicts without bias or favor to any side, and also without deception or dishonesty. In that sense *fairness* was fundamentally about not taking undue advantage of other people. As early as the fifteenth century it variously described a process, or a result, or both together, but always in forms that *fair-minded* people would be willing to accept as legitimate.

Fairness functioned as a mediating idea. It was a way of linking individuals to groups, while recognizing their individuality at a surprisingly early date. Always, fairness was an abstract idea of right conduct that could be applied in different ways, depending on the situation. For example, in some specific circumstances, fairness was used to mean that people should be treated in the same way. But in other circumstances, fairness meant that people should be treated in different ways, or special ways that are warranted by particular facts and conditions, such as special merit, special need, special warrant, or special desire. [50]

Fairness was a constraint on power and strength, but it did not seek to level those qualities in a Procrustean way.[51] Its object was to regulate ethical relationships between people who possess power and strength in different degrees—a fundamental fact of our condition. A call for fairness was often an appeal of the weak to the conscience of the strong. It was the eternal cry of an English-speaking child to parental authority: "It's not fair!" As any parent knows, this is not always a cry for equality.

Modern Applications of Fairness:
Their Consistent Core of Customary Meaning

Vernacular ideas of *fairness* and *fair* have changed through time, and in ways that are as unexpected as their origin. In early ethical usage, these words referred mostly to things that men did to one another—a *fair fight, fair blow, fair race, fair deal, fair trade.* They also tended to operate within tribes of Britons and Scandinavians, where they applied to freemen in good standing. Women, slaves, and strangers from other tribes were often excluded from fair treatment, and they bitterly resented it.

The tribal uses of *fair* and *fairness* were full of historical irony. These ideas flourished on the far fringes of northwestern Europe among groups of proud, strong, violent, and predatory people who lived in hard environments, fought to the death for the means of life, and sometimes preyed even on their own kin. Ideas of fairness and fair play developed as a way of keeping some of these habitual troublemakers from slaughtering each other even to the extinction of the tribe. All that might be understood as the first stage in the history of fairness.[52]

Something fundamental changed in a second stage, when the folk cultures of Britain and Scandinavia began to grow into an ethic that embraced others beyond the tribe—and people of every rank and condition. This expansive tendency had its roots in universal values such as the Christian idea of the Golden Rule.[53] That broader conception of fairness expanded again when it met the humanist ideas of the Renaissance, the universal spirit of the Enlightenment, the ecumenical spirit of the Evangelical Movement, and democratic revolutions in America and Europe. When that happened, a tribal idea gradually became more nearly universal in its application.[54] Quantitative evidence suggests an inflection at the end of the eighteenth century. The frequency of *fairness* in English usage suddenly began to surge circa 1800. The same pattern appears in the use of the expression *natural justice*.[55]

Then came a third stage in the history of *fairness*, when customary ideas began to operate within complex modern societies. In the twentieth century, *fairness* acquired many technical meanings with specific applications. One example regulated relations between government and modern media ("the fairness doctrine"). In another, fairness became a professional standard for people who were charged with the management of other people's assets ("fiduciary fairness"). One of the most interesting modern instances appeared among lawyers as a test of "balance or impartiality" in legal proceedings, or a "subjective standard by which a court is deemed to have followed due process," which began to be called "fundamental fairness" in law schools. Yet another example was "fair negotiation," which one professional negotiator defined as a set of rules for "bargaining with the Devil without losing your soul." One of the most complex applications is emerging today as an ethic of "fairness in electronic commerce." These and other modern applications of *fairness* appear in legal treatises, professional codes, and complex bodies of regulatory law.[56]

Even as modern uses of *fair* and *fairness* have changed in all of those ways, they also preserved a consistent core of vernacular meaning that had appeared in Old English, Norse, and Scandinavian examples and is still evident today. To summarize, *fair* and *fairness* have long been substantive and procedural ideas of right conduct, designed to regulate relations among people who are in conflict or rivalry or opposition in particular ways. *Fairness* means not taking undue advantage of others. It is also about finding ways to settle differences through a mutual acceptance of rules and processes that are thought to be impartial and honest—honesty is fundamental. And it is also about living with results that are obtained in this way. As the ancient Indo-European root of *fagrs* implied, a quest for fairness is the pursuit of practical solutions with which opposing parties could "be content." These always were, and still are, the fundamental components of fairness.[57]

Fair and Fairness in Translation

The surprising complexity of these English vernacular words *fair* and *fairness* appears when people try to translate them into other languages. In French-English dictionaries, the nearest French equivalents to the English word *fair* are usually given as *équitable, juste,* or *légitime,* which are not true equivalents. *Fairness* ("to be content") exists in the eye of beholders—unlike *justice,* which refers to an external standard of law, or *equity,* which implies an external and even empirical test of being even, straight, or equal by some objective measure. These three ethical ideas often overlap, but they do not coincide, and each has its own distinct center. The center of fairness (in customary usage) is about not taking undue advantage of others in dynamic conflicts, competitions, or rivalries; or in two words, *fair play.* The center of justice (and the original meaning of *ius*) is about the rule of law. The center of equity (and its ancient root, *aequitas*) is about a solution that is equal, level, or even-handed. Their relationship to one another might be represented as three overlapping circles in a Venn diagram. To think of *fairness* as synonymous with *justice* or *equity* is not true to the origins of these words, or to their literal meanings, or to predominant patterns of vernacular use. Translations that blur these different ideas are not accurate to their English meanings.[58]

Other translations are even more of a stretch. Several French dictionaries render *fair* as *permis* (literally, allowed); or *loyal* (which often means honest, upright, and straightforward, as well as loyal in its English sense). The English idiom *fair and square* is translated as *franc, franche et loyal* by the *Oxford French Dictionary.* To *play fair* in French is *jouer franc jeu,* and the noun *fair play* is translated as *loyauté* or *bonne foi.* None is a close match for *fair. Fairness* is rendered as *probité* in Langenscheidt's French-English dictionary. No cognate or exact synonym for *fairness* existed in French until the late twentieth century, when a new idiom appeared in French soccer slang: "*c'est pas le fairplay.*"[59]

Other Romance languages have similar problems. In English-Italian dictionaries, *fair* and *fairness* are translated as *giusto, giustizia, imparziale, onesto,* or *equità.* But in English vernacular usage, the words *just, justice, impartiality, honest,* and *equitable* are different from *fair.* Here again, meanings overlap but do not coincide. *Fair play* in Italian becomes *lealtà* (loyalty, trustworthiness, faithfulness) or *giuoco pulito* (literally, clean play). Spanish lexicographers struggle in a similar way: *fair* is translated in Spanish dictionaries as *justo* or *equitativo;* and *fairness* is *justicia* or *imparcialidad.*

In German dictionaries before the Second World War, the most common translation-terms for *fair* were *ehrlich* (equitable, honorable), *billig* (reasonable, just), *gleich* (equal, proportional), or *gerecht* (just, lawful, moral). None of these ideas is the same as fairness. After the Anglo-American occupation of Germany in 1945, a new word appeared in German dictionaries: the anglicism *die Fairness,* and new expressions such as *das ist nicht fair,* because there was no German equivalent. And even in modern English-German dictionaries after 1945, common terms of translation for *fairness* are *gerechtigkeit* (justice) and *unparteilichkeit* (impartiality). The simple English exclamation *fair enough* required six words in one German translation: *das ist nur recht und billig,* literally "that is only right and proper," and even so it missed the meaning.

Anglo-Dutch dictionaries translate *fair* as *billijk, eerlijk,* or *behoorlijk,* which literally mean decent or proper—not the same meaning. Cognates for *fairness* did not exist in most other European, Asian, Middle Eastern, African, or Native American languages before borrowings were introduced from English in the late twentieth century.[60]

Fairness in Other English-Speaking Countries

Wherever English is spoken, *fair* is in daily use. Quantitative frequencies are similar throughout the anglophone world.[61] But qualitative usage varies from one country to another. In regard to fairness as the organizing principle of an open society, two countries are similar to New Zealand: Canada and Australia. Australian writer David Malouf observes, "The one word that sums up what Australians demand of society, and of one another, is fairness, a good plain word that grounds its meanings in the contingencies of daily living. It is our version of liberty, equality, fraternity and includes everything that is intended by those grand abstractions and something more: the idea of natural justice, for instance. It's about as far as most Australians would want to go in the enunciation of the principle."[62]

Australians believe that fairness derives from the beginning of their nation. Historian Babette Smith thinks that "the sense of fairness dates from the First Fleet. . . . [W]hen the settlement at Sydney Cove was starving, Governor Arthur Phillip ordered equal rations for everybody. . . . [I]t became the basis of values that still shape society." In that example and others, Australian usage is similar in strength to usage in New Zealand and Canada, but different in its substance. For one, it tends to be more egalitarian. For another, Australians believe that their ideas of fairness are not strongly linked to laws and rules. Adrian Walsh writes, "We don't worry about illegality but we worry when things are unfair." He adds, "In sport we are less rule-bound but have a sense of its ethos." Australian philosopher Gerard O'Brien agrees: "Our sense of rules is not as strong as our sense of fairness."[63]

In Canada, fairness is also important as an organizing principle of this open society, but with different shades of meaning. Qualitative patterns of usage reflect the unique character of this nation. We find in the history and life of Canada a coexistence of ethics with distinct historical origins. One of them is an ethic of humanity that has deep roots in the vernacular cultures of New France—Québecois, Acadien, and Métis.[64] Another culture developed from Tories who were hostile to the American Revolution and migrated in large numbers to Canada after 1776, with strong bonds of loyalty to the empire and to each other.[65] A third grew in the nineteenth and the twentieth centuries, from a larger flow of British immigrants who had the same strong consciousness of fairness that went to New Zealand. A fourth derives from cross-border movements between the United States and Canada, which spread American ideas of liberty and freedom. The cultures of "first nations" are also very important in Canada, and other ethics multiplied as Canada became increasingly pluralist.

Canadian ideas of fairness have a strong association with rules of law that hold this country together. An example is the Canada Revenue Agency (CRA), similar to the American Internal Revenue Service (IRS). Every taxpayer in Canada has a legal right to a "fairness review" by a formal "Fairness Committee" in the CRA.[66] A second example is a law introduced by the Conservative Party in 2010, the Fairness at the Pumps Act, which required fair play in gas stations as a matter of federal law. A third is the Law Society of Upper Canada, the governing body for lawyers and paralegals in Ontario, which has a formal "Office of Fairness Commissioner" to protect the rights of individuals. When Queen Elizabeth II visited Canada in 2010, she celebrated "the country's values of freedom, fairness and the rule of law." That phrase captured Canada's pluralist and legalist tradition of fairness as an organizing principle of an open society, which was different from Australia.

In Britain, also, ideas of fairness are prominent in public life, and have grown more so. During a general election on April 29, 2010, party leaders David Cameron (Conservative), Gordon Brown (Labour), and Nick Clegg (Liberal Democrat) met in a national debate. Together they invoked the words *free* five times, *freedom* two times, *liberty* not at all, and *fair/fairness* twenty-two times.

Labour's leader Gordon Brown spoke in general terms of a "fair society," asserted that "fairness is in the British people's DNA," and promised "a future fair for all." Liberal Democrats talked of "fair taxes, a fair chance, fair future and fair deal," and fair elections with proportional representation. Conservative David Cameron offered a third idea: a fair society was one with "everyone doing their fair share." He insisted that "fairness means giving people what they deserve—and what people deserve can depend on how people behave." Altogether, this exchange was similar to political discourse in New Zealand, with a harder edge on the right, a softer touch to the left.

.At the same time, Britons of all parties cultivated another vernacular idea of fairness that had a unique intensity in the United Kingdom and was a product of its history, as vernacular ideas tend to be. Journalist John Kay summarized it in a sentence: "For the British, the epitome of fairness is shared adversity." No other English-speaking people had such a sustained experience of adversity in the Second World War. None responded with more unity and strength. They were able to do so in large part because they believed that the burden of adversity was shared fairly among themselves. John Kay observes that Winston Churchill understood this idea, and had it pitch-perfect on May 13, 1940, when he promised everyone in the realm the same ordeal of "blood, toil, tears and sweat." In the same spirit, King George VI and his family made a point of living in London during the Blitz, even as bombs were falling on Buckingham Palace. These were not small gestures but instrumental acts. Together they reinforced an ethic of fairness as the sharing of adversity, and Britons muddled through.

This British tradition is specially interesting in several ways. It had particular strength in a highly stratified society where many other things were deeply unfair. And it also demonstrated the extraordinary power of fairness when put to work that way—a lesson for us all in America.[67]

Fairness in American Usage: A Pattern of Cultural Ambivalence

In August 2010, an Australian traveler named Sophie Reynolds was in the United States, flying from Pittsburgh to Atlanta on Sky West Airlines. She asked an attendant for pretzels, was told there were none, and replied with a complaint that ended in the words *fair dinkum.* The attendant had never heard that expression and took offense. Another attendant demanded to see Reynolds's passport and took down her name. In Atlanta she was met by three police officers, who told her, "You swore at a hostess and there are federal rules against that." They interrogated her on the meaning of *fair dinkum,* learned that it was not a curse or a threat, and released Sophie Reynolds into the Land of the Free. Journalists who covered the story also had difficulty explaining to Americans what *fair dinkum* actually meant. One account quoted President George W. Bush on his meeting with Australian Prime Minister John Howard. "I called him a 'man of steel,' " said Mr. Bush. "That's Texan for Fair Dinkum."[68]

The word *fair* itself is very common in American usage. In daily discourse, it has always held an important place in the American pantheon of private virtues. But New Zealand's and Australia's highly developed vocabulary of fairness is alien to American speech. Americans tend to be divided and deeply ambivalent on the importance of fairness as an organizing principle of their open society.

From time to time it has become prominent in public discourse. Several major leaders in the United States shared a deep concern for fairness as a civic principle. George Washington did so when he urged fair treatment for Hessian and British prisoners in 1776, and again for the Whiskey Rebels who were arrested in 1794, and once more for Indian nations in the West, and later in the manumission of slaves at Mount Vernon. His Farewell Address urged Americans to give their republican institutions "a fair and full experiment," and advised them to follow a policy of fairness in foreign relations and domestic affairs. A sense of fairness was a fundamental strength in his character and leadership. It helps us to understand why so many people trusted him, and why they chose him to be commander-in-chief of the Continental Army, president of the Constitutional

Convention, and president of the United States, all by unanimous vote, a record without equal in American history.[69]

President Abraham Lincoln also showed a very active interest in fairness. He described the Union war effort as a "people's contest to afford all an unfettered start and a fair chance in the face of life." Substantive and procedural ideas of fairness were prominent in many of Lincoln's speeches and state papers. He wrote repeatedly that "fair play is a jewel," and that discourse should be shaped by "truthful evidence and fair argument." In his speech to the 166th Ohio Regiment on August 22, 1864, Lincoln spoke of freedom and fairness together as the primary purposes of the war. "I happen temporarily to occupy this big White House," he said. "I am a living witness that any one of your children may look to come here as my father's child has. It is in order that each of you may have through this free government which we have enjoyed, an open field and a fair chance for your industry, enterprise, and intelligence.[70]

Another president with a highly developed sense of fairness was Theodore Roosevelt. In 1903, he framed his promise of a "Square Deal" around "the old familiar watchwords of honesty, decency, fair-dealing, and common sense."[71] During the election of 1912, he spoke at length about fairness. His most important speech, "The New Nationalism," placed it at the center of his campaign. "I stand for the square deal," Roosevelt proclaimed, "not merely fair play under the present rules of the game," but for "new and fair rules, and a fair game." In "We Stand at Armageddon," another major speech, he talked of "honesty and fairness" for citizens and corporations, and regulations that would put an end to "unfair money getting."[72]

Woodrow Wilson also wrote often of fairness when he ran for governor of New Jersey in 1910 and for president in 1912. In his first inaugural address, Wilson promised a policy "with an eye single to the standards of justice and fair play."[73]

Twenty years later, Franklin Roosevelt also invoked ideas of fairness and fair play. His secretary of labor, Frances Perkins, knew him well, and wrote that he had no formal ideology in the usual sense, but that everything in his thinking came down to three words: "free, fair, and decent."[74] The New Deal rested largely on those principles, to the genuine bewilderment and deep displeasure of egalitarian radicals on the left and libertarian conservatives on the right. One of his last major reforms was the Fair Labor Standards Act (1938), which ended child labor and introduced a minimum wage of forty cents, with a workweek of forty hours.

Roosevelt also gave strong support to his Fair Employment Practices Committee (FEPC), which he created in 1941 to combat job discrimination by race and religion.

Harry Truman made fairness into the rallying cry of his presidency. On September 6, 1945, Truman told Congress that "every segment of our population, and every individual, has a right to expect from his government a Fair Deal." That sentence became the keynote of his administration.[75]

When Americans rank their presidents, they usually identify the top three as Abraham Lincoln, George Washington, and Franklin Roosevelt. Not far behind are Theodore Roosevelt, Woodrow Wilson, and increasingly Harry Truman. Most of these leaders led from the center. This was the case both for Franklin Roosevelt, who described himself as a little to the left of center, and George Washington, who was more than a little to the right of center. Both of these leaders deliberately governed from the middle, and surrounded themselves with colleagues to the right and left, as Washington did with Hamilton and Jefferson. Centrist ideas of fairness were a source of strength that way.

But the attitudes of these fair-minded men were not typical of American politics as a whole. A congressional coalition of southern Democrats and northern Republicans defeated most of Harry Truman's Fair Deal legislation. After Truman left office in 1953, not much was heard about fairness in American politics for an extended period. A new school of hard-right conservative Republicans had little interest in the subject. A new generation of Democrats cultivated a spirit of "tough-minded liberalism" that was very different from the thinking of Washington, Lincoln, Wilson, both Roosevelts, and Harry Truman on the subject of fairness.

A case in point was an event that happened in the presidency of a consciously tough-minded liberal, John F. Kennedy. During his administration, veterans of two wars were called up for a third time to serve in Vietnam. Some protested that they had done more than most, and that it was "unfair" of the president to ask them to serve yet again when many others had not served at all. Kennedy replied, "There is always inequity in life. Some men are killed in a war, and some men are wounded, and some men never leave the country. . . . It's very hard in military or personal life to assure complete equality. Life is unfair."[76]

But the veterans were not asking for "complete equality," or even for equality at all. They were appealing to an idea of fairness that Kennedy's response confused with equality. He dismissed it out of hand, and issued an executive order that made life a little more unfair. President Kennedy did not invent the idea that "life is unfair," but he gave it wings, as presidents can do. From the 1960s to the 1990s, Americans made a cliché of John Kennedy's cynical thought that "life is unfair." By and large, they did not expect the government to do much about it.

Some Americans went farther. They rejected the very idea of fairness, and some justified the existence of unfairness as a positive good. Conservative journalist William Safire elevated unfairness into a theological doctrine, and linked it to liberty and freedom. He wrote, "The icon-busting Book of Job teaches that God does not micromanage the universe, and that free-willed human beings are responsible for actions and injustices. That's why life is unfair." For Safire, unfairness was inseparable from liberty, freedom, and human responsibility.[77]

Other Americans have argued that unfairness is a strength and even a virtue. In 1997, for example, a magazine called *Golf Digest* was competing fiercely against its rivals. It recruited as a "player editor" the young prodigy Tiger Woods, at that time one of the most popular golfers in the United States. The magazine's editor announced his coup in the *New York Times* with a full-page advertisement. It consisted mainly of an eight-column photograph of the editor himself looming over Tiger Woods, as the young golfer signed a contract to write for the magazine every month. The caption boasted: "Signing Tiger Woods. That's An Unfair Advantage." As if that were not enough, the *Golf Digest* copyrighted the phrase "The Unfair Advantage" as a corporate motto.[78]

Other Americans celebrated unfairness in general as a positive good. A conservative business journalist, Hiawatha Bray, published an essay in the Boston *Globe* called "Unfair Is Fine." Bray wrote, "Life is unfair, thank God. If nobody was richer, tougher, or smarter than me, I'd be sitting in a cave somewhere. All of us benefit from unfair advantages held by others." In this way of thinking unfairness became a moral imperative.[79]

Similar attitudes appeared in a book called *Never Fight Fair! Navy SEALs' Stories of Combat and Adventure.* It celebrated their ruthlessness, taking its title from a comment by Lieutenant Commander T. L. Bociljevac, USN, who said, "There is no such thing as a fair fight. Never plan a fair operation." That attitude differed from the thinking of George Washington, Abraham Lincoln, and Franklin Roosevelt. The strongest and most successful commanders-in-chief in American history believed that fairness was a source of their strength and success. It also differed from memoirs by other Navy SEALs such as

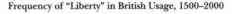

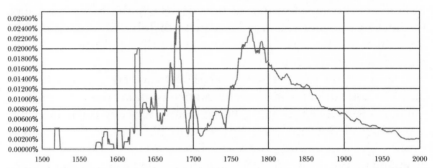

High frequencies of "Liberty" in English usage coincide in time with the founding of British colonies in what is now the United States; surging from 1600 to 1775 and declining thereafter in England but remaining very prominent in the United States. Here is a classic example of a founder effect in settler societies. The evidence derives from word counts in a corpus of one million English books, through Google Labs and Google Ngram viewers.

Eric Greitens, who stresses the importance of "thoughtful, disciplined and proportional" choices in the use of force, as central to SEAL missions: "Warriors are warriors not because of their strength, but because of their ability to apply strength to good purpose."[80]

In the early twenty-first century, American attitudes were very mixed on the subject of fairness. Some groups, mostly to the right, turned strongly against this idea, in large part because they were strongly committed to other values. A leading student of American political thought, Mark Lilla, wrote in 2010, "Many key words of our political vocabulary have been copyrighted by Republicans over the past thirty years, notably freedom . . . but there is still a powerful symbol the Democrats could capture because today's Republicans explicitly reject it: fairness." He added, " 'Life isn't fair' is a refrain you hear constantly from the right. Yet there is a strong sense in the nation today that things are rigged, especially at the top of the economic ladder."[81]

In 2008, leaders in the Democratic Party were keenly aware of all that, and made a major issue of fairness. The party platform in the presidential campaign used the words *fair* and *fairness* thirty-one times in a brief document.[82] The first law that President Barack Obama signed was the Lilly Ledbetter Fair Pay Restoration Act. Mr. Obama's opponents responded with strong attacks, not only on the new president, but on the idea of fairness itself. Conservative journalist Cliff Mason wrote angrily, "Fairness will be the death of us. . . . The notion of fairness, or rather the plan's fundamental unfairness, comes up again and again. . . . I say so what? Who cares if it's fair? . . . We've got bigger fish to fry."[83]

Frequency of "Fairness" in British Usage, 1500–2000

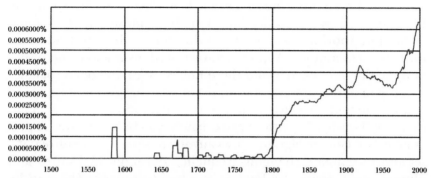

High frequencies of "Fairness" in English usage coincided with the period of British coloniza-
tion in New Zealand. The use of "Fairness" fluctuated at comparatively low levels to 1800,
then surged to high levels ca. 1840 and have continued to rise ever since. The evidence
derives from word counts in an entire corpus of one million English books, through Google
Labs and Google Ngram viewers.

Other Americans on the right believe that ideals of fairness and fair play are hostile to capitalism, destructive of national security, and dangerous to liberty. At the same time, ironically, others on the left believe that fairness undercuts the pursuit of equality. Both of these groups are minorities. Most Americans are in the center. They believe in the idea of fairness and have been demanding more of it. The frequency of the word *fairness* has been increasing in American usage during the twentieth century, though far below *freedom* and *free*.[84] Even so, few Americans think of fairness as the organizing principle of their open society.

Ethical Choices and Open Systems

The United States and New Zealand are both open societies, and have been so for many generations. Each in its own way has a democratic polity, a mixed-enterprise economy, a pluralist culture, a strong commitment to human rights, and a firm belief in the rule of law. Both of these open systems encourage individual people to make their own choices. They also share many values in common, including liberty and freedom, fairness and justice.

But they have drawn differently from that common stock. In America, liberty and freedom were the founding principles of the great republic. Most Americans today agree on the central importance of those ideas, even as they understand them in different ways—sometimes in opposite ways.[85] New Zealanders went another way. They gave central attention to values of fairness and "natural

justice," which explicitly appears in their Bill of Rights. Ideas of freedom and liberty were never absent from New Zealand's culture.
Ideals of fairness and justice have long been present in the United
States. But priorities have been very different in these two countries
for many generations. A question for historians is about the origin
of these differences. Why did these English-speaking open societies
develop in different ways? An important clue has recently appeared
in a new tool of historical inquiry—the digitization by Google Labs
of 5.2 million books, with approximately 500 billion words. A program called Google Ngram allows anyone to search that entire dataset and to estimate changing frequencies of individual words and
phrases, over periods as long as five hundred years. This can be
done for many modern languages, and within English for American
English, or British English, or all English-language books.

The use of the words *liberty* and *freedom* both show striking patterns of change through time. Usage of these words increased in a
series of sharp surges during the period from 1600 to 1800, which
brought them to their highest frequencies in that period of modern
history. Very different patterns appeared for words such as *fairness* and
natural justice. Both fluctuated at very low levels from the sixteenth
century to the late eighteenth century, when Britain's American colonies were settled. Then, from about 1800 both *fairness* and *natural
justice* surged to very high frequencies in English usage and reached a
peak from 1800 to 1850. This was the period when British cultures
were established in New Zealand. The huge Google dataset clearly
shows that one set of values was very dynamic and expansive among
English speakers when Britain's American colonies were founded, and
at its core were ideas of liberty and freedom. Another constellation of
values was predominant among English speakers when Britain's New
Zealand colonies took root, and it centered on fairness and justice.[86]

This evidence, for all its massive empirical base, is only a clue—
not a conclusion. But it invites us to take a closer look at the values
that English-speaking people carried with them to different places—
and in different periods. To do so is to discover that these values did
not flow from fixed and rigid determinants. They emerged from a
web of individual choices. Here we might move beyond determinism
and search for a more open cause. That became the next stage in
our inquiry.

PART I

ORIGINS OF OPEN SOCIETIES

SETTLER SOCIETIES

Founding Visions, Enduring Dreams

> Journalist: Do you think New Zealanders have developed separate national characteristics?
>
> George Bernard Shaw: No, it is the other way about. The characteristics of the British Islanders have changed so much in this century. They no longer resemble the Englishmen of the nineteenth century. New Zealanders resemble them very strongly, and consequently there is now a marked difference, but it is the Englishman who has changed, not the New Zealander.
>
> —G. B. Shaw, *What I Said in New Zealand*, 1934

MOST VISITORS to New Zealand fly into the city of Auckland. At first sight the scale of this metropolis seems inconsistent with its size. Auckland has been called the "city of a hundred hamlets."[1] Many neighborhoods have the air of small villages, nestled comfortably between long arms of the sea.

Our friend Kay Irwin met us at the airport and drove us to the village of Parnell on a coastal road that runs along Waitemata Harbour. Along the way we noticed a small building on a steep green hillside, high above the water's edge. Its glossy white paintwork gleamed as bright as a beacon in the strong Pacific light. Coming closer, we made out the low belfry, high-pitched roof, and Gothic windows of an early Victorian church. Kay told us that it was Saint Stephen's Chapel, built by English founders of Auckland in 1857 and still in active use today. On later visits we always found fresh flowers in the vases, hymnals on the racks, and embroidered cushions on the

pews. Outside we walked among the carefully tended graves of early
settlers. The stones are edged in English ivy and sheltered beneath
English shade trees, half a world from home.[2]

The setting of St. Stephen's Chapel in Auckland brought to
mind another Anglican church, St. Luke's in Virginia, built by English settlers in the seventeenth century near an arm of another sea,
and also still in service as a place of worship. Many of these sacred
buildings survive in North America: the Puritans' Old Ship Meetinghouse in Hingham, Massachusetts; the Friends' Old Meeting in Mer-
ion, Pennsylvania; the Catholic Mission of San Miguel in Santa Fe;
and Touro Synagogue in Newport, Rhode Island. All were built by
early settlers in the seventeenth or early eighteenth century and are
still serving their original purpose in our time.

It is much the same in New Zealand. In its many regions we found
old chapels and churches that are still functioning as houses of faith and
temples of memory. Separately, each of these buildings has a story to tell
about settlers in a strange land. Together, they testify to the importance
of small beginnings in the history of great nations. They also remind us
that first choices can make a difference in our decisions, even today.

The United States and New Zealand are prime examples of "settler societies," founded by colonists in the presence of much larger
indigenous populations. Many other nations had similar beginnings.
At last count, the United Nations recognized 227 sovereign states
and "areas of special sovereignty" in the world. Of that number about
a hundred began as settler societies in the modern era.[3]

St. Stephen's Chapel, built by founders of
the village of Parnell in 1857, is now part
of Auckland in New Zealand. Many similar buildings are lovingly preserved and
actively in use throughout New Zealand,
the United States, and other settler societies.

Part of this large process was the migration of English-speaking people, in relatively small numbers but on such a global scale that the speechways of their home islands have become the most widely spoken primary and secondary languages in the world. These British colonies did not grow from the imperial designs of strong rulers or great states, but from the choices of small groups and solitary emigrants.

In what is now the United States, these early adventurers were very diverse. Many were rebels, dissenters, and nonconformists. They felt themselves to be victims of tyranny and persecution, and shared an obsession with liberty and freedom. Some of them would later demand liberty to enslave others, or rights to become persecutors in their turn. But they began with a dream of living free, which has endured for many generations.

New Zealand's British settlers in the nineteenth century also tended to be dissenters and nonconformists, but in a different way. By their time, liberty and tyranny were no longer the most urgent issues in the United Kingdom. A new generation of English-speaking people had grievances of another kind. Many felt themselves to be victims of social injustice, gross inequity, and deep unfairness not merely in individual acts but in the systemic operation of an entire society. They hoped to build a better world that offered "a fair field and no favor."

These English-speaking emigrants to North America and New Zealand shared a sense of grievance, a consciousness of rights, and a tradition of autonomous action. They were driven by founding visions, similar in strength and stamina, but different in substance—as Britain itself was different in the seventeenth and nineteenth centuries.

Habits of Autonomy: American Mavericks, New Zealand Manings

In North America, the first English-speaking settlers arrived as early as the sixteenth century. Fishermen from West Country ports such as Bristol were summering on the American coast, and some were wintering in northern waters by the 1570s, probably earlier. Others followed in such number and variety that at least twenty-five small British settlements were planted in the neighborhood of what is now New England before the Puritans arrived.[4]

These earliest English adventurers contributed little to the peopling of America, but much to its folklore and history. An example was the Maverick family in Massachusetts Bay. Its American adventures began with Samuel Maverick (1602?–76?), the dark sheep of a

Devon family who built a small fort on an island in what is now Boston Harbor and occupied it with his family and four servants. Samuel Maverick was a kindly gentleman of engaging eccentricity. He nursed the Indians through smallpox epidemics and fed the Puritans when they first arrived. One early visitor to Massachusetts remembered that he was "the only hospitable man in the colony."[5]

The Puritans made Samuel Maverick a "freeman," but he was not comfortable in their Bible Commonwealth. A Calvinist described him as a "man of a very loving and courteous behavior, yet an enemy to the Reformation in hand." When he spoke out for freedom of conscience, Maverick was encouraged to leave the colony. But as Puritan leader John Cotton told another wayward soul, "banishment in this country is a kind of enlargement." In that spirit, many generations of Mavericks enlarged themselves across America for the better part of four centuries. Among them was another Samuel Maverick, who found his way to Texas, became a stockman, and stubbornly refused to brand his cattle on the open range. The unmarked yearlings were called mavericks by other stockmen. The name began to be applied to all animals that bore no man's brand—and to free-spirited loners who went their own way.[6]

Many such "mavericks" made their way to North America. Entire families such as the Balchs and Conants in New England and Claibornes in the Chesapeake arrived at an early date. Their offspring gained a reputation for autonomy through many generations. Like the first Samuel Maverick, they became symbols and carriers of an independent spirit that was much older than the Declaration of Independence. They helped to shape America's idea of itself.

In New Zealand, solitary English settlers began to arrive as early as 1792, probably earlier, also with no approval from higher authority. Some were the human flotsam and jetsam who wash up on saltwater beaches around the world. Others were whalers, sealers, kauri cutters, bird hunters, fugitives, deserters, romantics, rogues, missionaries, and a gang of escaped Australian convicts led by a desperado called Duce. The settlements were small, but numbers were large. By 1838, two thousand English-speaking people were living in New Zealand.

More than a few were villainous characters. One writer has described them as "unleashings of darkness unparalleled in the work of, say, Conrad." Others were very appealing, as in the glimpse we get of escaped convict Catherine Hagerty, an Irish lass with a "fresh complexion, much inclined to smile." Another was Charlotte Badger, a fugitive from Botany Bay, "very corpulent, with an infant child."

In New Zealand she became the faithful *wahine* of an Nga Puhi headman and refused to be "rescued" by Europeans. She and others like her began to know themselves as Pakeha, the Maori call-name for a paleface.[7]

A third was Frederick Maning (1811?–83), a well-heeled Anglo-Irish adventurer who arrived in 1833, settled at Hokianga, a hundred miles north of Auckland, took a Maori wife, and lived in New Zealand for nearly fifty years. Later he published a joyous book called *Old New Zealand . . . by a Pakeha Maori.*[8] Maning wrote that these early Pakeha-Maori "lived in a half-savage state, or to speak more correctly, a savage-and-a-half state, being greater savages by far than the natives." He was delighted to be among them. "Those were the times," Maning remembered happily, "the good old times before Governors were invented, and law, and justice, and all that. When everyone did as he liked—except when his neighbors would not let him (the more shame for them)—when there were no taxes, or duties, or public works, or public to require them."[9]

Frederick Maning hated government, quarreled endlessly with Maori and Pakeha authorities, battled missionaries and magistrates, fell out with his own children when they told him what to do, and left the country when he felt it had grown too crowded. Maning died in London, but he so loved New Zealand that his body was carried halfway round the world and buried in Auckland, where he is fondly remembered today.

Frederick Maning, a gentleman adventurer who made his own way to New Zealand, lived the independent life of a "Pakeha Maori," in his phrase. He wrote one of the classics of New Zealand literature and symbolized a spirit of individual autonomy that was strong in New Zealand and the United States.

In 1959, New Zealand's great poet-scholar Keith Sinclair placed Pakeha-Maori such as Frederick Maning at the center of a brilliant new history which argued the then heretical, now orthodox thesis that his country was not another Britain but a Pacific nation. Keith Sinclair was right about that, but ironically he fastened on a quality of British colonization to make his Pacific point. The Manings of New Zealand and Mavericks of America became cherished symbols of individual autonomy. They also added bright threads of color to the fabric of two nations. In that respect, New Zealand and the United States are much alike—and very British in their beginnings.[10]

Customs of Self-Rule: Plymouth and Kororareka

After the first solitary adventurers in North America and New Zealand, a second stage of colonization began when associations of English-speaking people organized small communities in new places. Their purposes were very mixed. Some came in search of honor and fortune. Others arrived on spiritual missions. More than a few were utopians in America and the South Pacific. Whatever their goals, these small groups began to impose English ideas of order on strange new worlds. In North America these collective ventures began with Sir Humphrey Gilbert's ill-fated colonial schemes (1578–83), which combined piety and profit with an Elizabethan spirit of adventure. Gilbert's missions ended abruptly when their leader was lost at sea. His men last saw him on the deck of a small vessel in a great gale on the North Atlantic, shouting across the stormy water, "We are as near to Heaven by land as by sea!" It was a gallant English failure that inspired other Englishmen. More disasters followed at Sir Walter Raleigh's Lost Colony of Roanoke, which mysteriously vanished after 1587, and Sir John Popham's settlement at Sagadahoc, which was largely abandoned after a cold Maine winter.[11]

Then at last came the first successes. A London joint stock company planted a commercial colony at Jamestown in Virginia (1607), in the expectation of extracting great riches from America. A pious band of Mayflower Pilgrims built a fortified village at Plymouth in New England (1620), in hope of practicing their faith without persecution. Much went wrong in these struggling settlements. In the first year, both were nearly destroyed by famine and disease, which killed three-quarters of the Jamestown colonists and half of Plymouth's Pilgrims.[12]

But these two colonies survived, and it is interesting to see how they organized themselves. At Plymouth, heads of families and independent men drafted a document called the Mayflower Compact. They agreed to "covenant and combine ourselves together into a civil body politic . . . to enact constitute and frame just and equal laws." These "compacts" were routine among English travelers, who were in the habit of managing their own affairs.[13] In 1636, the Mayflower Pilgrims also wrote a "Constitution and Declaration of Rights." They began by proclaiming that "as free-borne subjects of the State of England we hither came indued [endowed] with all and singular the priviledges belonging to such." The first "priviledge" was that laws should be made by "consent of the body of freemen or associates, or their representatives legally assembled, which is according to the free liberties of the free-born people of England." Every man was required to take his turn in public office. All the Mayflower Pilgrims bound themselves to defend the colony, and agreed to equip themselves with a musket, bandeleros, a sword, two pounds of powder, and ten pounds of bullets, on pain of heavy fines. They added other rights that Americans still cherish, and agreed to mutual obligations that some Americans have forgotten.[14]

Kororareka Beach, Bay of Islands, in 1836.

Kororareka Beach, now Russell, ca. 1836. This wide-open town was called by missionaries the "hell hole of the Pacific." Its inhabitants spontaneously created their own systems of self-government and law that were typical of British colonization in New Zealand and what is now the United States.

In early New Zealand, the largest English-speaking settlement before 1830 was Kororareka, now Russell in the beautiful Bay of Islands. Mariners throughout the South Seas knew it as "the Beach." Missionaries called it the "hellhole of the Pacific" and the "cesspool of the islands." Kororareka was crowded with grog shops, brothels, ship chandlers, and as many as five hundred European and Polynesian inhabitants, all chasing the main chance. In 1836, a traveler reckoned that it had "a greater number of rogues than any other spot of equal size in the universe."[15]

Kororareka was a rough town, but not without order. Its English-speaking inhabitants drew up a covenant called the Kororareka Association of 1838, which was remarkably similar to the Mayflower Compact of 1620. They agreed to elect a president and council, to live under "equal laws" enacted by their own consent, and to be judged by their peers in courts of their own creation. They also bound themselves to a web of mutual obligations. Every member of the association was required to arm himself with a musket, a bayonet, a brace of pistols, a cutlass, and sixty rounds of ball cartridge. The bearing of arms was a right and a responsibility.[16]

In many ways the adventurers of Kororareka and the Pilgrims of Plymouth could not have been more different, but in one way they were the same. Both were heirs to English traditions of self-government, individual rights, mutual responsibilities, and the rule of law. These small bands of British settlers introduced that heritage to North America and the South Pacific, and the world is much the better for it.[17]

Great Migrations and Regional Cultures

The first small settlements were followed by great waves of migration. Each wave was sharply defined in time and space and social circumstance. All were set in motion by events in the "mother country," but none were ordered by kings or controlled by parliaments. English-speaking emigrants made their own decisions. The character of these migrations rose from tensions between high ideals and hard realities of life in the mother country.

To compare these many folk-wanderings is to find what logicians call a problem of genus and difference. All of them happened in the modern era, but in different periods. All came from Britain and Northern Ireland, but different regions. Most of these migrants spoke English, but in different dialects. Nearly all were Christian and Protestant, but of different denominations. Most included large numbers of women by comparison with other colonies, but in different proportions.

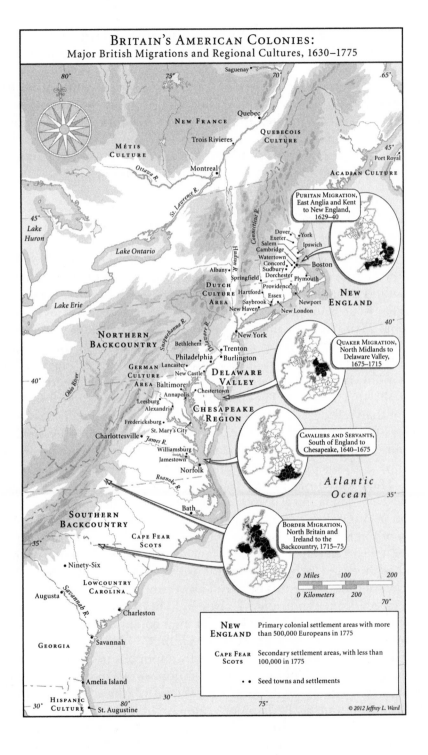

BRITAIN'S AMERICAN COLONIES:
Major British Migrations and Regional Cultures, 1630–1775

80°
75°
Saguenay
70°
65°

NEW FRANCE

Quebec

QUEBECOIS CULTURE

Trois Rivieres

MÉTIS CULTURE

45°

Ottawa R.

Montreal

Port Royal

St. Lawrence R.

ACADIAN CULTURE

PURITAN MIGRATION, East Anglia and Kent to New England, 1629–40

45°
Lake Huron

Lake Ontario

Connecticut R.

Dover
Exeter · York
Salem · Ipswich
Cambridge
Watertown
Concord · Boston
Sudbury
Dorchester
Plymouth

Lake Erie

Hudson R.

Albany

Springfield
DUTCH CULTURE AREA Hartford
Saybrook
New Haven
New London
Essex
Providence
Newport

NEW ENGLAND

40°

NORTHERN BACKCOUNTRY

Susquehanna R.
Delaware R.

New York

Bethlehem

Trenton
Philadelphia · Burlington

QUAKER MIGRATION, North Midlands to Delaware Valley, 1675–1715

40°

GERMAN CULTURE AREA

Lancaster
New Castle

DELAWARE VALLEY

Ohio River

Baltimore
Leesburg
Alexandria
Annapolis · Chestertown

CHESAPEAKE REGION

Fredericksburg
St. Mary's City
Charlottesville · James R.
Williamsburg
Jamestown

Norfolk

CAVALIERS AND SERVANTS, South of England to Chesapeake, 1640–1675

Roanoke R.

Atlantic Ocean

35°

SOUTHERN BACKCOUNTRY

Bath

CAPE FEAR SCOTS

BORDER MIGRATION, North Britain and Ireland to the Backcountry, 1715–75

35°

· Ninety-Six

LOWCOUNTRY CAROLINA

Augusta

Savannah R.

0 Miles   100   200

0 Kilometers   200

70°

Charleston

GEORGIA

Savannah

NEW ENGLAND — Primary colonial settlement areas with more than 500,000 Europeans in 1775

CAPE FEAR SCOTS — Secondary settlement areas, with less than 100,000 in 1775

· · Seed towns and settlements

· Amelia Island

30°

HISPANIC CULTURE

30°
80°
St. Augustine

75°

© 2012 Jeffrey L. Ward

Most of these settlers were in pursuit of material gain, but they also had other purposes in mind. Many were in flight from a British society that they felt to be tyrannical in the seventeenth century and unjust in the nineteenth—when judged by British standards. In America, every great colonial migration without exception was driven by a deep hunger for liberty and freedom that had been denied to them in Britain. In New Zealand most were inspired by visions of a better world, founded on ideas of fairness and justice. Let us look more closely at their similarities and differences.[18]

Puritan New England: John Winthrop's Idea of Ordered Liberty and Freedom, 1629–40

In America, the first of these great British migrations brought the Puritans to New England. This was a movement of about twenty thousand people, mostly from the east and south of England—East Anglia, Kent, and other counties where the Puritan movement was strong. Many were of middling rank in a highly stratified English society. About 75 percent paid their own passage; only 25 percent were servants. More than 90 percent came in family groups, which commonly included at least one member of a Puritan congregation (usually the mother). They multiplied at a mighty rate, founded more than a thousand towns in New England, and spread westward across the continent. Today most old-stock Yankee families in the United States are descended from Puritan forbears who splashed ashore in Massachusetts Bay within five years of the year 1635.[19]

Their leader was John Winthrop, an ascetic Puritan gentleman from East Anglia. As a lawyer he experienced at first hand the corruption of English courts. As a landowner he witnessed the oppression of English society. As a dissenter he suffered persecution within the English Church. Those experiences were shared by many of the twenty thousand people who came with him. Among them in the Great Migration were two hundred university graduates, mostly Puritan clergy from Cambridge University. They were leaders of high moral purpose who shared a vision of their colony as Saint Matthew's "candle in a candlestick, or a city on a hill."[20]

Liberty and freedom were urgently important to them, and in a very special way. The Puritan Migration of 1629–40 coincided exactly with England's "Eleven Years' Tyranny," when Charles I tried to rule without a Parliament, and Archbishop William Laud attempted to purge the Puritan movement from the Anglican Church. Many of New England's immigrants had direct experience

John Winthrop, leader of the Puritan Great Migration (1629–1640) and governor of Massachusetts Bay Colony, did much to shape the distinctive culture of New England. Its founding ideas of ordered liberty have left an enduring legacy in this region.

of oppression and persecution. John Cotton wrote that their purpose was "to breathe after greater liberty and purity." Others spoke of a hunger for the communion of "soul freedom" with other true believers. But they were not of one mind about the meaning of liberty and freedom. The great dissenter Roger Williams was for "liberty of conscience and conversation," and against what he called "soul-rape, which is the forcing of the conscience of any person." For that opinion, he was exiled from Massachusetts and founded a colony in Rhode Island that was open to many creeds.[21]

Other Puritans shared John Cotton's idea of "well-ordered liberty," which John Winthrop defined as the liberty to do "that only which is good." Nathaniel Ward, author of the *Laws and Liberties of Massachusetts*, wrote that "all Familists, Antinomians, Anabaptists, and other Enthusiasts shall have free liberty to keep away from us."[22] Dissenters were banished on pain of death if they returned. Three Quakers who came back were hanged on Boston Common.

Here is a sad fact about New England's history: victims of persecution became persecutors in their turn. Today Americans judge them harshly for denying to others what they demanded for themselves. But at the same time, New England Puritans were devoted to ideas of ordered liberty and freedom, from which many American rights descend. Five Puritan colonies in New England enacted formal codes of "fundamental law" and enlarged individual liberties far beyond any other government in the world at that time. They founded town meetings that embodied an idea of freedom as the right of self-rule. These complex principles of ordered liberty and freedom set New England apart from other cultures in America.[23]

Anglican Virginia: Sir William Berkeley's Idea of Hierarchical Liberty and Freedom, 1640–60

As the Puritan exodus ended, another great migration began. It went mainly to Virginia, from 1640 to 1680. When it started, that struggling colony was a sickly settlement of barely eight thousand souls. By its end, Virginia had grown to forty-five thousand people, with a distinct culture and society that persisted for three centuries.

Virginia's great migration began during the English Civil Wars, when Puritan Roundheads defeated Charles I and seized control of the country. Royalist refugees fled the country in many directions— Europe, the Indies, and some to Virginia. They came mostly from a triangle of territory in the south and west of England between London, Bristol, and Warwick, where Charles I had his strongest support. Less than 4 percent of Virginia's migrants came from East Anglia, and few from the Midlands or the north of England. They brought many laborers to work their land. Approximately 80 percent were indentured servants (compared with 25 percent in New England). About 15 percent were freemen of middling rank, and as many as 5 percent were younger sons of the gentry and aristocracy. Most were Anglican in their religion.[24]

Their leader was Sir William Berkeley (1606–77), governor for most of the period from 1641 to 1677. He was a staunch Royalist, devoted to the cause of Charles I, and driven by a vision for Virginia. At the critical moment, he dreamed that Virginia's beautiful countryside would become a Cavalier utopia, devoted to its Anglican faith, divided into great estates, and ruled by a small elite of birth and honor, which he largely created.[25] The Lees, Carters, Washingtons, Randolphs, Byrds, Warners, and Jeffersons did not descend from Jamestown's founding in 1607. Most arrived within ten years of 1650. Some were fugitives from the Puritans who won two civil wars, executed Charles I, and abolished Parliament. Others were younger sons in search of land and fortune. Many felt the sting of tyranny and persecution. Like most other Englishmen in the seventeenth century, these Cavaliers loved liberty and freedom. Sir William Berkeley himself wrote that it was "the libertye of the Collony and a right of deare esteeme to free borne persons . . . that no lawe could be established within the kingdome of England concerning us, without the consent of a grand Assembly here."[26]

Sir William Berkeley, long-serving Royalist governor of Virginia, modeled even his posture on King Charles I. Berkeley recruited an elite of younger sons who dominated Virginia, expanded an underclass of servants and later slaves, and promoted a culture of honor and hegemonic liberty that still survives in the American South.

Ideas of liberty and freedom in Cavalier Virginia were different from those in New England—less communal and more hierarchical. Even as Sir William Berkeley allowed all freemen to vote in Virginia, he believed that they should be ruled by a hereditary elite of honor, wealth, birth, and breeding. By Berkeley's design, a small Cavalier elite dominated Virginia's Royal Council, which controlled the distribution of land for many years. Every member of the council in 1775 was descended from a councillor who served in 1660.[27]

In a Cavalier utopia, Virginians possessed liberty in proportion to their rank. Gentlemen had many liberties. Yeomen had some liberties. Laborers and servants at the bottom had few liberties, or none. This hierarchical system was firmly in place by 1660. The great growth of African slavery came later. Slavery did not create this system in Virginia, but was created by it.[28] Hegemonic liberty in Virginia was thought to be entirely consistent with the keeping of slaves, which was justified in terms of a freeborn master's right to enslave others (*laisser asservir*). Edmund Burke wrote that "freedom is to them not only an enjoyment, but a kind of rank and privilege. . . . [I]n such a people, the haughtiness of dominion combines with the spirit of freedom, fortifies it, and renders it invincible."[29]

Quaker Pennsylvania: William Penn's Idea of Reciprocal Liberty and Freedom, 1675–1725

North America's third great migration brought about twenty-five thousand people to the Delaware Valley, in several waves during the years from 1675 to 1725. They came in large proportion from the North Midlands of England and the hill country of Wales. In early years, many had an association with the Society of Friends and were in flight from religious persecution. Others were sympathetic to that sect—"not a Friend, but Friendly," as one described himself. Many were very poor, but among them was a Quaker elite who would dominate the Delaware Valley for more than a century. They first settled at Burlington in New Jersey (1675), then planted the colony of Pennsylvania (1682) and organized "the three lower counties," which are now the state of Delaware.[30]

Their leader was William Penn (1644–1718), a great figure in the history of Christianity. Born to high estate, Penn joined the Society of Friends and was several times imprisoned for his Quaker faith. He converted his jailer and wrote many great works in defense of freedom and his faith. A charming man, he also became a good friend of Charles II, who gave him the colony of Pennsylvania.[31]

Quakers were like Puritans and Cavaliers in their obsession with liberty and freedom, but different in their understanding of those ideas. The center of their social thought was Christ's Golden Rule: "As ye would that men should do to you, do ye also to them."[32] Quakers reasoned from that rule to an idea of reciprocal liberty and freedom. More than any major group in modern history, they extended to others the rights they demanded for themselves. At the start there were exceptions to that rule. Some early Quakers and William Penn himself were keepers of slaves, but they became the first people in the world to join together against slavery.[33] Altogether the Quakers of the Delaware Valley were remarkably true to their ideal of reciprocal liberty. Its symbol was a great bell, commissioned by Quakers in the

William Penn, a high-born English Quaker, friend of kings, founder of West Jersey and Pennsylvania in the Delaware Valley, and a transcendent figure in the history of Christianity. He believed deeply in ideas of spiritual equality and reciprocal liberty. More than any other group, Quakers extended to others the rights they claimed for themselves.

Pennsylvania legislature to mark the fiftieth anniversary of William Penn's Charter of Liberties, and inscribed with a quotation from Leviticus: "Proclaim Liberty throughout the land, unto All the Inhabitants thereof." Here was an emblem of reciprocal liberty for all the people in Pennsylvania. It made a striking contrast with the ordered liberty of Massachusetts and the hierarchical liberty of Virginia.[34]

British Borderers in the American Backcountry: Patrick Henry's Idea of Natural Liberty, 1715–75

After the Quaker exodus, a fourth great migration flowed from the borderlands of North Britain: the lowlands of Scotland, the six northern counties of England, and northern Ireland. In the years from 1715 to 1775, as many as 250,000 colonists left those troubled territories and settled in the American backcountry from western Pennsylvania south to Maryland, Virginia, the Carolinas, and Georgia. They were led by a border "Ascendancy" of Houstons, Calhouns, Polks, Jacksons, and many other proud families. These were a warrior people, very mixed in ethnic origin, but they shared a common culture that was shaped by their history. It grew from a thousand years of brutal strife in the borderlands. For ten centuries the kings of Scotland and England fought incessantly over that broad region. The borderers who lived there suffered severely from this constant violence. They became passionately attached to their own idea of liberty, which they understood as a right to be left alone by governments in general, after having been abused by so many of them.[35]

Many North British borderers came to America shortly before the Revolution began. Most supported it. Their eloquent spokesmen

Patrick Henry was the son and grandson of emigrants from the borderlands of North Britain and Ireland. For a thousand years, their ancestors had suffered from the violence and tyranny of rival governments. They despised government in general, detested taxes, and shared an idea of natural liberty that was cast in the first person singular, "Give Me Liberty!" "Don't Tread on Me!" Their descendants are very active today in the southern and western United States.

was Patrick Henry, son and grandson of North British immigrants. The backsettlers who went to war in 1775 inscribed their hunting shirts with Patrick Henry's words, "Give ME Liberty or Give ME Death." Their symbol of liberty was a timber rattlesnake with the motto "Don't Tread on ME." These were among the first ideas of American liberty to be cast in the first person singular. They were a vision of natural liberty, an individual's right to be left alone, free from interference by government, but always among friends and family.[36]

Founding Ideals and New World Realities: Ironies of Open Space and Closed Enclaves in Early America

In America, these four great British migrations became the nucleus of large regional cultures in New England, the Middle States, the coastal South, and the backcountry. In the first U.S. Census of 1790 each region had about five hundred thousand inhabitants in a nation of about four million people. Another eight hundred thousand were African slaves, who had their own visions of living free.[37] Much of American history was a collision between these ideas of liberty and freedom. Always we find a sustained altruism in the culture of every American region, and everywhere the reality was something else again. Every American colony was founded on an idea of liberty and freedom, but all of them practiced slavery. Every colony preached an ideal of a free society, but most of them denied liberty and freedom to those most in need. John Roche observed that early America was an open continent dotted with closed enclaves—an American irony.

But that was not the end of it. In every colony, some people believed deeply that slavery and other forms of tyranny were violations of founding principles. Others listened and responded. The existence of unfreedom in their world inspired many Americans to enlarge their founding ideas. The result was a dynamic process in which the limits and failures of liberty and freedom inspired a continuing growth of those ideas through American history.

New Zealand's Great Migrations, 1839–66: Wellington and the Wakefield Colonies

New Zealand's great colonial migrations came mainly in a period of three decades. As in America, they planted settlements in different parts of the country, which grew into regional cultures. Here again the great waves began by voluntary effort. In the critical period, British rulers did not control the colonization of New Zealand, and sometimes actively opposed it. A primary instrument was a private corporation called the New Zealand Company. Founded in 1838, it resembled the Virginia Company and the Massachusetts Bay Company in many ways. One goal was to replace the "raffish free-for all of old New Zealand" with a "new Old England." Another was to found new societies as models for reform in the old.[38]

The driver was Edward Gibbon Wakefield (1796–1862), "a florid John Bull figure . . . with the air of a prosperous farmer" and "a pack of well-bred dogs at his heels." Opinion on him will always be divided. Many knew him as a humanitarian, utopian, and idealist who sympathized deeply with victims of injustice. Others complained of his dishonesty, treachery, and cruelty, and profiteering. Thackeray called him "a rogue if ever there was one." All of these judgments are correct. None alone can explain this extraordinary man.[39]

Gibbon Wakefield inherited three reform traditions. He was born into a family of Quaker reformers and raised near London, where his father was an Enlightenment reformer, and family friends were Utilitarian reformers James Mill and Francis Place.[40] During a wayward youth, Gibbon Wakefield rebelled against them all. He was expelled from the best schools in Britain, then eloped with a sixteen-year-old heiress and settled down for a few years. When his wife died after childbirth, he took up the reckless life of a Regency rake with

BRITAIN'S NEW ZEALAND COLONIES:
Cultural Migrations, Major Settlements, and Regions, 1840–61

Pacific Ocean

170°   175°

35°   35°

Australian, British,
Irish Settlers

Auckland, 1840

Plymouth Company from
the west of England

NORTH ISLAND

New Plymouth, 1841

Hawkes
Bay

40°   Tasman Sea   Wanganui, 1840   40°

Nelson, 1842

Wellington, 1840

Wakefields'
New Zealand Company
Home Counties
of England

SOUTH ISLAND   Lyttelton, 1850

Canterbury,
1850

Canterbury Association from
the south of England

Otago,
1848   45°

Southland,
1861

Otago Association,
from central Scotland

0 Miles   100   200

0 Kilometers   200

Stewart Island

© 2012 Jeffrey L. Ward   170°   175°   180°

Young Edward Gibbon Wakefield, ca. 1823. This regency rake was converted to the cause of moral reform and social justice by a term in Newgate Prison. He invented the Wakefield System and became a prime mover of colonization in New Zealand.

much drinking, dueling, gambling, dissipation, and worse. In 1826 he abducted another heiress who was barely fifteen. For that crime he was lucky to escape a hanging, and landed in prison.[41]

Three years in Newgate turned this Regency rake into a moral reformer. Wakefield discovered at first hand what he called the "gross injustice" of English institutions.[42] In confinement he began to write impassioned essays about the cruelty of corrupt judges who sentenced a child of eight to hang for stealing a cake, and executed a pauper for stealing a sheep to feed his starving family. Wakefield documented the systemic unfairness of courts where "the lower the rank of the accused and the more desperate the need . . . the more likely a hanging."[43]

Other writings were about the suffering of the working poor whom he had met in jail. One was a harrowing account about small boys who swept the chimneys of London. Another discussed the condition of English prostitutes. "Prostitution is one thing," Wakefield wrote, "prostitutes are another."[44] In 1830–31, he took up another cause of rural rebellions in East Anglia and Kent, where masked insurgents called themselves Captain Swing and burned barns and haystacks of the gentry. Wakefield wrote a pamphlet called *Swing Unmasked*. Its subject was the "misery and degradation of the bulk of the people."[45] In every case he described the shattering impact of systemic unfairness on the lives of individuals.

Wakefield was not a revolutionist. His remedy was colonization, and he began to study English colonies throughout the world. The history of Australia gave him a horror of penal settlements and a strong belief that colonization must be an open process. He studied the United States and judged it to be morally deficient in the condition of its least advantaged people.

Wakefield condemned the intolerance of New England's Puritan founders and the injustice of southern planters who demanded liberty to practice slavery. He also wrote with genuine sympathy for the suffering of slaves.[46]

As a remedy, Wakefield planned a new set of colonies for New Zealand, founded on a strong sense of social order and natural justice, where people would gain the rewards that their moral condition deserved. Nothing would be given to them, but much could be earned by industry, sobriety, and the Victorian virtues. Wakefield's object was to create a hierarchical society that was more just and fair than that of England. His idea of fairness was about matching rank to merit, and wealth to virtue. Here was a principle of equity without equality.[47]

Wakefield believed that a material key to this idealized system was land policy. America's history persuaded him that free land encouraged slavery in the South and a disorderly, materialist, money-grubbing society in the North. His solution was a theory of "sufficient price," which artificially inflated the price of land in New Zealand. The object was to stabilize a social order, support a moral elite, encourage a propertied middle class, and assist migration of the deserving poor. To Americans it is an alien idea, but English reformers liked it.[48]

In 1837, Wakefield convened the first meeting of the New Zealand Colonization Association, which became the New Zealand Company. With energy and evangelical fervor, Wakefield himself drew in his brothers Arthur, William, and Daniel, and his son Edward Jerningham Wakefield. In Philip Temple's phrase, New Zealand became the family business, and the Wakefields pursued it on a grand scale.[49]

Gibbon Wakefield proposed to found separate colonies in New Zealand: one for a mixed group of moderate Anglicans; others for Methodists, High Anglicans, Scottish Presbyterians, Irish Catholics, and Jewish Zionists. The Catholic and Jewish colonies never materialized, but other settlements succeeded. They differed very much from one another and also from Wakefield's plans, but most shared some of the purposes that were close to his heart.[50]

In 1838, the New Zealand Company dispatched the ship *Tory* to explore the country and purchase sites for settlement from Maori. The most promising location was a large deepwater harbor on the north side of Cook Strait between New Zealand's North and South islands. Wakefield's associates thought it a perfect place for a commercial and administrative center. They named it Wellington, to

View of Wellington by Charles Heaphy, September 1841.

honor an eminent supporter and to cement "the association of the Mother Country with the future of the town."[51]

A year later, *Tory* sailed again in a fleet of four immigrant ships, and by June in 1840, nearly 1,500 British colonists had come ashore at Wellington. Their leaders were military men such as Gibbon Wakefield's brother Colonel William Wakefield. His home became Wellington's Government House, now the site of New Zealand's Parliament.[52] Another officer was Captain William Mein Smith, a "dedicated man with strong principles," who became surveyor general and laid out the town. These men were not liberal democrats. They valued order and discipline, and some were described as "totally autocratic." But they believed that the moral fiber of English society had been weakened by corruption and injustice. In Wellington they sought to combine order and hierarchy with equity and fairness.[53]

Wellington was highly stratified from the start, and dominated by a small elite with ties to the British gentry and aristocracy. Their names would echo through the history of New Zealand: Bannatyne, Barton, Beetham, Bidwill, Clifford, Crawford, Daniell, Featherstone, Fox, Goring, Holmes, Johnston, Martin, Mein Smith, Molesworth, Phillips, Riddford, St. Hill, Turnbull, Vavasour, Wakefield, and Waterhouse.[54] This ruling elite was very English, but more open than

England's. It accepted Nathaniel Levin and Abraham Hort, who were Jewish, and the O'Connor family, who were Irish Catholic.[55]

Below this gentry was another stratum of merchants and shop-keepers. And beneath that layer were what Victorians called the working class, about four hundred or five hundred people at the outset. Wellington also had a proletariat of discharged soldiers and seamen, and immigrants who had been recruited from London slums and rural poor rolls in the Home Counties.[56] By comparison with other settlements in New Zealand, Wellington's population was volatile, with high rates of emigration. From 1840 to 1870, the number of prosecutions for violence and drunkenness was twice as high as in other New Zealand colonies.[57]

Wellington also had a vibrant pattern of religious diversity, but within a narrow range. At an early date it had five Anglican churches of various inclinations, and congregations of Catholics, Wesleyans, Presbyterians, Independents, Primitive Methodists, and "perhaps one or two more."[58] Gradually a colonial society developed from these elements that mixed without merging. The settlement was divided by rank and religion, but united by its English identity. Wakefield's Wellington was New Zealand's imperial city, fiercely proud of its place in the British Empire.[59]

New Plymouth's West Country Migrants and the "Taranaki Mob," 1841–52

On the west coast of the North Island, near the high volcanic peak of Taranaki, a different sort of settlement followed in 1841. It was encouraged by the Wakefields but founded by a separate association called the Plymouth Company. Settlers came mainly from four counties in the west of England: Cornwall, Devon, Dorset, and Somerset. Many had suffered from a severe rural depression that persisted for a generation in the west of England. Its victims leaped at a chance to start over in New Zealand. The directors made a point of recruiting large groups from small hamlets, so that "instead of regret at leaving their native village," they would have "the pleasure of improving their circumstances among their own village friends and relations."[60]

They named their colony New Plymouth, after the Devon seaport whence they sailed.[61] Once on the ground, the founders labored under many difficulties. They had no safe harbor, and supplies had to be landed through heavy surf on a rocky lee shore. Capital was desperately short, and the company was compelled to cut wages.

Impoverished laborers found themselves worse off than in England, and they organized angry protests. The leaders were stung by complaints of injustice in their model colony. With help from Gibbon Wakefield, they responded by providing some with land and work, and others with a passage to Australia.[62] By 1845, the colony began to flourish. In the 1850s, it exported grain and firmly established itself as a prosperous farming community. From the start this was an agricultural colony with a strong West Country flavor. William Fox visited it and described it as "extremely picturesque, scattered up and down the sloping sides of easy hills, and more resembling an English village than any other in the colony."[63]

After the problem of unemployment was solved, most colonists were hardworking families of middling rank. One letter home reported in 1843, "Of absolutely idle people we have none, and the settlement has the appearance of a thriving and industrious community. It will be a beautiful *villagy* sort of country, wherein the population will be principally farmers and well-doing peasants, with a sprinkling of large landowners, professional men, and shopkeepers."[64]

After the first settlement, a small elite found its way to New Plymouth in the period from 1851 to 1856. Among them were six families

New Plymouth was a distinct settlement planted by West Country emigrants on fertile land around the great peak of Taranaki. It acquired a character uniquely its own.

who became one extended cousinage and called themselves the
Taranaki Mob. Their family names were Richmond, Atkinson, Wilson,
Hursthouse, Fell, and Stephenson Smith. Some came from Yorkshire
and Cheshire, where some of them were described by their historian
Frances Porter as "gentry in reduced circumstances" but proud of
rank and ancestry. Others had been merchants in London.[65]

These families brought to New Zealand a highly developed idea
of fairness and justice that grew from their own experience of oppression in England. Some were Unitarians who rejected the divinity
of Christ. Their beliefs excluded them from the Anglican Church
and also from full participation in English society. Unitarians of
wealth and cultivation could not attend England's leading public
schools or take a degree at Oxford or Cambridge. They could not sit
in Parliament or exercise political power. Some were forced off the
land, which they loved. Here again, yet another of New Zealand's
colonial elites shared a memory of institutionalized injustice and the
dream of a better world.[66]

The Taranaki Mob found New Plymouth much to their taste.
They felt at home in this reconstruction of a West Country farming
settlement, which Charles Hursthouse described as "a quiet little
community devoted to agricultural pursuits." But there was no
place in this vision of a "new old England" for Maori, except in the
role of a servile underclass, which a proud warrior people dis-
dained. One of the Taranaki cousins wrote, "Once the question of

*New Plymouth also attracted another group of immigrants who because of their Unitarian
religion could not enjoy full membership in English society. Their experience of unfairness
was a factor in their decision to move to New Zealand. The strongest figure in this tight-knit
group was Jane Maria Richmond Atkinson (left), the "mainstay" of the Taranaki mob.*

'land' is amicably settled with the natives, their presence in a district is highly advantageous every year affording a better supply of labour." Relations with Maori became deeply troubled. In the 1850s the Taranaki Mob took an active role in alienating land from Maori possessors and was largely responsible for transactions that led to a major war. The trouble began at Taranaki in 1860–61, then spread through the North Island. The Richmond-Atkinson connection was at the center of it.[67]

Even as they were very unjust to Maori, fairness among their own kind was important to these families. Within narrow bounds, the Unitarian elite of Taranaki shared a sense of equity as a tribal idea— among people like themselves. But once planted in a new place, even very limited ideas of justice had a way of growing. That growth process was fundamental to the history of New Zealand—and something similar happened in the history of the United States and Canada, all with strong altruist impulses but different kinds of altruism.

The Canterbury Migration:
John and Charlotte Godley's Anglican Utopia, 1848–55

Yet another New Zealand colony was planted at Canterbury on the South Island. It was technically a Wakefield settlement but with its own unique character, which set it apart from the purposes of Gibbon Wakefield himself. Canterbury was a product of the Oxford Movement, a high church Anglican awakening of broad importance in British history. Some have written that it was started by a sermon. On July 14, 1833, conservative churchman John Keble delivered from the university pulpit at Oxford a powerful message called "National Apostasy." He was unhappy about Catholic emancipation in Ireland, deeply distressed by liberalism, troubled by modernity, and sorely vexed by secular reform.[68]

John Keble's remedy was a return to faith, and a higher standard of worship and piety within the Church of England. He was a saintly character, much loved by those who knew him. Though he could have held high office, he set an example by becoming a country clergyman, devoted to the service of his parish. He inspired a movement that seated itself in Oxford's conservative colleges and spread swiftly through the Church of England. Keble's followers supported spiritual reform, and sought a refuge from modernity in romanticism and medieval revival. At the same time they sponsored missions in London slums, and among the rural poor of Britain and Ireland.[69]

Some of Keble's disciples looked abroad. They dreamed of a colony in New Zealand that might be a sanctuary for suffering people and a model for humankind. The leaders were John and Charlotte Godley, who lived very briefly in New Zealand but had a long reach in its history.

John Godley was born into the Anglo-Irish gentry. His wife, Charlotte, was of the English aristocracy. He went to Christ Church College and was caught up in the Oxford Movement. She was inspired by the Evangelical Movement in North Wales.[70] In 1839, John Godley was called to the Irish bar, but he did not have a lawyer's temperament and described himself as a "briefless barrister." He took another job as high sheriff for the county of Leitrim, and it was the turning point of his life. In the Irish countryside he witnessed a depth of suffering that caused him to devote his life to reform at home and colonization abroad.

Godley, like other early leaders in New Zealand, was also no Democrat or Liberal. On a visit to the United States, he was appalled by what he called its "leveling spirit," and by what he took to be its excess of liberty and freedom. He reacted very strongly against the principles of the American and French revolutions, and also against some of the values of the Enlightenment. In

John and Charlotte Godley led the founding of Canterbury, another settlement with its own distinct origin and character. They were only briefly in New Zealand, but their distinctive values and purposes had a long reach.

particular he detested the utilitarian ideas of Jeremy Bentham and Benjamin Franklin as mere materialism, "the last degradation of political thought."[71] But Godley also did not approve of what England was becoming, with its factory towns, urban slums, rural poverty, and modern plutocrats. He was a staunch conservative—so staunch that he regarded even Tory leader Sir Robert Peel as an "old Whig at heart," but he added, "Better an old Whig than a new radical."[72]

John Godley worked out his own theory of conservative reform. He wrote that the error of the Whigs was "derivation of power from below." Godley believed that "principles of conduct should be founded upon morality, not upon natural rights." Here was another vision of the good society, one in which justice, fairness, and equity were more important then freedom, liberty, and democracy. Increasingly he was drawn to colonization in New Zealand as a vehicle for his ideas. Godley began to think in terms of founding a colony that might relieve suffering at home, and also serve as a model for social reform. In five letters to the *Spectator*, he developed his conservative vision of New Zealand, which was very different from the liberal purposes of British officials such as Sir James Stephen. Godley complained that the only enemies of colonization were the Colonial Office.[73]

His purpose was to found a just and fair society based "on duties, not upon rights, and so upon revealed religion." To that end he organized a group called the Canterbury Association in 1848. Its fifty members included two archbishops and seven bishops who were leaders of the Oxford Movement. One-third of the Associates had gone to the same college, Christ Church in Oxford. Many were relatives of Godley, his wife, and her eminent brother-in-law Lord Lyttelton.[74]

Together this group began to plan a colony in New Zealand as an Anglican utopia. Not everyone could come. Each emigrant was required to submit a letter of recommendation from his vicar, testifying that "the applicant is sober, industrious and honest, and that he and all his family are amongst the most respectable of their class in the parish." Even ordinary respectability would not suffice for this band of "Canterbury Pilgrims." It was very much an Anglican enterprise. Wakefield wrote to Godley, "The plan somehow repels desperate and bad people, such as commonly form a large proportion of the materials in a new settlement. Those whom it attracts are circumspect, cautious, and slow to decide."[75]

Emigrants were carefully screened in other ways as well. All adults were required to have a medical certificate and to be less than forty years old, preferably in their twenties. Married couples were favored over single persons. Strong preference went to "farm servants, shepherds, domestic servants, country mechanics and artisans." The object was to create a rural population with gradations of social class. Surviving immigrant lists indicate that these rules were closely followed. Age limits were strictly observed, and the gender ratio was very near parity. Recruitment was run from Charing Cross and drew heavily on London and the Home Counties. Most emigrants came from a broad triangular area in southern England, from Kent to Cornwall and north to Northampton.[76]

The nucleus of the colony came in four emigrant ships and were thereafter remembered as the "old settlers" of Canterbury. Godley went out in advance as chief resident agent, reporting to the Canterbury Association in England. When the first fleet arrived in 1850, he was there to welcome them, with his wife at his side, fully engaged in the same cause. When they appeared, Charlotte Godley remembered, her husband didn't know whether to laugh or cry and "I believe ended by doing both."[77]

Other shiploads followed, and by 1855 the numbers had increased to 3,500 Canterbury Pilgrims. Godley named his capital

This ball in the earliest years of Canterbury captured something of the tone of society among its founding elite. Other settlers were quick to follow and created a more complex set of cultures.

Christchurch. "I hope that my old college is grateful to me," he wrote. He also laid out towns on the Canterbury plain, and encouraged pastoral leases for large landowners on generous terms to create an Anglican gentry in the colony. He also fought for self-government and said in 1851, "I would rather be governed by a Nero on the spot than by a board of angels in London, because we could if worst came to worst, cut off Nero's head, but we could not get at the board in London at all."[78]

Godley had difficult relations with Gibbon Wakefield, who did not approve of the Oxford Movement and thought it was moving in the wrong direction. Canterbury remained functionally separate from Wakefield's Wellington colony and was organized on different principles. A major presence was Charlotte Godley, who was very active in church affairs, worked actively with women in the colony, and had an impact on social relations.[79]

Another leader of similar values was James FitzGerald, the first man to leap ashore from the ship *Charlotte Jane* in December 1850. His career was similar to that of many other leaders in New Zealand. FitzGerald had failed to win a commission in the army. For two years he wandered through North Britain and discovered for himself the depth of rural suffering. After that encounter he took up the cause of colonization as a remedy. In Canterbury he became superintendent of the colony, traveled about in a four-wheeled dog cart, and worked energetically to promote the purposes of the founders. FitzGerald founded a college on the model of his alma mater, Christ's College in Cambridge. He was a strong advocate for fairness and justice to Maori and played a major role in enacting a Native Rights Act and Native Lands Act.[80]

Others in Canterbury did not share these high purposes. A leader of a different stripe was Joseph Thomas, the colony's surveyor and land agent. He took for himself some of the best land on the Canterbury Plain and was joined by immigrants who had little interest in Christian utopias or moral reforms. The grazing lands attracted Australian pastoralists called Shagroons who were contemptuous of the Canterbury Pilgrims.[81]

But even as Canterbury changed that way, the settlement continued to bear the impress of the visionaries who had founded it. It did so in its churches, schools, social institutions, and especially through the leadership of its women, who preserved the colony's first purposes. John and Charlotte Godley stayed until Canterbury was self-governing, then were forced to go home by his poor health, to their regret. It was a short stay, but their vision and example

were long remembered. Gladstone called John Godley "a king
among men," a generous and large-spirited leader, and Charlotte
Godley was his consort. Together they made a difference in New
Zealand.[82]

Otago's Scottish Migration:
The North British Utopia of Thomas and Jane Burns, 1848–60

Edward Gibbon Wakefield encouraged the founding of yet
another colony in Otago, south of Canterbury. It was different from
the rest. The sponsor was a separate colonization society called the
Otago Association, and its founding population was predominantly
Scottish. In its first twelve years, from 1848 to 1860, more than 80 percent of colonists to Otago were Scots. Only 16 percent were English
and Welsh (very few Welsh), and 2 percent Irish. All other nationalities
amounted to less than 1 percent.[83]

Otago's population came mostly from the central belt of North
Britain that stretched across the narrow waist of the country from
Glasgow to Edinburgh. The leading counties were Midlothian and
Lanarkshire. Emigrants came from every county in Scotland, but
comparatively few were from the northern Highlands, or from the
borderlands that contributed so heavily to the settlement of the
North American backcountry.[84] The 350 "old settlers" of 1848 were
mainly Scottish farmers and crofters. Thomas Burns described
them as "the better educated and more religiously disposed of the
lower and middle classes of our home population, who valued religious principles so highly, and coveted education for their children." Nearly half were women or girls. In 1852 the gender ratio
was 126 males per 100 females, very near to parity for a colonial
migration.[85]

The leaders of this enterprise encouraged their Scottish Pilgrims to migrate in families, and 80 percent did so in the early
years. They also encouraged settlement in clan-groups. One leader
wrote, "The clanship of the Scotch will here find its best use. Neighbor will act upon Neighbor. . . . [T]he colony will, in very deed, be
a mere outlying province of Caledonia."[86] The clan structure of
Scotland was no invented myth, as some English relativists have al-
leged.[87] It was transplanted to Otago, with its proud piping traditions, its birth and burial practices, its New Year celebrations, and its
taste for food and drink. The culture and customs of Scotland were
carefully nourished through much of Otago and Southland. In the
high country, shepherds continued to speak Gaelic for many years.

The Presbyterian Kirk was at the center of society. If anything, Scottish identity grew stronger when it was carried to the South Pacific. Later in the nineteenth century, the Caledonian Societies and Burns Societies flourished throughout Otago and Southland, and kept the flame alive.[88]

Otago was at first tightly controlled by a small elite. In a letter of April 14, 1844, on plans for schools and the land system, Thomas Burns wrote to James MacAndrew, "I quite agree with you that, had time and other things permitted, it would perhaps served some good purpose if three or four of us could have had some viva voce discussion with you . . . on certain subjects of importance to this colony."[89]

With Burns and MacAndrew, those three or four included John McGlashan, Captain William Cargill, and later William Bannerman. All were Scots. Most went to the University of Edinburgh and joined the Free Church of Scotland. All were fiercely proud of their Scottish heritage, but they had suffered much in Scotland—some from the tyranny of circumstance, others from the cruelty of oppression, and many from both. William Cargill's father was an eminent Edinburgh lawyer who died when the son was fifteen years old; the family was plunged into suffering that was not of its making. Thomas Burns lost his living at the age of forty-seven when he joined a movement to reform the Church of Scotland. His family was turned out of its home, and his congregation was expelled from its church. They were forced to worship in the cold rain of New Prestwick and could find no hope of fair treatment in the Old World. These Scottish dissenters were driven by their enemies to think of emigration. As it was for so many of New Zealand's other early settler-leaders, their avowed purpose was to attempt a "godly experiment" by founding a more just and fair society on the other side of the world.[90]

In that respect the Scottish founders of Otago had something in common with the Wakefield Connexion, the Canterbury Pilgrims, and Taranaki's Unitarian Mob. Five of New Zealand's first "six colonies," as William Fox called them in 1851, were founded in that same large spirit. But they were different and even opposite in other ways. The Wakefields and Godleys had rejected the New England model in North America. Burns and Cargill embraced it, as a prototype for a society in which settlers shared a common religion and common values. They called it a "class settlement." Burns wrote, "If a colony starts on the same principles on which Otago and Canterbury started, as did the Puritans in New England, . . . there is no

Yet another major emigration flowed from Scotland to Otago. Its leader was the Reverend Thomas Burns (right), a victim of gross injustice in the Church of Scotland, along with his congregation. Another leader in Otago was Captain William Cargill (left), whose Scottish family suffered severely from misfortunes and oppressions that were not of their making. In Otago they sought to found a new Scotland on principles of social justice. The culture of this region still preserves the spirit of its origins.

alternative but to start a class settlement, embracing only such individuals as will sincerely and cordially consent to live under the same law and worship in the same house."[91]

In other ways, the Otago experiment was far removed from Massachusetts. Even as Burns and his colleagues admired the New England model from a distance, when they actually met a New Englander they were appalled by his air of autonomy, democracy, liberty, and freedom. It happened on their arrival in Dunedin, when a pilot came aboard to guide them into the harbor. One of the Scots wrote, "We received him gladly; he was a Yankee from North America, and his air of independence rather astonished us." Thereafter they did not welcome Yankees to their Scottish utopia.[92]

Also excluded at the start were Roman Catholics, Socinians, Socialists, and Free Thinkers. The Scottish leaders went after H. B. Graham, publisher of the first independent newspaper, the *Otago News*. Graham was an independent-minded journalist. Worse, despite his

Scottish name, he was an Englishman from the border fortress town of Carlisle, which had launched many a raid on Scotland. When he freely expressed dissident opinions in Dunedin, the Scots who ran the colony bought him out, changed the name of the paper, and put it under a "committee of management." They made life miserable for settlers who challenged their political hegemony, or merely failed to fit in. Otago, like most other new settlements, attracted a good many free spirits, who were perceived by the Scottish leaders as "hordes of loose characters." By 1852, the session minutes of the Deacon's Court reported with an air of satisfaction that "most of them had removed themselves."[93]

The leaders themselves were a close group, and tightly inter-married. William Bannerman married Jane Burns, second daughter of Thomas Burns. MacAndrew and Cargill founded family dynasties, and their descendants became an extended cousinage. The moral arbiters of this society were their wives, especially Thomas Burns's wife, Clementina. Here again, as in the rest of New Zealand's first six colonies, strong women played leading roles in shaping colonial culture.[94]

The Otago Way was a mixture of light and shadow. Burns wrote of excluding other opinions, but he also insisted on the importance of educational opportunities for people of all ranks, and especially for the poor. The leaders of this colony founded New Zealand's first college, now Otago University, a first-class institution. They took the lead in the education of women.[95] The Scottish culture of Otago was narrow in its exclusive ideas of ethnicity and religion, but broad in its idea of equity among its own people. It was severe in its moral code, but serious in its intellectual purposes. That combination appeared in both the English Calvinists who founded Massachusetts and the Scottish Calvinists who went to Otago. They were tough, hard, diffi-cult people, but also upright and strong-willed, with a high sense of justice and moral purpose. Even as the population of Otago would later grew more diverse, the character of these Scottish founders entered deep into the culture of this New Zealand region.

The Open City of Auckland: John Logan Campbell's "Fair Land of Poenamo"

Not every New Zealand colony began with a Wakefield system, a Godley vision, a Burns experiment, or a Taranaki dream. Other set-tlements were more open, secular, and entrepreneurial. The leading example was the city of Auckland.[96]

Disapproving scholars have written of Auckland as an historical accident and have stressed its pluralism and "haphazard process" of growth. Part of that interpretation is true enough. Its settlers were more diverse than the founders of Wellington, Nelson, Canterbury, Dunedin, and New Plymouth. In 1851, Auckland's population was 31 percent Irish, a larger proportion than in most New Zealand settlements. So many were Australians that William Fox described Auckland as "a mere section of the town of Sydney transplanted to the shores of New Zealand, filled with tradesmen."[97] A large number of inhabitants were Maori, also actively engaged in trade. More than a few settlers in Hauraki Gulf were American entrepreneurs, like the fabulous Bully Webster from Portland, Maine, a successful entrepreneur. The population in Auckland was pluralist, highly acquisitive, and very quick to grow.[98]

William Fox was one of many New Zealanders who did not approve of Auckland. "As an instance of colonization," he wrote, "it was altogether rotten, delusive and Algerine." Other New Zealanders were appalled. H. B. Morton wrote, "I recall the disparaging tone in which Auckland was spoken of in the South. . . . [A]ll were alike distrusted."[99]

These hostile judgments were mistaken. Auckland was not an accident. It was open and pluralist because its founders wanted it that way. Even today, the culture of this city still remains an artifact of their intentions. Auckland may not have begun with a settled plan, but always it had a purpose. John Logan Campbell wrote to his father, "The whole and entire object of everyone here is making money, the big fishes eating the little ones."[100]

John Logan Campbell became the first citizen of Auckland, a settlement with a character unlike any other in New Zealand. He wrote to his father that the "entire object of everyone here is making money, biggest fishes eating little ones." To that end, he and his friends deliberately created a society that was open, pluralist, dynamic, and with an aggressive spirit of enterprise.

The biggest fish was Logan Campbell himself. He was present at the creation, pitching a tent in 1840 near the water at what is now the bottom of Queen Street. After many adventures he died in 1912 at the age of ninety-four, a blind patriarch with a flowing white beard. Even in his last years he was the leader of a city that revered him as "the father of Auckland."[101]

Campbell had been born in Scotland, the grandson of a baronet in a family of high rank and small resources. He came of age in a time of scarcity and had to find his fortune elsewhere. His father mort-gaged the family home to raise a capital of a thousand pounds, and in 1839 Campbell resolved to try his luck in the Australian sheep busi-ness. He was appalled by what he found there. A pivotal moment was a night in an Australian tavern, where he watched in horror as a coffle of convicts were made to dance, shuffling in their shackles and chains to the screech of an ill-played fiddle. Looking on was a drunken crowd with what he described as "well-marked countenances of the true con-vict's stamp." That sight, and a discovery that Australian sheep barely brought ninepence a head, persuaded Campbell to "forswear the Great Convict Land." He started over in New Zealand.[102]

Logan Campbell sailed to the Gulf of Hauraki and came ashore in what is now Coromandel Harbour. On the beach he found a small cluster of fern shelters, log huts, and rough buildings inhabited by an "extraordinary assemblage of characters," Australian, Irish, Ameri-can, Maori, and three ambitious young Scottish capitalists. The Scots learned that the governor of New Zealand was about to select a site for his capital, and they guessed that he would choose the narrow isthmus of Tamaki, between Waitemata Harbor, which looks north-east to the Pacific, and Manukau Harbour, which opens to the south-west and the Tasman Sea. Campbell wrote that he and his associates had "one fixed determination, and that was to become purchasers of town lots in the new capital and settle down there, acting as very small landsharks."[103]

That gamble paid off handsomely, and they invested their profits in commerce, which also brought a large return. Logan Campbell and his Scottish friend William Brown founded the most successful mer-chant firm in the young town. With capital from a silent partner in Scotland, they did well in trade and better in real estate, the quickest way to wealth in new settlements. It was an economy of boom and bust, and very few survived. Years later Campbell remembered that "nearly every one of the young capital's first merchants came to grief and were blotted out." His firm survived by diversifying and by adding breweries and distilleries, which did a "thundering business" in down times.[104]

Logan Campbell was a landshark, but with a social conscience. He led many civic movements to make Auckland into a functioning city. In 1853, when Auckland acquired an elective government, his Scotch Clique took the name of the Progress Party and became active

Campbell led in making many civic improvements, such as this park with One Tree Hill which he donated to the city. He died in 1912, a blind patriarch with a flowing beard who was revered as the "father of Auckland."

in politics. They created the financial institutions that the city needed: the Bank of New Zealand, the New Zealand Insurance Company, and the New Zealand Loan and Mercantile Company. Altogether Logan Campbell served on more than forty standing committees, boards, trusts, or directorates in Auckland.[105]

He became a linchpin for Auckland's many elites and helped to create a structure that set it apart from other cities in New Zealand. From the beginning of its history, power was divided in Auckland. New Zealand's governors made it their early home and slowly increased their authority. Many governors got on better with Maori than with Pakeha and had their own imperial base. Also in early Auckland were New Zealand's chief jurists and lawyers such as William Martin, Attorney General William Swainson, and Registrar Thomas Outhwaite, who lived at Judges Bay and Taurarua.[106] Religious leaders such as Bishop George Augustus Selwyn were often there as well, and they built many churches and chapels that still stand today.[107] Once again many cultural leaders were women, such as Mary Ann Martin, wife of the chief justice.[108] The British Army and Royal Navy were also an important presence in Auckland. Their officers also became active in sponsoring the first racecourses, cricket clubs, and other associations. In Auckland all of these groups intersected with Logan Campbell's "Limited Circle" of like-minded businessmen.[109] Campbell also led civic campaigns of his own. More than any other individual he gave the city its parks, especially One Tree Hill, which became a symbol of Auckland, and insisted that the parks should provide sporting grounds and recreation for its people.[110] He also made a special point of recognizing Maori, whom he greatly respected. From the start their culture became an important part of the city's diversity.[111]

Auckland was never a single consolidated community, but with Logan Campbell's leadership it became a functioning society with a strong sense of its own character—as open and pluralist as he meant it to be, as restless and dynamic as he was himself. Even as Logan Campbell and his city were devoted to the pursuit of wealth, he was also driven by ideals of honor, equity, and fairness, in yet another meaning of that versatile idea.[112]

Constellations of Value in Settler Societies

In 1842, a correspondent wrote to the *Nelson Examiner*, "There is, sir, yet another class in those colonies—a class of men, who, though they cannot be said to have left their native land for conscience sake, as did the early American colonies, were yet not sorry to leave behind them the bigotry and uncharitableness of the old country. This class is not powerless, for that it belongs to no sect; but rather the more powerful, for that it belongs to all."[113]

In both New Zealand and what is now the United States, English colonization was similar as a process, but different in result. It created two complex constellations of cultural value that appeared in the early years of settlement and persist to our own time. Every major group in America's great colonial migrations shared a particular concern for liberty and freedom, and those founding purposes are still a national obsession. New Zealand's British colonists had a special concern for justice, equity, and fairness—three ideas, not one. From the start, the hard reality of life in these new settlements always fell short of the soaring ideals that inspired them. These many failings did not diminish those great principles but inspired a continuing growth of ethical traditions in generations that were yet to come.

TWO BRITISH EMPIRES

Imperial Systems as Ethical Schools

> While it treated them as a conquered people, it gave them so much liberty that they could easily rebel.
>
> —J. R. Seeley on the first British Empire

> This was the saving flaw of British imperialism, for this Empire did have an ideology after all: the High Victorian concept of Fair Play.
>
> —James Morris on the second British Empire

HISTORIANS draw a distinction between two British Empires. The first began in the seventeenth century, reached its climax after the accession of George III in 1760, and was shattered by the American War of Independence. The second British Empire rose on the ruins of the first. It began to grow in the late eighteenth century, reached its peak in the period from 1890 to 1945, and came apart very rapidly after the Second World War.[1]

These two great systems briefly became the largest empires in modern history, but by the measure of ancient Rome or imperial China they were very short-lived. Each British Empire lasted less than two centuries. Today not much remains of all their pomp and power except fading memories, forgotten monuments, and piles of paper. But both British Empires still make a difference in the world. Their cultural importance continues to increase, long after their power has declined. The language that English-speaking people established on every continent (even Antarctica) has become a cultural imperium in its own right. English traditions of law and self-government have taken root in many nations and are flourishing in new forms. The largest, most stable, and most dynamic open societies in America, Asia, Africa, and Oceania all have grown from British colonies.[2]

In some ways the two British Empires were similar, and many people think of them as one. But in many important traits they were profoundly different. They were founded in different eras, organized on different principles, and governed in different ways, and they have left different legacies in the world. The United States and New Zealand are cases in point. We are cultural cousins, because we both began as British colonies. But we are second cousins twice removed, because our imperial origins were not the same.

America and the First British Empire: A School of Liberty and Freedom

The special character of the first British Empire was created by a clash of dynamic opposites: aggressive rulers, and assertive colonists who did not take kindly to being ruled. That collision was strong and violent in North America. As we have seen, Britain's mainland colonies were settled mostly by voluntary migration. There were major exceptions in many thousands of British convicts and four hundred thousand African slaves. But more than a million immigrants came to North America as volunteers before 1776. A majority found their own way to the New World, and many paid their own passage. Most had been victims of persecution, tyranny, and exploitation in their native countries. Many chose to emigrate, in search of religious freedom, political rights, and economic opportunity. As a result, British America acquired a more diverse population than other European empires. It was also more open and very quick to grow. From the start its freeborn colonists were accustomed to managing their own affairs. They tended to be autonomous, enterprising, and very difficult to control.[3]

These qualities caused deep concern in London. British leaders presided over the most dynamic empire in modern history, but they looked upon other imperial systems with admiration, and even with envy. New Spain and New France appeared (from a distance) to be models of order and control. From 1634 to 1783, and especially after 1760, authorities in London tried many times to impose similar controls on their own colonies. All of their efforts failed—and thereby hangs a tale.

Imperial Dysfunction and Colonial Autonomy, 1634–85

The first attempt to control Britain's American colonies was made by Charles I, who attempted to fasten a system of royal absolutism on his subjects. From 1629 to 1640, he launched a new experiment in government and tried to rule England without a Parliament. At the same time he ordered Archbishop William Laud to enforce religious conformity on English Puritans. That effort drove many dissenters to America, where they defiantly governed themselves.

The king tried to curb the autonomy of his colonies (especially Puritan New England) by creating a Commission for Foreign Plantations in 1634. He appointed Archbishop Laud as its head, with orders to reduce the Puritan colonies to conformity, by force if necessary. A "great ship" was built for that purpose. The people of New England made ready to defend themselves, but before the ship could sail, Charles I ran short of money. He was compelled to call Parliament into session, and one of its first acts was to order the execution of Archbishop Laud. The Commission for Foreign Plantations disappeared, and the American colonies continued to run their own affairs.

When the English Civil War began between Parliamentary Roundheads and Royalist Cavaliers, a resurgent House of Commons claimed the right to regulate the colonies and created its own Commission for Plantations in 1643. Its purpose was to impose order on

Archbishop William Laud, implacable enemy of the Puritan movement, was the choice of Charles I to head his Commission on Foreign Plantations in 1634, with orders to bring New England to obedience. He succeeded only in driving it toward independence in its earliest years.

the growing empire. But before it could act effectively, Parliament was overthrown by Puritan general Oliver Cromwell, who had grown weary of its debates and imposed a dictatorship on England with himself as "Lord Protector." The Parliamentary Commission on Plantations collapsed, and the colonies continued to go their own way.

After 1653, Cromwell's Protectorate attempted yet again to control the colonies, much as the king and Parliament had tried to do. Two new imperial bodies were established by the Protector's Council: a Committee for Foreign Plantations (1655) and a Committee for America (1656). The colonies resisted, and a military expedition was mounted against Royalists in Virginia. Oliver Cromwell's death in 1658 put an end to this effort. Once again, the colonies preserved a large measure of autonomy.

The restoration of Charles II in 1660 was followed by a more sustained effort to create an imperial system. The King's Privy Council invented another new body called the Committee for Trade and Plantations, or the Lords of Trade (1660). Various other councils and committees also functioned in a fitful way, but the fragility of England's restored monarchy and the caution of the king himself prevented strong measures, except in Virginia after Bacon's Rebellion. Once more the colonies retained their habit of self-government, and exercised it for many generations.[4]

Failed Tyrants as Teachers of Liberty and Freedom: Edmund Andros and Francis Nicholson

The dynamics of this first British Empire appeared most clearly in the events that followed the reign of Charles II. In 1685, his elderly brother James II came to the throne and tried to lead Britain toward Roman Catholicism and Royal Absolutism. He appointed a viceroy for America, Sir Edmund Andros (1637–1714), an energetic English Royalist who governed most of the mainland colonies in the course of his long career. Most Americans have never heard of him, but he had a major impact on their history.

In 1685, James II resolved to curb the autonomy of the American colonies, by consolidating all of them from Maine to Delaware into a new body called the Dominion of New England. The king appointed Sir Edmund Andros as its royal governor. His orders were to abolish assemblies, make the laws himself, levy taxes with a council of his choosing, "judge any offender" in capital or criminal cases, and "put to death or keep and preserve alive, at your discretion" anyone who resisted him. His authority in America exceeded that of the king himself in England.

In office, Sir Edmund Andros became even more arbitrary than his powers. He arrived in Boston with a British warship and the first red-coated Regulars that the town had seen. Andros appointed his own sheriffs and jailers, suspended habeas corpus, arrested people at will, convicted them without indictment, and imprisoned them without trial. He vacated land titles by fiat and gave them to his friends. He imposed new taxes, raised fees to unprecedented levels, and fastened new charges on commerce. A Congregational meetinghouse (Old South in Boston) was taken for his own Anglican services every Sunday while its Puritan congregation was ordered to wait in the street. Andros banned town meetings, except one a year to execute his laws. He silenced even his own council. When constables complained of disorders by his soldiers and sailors, the governor "fell into a great rage, and did curse them, and said they ought to be sent to Gaol." His enemies agreed that Andros was brave and energetic. Even his friends allowed that he was "passionate," "hasty in speech," "rude," "insolent," and in a word tyrannical.[5]

Finally the people of New England grew weary of this man. On the morning of April 18, 1689, Sir Edmund Andros awoke to find two thousand men with weapons in their hands, on a ring of rising hills around the town of Boston. The colonial leaders of Massachusetts proceeded with practiced skill and implacable purpose. They found a way to disarm the red-coated Regulars without firing a shot, disabled the governor's warship without a fight by removing her

Sir Edmund Andros was appointed in 1685 by James II as his virtual viceroy for all the American colonies from New England to Pennsylvania. Andros vacated colonial charters, abolished assemblies, levied taxes by fiat, and violated most of the protections that later appeared in American bills of rights. The results were the American revolutions of 1689, which overthrew Andros. His failed tyranny deepened American ideas of liberty and freedom.

sails, and confined Sir Edmund's officers in the Boston jail, along with the former jailer, "for their protection." The governor himself was persuaded to submit to house arrest "for his own safety." All this was done by restrained application of overwhelming force, and no loss of life.[6]

In 1689, New England's rebel leaders also appointed a Council of Safety, much as their ancestors had done in the English Civil War, and their descendants would do again in the American Revolution of 1775. The people of Massachusetts recovered their government, and similar revolutions occurred in five other American colonies. At the same time a parallel event happened in Britain, where it was long remembered as the "Glorious Revolution." This great rising removed James II from power and replaced him with a Protestant dyarchy of Mary Stuart and her Dutch consort, William of Orange. It laid the foundations of a stable government in England, with a many-headed sovereign who was called the "King-in-Parliament."[7]

Sir Edmund Andros remained a prisoner in Massachusetts for nearly a year, then returned to England, where he was set free. To the amazement of American colonists, he was sent back to the New World as royal governor of Virginia and Maryland. There he became embroiled in bitter conflicts with the great Chesapeake planters, and even with Virginia's Anglican ministers. Sir Edmund was recalled just in time to prevent another colonial revolution, and given a job as governor of Guernsey in 1704, where the people of his own native island also turned against him. He retreated to the sanctuary of the Court in London and died in 1714. By the test of his own purposes, Sir Edmund Andros had been a spectacular failure, but he succeeded remarkably in teaching many unintended lessons in liberty and freedom to American colonists. He also taught them that their actions could make a difference in the world, and that they could triumph over tyranny, as they had done over him.

What is astonishing about the first British Empire is how many tyrants were dispatched to America, and how incompetent were their tyrannies. One more example might make the point. When Sir Edmund Andros came to Boston, his British soldiers were commanded by Captain Francis Nicholson (1655–1728), a fierce defender of royal prerogative. Later he became governor or "lieutenant governor-in-chief" of five American colonies in New York, Virginia, Maryland, Nova Scotia, and South Carolina. Nicholson made himself much hated by his wild rages and tyrannical

Francis Nicholson became governor of five American colonies. His repeated acts of tyranny challenged Americans to defend their liberty and freedom in conflicts that the colonists usually won.

manner. Virginians long remembered an episode when he courted a beautiful and spirited young heiress. She spurned him, and Governor Nicholson swore that if she dared to wed another, he would cut the throat of the groom, kill the clergyman who performed the service, and execute any justice who licensed the marriage. This and other quarrels with the great planters on the Virginia Council ended in his transfer to South Carolina, where more tempests followed.[8]

Imperial tyrants such as Edmund Andros and Francis Nicholson repeatedly challenged American settlers to defend their rights, by violating them in ways so outrageous and yet so ineffective that the colonists usually won. American traditions of liberty and freedom grew stronger with every test. The deep and impassioned American belief in liberty and freedom derives in large part from forgotten colonial conflicts that continued for nearly two centuries.[9]

Spiritual Imperialism: Bishop Secker's Blundering Tyranny

For many Americans, political and economic challenges by imperial officials seemed less threatening than other imperial threats to their religious freedom. The central figure was Thomas Secker (1693–1768), an Anglican clergyman who never came to America,

*Archbishop Thomas Secker's blundering
ecclesiastical imperialism in the 1760s
gave many American colonists a motive for
revolution that was more powerful than
issues of taxation and representation.*

but did much to provoke its revolution.[10] Secker was born to a Puritan family in Nottinghamshire. He converted to the Church of England and embraced its high church doctrines with evangelical zeal. As Bishop of Bristol and Archbishop of Canterbury, he confirmed vast crowds of Anglican believers by the evangelical methods of dissenting ministers.[11]

Secker also became the head of the Society for the Propagation of the Gospel in Foreign Parts, an Anglican missionary society that became very active in the colonies. He believed that the colonists were "wicked, and dissolute, and brutal in every respect" and thought it his duty to bring them to civilization and the Church of England, which he regarded as one and the same. The colonists had thought that the Society for the Propagation of the Gospel would proselytize Indians and Africans, but Secker built a mission next to Harvard College, where his heathens were Congregational undergraduates, whom he sought to convert to his Anglican faith. New Englanders were appalled.

Secker also announced his purpose of consecrating an Anglican bishop for America, and sought to establish the Church of England as the official religion in every colony, complete with the imposition of church taxes and church courts. He succeeded only in uniting every American denomination against him, even low church Anglicans, and he inspired a sense of urgent concern for religious liberty in the colonies. Many Americans felt more deeply threatened by religious tyranny than by taxation without representation. Jonathan

Mayhew wrote, "Is it not enough that they persecuted us out of the old world? Will they pursue us into the new?"[12]

The Legacy of the First British Empire:
America's Obsession with Liberty and Freedom

These many imperial conflicts are little remembered in the United States, but together they had a major impact on its history. From Sir Edmund Andros and Francis Nicholson to Archbishop Secker, six generations of American colonists were repeatedly challenged by imperial leaders to fight for their rights. The American obsession with liberty and freedom was in large part a product of that long experience. The people of the United States are today its heirs.

Altogether, conflicts within the first British Empire also shaped the substantive meaning of American liberty and freedom. They encouraged colonists to link liberty and freedom to rights of representative government. Imperial leaders attempted to suppress or abolish representative assemblies, as Andros did in the Dominion for New England, and Lord North and George III tried to do in the Coercive Acts of 1774. Royal governors prorogued colonial assemblies at pleasure, refused to call elections, and rejected requests to summon assemblies into session. Authorities in London disallowed colonial statutes and tried to limit the colonies' legislative powers in other ways. But the assemblies kept meeting, and the only effect was to deepen American ideas of liberty and freedom as inseparably linked to inalienable rights of self-government.

Imperial officials also greatly stimulated an idea of American liberty and freedom as a web of individual rights, mainly by the process of repeatedly infringing them. The many state bills of rights that followed independence were long lists of particular liberties that had been explicitly attacked by imperial officials before 1775. The federal Bill of Rights is itself in large measure a summary of specific grievances against imperial leaders from 1760 to 1775. Most of its major provisions were direct responses to acts of tyranny by British officeholders.

The tyrannical administration of the first British Empire also encouraged Americans to think of liberty and freedom as anchored in written constitutions. British officials repeatedly granted charters to American colonies, then arbitrarily took them away again. The result was an American tradition of liberty and freedom that would always be grounded in fundamental written documents. This was very different from constitutional traditions in England itself. It grew stronger in the colonies from a repetition of ineffectual challenges by imperial officials.

The rulers of the old empire, against their own intent, also greatly stimulated an idea of federal government in America. When America colonists tried to league together in the eighteenth century, imperial officials responded with intense opposition. A colonial congress at Albany in 1754 was perceived as dangerous to the empire, even when the American colonists were coming together to support it. This also had major consequences for American ideas of free institutions.

The regulatory acts of imperial authorities also encouraged American ideas of economic liberty as free trade. Economic policies in the empire were strongly mercantilist, from the first Navigation Acts to the outbreak of the American Revolution. The empire was organized as a closed economic system, with sweeping regulations of industry and commerce, all designed primarily to increase the prosperity of the mother country. The experience of living in such an economy greatly encouraged an idea of economic liberty in America.

In all of these ways, the first British Empire became a school of liberty and freedom, with incompetent tyrants as master teachers. In London, J. R. Seeley observed that "it claimed to rule the colonists because they were Englishmen and brothers, and yet it ruled them as if they were conquered Indians. And again while it treated them as conquered people, it gave them so much liberty that they could easily rebel."[13] This continued for more than 150 years, through six generations of strife between the colonies and the mother country. From that long experience Americans developed an obsession with liberty and freedom. That habit of mind found a permanent place in American ways of thinking about the world.

New Zealand and the Second British Empire

The people of New Zealand had a very different imperial experience, mainly because the second British Empire (that part of it with British colonists) was founded on new principles and managed in a different spirit. In the mid-nineteenth century its administrative center was a very odd building at 14 Downing Street in London, a few doors away from the present residence of the prime minister.

Number 14 was a large, clumsy structure, made of several houses that had been cobbled together without a central plan or symmetry. Large windows and heavy gables were pitched this way and that, and

The British Colonial Office at 14 Downing Street, London, was the seat of the second British Empire until 1876. Its rambling architecture symbolized the structure of imperial administration in that era.

a profusion of doors offered no obvious point of entry or departure. The architecture was awkward and very austere, but it was a bluff and honest building, with a character distinctly its own. Until it was pulled down in 1876, this ramshackle structure was the Colonial Office of the United Kingdom. It was also a fitting architectural symbol of the second British Empire.

The building at 14 Downing Street held the office of Sir James Stephen (1789–1859), counsel to the Colonial Office from 1813 to 1834 and permanent undersecretary from 1836 to 1847. For a leader in public life, he made an unexpected impression. A colleague described him as "shy as a wild duck." But he was a man of strict integrity, high moral principle, and an abiding concern for equity, justice, and fairness. Sir James Stephen was a formidable figure, more powerful than the ministers who were nominally above him. Privately they called him the "permanent oversecretary." During his tenure, he became a figure so dominant in the second British Empire that he was also known as "Mr. Mother Country."[14]

One persistent problem that landed frequently on Sir James Stephen's cluttered desk was the status of New Zealand. He had never been there, but knew quite a lot about it from several kinsmen who had served in the South Pacific. Stephen did not wish to add New Zealand to the empire, mainly because he believed that it rightfully

Sir James Stephen held many positions in the Colonial Office from 1813 to 1834, was permanent undersecretary to 1847, and played a major role in shaping the character of New Zealand. He was a man of strict integrity, with a deep concern for justice and fairness, especially to Maori.

belonged to its Maori inhabitants, whom he regarded as an admirable people. But events led him to change his mind. In 1839 he wrote, "The colonization of New Zealand is if not an expedient, at least an inevitable measure. It is, in fact, colonized already by British subjects of the worst possible character, who are doing the greatest possible amount of evil with the least possible amount of good."[15]

Stephen summarized his purposes in a single sentence: "The two Cardinal points to be kept in view in establishing a regular colony in New Zealand are, first, the protection of the aborigines, and secondly the introduction among the colonists of the principle of self-government, to the utmost extent in which that principle can be reconciled with allegiance to the crown."[16]

Here was an attitude profoundly different from that of the leaders of the first British Empire. When Sir James Stephen came into his office, three decades had passed since American independence, and a great tide of change had transformed the Western world. The American and French revolutions had set in motion new ideas of liberty, equality, and democracy. Stephen himself had been strongly supportive of the American cause.

After the War of Independence, Parliament never again attempted to tax British colonies primarily for a flow of revenue to London. For a while it maintained the old machinery of imperial control and economic regulation, but the Canadian Rebellion of 1837 made clear that something more was necessary. The report of Lord Durham on Canada at last persuaded Parliament that Britons abroad should be granted the same rights and powers that they possessed at home. The same idea was not extended to people of other cultures, but a new standard of self-government was established for British settlers. Stephen took the lead in developing this new policy.

Another major event of profound importance was the evangelical movement, which transformed the religious life of Protestant nations in America and northern Europe. It had a major impact on Britain's ruling elites, and on Sir James Stephen in particular. In combination with the values of the Enlightenment, the evangelical movement changed British attitudes toward other people throughout the world.

In Britain that new attitude appeared in the formation of the Aborigines Protection Society and the Church Missionary Society, which fiercely defended the rights of Maori in New Zealand. Members of the Church Missionary Society included Sir James Stephen himself and Lord Glenelg, secretary of state for the colonies. Stephen observed in 1839 that "the opposition of the great Missionary Societies . . . would be fatal to any project of colonizing New Zealand." He was careful to seek their support.[17]

Yet another factor was a radical transformation in British attitudes toward slavery. A nation that had taken a leading part in the African slave trade during the eighteenth century had now become the world leader in its abolition. In 1833, Parliament abolished slavery in the British West Indies and put slaves on a path to freedom through much of the British Empire. Stephen himself drafted the Abolition Act in 1833. At the critical moment he dictated a bill of sixty-six sections in a legislative marathon of forty-eight hours. Stephen also wrote many abolitionist tracts in his youth and strongly opposed anything resembling slavery and the slave trade throughout the empire.

Under his direction, New Zealand was founded in the spirit of these new trends. It was one of the very few colonies in any empire that had no system of race slavery, no penal settlements, no plantation serfdom, no encomienda, no indentured servitude in the eighteenth-century sense, and no contract bondage, which was spreading widely through the world in the nineteenth century. This new tendency was not a function of New Zealand's climate, terrain, or any material condition. It was a deliberate act of moral choice by British statesmen. Systems of forced labor never developed in New Zealand, because by the time it was colonized, slavery was strongly opposed by British governments in general, and by Sir James Stephen in particular. New ideas of nationalism also made a difference in the administration of the second British Empire. In its youth, nationalism was more liberal than conservative. It was often linked to ideas of democracy and self-determination. A policy of the second empire was to encourage unification or confederation of British colonists into incipient English-speaking nations. This happened in Canada, Australia, and New Zealand during the nineteenth century, but not in India or Africa until the mid-twentieth. Before 1776, imperial leaders in London had opposed attempts at colonial confederation in America, even resisting the Albany Congress, which was an attempt to support the empire. After 1783, British leaders acted very differently. Economic attitudes in the second British Empire were also different from those in the first. In the nineteenth century many British statesmen turned away from the dogmas of mercantilism on which the first empire was founded. They were converted to the economic gospel of free trade and embraced the principles of classical economics.

Perhaps the most important change was a new idea of social justice that was developing in Victorian Britain, despite the harsh and cruel reality of British society in that era, and in some ways as a reaction against it. These ideals took many forms. One version was utilitarianism, an idea of social justice as the greatest good for the greatest number. Another was an ideal of fairness and decency and social justice, which was all the stronger for its contrast with the unfairness of social conditions at the same time. An ideal of fairness was deployed in the novels of Charles Dickens, mainly by the method of harrowing descriptions of unfairness in England.

Those ideas of fairness and social justice were put to work in New Zealand by men such as Sir James Stephen, even as he never went there. They were both substantive and procedural ideas. In the administration of New Zealand they appeared most clearly in the character and acts of the men who were sent to govern the colony and to shape its institutions. The result, for better and for worse, was an imperial system in New Zealand that became a school of natural justice and fairness during the second British Empire. It happened in several ways at once. One was through the spread of the social ideals in which Sir James Stephen deeply believed. The other was a pattern of imperial response to continuing acts of unfairness and injustice perpetrated by British settlers against Maori, and also by Britons against each other.

Here again we find the same double irony that had appeared with regard to liberty, freedom, and slavery in the United States. The first irony was that realities always failed to match contemporary ideals. A second irony was that failures reinforced concern for the ideals themselves, and inspired others to achieve them, and to enlarge them in unexpected ways. That process led to more failures and further inspiration. This dynamic process converted an early idealist impulse into an ongoing tradition of extraordinary tenacity. It happened with regard both to liberty and freedom in the United States and to fairness and justice in New Zealand.

Imperial Leaders in New Zealand

Among the first carriers of that tradition were imperial officers who introduced the policies of Sir James Stephen to New Zealand. They were a small group. Chief among them were the early governors and their lieutenants: William Hobson, Robert FitzRoy, and Sir George Grey.

In the historiography of New Zealand these men are remembered and judged as individuals, but they were also a group who shared much in common. They came from England's upper middle class and the fringes of its aristocracy. Many knew one another before they came to New Zealand. Some were related by birth and marriage. Their fathers had been officers in the army and navy, as they themselves would be. The oldest had their schooling in the gunrooms of British warships or around the mess tables of British regiments. The youngest went to the Royal Naval and Military Colleges at Portsmouth, Dartmouth, Sandhurst, and Woolwich. They were raised to ideals of a gentleman's honor, an officer's duty, and a warrior's courage. They were trained in habits of firm command and decisive action.

As young men they saw much of the world. Many learned to speak languages other than their own. They fought in Europe and America during the great wars of the Napoleonic era. After Waterloo, they played active roles in the suppression of piracy in the West Indies and the interdiction of the Atlantic slave trade. They led missions of exploration and scientific research to remote corners of the world. Many shared a buoyant sense of confidence and optimism that was born of victory in the Napoleonic Wars. Most possessed that special combination of toughness and idealism that was highly developed in the early Victorian era.

Ethical Imperialism: William Hobson (1792?–1842)

A leading example was New Zealand's first royal governor, William Hobson. He was born in Waterford, the third son of an Anglo-Irish barrister with few connections and little wealth. At the age of ten, William Hobson was sent into the navy. He saw much service in the Napoleonic Wars and the War of 1812, and was given command of small vessels fighting piracy in the West Indies. Once he was captured by pirates, made a heroic escape, and hunted his captors to their deaths. Hobson was noticed as an officer of "great merit and intelligence" and promoted to commander. A superior called him "an officer who to the most persevering zeal unites discretion and sound judgment." But still he had few connections. In midcareer his health had been damaged by West Indian fevers, and the navy was cutting back. His ship was paid off in 1828, and he came home with his West Indian wife, Eliza. For six years he held no command and lived with relatives. His career seemed at an end.[18]

Then, in 1834, a new government came to power. The formidable Earl of Auckland became First Lord of the Admiralty. Men of energy and judgment were wanted again. Hobson was given a frigate, HMS *Rattlesnake*, and sent to the East Indies. He surveyed the south coast of Australia and helped to lay out the town of Melbourne. In 1837, when British resident James Busby reported that British lives were threatened in New Zealand by wars among the Maori, Hobson

Captain William Hobson became New Zealand's first governor in 1839, with orders to pursue "fair and equal" policies with regard to Maori and English settlers. The result was the Treaty of Waitangi in 1840. In 1841 New Zealand became a crown colony, closely watched by Sir James Stephen.

and HMS *Rattlesnake* were sent to keep the peace. His mission was a success. Hobson met many Maori leaders and won a reputation among them for courage, honesty, and fair dealing. At first he also got on with European settlers, and he submitted a report recommending the establishment of trading settlements in New Zealand on the Indian model. The idea was much noticed in London, and in 1839 Hobson was appointed consul and lieutenant governor in New Zealand, with instructions to obtain small tracts of land from the Maori by "fair and equal contracts."[19]

Hobson was in poor health and looked much older than his forty-seven years, but he had deep spiritual resources, absolute confidence in the rightness of his cause, and a remarkable power of will. Hobson was driven by a sense of duty and sustained by his deep Christian faith. He applied his spiritual energy and "persevering zeal" to the creation of a British colony in New Zealand.[20]

Also, he moved with astonishing energy and speed. On Christmas Eve 1839, he arrived in Sydney and concerted plans with British officials. On January 10, 1840, he met with the leading merchants of New South Wales and established a rapport with them. He was in New Zealand by January 29, 1840, read his commission on January 30, met with the missionaries, and on February 5 organized a gathering of Maori chiefs at the place they called Waitangi, "water of weeping."[21]

The very next day, February 6, 1840, the Treaty of Waitangi was discussed with Maori leaders, and it was signed on February 7. For some Maori chiefs, it was partly an expression of trust in Hobson himself. The Maori leader Tamati Waka Nene said to him, "Remain for us a father, a judge, a peacemaker. You must not allow us to become slaves. You must preserve our customs, and never permit our lands to be wrested from us. . . . Stay then, our friend, our father, our Governor."[22]

There would be much discussion in later years about misunderstandings and betrayals, and we shall examine the event at Waitangi more closely below. But Hobson's idea of the treaty was crystal clear, completely candid, and highly consistent. The Waitangi agreement was for him a vision of harmony, coexistence, justice, and mutual respect between British and Maori. With those purposes in mind, he moved decisively to establish British sovereignty over New Zealand, with explicit guarantees of a large measure of self government for Maori, along with guarantees that they would receive the same rights as British subjects and that no land would be taken without their agreement.[23]

His major conflicts were not with Maori but with other Europeans. Hobson acted with dispatch to establish hegemony over French
settlers at Akaroa and American whalers and sealers, as well as the
British colonies of the New Zealand Company who assumed sovereign powers. On September 18, 1840, Hobson hoisted the Union
Jack over a small settlement at Waitemata Harbour and named it in
honor of his patron, the Earl of Auckland. When the New Zealand
Company complained of Hobson's activities, the British government
firmly supported him. On May 3, 1841, New Zealand became a
Crown colony separate from New South Wales, with Hobson as its
first royal governor.[24]

Hobson did not believe in democracy. He ruled New Zealand as
if it were a man-of-war. When the *New Zealand Herald and Auckland
Gazette* criticized his administration he shut it down, and he dealt
summarily with community leaders who opposed him. But he was a
leader of high probity, and he recruited able and honorable men to
serve in the colony. Among them was William Martin, who organized
a system of courts for the colony. Hobson also had a highly developed sense of justice and fairness to the Maori, and appointed
George Clarke to a post called Protector of Aborigines. He sought to
govern New Zealand in that spirit until death came very suddenly
from a stroke in 1842.[25]

Humanitarian Imperialism: Robert FitzRoy

Hobson's successor, Robert FitzRoy (1805–65), was of the British aristocracy, but the third son of a second son, and a title was not
within reach. He was sent to the Royal Naval College at Portsmouth,
where he won the First Medal for his character and intellect. He was
an able officer, a good navigator, and a strict disciplinarian. His temper was so strong that his nickname in the navy was "coffeepot" for
the frequency with which he boiled over. FitzRoy received his first
command in 1830, a small survey ship that was destined for immor-
tality. She was HMS *Beagle*, the vessel that carried Charles Darwin on
his voyage to the Pacific. FitzRoy and Darwin together wrote a three-
volume history of their voyage, for which FitzRoy won a gold medal
and great distinction.[26]

In 1843, FitzRoy was appointed governor of New Zealand to
follow Hobson. He was given no money, no warships, no soldiers,
and only a few policemen from New South Wales to keep order. He
found the colony in disorder after Hobson's sudden death. Maori
were demanding return of lost land. English settlers wanted more of

Captain William FitzRoy RN was New Zealand's second governor. His rule was also marked by an explicit and very active policy of "fairness and justice."

it, and asked for hard measures against the natives. FitzRoy strongly supported Maori land claims and refused to protect settlers who had moved beyond the major settlements. He also worked actively to make peace among warring Maori tribes. In the North Island FitzRoy took strong action against the Maori war leader Hone Heke, which made the governor more popular with the colonists, but less so in the colonial office. His biographer writes that "his determination that the Maori should be treated with fairness and justice, while European settlers should discover their new life in peace and harmony, constituted a major contribution to the life of the new colony."[27]

FitzRoy was always driven by his conscience, and guided by his principles. In 1844, he abolished customs duties, claiming to be the first in the world to establish the "true and beautiful" system of free trade. Desperately short of funds for his administration, he took it upon himself to issue debentures to pay the cost of his government. For this principled disregard of authority, and for other troubles in New Zealand that were not of his making, he was recalled and removed from office in 1845.[28]

FitzRoy returned to England and the navy, and rose to the rank of vice admiral. In 1854, he also became the head of the first British Meteorological Office. In that office he did more than anyone else to create the science of "weather forecasting," a term of his invention.

FitzRoy applied himself to the daunting task of predicting British weather with the same sense of responsibility that he had shown in New Zealand, but with less success. A report concluded with regret that his forecasts of British weather were "more often wrong than right." So strong was his sense of duty, and so complete was his feeling of failure, that he slipped into deep depression and on a dark day in 1865 committed suicide. Even in the depth of despair, Robert Fitz-Roy remained a noble character, driven by an intensity of moral striving that was common in his generation.[29]

Spiritual Imperialism in the Second Empire: Bishop Selwyn and the Cambridge Connexion

During the administrations of Hobson and FitzRoy, another group of high-minded English imperialists seated themselves at Judges Bay, near the Auckland neighborhood of Parnell. They had strong connections in England. Many had belonged to one of the happiest of colleges, St. John's in Cambridge.

The Judge of Judge's Bay was William Martin, son of a Birmingham industrialist, and the leading spirit of that settlement. His presence attracted other graduates from St. John's to the colony. Among them was Thomas Whytehead, first head of a new institution called St. John's College in New Zealand. It included not only a college but also an institute of theology, a boys' school, a teacher training institute, an infant school, an orphanage, and a hospital.[30]

Another member of this Cambridge Connexion was Bishop George Augustus Selwyn. Like William Martin and Thomas Whytehead a member of St. John's College in Cambridge, he became Anglican bishop of New Zealand from 1841. Selwyn was a muscular Christian of extraordinary physical strength and energy. The Hocken Library in Dunedin has five manuscript volumes of his New Zealand journals. One journal for 1842–43 describes travels that totaled 2,277 miles in New Zealand during that one year alone. Selwyn walked across much of the North Island and sailed his own boat through a large part of Melanesia. One crusty old salt said that "to see the Bishop handle a boat was almost enough to make a man a Christian."[31]

Selwyn's biographer Warren Limbrick writes that he was "a high-principled idealist as well as a far-sighted man of action." Chief among his principles was a broad ecumenical version of Christianity, which in New Zealand became linked to an idea of racial equality and justice between Pakeha and Maori. One of his sermons preached

Bishop George Augustus Selwyn in the second empire made a dramatic contrast with Laud and Secker in the first. Selwyn became a fierce defender of Maori rights. He pursued a policy of humanity, civility, and justice toward British colonists, French settlers, and even Americans, whom he described as his greatest challenge.

in New Windsor was called "Unity of the Church." He took his text from the patron saint, John 7:21, "That they all may be one." Selwyn worshipped a God of mercy. The first sermon in his collective works was called "The Forgiveness of Sin." It celebrated the "merciful wisdom of God," and was very different from the Calvinist idea of divinity that was shared by Puritans and many Anglicans in the seventeenth and eighteenth centuries.[32]

Selwyn was no egalitarian. Another of his sermons was called "The Master's Duty and Servant's Right." He believed that "Christianity was intended by our Lord to make all men brethren, not by leveling all the distinctions of society, but by raising all men to the enjoyment of the same spiritual privileges. Christ does not say that there should be none great, or none having authority and dominion; but he commands that those who have authority and are in dominion, should in spiritual things be ministers and servants of their poorer brethren." Here was an idea of equity that made sense to a Christian gentleman. Selwyn celebrated what he called "the spiritual equality of all the members of the church of Christ."

Selwyn's idea of spiritual equality was deeply offended by the way that Maori were treated by some of his English brethren, and he became a fierce defender of Maori rights. His vision of New Zealand was one of Maori and Pakeha living together in harmony. "In this country," he wrote, "English settlers and natives will live side by side." Selwyn ordered all his parish clergy to learn Maori and compelled every missionary to serve English immigrants (which some were loath to do).[33]

This vision of Christianity embraced all humanity—even Americans, a severe test of Selwyn's ecumenical spirit, as he noted in his third journal. On a quick trip from Auckland to Stewart Island a thousand miles away, he found two American whaling ships riding at anchor in Horseshoe Bay. Selwyn wrote, "Remembering the Bishop of New Jersey's conversation at Eton on the unity of our Churches, I determined to send in the morning to offer to perform Divine Service on board." The whalers were probably Yankee Congregationalists or New Bedford Quakers who had no wish to join the Church of England. Selwyn wrote, "They disappointed me by sailing at break of day," and the American vessels disappeared over the horizon, steering in the general direction of Antarctica, which was the only way to escape the ecumenical attention of the Bishop of New Zealand.[34]

Selwyn ministered to the French at Akaroa and noted that he was received with civility. He visited the dour Scots of Dunedin in their first few weeks ashore, and he found them living in long sheds through weeks of driving rain, helped repair the roofs, and won the respect even of these Scottish Calvinists. Selwyn preached against the "sin of swearing" in fishing stations. But mostly he took delight in working with Maori. He liked and respected them very much. "The whole population," he wrote, "almost to a man, has at least some regard for the laws of man." Selwyn also celebrated their kindness and hospitality, and had great *mana* among them. He pursued sinners in the bush and wrote in his visitation journal that "the work of a missionary in New Zealand is like hunting a partridge in the mountains."[35]

Selwyn had a pantheistic idea of nature as God's design for the world, and he believed that part of his duty was to preserve the environment of New Zealand from all forms of pollution. A story was told of Selwyn in his youth, punting with his fellow Etonians on the River Thames in England. One of them spat into the river, which Selwyn regarded as an act of spiritual pollution. "If you must spit," he said to the offender, "spit *into* the punt!" Altogether Selwyn brought a large and generous spirit of Christian imperialism to New Zealand. Most of all this was a proud imperium of justice, fairness, and equity.[36]

Whig Imperialism: The Strange Career of Sir George Grey

In Hauraki Gulf, thirty miles above Auckland, there is a small island called Kawau. On it stands a large house that was the home of Sir George Grey, the most important of New Zealand's imperial

*Sir George Grey was the strongest of New
Zealand's early governors. He was an
English Whig who with little consultation
gave the colony its first constitution. It was
similar to American models and proved un-
congenial to the values of New Zealanders,
who later went another way. He was deeply
interested in Maori culture but did more
than anyone else to take their land.*

administrators, and also the most controversial. One historian
observed in 1980, "In recent years, Grey's reputation as Governor
has tended to decline while that of his predecessors, Governors
Hobson and Fitzroy, is rehabilitated."[37]

George Grey entered the world as the posthumous son of a
British officer, Lieutenant Colonel George Grey of the 30th Foot,
killed in the storming party at Badajoz in Spain. His wife was in a
hotel in Lisbon and overheard from her veranda two officers
speaking of the death of her husband. The shock brought on the
premature birth of George Grey. He was raised to privilege in an
aristocratic family, and schoolmasters judged him "clever but idle."
At the age of fourteen he was sent to Sandhurst. Three years later he
was an ensign in the 83rd Foot, serving in Ireland. That experience
changed his life. He was appalled by the suffering that he found
among the Irish people: "I saw enough there to give a bias to my
mind forever as to the necessity for change and reform."[38]

One day he was ordered to lead a detachment "under orders
to protect a tithe collecting expedition," which compelled the Irish
Catholic peasantry to pay a tenth of their meager harvest in taxes
to the Protestant Church of England. Later he wrote, "My heart
was wrung at what I witnessed. . . . To me it appeared wrong,
shameful, un-Christian, that money for a Church which preached
the love of God and His son towards mankind, should be wrung
from people by armed soldiers." That experience of serving as an

instrument of English oppression in Ireland turned Grey against established churches and large landed estates with an exploited peasantry.[39]

Something similar happened when Grey was sent to keep the peace in Australia. There he identified very much with aboriginal peoples, even as it was his duty to fight them. In one encounter he was severely wounded by an aborigine, who transfixed him with three spears in quick succession. Grey pulled them out of his flesh, charged the aborigine, shot him, and then was stricken with grief for the man he had killed. "I already felt deeply the death of him I had been compelled to shoot. . . . [T]hrough the woods came the piercing shrieks of wailing women and the mournful cries of native men, sorrowing over him who had fallen that day by my own hand. These cries rang in my ears all night." Grey's physical and spiritual wounds never fully healed. He sought relief from his suffering in laudanum and was said to have become addicted to opiates through the rest of his life.[40]

Grey was very much a loner. He preferred to live on his island, separate from his wife and protected by a staff sympathetic to his purposes. His biographer Rutherford writes, "Grey kept his own counsel, questioned and listened, but was rarely frank or outspoken. He was a lonely man in his own mind. His geniality was a little forced and patronising."[41]

As governor of New Zealand, Grey began by putting the colonial government on a sound fiscal footing. He was strenuously hostile to speculators and suspicious of missionaries. It was said that he "ruled New Zealand as a complete autocrat, obeying or disobeying instructions from England to suit himself, dominating his official staff and contriving to overrule, though not to silence, all local opposition, . . . and regularly put his decisions into immediate effect by proclamation." Where colonial leaders such as Godley sometimes turned Whiggish means to Tory ends, Grey often used Tory means to Whiggish ends.[42]

Then he dealt with Maori, and in a very complex way. Grey identified very much with them. He learned their language, and even wrote a book in Maori of their legends and traditions called *Nga Mahi a Nga Tupuna* (1854), later translated as *Polynesian Myths* (1855). His purpose was to govern wisely an inferior people: "I believe that the ignorance which has prevailed regarding the mythological systems of barbarous or semi-barbarous races has too generally led to their being considered far grander and more reasonable than they really were."[43]

Grey's purpose was to establish unequivocally an English hegemony over New Zealand, and he struck at the heart of Maori resistance. He cut off the flow of muskets and captured the great fortified
Pa at Ruapekapeka. Grey was keenly aware that Maori were formidable in battle. As a rule he did not fight the leading Maori warriors
but isolated them, destroyed their *mana,* and turned their chivalry
against them. Grey also took more land from Maori than anyone
else in the history of New Zealand. He bought title to thirty million
acres in the South Island and three million in the North.

Sir George Grey and New Zealand's Constitution

In his old age, Sir George Grey was asked how New Zealand got
its first constitution. He answered with a story. The colonists, he said,
had long asked for such a thing, and by the year 1849, their desires
had grown into demands. The Executive Council refused to agree,
and the governor was caught in between. To escape these various
pressures, Grey decided to retreat into the interior of the North
Island. He climbed the snowy slopes of Mount Ruapehu, one of the
highest mountains on the North Island. There, according to his own
account, he drafted a constitution for New Zealand in lofty solitude.
"A few Maoris accompanied me to carry the baggage; nobody else,
for I could not have drawn the constitution with a cloud of advisors
about me. Where did I get my inspiration? Oh, by talking to the hills
and trees, from long walks, and many hints from the United States
Constitution. I sought a scheme of government which should be
broad, free, charged with a young nation's vitality."[44]

An historian warns us that "this is an old man's humour running towards romance." The New Zealand Constitution was not literally handed down from the Olympian heights of Mount Ruapehu.
But in a broader sense, something similar actually happened. The
Constitution Act of 1852 was drafted by George Grey. It was approved by the British government, ratified by Parliament in London
with a few revisions, and imposed upon New Zealand from above. It
remained in force for 134 years, and it was not replaced until 1986
by a document of New Zealanders' own making.[45]

The New Zealand Constitution was made in a manner very different from the framing of the Constitution of the United States, but
the American system was clearly a model for Grey. He created a
quasi-federal system—a general government consisting of an
appointed governor with strong powers, an appointed or "nominated" upper house, and a house of representatives elected by the

people for five years. Below this general government were provinces, each governed by a superintendent and an elective council. There were also local or municipal governments. New Zealand's provinces were created from above, and were always less autonomous than American states. The governor could disallow provincial laws.

Grey did not get all he asked from Parliament in London, and his bill was changed in several ways. But his constitution-making had a profound and permanent impact on New Zealand, not so much in its substantive provisions as in the way that it was done. Self-government and the rule of law came to New Zealand from above. These great principles were ordained by imperial authority. The result, to paraphrase Tocqueville, was that New Zealand was born free without having to become so. It never had to fight for self-government, or win its rights by armed struggle. As a result, freedom and self-government were not problematical in the way that they had been in America. By comparison with other empires, including the first British Empire, tyranny was not a major problem for British settlers. But always there were contested questions about equity and fairness within this imperial system. Here was the unfinished business of the second British Empire in New Zealand, and work for generations to come.

The Second British Empire and the Ethos of New Zealand

All of these British imperialists—Stephen, Hobson, FitzRoy, Selwyn, Martin, Grey, and many others like them—contributed much to the making of New Zealand, and to the construction of its unique culture. Their ideas were not the same, but in various ways they introduced interlocking elements of a distinctive ethos. It was highly principled and deeply Christian, with an elaborately developed sense of justice and equity. In the early twenty-first century it is fashionable to mock the altruism of such men. In truth, their acts often fell short of their ideals. But there was a constancy of striving in their lives, and they planted the seeds of an ethical system that kept growing long after they were gone.

Today, most inhabitants of former British colonies are very mixed in their memories of what was once the mother country. They regard some aspects of British culture with respect and affection, but they remember a distance between British ideas and imperial acts, and are not overwhelmed with a sense of gratitude, to say the least. This was dramatically the case in the first British Empire, where the major conflict was between ideas of liberty and freedom on the one hand and tyrannical acts on the other. That tension persisted through five generations, and became a coiled spring at the heart of American culture, even to our own time.

In the second British Empire, attitudes were different. Questions of liberty and freedom were not so prominent. There was another sort of resentment against a society that laid claim to ideas of fairness and justice but in practice was often unjust and deeply unfair. Its rulers preached these great ideas but sometimes failed to practice them. People throughout the second British Empire doubly resented that hypocrisy. As a consequence, the second British Empire became a school of equity and social justice, in which colonial people condemned their imperial rulers by the ethical standards the rulers themselves had taught.

After the experience of English rule, many were left with a strong feeling of distrust for their former masters. In New Zealand, political leader Tim Shadbolt remarked that "the British Empire was described as the Empire on which the sun never sets because God didn't trust the poms with the lights out."[46] But it is interesting that he (and many other iconoclasts) condemned British imperial rulers by invoking the principles that the rulers themselves had proclaimed. The irony of British imperial rule was that it inculcated its ethical ideals by failing to live up to them. As early as 1913, American writer Edgar Watson Howe observed, "When you see a man who is exactly like an Englishman, but who abuses the English, you may know he is from New Zealand or Australia."[47]

This happened both in North America and in New Zealand, but in different ways. In Britain's first empire, the great ethical questions centered on power, liberty, and freedom. In the second British Empire, they were about power, justice, and fairness. Many generations later, the people of the United States are still actively engaged in the pursuit of liberty and freedom. The people of New Zealand are still absorbed in problems of fairness, equity, and natural justice. In large measure, two very different British Empires helped to make them that way.

INDIANS AND MAORI

Native Cultures and National Values

Let me be a free man—free to travel, free to stop, free
to work, free to trade where I choose, free to choose my
own teachers, free to follow the religion of my fathers,
free to talk and think and act for myself.

> —Hinmaton-Yalaktit (Chief Joseph), chief of the
> Nez Perce, 1877

This is a request of ours . . . deal fairly with the Maori
people, and with their lands.

> —Te Kooti Arikirangi Te Turuki, leader of the
> Rongowhakaata, 1892

VISITORS to New Zealand are quick to notice the vital presence of Maori culture in the life of this nation. On our first
flight with Air New Zealand, the modern aircraft bore an
ancient Maori name, proudly blazoned in blue-green letters on a
white fuselage. The interior was decorated with Maori motifs, and
the cabin crew greeted us in Maori and English. One of them was
Maori. The other identified herself as Pakeha, an old Maori word
for weird spirits in strange white skins. New Zealand may be the
only settler society where Europeans call themselves by a name the
natives gave them.[1]

We learned more about the functional importance of New
Zealand's Maori heritage at an academic conference in Auckland.
The meetings began with a ceremony of welcome called a *powhiri*
(pronounced "powfree"). Everyone was led into the university's

marae, a sacred Maori meetinghouse. We took off our shoes and sat facing one another on mats and benches while Maori and Pakeha hosts exchanged songs and speeches in both languages. Then we rubbed noses in the *hongi*, a Maori ritual that symbolizes friendship, harmony, and creativity. At American conferences, scholars also rub each other's noses, but in another spirit.[2]

These Maori ceremonies were more than gestures. They set a tone for events that followed. In substance the meetings were highly professional, but in spirit they seemed more like a family gathering. We witnessed some heated family arguments, yet also a sense of kinship that rarely appears in big American conferences. Colleagues in New Zealand managed their disagreements in a spirit of reciprocity that is important to this nation. Maori rituals were instrumental to that end.

As the conference went on, the Maori heritage was prominent in other ways. In discussions of subjects far distant from New Zealand, Pakeha scholars deployed Maori phrases for emphasis, or for shades of meaning, or for thoughts not easily rendered in English. More often, the purpose was to explore a serious difference in a spirit of comity and mutual respect. We greatly admired that custom.

The expanding importance of the Maori heritage is not only to be found in academe. We also met it in the camaraderie of military men who were proud of their service, conservative in social attitudes, and contemptuous of academic "maoriolatry," as one called it. But when the conversation turned to World War II, Pakeha soldiers celebrated the Maori Battalion and used Maori phrases that are not much heard in scholarly circles.[3] It is the same again in New Zealand sport. At rugby matches, Pakeha players routinely begin with a Maori dance of challenge called the *haka*. Maori athletes observe Pakeha rituals of fair play that migrated from the playing fields of England.[4]

On another level, these attitudes also appear in major works of New Zealand literature. Pakeha authors mock the inauthenticity of the "Bone People," as Keri Hulme contemptuously called Anglo-Saxon ladies who adorn themselves with jewelry of Maori bone and jade. But writers who mock this custom also adorn their prose with Maori flourishes that are rhetorical equivalents of jade and bone. We found that both Anglo-Saxon ladies and Pakeha literati are authentic in their love of Maori culture and genuine in their respect for Maori ways.[5]

This dual heritage is highly developed in the work of three New Zealand writers who have devoted their careers to bicultural study of their country's Maori and Pakeha culture. Michael King, before his death in a car crash at the age of fifty-eight, published forty books mostly with one mission in mind. *Being Pakeha* (1985) sought to explain Maori ways to Pakeha; *Being Pakeha Now* (1999) tried to explain Pakeha ways to Maori. His last major work, *The Penguin History of New Zealand* (2003), rejected the fashionable idea of a "fatal impact" when European settlers met native people. King believed that New Zealand's history has been a continuing engagement of two dynamic groups who borrowed and learned from each another, often in a constructive and tolerant spirit. Some New Zealanders do not agree, but many believe that Michael King's theme is correct and that his writings have done much to make it so.[6]

Another major contribution is James Belich's *Making Peoples: A History of the New Zealanders.* It begins with two small immigrant ships, freighted with families and ancient Gods. One ship is Polynesian, headed for New Zealand. The other is Viking, bound for Britain. Belich's history becomes a braided narrative of two cultures, Maori and Pakeha. A second volume continues through the twentieth century, with brilliant flashes of insight on the interplay of two cultures.[7]

A third body of literature comes from anthropologist Anne Salmond, who writes beautiful books of deep learning and graceful prose about early encounters between Maori and Pakeha, always with empathy for both people. She gives us a unique idea of history. It centers on a Maori image of the *pae*, the horizon of earth, water, and sky, "where people and ancestor gods enter into exchanges that separate and bind them." This, for Anne Salmond, is "a place of action where history is made." Her model of historical change is a spinning spiral—a favorite motif in Maori art. She writes of our time, "the spiral is still spinning . . . the past never ends."[8]

Anne Salmond's image might perhaps be understood as two spirals—a dynamic double helix that is the cultural DNA of this nation. This complex Maori and Pakeha heritage sets New Zealanders apart from all others in the world, as do Indians in America.

Maori and American Indians

In 1969, the Ford Foundation sponsored an exchange program that brought ten Maori leaders to meet American Indians in the United States and sent ten Indians to live among Maori. Among the Americans was Joe Sando, a Jemez Pueblo leader who visited the Wanganui Maori. He was what Maori of that generation called a

Dr. Joe Sando, a prominent Jemez Pueblo leader, was part of a Ford Foundation program in 1969 that invited ten Indians and ten Maori to live in each other's communities. Joe Sando formed a strong identity with his Maori hosts.

"hard man," a veteran of the war against the Japanese, and a fighter for his people in North America.[9]

When Joe Sando returned to the South Pacific on a mission of peace, this hard man was overwhelmed by the welcome he received from his Maori hosts. "We were touched at the depth of our hearts," he wrote. More than that, Joe Sando felt that the Maori shared much in common with his own people. "I changed the word Maori to Indian, and one or two Maori words, and thus every word . . . applied," he said.[10]

In the course of his visit, Joe Sando came to believe that American Indians and New Zealand Maori are one people, similar in "outlook, philosophy, and customs."[11] He told the Wanganui Maori that he felt the stirring of the same "Great Spirit, that you call Io and my people call Yo." Other Indians and Maori in that exchange program shared Joe Sando's sense of kinship. One of them wrote, "Many questions sprang to mind as I talked and listened to people. What's different and what's the same about Indians and Maori?"[12]

Numbers and Proportions

A good starting point is demography. New Zealand's census of 2001 counted 526,281 people who identified themselves as of the "Maori ethnic group," in a nation of 3.7 million. In the United States, by comparison, the census of 2000 enumerated 2,664,000 American Indians in a population of 281 million.[13]

In absolute terms American Indians were five times more numerous than New Zealand Maori. But in relative proportions, the opposite was the case. American Indians in 2000 were a little less than 1 percent (0.9 percent) of the United States. New Zealanders of Maori descent in 2001 were 14.7 percent of their nation. Another 6.5 percent of New Zealanders in that year identified themselves as "Pacific peoples," who were defined in the census to include Samoan, Cook Island Maori, Nieuean, Tokelauan, Hawaiian, Tahitian, "and other Pacific Islanders." Correcting for overlap, census takers estimated that Polynesian people in New Zealand were nearly 20 percent of the nation in 2001. They are the second-largest ethnic group in a predominantly bicultural society. By contrast, in the United States more than twenty ethnic groups are larger than American Indians, in a more multicultural society.[14]

After contact with European settlements (especially European children), Maori and Indians suffered a catastrophic decline in numbers, which continued to about 1890. Thereafter both indigenous populations began to grow again, and they multiplied rapidly through the twentieth century. In the United States from 1980 to 1990, the nation as a whole grew by 10 percent; Indians increased by 38 percent in that decade. The trend was similar in New Zealand: total population went up by 7 percent from 1981 to 1991; Maori and Pacific Islanders rose by 23 percent. Thereafter, rates of gain for Maori and Indians fell a little, but remained above the national average.[15]

Much of this growth was driven by natural increase. Through most of the twentieth century, birthrates among Maori and Indians were higher than in the general population. In 1995, 60 percent of Maori were under the age of fifteen, and an astounding 85 percent were younger than twenty-five. The median age of Maori was half that of Pakeha, mainly because of higher fertility.[16]

Another factor was also important. Maori and Indians have long had very high rates of outmarriage. In the U.S. Census of 1990, nearly 80 percent of American Indians reported that they were of mixed ancestry. Brenda Manuelito, a Navaho expert on this subject, concludes that "American Indians are today the most exogamous group" in an elaborately interbred nation. Similar patterns appear among Maori.[17]

The effect of that tendency was reinforced by a third trend, which is very important. Today, Americans and New Zealanders of mixed ancestry increasingly identify themselves as Indian or Maori.

One demographic study in the United States found that "as much as 60 percent of the apparent population-growth of American Indians from 1970 to 1980 may be accounted for by such changing identifications." Behind those numbers is a revolution in ethnic attitudes.[18]

Languages: Indian Diversity, Maori Unity

When a New Zealander asked American Pueblo leader Joe Sando about cultural differences between the Maori and Indians, he answered, "One factor stands out in my personal evaluation. An obvious advantage that you enjoy is the common language spoken by all your tribal groups." He offered an example from his own experience. "In our Pueblo Indian organization," he said, "there are nineteen villages and out of this we speak three different languages: Keresan by seven villages, Zunian by one village, and Tanoan by eleven villages. This Tanoan language is further divided into three dialects: Tiwa spoken by four villages, Tewa spoken by six, and my language Towa spoken by one village. The rest of the American Indians are in similar situations." It was (and is) difficult for Indians to communicate among themselves in native languages, even within Joe Sando's own small pueblo. He added, "Many languages in one meeting can slow down the progress of a meeting, as we have to interpret for our elders and councilmen from English to our native tongues."[19]

American Indians have long been divided in this way. In the mid-twentieth century, linguist Mario Pei at Columbia University counted 2,796 languages throughout the world, and estimated that more than 1,200 were spoken by American Indian nations, "which mostly number only a few thousand or a few hundred speakers." His taxonomy of Indian languages is a matter of dispute between "lumpers" and "splitters." Mario Pei was a splitter in these statistics. Today most linguists are lumpers who count two hundred or three hundred Indian languages, with many more dialects. But lumpers and splitters agree that American Indian languages have long been extraordinary for diversity, in a large number of very small groups.[20]

These many Indian languages share important elements in common. The first person singular is *na* through much of North and South America. That similarity suggests a common origin. Through many millennia aboriginal speechways in America multiplied and moved apart. They also tend to be polysynthetic languages, in which "words have little if any individual status, but become meaningful only when placed in a sentence." Polysynthetic languages are extremely difficult for non-native speakers to learn. Their

AMERICAN INDIAN NATIONS AND LANGUAGES CIRCA 1600

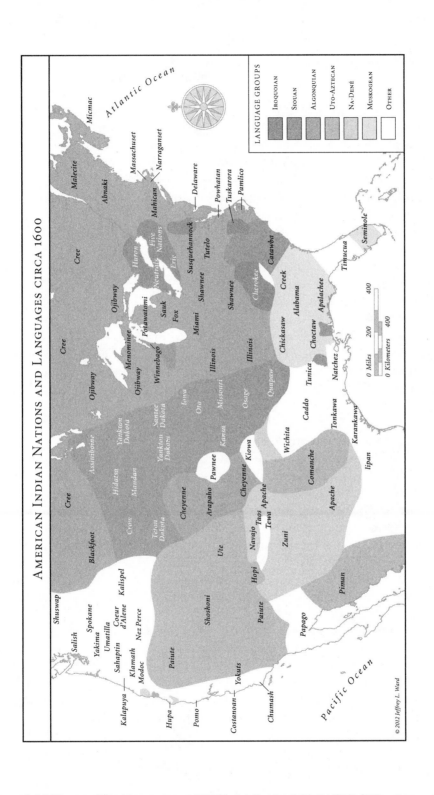

LANGUAGE GROUPS

IROQUOIAN
SIOUAN
ALGONQUIAN
UTO-AZTECAN
NA-DENÉ
MUSKOGEAN
OTHER

Atlantic Ocean

Pacific Ocean

Micmac
Malecite
Abnaki
Massachuset
Narraganset
Mahican
Delaware
Powhatan
Tuskarora
Pamlico
Cree
Huron
Five Nations
Neutral
Erie
Susquehannock
Tutelo
Catawba
Shawnee
Shawnee
Cherokee
Creek
Alabama
Apalachee
Chickasaw
Choctaw
Natchez
Tunica
Seminole
Timucua

Cree
Ojibway
Ojibway
Menominee
Potawatomi
Winnebago
Sauk
Fox
Ojibway
Miami
Illinois
Illinois
Iowa
Oto
Missouri
Osage
Kansa
Quapaw
Caddo
Tonkawa
Karankawa
Iipan
Comanche
Apache

Cree
Assiniboine
Hidatsa
Mandan
Yankton Dakota
Santee Dakota
Yankton Dakota
Pawnee
Wichita

Blackfoot
Crow
Teton Dakota
Cheyenne
Arapaho
Cheyenne
Kiowa
Ute
Taos
Tewa
Apache
Navajo
Zuni
Hopi
Shoshoni
Paiute
Piman
Papago

Shuswap
Salish
Spokane
Yakima
Umatilla
Coeur d'Alene
Kalispel
Sahaptin
Klamath
Modoc
Nez Perce
Kalapuya
Hupa
Pomo
Costanoan
Yokuts
Chumash
Paiute

0 Miles   200   400
0 Kilometers   400

© 2012 Jeffrey L. Ward

structure is an added barrier to mutual understanding. American Indians of different nations often communicated not by speech but by sign language.[21]

Maori did not have that problem. They also were divided into many *iwi*, or tribes, with different traditions. But unlike Indians they could discuss their differences in dialects that were mutually intelligible. This was so throughout Polynesia. When Captain Cook came to New Zealand he was accompanied by Tupaia, a Tahitian priest-navigator who was able to converse with Maori, even though their peoples had not been in contact for many centuries. Maori have preserved a linguistic unity. American Indians have long been divided by language.[22]

A related linguistic difference appeared in words that Maori and Indians used for themselves before European contact. The native people of New Zealand had a special name for their homeland, because they were aware of other lands before the first Europeans appeared. They called it Aotearoa, Land of the Long White Cloud, as it had first appeared from a distance to Polynesian navigators. Indians had no special name for America, which they long believed to be all the world, and no collective noun for themselves apart from others.[23] We asked a large group of Indian leaders what they wished to be called. Invariably they preferred to be known by the name of their own Indian nation.[24]

The literal meaning of these names is interesting. An example is the nation known to the English as the Delaware. They called themselves Lenapi, which meant the People, or the Human Race. The same meaning appeared in many such names: Anishinaabe (Ojibway), Dene (Chipawyan), Illiniwek (Illinois), Innu (Montagnais), Inuit (Eskimo), Ininiwok (Cree), Maklak (Klamath), Ndee (Apache), Numinu (Comanche), Nuutsiu (Ute), Tetwaken (Cayuse), and others. All meant something like the People, or the True People, or We, the People. They implied that Indians of other nations were not people.[25]

The nomenclature of Maori tribes differed from that of Indian nations in this way. Many *iwi* names begin with the common prefix *nga*, *ngai*, or *ngati*. They often end with a patronym such as *Ngati Tuwharetoa* or another word that variously refers to a line of descent, a place, a canoe, a war, or a conquest. Maori were named as subdivisions of a larger whole. In that way they are more like tribes than nations. Indian units were named as if they were entire to themselves, and are more like nations than tribes. These patterns of identity made a difference in relations with others.[26]

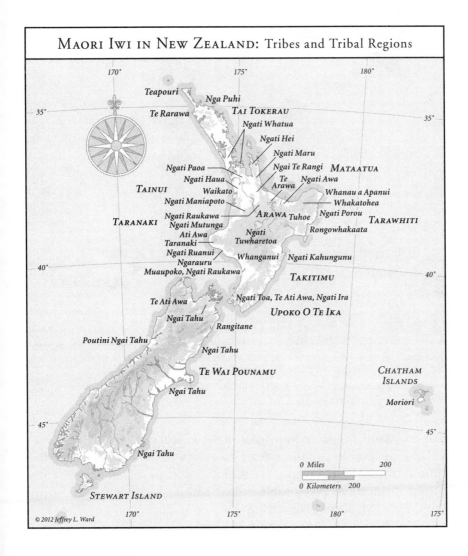

MAORI IWI IN NEW ZEALAND: Tribes and Tribal Regions

170° 175° 180°

35° 35°

Teapouri
Nga Puhi
Te Rarawa TAI TOKERAU
Ngati Whatua
Ngati Hei
Ngati Maru
Ngati Paoa Ngai Te Rangi MATAATUA
Ngati Haua Te Ngati Awa
TAINUI Waikato Arawa
Ngati Maniapoto Whanau a Apanui
Whakatohea
Ngati Raukawa ARAWA Tuhoe Ngati Porou
TARANAKI Ngati Mutunga TARAWHITI
Ati Awa Ngati Rongowhakaata
Taranaki Tuwharetoa
Ngati Ruanui Whanganui Ngati Kahungunu
Ngarauru
Muaupoko, Ngati Raukawa TAKITIMU

40° 40°

Te Ati Awa Ngati Toa, Te Ati Awa, Ngati Ira
Ngai Tahu UPOKO O TE IKA
Rangitane
Poutini Ngai Tahu
Ngai Tahu

TE WAI POUNAMU CHATHAM
ISLANDS
Ngai Tahu
Moriori

45° 45°

Ngai Tahu

0 Miles 200
0 Kilometers 200

STEWART ISLAND

© 2012 Jeffrey L. Ward 170° 175° 180° 175°

Origins and Memories: Maori and the Sea; Indians and the Land

Maori and Indians formed contrasting identities in another way. Both groups made epic migrations to a new world. Polynesians came by sea in long voyages across open water in the Pacific Ocean. The first journeys took them from Asia to an island home in the central Pacific that they called Hawaiki. Scholars believe that Hawaiki lay somewhere within a huge "Polynesian triangle," nearly four thousand miles on each side, from its northern apex in Hawaii to Easter Island in the southeast and New Zealand to the far southwest. Some historians think that Hawaiki may have been the Marquesa Islands,

This East Polynesian double canoe, carefully drawn by Hawaiian artist Herb Kawainui Kane, is typical of vessels used in the epic Polynesian migrations to New Zealand. Maori proudly thought of themselves as a people of the sea. American Indians proudly knew themselves as the people of the land.

five thousand miles east-nor'east of New Zealand. From that base, Polynesian families made ocean crossings to New Zealand in the thirteenth and fourteenth centuries. Some were deliberate colonizing missions in big double-hulled canoes—heroic feats of shipbuilding, navigation, seamanship, and courage.[27]

Today, eight centuries later, Maori vividly recall those great voyages. The names of the canoes have passed from parent to child through thirty generations. Children of the Ngati Raukawa learn to chant them in a nursery rhyme:

> I am but a child,
> A child of little knowledge
> Tainui, Te Arawa, Mataatua,
> Kurahaupo and Tokomaru
> These were the canoes of my ancestors.[28]

Pakeha also cherish these sagas as part of their identity as New Zealanders. As early as the 1840s, Governor Sir George Grey learned to speak Maori and worked closely with Arawa chief Te Rangikaheke to record these ancient traditions.[29] In the next generation Percy Smith, a founder of the Polynesian Society, worked with Maori friends to collect canoe legends and published them in versions that were sometimes inaccurate but always accessible.[30]

Scholars and scientists have corrected Percy Smith's errors, but they have also confirmed some of the main lines of the canoe legends by empirical research. A team of geneticists led by Rosalind Murray-McIntosh studied the mitochondrial DNA of Maori in the twentieth century and found that New Zealand's Maori population (half a million in 1997) was descended from approximately seventy Polynesian women who had arrived thirty generations earlier, circa 1200–1400. She concluded that these results were "consistent with a general understanding of Maori oral history."[31]

The evidence of archaeology also supports the accuracy of Maori memories. In New Zealand, most of the earliest remains of human settlement and forest-clearing have been carbon-dated to the thirteenth and fourteenth centuries.[32] Independent research in climate history and isotope geochemistry has added further evidence in an ingenious way. New Zealand chemist Alexander Wilson and his colleagues constructed deep chronologies of climate (temperature and precipitation) for the South Pacific. They worked from oxygen isotope ratios in deposits of calcium carbonate on stalagmites in New Zealand caves. Those data yielded evidence of periods of climate change and very violent storms in the Pacific, before and after Polynesian voyages to New Zealand, like other periods of violent weather in the early twenty-first century. These findings may explain why Polynesian voyages to New Zealand started and stopped when they did.[33]

All of this evidence makes clear that the canoe legends refer to events that actually happened. These memories are important to the identity of New Zealanders, Maori and Pakeha alike. Always, Maori continue to remember their maritime past with pride. Their gods were navigators. Their ancestors were seamen of surpassing skill and courage. In New Zealand, Maori have thought of themselves as an immigrant people, and they did not regard the arrival of others as illegitimate. These origins may have made a difference in their responses to Pakeha settlers.

American Indians remember their origins differently. On that subject we were invited to meet a large number of Indian leaders who were not happy about the way that scholars in the United States were writing about their history and culture. We expected the discussions to center on issues of land-taking, but the primary concern was about something else. Indian leaders of many tribes wanted histo-rians to give more respect to their culture, and especially to their memory of origins.[34]

The memories of Indian nations varied in detail, but many shared a central theme. Indian children were taught that their an-cestors came from the dark womb of mother earth, and were born into the sunlight and traveled through the land to their "central place." At the time of European contact, their own histories (with some exceptions) centered on the assumption they had always lived on the land. This idea of origins sustained a strong proprietary sense of place, and a sense of difference from Europeans who came by sea.[35]

Scientists and scholars do not agree with part of this tradition. They conclude from empirical research that the ancestors of Indians were also immigrants, who traveled long distances eastward across the great land mass of Asia toward the North Pacific. These great wanderers made comparatively short water crossings to their new world, and then more long marches through the huge continents of North and South America.

There is a lively debate about when and how these Indian immi-grants passed from Asia to America. Scholars increasingly think that they came by boat in short coastal journeys around the northern rim of the Pacific Ocean. Others hypothesize that Indian immigrants made passages across the Bering Strait, now fifty-six miles of water between Siberia and Alaska, with the Diomede Islands in between. Some scientists favor a third hypothesis, that Indians crossed on a "land bridge" that might have connected Asia and America during glacial periods when sea levels were low. If so, they would have been the only American immigrants who walked to the New World. How-ever these movements were made, water crossings were a small part of longer overland migrations.[36]

These first immigrant-forebears of Indians reached America much earlier than did Maori in New Zealand. Archaeologists have found evidence that Indians were living in both North and South America at least fourteen thousand years before the present. The progress of archaeology continues to move these estimates back in time. Some scholars think that the first crossings from Asia to America may have happened as early as fifty thousand years ago.[37]

Many American Indians remember that their ancestors have always lived on the land. They believe that the land had been a sacred gift from the Great Spirit to them alone in the moment of creation. One of their deepest beliefs is that the land where they lived was theirs, and nobody else had a right to it.[38] Maori are similar in one way. They also have a very strong attachment to the land in New Zealand. They call themselves *tangata whenua*, people of the land. This is not precisely a proprietary idea. Judge Edward Durie, chairman of the Waitangi Tribunal and himself Maori, explains that "one did not own land. One belonged *to* the land." New Zealand's Maori and Pakeha have had many conflicts over land, and much tension exists today, to say the least. But even in the midst of these troubles, Maori and Pakeha have accepted an idea of coexistence that was not always evident among Indians and Europeans in America.[39]

Material Conditions: Unstable Abundance; Growing Scarcity

Other differences appeared in patterns of material life. Before European contact, Maori and American Indians both developed neolithic economies that combined hunting and gathering, fishing and farming, manufacturing and exchange in material cultures of high complexity. But they did so in different ways. Hunting continued to be more important for a longer time in North America, which offered a vast abundance of deer, beaver, buffalo, bear, and other large mammals that did not exist in New Zealand.[40] Many American Indians were also skilled farmers. Their leading crops were corn and beans, which they cultivated with high success. As late as 1779, when New England troops invaded Iroquois country, they discovered that the corn farming of this Indian confederacy was much superior to European agriculture in breeding stocks and crop husbandry, six generations after British settlement.[41]

In America, overall patterns of ecological change were complex. Indians migrated through the hard environment of the subarctic region into temperate and tropical zones, which offered increasing abundance as they spread through the Americas. They hunted some species of animals to extinction, but so vast were the resources of the Americas that many animals remained. Before the Europeans arrived, American Indians lived in ecocultural regimes of unstable abundance. Through the eastern woodlands and the Mississippi Valley, they hunted in small bands of a size that matched their resources, and moved through space in annual rhythms of transhumance that were adapted to their environmental opportunities.

In the period before European settlers arrived in North America, this unstable condition of material abundance had an impact on the history of American Indians. In the eastern woodlands they were able to deal with ecological challenges (which were many) by living in units that were comparatively small, open, mobile, and free. Their material problems could be solved, or eased, by more freedom. The first Europeans to live among them were quick to notice. The founder of New France, Samuel de Champlain, observed that the Indians in the American forest lived lives of liberty so extreme that he called it "*la vie anglaise.*" English settlers agreed in the fact if not the judgment. In time American Indians became living symbols of liberty and freedom.[42]

It was another story in New Zealand, where abundance and scarcity had a different history before the Europeans. For several centuries, Maori flourished in a plentiful environment. They were efficient hunters, skilled gatherers, and expert fishermen. Their favorite prey were moa, big flightless birds, some twice the height of a man. Within a few hundred years the Maori hunted every species of moa to extinction, and forty other species of birds, and many lizards and frogs. They greatly diminished seal populations on the coast.[43]

As hunting became less productive, agriculture grew more important. The leading Maori field crop was kumara, a plant similar to sweet potato that is still widely favored in New Zealand. It often appeared on our table while we were in the country. Maori also cultivated gourds, cabbage trees, flax, some varieties of fern, and other crops. This system of farming was a challenge in many ways. A Polynesian regime of tropical agriculture was adapted with great difficulty to a temperate climate under severe pressure.[44]

Those stresses had an impact on social systems. As problems of scarcity developed, competition for resources caused increasing violence. Warfare became endemic. Cannibalism developed in New Zealand, as on other Pacific islands, the result of desperate conditions that also caused incessant fighting between groups.

At the same time, military security and sedentary agriculture required cooperative institutions within the group. Maori colonists had carried from tropical Polynesia highly developed systems of social integration in the *whanau* (extended family), *hapu* (clan), and *iwi* (tribe). The words *hapu* (literally, from the same womb) and *whanau* (bound by birth) acquired strong communal meanings that spread through Maori culture and are used today by Pakeha.[45]

Material scarcity in New Zealand had an impact on these Maori institutions. It caused increasing conflict between Maori groups, and growing cooperation within them. Tribal became more important than *hapu* clans, and units of settlement grew larger. Early European visitors described Maori villages with hundreds of houses, protected by complex fortifications. Resource limits imposed increasing constraints on Maori. It required them to live and work more closely together if they were to survive.[46]

In these material conditions, Maori developed a constellation of moral principles within primary groups. Near the center is *whakapapa*, often translated as genealogy, but it means much more than that—a highly developed idea of an ethical imperative based on belonging to an ancestral group. Those groups were (and are) also held together by a strong idea of *tauutuutu*, reciprocity. There is a Maori saying, *He tauutuutu kai te manawa o to tatau Maoiritanga,* "Reciprocity is at the heart of our Maori culture." Another vital idea is *kotahitanga*, unity. Maori say, *Ma te kotahitanga e whai kaka ai tatau,* "In unity we have strength." This ethos was complex, dynamic, and always changing. It was highly developed before European contact and made a difference in events that followed.[47]

First Encounters with Europeans

When English-speaking settlers and Indians met in seventeenth-century North America, they often began by fighting. It happened in Virginia on April 26, 1607, when the founders of Jamestown were attacked on their very first night, by "savages creeping upon all fours from the hills like bears, with their bows in their mouths." One of the English settlers remembered that the Indians "charged us very desperately," wounded two people, and were driven off in heavy fighting.[48]

The same thing occurred in New England when the Pilgrims first came ashore on Cape Cod, December 6, 1620. William Bradford remembered that early on the first morning they were attacked without warning by Indians, and "arrows came flying." The Pilgrims ran for their weapons and returned fire until the Indians retreated. The site is preserved today as First Encounter Beach.[49]

It was the same again on Manhattan Island, October 1–2, 1609, when Henry Hudson's Anglo-Dutch crew fought a battle with the Indians on the first day of contact near "Manna-hatta." Many Indians were killed. Rare exceptions in North America were the first permanent French settlements led by Samuel de Champlain, who went another way, and the Quakers in the Delaware Valley, and the Providence Plantations of Roger Williams in what is now Rhode Island.[50]

Violent first encounters at other British settlements were followed by periods of wary exchange and more violence. In early wars, American Indians attempted several times to expel English-speaking

In seventeenth-century Virginia and New England, the founders of Plymouth and Jamestown were fighting with the Indians on the very first day of contact. The spirit of these encounters was captured in this image of Captain John Smith, taking prisoner a chief of the Powhatan confederacy at pistol point.

settlers altogether. This happened at Virginia in the great massacre of 1622, and nearly succeeded. It happened again in New England during King Philip's War in 1676, one of the bloodiest struggles in American history, in the proportion of people killed on both sides. Similar purposes were shared by the great Ottawa war chief Pontiac during the eighteenth century and by the Shawnee warrior Tecumseh and prophet Lalawethika in the early nineteenth century. On the other side, as we shall see, many generations of English-speaking people in the United States explicitly denied to American Indians the rights of citizenship, the most elemental rights of humanity, and basic protections of law until the twentieth century.[51]

The result was an escalating cycle of hostility and violence in North America, as people on each side rejected the legitimacy of the other. The fighting was cruel and bitter. Settlers and Indians were not merely killed in battle but murdered in horrible ways. Land was taken by brute force. The founders of New England were very proprietary about the land, more so than the founders of New France. At Tadoussac, French leaders such as Samuel de Champlain began by asking permission to plant a settlement. In Massachusetts, English Governor John Winthrop declared that "most land in America is *vacuum*—legally waste because the Indians have not subdued it." He concluded that the Indians had "no proprietary rights in the land."[52] These attitudes reinforced a judgment among Native Americans that English settlers had no right to be there. At the same time, New England's leaders believed with equal fervor that Indians had no right to remain. These ways of thinking left little room for coexistence, even in a very large continent.

In New Zealand, it is interesting to observe that the very earliest recorded European contact was as violent as were events in Virginia and New England, and at about the same time. At sunset on December 18, 1642, Dutch explorer Abel Tasman entered the beautiful bay of Taitapu (Golden Bay) on the northwestern tip of the South Island. Maori canoes approached in twilight and greeted (or warned) the newcomers with "loud shouts and ritual blasts of a shell trumpet." Tasman wrote, "We could not in the least understand any of it." The Dutch replied with their own shouts and two trumpets and fired a cannon. Maori "raged terribly" and retreated. The next morning more Maori canoes appeared. The Dutch warily offered gifts of cloth and knives and launched small boats. Suddenly Maori warriors paddled rapidly toward a Dutch boat, rammed it with great force, mortally wounded four sailors with quick blows of their short clubs, and paddled back to shore with what the Dutch described as "unbelievable skill." More canoes came out, led by a man holding a large white

The English founders of Jamestown kept the Indians at a distance. They built a pale around the area of settlement, and forbade Indians to enter without a passport such as these silver badges. Here again we see a difference between seventeenth-century Anglo America and nineteenth-century New Zealand.

*How do we explain differences in relations
between Europeans and native peoples
in seventeenth-century America and
nineteenth-century New Zealand? Part
of the answer appears in the career of this
great leader, Captain James Cook, a man of
the enlightenment who regarded all people
as sharing a common humanity. His early
contacts were guided by that principle.
The key here was a factor of time. Virginia
and New England were founded before
the enlightenment. Major contact in New
Zealand came afterward.*

flag, perhaps as a sign of peace. The angry Dutch replied with their great guns, shot the flag-bearer, and sailed away. They named the place Murderers' Bay—not a hopeful start.[53]

A century later, first encounters between English and Maori also threatened to begin that way. But these contacts developed differently, in large part because of the acts and choices of two extraordinary leaders. One was Captain James Cook, a man of the Enlightenment. The other was his Polynesian companion and friend, the Tahitian scholar-priest Tupaia. In the fall of 1769 they sailed along North Island and found Maori ready and even eager to fight in many places. Cook responded with a combination of restrained force, gestures of peace, and patient communication through Tupaia. Near the Ngaruroro River in Hawke's Bay, on October 14, 1769, large canoes of Maori warriors converged on Cook's ship, *Endeavour*, shouting war cries and brandishing weapons. Cook fired grapeshot across their bows. They retreated, and more canoes approached. Tupaia called out to them to leave their weapons in another vessel and come alongside, which they did. They talked together of history and geography, "exchanging the names of kings and countries, etc." Communication was the key. Cook, Tupaia, and Maori leaders were able to establish peaceful contact in many parts of New Zealand because they could talk together.[54]

Comparative Chronologies: Timing and Sequence in Early Encounters

Cook and Tupaia were followed by scattered settlers and traders, most of whom managed to live in peace with Maori, with some very violent exceptions such as the massacre of passengers and crew aboard the ship *Boyd* at Whangaroa in 1809. Michael King writes, "Most Maori had welcomed European settlers when they first encountered them. . . . Many chiefs spoke with pride of 'their' Pakeha." At no point did they make a sustained attempt to expel Pakeha settlers, even in early years when the disparity in numbers was great.[55]

Then came the Christian missionaries who settled in small parties before the great migrations—an important fact. Anglicans led by Samuel Marsden arrived in 1814. Methodists were at Whangaroa in 1822, and Catholics at Hokiango in 1838, and Moravians in the Chatham Islands by 1842. Missionaries were converting Maori leaders to Christianity by the 1830s. Many Maori had been proselytized before European migration and settlement began on a large scale in 1840. Here was an important difference of chronology in America and New Zealand.[56]

Some of these missionaries were themselves much changed by Maori, and at an early date. In 1822, missionary Thomas Kendall wrote of Maori beliefs that their "apparent sublimity almost completely turned me from a Christian to a Heathen."[57] In Northland, Maori and Pakeha leaders began to integrate elements of Christian belief and Polynesian culture. These were profoundly different ways of thinking. Abstractions were not easily translated from one language to the other. Even so, early leaders found many possibilities for ethical conjunctions. On one side was the Maori ethos of *kitihitanga* (unity), *mahinga tahi* (cooperation), *tauutuutu* (reciprocity), and *utu* (often understood as revenge, but more fundamentally an idea of an appropriate return or balance), all within the frame of *whakapapa* (ancestry) and *hapu* (extended family). On the other side was the example of Jesus, the teachings of the four Gospels, the Golden Rule, and secular concepts of equity, justice, and fairness.[58]

From the start, before the large settlements, British missionaries and imperial leaders in New Zealand formed very positive ideas of Maori. Samuel Marsden wrote, "The more I see of these people, the more I am pleased with and astonished at their moral ideas, and characters. They appear like a superior race." Many British leaders made similar statements of respect and empathy for Maori—and vice versa—in part because some important elements of two ethical systems could be reconciled.[59]

Attitudes toward Maori among major figures such as Marsden were very different from those of early English leaders toward Indians in North America. The cause was complex, but a vital factor was time. In the fifteenth and sixteenth centuries, Europeans perceived American Indians as the Devil's children. Leading examples of this thinking were Christopher Columbus (1451–1506), his brothers Bartolomeo and Giacomo, and his son Diego in the Caribbean. Similar attitudes appeared among Francisco Pizarro (ca. 1475–1541) and his brothers in Peru, Hernán Cortes (1485–1547) in Mexico, and Juan Ponce de Leon (1460–1521) and Hernando de Soto (d. 1542) in Florida.

These men were very brutal to the American Indians. So were the African-Portuguese explorer Estévan Gomez (fl. 1490–1525), the Danish pirates Pining and Pothorst (fl. 1494–1510?), the French captain Jacques Cartier (1491–1557), and the English explorer Martin Frobisher (ca. 1535–94). These early explorers kidnapped Indians and took them home as specimens and slaves. Frobisher's English seamen killed natives for sport and stripped an elderly Indian woman of her clothing to see if she had cloven hoofs. They did not recognize her as human. In Maine, when the English captain George Weymouth and his brutal seamen grew "weary" of the American Indians, they set flesh-eating English mastiffs on them. In all of these early encounters the "Black Legend" was firmly founded in fact, but it described an era rather than a nation. From the fifteenth to the mid-sixteenth centuries, with exceptions such as Bartolomé de Las Casas, Europeans did not treat American Indians humanely.[60]

Attitudes began to change in the late sixteenth and early seventeenth centuries, among men such as Samuel de Champlain (1570–1635), Pierre Dugua, Sieur de Mons (ca. 1560–1628), and several groups of French humanists in North America, all inspired by their king Henri IV. Other strains of humanist thinking also appeared among a few English Puritans such as John Eliot (1604–90) and Roger Williams (1603?–83), and many Quakers such as George Fox (1624–91) and William Penn (1644–1718). But they were exceptions in their time.[61]

By the time that Captain Cook explored New Zealand in 1769–70, a thought-revolution had occurred in the Western world. The values of the Enlightenment inspired a universal idea of humanity. Before New Zealand's great colonial migrations began in 1840, the Evangelical Movement also overswept the Protestant nations. New Zealand historian Erik Olssen was one of the first to observe the importance of timing in attitudes and settlements.[62]

All of this made a difference for Indians and Maori. The first encounters between Europeans and Indians happened in America before the spread of humanist ideas from the Italian Quattrocento, and long before the Enlightenment and the Evangelical Movement. First encounters between Maori and British explorers came after these great ethical events. Anne Salmond's study of Captain Cook's first encounter with Maori and Polynesian people found that the English approach was "based on the perception, shared by James Cook himself, that in his journeys of Pacific exploration, Europeans and 'natives' alike were only human." Further, Salmond found that Cook always was "determined to act as an enlightened leader during his first two voyages." Sometimes he had trouble doing so, especially after a violent encounter at Queen Charlotte Sound in 1777, but he preserved a spirit of humanity and enlightenment to the end of his life.[63]

A second vital factor (linked to the first) was communication. In North America Samuel de Champlain got on with the Indians because he could talk with Anadabijou of the Montagnais, Bessabes of the Penobscot, Membertou of the Mi'kmaq, and many others.[64] The same thing happened on the coast of New Zealand in 1769 when Captain Cook could speak to Maori through his Tahitian companion, Tupaia, who was one of the pivotal figures in the history of New Zealand. More important, these men could listen. In these exchanges Maori leaders acted in a reciprocal spirit, as did the stately chiefs of Anaura in their red feathers and white dogskin cloaks near Poverty Bay, and the high chief Te Whakatatare-o-te-Rangi at his school of learning in Tolaga Bay, and the high chief Tapua in the Bay of Islands.[65] The timing and sequence of these early contacts made for a major difference between New Zealand and North America.

Treaties

After the first encounters came the treaties. In North America, hundreds of treaties were made between American Indians and anglophone settlers. It has been said that American Indian nations were "treatied almost to death."[66] Many were broken even before the ink was dry. Indians were driven off their land, sometimes with extreme violence, by land-hungry settlers, state authorities, and the federal government. An example was the Trail of Tears in the 1830s, when the "civilized tribes" of Cherokees, Creeks, Chickasaws, and Choctaws were forcibly removed from their ancestral homes by settlers and the United States Army, and driven west on winter marches that killed many women and children. On forced marches of thirteen thousand Cherokees in 1838, four thousand died of hunger, exposure, cruelty, and callous neglect. The mortality rate on that Trail of Tears was greater than on the Bataan Death March, and one group of Americans inflicted it on another. It was not the worst.[67]

New Zealand's record was far from perfect, but it went another way. Where Americans made many Indian treaties and forgot them, New Zealanders made one treaty and remembered it: the Treaty of Waitangi, February 6, 1840. Since 1974, that day has become New Zealand's national holiday. Many New Zealanders—Maori especially[68]—remember the Treaty of Waitangi as "significant"

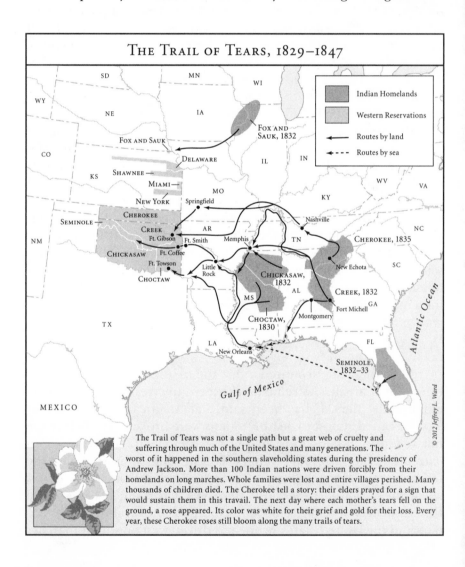

THE TRAIL OF TEARS, 1829–1847

	Indian Homelands
	Western Reservations
→	Routes by land
◀---	Routes by sea

The Trail of Tears was not a single path but a great web of cruelty and suffering through much of the United States and many generations. The worst of it happened in the southern slaveholding states during the presidency of Andrew Jackson. More than 100 Indian nations were driven forcibly from their homelands on long marches. Whole families were lost and entire villages perished. Many thousands of children died. The Cherokee tell a story: their elders prayed for a sign that would sustain them in this travail. The next day where each mother's tears fell on the ground, a rose appeared. Its color was white for their grief and gold for their loss. Every year, these Cherokee roses still bloom along the many trails of tears.

and "meaningful" for them. Some do not. A few think of it with pain, and even with anger. There was also a dark period in the nineteenth century when corrupt and racist Pakeha judges in New Zealand decreed that the Treaty of Waitangi was not the law of the land. But that attitude changed again during the twentieth century. The Waitangi Treaty has become a central part of New Zealand's cultural identity, even as people disagree on its meaning.[69]

An important fact about the Treaty of Waitangi is that Pakeha and Maori made it freely together. It was an act of deliberate choice on both sides. In 1840, both British and Maori leaders were deeply troubled by conditions in the islands. Some worried about the New Zealand Company and Edward Gibbon Wakefield, who were buying land on both islands in 1839 and acting as if they were a law unto themselves. Individual Maori sold land they did not own, and Pakeha bought it with promises they did not keep.

And the French were moving in. A colorful adventurer who called himself the Baron de Thierry arrived with colonists in 1837 and claimed to be Feudal Proprietor of New Zealand. American whalers and sealers were swarming on the coast, with no imperial ambitions but a hunger for anything that could be turned into a Yankee dollar. Most worrisome to Maori was their own internal disorder. The Musket Wars had been raging among their own people since 1807—thirty years of escalating violence, vengeance, enslavement, and cruelty beyond description, with hundreds of battles and an estimated twenty thousand deaths.[70]

In the 1830s the Musket Wars were still going on, and some tribes were arming themselves with artillery. It was madness, but Maori leaders could not end it, and the British Colonial Office was increasingly concerned. To keep the peace it sent a forward-looking young British Resident named James Busby who built a house at Waitangi, and planted New Zealand's first vineyards and tree nurseries. In 1834 and 1835, he and a party of missionaries and merchants persuaded a group of Maori chiefs to adopt a flag for New Zealand, issue a Declaration of Independence (with an eye to the French), form a tribal confederation, and frame a government. The government failed, but Busby urged Maori leaders to meet and talk together.[71]

That effort opened the way for New Zealand's first governor (officially lieutenant governor), William Hobson. He arrived in 1840 aboard Her Majesty's frigate *Herald*, with instructions to make a treaty with Maori chiefs and persuade them to accept British sovereignty in return for a guarantee of their lands, rights, and self-rule.[72]

THE SIGNING OF THE WAITANGI TREATY, 1840

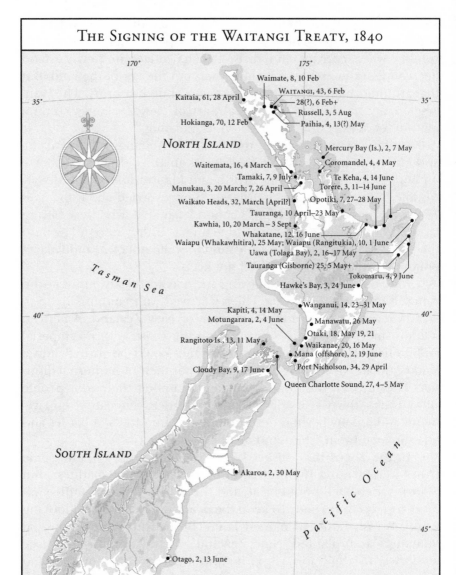

Waimate, 8, 10 Feb
WAITANGI, 43, 6 Feb
Kaitaia, 61, 28 April
28(?), 6 Feb+
Russell, 3, 5 Aug
Hokianga, 70, 12 Feb
Paihia, 4, 13(?) May

NORTH ISLAND

Mercury Bay (Is.), 2, 7 May
Coromandel, 4, 4 May
Waitemata, 16, 4 March
Tamaki, 7, 9 July
Te Keha, 4, 14 June
Manukau, 3, 20 March; 7, 26 April
Torere, 3, 11–14 June
Waikato Heads, 32, March [April?]
Opotiki, 7, 27–28 May
Tauranga, 10 April–23 May
Kawhia, 10, 20 March – 3 Sept
Whakatane, 12, 16 June
Waiapu (Whakawhitira), 25, May; Waiapu (Rangitukia), 10, 1 June
Uawa (Tolaga Bay), 2, 16–17 May
Tauranga (Gisborne) 25, 5 May+
Tokomaru, 4, 9 June
Hawke's Bay, 3, 24 June

Tasman Sea

Wanganui, 14, 23–31 May
Kapiti, 4, 14 May
Motungarara, 2, 4 June
Manawatu, 26 May
Otaki, 18, May 19, 21
Rangitoto Is., 13, 11 May
Waikanae, 20, 16 May
Mana (offshore), 2, 19 June
Cloudy Bay, 9, 17 June
Port Nicholson, 34, 29 April
Queen Charlotte Sound, 27, 4–5 May

SOUTH ISLAND

Akaroa, 2, 30 May

Pacific Ocean

Otago, 2, 13 June

0 Miles 100 200
0 Kilometers 200

Ruapuke, 3, 10 June

STEWART ISLAND

The Waitangi Treaty was signed by more than 500 Maori leaders throughout New Zealand, from February 6 to September 3, 1840. This map shows the dates, places, and approximate numbers of signers. It is compiled by Claudia Orange from manuscript treaty sheets in New Zealand's National Archives.

© 2012 Jeffrey L. Ward after Claudia Orange

At Hobson's invitation, Maori and British imperial leaders came together at James Busby's house near Waitangi, on February 5, 1840. It was one of the great scenes in modern history: a "particularly fine day" in midsummer, on a long green lawn looking outward across a broad sheet of blue water to Bay of Islands. HMS *Herald* lay at anchor, with her boats moving to and fro. Other vessels were moored nearby, British and American, with colors flying. Hundreds of Maori leaders arrived in "numerous canoes gliding from every direction . . . rowers straining every nerve to gain and keep the lead, whilst their paddles kept time with the cadence of the canoe song of the *kai-tuki* [canoe singer], who standing conspicuously erect in the midst of each canoe, and often on the thwarts, animated the men by his gestures as well as his voice."[73]

Herald's seamen rigged a huge tent of sailcloth above the lawn and dressed it with bright bunting from the frigate's flagbags. A big crowd assembled in the tent, perhaps seven hundred in all. Most were a great gathering of Maori leaders, some in dogskin mats, others in cloaks "of every shade of striking colour," a few in European suits or "common native dress." In the center stood Hakitara, the very tall chief of the Rawara, in a "large and handsome silky white *kaitaka* mat," the "sunlight streaming down from an aperture in the top of the tent on this beautiful white dress." Around the edges, Europeans and Americans were looking on, and young Midshipman Henry Comber of the Royal Navy was taking notes. He specially noticed that "200 Maori women and children were present," and "the women were very pretty."

At the front of the tent was a raised platform for Governor Hobson and his staff. Before him was his total military strength, a corporal's guard of eleven mounted police from New South Wales in scarlet tunics. The French military bishop Jean Baptiste Pompallier in his purple robes stood to one side, and British Protestant clergy in black gathered on the other.[74] Governor Hobson rose, spoke briefly to the Europeans, then turned to the Maori chiefs and talked at length in English, while missionary Henry Williams translated his words into Maori. Hobson impressed the Maori by his upright military manner, straight talk, and an entire absence of guile and vanity. He said that Queen Victoria was "always ready to protect her subjects, and is also always ready to restrain them." She wished "to do good to the chiefs and people of New Zealand, but only with your consent." Hobson reminded them that "you yourselves have often asked the king of England to extend his protection to you. Her Majesty now offers you that protection in this treaty." His words were repeated in Maori, as everyone listened "in profound silence."[75]

The treaty itself was a very brief document with three short articles. The first gave the queen "all the rights and power of sovereignty" in the English text and *te kawanatanga katoa* in Maori, literally "complete government over the country." Article II gave Maori *te tino rangatiratanga,* literally in Claudia Orange's translation "the unqualified exercise of chieftainship," and also guaranteed to Maori "exclusive and undisturbed possession" of lands and estates, forests, fisheries, and other properties," as long as they wished to keep them. It provided that lands must be sold to the Crown, not to private purchasers unless the Crown refused to buy them. Article III, profoundly important in the larger scheme of things, extended all the "rights and privileges of British subjects" to "all the Natives of New Zealand."[76]

Hobson proposed that the Maori chiefs start with five hours of debate among themselves on the treaty, then take a night to reflect, and have another debate the next day before making a decision— and with more time if they wished it. At first, several Maori responses were hostile to the treaty, though respectful of Hobson as he was of them. Some Maori predicted that they would lose their land and become slaves; others expressed deep suspicion of British missionaries and settlers. But equally strong views were freely expressed in support of the treaty. One chief asked, "What did we do before Pakeha came? We fought, we fought continually. But now we can plant our grounds, and the Pakeha will bring plenty of trade to our shores." Another urged the chiefs to think "how much the character of New Zealanders had been exalted by their intercourse with Europeans."

They spoke about the ambitions of the Americans and the French, who were both present in the tent. In 1840, Maori leaders were well informed about the world. Many had been to Australia, and some to Britain. They had witnessed chain gangs of convict laborers in New South Wales, and some feared that they themselves might be "reduced to the condition of slaves and compelled to break stones on the roads." Major factors were Bishop Pompallier's French priests, who circulated freely on the lawn at Waitangi, urged Maori not to make a British treaty, and in the process offered evidence of why they should.[77]

After long discussion, most Maori leaders decided to sign the Waitangi Treaty. Some hoped it would bring peace among their people, and an alliance with the British. Others thought it might keep the Americans and French away. Many chiefs also feared that the treaty would increase land-taking by Englishmen, but most decided that the strengths of the treaty were greater than its weaknesses. The meeting at Waitangi was followed by gatherings throughout New Zealand. More than five hundred Maori chiefs agreed to sign.

Hobson and the Maori chiefs succeeded not by force or by fraud, or even by persuasion, but by finding a mutuality of material interest and a harmony of ethical principles. The central principle was a creative tension between two elements. One was British "sovereignty," or *kawanatanga* (governance) in the Maori text. The other was the guarantee of *te tino rangatiratanga*, which meant not only "unqualified exercise of chieftainship" but, more broadly, "Maori control over Maori things." At the heart of the treaty was an idea of divided powers—a concept fundamental to governance among English-speaking people. Maori chiefs were not stupid, ignorant, or innocent natives. They believed that the treaty, even with its flaws, was the best way for them.[78]

Early British governors genuinely tried to respect the treaty and sought to do justice to the Maori, particularly on questions of land-taking. Maori historian Ranginui Walker writes, "Hobson and Fitz-Roy took seriously their first duty to protect the rights of the Maori from settler land hunger." Both became unpopular among British settlers, largely because of their attention to Maori rights under the treaty and their appointment of officers called Protectors of Aborigines. Some of the governors who followed them were not so scrupulous, and several went a different way.

Maori chiefs and British officers established a frame of law, and an idea of divided powers between *te kawanatanga katoa* for the queen and *te tino rangatiratanga* for Maori. Together they created the possibility of balance, justice, and fairness. Bad things would happen in years to come, and those ideals were never fully realized.[79] But even so, the first British leaders set a high ethical standard. When Captain James Cook embarked on his first voyage to the South Pacific, he carried strict orders from the Earl of Morton, president of the Royal Society in London. Cook was told in no uncertain terms that the native people of the Pacific were to be recognized as "the natural, and . . . legal possessors of the several Regions they inhabit," and that any use of their lands required free and full consent. New Zealand's historian John Wilson observes that "a line can be drawn from Cook's first voyage to the Treaty of Waitangi."[80]

The Taking of the Land

The first British governors of New Zealand tried to respect those rules, but many settlers did not. They started a long process by which most of the lands were taken from Maori, in defiance of the Earl of Morton and the Waitangi Treaty. In 1800, the area of New Zealand was approximately 26.9 million hectares (65.6 million acres). All of it belonged to Maori before the first Europeans arrived. By the year 2000, Maori lands had fallen to 1.3 million hectares (3.2 million acres). In two centuries, Maori lost 95 percent of their land.

Most of it happened in sales of large tracts for small prices. Big blocks of land were bought by the New Zealand Company for its colonies, circa 1839–44. Then came another round in which the prime mover was Governor Sir George Grey (1845–53), a very complex figure. Maori respected his *mana* and valued his genuine interest in their culture. But as we have seen, there was another side to George Grey. He abolished the Protectors of Aborigines and accelerated the acquisition of Maori land. From 1846 to 1860, Governor Grey's land agents persuaded the great Ngai Tahu tribe to sell nearly all of the South Island and Stewart Island as Crown land in eleven big blocks for 14,800 pounds sterling. It was done with much sharp practice, chicanery, and outright fraud. The Nagi Tahu were promised 10 percent of the land for their use, and the promises were broken by fraud and force. In that one set of transactions, Maori lost nearly 60 percent of the land in New Zealand.[81]

Lands in the North Island were taken in more complex ways. Purchases of 7 million acres were made before Grey, often in fraudulent transactions. When the Maori refused to part with their land, Grey authorized the seizure of 3.3 million acres without pay or permission, a direct breach of the Treaty of Waitangi. About 1.6 million acres were actually taken. Maori lost their best lands and many were driven from some of their most sacred places. In James Belich's phrase, Grey became "a philo-Maori hammer of the Maori."[82]

After Grey, more tracts of Maori land were taken by legal proceedings from 1865 to 1890, in what Maori called the Land-Taking Court. Another 2.7 million acres were seized by preemption and forced purchase from 1891 to 1914. By 1914, Maori retained title to only about 8.8 million acres, and even that was not the end of it. From 1914 to 1975, another 5 million acres were lost in many small sales, preemptions, and confiscations for nonpayment of taxes under parliamentary statutes that were enacted from 1865 to as late as 1967. By 1975, only about 3 million acres remained.[83]

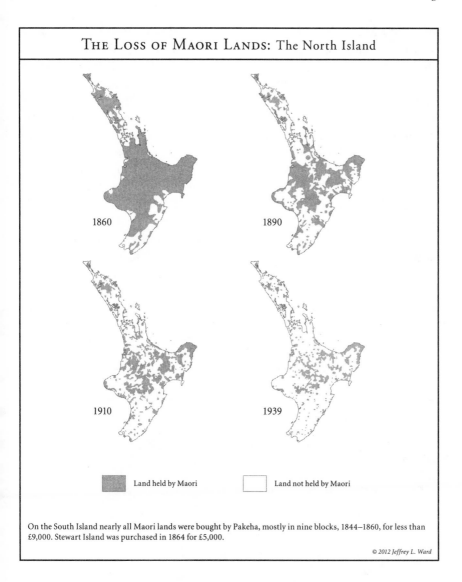

THE LOSS OF MAORI LANDS: The North Island

1860

1890

1910

1939

Land held by Maori   Land not held by Maori

On the South Island nearly all Maori lands were bought by Pakeha, mostly in nine blocks, 1844–1860, for less than £9,000. Stewart Island was purchased in 1864 for £5,000.

© 2012 Jeffrey L. Ward

After 1868, much of this long process was in direct violation of the Treaty of Waitangi, a betrayal of promises made in good faith by Hobson and FitzRoy in New Zealand and by the Earl of Morton and Sir James Stephen in London. Much of it was outright theft. The rationale was cast in terms of race: land was wasted on Maori, Britons could put it to use. Here was the greatest act of unfairness and injustice in New Zealand's history.

Some New Zealanders struggled to protect native rights. One part of the Treaty of Waitangi had introduced a principle of justice in which Maori had the same rights as British subjects. As early as 1856, Donald McLean recommended that Maori should be given the right to vote. That proposal was revived by James Edward FitzGerald, who insisted that Maori were entitled to "all political rights" and "fair representation" in Parliament.[84] One result was the Native Rights Act of 1865, which guaranteed full rights to Maori men. Another was the Maori Representation Act of 1867, which created four Maori seats in Parliament and gave universal male suffrage to Maori before it was granted to Britons in the United Kingdom. The first elections followed in 1868, and Maori were appointed to the Legislative Council in 1872. All this was far in advance of other English-speaking countries.[85]

Worse things happened in the United States, where even more land was taken and few legal rights were given to Indians until the twentieth century. The total land area was not 65.6 million acres, as in New Zealand, but 2.3 billion acres. It should have been enough for coexistence, and yet an even larger part of it was taken from native people. By 2010, Indians retained only 2.3 percent of the land

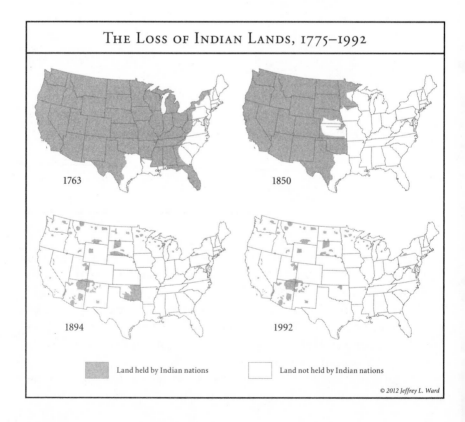

THE LOSS OF INDIAN LANDS, 1775–1992

1763

1850

1894

1992

Land held by Indian nations

Land not held by Indian nations

© 2012 Jeffrey L. Ward

they had once possessed, and much of that small remnant was the most miserable land in the country.

On top of that, American Indians were denied legal rights and protections under the United States Constitution. They were refused rights of citizenship until Congress passed the Snyder Act in 1924, more than three hundred years after the first permanent English settlements. New Zealand's record was better in that respect. Other rights embedded in the Waitangi Treaty have ebbed and flowed for many generations, but always they were there. The treaty proclaimed an idea of fairness, equity, justice, and the rule of law, even when these ideas were honored in the breach.

The Experience of War

Conflicts over land led to much fighting in both the United States and New Zealand. Indians and Maori were formidable in war. They won many battles, but lost the campaigns and were defeated by technology, logistics, and the weight of numbers. The results were similar in both countries.[86]

But the wars were conducted differently. In the United States, clashes flared suddenly, often from individual acts by European settlers and Indian braves. Retaliation followed quickly in an escalation of violence. That process reached its deadly climax in the American West during the late nineteenth century. The great warrior Geronimo remembered how it was with his own people, the Chiricahua Apache. A white child was kidnapped by a small band of Indians. The United States Army arrested another band who were innocent, hanged them, and left their bodies to rot at a rope's end, a fate worse than death itself for that proud warrior people. Horrific acts of vengeance followed on both sides and grew into full-scale wars.[87]

It was different in New Zealand. An early example of the New Zealand Way was the Wairau Affair (1843), in which two Maori warriors, Te Rauparaha and Te Rangiheata, tried to stop a surveying party of the New Zealand Company: first by warnings, then by pulling up surveyors' stakes, and by burning a hut after British property inside had been carried to safety. The New Zealand Company sent out an armed party. As discussions began, a musket shot rang out and a native fell dead. The infuriated Maori attacked, and killed twenty-two Europeans.

What happened next was what made the difference. New Zealand's Governor Robert FitzRoy intervened. He condemned the violence of the Maori but declared that the British had been in the wrong, and he guaranteed Maori title to their lands. FitzRoy was much criticized by Pakeha settlers, but he acted with firmness and affirmed an idea of justice and fairness.[88]

Another precedent was set by the acts of two Maori leaders in Northland. The first was Hongi Hika (1772–1828), a Nga Puhi chief who welcomed European seamen, merchants, and missionaries and protected them from other Maori. Early mission stations were founded with his protection at the Bay of Islands, Kerikeri, and Waimate. Hongi Hika imported metal tools and wrought a great change in Maori farming. In 1820, he visited England, met King George IV, and helped Cambridge scholars compile the first Maori dictionary. He was given a suit of armor and many presents, which he carried to Sydney and sold for muskets and gunpowder, using his new weapons to make war against other Maori on the North Island.[89]

In 1826, Hongi attacked the Ngati Uru and Ngati Pou, who had shown hostility to Methodist missionaries at Whangeroa, and was shot in the chest. On his deathbed he told his people, "Children and friends, pay attention to my last words. After I am gone, be kind to the missionaries. Be kind also to the other Europeans. Welcome them to our shore. Trade with them, protect them, and live with them as one people; but if ever there should land on this soil a people who wear red garments, who do not work, who neither buy nor sell, and who always have arms in their hands, then be aware that they are a people called soldiers, a dangerous people, whose only occupation is war. When you see them, make war against them. Then O my children, be brave! Then, O friends be strong! Be brave that you may not be enslaved, and that your country may not become the possession of strangers."[90]

Hongi Hika's words were heard by his son-in-law, Hone Wiremu Heke Pokai (ca. 1807?–50), another great Nga Puhi warrior of high character and purpose. He was educated at a British Mission School at Kerikeri and baptized with the Christian names Hone (John) and Wiremu (William). Hone Heke formed a friendship with Anglican missionaries, and also with the United States consul in the Bay of Islands, J. B. Mayhew. His American friends told him about their War of Independence against Britain and gave him an American flag, which Hone Heke flew from the sternpost of his canoe as an emblem of freedom and independence. Even as he remained friendly to British settlers, he was concerned about the increasing exercise of British control in the Bay of Islands. A symbol was the raising of the Union Jack on a pole above Korarareka.[91]

The acts and choices of Maori leaders also made a difference. An example was Hone Heke, proud defender of Maori rights and a seeker after mutual fairness and justice in relations with Paheka. In this painting (1846) his wife Hariata wears European dress, and Heke is in Maori clothing. His ally Kawiti carries a traditional taiaha, while Hone Heke holds a musket.

On July 8, 1844, Heke's followers cut down the British flagpole in Kororareka. One New Zealand historian has called that act a Maori "Declaration of Independence." The British replaced the pole, and Hone Heke pulled it down again. The British put it up once more, posted guards, and put a price on the head of Hone Heke. He replied, "Am I a pig that I am bought and sold?" With what one scholar describes as "magnificent bravado," he returned to the flagpole, contemptuously pushed the guards aside, and pulled it down yet again. The British brought in troops, and Hone Heke defeated them on March 11, 1845, in what was described by a Pakeha historian of the old school as a "fair fight." British reinforcements were summoned from Australia. Hone Heke enticed the British troops into a bayonet assault on a heavily fortified position at Puketutu, and defeated them yet again in a brilliant campaign.[92]

The combat was intense, but Heke insisted on strict rules of engagement. Fighting only happened in daylight, and Hone Heke

drew a line that protected the missions of both Anglicans and Roman
Catholics. He safeguarded a printing press, ordered his warriors not
to harm noncombatants, arranged truces to protect the wounded,
and brought in missionaries to bury the British troops he killed.

The British sent more troops against him and recruited other
Maori to help them. Hone Heke switched to Fabian tactics. After
another campaign that ended with a British success but no decisive victory, a peace was negotiated. Both sides agreed to respect
the Treaty of Waitangi. Hone Heke continued to maintain friendly
relations with Europeans who came in peace, but fiercely defended
Maori rights. The British were very careful not to erect another
flagpole at Korarareka, until Maori themselves raised one on their
own terms many years later. A great flagstaff still stands there today,
without a flag when we were there, a fitting monument to Hone
Heke.[93]

Not all New Zealand wars were conducted in the spirit of Governor FitzRoy, Hongi Hika, and Hone Heke. Later campaigns in
Taranaki and the Waikato Country (1860–72) were sometimes very
brutal. The tone was changed by officers such as the regrettable Captain Lloyd of the 57th Foot, an officer "new to Maori warfare," who
advanced recklessly into the bush and laid waste to Maori fields in
Taranaki, while exposing his command in a vulnerable position. The
infuriated Maori struck back, broke the British force, and killed its
commander near New Plymouth on April 6, 1860. Captain Lloyd's
head was cut off and "preserved in the native fashion by baking with
leaves, etc., and carried by war parties as a trophy, to incite the natives." It was also a warning to the Pakeha, on how they should conduct their wars. This episode was regarded by General James
Alexander as a lamentable lapse of British leadership and a splendid
feat of soldiering by his Maori opponents.[94]

Other British lapses in Taranaki involved Colonel Trevor Chute,
a stupid and sadistic man who allowed his troops to murder Maori
prisoners, kill noncombatants, and behave with savagery far beyond
the acts of people he called savages. But Captain Lloyd and Colonel
Chute were very much exceptions. More typical British leaders in
New Zealand were officers such as Duncan Cameron and James Alexander, men of character and humanity. They admired the courage
and skill of the Maori warriors, and what Alexander described as
their sense of "fair play." Alexander celebrated a document sent by
the chiefs of Tauranga that proposed "laws for regulating our fight":
no killing of unarmed Pakeha, no murdering of wounded, and sanctuary for any soldier who fled to the house of a priest.[95]

A memorable exemplar of Maori ethics was Taratoa, a teacher and a great warrior of the Ngai Te Rangi. In the Waikato War of 1863–64, he fought fiercely for his lands and his people. He also drew up another code of conduct for Maori warriors that combined Christian and Maori principles. One of his rules came from Romans 12:20: "If thine enemy hunger, feed him. If he thirst, give him drink." During the war, Taratoa's warriors severely wounded a British colonel. Taratoa himself carried a calabash of cold water to the British officer at risk to his own life. Shortly afterward he was killed at the battle of Te Ranga and was buried in a rifle pit on the field. For many years, even into the twentieth century, as we shall see, the example of Taratoa inspired Pakeha New Zealanders. British soldiers remembered him for an ethic of right conduct, justice, and fair play that engaged the values of two cultures. When Bishop Selwyn returned to England as Bishop of Lichfield, he commissioned a stained glass window in memory of Taratoa.[96]

All this made a striking contrast with Indian wars in the United States. Americans of European descent also honor the memory of great Indian warriors. We remember Pontiac and Tecumseh, who came closest to uniting the Indian tribes against the Europeans, for their eloquent defense of Indian freedom. We celebrate the superb defiance of Osceola, the great Seminole chief who said, "They could not capture me except under a white flag. They could not hold me except with a chain." We respect Sitting Bull, who

Taratoa became a hero to Maori and Pakeha alike. He was a formidable warrior who fought for his people and also a teacher who drew up a code of conduct that combined Maori and Christian principles. On the battlefield he risked his life to take a calabash of water to British wounded. Long afterward he was remembered for his courage in combat and for his ethics of right conduct, justice, and "fair play."

hated whites with a passion and fought bravely for the rights of his people. We honor Geronimo and great leaders of his nation, not for the ethics of Apache warfare, which were cruel beyond imagining, but for their fierce and stubborn struggle for independence.[97] And Americans cherish the memory of Tashunca-uitco, or Crazy Horse (ca. 1849–77), named after a solitary wild pony who galloped through the village when he was born. He was an Oglala Sioux warrior who refused to live on reservations. A brilliant tactician, he defeated a much larger U.S. force at Rosebud and was instrumental in Custer's defeat at Little Big Horn. He demanded the right to live free.[98]

The spirit of these American conflicts was different from the fighting in New Zealand. Many citizens of the United States, civilians perhaps more than soldiers, shared the view of Major General Philip Sheridan that "the only good Indians I ever saw were dead." That remark spread widely through the West and was repeated in many variations, of which the best known was "The only good Indian is a dead Indian." It was an attitude that rejected the humanity of American Indians, and denied even their right to life itself.[99]

One might compare General Sheridan with an eminent military leader in New Zealand, General Sir James Alexander, who served in

Many Americans honor the memory of the great warrior Geronimo, not for his ethics of Apache warfare, which were cruel beyond imagining, but for his fierce and stubborn struggle to defend the independence, freedom, and liberty of his people.

the Maori Wars of the 1860s and published two books about his experiences: a popular history called *Incidents of the Maori War* (1863) and a professional monograph called *Bush Fighting* (1873). In both works General Alexander described himself as "an aborigines protectionist," and he praised the moral character of what he called "the fine race of Maoris." He wrote of "our duty to preserve aborigines and not destroy them, God's creatures, given an earthly inheritance as well as ourselves." General Alexander urged New Zealanders to think of their nation as embracing both Pakeha and Maori in a fair-minded way: "We are too apt to legislate as if for a white colony, quite forgetting the rights and claims of the original lords of the soil, a noble race of aborigines physically, and a great number of them with very acute intellects."[100]

The range of attitudes was similar in both countries. General Alexander observed that "in every community there are men of low minds, usually also cowardly, who seem to take pleasure insulting those whom they think inferior to themselves, particularly if the skin is of a darker hue." But the balance of judgment was not the same. A long road remained ahead in both countries. Much of it is still untraveled.[101]

Demographic Decline

After contact with large numbers of Europeans, Maori and Indian populations began a long decline. The cause was complex, but the major part of it was a rise in mortality among indigenous people. In the United States, numbers of American Indians shrank very rapidly. Before 1492, at least several million American Indians lived north of the Rio Grande. Some think more, but all agree that the nadir was reached circa 1900 when the U.S. Census counted 237,000 Indians in the United States.

In that year, the total population of American Indians had declined by at least 90 percent. Maori population of New Zealand reached its low point in 1896, at 42,000. Many observers believed that Maori were destined for extinction. Similar predictions were made for American Indians. Much the same trend also appeared among African Americans in the United States. As late as 1860, they had been 18 percent of the American population. By 1890, they were 9 percent of the nation. In the 1930s, about 3,000 former slaves were interviewed at length about their lives. Many testified that slavery was very bad, but that the period after emancipation was worse, as we shall see.[102]

Spiritual Renewal and Ethical Ideas among American Indians

Indians and Maori were not passive victims. During the long decline in the nineteenth century, countermovements of great power developed. Even in this most difficult era, people of these three groups began an extraordinary process of renewal. It started with a spiritual revival. In the United States many leaders emerged among the American Indians. Among them was a Shawnee medicine man who took the name of Tenskwatawa (1768?–1834). Another was an Iroquois war chief known by his title of Ganeodiyo, or Handsome Lake (1735?–1815). Both were highborn within their nations. Handsome Lake was the brother or half brother of Cornplanter, the great Iroquois leader. Tenskwatawa was said to be the twin brother of Tecumseh. Both experienced military defeat that broke the power of their nations: the Iroquois during the "War of the Thirteen Fires," as they called the American Revolution; the Shawnee at the Battle of Fallen Timbers in 1794, which forced them to leave their homeland. Both suffered through a time of moral collapse that followed. Both lost their way, turned to drink, fell deathly ill, and slipped into a coma from which signs of life disappeared.[103]

For Handsome Lake the crisis came in 1799, when he suffered a total collapse. His breathing and pulse appeared to cease, and he was said to turn deathly cold except for a small spot of warmth in the middle of his chest. Then suddenly he awakened and described a vision in which spirits visited him with messages from the Creator. Something similar happened independently to the Shawnee

Another spiritual leader was Sequoyah, a Cherokee hunter who invented a unique system of writing for his people, taught them to read and write it, and published many works about the traditional beliefs of his nation.

medicine man, who fell ill and appeared to die in the spring of 1805. On the eve of his funeral he revived and said that he had been visited by spirits who revealed to him the wishes of the Master of Life, and he took the name of Tenskwatawa, "the Open Door."[104]

These men became prophets, and some of their teachings were very similar. They attacked whiskey, promiscuity, theft, crime, and witchcraft. They preached devotion to family, honor, and integrity. Both urged their people to return to the ways of their ancestors, and to the spirit-teachings of the Creator. But in other ways their messages were very different. Handsome Lake was a warrior who became a prophet of peace. He drew upon some elements of Christian theology such as its ideas of heaven and hell to rebuild a religion for his people.[105]

Tenskwatawa was a medicine man who became a prophet of war. He worked to unite the Indian nations against the white man, and promised that the return of the Spirit would be proof against musketry and cannonballs. He gained credit by predicting an eclipse, and announced that when the soldiers came against them another darkness would destroy these attackers.[106]

A third great spiritual leader was the Cherokee hunter and warrior Sequoyah (1770?–1843). His mother was Cherokee; his father may have been the white Indian trader Nathaniel Gist. In the late eighteenth century, he was with a war party that captured a white soldier and took from him a letter. They were fascinated by it. Many years later Sequoyah recalled that "the question arose

Tenskwatawa, The Open Door, also called the Shawnee Prophet, was one of many spiritual leaders who appeared in Indian nations during the nineteenth century. They reconstructed the old ethics and beliefs of their people and created new ethics that resisted alcohol and other corruptions. In a dark period, they nourished the spirit of their people.

among them, whether this mysterious power of the talking leaf was the gift of the Great Spirit to the white man, or the discovery of the white man himself?" Sequoyah invented a system of writing for his people. At first he tried to do it with a sign for each word. When that failed, he invented a syllabary of eighty-five or eighty-six terms. Many Cherokees learned to read and write their own language, and soon books and newspapers began to stream from Cherokee presses. Sequoyah's syllabary was preferred by his nation to other Cherokee alphabets and vocabularies created by white missionaries and teachers. Most of the texts that were written in Sequoyah's syllabary were about the traditional spiritual beliefs of the Cherokees. Theda Perdue writes, "The syllabary was, without doubt, a major factor in the early nineteenth-century political regeneration of the Cherokee."[107]

Many other spiritual leaders emerged in the Indian nations during the nineteenth century, and they deserve to be remembered by all Americans: men such as Smohalla, Tavibo, Wovoka, and Kennekuk. Some urged their people to learn some of the ways of the white people while preserving their own. Others such as Smohalla went the opposite way. A few embraced violence; most rejected it. Common themes were the reality of the spirit world, the truth of dreams, the power of prophecy, the importance of ritual and dance, and the organic unity of people and the earth.[108]

Chief Joseph of the Nez Perce linked the ways of his people to ideas of liberty and freedom. Another leader observed that this "certain feeling for freedom" became "the song of every Indian."

Many American Indians framed these spiritual movements in terms of an ethic of liberty and freedom—liberty to be left alone and go one's one separate way; freedom to become one with their people and with the Spirit. In Indian sign language, the sign for liberty also meant alone, by oneself, in solitude. When combined with a gift it meant that nothing was wanted in return.[109]

Indians understood these ideas in different ways. In 1832, Black Hawk said, "We told them to let us alone and keep away from us; but they followed on, and beset our paths, and they coiled themselves among us, like the snake. They poisoned us by the touch. We are not safe. We live in danger."[110] Another meaning was that of Chief Joseph of the Nez Perce, who said, "Let me be a free man—free to travel, free to stop, free to work, free to trade where I choose, free to choose my own teachers, free to follow the religion of my fathers, free to talk and think and act for myself."[111] In 1967, Kiowa-Navaho John Belindo, executive director of the National Congress of American Indians, testified to Congress, "I think this is essentially the song of every Indian and Indian tribe, a certain feeling of freedom, a chance to be free to manage their own affairs."[112]

In the 1870s the Ponca nation was driven off its land in Nebraska. Their war chief, Standing Bear, had often fought the white man, but this time he went to a federal court and sued the government, winning his case in 1879. His ally was Bright Eyes, Suzette La Flesch, an Indian woman of the Omaha nation. In 1879 she organized a public relations campaign, with such success that the federal government decided not to appeal the court decision.

In America, this Indian movement was not a single organized effort, but many separate efforts by associations, tribes, states, courts, individuals. A pivotal moment occurred in 1879. The Ponca Nation had been removed from their land in Nebraska and driven south on their own trail of tears to Oklahoma. Many died. Their leader, the warrior Standing Bear, lost his son, and led his people on a long march home, where they were rounded up for removal once again. Standing Bear thought about war, but then he went another way. He and others of the Ponca nation brought suit against the federal government and sought to win their freedom in court. To the amazement of many they won their case. The judge ruled that an Indian was "a PERSON within the meaning of the laws of the United States" and had a right to sue for habeas corpus when "restrained of liberty in violation of the Constitution." Further, he found that the government had no right to take the land of the Poncas and added that Indians had "an inalienable right to life, liberty, and the pursuit of happiness." Here again, it was the oppressed who fought against their oppression. They expanded the idea of liberty and freedom as universal rights for all humanity.[113]

Spiritual Revival and Ethics of Justice Among Maori

Maori also had strong movements of spiritual revival, which were similar to and different from those of American Indians. From the start, English men and women who met the Maori were much impressed by their ethical beliefs. Governor Robert FitzRoy wrote, "While, on the one hand, no people are more commercially inclined than the New Zealanders, or more keenly intelligent; on the other, no men are more alive to a sense of justice."[114]

Maori had ethical beliefs of high complexity, which changed through time, in part by interaction with European cultures. To the old imperatives of *wakipapa, hapu, tauutuutu,* and *kotihitanga,* others were added, or took on new meanings. One important part of Maori ethos appeared in the word *tika,* which means literally "straight," or "the straight path," but like other ethical ideas took on many meanings. In dealings with Pakeha, it also came to mean just, right, and fair.

Another important concept in the Maori ethos is *mana.* Today, it is often translated as "power" by secular New Zealanders. But Frederick Maning wrote, "Mind you do not translate *mana* as power; that won't do; they are two different things entirely." Maning observed that the English language has no exact equivalent for *mana.* "*Virtus*, prestige, authority, good fortune, influence, sanctity, luck, are all words which, under certain conditions, give something near the meaning of mana, though not one of them gives it exactly." Chiefs and warriors had *mana.* Great chiefs had great *mana.* Ideas and things could have *mana* as well. *Mana* is "the accompaniment of power, but not the power itself," said Maning. "*Mana* is a spiritual and moral idea. A man must be in the right to have great *mana.*"[115]

All of these ideas gained a new depth of meaning in the nineteenth century, when Maori leaders joined their traditional ways to the ethics of Christianity. One of these men was Matiu Parakatone Tahu, *tohunga* of the Ngai Te Rangi in Tauranga, who became an intermediary between the missionaries and his people. He said to a missionary in 1846, "You are not satisfied with us, and you often express a fear that our religion is only lip service, and that it has no root in our hearts. You forget what we were and what we have thrown away—our cannibalism, our murders, our infanticide, our tapus, which were Gods to us." Here was an agent of change in Maori ethics.[116]

Another was Tarapipipi, sometimes called by his Christian names Wiremu Tamihana or William Thompson. He led the Ngati Haua, stopped a war between Maori tribes with a Bible in his hand, built a chapel that seated a thousand people and became the "largest native house in New Zealand," established a code of laws, and played a major role in establishing a Maori monarchy. He confirmed Te

Many spiritual leaders appeared among Maori in the late nineteenth century. They revived the ways of their people and organized new ways of striving for justice. Tarapipipi made peace among Maori tribes, founded a Maori monarchy, and informed angry Pakeha that his purpose was an alliance between the English queen and Maori king, with God over both.

Wherowhero as king by holding a Bible over his head. Tarapipipi was much resented by Pakeha who accused him of violating the Waitangi Treaty, which he denied. He insisted that he was cementing an alliance between the English queen and the Maori king "with God over both." This in his mind was the meaning of a central idea in the Treaty of Waitangi: *te tino ringatiratanga.*[117]

Tarapipipi did not abandon Maori beliefs but combined them with the teachings of Christ. Evelyn Stokes writes that "he lived by the principles of Te Whakapono, Te Ture, Te Aroha: be steadfast in the faith of God, uphold the rule of law, show love and compassion to all." In these beliefs he combined Maori and Christian elements in his ethic of faith, love, law, and justice. All of this became part of Maori striving for justice.[118]

New Zealand Maori and American Indians both renewed the deepest ethical principles of their own cultures. At the same time, they integrated some ethical ideas that were widely shared among European settlers.

These processes were similar in the United States and New Zealand, but the principles were different, in ways that reinforced the character and purposes of both nations.

FRONTIER AND BUSH

Material Conditions and Moral Choices

> From this hour I ordain myself loos'd of limits and
> imaginary lines.
> Going where I list, my own master total and absolute. . . .
> I inhale great droughts of space,
> The east and west are mine, and the north and the
> south are mine.
> I am larger, better than I thought.
>
> —America's Walt Whitman, "Song of the Open
> Road"

> Did it go wrong just about a hundred years ago? A
> ramshackle self-appointed cast-off élite of first comers,
> promoters, bent lawyers and sham doctors, set it up for
> themselves, a gentry of sorts, saw it collapse and crept
> away with slim gains. . . . Something had to be done.
>
> —New Zealand's W. H. Oliver, "Counter-
> revolution"

WEST OF WELLINGTON, very near the city's center, is a suburb called Karori. Before the Europeans arrived it was what New Zealanders call bush: a dense green tangle of forest, fern, and shrub. Overhead was a canopy of magnificent old trees that are unique to these islands. Merely to recite their Maori names is to make a poem: rimu, rata; kahikatea.

When the Wakefield settlers arrived at Wellington, the hills of Karori were covered with these ancient trees. An English settler

named Henry Smith Chapman found a rimu that was thirty-one feet
in circumference. Chapman did what American pioneers had done
when they met a very large tree. He cut it down and counted the
rings: 302 rings altogether. Then he found a kahikatea that was
even larger. It met the same fate: 367 rings. Some of Karori's old-
growth trees survived Henry Chapman's curiosity. A few still stand
today in a preserve named Job Wilton's Bush, after a thoughtful
farmer who protected them. A giant rimu still grows there, with
three times the girth of Henry Chapman's trees. It is eight hundred
years old.[1] In the nineteenth century most of these old trees were
cut down. Karori was shorn of its bush and became an orderly landscape of farms, fields, and pastures. Then the farmland disappeared,
and Karori was divided into suburban house lots for Wellington
commuters.[2]

   The clearing of Karori was part of a world process that Americans know well, or think we do until we study it in other places. To
learn more about it, we went to Karori in 1994 and met an expert
on the subject. He was Rollo Arnold, now in his grave and much
missed by colleagues around the world. He was a great historian of

*This image captured the density of New Zealand's primeval bush, with its great trees, enormous
ferns, and thick undergrowth. Many patches still exist today.*

migration and a close student of settlement and bush-clearing in New Zealand. I discovered his work while teaching at Oxford, where Arnold's books and essays were admired for their meticulous scholarship, large spirit, and deep insight into great problems.[3]

One day when we were in Wellington, we called Rollo Arnold and asked if we could get together. He and his wife, Betty, invited us to their home in Karori and warmly welcomed two wayfaring strangers. We talked in their living room about books and life in New Zealand and America, and began to understand what made his work so special.

Rollo Arnold had been raised in a small settlement on what he called the "bush fringe" of Nelson, near the top of New Zealand's South Island. When he was a child, his family lived in a house with no running water, no electricity, and no telephone or radio. In his youth he cleared the bush with his own hands, broke the stubborn land to the plow, and farmed the virgin soil. At night he studied for a diploma in a correspondence school. Later Rollo Arnold went to university and made a career of scholarship, but first he lived the history that he wrote, and came to know it with a depth of understanding that one can gain no other way. He also brought to his work an abiding love of the land and a respect for the people who cleared it—a rare and happy combination.

From his own experience, Rollo Arnold told us many stories of the New Zealand bush. Some were similar to tales we had heard in childhood about the American frontier, but his stories were not the same as ours. As we listened to his words, we began to realize that our two nations had both participated in the same global process of land-taking and land-clearing, but not in the same way. For an historian, the first problem is to find an axis of comparison. How might we study people on the land in America and New Zealand? In what ways were their acts and choices similar? How were they different?

Models: The Frontier Thesis and Settler Capitalism

A large historical literature has been written on this subject. Much of it centers on two models: Turnerian and Marxist. In 1893, historian Frederick Jackson Turner published an essay called "The Significance of the Frontier in American History." He summarized his thesis in a sentence: "The existence of an area of free land, its continuous recession, and the advance of American settlement westward, explain American development."[4]

For Turner, "free land" meant an abundance of land that was free for the taking, by people with weapons in their hands. His American frontier was nothing like a European boundary between sovereign states. He thought of it as the edge of the unused. Turner measured the frontier by density of population and defined a frontier as a place with fewer than two people per square mile. Drawing on the work of Italian social scientist Achille Loria, he argued that "so long as free land exists, the opportunity for a competency exists, and economic power secures political power." On that assumption, Turner concluded that "the frontier is productive of individualism" and that "frontier individualism has from the beginning promoted democracy." In that way, he believed, the free land on the American frontier created a nation of free people and supported the growth of democracy, capitalism, liberty, and individualism.[5]

Turner's frontier thesis ignited a controversy that continues to this day. Many attacked it, others supported it, and some applied it to other nations around the world. Several scholars argued that New Zealand and the United States were both part of the same global "great frontier," fundamentally similar in the abundance of land and its social consequences that Turner himself had experienced as a child on the frontier of Portage, Wisconsin.[6]

Others who came after Turner strongly disagreed. A very different approach to the same subject was taken by Marxists, who believe that history is driven by change in the organization of the means of production, that the great problem is the growth of inequality in the world, and that the urgent need is revolutionary action to put it right. Within that frame some Marxist historians seek to understand the taking of land in societies such as New Zealand and the United States as part of a world-historical process that they call "settler capitalism." This approach was popular among historians in Canada, New Zealand, and especially Australia during the 1970s and 1980s.[7]

This school of interpretation appeared in the United States as the "new western history." It was written by angry young radicals who began to call themselves American Marxists, shortly before the collapse of the Soviet Union. They rejected the Turner thesis out of hand. One new western historian, Patricia Limerick, dismissed Turner's frontier as the "f-word," an unmentionable obscenity. In their books, Turner's happy story of democracy, freedom, and individualism became a Gothic tale of human exploitation, environmental degradation, cultural imperialism, social inequality, and old-fashioned greed. This was their idea of American history. It had strong appeal to a troubled generation that came of age in the era of Vietnam and Watergate.[8]

By the turn of the twenty-first century both of these approaches—frontier history and settler capitalism—were running thin. A question for historians was what next, how to move forward. Clues appeared in the weaknesses and strengths that Turnerians and neo-Marxists shared. Both tended to be materialist and determinist. They wrote of people as its objects of history, rather than agents. Since the 1980s, many scholars have been moving toward another idea of history as a more open process in which people make choices, and choices make a difference in the world. Interesting results were obtained when Rollo Arnold combined that approach with his method of careful study, close attention to the evidence, and full respect for the varieties of individual thought and action.[9]

Another way forward might be found in a strength that Turnerians and neo-Marxists had in common. Both groups became very interested in writing comparative histories of frontiers and settler capitalists. A work of major importance is John Weaver's *The Great Land Rush*, a comparative history of land-taking in the modern world. Weaver centers his inquiry on the interplay of "private initiatives" and "ordered state-backed certainties of property rights" in five settler societies throughout North America, the South Pacific, and South Africa. His close comparative analysis of land hunters, speculators, squatters, survey systems, land titles, and land markets puts the entire subject on a new foundation.[10] A particular opportunity is to combine these methods of inquiry into a study of material conditions and moral choices that people have made in different times and places.

Material Structures: Climate, Water, Land

Let us begin with a comparison of material and environmental conditions in which choices were made. In some ways, New Zealand and the United States are similar in their environments. Both countries have pleasant and productive climates in the temperate zone. The range of heat and cold is greater in the continental land mass of North America than in New Zealand's maritime climate, but mean temperatures in New Zealand's Southland and Northland are not very different from conditions in New England and the American South. Without going anywhere near the environmental determinism of Ellsworth Huntington or Arnold Toynbee, or the materialism of Turner and Marx, one might observe that temperate climates in New Zealand and North America were powerful incentives to settlement and economic growth. They inspired choices, and rewarded them.[11]

Both nations are also broadly similar in their supply of water, always a vital material factor, and rarely studied by historians. Most regions in New Zealand and the eastern and central United States have rainfall above 1,000 millimeters, or 40 inches, a year. Large exceptions were in the arid western reaches of the United States beyond the 100th meridian, and some of the dry leeward slopes of New Zealand's South Island. But by comparison with other nations these two countries are blessed with abundant supplies of water, and they consume it at a prodigious rate. Around the year 2000, New Zealanders used 371 gallons of fresh water per capita every day. Americans were almost the same: 374 gallons.[12] In both countries, 75 to 80 percent of this extravagance went for agricultural and pastoral uses. The distributive abundance of available water, and relative stability in its supply, are vitally important to the growth of open systems in these two nations, as scholars have discovered when studying other countries that are not so fortunate.[13]

New Zealand and the United States also have an abundance of land in proportion to their populations. Even today they are thinly settled by world standards. In 2006, the density of people per square mile was 39 in New Zealand and 82 in the United States. Comparable numbers were 365 in China, 611 in Germany, 968 in India, and 2,850 in Bangladesh. Turnerians believe that the ratio of people to land (and resources) is the fundamental determinant of a free and open society, but that is not invariably the case. Opposite patterns in two directions appear when we compare the Netherlands and Somalia, to name but two examples. But an abundance of land was vitally important to the development of the United States and New Zealand, especially in the early generations of European settlement.[14]

A more complex problem is to compare the quality of land, and the proportion that is potentially useful for farmland, pasture, range, and forest. New Zealand's mountainous terrain greatly reduces the proportion of usable land—more so than in the United States. More than half of the land in New Zealand has a slope greater than 30 degrees. But the surface area of the United States also includes vast areas of mountain, desert, tundra, swamp, and inland seas. In 2001, after many centuries of settlement in the United States, only 5.5 percent of its surface area had been developed. New Zealand has a larger proportion of land that is developed in one way or another, but we were unable to make an exact comparison. Still, the main lines are clear.[15]

Quantity of Land: Scale, Magnitude, and Growth

In another respect, a major material difference appears in the landed resources of both two nations. It is partly a matter of scale. New Zealand covers 109,000 square miles (300,000 square kilometers).

Land clearing happened rapidly in both countries and often paid for itself. Here New Zealand loggers in northern Whangarei are felling a Kauri tree and sending it to market by bullock team and timber ship. In the American colonies, the great mast pines of New England and the live oak and cypress of the South were harvested in the same way.

The United States has a land area of approximately 3.7 million square miles (9.6 million square kilometers).[16]

As a consequence, the taking of land in America continued for a much longer time. This process began with the first fishing settlements on the Atlantic coast in the sixteenth century. Frederick Jackson Turner believed that it ended around the year 1890, when the superintendent of the census announced that he could no longer find a clear line of advancing settlement on his population maps. On that basis Turner announced in 1893 that "the American frontier was closed." He was mistaken. The taking of "virgin land" in the United States continued long after that date. In quantitative terms, the high point of new settlement on "vacant lands" in the United States came a generation later in the twentieth century. The peak year was 1910, and land-taking through the nation continued at a very high rate through the 1920s. In parts of the arid West beyond the 100th meridian, it persisted into the 1990s. During the early twenty-first century it still goes on in Alaska, and on what might be called pocket frontiers in long-settled states. And a second wave is now happening in parts of the country such as New England and the South, where land was taken, cleared, farmed, and abandoned many years ago. The forest reclaimed the ruined soil and revived it in some degree, and now the land is being taken again, and cleared once more, and put to work by another generation of American

Forest and bush were swiftly stripped of small growth, which also went to market, as in this busy New Zealand scene. In New England and New York, pioneers sugared their trees, felled them for lumber, burned brush into potash, and sent three products to market before the first crops were in.

pioneers—an extraordinary phenomenon, and one that has yet to find its historian. Altogether, this very long process of North American land-taking has continued through five centuries from the sixteenth century to the twenty-first, and it is still strong today—a fundamental fact of American history.[17]

In New Zealand, the occupation of the land by European settlers was compressed into a shorter period. Most of it happened in fifty years, from the 1840s to the 1890s. Here too, the actual labor of land-clearing was more protracted. Much of the bush remained to be cleared after 1890. Rollo Arnold was clearing it in Nelson during the 1930s. But the fundamental fact remains: the taking of the land was mostly done by two generations of New Zealanders. In the United States it has continued through sixteen generations and is still under way.

Quality of Land: The Geography of Fertility and Dynamics of Change

In the full span of American history, ideas of abundance have tended to grow stronger through time. That growth process was reinforced from an early date by another material and environmental factor. This was the geographic distribution of soil resources, which operated differently in the histories of New Zealand and the United States. In some parts of eastern Massachusetts, the topsoil is less than an inch deep, and the undersoil is a thin stony loam that offers small encouragement to a farmer. Every year, when the frozen ground thaws in the brief muddy moment that New England calls spring, the land throws up a fresh crop of granite, which adds much to New England's scenery but little to its fertility.

A thousand miles to the west, the topsoil in parts of Iowa is as much as seventeen feet deep, a fact of high importance in American history. As Americans moved west from the Atlantic coast into the Mississippi Valley, the fertility of their land increased. A given unit of capital or labor, when transferred from an acre in Massachusetts to an acre in Iowa, brought greater returns without any change in "factor-inputs" other than the land itself. The result was a large gain in the productivity of capital and labor, and more rapid rates of economic growth.

In New Zealand, that trend ran in reverse. Soil maps are highly complex in both nations. As in the United States, some of New Zealand's soils are deeply fertile, and they have supported intensive farming and grazing for many generations. Other soils are thin and nearly useless for agriculture. That diversity was broadly similar in the two nations, but the sequence of land-taking in New Zealand was the opposite of the American pattern. New Zealanders occupied most of the best lands first. Much of the most fertile farmland in the South Island was on the Canterbury Plain, and also near Nelson and Blenheim. On the North Island, some of the best land was just inland from Hawke's Bay, and southwest of Napier, and in the Wairarapa northeast of Wellington, and around Taranaki. This land was occupied by the first settlers. Other prime land in Waikato remained unoccupied by Europeans until after the New Zealand Wars (1860–72). But in general much of the most fertile farmland was occupied at an early date.

Something similar happened with both arable and grazing lands. A survey for the New Zealand Atlas concluded that "practically all the open country suitable for grazing in both the South island and the southern half of the North island was occupied and stocked" by the 1860s. The process of land-taking took another generation in parts of the North Island, but by the 1890s only the less productive lands remained. Returns to labor and capital diminished as inferior lands were brought into cultivation. The net result was a negative weight on rates of economic growth in New Zealand. Here again, these opposite tendencies in the United States and New Zealand further reinforced a sense of opportunity in one country and constraint in the other.[18]

Material Conditions and Moral Choices

That difference has had a profound effect on the development of economies, cultures, worldviews, and local choices. In the United States, the frontier experience has been a continuing presence in American life for a very long time. The idea of the frontier is still strong in the United States—stronger than ever, after failed attempts by new western historians and neo-Marxists to explode it. The more that iconoclasts attack what they call the myths of the westward movement, the stronger those images grow in American culture. All of this has reinforced what John Higham calls the idea of boundlessness, a world without limits in the United States. Other evidence shows that this part of the American Dream is still widely shared in the United States, even during periods of economic recession. Surveys reveal that many Americans still have a strong sense of boundlessness, and many persist in believing that they live in a universe without limits.[19]

In both countries, a major question was how to create a society that offered equitable opportunities to people in search of land. The American solution was expansion and continuous acquisition of vast new supplies of land, which promised to reconcile freedom and liberty with an idea of equity. An example of that spirit is this broadside for new lands in Iowa and Nebraska (1872).

This attitude and its material base have had a major impact on ideas of social justice and on the ethical foundations of open systems. Even in the troubled years of the early twenty-first century, the United States has continued to be an open society where economic growth remains positive during periods of economic slowdowns. Over the long run, annual growth rates of domestic product per capita in constant dollars tend to fluctuate in a fixed range of 1.3 to 1.7 percent—not an impressive number in itself, but large enough for national product per capita to double every thirty-four years or so, and this comes on top of population growth, which remains higher in the United States than in most other developed nations.

Where growth is positive, and material limits are less constraining, it seems reasonable to believe that one person can become rich and prosperous without impoverishing another. On that assumption, American ideas of liberty and freedom, especially freedom of opportunity, became plausible ways of achieving fairness and natural justice. Not all Americans share that way of

This American ethos of equity through liberty, freedom, and boundless expansion was also a vision of eternal improvement. An image of this idea was this celebratory painting of the westward movement as the march of progress for all, except the American Indians in the foreground.

thinking, but many do so—especially those who have been successful in their own lives.

The great majority of Americans strongly oppose policies of wealth redistribution. When the Democratic Party nominated Senator George McGovern for president in 1972, he campaigned in part for the redistribution of wealth in the United States. Most Americans—white collar and blue collar, rich and poor—rejected that idea out of hand. Even people of very modest means condemned it as unjust to hard workers. Americans liked George McGovern and thought he was a kind and decent and caring man. But he was defeated in forty-nine out of fifty states, because he had lost touch with the American Dream. Americans don't dream of equality. They dream of wealth. They don't want to get even; they want to get ahead. And they deeply believe that in this dynamic society one person can become a millionaire without beggaring another.

In New Zealand, attitudes are very different. The land was taken long ago. Within two generations of settlement, a growing nation began to run up against its physical limits. In such a setting, most ideals of social justice could not be realized simply by freedom of opportunity. They required intervention, planning, and even the redistribution of limited resources and material possessions such as land. New Zealanders began to act on this assumption as early as 1890. Many support that idea today, even after a period of free-market restructuring, and in some degree because of it.

Here, in these two open societies, one finds two different ethics. In a world of abundant resources, Americans could reasonably believe that the path to equity and justice lay in the expansion of liberty and freedom. In New Zealand, material constraints led people to believe that social justice required the active pursuit of fairness and equity through the redistribution of limited resources.

Land Policy as an Instrument of Social Purpose

In early America and New Zealand, the leaders of every great migration actively used the distribution of land as an instrument of various social purposes. But here again the two countries were different, and each major region went its own way.

New England Puritans deliberately used land to encourage the growth of towns and middling freehold farms for yeoman families. Individuals were forbidden to acquire land directly from the Indians. Only the commonwealth could do so, and the land was granted by the General Court to groups called proprietors, who tended to be yeoman farmers. They distributed the land in middling tracts to people like themselves. Further, the land was held in fee simple, which meant that owners could buy and sell it freely, and in cases of intestacy it passed to children by a system of double partible inheritance. The first-born son got a double share, but other sons received land as well. Behind this process lay an idealized vision of a social order that actually developed in New England.

Virginia was another story. Access to the land came through the governor's council, a small group composed of Sir William Berkeley's Cavalier elite. They granted the best ground in large units to a small number of large landowners like themselves. Members of the council themselves and their friends and relations got the lion's share. Land policy was used to build a hierarchical social order. Moreover, land was granted not in fee simple but in fee tail. It was entailed from one generation to the next and could not be taken for debt. The purpose was to stabilize dynastic families and large estates. Within the estates, various forms of tenancy and leasehold also existed, especially on the Northern Neck of Virginia, much of which was a fief of the Fairfax family. All this was part of a concerted effort to construct a material base for a hierarchical society in Virginia's Cavalier utopia. In general, it succeeded in achieving its ends through eight generations, and in some parts of Virginia even to our own time.

In the Delaware Valley, the Quaker colonists who settled eastern Pennsylvania, northern Delaware, and western New Jersey went a third way. William Penn used land as a source of capital for his colony, and he and other Quakers actively encouraged a more equal distribution of land than in New England or Virginia. In parts of colonial Pennsylvania, the wealthiest 10 percent of landowners held only 20 percent of the land—one of the lowest levels of wealth concentration that has ever been measured in the Western world. It was much in keeping with the egalitarian ethic of the Society of Friends.

In the Southern backcountry, title to the land was acquired by a few large owners and Gini ratios were the highest (most unequal) in early America. But the land was often occupied by squatters who moved in and sorted out land titles later. Many came from the borderlands of North Britain. They tended to build separate farmsteads along small creeks, where neighbors became kin groups and strangers were not welcome. An example is this settlement map for the Catawba River Valley in North Carolina. Other distinctive land

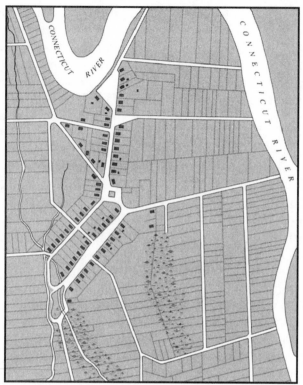

Land use in settler societies was shaped not only by material determinants but also by cultural values and social purposes. In New England, land was granted to proprietors who were mostly yeoman farmers. They used it to found nucleated towns of yeomen such as themselves, with an equitable (but rarely equal) distribution of different types of land to most families. An example is this plan of Wethersfield in Connecticut.

policies developed in the Carolina lowcountry, Dutch settlements in the Hudson Valley, New France, and New Spain.[20]

In New Zealand, land distribution was also an important instrument of social policy in all six initial settlements (Wellington, Nelson, Canterbury, Otago, New Plymouth, and Auckland). All but Auckland attempted to enact something like the Wakefield system of "sufficient price," in which land prices were kept artificially high for two purposes. One object of each colonizing association was to create a flow of revenue that could subsidize emigration from England. Another goal was to re-create an improved idea of English or Scottish rural society, with close settlement, mixed farming, and social hierarchy. This policy was introduced in Wellington, New Plymouth, Nelson, Canterbury, and Otago, with varying degrees of success. Only Auckland went a different way.

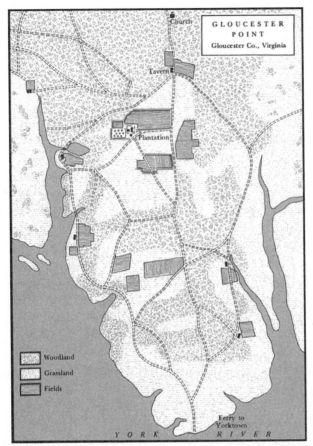

Very different was land use in Virginia. Here land was distributed by the Virginia Council, which consisted of a small number of large landowners. The best land went to themselves and others of the same rank. The result was a pattern of land use such as this one on Gloucester Point in Virginia.

Land-taking as an Instrument of Individual Gain in America

Land had a double importance in settler societies. It was arguably the most important instrument for the shaping of a social order. At the same time, it was perceived as the primary way to individual wealth.[21] These two purposes were often at odds, increasingly so. Small settlers and new generations grew very unhappy with the social purposes of the founders. Many registered their unhappiness by moving away from the earliest colonial settlements, and by carving out their own holdings in new ways that did not conform to older designs. This was the case in every American region, as more land was taken from the Indians and small coastal settlements rapidly expanded.

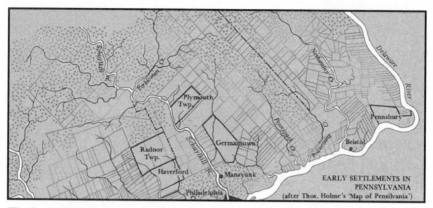

The Quaker leaders of Pennsylvania went another way. An object was to support large families and small hamlets, in a process that was shaped in large part by Quaker beliefs and values. The result was a pattern of landholding and land use that was more nearly equal than in other colonies.

As they did so, the founders began to lose control. Patterns of land-holding changed, and so did the forms of land use. The old purposes were never entirely lost, and always made a difference, but they were modified in important ways. In New England "outlivers" began to oc-cupy their own land away from town centers, often against the collec-tive will of the town meeting and its selectmen. New "uncovenanted" towns began to spring up that had a more open texture.[22]

The land system in the American backcountry became very dis-orderly in the eighteenth century. In the southern highlands, people staked their claims as best they could by individual effort. Land was taken by the "metes and bounds" system, in which men marked claims by blazing trees with tomahawks, and the lines between the blazes became the boundaries of the property. The result was a pat-tern of landholding that looks like a crazy quilt when seen from the air. In this system, claims overlapped like shingles on a roof. A tangle of counterclaims created another sort of opportunity in litigation, and a handful of the fiercest competitors came out on top. Many families got no land at all, and others squatted on property that they did not own. Some were able to make good a squatter's claim with the help of backcountry courts that recognized what was called "the right of the first trespass."[23]

Land-taking and Individual Gain in New Zealand

Something similar happened in parts of New Zealand, for a time. Wellington's founding was followed by new settlements at Wanganui on the west coast and Hawke's Bay to the east. Nelson's congested settlements at the top of the South Island spread eastward to create the province of Marlborough, with its capital at Blenheim. In the North Island, settlers moved south from Auckland into Waikato after the Maori Wars, and east to Gisborne, and north to Whangarei and Kaitaia. Emigrants from Otago founded Southland, with its capital of Invercargill, and a rural countryside that became more fiercely Scottish than the Scots of Dunedin itself. The western reaches of Canterbury Province beyond the Alps became the separate region of Westland, with a mining economy and an Australasian culture.[24]

All this led to a change in landholding. A case in point was the colony of Nelson on the northern end of the South Island, where the Wakefield colonists began to run against the limits within a few years of settlement. The immediate problem was not the shortage of land itself but the terms under which it was held. The price of land was kept artificially high, and much of it belonged to absentee owners. As a consequence of Wakefield's social policies and his economic theory of sufficient price, only 80 of 920 men who lived in Nelson were able to own land. Landless men had little opportunity to get farms of their own, or landed families to expand their holdings.[25]

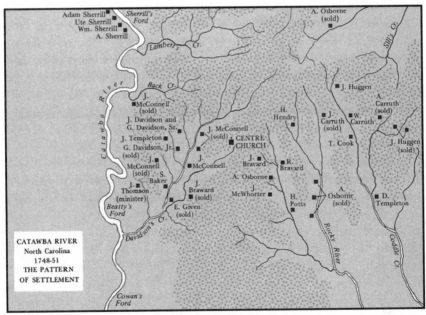

In the Southern backcountry, title to the land was acquired by a few large owners and Gini ratios were the highest (most unequal) in early America. But the land was often occupied by squatters, many of whom came from the borderlands of North Britain. They tended to build separate farmsteads along small creeks, where neighbors became kin and strangers were not welcome. An example is this settlement map for the Catawba River Valley in North Carolina.

To the south and east of Nelson's first settlements, beyond a very rough barrier, were large tracts of grasslands in the Wairau, Awatere, and Clarence valleys, all excellent grazing country. That opportunity was seized by an interesting group of men. Charles Clifford, Frederick Weld, William Vavasour, and Henry Petre were an Anglo-Catholic cousinage with aristocratic connections in the west of England. They were recent immigrants, men of wealth who had been penalized for their faith, and carried with them yet another memory of injustice and unfairness in Britain. In 1846, they met together at Barrett's Hotel in Wellington and talked of the "splendid grassland" in the Wairau. They went to New South Wales, bought three thousand sheep, and drove them to the Wairau River in the midst of a wild storm. On arrival, one of these adventurers laconically noted that the men were "half dead, sheep ditto." These pioneers were followed by others, and a large part of Wairau's pastureland was quickly taken by a few families.[26]

In 1856, a struggle for power occurred in Nelson. A faction of landholders who called themselves the Supper Party put up their own candidate for superintendent—Dr. David Monro, a strong conservative. He observed, "The great question of all others appears to be—are we to take American or British institutions as our model; are we to say with the Yankees that the people are the sole source of power or are we to follow the English plan, which recognizes the existence of another source of power and in its practical working gives a weight to intelligence and property, and does not merely count heads." Dr. Monro had strong support from landed gentry, but his electoral prospects in Nelson were not bright. He wrote to a friend, "A very large proportion of the Electors are as you are aware most ignorant men, and with them one of the dominant ideas is that they will best be served by putting in a man of their own class."[27]

The electors of Nelson did not take kindly to Dr. Monro's attitude and turned to a "man of their own class," John Perry Robinson, a mechanic from Birmingham, who had been linked to John Bright's radical liberalism in England. Robinson favored low land prices and the opening of lands to the "the man of small means." He carried the election by sixteen votes, with support from Maori and Pakeha laborers, and later won reelection for a second term. The big run-holders of Wairau responded by seceding from Nelson and forming a new province of Marlborough.[28]

Other secessions happened at about the same time: Hawke's Bay from Wellington in 1858; Marlborough from Nelson in 1859; Southland from Otago in 1861; Westland from Canterbury in 1873. Many of New Zealand's secondary settlements were made by pastoralists who converted large stretches of the country into sheep runs. Often they did so on terrain that was unsuitable to field husbandry but lent itself to sheep farming. From 1849 to 1851, the Crown Land Ordinances opened large areas that were suitable for grazing. By 1900, New Zealand was inhabited by eight hundred thousand people and twenty million sheep on large tracts of grassland. Frederic Lloyd wrote, "Modern New Zealand is built upon grass."[29]

Growing Inequality in New Zealand and the United States

In both countries, the result was a rapid growth of wealth inequality, which increased sharply in the United States during the period from 1780 to about 1840. One of the ironies of American history was the expansion of political democracy and the concentration of wealth-holding at the same time in the early republic. This trend appeared in every American region. In New England, large holdings throughout New Hampshire and Maine came into the hands of speculators and land companies during the late eighteenth century. Similar patterns appeared in western New York and central Pennsylvania, and much of the Ohio Valley. The same trend appeared earlier in the coastal South and advanced farther. And the highest levels of concentration were (and still are) to be found in the southern highlands, the lower Mississippi Valley, Texas, and the Old Southwest. These trends advanced very rapidly during the American Revolution, the early republic, and the age of Jefferson and Jackson.[30]

At a later date the same thing happened in New Zealand, where rural inequality rose to high levels during the decades from 1860 to 1890. One study by Tom Brooking found that in the year 1890, 422 individuals and companies owned 8 million acres of freehold land out of a total of 12.5 million acres in use throughout New Zealand. Approximately 1 percent of freeholders owned 64 percent of freehold land in the country. Exactly the same results were obtained in Margaret Galt's careful study of estates in probate: the top 1 percent owned 65 percent of the wealth.[31]

This top 1 percent acquired not merely the most land but also the best land. They were not overscrupulous as to means and made heavy use of illegal devices. One was called "gridironing." A wealthy investor acquired a checkerboard pattern of landholdings in alternate blocks of perhaps eighteen acres in areas reserved for settlement in twenty-year lots. The remaining lots were too small for occupation and could be acquired later at little expense, or not acquired at all but merely used. This method was widely used in Canterbury. Another device was called "spotting," or "peacocking," in which lands near rivers were acquired. This practice isolated other blocks from communications and made them useless, a common practice in Marlborough and Hawke's Bay. Much illegal trafficking in Maori lands also occurred throughout the North Island.[32]

Inequalities of landed wealth varied from one part of New Zealand to another. The highest levels of concentration were in Canterbury, where a few runholding families controlled most of the good grassland that was suitable for extensive grazing. Much of this land was kept in large leaseholds of ten thousand acres or more. The leaseholding families lived in stations, with their shepherds and station hands.[33]

The largest individual holding belonged to a character called Ready Money Robinson, the self-made son of a Lancashire tenant farmer, who built an estate of 93,000 acres in freehold, of which 84,000 were on one great estate called Cheviot Hills. Almost as large was G. H. Moore's Glenmark, about 75,000 acres of freehold, plus another 75,000 acres of leasehold. This system reached its peak in the period from 1870 to 1890, and some big runholders did well even in the "Black 80s," which were very hard on small farmers. In 1886, Cheviot Hills was running more than one hundred thousand sheep, and its wool clip brought £20,000 ($100,000) a year to that one estate alone. Even so, Ready Money Robinson lived beyond his means, as did many of the sheep-running gentry, flaunting their wealth in great houses, blooded horses, squadrons of servants, conspicuous consumption, and big loans from the Bank of Australia. Something similar was happening in other parts of New Zealand. Jim Gardner writes, "The 1880s were traditionally regarded as the decade of runholders and land monopoly." There were increasing complaints

Much land in New Zealand was held in large estates such as Cheviot, here with its great mansion house.

against the unfairness of a regime in which "much of the best land was indeed gathered into the hands of a few."[34]

The American Solution: Expansion, Liberty, and Freedom

These trends in wealth concentration were regarded with concern by leaders in both countries. An important question was how to preserve freehold properties for middling families in the face of rapid wealth concentration.

Americans tried to solve the problem through the nineteenth century mainly by rapid acquisition of vast new supplies of land. The Louisiana Purchase (1803), the annexation of East Florida (1810–12), and the purchase of West Florida (1819) doubled the land area of the country in the presidencies of Thomas Jefferson, James Madison, and James Monroe. The annexation of Texas (1845), the Oregon Treaty (1846), and the Mexican Cession (1848) nearly doubled it again during the administrations of Tyler and Polk. Another huge territory came with the purchase of Alaska by the diplomacy of William H. Seward, the rhetoric of Senator Charles Sumner, and the secret-service money of Russian minister Baron Edouard de Stoeckl, who bought the necessary votes in Congress.

American land legislation in the nineteenth century was an attempt to make this land accessible to freeholding farmers, planters, and ranchers as rapidly as possible. State laws and federal legislation served this goal by encouraging land sales at very low prices. They also did it by subdivision of new lands into smaller and more affordable units, by accessible land offices, and by quick surveys. They allowed rights of preemption, warrants for veterans, lotteries, and outright gifts of land.

Here again these processes varied by region in the United States, in ways that reinforced old cultural differences. In the South, large landlords were more numerous and more powerful than in the North. Inequality was much greater on the southern frontier than in other parts of the nation. Southern votes in Congress blocked federal homestead laws, which failed of enactment until the southern states left the Union in 1861. The northern pattern became predominant with the Homestead Act of 1862 and other federal and state laws that virtually gave land away to small freeholders. Other large land grants were given to canal companies and railroad corporations in the expectation that they would open large areas to settlement.

The American system of abundant and accessible land worked for many generations to create a majority of independent property holders. Many minorities were not able to share in this process—former slaves

ACCESS TO LAND IN THE UNITED STATES:
Acquisition of New Territory, 1763–2000

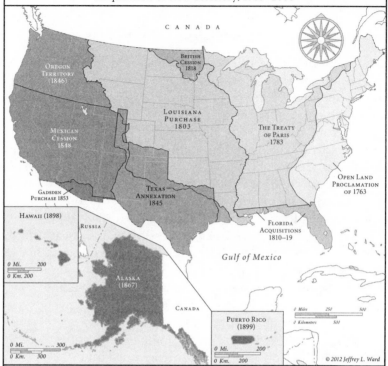

LANDS OPEN FOR SETTLEMENT IN WHAT IS NOW THE UNITED STATES

	LAND AREA SQ. MILES		POPULATION PER SQ. MI.
	ADDED	TOTAL	
Open Land Proclamation of 1763		233,961	6.8 (1760)
The Treaty of Paris, 1783	654,994	888,685	4.5 (1800)
Louisiana Purchase, 1803	827,192	1,715,877	
Florida Acquisitions, 1810–19	58,586	1,774,463	4.3 (1810)
Other Areas, 1810–19	13,443	1,787,906	
Texas Annexation, 1845	390,143	2,178,049	7.4 (1840)
Oregon Settlement, 1846	285,580	2,463,629	
Mexican Cession, 1848	529,017	2,992,646	7.9 (1850)
Gadsden Purchase, 1853	29,640	2,992,646	
Alaska Purchase, 1867	586,412	3,579,058	11.2 (1870)
Hawaii, 1898	6,450	3,585,508	
Puerto Rico, 1899	3,435	3,500,943	21.5 (1900)
Added and Reclaimed, 1900–2000	205,140	3,794,083	
Total, 2000		3,794,083	79.6 (2000)

Sixteen generations of Americans have exploited new land and untapped resources from 1607 to 2010. This process was sustained by the acquisition of new territory, which multiplied land area 15-fold from 1763 to 2000. The peak period of individual land-taking was the 1920s. New lands and resources are still being occupied in the 21st century. This process has sustained a sense of boundless opportunity, which is fundamental to American ethics of liberty and freedom.

In the late nineteenth and early twentieth centuries, this process of opportunity through expansion was beginning to meet its limits, but still it went on. Examples were the Oklahoma Land Rushes (1892–1907). The Cherokee Strip and other lands were taken from Indian owners for a pittance, and at appointed hours the land was opened to galloping hordes of landseekers. These were scenes of increasing demand and diminishing supply. But still the process continued, and the ethos was deeply believed through the twentieth century.

and servants in the South, Indians in the West, and new immigrants in the North. But for the majority of the American people, freehold farming remained the rule, even as wealth inequality increased. From 1790 to as late as 1930, this system was maintained by open access to new lands. The most dramatic examples of this process were the great land rushes in Oklahoma, where men on galloping horses raced each other to the land, then tested the strength of their claims by fists and firearms. Processes of settlement were more orderly in other regions such as the Old Northwest, but in general a system of freehold farming grew by a process of open access to vast supplies of the land. A system of social equity was supported by freedom of opportunity in much of the United States.[35]

New Zealand's Solution: Redistribution, Fairness, and Natural Justice

In the late nineteenth century, New Zealand went a different way. W. J. Gardner writes that by the 1880s, "in some land-hungry areas settlement had almost dried up for lack of suitable land." The national economy slipped into a steep decline. It was widely believed that a leading cause was lack of good land for new settlement. There was also much concern about the concentration of land in large estates. Freedom of opportunity could no longer sustain the expansion of freehold farming in New Zealand.[36]

In January 1891, a new Progressive Lib-Lab government came to power and made a major effort to solve the land problem. One of the central figures was Premier John Ballance, who had long been interested in land reform and was attracted to John Stuart Mill's idea of using tax policy as a tool for redistribution. Another leader was Jock McKenzie, minister of lands in the Lib-Lab coalition. He himself lived on a small farm in northern Otago, and land reform was a sacred cause to him. His supporters were smallholders like himself, "cockatoos," as they were called in the South Pacific, or "cockies" for short. His purpose was to put more small farmers on land of their own. McKenzie's slogan was "Millions of hands want acres, and millions of acres want hands." A third was William Pember Reeves, who described large estate holders as "social pests" who were a burden on the nation.

Working together, they enacted many land reforms in the 1890s. The Land and Income Tax Assessment Act (1891) discouraged large holdings by imposing a tax on unimproved lands, a graduated estate tax, and a surcharge on absentee landlords. It added a system in which an owner could request a lower valuation, and the commissioner of taxes had an option to purchase at that price. Under its terms, the government acquired one of New Zealand's largest pastoral estates, Cheviot in North Canterbury. The reformers worked hard to make the transaction a model that would be acceptable to all parties. The heirs were happy to sell on terms of advantage to them. Its 84,000 acres were divided into 447 holdings, which made many others happier. The "bursting" of the big Cheviot estate was received with enthusiasm by New Zealanders.[37]

On the strength of that success, McKenzie and the Lib-Lab coalition did very well in the next election, and they used their majority to expand the program. The Lands for Settlements Act (1892) created funds for acquisition of other larger estates. An Advances to Settlers Act (1894) helped small purchasers with government loans for improvements on their properties. A Compulsory Purchase Act gave the government power to take land at a fair market price; and a Lease in Perpetuity Act introduced a new system of leasehold tenure for 999 years, which "gave the rights of freehold in everything but name," but also protected holders against loss to private creditors.[38]

Altogether, the government bought 223 large estates in every region of New Zealand during the twenty years from 1892 to 1912.

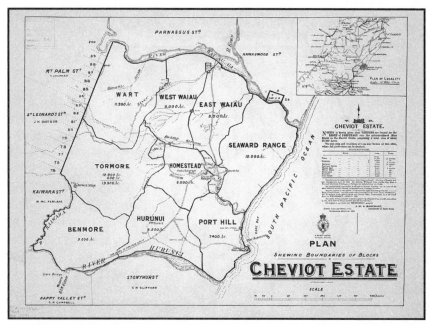

In two generations most of the land in New Zealand was taken. In 1890, a new government came to power and sought a remedy by "bursting the big estates," such as Cheviot and dividing them into small holdings.

A total of about 1.3 million acres were acquired for about 6 million pounds sterling, and 22,000 families were settled on land previously owned by 200 people. At the same time, the government helped another 27,000 families to acquire Crown land in long leasehold or freehold.[39]

On balance this part of the program was a great success. A careful inquiry by Tom Brooking concludes that "McKenzie kept his promise of treating sellers fairly," perhaps more fairly than sellers treated the government. This great reform helped to create what Brooking calls a "revitalisation of the countryside between the 1890s and 1914." In the process it changed the distribution of landed wealth in a significant way. Brooking estimates that "the gross inequalities of 1891 had largely disappeared by the new century.[40]

Consequences: Land Tenure in Britain, America, and New Zealand, 1880–1950

The results of these policies appear in another important study by Tom Brooking of land tenure in three countries: Britain, the United States, and New Zealand. At an early date, both Americans

ACCESS TO LAND IN NEW ZEALAND:
Bursting the Big Estates, 1890–1940

NORTH ISLAND

SOUTH ISLAND

Tasman Sea

Pacific Ocean

CLANDON

Auckland
MANGATEPARU
REWI
MATAMATA
KARAPIRO
TAUTARI SELWYN
KANAKANIA
NGATAPA
CLYDEBANK

RANGIATEA
MANGAWHERO
AND TE HANGA
WAIMANA
WIGAN
Gisborne
TE ARAI

MANGATAHI
ARGYLL
Wanganui FOREST GATE
OHAKEA
MANGAWHATA
CARRINGTON
TANGOIO
ELSTHORPE
LINDSAY
POURERERE
RAUMATI
MANGA-A-TORO
KUMEROA
LANGDALE
HIKAWERA
DYER

Nelson

WANGAPEKA
NORTHBANK
Wellington
BRAEBURN
FLAXBOURNE
LYNDON STARBOROUGH
KOKATAHI CULVERDEN
ANNAN
POERUA CHEVIOT
ASHLEY
GORGE HORSLEY DOWNS

SHERWOOD DOWNS HIGHBANK MORICE
KINLOCH
PUNAROA
CHAMBERLAIN TRIPP
ROSEWILL
MATAKANUI OTEKAIKE OTAIO
WAIKAKAHI
MAEREWHENUA STEWARD
EARNSCLEUGH ARDGOWAN
MEADOWBANK TOTARA
POMOHAKA ST. HELENS, KAUROO
BEAUMONT DOWNS GREENFIELD MAKAREAO, MAKAREAO EXTENSION
OTAHU PUKETAPU
Dunedin
TAUMATA
CONICAL HILLS
GLENHAM
EDENDALE

Stewart Island

Large holdings acquired and redistributed

© 2012 Jeffrey L. Ward

After two generations (1840–1890), New Zealanders were running short of good land. By 1890, the supply was highly concentrated in a few hands: 422 families and companies (1 percent of owners) held 64 percent of freehold estate. A new coalition of Liberal and Labour leaders responded with the Lands for Settlement Act (1892), for the acquisition of all large estates and their redistribution in small holdings. From 1890 to 1940, 669 large estates were bought from willing sellers, and 2 million acres were distributed in smaller units. New Zealanders strongly supported this program, rich and poor alike. Less fair was the forcible seizure and distribution of Maori lands.

and New Zealanders had introduced a mixed system of freehold and leasehold such as had existed in Great Britain. The legal categories were similar, but pattern of actual holdings was very different from the mother country. Tenancy continued to be predominant in Britain. As late as 1880, only 15 percent of landholdings were occupied by their owner in the United Kingdom; 85 percent were occupied by tenants and owned by large landholders.

In America and New Zealand, English forms of land tenure were preserved, but the patterns of landholding were revolutionized. Tom Brooking shows that the mix of landholding in the three countries varied as a percent of total holdings (see table).[41] In the United States, most rural lands were occupied by owners in the late nineteenth century. As late as 1880, nearly three-quarters of American farms were owned as freeholds by the families that occupied them. Americans were lords of their land, with virtually unlimited rights to use it as they pleased, and to alienate it however they wished. State and Federal governments intervened mainly to encourage settlement by small farmers on western lands through homestead legislation, preemption rights for small farmers, grants to veterans, and land grants to immigrants. Otherwise, with the exception of land taken for public use by eminent domain and compensated under the Constitution, the states and the nation allowed the untrammeled free market to operate without restraint or redistribution. Less than 23 percent of American landholdings were in the hands of tenants. This included former slaves who became tenants after emancipation.

In New Zealand, the pattern was very similar. Freehold farming also predominated, and in approximately the same proportion as in the United States. In 1880, the proportion of owner-occupied holdings was 71 percent in New Zealand, compared with 74 percent in the United States, very nearly the same.

But the dynamics were different. New Zealand after 1891 began a sustained program to redistribute its lands. It did not confiscate estates from families of great wealth, but when large holdings came on the market, the government purchased them and broke them into smaller units, then sold them at attractive prices to farming families as freeholds. In that way, the government of New Zealand played a major role in wealth redistribution, and with much success. Dramatic evidence of the results appeared in Margaret Galt's study of wealth concentration in probated estates. The proportion of wealth held by the top 1 percent of estates fell from 65 percent in 1893 to 30 percent in 1912, then fluctuated under more conservative governments in a range of 42 to 24 percent from 1912 to 1935.[42]

Landholding in Three Nations: Percentage of Land Occupied by Owners,
Lessees, and Tenants in Great Britain, New Zealand, and the United States,
1880–1950

Year	Great Britain		New Zealand		United States	
	Owners	Lessees	Owners	Lessees	Owners	Tenants
1880	15	85	71	29	74	23
1900	20	80	68	32	61	38
1910	20	80	64	37	58	41
1930	36	64	64	36	51	48

Source: Tom Brooking

In the United States, federal, state, and local governments did
not attempt redistribution, not even in the Progressive Era. As a consequence, inequality increased, and tenancy grew rapidly in the
United States, more than doubling (109 percent) in the half century
from 1880 to 1930. In New Zealand tenancy also rose, but only by 24
percent. Most American families continued to own their land, but
the proportion fell from 74 to 51 percent. As late as 1930, a bare
majority of Americans still owned the real estate on which they lived,
but the proportion of freeholds was diminishing, and so was the proportion of farmers who were freeholders. Liberty and freedom were
maintained, and government activity was kept low, at a heavy cost in
equity and fairness.

Another interesting pattern emerges when we add a third comparison. The United States and New Zealand, for all their differences, were closer to one another than either was to Great Britain,
where patterns of landholding were even more grossly inequitable.
From 1880 to 1910, 80 to 85 percent of British landholders were
lessees, and not owners. Landed property was heavily concentrated
in a few hands, and that pattern changed only a little from 1910 to
1930. The United States and New Zealand both preserved much
more equity in landholdings than did Great Britain, but they did so
by different means. In North America as late as 1930, we see a strong
residual effect of a vast abundance of land. Large supplies of cheap
land persisted for half a century after Turner declared the frontier to
be closed. Many Americans were able to take advantage of these possibilities—but not so many Afro-Americans or Indians or desperately
poor new immigrants could do so. That injustice in time would lead
to another great reform movement, but it centered on justice through
freedom of opportunity rather than justice through redistribution.

New Zealand went another way. As early as the 1890s it had to expand the possibilities for social justice by an active program of redistribution. It did so with great success for many Pakeha families, but not for Maori. A majority of New Zealanders did well, and many did better than ever. Maori did worse. Still, even in the face of that failure, New Zealand's ideals of social justice and fairness persisted, and so also did policies of redistribution. The continued presence of gross inequities for a minority in New Zealand gave rise to new reform movements and redistributive programs in the next century.

Failures: The Denial of Fairness for Maori and Freedom for Indians

In 1892, New Zealand's program for fairness and justice through redistribution also had a darker side. At the same time that it divided large estates into small tracts, it also redistributed very large holdings of undeveloped land from Maori tribes to the Crown, and in turn to individual Pakeha farmers. McKenzie revived Crown preemption and used it to acquire 3.1 million acres of land from Maori during the period from 1890 to 1911, plus another 500,000 acres in private sales. This was done on terms that were very unfavorable to Maori. Owners of big estates had received 84 shillings an acre and were allowed to keep 640 acres of prime land. Maori received 6 shillings an acre, and individual families got 50 acres.[43]

Worse, Maori were excluded from the Advances to Settlers Program, which helped many Pakeha smallholders. For many individual Maori the choices were stark and cruel. They could work as a rural peasantry on land they could not buy, or they could move to the cities as an urban proletariat.[44] Tom Brooking observes that "the great estate owners were successfully integrated back into the political system and the broader society, while Maori became even more excluded."[45]

A major act of injustice was done to Maori in the cause of a more fair distribution of land among Pakeha. But that was not the end of it. Larger ideas of justice, fairness, and equity had taken root in New Zealand, and traditional Maori ideas of right and wrong had continued to develop. Many people in New Zealand were quick to challenge the taking of tribal lands. Maori leaders took the lead. Holders of Maori seats in Parliament spoke out. Other leaders of the rival Kingitanga (Maori Sovereignty) and Kotahitanga (Maori Unity) movements joined together to protest against the alienation of Maori lands.

One man in particular did something about it. He was James Carroll, the son of an Irish father and a formidable Maori mother.

Carroll became fully a part of both cultures. He was elected to Parliament by Maori voters in a Maori seat. In 1892, he became a cabinet member in the Lib-Lab government, received the portfolio of minister of native affairs in 1899, and became acting prime minister of New Zealand in 1909 and 1911. Carroll and a circle of Maori leaders sought justice for their people by a double strategy that one of them described as "one foot on the Pakeha brake and the other on the Maori accelerator." It began to get results. Carroll opposed the taking of Maori lands. He was unable to stop it, but greatly reduced it. Maori lands had been taken at 360,000 acres a year in the 1890s. Historian James Belich calculates that "in the 1900s, with Carroll's foot firmly on the brakes, it sold at about 50,000 acres a year."[46]

Other wrongs were righted. Maori were admitted to the Advances to Settlers Act, but not until the 1920s. Carroll enacted laws that gave Maori more control of their tribal property. He and his friends founded Maori farms, Maori collectives, Maori corporations, Maori schools, and Maori political organizations. Some Pakeha leaders awakened to Maori rights. In the Lib-Lab coalition Richard Seddon did so, to the surprise of others. And in the conservative National Party, Gordon Coates became a steadfast supporter of Maori rights.[47]

That was the way New Zealand's tradition of social justice and fairness developed through many years. First came the ideals of fairness

Reformers also seized much Maori land and distributed it to Pakeha farmers. Maori minister James Carroll struggled against this injustice and won some victories, but the land continued to flow out of Maori hands.

themselves, transplanted to New Zealand at an early date, proclaimed in good faith, but honored in the breach. The pursuit of justice and fairness was always more limited than the ideals themselves. Then came the material stresses and moral failures that led to acts of gross injustice. They in turn triggered a response. Others worked to revive the tradition of fairness and justice. In that process they also enlarged it and put it to work in new ways.

New Zealand's tradition of fairness and social justice was not a simple story of continuity but a complex process of invention and rejection, achievement and failure, assertion and denial, reinvention and defeat, transformation and revival. At the same time, it kept growing. This was a living tradition, an organic process that derived its dynamism from the creativity that is embedded in its history. The longer it continued, the deeper were its roots, the more potent its strength, and the greater its resilience. Its future will always take us by surprise.

In the United States, a complex and pluralist tradition of liberty and freedom has had a similar history. Here we find an even longer story of light and darkness, victory and defeat, triumph and disaster. The brightest moments in American history were the struggles for liberty and freedom in the American Revolution, the invention of a new republic "to secure the blessings of liberty," the emancipation of slaves in the Civil War, a "larger idea of liberty and freedom" in the New Deal, and leadership in a world struggle for free and open societies against mortal enemies to the left and right. The dark moments in American history were the hanging of Quakers for the "soul liberty" of their Puritan persecutors, and the destruction of the American Republic in 1861 to secure the liberty to keep a slave. All that is America. In the short run things often get worse, but in the long run they tend to get better. Winston Churchill had us right when he said, "The Americans can always be trusted to do the right thing, once all other possibilities have been exhausted."[48]

PART II

NATION BUILDING AS
OPEN PROCESSES

FEDERALISTS AND CENTRALISTS

Two Open Governments

We are all republicans—we are all federalists. . . .
Would the honest patriot, in the full tide of successful
experiment, abandon a government which has so far
kept us free and firm?

—President Thomas Jefferson, March 4, 1801

For more than twenty years we have tried Provincialism. . . . We have given it a fair and independent trial,
and we have found that it has not supplied throughout
the colony good and fair government. Some parts of
the colony have been rolling in wealth, while others
have been reduced almost to starvation; and so long as
we have to put up with Provincialism, so long will that
be the case.

—Premier Harry Atkinson, September 19, 1876

TO AN AMERICAN VISITOR, New Zealand's capital city of
Wellington calls to mind San Francisco or Seattle, but with a
character uniquely its own. Like those other Pacific cities of
similar age, Wellington sits on a range of hills around a handsome
harbor. Close-built neighborhoods of old-fashioned wooden houses
rise one above another on steep slopes that overlook the water. The
vernacular style runs to nineteenth-century urban villas, with high-
pitched gables and an abundance of Carpenter's Gothic. Their
antique facades are often painted in bright contemporary colors—a
happy combination.

New Zealand's Beehive holds the executive offices of Parliament in Wellington. Its centripetal design is emblematic of a democratic polity that is the most centralized of all the English-speaking nations.

Downtown, where Bowen Street begins its long climb to the botanical gardens on the Tinakori Road, the architectural mood is broken by an extraordinary modern building. It is big and round, with an exterior that is honeycombed by many layers of small dark windows. New Zealanders call it the Beehive, which accurately describes its appearance, if one can imagine an enormous beehive of steel and concrete, soaring ten stories above a busy swarm of city traffic.[1]

The Beehive is familiar to every New Zealander. It holds the executive offices of Parliament and is at once the seat of government and a symbol of national sovereignty. At the same time, it is emblematic of New Zealand's political system in another way. The building's design is tightly centered and compressed upon itself in a way that creates a strong centripetal feeling. Its architecture is a perfect symbol for a system of democratic self-government that is the most centralized and consolidated in the English-speaking world—much more so than Australia, Canada, or the United States.[2]

In that symbolism, the Beehive is to New Zealand as the Capitol building is to the United States. Strangers in the city of Washington have a similar sense of surprise and wonder when they visit the great structure that sprawls across the top of Capitol Hill. From the outside, this building presents a spectacle of complex symmetry, with two very

The United States Capitol Building is the seat of Congress and an emblem of the American political system. On the outside it presents an image of complex symmetry with countervailing checks and balances. Its interior is a mix of public spaces and private passages that are closed to the people but wide open to lobbyists.

large wings that meet beneath an enormous iron dome. Inside, the grand corridors and public function rooms are surrounded by a maze of small chambers, secret hideaways, narrow passages, hidden doors, and private stairs. Members of Congress like to call it the People's House, and part of it is so, but much of it is closed to the people, and wide open to lobbyists who grease the rusty wheels of the republic.[3]

Even so, the Capitol is much loved in the United States as a symbol of democracy, federalism, and especially of liberty and freedom—the great values that Americans hold most dear. The building itself is also an expression of a unique republican system—a complex set of countervailing institutions, carefully designed to check and balance one another (which sometimes they succeed in doing all too well). And the internal architecture of the Capitol also symbolizes a conflicted political culture that combines soaring ideals with systemic corruption.

As these buildings suggest, the United States and New Zealand are both democracies, but in very different ways. New Zealand has been called the "purest example of the Westminster model of government in the world," more so than Westminster itself. The United States is a leading example of mixed government, with its checks and balances. The contrasts between those two systems are many and complex: centralism and federalism, prime minister and president, parliament and congress, unicameral and bicameral legislatures, "responsible government" and executive independence, proportional representation in New Zealand and winner-take-all in the United States. Another contrast captures two ironies in these open societies. The United States is a large multicultural system, with hundreds of ethnic groups and only two major political parties. New Zealand is a smaller bicultural system with two predominant ethnic groups and many political parties.[4]

These democratic systems were deliberately invented to serve different purposes. American institutions were created primarily to preserve liberty and freedom, and to mediate among many rival conceptions of those contested ideas.[5] Ideas of justice, equity, and fairness are also important in the United States, but are thought to flow from free institutions. By contrast, New Zealand's national institutions were designed to promote fairness, equity, and "natural justice" throughout the nation. Freedom and liberty are also valued, but are thought to grow from a system that is just and fair. The same ethical elements exist in both cultures, but priorities run in reverse.

Colonial Self-Government: Two Traditions

These institutions developed in different processes of nation-building, but in one fundamental way their beginnings were the same. In both countries, English-speaking colonists from Britain began to govern themselves in accustomed ways long before they became independent nations. They also began to construct governing systems for open societies—some of the first open societies in the modern world.

In North America, all of the original British colonies founded representative assemblies, which were as many as six generations old by 1776. A vernacular tradition of self-government was firmly established before the War of Independence. The sequence of those events was different from the history of New France, New Spain, New Netherland, Brazil, and from most settler societies in the modern world.[6]

In the mainland colonies of British America, many different forms of local government were invented. A system of town meetings in New England was functioning by 1635, under the Massachusetts Town Act. The Quaker colonies created a different system of commissions and order keepers that was functioning from the start. Virginians developed yet another structure of county courts and parishes. The variety of these local institutions is evidence of their spontaneity and autonomy.[7]

On a higher level, the thirteen colonial governments were similar in structure, though not identical. Before 1776, the power to make laws was shared by an elected assembly, an appointed council, and a governor. This system of divided or balanced government had deep roots in Western culture. It had appeared as a design in Aristotle's *Politics* and was put to work in medieval polities, Renaissance city-states, and the English joint-stock companies from which many colonies derived. The leading example was the government of England itself, with its divided government of a Monarch, Lords, and Commons, each with its role in legislation by "King-in-Parliament." This mixed British system reached its highest level of development when the American colonies were young. Its architecture was closely linked to ideas of English liberty and freedom in the early modern era. All thirteen American colonies adopted this system of government in various forms.[8]

In New Zealand, English-speaking people also founded small colonies that were autonomous in high degree. In 1851, William Fox published a book called *The Six Colonies of New Zealand*. He discussed Auckland, Canterbury, Nelson, Otago, Plymouth, and Wellington as if they were separate states. He observed that by many tests, the original "six colonies of New Zealand" had stronger ties to Britain and Australia than they did to one another. At first these little settlements did not much associate with one another.[9] That year, for example, Governor George Grey noted the arrival of shipping in Auckland: 472 vessels from the Bay of Islands and settlements near Auckland; 46 from Australia and Britain; and only 6 from all other "principal settlements in New Zealand."[10] William Fox also observed in 1851 that Nelson had had no contact with Wellington for three months when major decisions were being taken in both places. The two settlements were only 150 miles apart.

In those circumstances, all of New Zealand's original "six colonies" began by improvising their own governments, with varying degrees of success. The founders of New Plymouth were typical that way. On January 21, 1842, they came together in a chapel to organize their first "public meeting," where "holders of Land Orders" settled questions by majority vote.[11] In Dunedin, the settlers improvised spontaneous "town meetings," and the congregation of the Presbyterian Kirk elected elders to enforce order and administer welfare.[12] Wellington held elections for a "Borough Council" as early as 1842; every adult male who enrolled as a "burgess" and paid one pound could vote; 93 percent did so.[13] Canterbury was run by a "committee of management" of all land purchasers in "general meetings" that adopted parliamentary rules of debate and ballot.[14] Auckland's settlers were ruled by an unpopular oligarchy called the Official

Land-Jobbing Association.[15] Nelson in its early years was riven by strife among company officials, absentee landowners, angry laborers, and infuriated Maori.[16]

Imperial officials complained of disorder in these local polities. A leading purpose of George Grey's constitution was to convert six settlements into a united colony, with self-governing "provinces" and uniform systems of representative government. Under the Constitution of 1852, each province was given a council and a superintendent elected by the people. The councils had broad powers to make laws "not repugnant to the law of England." They were forbidden to legislate on foreign affairs, trade, Crown lands, coinage, and sovereign prerogatives but had authority to deal with immigration, land, schools, public health, and public works.[17]

Unlike America's bicameral governments, New Zealand's first provincial systems had unicameral councils. In four new provinces that followed the first six, each council elected a superintendent by majority vote. He sat with them and functioned as a provincial premier. There were few checks and balances of the sort that had been customary in England and the American colonies during the eighteenth century. Like English-speaking Americans before them, New Zealanders modeled their political institutions on British practices in their own time. Their prototype was Britain's nineteenth-century parliamentary system, with a prime minister as head of government and a monarch as head of state. This was a very different polity from the mixed or balanced government of Britain's "Eighteenth-Century Constitution."[18]

Two Paths to Independence

Another major difference between New Zealand and the United States appeared in the ways that they achieved nationhood. The American republics won their independence in a long armed struggle. The War for Independence rose from a bitter conflict between American settlers and British leaders over many issues, but mainly about the status of colonial governments in relation to Parliament. American colonists insisted that their assemblies were parliamentary bodies, co-equal with Parliament on internal questions, with parliamentary privilege for their members, rights of election for freemen, and full powers of legislation on domestic subjects. Imperial officials in London emphatically disagreed. They believed that American assemblies, like English municipal councils, were subordinate to Parliament.[19]

In the Stamp Act Crisis in 1765, Parliament asserted the right to tax the American colonies, then backed away under heavy pressure from American colonists and British merchants. In 1766, Parliament asserted the right to legislate for America in "all cases whatsoever," and attempted to do so with increasing frequency on many aspects of colonial life.[20] Finally, when British imperial authorities attempted to curb colonial institutions of self-government and even to destroy them in the Coercive Acts (1774), the colonies took up arms.[21] American independence was won on the battlefield in a hard-fought war that continued longer than the Civil War and American participation in World War II combined. The memory of that armed struggle is still very strong in the United States three centuries later.

New Zealand's independence happened in another way. Historian David McIntyre writes, "When and how their country gained their independence is not a question New Zealanders ask themselves. If they did, few would have an answer. Unlike Americans with the Declaration of Independence, or Indians with the 'transfer of power,' New Zealand was a British colony which became an independent nation very gradually. . . . The landmarks are not dramatic and the process is suffused with paradox and ambiguity."[22]

New Zealanders always exercised a high degree of self-government without issuing a declaration of independence. Their national institutions formed slowly by a gradual process of evolution. Milestones on that very long journey were George Grey's Constitution of 1852, the calling of New Zealand's first General Assembly in 1854, and the beginning of what New Zealanders call "responsible government" in 1856, by which they mean ministers who are responsible to a parliamentary majority and ultimately to the electorate. Other important events were the Secret Ballot Act in 1869, universal manhood suffrage in 1879, women's suffrage in 1893, the Dominion System in 1907, the Statute of Westminster in 1931, its very belated Ratification in 1947, and New Zealand's Constitution Act of 1986.[23]

A sense of national identity grew slowly. A case in point was New Zealand's response to the Statute of Westminster (1931), in which Britain's Parliament granted full legal independence to New Zealand, Canada, Australia, South Africa, Newfoundland, and the Irish Free State. All were quick to ratify its terms except New Zealand. Historian Peter Gibbons observes that both the National and Labour parties "accepted some autonomy but felt no need to proclaim it." Not until twenty-six years later did New Zealand ratify the Statute of Westminster, and even then added strong expressions of identity with Britain and the Commonwealth.[24]

Many individual New Zealanders told us that a sense of national independence did not fully emerge until the late twentieth century. Some believe that the major break came on January 1, 1973, which James Belich calls "a black-letter day in New Zealand history." It was the date when Britain entered the European Economic Community and unilaterally ended long-standing economic relations with her colonies.[25] As late as 1950, Britain had bought nearly 70 percent of New Zealand's exports. After Britain joined the European Community in 1973, that number fell to 7 percent. New Zealand farmers found themselves competing at a disadvantage for markets in the "mother country" as Britain and other European economies aggressively subsidized their own farmers.[26]

Belich observes that "the EEC was far from the whole story," but that Britain's decision to join the European community had a profound effect on the thinking of New Zealanders.[27] Worse than the material injury was a deep sense of moral outrage against a "mother country" that so casually abandoned its own children. Twice New Zealanders had come to Britain's aid, in 1914 and 1939, at heavy cost. Now they felt themselves deserted, and at a very difficult time when the world economy was contracting.

The memory of these different experiences of independence had major consequences in both nations. Even today, many Americans vividly remember their long, hard struggle for liberty and freedom, almost as if they themselves had been there and done it. Every generation (nine generations to date) has dedicated itself anew to the noble and enduring values of the Declaration of Independence. The values of the American Revolution and the "founders" are continuing models even in the twenty-first century.

Memories are not the same in New Zealand. Even in the 1990s, we heard expressions of deep resentment over the British decision to break economic ties with its former colonies, and a feeling of profound injustice. The sense of perfidy and betrayal was most intense among New Zealanders who had been the most loyal to Britain and the empire. One leader told us, "We envy your Declaration of Independence from the mother country. As for us, our mother left home."

The Critical Period in the United States, 1783–89: A Conjunction of Crises

After the American War of Independence, the newly independent United States suffered through a troubled era that scholars have long called the Critical Period of American history. Some date it to the years from 1783 to 1789. Others think of it in broader terms, from 1776 to 1815, but most restrict it to the 1780s.[28]

This era was critical in more senses than one. It was a crisis in the journalist's sense of a moment when things went badly wrong. The newly independent American republics struggled through a time of troubles of a sort that follows every revolution, and often decides its fate. Most cities and much of the countryside had been ravaged by eight years of fighting. After the war, large areas of the country were still held by Britain and Spain in defiance of the peace treaty. The Continental Congress was incapable of functioning as a national government. The thirteen states were riven by internal conflict, incessant violence, and political instability. These problems were compounded by economic contraction and environmental stress in a time of severe worsening of world climate during the 1780s.

At the same time, this period of American history was also a crisis in the classical sense of ancient Greek drama—a moment when fate was hanging in the balance, and might have gone one way or another. Americans grappled with great problems in the years from 1783 to 1789. As they did so this era also became critical in the third sense of a time when some major problems of urgent importance were actually resolved. The result was critical in yet a fourth meaning

John Adams (right) thought of a republic as a system of checks and balances, primarily within the legislature, between the aristoi and demos, the few and the many. The role of the president was to maintain a balance between them and prevent either from establishing a tyranny. Alexander Hamilton feared the mob and disliked democracy. He believed that the republic could survive only in close alliance with its elites and with rapid economic growth.

of that complex word. It was an historical analogue to what physicists call a "change of phase," as when the molecular structure of H_2O suddenly (very suddenly) changes from water to ice.

In this difficult period, Americans framed a federal constitution and adopted a novel system of government that has endured for more than two centuries. The major decisions were made by a remarkable group of leaders, men of experience and enlightenment, men of reason and abiding faith, with large purposes and clear visions for America.[29]

The problem was that their visions were not the same. And they were also trying to do something that had not been done before—create a republic on a continental scale. To that end, they invented a variety of different models of a constitutional republic. A major task of the American founders was to mediate among these differences, and to construct a common frame for their coexistence.

John Adams designed a free republic on the Aristotelian model of a balanced constitution. He thought of it as a dynamic balance between monarchical, aristocratic, and democratic elements. A bicameral legislature was intended to represent the few and the many, to keep either one from tyrannizing the other. The role of an independent president was to maintain the balance by shifting his weight between the few and the many as circumstances required.[30]

The model republic of Thomas Jefferson (right) centered on the ward, or hundred, a small sovereign body of self-governing yeoman farmers that delegated limited power to the county, state, and national government. James Madison thought of a republic as a set of many groups, with opposing interests. His way of protecting freedom and liberty was to multiply these groups, so that none could establish a tyranny.

Alexander Hamilton preferred a free republic governed by elites under the rule of law. He sought stability by "binding the monied men to the government," and by keeping the people at a distance from power by various constitutional devices such as very long terms of office (he favored a life term for the president) and secrecy in government. He also believed that a very large republic with a strong central government would be remote from the people, in part because of its scale.[31]

Thomas Jefferson had another vision of a free republic in which sovereignty rested in self-governing "wards," or groups of independent farmers, small enough to assemble within the reach of a man's voice. Jefferson observed that any government was "republican in its proximity to this model." He believed that all power should be delegated from these small "wards" to counties, states, and the national government, in carefully limited ways, and that governments should be kept on a very tight leash.[32]

His friend James Madison preferred a large pluralist republic, on the theory that a free republic might become more stable as religions, factions, and parties multiplied. It was for him a question of political arithmetic: the greater the number of groups, the smaller the probability that any one of them could tyrannize over the others.[33]

George Washington believed in a republic of virtue, which he personified. He attracted able and virtuous leaders to serve with him and inspired others by his example. Benjamin Franklin was the oldest of the founders, also the most modern in many ways.

George Washington believed in a republic of virtue, led by men of independence who served others and the republic itself with integrity, honor, courage, wisdom, and stoic virtue. He served this ideal all his life, and won many Americans to it by the strength of his example. Others wondered where any republic could find such leaders. Washington found many of them in his time, and they modeled their conduct on him. It seemed a perfectly workable idea at the time.[34]

Benjamin Franklin, the oldest of these founders, had in some ways the most modern idea of a representative republic, as a community of opinion and judgment, sustained by the free flow of information and knowledge. These different visions (and there were many more) caused deep divisions in the new republic.[35]

American Federalism as a Framework for Liberty and Freedom

At the same time that the American founders developed these republican ideals, they also had another purpose. The experience of the War of Independence persuaded them that they needed a strong national government if their free republics were to survive in a very dangerous world. But the history of European states and empires also convinced them that strong local institutions were vital to the protection of liberty and freedom.[36]

To solve these problems, the architects of the Constitution invented a federal republic in which power was carefully distributed among local, state, and national governments. Through the full span of American history this complex system changed by becoming stronger in many of its moving parts. The national government gained strength, but states and local governments fiercely guarded their powers within the federal system, and even enlarged them. On both the national and state levels, the various branches of government also asserted their powers with success. Many presidents, especially Washington, Adams, Jefferson, Jackson, Polk, and Lincoln, increased the executive power of their office. Both branches of Congress expanded their legislative roles. National and state judiciaries asserted the power of judicial review, which appears nowhere in the federal constitution, and won it in the period from 1780 to 1820 without constitutional authority. Many Americans regard powers of judicial review in the Supreme Court as a palladium of liberty and freedom, even as they reserve their constitutional right to rage against the sitting justices, who never fail to infuriate a large part of the American people.

A FEDERAL SYSTEM FOR THE UNITED STATES:
Support and Opposition for the Constitution of 1787–89

In 1789, the thirteen original states adopted a Federal system after long debate. In support of stronger national institutions were southeastern New England (Massachusetts and Connecticut); the Delaware Valley (east Pennsylvania, New Jersey, and Delaware); tidewater Virginia and Maryland; and low country Carolina and Georgia. Opposed were upstate New York, Rhode Island, backcountry Pennsylvania, southside Virginia, the Southern Highlands, and Cape Fear Valley. Some of these alignments still exist today.

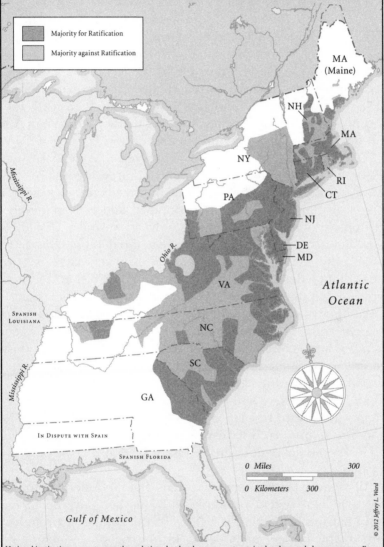

National institutions grew stronger through time, but local governments retained and expanded many powers. Every county had a busy shire town, and sometimes "half-shire towns." On each level Americans established intricate checks and balances, and kept their leaders on a short leash. Connecticut elected its legislature every six months. This mixed system was cumbersome and costly—a heavy tax on Americans who resented taxation in general. But they paid willingly for many layers of government, to protect local folkways and to safeguard liberty and freedom.

All of this created a complex federal system, with extensive separation of powers and multiple checks and balances. Through it all, the states retained much of their power as well. In America from 1776 to as late as 1861, *the United States* was commonly used as a plural noun, sometimes with *united* in the lower case and *States* in capitals. The Civil War transformed this federal system, but also preserved it. The Union victory made *the United States* into a singular noun, but the states retained their importance, and in some areas even increased it. Other transformations followed in the late nineteenth and twentieth centuries, especially in the Progressive Era, the New Deal, and the New Liberalism of the 1960s, which strengthened the national government while also reinforcing state and local governments. In the early twenty-first century, the federal system is stronger than ever before in American history, despite much rhetoric to the contrary.[37]

A vital factor in its existence was the size and scale of the system. The American Republic was born big, and grew bigger. In 1783, it was the only republic in the world that operated on such a scale. The vast area of the United States encouraged and even required the development of a federal system, as it did in Australia, Canada, and Russia. But many small nations also created federal systems: Switzerland and the Netherlands, for example. And very large ones have done without federalism. China is a case in point. Size and scale were important, but they were not fixed determinants of federalism.

Another vital determinant of federalism was ethnic and regional diversity, reinforced by fundamentally different cultural values, social structures, and economic systems. And one of the most important differences was about slavery. In 1776, every state was a slave state. By 1787, when the Constitution was written, seven states in New England and the Delaware and Hudson valleys had abolished slavery or were moving toward free labor systems. The states below the Mason-Dixon line all preserved slavery on a large scale, and most strengthened it. As colonial regions evolved into "sections," these differences increased.

All of those factors were important, but the American founders chose a federal system primarily with another purpose in mind. James Madison explained in 1788, "In the compound republic of America, the power surrendered by the people, is first divided between two distinct governments. . . . Hence a double security arises to the rights of the people."[38]

As the *Federalist Papers* explained over and over again, the federal system in the United States was created mainly to protect "the rights of the people," and to promote liberty and freedom. Many conflicts followed over the design of the system, but most of them, except the slavery question, happened within the framework of consensus that Thomas Jefferson described in his inaugural. With few exceptions, Americans have indeed been all republicans and all federalists—even as we disagree profoundly on many other questions.[39]

New Zealand's Critical Period

New Zealand also had its Critical Period, in the years between 1856 and 1876. As in the United States, it was critical in several ways at once. This was a crisis in a journalist's sense of a time when things went wrong. The mid-nineteenth century was an era of growth and instability, marked by intermittent boom and bust. It was a period of the largest wars between Maori and Pakeha, of painful political conflict, and of chronic dysfunction in existing political institutions. The provincial system was not working well. It failed to keep the peace, failed to serve the material welfare of the country, and failed ethical tests of justice, equity, and fairness that were so important in this society.

As New Zealanders responded to these problems, this Critical Period also became a crisis in the classical sense, a pivotal moment when the country might have developed in different directions. Much hinged on hard and painful choices. And as major decisions began to be made, this era became a crisis in a third sense—a founding era in which the acts and choices of New Zealanders framed their national institutions, which still endure. The result was the construction of a nation-state in New Zealand with a distinctive polity and national institutions even before it achieved full independence. In time these new institutions shaped a society, and also the national culture that exists in New Zealand today.[40]

Different as they were, New Zealand's leaders in its Critical Period shared much in common. Prominent among them were four men who became the movers of change in the country: Julius Vogel, Edward Stafford, Harry Atkinson, and James FitzGerald. All of them were immigrants, born in Britain or Ireland between 1818 and 1835, and raised with values that we associate with the Victorian era. All emigrated during the late 1840s and early 1850s, flourished in private careers, and became active in public life. Most were elected superintendents of their provinces, strongly supported the provincial system, and then moved into national politics. All had large visions for New Zealand. Their visions were not the same, but they shared a fundamental purpose. At the center of their thinking were explicit ideas of fairness and justice.

Edward Stafford (1819–1901) was a gentleman runholder in Nelson. He had been raised in Ireland among the Anglo-Irish ascendancy and migrated to New Zealand in 1843. A Chartist in British politics, he became a Gladstone Liberal in New Zealand, with a vision of a democratic nation and a growing interest in what he called "a fair measure of justice" for Maori and Pakeha alike. Stafford became Nelson's first superintendent and made his province a model in education, internal improvements, and forward-looking laws. He sat in the New Zealand Parliament for twenty-two years and served as premier for nine of them. The beginning of his first ministry as premier in 1856 transformed his political thinking. As he began to think in more national terms, this leading provincialist suddenly became a centralist. Later he recalled, "From that moment I determined to be a New Zealander. I determined neither to know Auckland nor Nelson, nor Wellington, nor Otago." He worked to strengthen the national institutions of New Zealand, not primarily for their own sake but as an instrument of large social and political purposes. Always prominent in Stafford's thinking was his persistent theme, "a fair measure of justice."[41]

Another leader was Harry Atkinson (1831–92), a gentleman farmer of New Plymouth and one of the Taranaki Mob. Born and raised in Cheshire, the son of a Unitarian architect and builder, he migrated to New Zealand in 1853 with many of his family and became a leading landowner in his province. In 1876, at the age of thirty-five, he became premier of New Zealand. Atkinson was a man

Edward Stafford, a gentleman runholder from Nelson, encouraged New Zealanders to think not in terms of justice to the provinces but justice to individuals. He put that idea to work in the cause of democratic reform.

of high integrity, known for honesty, simplicity, prudence, and moderation. His principles were also those of a Gladstone Liberal. He hated the waste and narrowness of the provincial system, felt that it had not given New Zealand "good and fair government," and spoke out for what he called a progressive and economical system.[42]

Harry Atkinson was a gentleman farmer from New Plymouth and a conservative Liberal. He disliked the waste and excess of the provincial system and worked for "progressive" and "economical" institutions. Most of all he spoke out for "good and fair government" in all of New Zealand.

A third main leader was James Edward FitzGerald (1818–96). Born in Ireland, schooled in England, a humanitarian and founder of the English Colonial Reform Society, he was the first colonist to come ashore at Canterbury. An amiable, very able, and large-spirited man, he was the first elected superintendent of Canterbury province. He is remembered in that role as the first to introduce "responsible government," in New Zealand's sense of an executive who was subordinate to the legislature. FitzGerald acted on that principle initially in Canterbury (1852–53) and then in New Zealand (1854–56), where he would have been the first premier had he not been in poor health. He became instead the comptroller and auditor general of New Zealand and devoted himself to honesty in politics, fairness in government, and justice for Maori.[43]

A very different figure was Julius Vogel (1835–99). He came from a London Jewish family, was educated in the Royal School of Mines, and followed gold rushes around the world. In 1852, he went to Australia in 1852, where he set himself up as an apothecary in the gold fields, attracting customers with a stuffed iguana. In 1860, he moved to New Zealand and became editor of the *Otago Daily Times*, New Zealand's first daily, which he made into a strong voice for provincial autonomy, and even for the independence of the South Island. Always he was consumed with ambition, for which he sought

*James Edward FitzGerald was the first
elected superintendent of Canterbury
province and a humanitarian reformer.
He is remembered as one of the leaders who
promoted "responsible government" in New
Zealand's special sense and also worked for
justice to Maori.*

a "fair field." In 1863, he went to the National Assembly and became colonial treasurer and premier, with a particular interest in economic development. In those new offices he became a strong centralist. Vogel was optimistic and enthusiastic, full of large plans and special purposes for New Zealand. He wrote to his friend William Reynolds that the political models in Britain and America did not apply there. Vogel devoted himself to finding another way and constructing a system that would promote rapid economic development in his new country.[44]

New Zealand's Turn Toward a Central System: "A Question of Fairness"

In the nineteenth century, these four leaders deliberately decided to create a highly centralized system of government for New Zealand. That decision was made only after an experiment with provinces and a quasi-federal solution had failed. In 1852, Governor George Grey and Britain's Parliament had given New Zealand a "general government" and uniform self-governing provincial governments, whether it wanted them or not. This very Whiggish plan was inspired by Grey's memory of eighteenth-century British

Julius Vogel was a principled entrepreneur who worked for a system of government that could promote rapid economic development and a "fair field for ambition." He combined that purpose with many other causes, such as the rights of women and justice for Jewish people throughout the world.

Sir Julius Vogel
Premier

institutions and by his admiration of the American Constitution. It included a chief executive, a bicameral legislature, and other elements that Americans had adopted in 1789. Grey's quasi-federal system began to function in 1854, and the number of provinces multiplied from six in 1854 to ten by 1873. But this "provincialism" did not work well in New Zealand.

Part of its failure was a function of scale. In 1870, New Zealand had a population of three hundred thousand, less than one-tenth the population of the United States in 1790. There was a general feeling that New Zealand's provincial system was cumbersome, complex, and too costly for the country. Anthony Trollope visited New Zealand in 1872 and wrote that "New Zealand is over-governed, over-legislated, over-provided with officials, and over-burdened with national debt." He was amazed by the buildings of the Otago Provincial Council, which were modeled on the Houses of Parliament in London. Trollope observed that they were more opulent than the government buildings of American states, which were many times larger. "The architecture, furniture and general apparel of these Houses," he wrote, "struck me as being almost grander than was necessary." Another British politician unkindly called it "a most Brobdingnagian Government for a series of Lilliputian States."[45]

Yet another factor was growing disparity of wealth among the provinces. Some had strong and independent governments, especially Otago and Canterbury. Others were so poor and weak that they were barely able to govern themselves at all. Vogel said, "Their doom was . . . that they could not raise their own revenues." The system was uneven, unjust, and very unfair to individuals.[46]

For twenty years New Zealanders struggled to make this system work. But the rich provinces jealously guarded their independence, and the poor provinces complained bitterly that needs were not being met. The General Assembly attempted to assume a larger role in public works, immigration, and social legislation. Both the provinces and the general government borrowed very heavily but were unable to serve the needs of an expanding population. Provincial leaders accepted some reforms but refused to cooperate on others. Every ministry was a fragile coalition, and premiers succeeded one another in rapid succession. Factional strife increased between centralists, provincialists, and outright separationists.

Gradually a new generation of young leaders emerged in national politics during the late 1860s and 1870s. Most had begun as strong supporters of the provincial system and had risen to high office within it. But when they went to the New Zealand Assembly, and struggled with problems on that higher level, they became centralists. One of the first to do so was Edward Stafford, who was working to strengthen the general government by the 1860s. At first he was strongly opposed by Julius Vogel, then a leading provincialist from Otago.

A turning point came in 1869 when Vogel became colonial treasurer and proposed a new budget with heavy borrowing and spending on public works and immigration. It met with mixed results, in both New Zealand politics and world money markets. In 1873, Vogel became premier and found himself increasingly embattled against the provinces. Just at that moment, a major credit crisis developed in North America and Europe. By 1874, New Zealand's agents had trouble getting large loans on good terms. Prospects for borrowing were even worse in 1875–76.[47] The political problem came to a head when Vogel proposed to use revenue from the sale of Crown lands for the construction of railroads throughout New Zealand. Provincialists wanted the revenue for their own governments and refused to agree. Worse, when three provinces on the South Island built railroads, they adopted three different gauges: a "broad gauge" in Canterbury, "standard gauge" in Southland, and a middling "new standard gauge" in Otago. Yet another struggle followed, over Vogel's proposal for creating national forest reserves, which were also resisted by some provincial leaders.

These conflicts turned Vogel into a centralist. Working with his former opponent Edward Stafford, he proposed the entire abolition of all provincial governments on the North Island. Many of the poor provinces supported that idea, and the rich provinces could not unite against it. The measure passed. Another bill extended the new system to the whole of New Zealand. Vogel was out of the country when the proposed bill came to a vote, but Atkinson, with strong support by Stafford, managed to get it through. Provincialists from Otago and Canterbury fought it tooth and nail. Sir George Grey was passionate in his opposition. But a strong majority of representatives, especially from poor provinces, supported the centralists. In 1876, the new reform carried on the second reading, 52 to 17.[48]

The result was a landmark law called the Abolition of Provinces Act. The provinces were renamed "provincial districts," which functioned as arms of the central government and lost virtually all of their various roles. This reform eliminated a middle level of autonomous governments. It left New Zealand with a national government and local bodies such as municipal corporations (under a new act in 1867), borough councils, county councils, road boards, river boards, and the like. Through the years, Parliament divided the country into arbitrary "counties," and then sliced it into various sets of administrative districts for particular purposes.

The abolition of provinces in 1875 is little studied in New Zealand today. It is interesting to ask why it happened, when most English-speaking settler societies were going the other way. All four leading reformers explained their own purposes in terms of fairness and social justice, but they did so in different ways. Harry Atkinson, who guided the bill through the assembly, thought it was mainly a question of fairness for small provinces, as he came from one of the smallest. He said, "For more than twenty years we have tried Provincialism. . . . We have given it a fair and independent trial, and we have found that it has not supplied throughout the colony good and fair government. Some parts of the colony have been rolling in wealth, while others have been reduced almost to starvation; and so long as we have to put up with Provincialism, so long will that be the case."[49]

Stafford's thinking was similar, but he recast the problem in other terms. For him, the great question was fairness for the people,

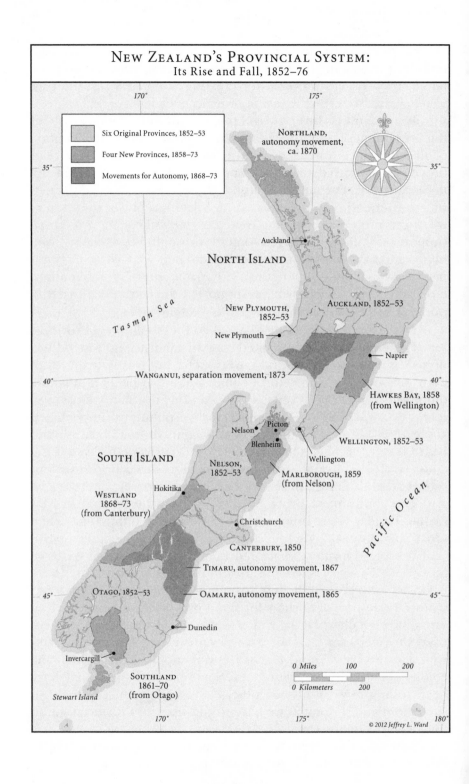

NEW ZEALAND'S PROVINCIAL SYSTEM:
Its Rise and Fall, 1852–76

Six Original Provinces, 1852–53

Four New Provinces, 1858–73

Movements for Autonomy, 1868–73

NORTHLAND, autonomy movement, ca. 1870

Auckland

NORTH ISLAND

NEW PLYMOUTH, 1852–53

AUCKLAND, 1852–53

New Plymouth

Tasman Sea

Napier

WANGANUI, separation movement, 1873

HAWKES BAY, 1858 (from Wellington)

Nelson   Picton

Blenheim

WELLINGTON, 1852–53

SOUTH ISLAND

NELSON, 1852–53

Wellington

MARLBOROUGH, 1859 (from Nelson)

WESTLAND 1868–73 (from Canterbury)

Hokitika

Pacific Ocean

Christchurch

CANTERBURY, 1850

TIMARU, autonomy movement, 1867

OTAGO, 1852–53

OAMARU, autonomy movement, 1865

Dunedin

Invercargill

0 Miles   100   200

0 Kilometers   200

SOUTHLAND 1861–70 (from Otago)

Stewart Island

© 2012 Jeffrey L. Ward

not the provinces. He declared, "If we heard less of the provinces and more of the people of New Zealand, our legislation would be more beneficial."[50] FitzGerald was often thinking about justice to Maori.

Vogel thought of fairness and justice not so much as ends in themselves but as means to other ends of economic growth and domestic peace. He wrote, "There can be no hope of freedom from conflict except in the symmetry and consistency of uniform legislation." This vision of "symmetry and consistency" and "uniform legislation" was yet another idea of equity.[51] Most New Zealanders agreed with one of these ideas or another. After the reform passed, a general election followed, and centralists gained another large majority. George Grey accepted the new regime, as did most provincial leaders in Otago, Auckland, and Canterbury.

The consequences of this pivotal reform were even more interesting than its cause. In a word, centralization brought a revolution in government. It was followed by a major change in suffrage. The Qualification of Electors Act enfranchised all adult males who had lived in New Zealand for at least twelve months. The proportion of registered voters rose from 71 to 91 percent. Newspapers gave more attention to public issues, and political associations multiplied. Elections became national events, and turnout surged. In Otago and Southland participation rose from 48 percent in 1879 to 85 percent in 1887. A large measure of power shifted from small provincial oligarchies to a national democracy. Working-class and middle-class voters were both empowered by this revolution. The old demands of conservative elites for retrenchment and low taxes continued, but new voices were heard, calling for expanding the role of the national government in the economy and social reform.[52]

In the United States something similar had happened in its federal system after its Critical Period. Universal suffrage for free white males spread through most American states during the early republic. By 1814, as many as 68 to 80 percent of adult white males were actually voting in most states. Democracy was not the achievement of Andrew Jackson, it was the medium in which he swam.

These two systems were both transformed in their Critical Periods. Both became functional democracies—the United States before the critical elections of 1800 and 1828; New Zealand before the pivotal election of 1890. Major reform movements followed. But these processes produced different results in America's federal system and New Zealand's central government.[53]

Social Consequences of Federalism and Centralism:
Systems of Order and Violence

In what is now the United States, the preservation of internal peace has always remained primarily the responsibility of local and state institutions, with a growing role for the national government. As a result, distinctly different systems of maintaining order and controlling violence developed in the regional cultures of early America. These differences persist even to our own time. Virginia and most southern colonies had relied mainly on county justices and sheriffs, who were Crown officers appointed from above. New Englanders preferred town constables, elected by their communities. In the Quaker colonies, religious societies disciplined their own members, and county officers called "order keepers" maintained peace among those many groups. After the Revolution, western settlements had roving peace officers called rangers, and in federal territories U.S. marshals and the regular U.S. Army kept order. Most of these peacekeeping institutions, except Quaker order keepers, have persisted through three centuries, even to our time.

In response to urbanization and industrialization, other peacekeeping institutions were created, mostly by state and local governments. After 1820, professional police forces developed in American cities, under the authority of state legislatures. Following the Civil War, new bodies called "state police" were created. They were small professional forces, founded on military models, dressed in military uniforms, and designed to control violence and disorder that reached beyond local communities.

In the twentieth century, the increasing scale and complexity of criminal organizations in the United States led to the expansion of federal criminal law and federal enforcement agencies. By the year 2000, twenty federal agencies employed 100,000 peace officers, with powers to carry firearms and to make arrests. Even so, public law enforcement remained primarily the responsibility of 16,000 state and local governments, which employed 946,786 full-time police officers in 2000. Still more numerous in the United States were fast-growing forces of private police. More than a million guards and security officers worked for business corporations, neighborhood associations, universities, and many other nongovernmental organizations. Throughout its history, the United States has maintained a complex and highly decentralized system of social order.[54]

New Zealand went another way. In 1877, as a direct consequence of the abolition of provincial governments, it created a single national police force, funded by the central government and controlled by the Ministry of Justice. A national training depot was established in the capital at Wellington, and the same regulations applied throughout the country. This new force was founded on the British Victorian model of a civilian police that Robert Peel had given the city of London. New Zealand's national police were a small, highly professional force who were also called "peelers" or "bobbies," as in London.[55]

There were not many of them. In 1907, a New Zealand nation of one million people was served by 699 regular police, plus a few dozen "native constables" and several "police matrons." They did not carry firearms and were trained to keep order without the application of deadly force. Commissioner John O'Donovan wrote in 1920, "The letter of the law may be rigorous, but the administration of it may be beneficent. We keep a baton, but seldom use it; when we do its application should be scrupulously proportioned to need."[56]

There was a paradox in this system. New Zealand's police made less use of force in routine policing than did their American counterparts. Like British bobbies, New Zealand's peelers were distinguished by courtesy and restraint in the ordinary course of their constabulary duties. But they were also less constrained by constitutional protections accorded to people accused or suspected of crimes. Often New Zealand police were not respectful of civil liberties, especially in national emergencies, when they dealt with major problems of order by enlisting civilian volunteers who lacked professional training. This happened in periods of industrial violence in 1890, the Waihi Strike in 1912, and the General Strike of 1913, and other "unusual circumstances" such as the Hokianga Rebellion of 1898 and the Rua Expeditions against Maori in 1916.[57]

As time passed, New Zealand's police became more professional, with elaborate regulation, stringent qualifying examinations, rigorous training, more specialization of function, and modern methods of forensic science. National policewomen were added in 1938, after strong pressure by the National Council of Women. They at first worked in civilian clothes and were part of the detective branch of the New Zealand Police.[58]

Through all these changes, traditional methods of "preventive policing" persisted, with some important changes. In 1919, when Constable Vivian Dudding was killed by a Wellington Wharfie with an automatic weapon, Parliament responded with the Arms Act of 1920. The act imposed stringent restrictions on the sale, ownership, and use of firearms and explosives and banned automatic weapons.[59] In the United States the Second Amendment to the Constitution guarantees a right to "keep and bear arms." Attempts to regulate firearms are strongly opposed by the National Rifle Association, often working very closely with weapons manufacturers.

During the late twentieth century, New Zealand and the United States suffered from stresses that afflicted most nations throughout the world, but dealt with them in different ways. New Zealand preserved its tradition of preventive policing, and continued to do so with remarkable economy of force. The American response was to increase numbers of police, multiply law enforcement agencies, and give more attention to heavily armed "SWAT teams" and "rapid reaction forces" modeled on military units.

At the beginning of the twenty-first century, New Zealand maintained a single national police force, with 7,000 sworn officers: roughly 1 police officer for every 600 New Zealanders. By comparison, the American governments maintained 18,000 federal, state, and local law enforcement *agencies*, which employed 1.2 million officers, or 1 police officer for every 250 Americans—not counting private police, who doubled the absolute number and halved the ratio to 1 public or private order keeper for every 125 Americans.[60]

Patterns of crime and punishment were also very different in the two countries. In general, violent crimes occurred much more frequently in the United States. In 1995 (a peak period), 21,610 homicides were reported in the United States, a rate of about 8 per 100,000. New Zealand in 1996 reported 119 homicides, or 3 per 100,000. An even greater difference appeared in reported rates of aggravated assault—418 per 100,000 in United States, 62 in New Zealand.[61]

The most striking differences between the two nations appeared in variations in the regional distribution of violent crime. In New Zealand homicide rates varied comparatively little by region. American regional differences in violence have always been very large. New England states in 1995 had a homicide rate of 3.4 per 100,000, very similar to New Zealand in that year.[62] By contrast, the homicide rate in the state of Louisiana was 17 per 100,000, five times greater than New England. Texas, Oklahoma, and the lower Mississippi Valley all had very high rates of violent crime.[63]

These regional differences were highly persistent. They had appeared in vernacular traditions of order and violence that had appeared in their founding. People in Texas, Louisiana, and Oklahoma were more apt to own firearms than their counterparts in New England. Cultural ideas of justice in the southwestern states ran to a traditional idea of justice as *lex talionis*, the rule of retaliation. Andrew

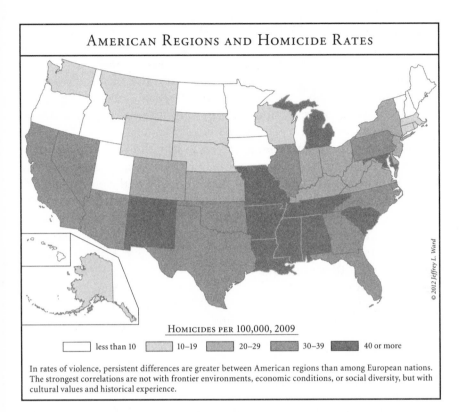

AMERICAN REGIONS AND HOMICIDE RATES

© 2012 Jeffrey L. Ward

HOMICIDES PER 100,000, 2009

less than 10   10–19   20–29   30–39   40 or more

In rates of violence, persistent differences are greater between American regions than among European nations. The strongest correlations are not with frontier environments, economic conditions, or social diversity, but with cultural values and historical experience.

Jackson's mother told her son never to go to law over slander and assault, but "always settle them cases yourself." Courts enforced this rule of *lex talionis* in that region even to the late twentieth century. A study in 1993 found that American rates of justifiable homicide were highest in Texas, Louisiana, Oklahoma, Tennessee, South Carolina, and Georgia. They were very low in New England.[64]

Similar disparities appeared in the use of capital punishment. New Zealand abolished the death penalty in 1941, restored it in 1950, suspended it in 1958, and removed it from its criminal code in 1989. Throughout the United States, the death penalty currently exists in thirty-seven of fifty states. The number of people executed under civil authority in the United States from 1930 to 2006 was 5,076. Rates of execution varied by state and region in the same way as did homicides. They were very high in Texas and zero in New England, with regional patterns throughout the country that were similar to those for the commission of violent crimes.[65]

Large differences between the two nations, and also between American regions, appear in the frequency of imprisonment. In 1996, the prison population in the United States was 1,085,100 (a rate of 411 per 100,000). In New Zealand it was 5,150 (137 per 100,000).[66] This disparity was also growing larger. From 1996 to 2006, rates of violent crime declined in the United States, but rates of imprisonment greatly increased. An international survey in 2008 found that the number of American prisoners had risen from about 1 million in the early 1990s to 2.3 million in 2006, a rate of 760 per 100,000, the highest rate of imprisonment among 216 nations in the world. Rates of incarceration also varied greatly by region: five times higher per capita in Louisiana and the deep Southwest than in Maine and New England.[67]

These trends had a complex cause. Regional differences developed first in American history, then called the American federal system into being. Federalism in turn reinforced regional differences and perpetuated them. New Zealand, by contrast, has a highly centralized system of order and violence. Its ethnic groups possess different ideas and traditions, but they live under the same national institutions of law and order. Patterns have tended to converge in a centralized system, which seeks to support an idea of fairness, equity, and natural justice, and to enforce it throughout the nation in the same way.

Cultural Consequences of Federalism and Centralism: Education

Federalist and centralist systems also had an impact on social institutions in both countries. An example appears in the comparative history of education. In English-speaking colonies, schools began as local institutions that were founded and supported by the people they served. In America they varied by region. Virginia's Cavalier gentry supported grammar schools and a college for the training of colonial elites, but they had little interest in broad systems of primary education. Pennsylvania Quakers went the opposite way. They strongly encouraged primary schools, but did not establish a college until the nineteenth century, the last major Protestant denomination to do so in the United States. New England Puritans supported schools on every level. They required compulsory education within all families from 1642, compulsory maintenance of schools by all towns in 1647, and support for a college from 1636. The North British borderers in the American backcountry, with their inherited hostility to government and taxes, had the weakest schools and lowest levels of education.

That American pattern of local control and regional variation has persisted to our own time. As early as 1820, students in Connecticut received an average of ten years' schooling. In the southern backcountry at the same date, free white students received less than two years of schooling on the average.[68]

After independence, many Americans believed that education was fundamental to a free republic and to ideas of ordered freedom. New Englanders required compulsory taxation for the support of free public schools. In the southern and western states, many Americans refused to pay for the schooling of other people's children, which they perceived as a violation of their own individual liberty and freedom. That attitude still persists in Texas, where high executives of the ill-fated Enron Corporation demanded an exemption from having to pay school taxes.

New Zealand at the start was similar to the United States in terms of local control of education and regional diversity. Otago created a sectarian system of Presbyterian schools in the Scottish tradition, which rapidly became the best educational establishment in New Zealand. Canterbury also founded a strong system of public schooling. Nelson's system was very creative in its Education Act of 1856. It called for a strong central board of education, levied a school rate of one pound on every householder, and imposed a head tax of five shillings on every child of school age—an attempt at fairness in the distribution of costs and benefits. The schools of Nelson were nonsectarian: "Any religious instruction given in such schools shall be free from all controversial character, and imparted at such hours that any parents objecting thereto may be able to withdraw their children." Religious minorities in any district were allowed to retain their school rates for their own "separated schools." Nelson was distinctive in its combination of compulsory provincial rates and nonsectarian teaching.[69]

In other provinces, schools were not as strong. Private schools multiplied in Auckland, with strong schools for the few and weak schools for the many. Standards at Wellington's schools became a public scandal in 1866–69. Small impoverished provinces lacked resources and lagged behind. The result was a wide disparity of support and opportunity throughout New Zealand, which became evident to all by 1870.[70]

These disparities in education contributed to growing discontent with provincial governments. Individual provinces tried to move in the direction of the Nelson system. Wellington in 1871 copied the Nelson acts. Auckland went that way in 1872, adding a bachelor tax on males who were not liable for household levies. Otago made concessions to Anglicans and Catholics and allowed parents of other denominations to withdraw their children from predominantly Scots Presbyterian schools. The new province of Westland, where

FEDERALISM AND THE PERSISTENCE OF CULTURAL DIVERSITY:
Regional Language Patterns in the United States, 1950

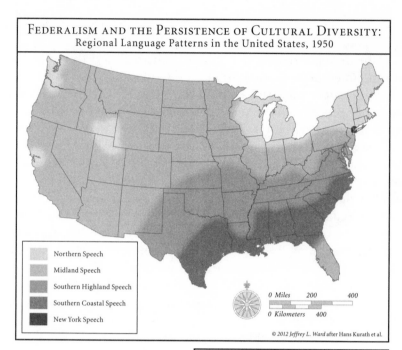

- Northern Speech
- Midland Speech
- Southern Highland Speech
- Southern Coastal Speech
- New York Speech

0 Miles   200   400
0 Kilometers   400

© 2012 Jeffrey L. Ward after Hans Kurath et al.

In the mid-20th century, a massive project of field research led by Hans Kurath found four broad speech regions in the United States. They rose from four cultural hearths in southeastern New England, the Delaware Valley, the lower Chesapeake Bay, and the southern "Backcountry" in the 18th century. All spread across the continent by migration. A large component of New England speech was carried overland to the Great Basin of Utah, and by sea around Cape Horn to Puget Sound and the California Bay area. More recently, Great Basin speech has expanded into four surrounding states, and large areas of Hispanic speech have developed along the southern borders. Another speech region exists in greater New York City, a cultural hearth without a hinterland. Research by New Zealand linguists suggests that children of school age are carriers of these speechways, and often the drivers of change. In New Zealand, where school systems were more centralized, regional variations tended to grow faint by contrast with the United States.

Similar regional patterns appear in Henry Glassie's work on forms of American material culture and vernacular architecture. Here again we find four major cultural regions in the eastern United States.

Vernacular Architecture, Regional Patterns: 1790–2010

North

Mid-Atlantic

Midwest

Upland

Upland South

Lowland South

0 Miles   200   400
0 Kilometers   400

© 2012 Jeffrey L. Ward after Henry Glassie

Catholics comprised more than 30 percent of the population, also attempted to follow the Nelson model, with mixed results.[71]

The opportunities for children throughout the country seemed very unfair to New Zealanders. In 1869, Thomas Ball introduced a bill "to terminate the unequal distributions and lack of harmony which obtains in the administration of educational agencies under the independent action of the provincial governments, by the introduction of a comprehensive scheme of Public schools."[72] The bill died, but the question remained alive. Other bills were introduced by James Richmond in 1870, Fox in 1870 and 1871, and Vogel in 1873. All were defeated, but the problem of inequity in education persisted.

The major change came after the abolition of provinces in 1876. The very next year, Minister of Justice Charles Bowen designed a national system of primary education, and it passed.[73] The Nelson schools, once again, were the model. The Bowen Act created a Ministry of Education that supervised local school boards and subsidized them with a grant for every child, abolished fees, and introduced compulsory attendance for all European children.

The result was a very large increase in education throughout the country. In 1871, only 27 percent of New Zealand children (aged five through fourteen) went to school, which meant an average of two or three years' schooling. By 1886, 73 percent did so, for an average of about six or seven years. The numbers kept rising.[74]

After the Bowen Act, a national Education Department began to develop in Wellington. Local boards retained powers to appoint or remove teachers, but other centralizing measures followed. Secondary and tertiary education were brought into the national system. Schooling became compulsory for Maori children in 1890. Another major reform was the Education Act of 1914, which created a centralized system of school inspectors. A standard national curriculum developed for the entire country.[75]

In short, New Zealand adopted a centralized public educational system explicitly in the cause of fairness and equity for children throughout the country. The United States maintained local control of public school systems throughout the country to support an idea of a free republic and local self-government.

Conclusion

America's federal system was called into being by the size of the country, by its regional diversity, and by its concern for liberty and freedom. Its effect has been to reinforce all of these characteristics.

The United States was born big, and grew bigger in many dimensions. It was diverse from the start in its regional and ethnic cultures, and that diversity has increased through time. The American people, for all their variety, are deeply devoted to those enduring ideas of liberty and freedom—even more so today than in 1776. They have also maintained a creative diversity of those ideas.

New Zealanders tried a federal system in Sir George Grey's constitution and a provincial system from 1854 to 1876. They deliberately decided to replace it with a central system. Federalism seemed wrong for the scale of the country—an important factor. But also important were values and purposes. The provincial system was tried and found wanting on grounds of justice, fairness, and equity. Atherton thought it was unjust to the provinces. Stafford felt that it was unfair to individuals. Vogel believed that it undercut economic development. FitzGerald was concerned about Maori material development.

The effect of a federal system in America, and a central system in New Zealand, was to reinforce the ideas and purposes that called them into being. Federalism has made Americans more conscious of liberty and freedom. Centralism has made New Zealanders more attentive to fairness, equity, and natural justice. They both strengthened democracy and open systems, but did so in different ways.

From these many differences we all might have something to learn. American Senator J. William Fulbright wisely observed in 1964, "We are inclined to confuse freedom and democracy, which we regard as moral principles, with the way in which they are practiced in America—with capitalism, federalism, and the two-party system, which are not moral principles, but simply the accepted practices of the American people."[76] The accepted practices of New Zealanders are something else again. In the larger scheme of things, Yanks and Kiwis are not so very different in other ways. But as the French say on another subject, *Vive la différence!*

IMMIGRANTS, VOLUNTARY AND ASSISTED

The Peopling of Two Nations

Ubi panis et libertas, ibi patria. Where there is bread and
liberty, there is my country.

—Motto of Hector St. John Crèvecoeur,
immigrant to the United States, 1787

A fair field and no favour.

—Motto of Alfred Simmons, immigrant to
New Zealand, 1879

IN NEW ZEALAND and the United States, everyone is an immigrant or a descendant of immigrants—Maori and Indians included. That heritage is something we all share. But the process of migration took different forms in the two countries, and it has changed very much from one generation to the next.[1]

In that regard, historians draw a useful distinction between colonists and immigrants. Colonists came early and their numbers were few. Immigrants came later and their numbers were many. Colonists founded new societies and established cultural hegemonies in new worlds. Immigrants joined societies in being and adapted themselves to established cultures. In English-speaking settlements, colonists largely controlled the flow of immigration, but not just as they pleased. At the same time, immigrants changed the colonial societies, but not always as they wished. All of these things happened in New Zealand and the United States, but not in the same way. The differences were surprising to this historian, even startling in their substance and results.[2]

Numbers, Rhythms, Trends

As always, a major difference between the two countries is a matter of scale. Altogether, the area that is now the United States has attracted approximately ninety million immigrants in four hundred years. New Zealand received about three million immigrants in two hundred years.[3] In absolute numbers, immigration to the United States has been the largest folk movement in modern history.

But in relative terms, another pattern appears. When we measure the total number of the immigrants as a proportion of present population, the flow of migration to New Zealand has been even larger than to the United States, and by a broad margin. In four centuries, total immigration to the United States was about 30 percent of the resident population in the year 2000. By contrast, total immigration to New Zealand during the past two centuries amounted to 75 percent of the population in 2001. The difference was due to higher rates of fertility in early America, a longer run of natural increase in the United States, and greater rates of emigration from New Zealand, much of it as part of a very large flow of traffic to and from Australia.[4]

In both the United States and New Zealand, immigrants tended to come in waves.[5] But comparative analysis brings out fundamental differences in the character and cause of these movements. Through the eighteenth, nineteenth, and early twentieth centuries, American immigration surged during periods of economic prosperity in the New World, during the early 1770s, 1820s, 1850s, 1880s, and the first decade of the twentieth century. Invariably, American immigration diminished during major wars and economic depressions.[6]

Immigration to New Zealand during the nineteenth century also correlated with economic conditions, but in different and even opposite ways—which tell us much about the peopling of both nations. From 1840 to 1900, migration increased during periods of economic stress in Britain: the "hungry forties" (especially 1840–42 and 1847–50), the deep agricultural depression of 1873–79, and the world depression of the 1890s. That rhythm persisted for many years.[7] It was interrupted only by the New Zealand gold rushes of the 1860s.[8]

Altogether, the rhythm of immigration to New Zealand and the United States during much of the nineteenth century made a complex counterpoint. The peopling of North America before 1900 correlated primarily with the "pull" of good times in the New World.

Migration to New Zealand before 1900 was driven mainly by the "push" of hard times in the Old World.

In the twentieth century, those contrasting patterns began to change. As the world became more integrated, rhythms of migration in both nations began to rise and fall together. From 1901 to 1914, the United States and New Zealand both experienced great waves of migration, larger and more sustained than any previous surge in their histories.[9] Those very powerful movements ended abruptly with the start of the First World War. Migration fell sharply in many nations, including the United States and New Zealand, and remained at low levels through the war years (1914–18). The Armistice was followed by a steep increase immediately after the war. In the United States, that trend was suddenly and very deliberately halted in 1921 and 1924 by laws that severely restricted immigration. But movement to New Zealand continued through the 1920s, fluctuating with economic conditions as before.

Then came the dark years of the Great Depression, and net migration to both countries fell below zero. In the cruelest years (1932–34), more people left the United States and New Zealand than arrived. That reversal was not unprecedented, but it happened rarely in the history of both nations. When conditions began to improve after 1935, immigration surged in New Zealand and revived a little in the United States, but it was kept in check by immigration-restriction laws. With the coming of the Second World War, immigration fell in both countries and began to revive with the coming of peace.

After the war, very strong new waves developed, especially in the United States, with a strong increase during much of the 1960s and a decline during the difficult times of the 1970s. As American economic conditions improved in the mid-1980s and 1990s, immigration surged enormously at the end of the twentieth century in both New Zealand and the United States. The early years of the twenty-first century brought the largest flows of immigrants in the history of both nations.[10]

These fluctuations in migration between 1901 and 2010 were complex in their cause. Major determinants were world wars, economic trends, political events, and social conditions. An even more powerful factor was the role of government. In both countries, policy decisions explained many twists and turns in the flow of immigration. These broad trends flowed primarily from choices by policy makers, and by migrants themselves. It has always been so, from the earliest great migrations to our own time.

Immigration Policy in Early America: Variations by Region

The formation of immigration policy has itself varied through time and space. In early America, the process was regulated by colonists who got there first and shaped it to their own ends. British imperial authorities had an impact, but less than one might imagine. People who lived in the colonies themselves had more effect. As a consequence, patterns of immigration differed very much from one colonial region to another.[11]

In New England immigration policy was driven by religion. Calvinists of every creed and country were generally welcome. English Puritans got on with French Huguenots such as the silversmith Apollos Rivoire, who flourished in Boston and changed his name to Paul Revere "on account that the bumpkins could pronounce it easier." Puritans were intolerant of others and did all in their considerable power to keep strangers at a distance. People of different faiths were encouraged to go elsewhere.[12]

This policy continued until the later decades of the colonial era, when old-stock New Englanders began to lose control. In the eighteenth century, land speculators encouraged German immigrants to settle the town of Waldoboro and created an enclave of German cultures on midcoast Maine. Scots-Irish immigrants also founded New England towns that still preserve distinct ethnic identities, such as Londonderry and Antrim in New Hampshire, and Colrain in western Massachusetts.[13]

But by comparison with other American regions, ethnic minorities remained very small in the Puritan colonies. Roman Catholics stayed away for six generations. Jewish immigrants tended to keep clear of the Puritan settlements in Massachusetts, Connecticut, and New Hampshire. Quakers who tried to convert Puritan neighbors were banished from the Bay Colony on pain of death. American Indians were kept at a distance, and comparatively few African slaves were imported. As a result, Puritan New England became one of the more homogeneous colonial populations in America, and remained so into the early nineteenth century.[14]

In the Chesapeake region, the "first gentlemen of Virginia" adopted another immigration policy. They were mainly interested in recruiting a servile underclass to support their Cavalier utopia. During the seventeenth century, indentured servants were more than 75 percent of total arrivals to Virginia, and less than 25 percent in New England.[15] This flow of English servants to the Chesapeake diminished after 1700. They were followed by larger numbers of

African slaves, mostly from 1715 to 1775. Altogether, approximately four hundred thousand African slaves came to the mainland British colonies and made up 20 percent of the total population before independence. To be of African ancestry in the United States today is in most cases to be descended from an immigrant who arrived within thirty years of 1745.[16]

Many British convicts were also transported to the Chesapeake colonies of Maryland and Virginia.[17] A small but important emigration of the younger sons and daughters of British gentry and aristocracy continued to replenish the ranks of the Chesapeake elite and reinforced the hierarchical culture of this region. This pattern prevailed to 1776, except in the highlands.[18]

Other colonies had very different attitudes toward immigration. In the Delaware Valley, William Penn and Quaker leaders welcomed newcomers of many faiths and nationalities. Penn himself made a major effort to recruit settlers from European states, especially Christian groups who were spiritually akin to the Society of Friends. The result was an influx of Amish immigrants from Switzerland, Moravians from Czechoslovakia, Mennonites, Pietists and Lutherans from many parts of Germany, and groups from other nations.[19] Jewish immigrants were encouraged to settle in Pennsylvania, as also in colonial Rhode Island, New York, South Carolina, and Georgia. Before 1775, thriving Jewish communities took root in those five colonies, which adopted more pluralist policies than New England and Virginia.

National Policy in the United States, 1789–1921: Voluntary Immigration, with Some Restrictions

After Independence, the new federal government compelled New England and southern states to abandon their traditional immigration policies. In 1790, the first Congress enacted a national law that allowed any free white male to become a citizen after two years in the country. Congress also prohibited the foreign slave trade in 1807, the earliest date when it could act under the Constitution. Migration of slaves from abroad came to an end, except for a small illegal commerce in the Deep South, which demographers have reckoned at about a thousand slaves each year. With these changes, an open and voluntary national system of immigration took root in the new republic.[20]

The Supreme Court allowed states to regulate immigration in specific ways, and to keep out criminals, paupers, vagabonds, and convicts, but it also firmly established a larger frame of free access for voluntary immigrants. A landmark case was *City of New York v. Miln* (1837). Many states exercised their powers under that double-acting rule. They also competed actively for immigrants with recruiting offices, cheap land, blue-sky literature, and the occasional small subsidies. But in general, American immigrants in the nineteenth and twentieth centuries paid their own way or were supported by families and friends.[21]

As a result, colonial Pennsylvania's pattern of an open door, free migration, and ethnic pluralism spread rapidly through the northern United States. After 1815, the ethnic structure of New England was transformed by the departure of Yankee families for the western states and by the arrival of four large Catholic populations: Irish, Italian, French Canadian, and Polish. These new immigrants settled in such numbers that by 1950 every county in all six New England states had a Catholic plurality, with the sole exception of Hancock, Lincoln, and Waldo counties in downeast Maine. Many smaller ethnic groups also made a large contribution. In Massachusetts, examples included East European Jews in Boston's North End, Swedish metalworkers in Worcester, Albanians in Natick, and Armenians in Watertown.[22] Something similar happened in New York, the middle states, the Midwest, and border cities such as Baltimore, Cincinnati, Louisville, and St. Louis. Throughout the northern states in the nineteenth century, this complex process of migration and settlement created a cultural pluralism that was both ethnic and regional in its dynamics.[23]

The slaveholding South was increasingly a region apart. The persistence of slavery itself was a discouragement to the immigration of free labor. By 1860, free people below the Potomac and the Ohio rivers comprised less than a third of the free population of the United States. As Thomas Jefferson remarked, they had "the wolf by the ears."[24]

Other social problems developed from migration to the free states. Some Americans became unhappy about the huge flow of voluntary immigrants. Often these "nativists" were recent immigrants themselves, deeply resentful of others who came after them. Even before the American Revolution examples of this attitude appeared in Pennsylvania. Benjamin Franklin, himself an immigrant to Philadelphia from New England, expressed intense hostility to German and Scotch-Irish immigrants who followed him. That prejudice was widely shared, but new immigrants continued to multiply, and their diversity greatly increased.[25]

In the early republic, leaders of the Federalist Party were hostile to new immigrants, who tended to vote for Democratic Republicans. In 1798, Federalists tried to restrict citizenship to native-born

Americans. They failed in that goal but succeeded in making naturalization more difficult.[26] Individual free states also sought to restrict the flow of immigration in ethnic and racial terms. Among the most extreme were Ohio, Indiana, and Illinois, which entirely prohibited the entry of African Americans, but they were unable to enforce their own laws. In California, a majority of white legislators imposed a prohibitive tax on nonwhite immigrants, mainly in an effort to keep Asians away, but the law was overruled in 1857.

Throughout the northeastern states, nativist parties multiplied in the 1850s. Many of these nineteenth-century nativists sought not to exclude immigrants from the country but to deny them the right to vote. The largest group was the secretive Native American Party, whose members called themselves "Know Nothings" (when asked about their party they were required to say "I know nothing"). They were supported by recent German Protestant immigrants who took the name of *Sag Nichts* and joined the nativist movement before they were in the country long enough to learn English. Often these German Protestants wished to exclude German Catholics. In 1854–55, a peak period for both immigration and nativism, Know Nothings grew strong enough to gain control of the state government in Massachusetts and were powerful in many other states. They contributed much to ethnic and religious conflict in American politics but could not stop the huge flow of new arrivals. Through that turbulent era, American immigration continued to be free and open.[27]

In the late nineteenth century, ethnic and racial prejudice grew more intense. The courts expanded federal power over immigration policy, and nativists in Congress found ways to close the open door.[28] In 1882, Congress yielded to heavy pressure from California and passed the Chinese Exclusion Act. In 1885, the Foran Act forbade recruitment of laborers by advance contracts and payments for passage costs, after heavy lobbying by American labor unions. In 1891, chronically ill immigrants, paupers, and polygamists were excluded. Elaborate systems of inspection were established at new immigration stations such as Ellis Island in 1892. Ellis Island had a double purpose. It was founded to speed the arrival of "desirable immigrants" but also to stop all who were thought to be undesirable in one way or another. Millions were admitted; thousands were sent away.[29]

America's political parties have always divided on immigration policy. In general, Federalists, Whigs, and Republicans tried to keep people out, or stop them from voting. Democrats wanted to let them in, and marched them to the polls. Grover Cleveland and Woodrow Wilson both vetoed exclusion laws, but nativist majorities in Congress

This image of an arriving family in New York harbor captured the driving purpose of American immigrants in every generation—material gain, a better life for the children, and an abiding dream of liberty and freedom.

enacted federal statutes that excluded radicals, beggars, and the seriously ill. Asian immigration was curtailed by national exclusion laws in 1902, 1908, and 1917.

The Closed Door: An Era of Restricted Immigration, 1921–65

The tightest restrictions came after the First World War, when two very conservative Congresses placed broad limits on American immigration in the Quota Act of 1921 and the Johnson-Reid Act of 1924. The 1924 law tried to freeze the ethnic composition of the United States. It set immigration quotas by national origins in proportion to the size of groups in 1890. The effect was to reduce immigration from southern and eastern Europe from 700,000 before the First World War to 158,000 under the Act of 1921 and 21,000 after the Act of 1924. Republican President Herbert Hoover also issued an executive order, which denied entry visas to anyone who might become a public charge.[30]

Immigration stations at Ellis Island (1892) and other ports of entry had two functions. One was encourage "desirable immigrants" who were able to do well in an open society and who shared American values of liberty and freedom. Another goal was to exclude others who failed to meet these tests. Here again the immigration process functioned as a filter that reinforced the character of American society, and strengthened its dominant values.

That policy of restriction persisted through the Great Depression and the Second World War, with limited exceptions for displaced persons, war brides, and refugees. It was extended during the Cold War by the McCarran-Walter Act (1952), which renewed the quota system and gave restriction a new edge by excluding "subversives" and authorizing the deportation of "dangerous aliens." A driver of nativism in Congress was Senator Pat McCarran of Nevada, himself the son of Irish Catholic immigrants.[31]

These laws succeeded in reducing the flow of immigration to the United States for more than forty years, from 1921 to 1965. But even through that era of restriction, voluntary immigrants continued to find their own way into the country. As always, they were drawn by dreams of liberty, freedom, and opportunity in an open society.

The Door Reopens, 1965–2012

Then came the 1960s, one of the few moments in American history when liberals and progressives gained control of every branch in the federal government. The Hart-Cellar Act (1965) revised national quotas, increased total numbers of immigrants, and admitted them from the Western Hemisphere on a first-come basis. The result was an enormous flow of legal immigrants in the late twentieth and twenty-first centuries, the largest wave of migration in American history.

It was also unlike any earlier wave in its composition. These immigrants came mainly from Latin America, Asia, and Africa. In terms of social class, this movement tended to be bimodal: many highly skilled and wealthy immigrants, vast numbers of very poor people, and comparatively few from the middling strata—a fundamental change from earlier patterns. Another change occurred in gender. Early American immigrants were mostly male; in the late twentieth century a majority were female.[32]

Illegal migration also increased rapidly. A nativist backlash led to the Immigration Reform and Control Act (1986), which penalized employers who knowingly hired unlawful immigrants, and also offered amnesty to illegal aliens in the country. The net result was a huge increase in immigrants and new citizens. During the early twenty-first century the United States admitted more immigrants to lawful residence than any other developed society in the world, and illegal migration continued at even higher levels. Tens of millions of unlawful aliens were in the country in 2010. Many efforts at regulation by Congress from 1990 to 2010 failed. [33]

Throughout this long history, most immigrants to the United States shared important traits. With the major exceptions of African slaves, British convicts, and indentured servants, the great majority made their own way to America or were helped by families and friends. Except in the period of exclusion from 1921 to 1964, immigration was free, open, voluntary, autonomous, and self-propelled—a fundamental fact of American history.

Immigration Policy in New Zealand: Assisted Migration, with Many Exceptions

The peopling of New Zealand was also free—in one important way, the most free in the world. It had nothing like the slave trade in the Americas, the flow of convicts to Australia, the movement of conscripts to Quebec, or the traffic in contract laborers to Africa and Pacific islands. New Zealand also had no institutions of forced labor comparable to plantation slavery in the American South, the encomienda of New Spain, or serfdom in eastern Europe. Among major settler societies in the modern world, New Zealand's history is unique that way.

But New Zealanders who wished to encourage free immigration had a major problem of another kind. The cost of passage from Britain to the South Pacific was five times greater than to North America, and far beyond the ability of most people to pay. By necessity, a large part of population movement to New Zealand was "assisted migration," as it came to be called. From the mid-nineteenth century to the late twentieth, many immigrants to New Zealand were actively recruited and heavily subsidized by colonizing companies, the old provinces, the new central government, the churches, and even the British Army.[34]

Assisted migration to New Zealand began with the first great waves of colonization during the 1840s. Edward Gibbon Wakefield had intended to use revenue from land sales for the "conveyance of British labourers to the colony, free of cost." His plan was never fully realized, but it had a major impact. To qualify for support, assisted colonists had to be young (under forty), in good health, and of high moral character. Certificates from physicians and letters of recommendation from clergymen were sometimes required. Families were especially encouraged, and the company tried to maintain the balance of males and females among single passengers.[35]

Much of this human flow to New Zealand in that period was divided in two groups called "colonists" and "emigrants," with meanings different from other settler societies. Colonists were cabin passengers who paid their own way (about thirty pounds or higher). Emigrants went in steerage, mostly with subsidized passage. The proportions of these two groups varied from one part of New Zealand to another. In high-toned Canterbury, self-supporting colonists comprised nearly 25 percent of the whole, the largest proportion. They were less than 15 percent in the Wakefield settlements. Overall, a majority of early emigrants from Britain came in steerage, with help from colonizing associations.

Recent estimates indicate that about 27,000 immigrants came to New Zealand in the first wave from 1840 to 1852. Most were assisted immigrants, who received subsidies. The cost of their passage was paid by the New Zealand Company and similar groups, who sent out about 11,800 settlers to the Wakefield colonies alone from 1840 to 1854. Another 3,200 went to Canterbury, and about 700 to New Plymouth. Numbers are uncertain for Otago and Auckland.[36]

After 1852, the provincial governments of New Zealand took over from the colonizing companies and ran their own programs of assisted migration. They sent agents to Britain, who recruited migrants and paid their passage in whole or part. The cost was supported by land sales, somewhat as Gibbon Wakefield had envisioned. Special encouragement was given to families and single women of childbearing age. Local clergy and heads of families in Britain were invited to "nominate" prospective immigrants and "certify" their moral character. The process of certification is said to have been less rigorous under the provincial governments than under the companies, but it continued. Altogether, in this dynamic period of gold rushes and land booms from 1852 to 1870, about 250,000 immigrants came to New Zealand. Of that number, about 100,000 left again, and 150,000 settled in. In Canterbury, where the best records survive, assisted immigrants were nearly two-thirds of all who settled there. The gold fields were a different story. More people came to the gold fields without assistance, but most soon departed for other El Dorados. As before, assisted immigrants were more likely to remain.[37]

After 1870, another era began when the new central government of New Zealand assumed control of immigration. Premier Julius Vogel created a much larger system of assisted migration than ever before in the Immigration and Public Works Act. One part of this system was a process of "nominated migration," with application forms and certificates, by which any resident of New Zealand could propose a relative or friend. Other systems of assisted immigration were created for people without acquaintances in New Zealand. Private organizations also took a hand. In England, the National Agricultural Laborers Union was one of the most important. It actively assisted emigration in hope of relieving unemployment in Britain.[38]

These national programs grew very large. In 1872, New Zealand employed 137 recruiting agents in Britain and Ireland, and they were busy. In a single year, 1874, for example, 43,965 immigrants arrived in New Zealand. Of that total, 31,774 were officially classified as "assisted immigrants," and the true number is thought to have been closer to 34,000. Others were assisted in less formal ways.[39] New Zealand historian Jock Phillips writes that "the migration of the 1870s was the most significant in New Zealand history." Total numbers of immigrants from 1871 to 1884 were 289,026, more than the total non-Maori population in 1871. Phillips observes, "The main reason for this flood was the free or assisted passages offered by the New Zealand government." Overall, during the peak decade of the 1870s, 70 percent of New Zealand's immigrants from Britain and Ireland were assisted or nominated. Most made New Zealand their permanent home.[40]

Vogel's national system of assisted immigration to New Zealand ended in 1891. After a brief intermission, yet another program was established in 1904 and continued until 1927—not quite as before, but large enough to make a difference. In peak years from 1901 to 1915, 300,000 people traveled from the United Kingdom to New Zealand. About one-third were assisted immigrants. This was one of the few periods in the history of New Zealand when most immigrants paid their own way. Once again, many came by way of Australia. But even in this era, a large proportion of New Zealand's immigrants were assisted and carefully selected.[41]

The flow of migration was broken by the First World War, and it resumed immediately after the Armistice. From 1919 to 1927, 120,000 people moved from the United Kingdom to New Zealand. Of that number, 70,000 were assisted immigrants. In the immediate postwar years, many assisted immigrants were wives or children of New Zealand soldiers who had served overseas and were assisted jointly by the British and New Zealand governments. Others were "nominated" by New Zealanders who became responsible for finding them jobs.[42]

After another interruption during the Great Depression and the Second World War, assisted immigration to New Zealand revived yet again, but on a smaller scale. From 1951 to 1967, assisted immigrants were only about 20 percent of the total flow, or 47,000 out of 234,000 people. Even so, assisted migration continued to be carefully controlled. Comparable programs existed in other countries, but in the words of historian Megan Hutching, "unlike the similar schemes run by the Australian and Canadian governments, immigrants [to New Zealand] were carefully selected with regard to their occupation, health, marital status, and age." They were also required to work for two years in a job chosen for them by New Zealand's Labour Department.[43]

In this period, a growing proportion of assisted immigrants were not of British origin. During the late 1940s and early 1950s, many came from the Netherlands and the former Dutch East Indies and were given subsidized passages. Other flows brought Greeks, Cypriots, Lebanese, and emigrants from eastern Europe. But the majority of assisted immigrants were British; the next largest group were Australians.

Through the full span of New Zealand's history, assisted migration also took other forms. During the land wars, men with military

To single men and women

GOOD JOBS

GOOD PAY

GOOD LIVING

Emigrate to **NEW ZEALAND**

..for a *NEW* way of life

New Zealand has a place for **YOU** in her future development. There are many jobs awaiting the new settler.

For MEN—Building, Engineering, National Development and Farming.

For WOMEN—Nursing, Factory, Domestic and Office.

If you are under 36 **enquire** about the Free and Assisted Passages being offered to **single** British men and women by calling on or writing to the **Chief Migration Officer, New Zealand Government Offices, 415 Strand, London, W.C.2**

Assisted migration made a major difference in the history and culture of New Zealand. It operated as a social and cultural filter, with results very different from migration to America.

experience were given free passage for themselves and their families, and fertile land for farms, if they agreed to settle between Maori and Pakeha. In 1847–48, they were called "New Zealand Fencibles," and 2,500 men, women, and children came to New Zealand as part of this program. Most settled south of Auckland. The expense of transport and settlement was borne by the Crown. The Fencibles saw little military service, but in the words of Ian Ward the program led to "the establishment of a considerable number of landed proprietors in a fertile country."[44]

A larger group was the Waikato militia in the period from 1863 to 1867. They were recruited in Australia, England, Scotland, Ireland, and South Africa. Most had served in British regiments; many were Irish and Scots. Some 5,397 men were settled in the Waikato Country, at sites that would become the city of Hamilton and the town of Cambridge. Others went to Tauranga and perhaps 2,000 more to Taranaki, Hawke's Bay, and the Bay of Plenty, all in the 1860s.[45] Still other military migrants arrived with British regiments, were discharged in New Zealand, and settled in the country. James Belich observes that "the British army ranks next to Wakefield and Vogel as an agent of organised immigration."[46]

Though many immigrants to New Zealand were assisted, it is important to observe that a large number were not. The latter included cabin passengers to Canterbury, miners to Otago and Westland, and independent families from Cornwall and the Shetland Islands who paid their own passage. Jewish immigrants also made their own way. Among them was Dove-Myer Robinson, who started as a peddler and became mayor of Auckland. These unassisted Jewish migrants were attracted by the comparative weakness of anti-Semitism in New Zealand and the strength of material opportunity. Immigrants of other ethnic origins also came without assistance from Australia, though more than a few had originally been assisted immigrants to Victoria, New South Wales, and South Australia. These arrivals tended to be mostly solitary males. They were often Irish and Roman Catholic.[47]

For many years access to New Zealand was entirely open to immigrants from Britain, Australia, and North America. But in 1881, racial and ethnic restrictions began to grow, much as in the United States. A series of increasingly severe Chinese Immigration Acts limited the number of Chinese that any ship could carry and levied a head tax on each arrival. Other measures restricted the flow from India and South Asia. New laws required Chinese immigrants to be able to read a hundred words of English—a rule that was not applied to Britons.

A more general Immigration Restriction Act in 1899 forbade entry to immigrants not of British or Irish parentage who were unable to write, or read or speak English or another European language. A conservative government passed an even more rigorous Restriction Act in 1920. It required all immigrants not of English or Irish birth and ancestry to apply in writing. The Customs Service could reject anyone at its discretion. Prime Minister William Massey candidly explained that the goal of this policy was a "white New Zealand." It also closed the country to anyone who was "disaffected or disloyal" or in any way "injurious to the peace, order and good government of New Zealand," or merely "unsuitable."[48]

Not until 1974 did New Zealand change its immigration policy in a fundamental way. The special relationship with Great Britain ended in that year. New Zealand continued to control the flow of people into the country but shifted its criteria from race and nationality to individual skills, money, merit, family relations, and humanitarian need. British migrants were judged by the same standards as everyone else. Under new rules (enacted in 1974, 1987, and 1991), economic tests were applied to people of all nationalities. Employment was the critical issue. Migrants who threatened the jobs of New Zealanders were not encouraged; those who seemed capable of creating employment were welcome. In practice, about half of New Zealand's immigrants were business people who were required to bring a capital of at least NZ$150,000 (later raised to NZ$1 million for investors). Exceptions were made for others in various ways. About a third of immigrants in this period were joining family members, and 10 percent were admitted on humanitarian grounds.[49]

In the years from 1990 to 2003, the total annual flow of newcomers surged to the highest absolute levels in New Zealand's history, peaking at nearly 100,000 permanent and long-term immigrants in 2003, twice the numbers in 1990. The balance of inflow and outgo, negative in the difficult years of the 1980s, became strongly positive.[50] Countries of origin also changed in this period. Immigrants from Great Britain fell from more than 90 percent in earlier years to 10 percent of citizenship approvals in 2005. At the same time, immigration from Asia went up in a series of surges, 1990–91, 1996–97, and 2003–04, and very little of it was assisted.[51]

Altogether, through the full span of New Zealand's history, a majority of immigrants who remained in the country were assisted or subsidized or nominated in one way or another. For many years, New Zealand historians of an earlier generation, such as J. B. Condliffe, W. P. Morrell, and Keith Sinclair, tended to play down the importance of assisted migration. More recently Rollo Arnold, Jock Phillips, Terry Hearn, Erik Olssen, and Marcia Stenson have demonstrated that the numbers of assisted immigrants were larger than had been assumed. So, also, was their contribution to the peopling of New Zealand.[52]

Consequences: Migration as a Process of Social Filtration

Assisted immigration produced a flow of people that was distinctive to New Zealand and very different from migration the United States. For many years it was carefully designed to encourage movement from Great Britain. Leaders such as Vogel tried to recruit assisted immigrants from Europe, but at least 93 percent of assisted migrants were British or Irish. This system was used very deliberately to recruit by ethnicity, class, occupation, gender, religion, and ideas of moral character. Rollo Arnold found that assisted emigrants were mostly laborers in humble circumstances from the English countryside and small villages. Few came from large cities. Nearly half were female. Most were Protestant in their religion. Many were required to submit letters of recommendation and to supply other evidence of good character.[53]

An example was the wave of assisted immigration to New Zealand from 1947 to 1975. Candidates were carefully screened in the London offices of New Zealand's High Commission. At the start candidates were required to be single, between the ages of twenty and thirty-five, and "of European race and colour." Later, families with no more than two children were allowed to come. Skilled artisans were preferred, and good work records were required. In the 1940s they were required to pay ten pounds, unless they were veterans, and were called "Ten Pound Poms" in New Zealand. But even this small sum was found to be onerous, especially for young women, and it was abolished in 1950.

All were asked to submit birth certificates, character references, statements from employers, records of military service, and medical reports. A personal interview was also mandatory. Applicants were judged for "character" and "bearing," and many were rejected. Admitting officers in New Zealand's Immigration Branch complained that "the wrong type" too often applied. Wrong types included "semi-professional men," "junior executives," and "small traders"—an attitude opposite to that in the United States. One observer remarked that it was harder to get into New Zealand than to join a gentleman's club in London.[54]

Consequences for Cultural Values

Immigration as a process of social filtration had other important consequences for both New Zealand and the United States. In some ways its effects were diametrically opposed. In New Zealand, Megan Hutching did a survey of assisted immigrants and found that "in the end, people often chose New Zealand because it seemed non-threatening." One woman explained that she selected New Zealand because it was "small and comfortable."[55]

All of this was very different from American immigration. In the United States, a voluntary and largely self-driven process selected immigrants who were restless, autonomous, ambitious, aggressive, entrepreneurial, and highly individuated. They tended to be more tolerant of risk, in the hope of greater profit. America's open and voluntary system of immigration selected a population that lived for liberty and freedom.

In New Zealand, fairness was a frequent theme. Programs of assisted migration were founded with the explicit purpose of giving people a fair chance that was denied to them in Britain. The Salvation Army organized schemes for young people of good character from the densely crowded slums of England and Scotland. Its object was to give them a fair go in New Zealand. Another association, called Flock House, assisted the children of British seamen who had been killed or crippled in the First World War.[56] A third program was founded by William Ranstead, a self-made businessman and Fabian socialist who published a newspaper called *Clarion*, in which he celebrated New Zealand as a "socialist Canaan." In 1900, Ranstead led four shiploads of "Clarionites" and "Canaanites" in search of social justice and fairness. He urged those who were able to pay their own way; others were assisted. Altogether, Ranstead is thought to have helped a thousand people migrate to New Zealand. Among them were many founders and supporters of New Zealand's Labour Party.[57]

In New Zealand's migrations, one finds many variations on a theme of fairness. Rollo Arnold discovered that much of New Zealand's immigration in the 1870s was linked to the "revolt of the fields," a rebellion of farm workers against landowners in rural England during the difficult period from 1872 to 1879. This movement rose from the grass roots and became highly organized, producing agricultural unions, which demanded fair pay and more favorable conditions. Arnold turned up much evidence that the revolt of the fields was ruthlessly suppressed by England's rural gentry and strongly opposed by country clergy of the Anglican Church. Some leaders were "locked out" by employers. Many began to look abroad.

Rollo Arnold read the literature of rural protest in Lincolnshire, Oxfordshire, and Kent and the letters of those who departed. Two complaints led the list: "unfair working conditions" and starvation wages. There were some references to freedom. In a letter home from New Zealand to the Kent Union in 1874, one emigrant wrote, "Father says you are not to stay in England to be transported, but you are to come out here; he says he was transported all the time he was there, but now he is free again." But the central theme was something else. The author of the letter believed that New Zealand was a place where a man could find fairness and justice. Another immigrant wrote home, "The masters are not like they are in England, and you don't see them with kid gloves on. They take hold of the pick and shovel, the same as other men."[58]

In 1879, one of these immigrants published a book called *Old England and New Zealand*. Its author, Alfred Simmons, led a party of five hundred people from Kent and Sussex. Simmons described them as "locked out laborers" and their families. Most were religious dissenters. Not one in fifty had Church of England prayer books. They assembled in Maidstone, left by special train to Plymouth, and sailed from that port for New Zealand. There they landed at Port Lyttelton and were greeted by Kentish friends who had settled on the Canterbury Plain.[59]

Like many others, Alfred Simmons had mixed memories of England. He despised the aristocracy and gentry and hated "land-sharks" and entrepreneurs who preyed upon the working poor. At the same time, he felt great pride in his English origins and contempt for others in proportion to the pigment in their skins. This leader from the English working class disliked British aristocrats, African natives, Australian aborigines, and New Zealand Maori in equal measure. He regarded the French and Spanish and Portuguese as "colored races." His sense of self was shaped by a strong consciousness of race, class, religion, and nationality. He was proud to be working class, white, Christian, and, especially, English.

In one way these prejudices set him apart from some of New Zealand's early colonizers, who had sympathy and respect for Maori, which Simmons did not. But in another important way, the values of colonists and immigrants were much the same. Simmons began his book with an epigraph on the title page, in italic capitals: "A fair field and no favour."[60] Six generations of colonists and immigrants to New Zealand were not of one mind on these questions. Still, all of them gave high importance to ideas of equity, rules of right, and various conceptions of fairness. These attitudes brought them together, and also set them apart from colonists and immigrants to the United States.

Jock Phillips observes that the expectations of immigrants were reinforced by efforts to attract them. New Zealand officials advertised their country in ways that "inclined the new immigrant to look favourably on the state and come with expectations about New Zealand as a fair society." This was very different from the United States, where, as Phillips points out, the "the use of land grants as an immigration carrot in America placed emphasis on individual economic opportunity."[61]

Most immigrants came voluntarily to America in search of liberty and freedom in one form or another. Some sought religious freedom. Others were in flight from political oppression: Irish rebels, French émigrés, German 48ers, Jewish refugees from Russian pogroms. In the twentieth century, many were victims of Prussian militarism, Fascist brutality, Communist tyranny, and Islamic oppression. Most were in search of economic liberty, and freedom of opportunity. In all of these different ways immigrants were driven by dreams of living free—dreams that became a central part of American culture, and remain so to this day.

Ethnic Consequences

Processes of immigration in New Zealand and the United States also made another major difference in the ethnic composition of the two nations. In New Zealand, the predominance of British stock was very large, more so than in Canada, Australia, the United States, and other English-speaking settler societies. The largest group came directly from Great Britain—nearly half of the total flow. A second and smaller group came from Australia, the United States, and Canada and were also mostly of British stock. A third group, the smallest and very diverse, came from everywhere else.

Through many generations in New Zealand, major efforts were made to maintain the homogeneity of the immigrant population and the hegemony of British stock. Respectable immigrants of British ancestry were allowed to enter freely; people of other ancestry were not so actively encouraged, and sometimes forbidden outright. In the census of 2001, 80 percent of New Zealanders identified themselves as of European origin; of that number at least 80 percent reported that they were of British ancestry (about 60 percent of the total). The great majority descended from English-speaking settlers who emigrated within three decades of the year 1870. Nearly 20 percent were Maori and Polynesian. Another 20 percent were everybody else.

Many other ethnic groups settled in New Zealand. A French colony, as mentioned earlier, had been founded at Akaroa in 1840. Other French immigrants were encouraged to settle in the 1870s, and one group of French mechanics turned itself into a ballet company—to the horror of the Victorian authorities who had assisted their migration. Groups of Italians settled at Jackson Bay but hated the climate and refused the work that was given them. More successful were Germans, who settled near Nelson as early as 1843; Bohemians in Puhoi from 1863; and Scandinavians, who founded Dannevirke and Norsewood and other towns near Palmerston North in the 1870s. Some 3,500 Scandinavian settlers, more familiar with the ax than were British colonists, cleared much of the 70-Mile Bush. During the 1880s, Dalmatians settled North Auckland as diggers of kauri gum. Some of their descendants are flourishing vintners today. They were joined by parties of Croats and Yugoslavs. After World War II, Dutch immigrants arrived from Indonesia.

Romanians and Poles came from eastern Europe, and in 2005 a sizeable movement flowed from South Africa.[62]

Important elements of ethnic diversity operated differently in New Zealand and the United States. A case in point, much studied by scholars in both countries, is the ethnic history of Irish immigrants. In New Zealand's census of 2001, Irish Catholics were the fourth-largest ethnic group, after English, Scottish, and Maori. They were about 9 percent of New Zealand's inhabitants. By comparison, Catholic Irish comprised 20 percent of the United States' and 30 percent of Australia's population—all by self-reported data. New Zealand's Irish immigrants came largely from Cork and Kerry in the southern reaches of the Irish republic, mostly within a span of two generations. They had similar social origins, but once in New Zealand they scattered across the country and never formed ethnic ghettos comparable to South Boston or the Irish neighborhoods in New York City.[63] In America, even as the Irish moved into the middle class, many tended to flock together. In Massachusetts they settled heavily not only in Boston but also in "lace-curtain suburbs" such as Wellesley, west of Boston, which became very heavily Irish Catholic. Others went to the town of Scituate on the South Shore of Massachusetts, sometimes called the "Irish Riviera." New Zealand's Irish immigrants became less visible as a group and intermarried rapidly with English and Scottish neighbors.

The story was much the same among the French of Akaroa, the Dalmatians of Northland, and East Europeans who arrived after the Second World War. Their folkways survive in the picturesque street scenes of Akaroa and the festivals of Puhoi and Dannevirke. All of these groups enriched the culture of New Zealand, but their numbers were small by comparison with Australia, Canada, and especially the United States. There was a fundamental difference of scale in New Zealand's ethnic diversity. Most ethnic groups other than the British and Maori had nothing like the strength, size, coherence, and persistence of ethnic groups in the United States. They intermarried with New Zealanders of British stock, who constitute an overwhelming majority of the population—more so than in any other English-speaking nation except Britain herself, which also is increasingly diverse. Overall, the proportion of New Zealanders whose ancestors came from England, Wales, Scotland, and Protestant Ireland today is about 65 percent.

In the United States, by contrast, the Census Bureau finds that between 19 and 25 percent of the American people report having some British ancestors. The largest ethnic group is not British but

German. The same surveys found that people with some self-reported German ancestry constitute between 25 and 30 percent of the American population. The Germans, in turn, are divided into Protestants of many denominations, German Catholics, and a small population of German Jews. There is little sense of ethnic solidarity across these religious lines. After Germans, the next largest groups are, in order, British, Irish, and Africans. They are followed by hundreds of other ethnic groups. Some are nearly extinct in their native lands and flourish in America. East Texas has a large population of Wends (or Lusatian Sorbs), who take great pride in their ethnic heritage, as do their kin in eastern Germany. Vibrant communities of Volga Tatars live in New Jersey, Bashkirs in Brooklyn, Basques in Nevada, Frisians in Iowa, Cape Verdeans in New Bedford, Kalmyks in New Jersey, and Kurds in the District of Columbia. With few exceptions, these groups are fiercely proud of their identity—in some cases, more so than in their own homelands. Militant Irish Fenians in the nineteenth century and the Irish Republican Army in the twentieth century had stronger support in the United States than in Ireland itself. The same thing happened among Albanians in Massachusetts, Italians in Queens, Poles in Buffalo, Slovaks in Cleveland, and Jews in Brooklyn. Many leaders of national movements throughout the world, such as Eamon de Valera in Ireland and Golda Meir in Israel, came to prominence in the ethnic politics of the United States.

The construction of ethnicity in the United States owes its power to this multiplicity of ethnic groups. In the country at large, every American belongs to an ethnic minority. The number and variety of these groups continue to grow geometrically, as the total population increases arithmetically. The ethnic structure of the United States is changing rapidly and becoming more complex.

But at the same time, members of these groups are rapidly intermarrying. Most Americans today are of mixed ethnic ancestry, and they tend to maintain multiple identities with great pride. They also have strong regional affiliations. The Wends of Texas are as loyal to the Lone Star State as they are to their Wendish heritage. The Boston Irish cherish their New England heritage equally with their Irish identity.

Americans, in short, borrow freely from other ethnic cultures. Most of us speak something like English. Many of us are increasingly African in our musical tastes. Americans of all faiths have absorbed much Jewish culture from the media and often use Yiddish slang. On St. Patrick's Day most Americans wear something green and celebrate the cultural heritage of Ireland with high enthusiasm.

In Boston discotheques, Irish, Jews, and Anglo-Saxons dance together to music with an African beat and then go out for sushi. The result is an existential pluralism of high complexity.

But it is not a story of atomization, disintegration, fragments, or fractures. Nearly all Americans, no matter what their origins, share a common allegiance to the founding ideas of the republic—and most of all, to liberty and freedom. At the same time, most of them exercise their sovereign right to rage against the government, no matter who is in power. Ethnic pluralism in America operates within a consensual republican frame, and it rises from the conditions of a free society. It has grown from liberty and freedom. These great principles in turn are reinforced by an ethnic diversity that expresses itself not only in a multiplicity of groups but in a pluralism that is internal to individual Americans. Much of this flows from a long history of migration in the peopling of the United States. And another great process of creativity has happened in the peopling of New Zealand.

WOMEN'S RIGHTS

Two National Traditions

> The history of mankind is a history of repeated injuries and usurpations on the part of man toward woman, having in direct object the establishment of an absolute tyranny over her. . . . Woman herself must do this work; for woman alone can understand the height, the depth, the length and the breadth of her degradation.
>
> —Elizabeth Cady Stanton, Seneca Falls, July 19, 1848

> The real power of the women's vote in New Zealand is not in opposition, but in its harmony and co-operation with the men's vote.
>
> —Anna Logan Stout, Wellington, August 22, 1895

I N NEW ZEALAND and the United States, the history of women's rights has been similar but not the same. From the start, both open societies shared the same broad range of gender roles. Both had very strong women's movements, with much the same goals but different methods and results.

One difference in particular poses an interesting question. Women in the United States were among the first in the world to seek the vote. They began to exercise it in state elections as early as 1787, but they did not win the right to vote in national politics until 1920. The American movement had an early start, but it was slow to win the decisive victory. In New Zealand, it was the other way around. The movement for women's rights had a late start and won the earliest national victory in the world. New Zealanders enacted women's suffrage in national elections in 1893—the first country in the world to do so. A goal that eluded American women for more than a century was achieved by New Zealanders in less than thirty years. Something similar happened in campaigns for equal rights during the late twentieth century, and also in the election of women to the highest public offices. The question is why.

Many answers come to mind. For one, the bar of success was set much higher in one political system than in the other. To enact this national reform, New Zealanders needed a simple majority in Parliament. Victory in the United States required a constitutional amendment, two-thirds majorities in both houses of Congress, and approval by three-quarters of state legislatures. But other factors were also involved. This inquiry will consider the causal role of cultural values in two open societies.

Women's Traditional Roles and Rights in British Colonies

In early English-speaking settlements, more than in most other cultures throughout the world, the condition of women was framed by two traditional ideas that were always in tension, and often in conflict. One was a highly articulated sense of women's primary role as "goodwives" to their husbands in seventeenth-century New England and "helpmeets" in nineteenth-century New Zealand. Their primary responsibility was to occupy a domestic role in patriarchal households that were the building blocks of colonial societies.[1]

The other idea was an ancient folk tradition in English-speaking cultures that freeborn females have rights of their own. As early as the seventeenth century, Anglo-American women often asserted their claims to liberty and freedom. At first they did so not on grounds of equal rights, but the opposite. They claimed special privileges that flowed from the superiority of their Christian faith, social rank, and British origins. One plantation mistress in early Virginia proudly called herself a "she-Briton." She asserted her prerogatives as a member of that tribe over males of other origins.

Similar claims to special privilege were made in a different way by Maryland's Margaret Brent, proud mistress of St. Gabriel's Manor. She required her tenants to do "Fealty to the Lady," and demanded a "Place and Voyce" in the colonial assembly as early as 1647, not on grounds of equality but by virtue of social rank. In Massachusetts, Anne Hutchinson asserted her superiority in spiritual terms as one of God's Elect, specially chosen to preach to depraved males whether they wanted to hear her or not.[2]

These traditional ideas of a freeborn woman's rights in English-speaking societies were recognized by non-English-speakers throughout the world in the early modern era. An example appears in the second act of Mozart's opera *The Abduction from the Seraglio* (1781). Two of the characters are a spirited she-Briton named Blonde and an Otto-man despot named Osmin who wishes to make her a sex slave. She tells him that he might be able to do that to other women, but not to her: "*Ich bin eine Engländerein,*" she says, "*zu freiheit geboren.* I am an English woman, born to freedom." That exchange continues in a duet. The enraged tyrant Osmin shouts, "O Englishmen! What fools you are to let your women have their way." The freeborn Blonde replies, "A heart born to freedom will never slavishly take orders. And even when freedom is lost, she remains the monarch of all she surveys."[3]

In Mozart's opera, that attitude was perceived as something peculiar to English-speaking people and deeply rooted in a vernacular tradition of liberty and freedom. We also find it in ancient societies throughout northwestern Europe and especially Scandinavia. Norse sagas tell of Viking women who lived proud and free, and armed themselves with daggers in their girdles. The sagas tell of Viking warriors who returned from a wild rampage and treated a Viking woman as if she were a conquered province—a fatal mistake. Wherever this folk tradition came from, we know where it went—to North America in the seventeenth century and New Zealand in the nineteenth century.

The First Wave of American Feminism:
Origins in an Age of Revolution, 1776–95

Traditional ideas of a freeborn she-Briton's rights took on new meaning in the age of the American and French revolutions. This was the era when *ideology* was coined, and when "isms" began to multiply. Before 1776, "isms" in their modern meaning did not exist. By 1830, most had come into common use, including *feminism.*[4] Thomas Jefferson's ringing declaration that "all men are created equal" inspired women to demand rights for themselves in new terms of equality. Among the first to make that argument in a systematic way was a circle of New England women who included Abigail Adams, Mercy Otis Warren, and Hannah Winthrop. They knew each other, talked together, worked together, joined the Revolution, supported the War of Independence, and repeatedly reminded its male leaders to "remember the ladies." In a word, they became a feminist movement—the first in America, and one of the first in the world.

The first American feminists were a circle of New England women in the mid-eighteenth century. They supported the Revolution and spoke out strongly for the rights of women. Among them were Abigail Adams (left) and Mercy Warren.

Many American women in the revolutionary generation were part of it. Judith Sargent Stevens Murray, also of Massachusetts, was among the first to develop on paper an argument for this new egalitarian idea of women's rights. She published a series of essays "On the Equality of the Sexes" in the *Massachusetts Magazine* during the spring of 1790. These ideas spread rapidly. Two years later Mary Wollstonecraft published in Britain her *Vindication of the Rights of Women*.[5]

In the new American republic attitudes changed rapidly in many ways. In 1776, the state of New Jersey gave women the right to vote if they could meet a property requirement that was also imposed on men. As early as 1787, women were actually voting in New Jersey. (One man complained that a woman cast her ballot, changed her dress, and voted twice.) American women also gained the right to vote in some local elections, such as school boards in Kentucky. They also voted in female associations, and formed habits of self-government in that sphere. In early American republics, the law of divorce and property began to be liberalized, first in court decisions, then by statute.[6] Opportunities for employment opened outside the home for unmarried younger women, though rarely for wives and mothers.[7]

A younger leader in the first wave of American feminism was Judith Sargent Stevens Murray, shown here in a portrait by J. S. Copley. She was one of the first to develop a new egalitarian idea of women's rights, in essays titled "On the Equality of the Sexes" (1790).

The Aftermath of Revolutionary Feminism: Individual Achievement and Domesticity

The pursuit of women's rights never ceased in the modern era, but its volume and intensity ebbed and flowed in wavelike movements. Strong surges of feminism rarely continued for more than two or three decades. In 1807, for example, New Jersey ended women's suffrage in state elections after an experiment of twenty years and restricted suffrage to men only. But American women continued to vote in some local elections. Legal evidence provides good empirical indicators of these tidal movements.

As feminist passions cooled, circa 1810–25, women continued to assert their rights as individuals. Unmarried young women worked outside the home in larger numbers, taking advantage of opportunities that had begun to open during the Revolution. This was also a period when parents (often fathers) educated daughters in a new spirit. Leading examples were the American bluestockings Theodosia Burr Alston (1783–1813) and Margaret Fuller (1810–50). Both were young women of extraordinary gifts, raised by eminent fathers to be the intellectual equals of the most cultivated men in their age. Theodosia Burr Alston (daughter of Aaron Burr) was developing a literary career of high promise when she mysteriously disappeared at sea.[8] Margaret Fuller, schooled by her father, Timothy Fuller, mastered five languages at an early age and was given access to the library of Harvard College, though not admitted as a student. She became a leading figure in the Transcendentalist movement, wrote works on literature and social criticism, and went to Europe as the first female foreign correspondent for Horace Greeley's *Tribune*.[9]

In the early American republic, women also played leading roles that had previously been reserved for men. Among them was Hepzibah Clarke (1776–1825), Mrs. James Swan, who became a major figure in Boston, member of a real estate syndicate called the Mount Vernon Proprietors, and developer of Beacon Hill. Another was Catharine Greene (1755–1814), widow of Revolutionary War general Nathanael Greene, who ran southern plantations with much success and employed Eli Whitney to reinvent a revolutionary cotton gin. A third was Anne Royall (1769–1854), a leading investigative journalist, undeterred by an effort to convict her as a "common scold," and a prominent presence in national politics.[10]

A little later, other American women chose to strive for their rights within their domestic roles as wives and mothers. Among the leaders of this movement were Catharine Maria Sedgwick (1789–1867), who developed these themes in domestic novels such as *Hope Leslie* (1827), *Live and Let Live* (1837), and especially *Home* (1835). Also important were Sarah Josepha Hale (1788–1879), best known as editor of the *Lady's Magazine* and later *Godey's Lady's Book*, and Catherine Beecher (1800–78) in writings such as *A Treatise on Domestic Economy* (1841), a handbook of domesticity. A later generation of radical feminists marked them as the enemy, but they also expanded women's rights and roles as wives and mothers. Another object was to enlarge their civic power as controlling figures in a domestic sphere, and as guardians of virtue in the republic.[11]

The Second Wave: Romantic Feminism in America, circa 1840–60

In the mid-nineteenth century, that era of domesticity was followed by a new feminist movement. Many of its leaders had been active in the antislavery movement and found a model for militant reform in the example of the American Revolution. Yet another inspiration was the Romantic movement, which stressed expressive action, appeals to emotion, and absolute moral judgments. Many leaders in America combined confrontational tactics and combative rhetoric with uncompromising ideas of liberty and freedom.

A defining moment for this new feminism was the Seneca Falls Convention, organized in 1848 by Lucretia Mott and Elizabeth Cady Stanton. They issued a manifesto copied on the Declaration of Independence and called a Declaration of Sentiments. It demanded women's suffrage and equal employment as inalienable rights, attacked men as tyrants in language that the Continental Congress had reserved for George III, and then asked for their support.[12]

Stanton herself explained, "If I were to draw up a set of rules for the guidance of reformers . . . I should put at the head of the list: 'Do all you can, *no matter what*, to get people to think on your reform, and then, if the reform is good, it will come about in due season.' " An historian comments, "She did not care whether her efforts generated sympathy or antipathy, as long as they undermined public apathy."[13] Other leading American feminists in that era chose similar tactics. Of Lucy Stone, an admirer wrote that she was "independent in manner and advocates woman's rights in the strongest terms . . . scorns the idea of asking rights of men but says she must boldly assert her own rights and *take* them in her own strength."[14]

This second American feminist movement in the mid-nineteenth century succeeded in inspiring many women. It won important legislative victories, notably in the enactment of Married Women's Property Acts. But the adversarial tactics of romantic feminists offended many potential supporters who might have helped

Another American feminist movement formed in an age of romantic and religious reform. Among its leaders were Lucretia Mott and Elizabeth Cady Stanton, who worked together against slavery and for temperance, and introduced the militancy of those movements to feminism. Their Declaration of Sentiments at Seneca Falls, New York (1848), was modeled on the Declaration of Independence and made all men into tyrants on the model of George III.

them. For example, Elizabeth Cady Stanton alienated her own husband, Henry Stanton. Her father, whom she deeply loved, was so outraged by her angry attacks on men that he disinherited her. That act in turn deepened her anger, which reinforced his wrath.[15]

Radical reformers in nineteenth-century America (feminists, abolitionists, and others) also formed the habit of fighting with one another. Ideological causes led to tests of ideological purity that were deeply divisive. Examples were New York's early socialist feminists, who spoke of nonsocialist feminists as "enemy sisters." The conduct of these internal struggles also revealed a larger weakness. Instrumental action was often subordinated to expressive action, which undercut the purpose of the enterprise.

This historical sequence of movements for women's rights—a feminist movement with large ideological purposes, followed by a period of individual achievement, and then by an era of domestic reform, and in turn another wave of feminism—first appeared in the United States from 1776 to 1840. It was a rhythm that would recur many times in American history, and also in New Zealand.

The Rhythm of Women's Rights in New Zealand

The first major settlements in New Zealand were founded in an era of domesticity throughout the English-speaking world—a time of high Victorian celebration of family, hearth, and home. The material condition of settler societies modified this idea in some ways and reinforced it in others. Patterns of regional diversity developed from the start—at least many New Zealanders thought so. Regional stereotypes of gender roles appeared by the mid-nineteenth century and persisted for more than a century. As late as 1964, Auckland's John Cowie Reid supplied examples, in a spirit of universal condescension that could not have been better designed to infuriate women everywhere. He wrote, "If Dunedin is a stolid, wholesome Scots lassie, Christchurch a hockey captain-type of English girl, Wellington a slightly dowdy secretary, modern Auckland is a perky gold-digger, over-talkative but full of ideas, mildly interested in the arts and much in love with life."[16]

Behind these crude stereotypes were real differences among New Zealand's early settlements. Auckland, an atomized society from the start, offered more complex associational opportunities for women, who took an early lead in founding voluntary groups such as the Auckland Ladies Benevolent Society (1857), the first of its kind in New Zealand.

Canterbury had an exceptionally strong sense of social hierarchy, grounded in the values of its Anglican founders, and later in the growth of a purse-proud runholding gentry. Attached to this tradition was an ideal of moral authority in women of good estate. Examples appeared in the writings of Charlotte Godley (1821–1907), who on one occasion "begged two young bachelors on a Canterbury backblocks station to set up a dummy of a lady in their sitting room, and 'always to behave before it as if it were their mother, or some other dignified lady.'"[17]

Otago's Scottish population introduced a comparatively strong sense of gender equality—among Scots. The high walls of Dunedin's Early Settlers' Association, when we visited there, were lined with early photographs of the founders—hundreds of men and women in equal pairs, frowning down upon their posterity. These sturdy Calvinists had a deep interest in female schooling. A result was the rapid expansion of women's education in Otago, the home of New Zealand's first secondary school for females.

In the MacKenzie Country, and in outlying districts that New Zealanders call the "back blocks," women lived on isolated farms, sometimes with no other female for miles around. A tale was told about the Burgess family at Burke Pass, now a busy tourist route to Mount Cook National Park, but then so remote from human habitation that the children had never seen a woman other than their mother. One day another family came through, on its way to an even more remote sheep run at Sawdon Station. The children watched in amazement as a strange woman climbed down from a bullock dray. One ran home crying, "Mother! Mother! There is a man out here with your clothes on!"[18] Behind these examples was a pattern of regional variation on a theme of domesticity in New Zealand.

New Zealand's First-Wave Feminists: Maria Rye and the Three Marys, circa 1860–69

Even as domesticity flourished in these many forms, a wave-pattern began to appear in the history of women's rights throughout New Zealand, similar to America but not the same. The first wave began in the mid-nineteenth century. A leader was Maria Susan Rye (1829–1903), a woman of Quaker ancestry, born and raised in London, where her father was a solicitor and bibliophile. She educated herself in his large library, became an active feminist, wrote on women's issues, and dedicated herself to improving the economic condition of women. Working with a Society for Promoting the Employment of Women, she started her own business as a scrivener and created jobs for twenty women who engrossed legal documents. The business flourished, but she was looking for a larger solution.

To that end, Rye organized a Female Middle Class Emigration Society (1862) and came to New Zealand as a spinster (at the age of thirty-three). Instantly she threw herself into feminist work throughout the colony. One of her first tasks was to inspect Dunedin's miserable Prince's Street Barracks for unmarried female immigrants. When the authorities did not support her, she created such an uproar that the superintendent lost his job. The men who ran Otago were appalled, and something similar happened when she continued her work in Canterbury. Rye wrote home, "I am looked upon as a kind of ogre." But she kept at it, and things went better in Nelson, Marlborough, Wellington, and Hawke's Bay. She listened and learned to work with men rather than against them in a way that would become typical of New Zealand's feminists. Its object was to move forward, not by confrontation but by meetings, negotiations, and agreements with men in high offices throughout New Zealand. One male leader wrote that she "did not seem to despise the advantages of attractiveness in externals common to her sex" and wore "a jaunty hat fronted with flowers, a light blue mantle, [and] a pair of follow-me-lads," which were "a cascade of ribbons hanging over her shoulder."[19]

Maria Susan Rye has been called an imperial figure in every sense, an English feminist who came to New Zealand in 1862 and worked tirelessly to improve the condition of women in every major settlement except Auckland. After angry collisions with male leaders, she learned to work with them and achieved high success during her short stay in New Zealand.

"Follow me, lads" might have been the motto of her feminist movement. Rye worked in seven New Zealand settlements, started programs for female immigration, established female schools, and founded homes for single women who were ill or unemployed. She raised substantial sums for those purposes, four thousand pounds in Wellington alone. After 1864 she worked in Australia, Canada, and England. Charlotte Macdonald writes that "she was in more than one sense an imperial figure."[20]

Maria Rye was in New Zealand for only a year and a half, but it was a critical moment when the immigration of women was at a peak. Afterward she kept up her connections and recruited other feminist leaders for New Zealand women. Among her followers was Caroline Alpenny (1821–?) who worked to bring women and civilization to Dunedin, founded a woman's employment office, and lectured on "The Moral and Intellectual Influence of Women on Society." She is thought to have sent twelve thousand colonists to New Zealand, many of them young women. She was strongly supported—except when she sent a shipload of Irish Catholic women to live among the Scottish Presbyterians of Otago. Through Alpenny and others, Rye touched the lives of many women, and they in turn touched many more. Her short stay in New Zealand had a long reach.[21]

Among other figures in this first wave of New Zealand feminism were the "Three Marys" of New Zealand legend: Mary Ann Wilson Müller (1819/20–1901) in Nelson, Mary Taylor (1817–93) in Wellington, and Mary Colclough (1836–85) in Auckland. They were inspired by the example of Maria Rye and influenced by the writings of John Stuart Mill, especially his essay on *The Subjection of Women* in 1869, and had a relationship with Charlotte Brontë and other British literati. Most were motivated by their own struggles to support others, in and out of marriage. All reached a large public in New Zealand and Britain with essays on many feminist causes. Mary Ann Müller wrote under the pen name Femmina [*sic*] for the *Nelson Examiner* and published her first pamphlet on suffrage in 1869.[22] In the early 1870s, Mary Colclough published feminist essays in newspapers over the name of Polly Plum. Always, her "first and greatest concern" was about material issues of economic independence, employment opportunities for women, and control of property.[23]

The writings of the Three Marys had a very different tone from the Seneca Falls movement in America. Femmina appealed primarily to men for their support, in a moderate and reasonable tone. Polly Plum went out of her way to conciliate men and wrote, "I can speak favourably of the intelligence and kindness of men generally. I have

The first wave of feminism in New Zealand, like that in the United States, has often been forgotten. Among its leaders were the Three Marys: Mary Ann Wilson Müller in Nelson (seen here), Mary Taylor in Wellington, and Mary Colclough in Auckland. Their writings had a different tone from the Seneca Falls declaration, strongly assertive but conciliatory to men and cast in terms of appeals for justice and fairness rather than demands for liberty and freedom.

made many friends among the opposite sex by my advocacy of 'Women's Rights.' " Much of her appeal was cast in terms of justice, fair treatment, and the Golden Rule. These first New Zealand feminists gave more attention to inequity, unfairness, and injustice in the material condition of women than to liberty, freedom, and political disabilities.[24]

An Era of Individual Achievement

The first wave of feminism in New Zealand led to an expansion of possibilities for women. In 1871, Otago Girls' High School opened in Dunedin, the first such school in New Zealand. Others followed. Young women seized these opportunities and in the early 1870s sought admission to universities. The pioneers were three extraordinary women: Kate Edger (1857–1935) at Auckland College, Helen Brown Connon (1859?–1903) at Canterbury College, and Caroline Freeman (1855/56?–1914), first to graduate from Otago University.

They faced strong resistance, and it is interesting to see how they overcame it. Edger was explicitly ordered to enter class in Auckland with "downcast eyes." Freeman had a rough time with some of her teachers in Otago. It was said that had she been a soldier she would have been decorated for valor. They persevered, and excelled in their studies. In 1877, Edger became the first woman in the British Empire to earn the degree of bachelor of arts. Connon was the second, in 1880, and the first to add a master's degree, with a double

The first wave of activity in support of women created new opportunities especially in education. In the nineteenth century young women began to gain admission to New Zealand colleges. Among them was Helen Brown Connon at Canterbury, who with Kate Edger at Auckland and Caroline Freeman at Otago met initial resistance but won broad support. Connon made a career of expanding opportunities for other young women and attracted the support of men in that cause.

first in English and Latin. Freeman took the first women's degree at Otago and won the Bowen Prize, which was open to all students.[25]

New Zealanders, male and female alike, took pride in their success. Edger's commencement at Auckland drew nearly a thousand people. When Freeman graduated at Otago, male students gave her an ovation and threw flowers on the stage, and a member of the faculty delivered an oration on the importance of university education for women. These three New Zealand pioneers were much celebrated for the manner of their achievements. The Bishop of Auckland presented Edger with a white camellia for what he called her "unpretending excellence." Connon was much loved for what her biographer describes as "her quiet dignity and kindness as well as for her intellect." It was done in the New Zealand way.[26]

All of these women went on to distinguished careers in education and opened opportunities for others: Edger as principal of Nelson College for Girls, Connon as principal of Christchurch Girls' High School, and Freeman as founder and head of Girton College, a distinguished private school with branches in two cities. They held many other offices. Edger and Connon married and raised families while pursuing their careers. Only Edger was active in feminist groups, though she was described as "not strongly feminist in outlook." Their goal was individual achievement by women, and they helped others to pursue it with high success.[27]

New Zealand's Second Wave of Progressive Feminism: The Suffrage Movement, 1880–1914

Many scholars have noted that New Zealand's suffrage movements had a distinct character. In a study of international feminism, Melanie Nolan and Caroline Daley observe that the New Zealand story was "comparatively peaceful and quiet," with an absence of high drama that has caused it to be "underplayed in many suffrage studies."[28] A contemporary observer of a suffrage meeting in New Zealand noted that "a number of the delegates were quiet motherly-looking persons, quite unlike the shrieking sisterhood which male experience, very wrongly, had been led to expect."[29]

Four New Zealand women were among the leaders of this second wave. Kate Sheppard (1847–1934) was an immigrant of good family, highly educated by an uncle who was a minister in the Free Church of Scotland, and she married an affluent merchant in Christchurch. A contemporary observed that Sheppard was "the very opposite of the bogey 'advanced woman.'" She was described as "handsome, well proportioned, and in glowing health." One of her family remembered that "she never argued with men's opinion of women, but laughed and asked if they really thought women were like that." She gave the suffrage movement strength, reason, dignity, good humor, maturity, and success.[30]

The most prominent public figure was Anna Paterson Logan Stout (1858–1931). Stout was a native New Zealander, born and

Progressive feminists in New Zealand shared much in common with American feminists in the same era but with interesting contrasts in methods and results. Among the most prominent leaders was Kate Sheppard in Christchurch.

raised in Dunedin and married to Robert Stout, a successful bar-rister who became prime minister of New Zealand. Stout was remem-bered for her dignity, refinement, beauty, and especially her bright blonde hair that was said to shine like "spun gold." She combined a complete devotion to her domestic role as wife and mother of six children with outspoken feminism.[31]

Of equal prominence was Margaret Home Richardson Sievwright (1844–1905). Born in East Lothian, the daughter of a Scottish estate factor, she trained as a nurse with Florence Nightingale, worked with poor children in the slums of Edinburgh, emigrated to New Zealand in the 1870s, married Robert Stout's law partner, lived in a villa called Hjaltland (the Viking name for Shetland), with a squadron of ser-vants and gardeners, and involved herself in many social causes. At a public meeting in 1900 she asked, "What do women want? We want men to stand out of our sunshine. That is all." Her phrase still echoes in New Zealand.[32]

A generation older than those three leaders was Amey Daldy (1829?–1920). English-born, she married a wealthy businessman

Anna Stout (left) was another leader who was very traditional in her appearance and con-duct, and also a strong feminist. She enlisted her husband in the cause. He was Robert Stout, prime minister of New Zealand. Margaret Sievwright is remembered for saying at a public meeting, "What do women want? We want men to stand out of our sunshine. That is all." Her phrase has echoed through the history of women's rights in New Zealand.

and prominent political leader, William Crush Daldy, became a philanthropist in many causes, and emerged as a leader of feminism in Auckland. Daldy was a woman of courage, presence, and high intelligence. She was always careful to cultivate a very proper Victorian appearance, with high-collared dresses and a pristine-looking white lace bonnet that became her symbol. In methods and purposes, she advised women to be "wise as serpents, harmless as doves."[33]

A vital factor, highly variable in the history of feminist movements, was their attitude toward men. These four feminist leaders in New Zealand all actively enlisted men in their cause and persuaded their husbands to help them. Margaret Sievwright worked closely with William Sievwright, who published defenses of feminism and women's suffrage at a pivotal moment.[34] When Robert Stout, Anna Stout's husband, became prime minister he threw his considerable weight behind feminist legislation.[35] Amey Daldy's affluent husband went to meetings with her and helped to subsidize the feminist cause.[36]

New Zealand's experience was distinctive not only in the tactics of its feminists but also in responses of men. As early as the 1870s, Premier Julius Vogel defended the rights of women, though he had also declared that he was, "in general, opposed to exceptional reforms." In 1889, he published a prophetic feminist novel that compared the liberation of women to the emancipation of the

Amey Daldy recruited her husband, William Daldy, for the feminist cause. He was a wealthy Auckland businessman who went to meetings and helped to subsidize the movement. She advised New Zealand women to be "wise as serpents, harmless as doves." This New Zealand feminism, with its conciliatory methods and appeals to justice and fairness, proved highly effective. It won the first victory for women's suffrage in national elections anywhere in the world.

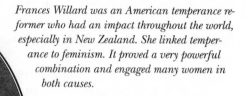

Frances Willard was an American temperance re-former who had an impact throughout the world, especially in New Zealand. She linked temper-ance to feminism. It proved a very powerful combination and engaged many women in both causes.

Jews.[37] Many of New Zealand's prime ministers actively supported women's suffrage. Harry Atkinson, a moderate conservative, was won over by his sister Emily Atkinson Richmond and sister-in-law Jane Richmond Atkinson. Sir John Hall on August 5, 1890, gave a highly effective speech for women's suffrage. Kate Sheppard remarked that it was important "not only for its strength and pointedness, but also for its moderation. . . . I feel sure that many will be won through its means."[38]

These men provided parliamentary leadership and worked in a spirit of cooperation with feminist leaders. The American feminist Frances Willard watched all this in amazement and contrasted it with her experience in the United States. "What fine men you must have in New Zealand," she wrote.[39] Through the combined efforts of women and men, women's suffrage in New Zealand was first enacted in local elections at an early date. The Municipal Corporations Act of 1867 did not restrict voting to men, and women were allowed to vote in Nelson and Otago. In 1875, women's suffrage in local elections was extended throughout the country, with strong support from Hall, Stout, Vogel, and Ballance.

In national elections it faced stronger opposition. In 1878, Robert Stout introduced a bill that gave women the vote in national elections and also the right to stand for Parliament. It was defeated on a technicality. Other bills—in 1879, 1880, and 1881—also failed.

The struggle gained a new dimension in 1885, when American temperance reformer Mary Clement Leavitt visited New Zealand and organized a National Woman's Christian Temperance Union. It grew rapidly, added a "Franchise and Legislation Department," sought women's suffrage as a way of enacting temperance laws, and attracted broad support. Its suffrage petitions drew 10,000 signers in

1891, 20,000 in 1892, and 31,871 in 1893—a quarter of all adult women in New Zealand. Opposition to women's suffrage also increased, much of it from brewers and publicans who feared that women's votes would enact prohibition.

In 1887, yet another a bill for women's suffrage was introduced by Julius Vogel. This time a majority were in favor, but Westland populist Richard Seddon defeated it by a late-night parliamentary trick at one o'clock in the morning, much to the outrage of women. Seddon's tactics added a new argument to their cause. In 1890, another majority supported women's suffrage, but more midnight maneuvers defeated it, putting the enemies of women's suffrage squarely on the side of procedural unfairness—a fatal error in New Zealand.[40]

Feminist leaders and many conservative and liberal politicians responded with appeals for fair play and carried the day. In 1893, New Zealand became the first nation to enfranchise women, and the bill was proclaimed as law within a week. Two weeks later, women were able to vote for members of Parliament. More than 80 percent of eligible Pakeha women turned out, and about four thousand Maori women.[41]

There is a debate over women's suffrage in New Zealand. Did it come as a gift or was it gained by struggle? Feminist leaders rejected both answers and took a third view. Anna Stout commented, "The real power of the women's vote in New Zealand is not in opposition, but in its harmony and co-operation with the men's vote."[42] Kate Sheppard said in 1894, "We asked for the suffrage, not on the ground that it could help us to advance social and moral reforms, but as an act of justice."[43] Afterward, Prime Minister Joseph Ward declared, "The main argument, however, which weighed with us, was that of right, of abstract right. If the foundation of the government is the consent of the governed, it appears monstrously unfair that one half of the population should not be represented or have any share in it."[44]

The consequences of women's suffrage were also much disputed. In 1909, the formidable American feminist Maud Park visited New Zealand. Her purpose was to study the social consequences of women's suffrage, which she believed to be profound. Every New Zealander who came within reach was relentlessly interrogated: "fellow travellers on railways and boats, women at afternoon teas, women in shops, the men who took me out to dinner, the conductor while I was waiting for the train to start, my hairdresser, the minister of education, the man who mended my shoes." To her dismay, 70 percent of respondents told her that women's suffrage had made no difference, except to shrink the number of places where liquor was sold.[45]

Her informants were mistaken. Women's suffrage made a profound difference. It led directly to other acts, including the repeal in 1910 of the Contagious Diseases Act, which had discriminated outrageously against women. The vote for women was instrumental in the passage of the Slander of Women Act, the Summary Separation Act, labor laws for women, the tightening of liquor licensing, an act to curtail smoking by minors, and increased expenditures for schools. The success of the suffrage campaign also inspired new organizations such as the National Council of Women in 1896. Kate Sheppard concluded that "generally, the result of women's suffrage has been to strengthen the movement for social and moral reform." She appears to have been entirely correct.[46]

Parallel Movements: Progressive Feminism in America

At the same time that women won the right to vote in New Zealand, another wave of feminism in America sought the same goal. The suffrage cause had long been active during the nineteenth century but had few victories to show for many years of effort. Several western states granted women the right to vote. Wyoming did so in 1869, and Utah in 1870. Western labor unions and farmers' alliances allowed women to vote, but more as a result of ethnic, class, and religious politics. In Utah Mormon men enfranchised women, who were mostly Mormons, to maintain their hegemony over non-Mormons. Other states did the same thing from fear of voting power among Asians, Africans, and European immigrants. These local events had little impact on the national level. In 1875, a very conservative Supreme Court ruled against women's suffrage on constitutional grounds, which meant that an amendment to the Constitution became necessary. Congress refused to act, and an amendment was defeated in 1878.[47]

A difficult problem was the diffusion of energy in progressive feminism among rival groups. In 1890, Susan B. Anthony succeeded in organizing the National American Woman Suffrage Association. Its leadership passed to a new generation of progressive feminists, and by the early twentieth century they began to gain ground. The movement presented two faces to the public. One of them belonged to Carrie Chapman Catt (1859–1947), a middle westerner who became president of the Woman Suffrage Association in 1900. A

A very strong American feminist movement formed in the progressive era and functioned on a new scale. A highly effective organizer was Carrie Chapman Catt, who quietly brought many women's groups together and worked to win the support of men with much success.

skilled organizer, Catt helped to build a broad coalition of women's groups. At the same time, she reached out to male progressives and appealed to principles that both women and men might support.[48]

Another face of the American suffrage movement was more militant. Its leader was Alice Paul, a New Jersey woman who followed the example of British feminists and chose the path of confrontation and provocation. She broke with Carrie Catt, seceded from the National American Woman Suffrage Association, and founded her own group in 1913. Paul launched furious attacks on male leaders in general and Woodrow Wilson in particular. During the First World War she compared Wilson to Kaiser Wilhelm, set fire to the president's speeches, and chained herself to the White House fence, seeking publicity by deliberately outrageous acts. The Wilson administration was predictably outraged. Paul and several followers were sent to prison. In confinement they went on hunger strikes. Wardens responded with brutal forced feeding. Stomach tubes were rammed down women's throats by male jailers in scenes of horror that Paul used as symbols of her cause.[49]

A later generation of radical feminists made Alice Paul into a heroine. But in her own time, most suffrage leaders did not approve of her tactics and worked within the pragmatic tradition of American progressivism. Their strategy was to get results by winning the right to vote, which they expected to be an instrument of other reforms. Their tactics were to seek persuasion rather than confrontation.

Progressive feminists agreed on many goals but were divided on means. Militant New Jersey feminist Alice Paul broke with Carrie Catt, adopted the confrontational methods of some British feminists, and mounted angry attacks on men in general and President Woodrow Wilson in particular. She and her supporters were jailed, brutally mistreated, and later celebrated as martyrs by radical feminists.

In 1917, Carrie Chapman Catt and most other suffrage leaders supported the Wilson administration in its decision to enter the war and invoked the president's rhetoric in their own cause. They demanded that rights of self-determination should extend to the women of America. The active participation of women in the war effort was used by the suffrage movement as another argument for their cause. In 1919, Congress at last passed the Nineteenth Amendment and gave women the right to vote. Strong support came from President Wilson and his administration. State legislatures in the North and West, but not the South, quickly ratified the amendment, and it became law on August 18, 1920, in time for the presidential election.[50]

An important question is about the effectiveness of these various tactics in the campaign for women's suffrage. Some historians believe that Alice Paul lost more support than she gained and gravely weakened the suffrage movement; others have come to the opposite conclusion. Jane Addams took a third view. She believed that the decisive factor was the conduct of American women in the First World War. Suffrage, she wrote, was "a direct result of the war psychology."[51]

Another Postfeminist Era: Emancipated Women in Two Nations

In both countries, the great wave of progressive feminism receded after the First World War. A period followed in which rhythms of change began to converge in both nations, with increasing global

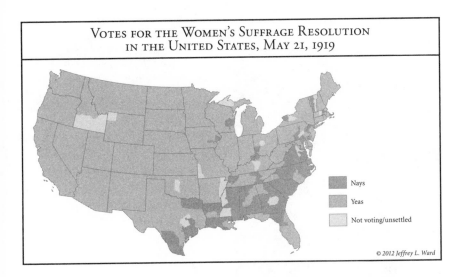

VOTES FOR THE WOMEN'S SUFFRAGE RESOLUTION
IN THE UNITED STATES, MAY 21, 1919

Nays

Yeas

Not voting/unsettled

© 2012 Jeffrey L. Ward

integration throughout the English-speaking world. In both the United States and New Zealand, women became less ideological about feminist issues but more active as individuals in asserting their rights. During the 1920s and 1930s, they entered many areas that been reserved for men, sometimes in spectacular ways.

New fields of endeavor offered many opportunities. Women became leading aviators in the 1930s, often employing men to work for them. Amelia Earhart in the United States and Jean Batten in New Zealand became major figures and role models, celebrated for their courage, skill, grace, and especially for their spirit of independence in long-distance solo flights that were symbolic of the New Woman, as this ideal began to be called. They were both bright, lively, attractive, and very feminine. Batten was called "the Garbo of the Skies." Earhart had a style and presence that were uniquely her own. Both had many admirers.[52]

Other New Women became journalists, photographers, foreign correspondents, and war correspondents, aggressively (and successfully) competing against male colleagues. Marguerite Higgins, Clare Boothe Luce, Margaret Bourke-White, and many other women became very prominent in the expanding mass media of the 1930s and 1940s.

Women began to enter politics and took prominent roles in public life. One of the most eminent was a Virginian, Nancy Langhorne, who as Lady Astor succeeded to her husband's seat in the British House of Commons and became the first woman to sit in Parliament. She was also the leading spirit of the right-wing Cliveden Set, a conservative clique that favored the appeasement of

As the wave of progressive feminism receded in the 1930s, many individual women claimed their opportunities equally with men, often in new fields. None did so with more grace and flair and strength and impact than the New Zealand aviator Jean Batten, who was celebrated as the "Garbo of the skies."

fascism in the 1930s. To the left of center was Eleanor Roosevelt, who transformed the role of the first lady into a public office of great prominence. In New Zealand the first women entered Parliament and the cabinet in the 1930s. A few of these high achievers were feminists. Amelia Earhart joined the National Woman's Party. Most did not identify themselves with feminist movements, but all were devoted to the pursuit of women's rights by other means. They succeeded in enlarging opportunities for women by example rather than precept. In some ways they were building on the achievements of feminists in the Progressive Era.

The Second World War reinforced these trends in some ways. It hugely expanded employment of women outside the home. In every combatant nation, women replaced men in jobs of every imaginable description. They did so differently from one nation to another. In New Zealand and Britain, they were conscripted into war work. In the United States, women were recruited in a free labor market, and went to work with an enlarged sense of their own agency.

The Revival of Domesticity, 1945–65

After World War II, and partly because of it, a great revival of domesticity occurred in New Zealand and the United States. This was an international trend, evident in a surge of marriage and fertility

Amelia Earhart in the United States was another aviator who inspired men and women alike by her many achievements. She appears here with navigator Fred Noonan on her last flight, an attempt to circumnavigate the globe, which ended in 1937 when they disappeared in the Pacific.

rates. It also appeared in declining numbers of women in paid employment, and in a reduction in the number of women entering professions such as law, medicine, and scholarship during the late 1940s and the 1950s.[53]

The age of domesticity was anathema to radical feminists who came after it. But it was a period of expansion in women's rights. Many things were happening within families, which were becoming less patriarchal in these years. Women increasingly expected equality of esteem, and even demanded it. They raised their daughters to be free and proud. This age of domesticity included an idealization of marriage as partnership rather than patriarchy, and new visions of family life that served the welfare of its individual members. All this was a reform movement in its own right, different from another sort of feminism that mocked it, and in some ways more sustained.[54]

But at the same time, the 1950s were also an era when choices for women outside the home were very restricted—more so than during the 1940s and 1930s. Gifted young women were encouraged to excel, only to discover that the best schools and careers and opportunities in many fields were closed to them. In the United States and New Zealand especially, with their great founding principles of freedom and fairness, these cruel inequities were bitterly resented.

Fourth-Wave Feminism in the United States: Women's Liberation

The result was another wave of feminism, an international movement with a character distinctly its own. This movement rose among women who possessed many fundamental human rights, more than most men throughout the world. By 1963, women in the United States received more formal education than men. They had the right to hold property, and more large fortunes were held by women than by men. They had the right to vote and were active in social causes and cultural organizations. Many worked outside the home, but conditions of employment were not equal. Women tended to be in jobs of lower status than men. And even in the same jobs, they received less pay than men, with fewer prospects for advancement. From 1950 to 1968, the median wage of women in the United States actually declined as a percentage of men's pay. Opportunities, even for women of high status and education, were limited. The correction of these material problems became a major goal of the new feminism in the United States.[55]

This movement had been growing quietly in the 1950s. A major international event was the publication of Simone de Beauvoir's treatise *The Second Sex* (1952), a restrained but powerful indictment of gender discrimination. Other events of high importance included a series of statistical studies by private foundations and public agencies. One of the first was the Ford Foundation's report *Womanpower*, in 1957. Another was the Kennedy administration's Commission on the Status of Women, which published its report in 1963. These inquiries documented the depth of the problem and concluded that discrimination against women was damaging to the entire society. Their arguments were addressed both to women and men.

The first chairman of the Commission on the Status of Women was Eleanor Roosevelt. In the years of her maturity, she became the face of American feminism and brought to it qualities of dignity, intelligence, seriousness, and strength that had great weight with all but the most rabid of Roosevelt-haters. She also had direct access to four presidents and used that advantage to great effect.

Another inspiration in the United States was the civil rights movement, which had an impact on a number of struggles for freedom, both in America and throughout the world. Among the first to be influenced by it was a new feminism, often through women who had worked against racial discrimination and then turned to gender discrimination.[56] Civil rights activism created a climate for change in the early 1960s, as important and far-reaching legislation was enacted in Congress. Most important was the Federal Civil Rights Act of 1964. Conservative southern Democrats tried to defeat the measure by adding a new section, Title VII,

In the late 1950s, Eleanor Roosevelt became the most important leader in the early stages of a new feminism. She commanded the support of men such as John F. Kennedy and linked women's rights to the central values of the republic. She also became the symbol of a larger idea of liberty and freedom, as in this happy cartoon by HerBlock.

which forbade discrimination by gender as well as by race. To their horror, it passed. The new statute created a growing body of law in support of women's rights. Commissions on Women were appointed in many states and met annually in Washington. These meetings addressed growing frustration with laws that were not enforced, reports that were not read, and recommendations that were ignored.[57]

Then came Betty Friedan's *The Feminine Mystique,* an extraordinary new book that made a difference in the way people thought about these problems. The author, a seemingly typical housewife— middle class and middle-aged with three children—wrote for other women like herself, about what she called a "problem that has no name." Friedan argued that women were the silent victims of a "feminine mystique" that deprived them of "personal identity and achievement" apart from their home-and-family roles as wives and mothers.[58] She drew heavily on the work of psychologists and psychiatrists such as Bruno Bettelheim, Olga Lengyel, and Eugen Kogon, who had been in concentration camps and survived to write about the psychological consequences of being subject to another will. This literature led Friedan toward a new idea of liberty and freedom as psychological liberation. She sought to improve the social and material condition of women, but mainly it meant to "raise consciousness," to elevate a woman's sense of self-esteem, and to transform her way of thinking about herself.[59]

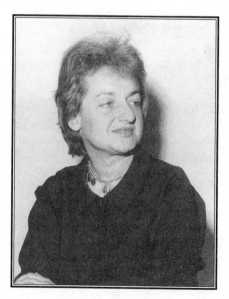

Betty Friedan gave the new feminism a depth of purpose in her extraordinary book, The Feminine Mystique *(1963), which centered on an old "problem that has no name" and a new goal of "raising consciousness" among women. To traditional ideas of liberty and freedom it added the idea of psychological liberation.*

These large purposes inspired a new National Organization for Women (NOW) in 1966, which came together in Friedan's hotel room at a National Conference of State Commissions on Women. Its primary goal was to increase pressure in Washington and to "raise consciousness" among women. It met with spectacular success. Friedan herself wrote that "the absolute necessity for a civil rights movement for women had reached such a point of subterranean urgency by 1966, that it took only a few of us to get together to unite the spark—and it spread like a nuclear chain reaction."[60]

That "chain reaction" in the early 1960s was the greatest achievement of the new feminist movement. It was the explosive growth of a new idea called women's liberation, and it spread at lightning speed everywhere. But its methods and goals varied from one nation to another in ways that reflected their culture and history. The United States and New Zealand were both caught up in this great movement at the same time but in different ways.[61]

In America, the movement for women's liberation became highly combative and confrontational. Many of its leaders had served in the civil rights movement, or the anti-war movement, or had been schooled in the ethnic politics of urban America. They were accustomed to the sound and fury of public life in the 1960s, when the decibels sometimes rose so high that only a scream could be heard. The result was a new style of in-your-face feminism. Its leaders were radicals and activists such as Bella Abzug, Ti-Grace Atkinson, Shulamith Firestone, Kate Millett, and Gloria Steinem. Its militant groups included NOW, Radical Women (1967), Red Stockings (1969), the Stanton-Anthony Brigade (1969), and Bread and Roses (1970?). These groups were not large. The biggest of them, NOW, had between five thousand and ten thousand members in 1971, and perhaps thirty thousand in 1973, making it far smaller than other organizations, such as the Women's Equity Action League, Federally Employed Women, and Human Rights for Women Inc. But in-your-face feminism attracted journalists and shaped the image of the women's movement out of proportion to its numbers. Its marches and demonstrations were designed to capture the front pages. In September 1968, it won headlines by organizing a protest against the Miss America contest. In a Rabelaisian demonstration, a sheep was anointed as Miss America, and brassieres and girdles and false eyelashes were ripped off and hurled into a "Freedom Trash Can." A Women's Strike for Equality on August 26, 1970, organized marches in many cities. Radical women carried signs that read "Don't Cook Dinner—Starve a Rat Today" and "End Human Sacrifice! Don't Get Married!!"

Gloria Steinem led a younger generation of angry young women, who increasing made the new feminism more combative and more hostile to men. They worked within a long American tradition of feminist militancy that had appeared in the rhetoric of Seneca Falls and the campaigns of Alice Paul. It was also typical of labor movements and other reformers in the United States.

Altogether, in-your-face feminism offers a textbook example of how not to organize a political movement for social change. In a middle-class nation, it delighted in outraging bourgeois sensibilities. In a society that firmly supported free enterprise and private property, it went out of its way to attack capitalism. In a nation strongly centered on marriage and the family, it picketed marriage license bureaus. In a democratic polity, it declared half of the electorate to be its inveterate enemy. In a world of mass communications, it furiously attacked journalists and organized demonstrations against major newspapers (putting up a picket line around the *New York Times*). While complaining about sexism, it expressed intense hostility toward all males. Much of the energy of radical feminism was absorbed in furious internal battles over ideological purity. While it succeeded in raising the consciousness of some women, it failed to achieve other goals.

The gravest defeat was the struggle for an Equal Rights Amendment, designed to prohibit discriminatory acts by the United States and by the individual states. The draft amendment provided that "Equality of rights under the law shall not be denied or abridged by the United States or by any state on account of sex." The ERA was approved by large majorities in Congress in 1972, signed by President Gerald

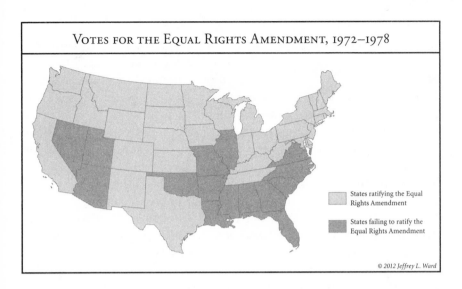

VOTES FOR THE EQUAL RIGHTS AMENDMENT, 1972–1978

States ratifying the Equal
Rights Amendment

States failing to ratify the
Equal Rights Amendment

© 2012 Jeffrey L. Ward

Ford in 1975, and sent to the states for ratification. Most also agreed: thirty-five out of fifty states; but thirty-eight states (more than 75 percent) were required. The amendment failed by narrow margins of a few votes in three states. Radical and adversarial feminists were widely seen as the cause of its defeat. More than a few opposed the amendment, because it did not explicitly prohibit all discrimination in every form everywhere. Others persisted in using tactics that alienated moderate supporters, both male and female, in a very close run contest.

The New Feminism in New Zealand, circa 1960–80

The same question was taken up in New Zealand, with different results. In 1959, Margot Roth published in the *New Zealand Listener* an essay called "Housewives or Human Beings?" In earlier pieces Roth had delighted her readers with witty observations on the passing scene, but this time she was not in a happy frame of mind. Roth was fed up with what she called "the homemakers' cult." She continued, "Quite obviously, our society's out of plumb somewhere. And I'm suggesting that one way of helping them to correct it is to get nearly half of it—the women—out of the mould of inferiority in which they're settling themselves more and more deeply."[62]

The *Listener* ran her piece with a sketch of women on the march. They held a banner that read "Unfair to Housewives." The editor commented that Roth's piece "sparked a thousand arguments in suburban living rooms," and probably many more in the kitchen. The point was much the same as Betty Friedan's, but the rhetoric was very different. Friedan argued that the home had become a domestic "concentration camp" that infantilized women and violated their inalienable rights. Roth expressed quiet indignation against practices that were "unfair to housewives." Roth appealed not to radical ideologies or to models of political revolutions for liberty and freedom, but to what she called a "better tradition which stems from the old liberal middle-class in New Zealand" and to ideas of fairness and social justice. The 1960s brought a rising chorus of voices like Margot Roth's. They were quiet voices, but strong and angry, and they were the true beginning of a new feminism that overswept New Zealand.

Some historians remember the origin of this new wave of feminism in another way, as a radical movement that "burst suddenly on New Zealand" in the early 1970s. They stress feminist figures such as Germaine Greer, who visited Auckland, made an incendiary speech, and got herself arrested and fined NZ$40 for using an obscenity ("bullshit") in a public place.[63] The newspapers had a field day, but that was not the start of the new feminism in New Zealand. When Greer's photo appeared in every newspaper, other women had been hard at work for a decade, building a movement that combined in an idea of "women's liberation" with the traditions of earlier movements in New Zealand.

These new feminists spoke with many voices. Sonja Davies was a trade unionist who linked that cause to a women's movement. Eva Rickard worked for Maori land rights and women's rights in Maoridom. Sandra Coney combined feminism with health issues. Sue Kedgley was a television journalist and producer who published major works on women's rights and environmental issues, and won many men to the support of both movements.[64]

In the years before Germaine Greer caused an uproar in Auckland, feminists and members of Parliament in New Zealand had worked quietly together to pass a series of Equal Pay Acts that were among the most sweeping reforms for gender rights in any Western nation. A measure that required equal pay for equal work in public employment was enacted in the Government Service Equal Pay Act of 1960. That law was extended to the private sector in the Equal Pay Act of 1972. It became a party issue. A conservative National government repealed equal pay for equal work in the private employment; Labour passed it again in 1990, and National repealed it quickly in the same year. But a Human Rights Commission Act (1977) prohibited discrimination by gender, race, or religion and established machinery for enforcement. The Matrimonial Property Act (1976) recognized the work of housewives and equity in a marriage. In

1979, welfare benefits were made equal by gender. Other laws in this period extended rights of free and fair trial to women without discrimination, as in the Evidence Amendment Act (1977).[65]

Overall, in regard to equal rights, this wave of feminism largely succeeded in New Zealand. One cause of its success was a difference in political institutions. Another was a difference in public values and cultures.[66]

Postfeminists Once More: An Era of Individual Striving

After about 1980, the new feminism lost momentum in both countries. It was a story of internal divisions, major defeats, growing opposition, and the alienation of its own base. By the early 1980s, even its leaders were beginning to speak of the new feminist movement in the past tense. Most observers agreed that a new era had begun, though they disagreed on its nature.[67] Surveys showed that 75 to 80 percent of women in the United States and New Zealand were alienated by the excesses of radical feminism and did not wish to be called feminists themselves. But the same surveys showed that most women were deeply committed to women's rights.[68]

Increasingly, attention shifted from collective efforts by formal organizations to individual gains. Measures of achievement included rapid rises by women in academe, private business, and other sectors of society. International surveys of political empowerment by women found that New Zealand's women had a stronger record of achievement than women in any other nation. By 2002, New Zealand's top four offices in politics and law were all held by women. The United States lagged far behind. In that year, when New Zealand women held 31 percent of seats in Parliament, American women held 13 percent of seats in Congress. But in both countries, proportions were rising.[69]

Women in high office were increasingly admired by New Zealand men for their success. The leading example was Helen Clark, a farmer's daughter from Waikato who became a university lecturer in the 1970s, won a seat in Parliament in 1980, headed the Labour Party in opposition, and served three terms as prime minister from 1999 to 2008. Clark came to be highly respected for her skill in leading complex coalition governments, and she kept growing in the esteem of her country. Sir Edmund Hillary said of Helen Clark, "She's always off climbing something. . . . New Zealanders admire that." As a striver and achiever and climber of political heights, still more for the manner of her striving, Clark made herself an example to many young people of both genders.[70]

Feminist and Non-Feminist Movements for Women's Rights: Rhythms of Change in the United States

---

Revolutionary Feminists
Abigail Adams, Mercy Warren, Hannah Winthrop, Judith Murray (ca. 1776–95)

Red Cloaks and Blue Stockings
Hepzibah Swan, Theodosia Burr, Catharine Greene, Anne Royall (ca. 1795–25)

Reform Domesticity
Catharine Maria Sedgwick, Catherine Beecher, Sarah Hale (ca. 1820–40)

Romantic Feminists
Elizabeth Cady Stanton, Lucretia Mott, Lucy Stone (ca. 1840–60)

Emancipated Women
400 Female Civil War Soldiers, Victoria Woodhull, Tennessee Claflin (ca. 1860–75)

Institutional Domesticity
Wellesley College Alice Freeman Palmer (ca. 1875–95)

Progressive Feminists
Carrie Catt, Alice Paul (ca. 1890–1920)

New Women
Mary Pickford, Amelia Earhart, Eleanor Roosevelt, Rosie the Riveter (ca. 1920–45)

Baby Boom Domesticity
Mamie Eisenhower, Grace Kelly (ca. 1945–1960)

Women's Lib Feminists
Betty Friedan, Kate Millett (ca. 1960–80)

Strivers and Achievers
Hillary Rodham Clinton (ca. 1990–2010+)

Feminist and Non-Feminist Movements for Women's Rights: Rhythms of Change in New Zealand

Settler Domesticity
Charlotte Godley,
Clementina Burns, the
Burgess Family
(1840–55)

Romantic Feminists
Maria Rye, Mary Ann
Wilson Müller, Mary
Colclough
(1855–70)

Emancipated Women
Girls' High School, 1871
Kate Edger, Helen
Connon, Caroline
Freeman
(1871–80)

Reform Domesticity
Jenny Wren (Jane Harris)
Adoption Act, 1881
Married Women's
Property Act, 1884
(1880–90)

Progressive Feminists
Women's Suffrage,
Kate Sheppard,
Margaret Sievwright,
Anna Stout
1890–1914

New Women
Te Puea, Jean Batten,
Elizabeth McCombs
(1920–45)

Baby Boom Domesticity
Hilda Ross, Mabel Howard
(1945–65)

Women's Lib Feminists
Consciousness Raising
Equal Rights Laws
Toni Church, Connie
Purdue
(1960–85)

Strivers and Achievers
Helen Clark
(1985–2010+)

In the United States a leading example is Hillary Rodham Clinton. Things were difficult for her in the 1990s. She was viciously attacked by conservative Republicans (as Eleanor Roosevelt had been, and Nancy Pelosi would be) but dealt gracefully and well with adversity, and she began to grow in the esteem of the country. She won election to the United States Senate from New York and earned the respect of male colleagues in both political parties. As secretary of state in the administration of President Barack Obama, she has distinguished herself for strength of intellect, character, and judgment. In 2010, her approval ratings were higher than those of any other major leader in either party.[71] Many other women in both countries also rose to high office. Few thought of themselves as feminists. Most worked for women's rights in other ways and were an inspiration to others by their example.

Conclusion

In both the United States and New Zealand, the history of women's rights developed through a similar sequence of stages. Feminist movements (four of them in North America and three in the South Pacific) each flourished for about twenty or thirty years and were followed by very different eras of individual achievement and in turn by periods of domestic striving.

In New Zealand and the United States, each movement for women's rights drew constructively on its own traditions and values. Through four centuries in what is now the United States, women were always striving for their rights. Their methods changed many times through many generations, but they all shared the heritage of liberty and freedom, and inspired its enlargement. This tradition of liberty and freedom is America's great contribution, and women in their search for equality have immeasurably strengthened it.

New Zealand made a contribution in another way. Raewyn Dalziel, formerly vice-chancellor at the University of Auckland, observed from her close study of women's issues in her country that "justice and natural right had always played a role." She added, "The message about women's suffrage that New Zealand conveyed to the outside world was not only about New Zealand women and New Zealand's political life, but about social and political justice." Dalziel wrote, "Not to be heeded has always been the fate of small nations." But through the years, many people around the world have been paying attention to New Zealand, and to its tradition of fairness, from which we all have much to learn.[72]

RACIST WRONGS

Struggles for Freedom and Justice

> Whenever men and women straighten their backs up,
> they are going somewhere, because a man can't ride
> your back unless it is bent.
>
> —Martin Luther King Jr., 1968

> I will fight the law if it is not justice.
>
> —Whina Cooper, 1981

O F ALL the many challenges to open societies, the most dangerous have been about race and racism. Perceptions of race are very old in the world. Ideologies of racism are something new, an error of modernity.[1] In one of the great ironies of modern history, the first sustained argument for innate racial differences appeared in 1776, when Thomas Jefferson and Thomas Paine proclaimed that all men are created equal. That same year Johann Friedrich Blumenbach published *On the Natural Variety of Humanity*, which argued that all were unequal. He divided humanity into five races, which he was the first to call Caucasian/white, Mongolian/yellow, Malayan/brown, African/black, and American/red. His thesis was that skin color and skull size correlated with variations in mental intelligence and moral judgment.[2]

By the mid-nineteenth century, Blumenbach's idea of race hardened into an ideology of racism. The major work was Joseph Arthur Gobineau's *Essay on the Inequality of the Human Races*, published in four volumes at Paris, 1853–55. The author argued that race is the driver of culture, that the "white race" is the creator of civilization, that the "Aryan race" is superior to other whites, and that inbred aristocrats such as Gobineau himself are the best of all possible Aryans. He also believed that race-mixing was the root of all evil in the world.[3]

Gobineau's book had two major consequences. It provoked a strong antiracist reaction from liberals such as Alexis de Tocqueville.[4] At the same time, it also inspired others to adopt racist ideas and to act upon them in horrific ways. An English translation in 1856 was much admired in the American South. Embattled defenders of race slavery became impassioned advocates of racism as an ideology. A German translation of Gobineau's work was sponsored by Richard Wagner's Bayreuth circle. It inspired four generations of German racists from Wagner himself to Adolf Hitler.[5]

The ideology of racism became a global epidemic. It infected both New Zealand and the United States and many other societies from the mid-nineteenth to the mid-twentieth century. Open societies, with their internal tensions and anxieties, were especially vulnerable. Racism caused some of their worst failures, crimes, and cruelties. It also inspired some of their greatest achievements, in heroic struggles against racism that were often led by its victims.

Racism in the United States and New Zealand, 1877–1920

The long American struggle against racism happened in two great stages. Each continued for more than a century. The first occurred from 1776 to 1865 and was primarily a campaign against race slavery. Its goal was the abolition of forced bondage and the emancipation of slaves. Its cause was liberty in the original sense of *libertas*, independence and autonomy from the will of others.

The founders of the American republic achieved the first general emancipations in the world, when seven states ended slavery after the American Revolution, and prohibited slavery in the Northwest Territories. They were unable to end slavery in the southern states, below the Mason-Dixon line and the Ohio River. That task required another century of struggle and a long and bloody Civil War. Slavery in the United States was finally abolished by the Thirteenth and Fourteenth Amendments to the U.S. Constitution, which were ratified in 1865 and 1868, respectively.

The end of race slavery was the beginning of a second struggle against racism in another form. Throughout much of American history, emancipation was followed by growth of formal segregation. It happened first in the northern states that ended slavery during the Revolution. In Boston, New York, and Philadelphia systems of segregation in

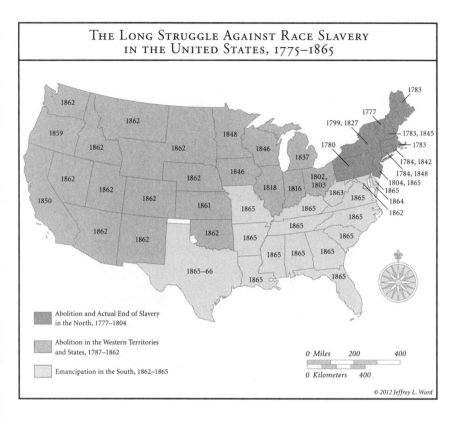

THE LONG STRUGGLE AGAINST RACE SLAVERY
IN THE UNITED STATES, 1775–1865

Abolition and Actual End of Slavery
in the North, 1777–1804

Abolition in the Western Territories
and States, 1787–1862

Emancipation in the South, 1862–1865

0 Miles   200   400

0 Kilometers   400

© 2012 Jeffrey L. Ward

housing, schools, and churches were created during the early republic. Former slaves in the North became the first victims of this new racism that was increasingly virulent, violent, and very cruel.

The same thing happened in the South after the Civil War and the failure of Reconstruction. Former slaves were compelled to live apart in separate neighborhoods, schools, churches, and social institutions. After 1890, segregation hardened into an elaborate structure. Southern courthouses had Jim Crow entrances, Jim Crow seating, Jim Crow elevators, Jim Crow drinking fountains, and even Jim Crow Bibles so that white and black hands and lips would not touch the same book. Jim Crow was costly, in more currencies than one. When it became too expensive, African Americans did without. In *Plessy v. Ferguson* (1896) the U.S. Supreme Court established the rule of "separate but equal." It was a contradiction in terms.[6]

Late in the twentieth century, Afro-American historian Rayford Logan looked backward across four centuries and observed that the "nadir" of race relations in the United States came not during the time of slavery itself but in the period from 1877 to 1920, from the

The U.S. Supreme Court ruled in 1896 that racial segregation was constitutional if public accommodations were "separate but equal." These drinking fountains in a county courthouse at Albany, Georgia (ca. 1962–64), made a mockery of that idea. Further, as the Court later ruled, racial segregation was "inherently unequal."

inauguration of Rutherford Hayes to the retirement of Woodrow Wilson.[7] In the 1930s, about three thousand former slaves were interviewed at length about their lives. Many testified that slavery had been very bad, but the long years after emancipation were worse.[8] In the period from 1877 to the 1920s, a depth of material deprivation took a heavy toll on the human spirit. So also did intolerance, segregation, hostility, hatred, and violence. All of this was rooted in racism, and it was not unique to the South, or to the United States.

Parallel patterns appeared in the treatment of "people of color" in every English-speaking society. Among its victims were people of African origin, Asian descent, and Indians in the United States and Maori in New Zealand. Alfred Simmons, an English immigrant to New Zealand, wrote with great sympathy for the suffering of his own people, but for Maori he had none. In 1879, Simmons observed of

Maori that "the race is fast degenerating, and even now is of little political importance. They will ultimately become a driveling herd of servile beings." In Canterbury he saw a gathering of Maori and described them as "a shabby, mean-looking chattering lot." He wrote that "nine-tenths of the assemblage were ragged and bore the stamp of laziness upon their every movement."[9]

That way of thinking was less common among colonists who met Maori earlier in the nineteenth century, but it became widespread among Pakeha in Simmons's generation, when Maori came to be called the "niggers of New Zealand." Richard Taylor wrote in 1868, "The Maori is constantly being called a nigger and black fellow to his face."[10] People of both cultures testified that Pakeha farmers turned their dogs on the "dirty Maori." Alfred Simmons referred to them as the "conquered and lazy remnant of the New Zealand blacks."[11]

Racism and the Struggle for Freedom in the United States

This time the American struggle against Jim Crow was not primarily for liberty, as the rights of autonomy. It was for freedom, as the rights of belonging in a society of other free people—the right to vote, to hold property, and to be a full citizen of the United States. And it was bitterly opposed by other Americans who were consumed by racism and race hatred. They created an elaborate system of discrimination and maintained it by brutal violence.

The victims fought back. In the United States during the worst years of the 1890s, even when lynching reached its peak of savage violence, former slaves worked tirelessly to organize their communities and to strive for their rights. In this very dark era of southern history, freedom as a universal idea continued to expand. Its primary defenders were African American people themselves. This side of the story is to be found in the chronicles of African American churches, newspapers, and schools.

African American ideas and symbols of freedom were different from those of white Americans. In Atlanta, Andrew Young observed that "no one in the Black community is really excited about the Statue of Liberty. We came here on slave ships, not via Ellis Island."[12] For them an American eagle was not a freedom bird but a predator. At New Bern, North Carolina, in 1896, a black housewife and journalist, Sarah Dudley Pettey, wrote that the American eagle sheltered "beneath his mighty wings all of his white children: while with his talons he ruthlessly claws all who are poor and especially those who trace their lineage to ebony hued parentage."[13]

African Americans adopted other images of freedom. A black newspaper in Charlotte, North Carolina, called itself the *Star of Zion*, a symbol of light. Spirituals celebrated the Star of Zion as the light of freedom.

> I've got the light of Freedom, Lord,
> And I'm going to let it shine!
> Let it shine, let it shine, let it shine!

Even in days of suffering and defeat, the Star of Zion symbolized victory and triumph in the long run, and its rays reached out to everyone on God's earth.[14] Former slaves of the Old South embraced an idea of universal freedom with a large and generous spirit, at a time when southern whites went the other way. While former masters of the South lost their way in the darkness of racism, former slaves sang of the light. The greatness of America's dream passed to them, and was nourished by a forgotten generation of black Americans who lived in the valley of the shadows, between the Civil War and Civil Rights.[15]

Racism and Movements for Maori Justice in the Nineteenth Century: Te Whiti and Tohu

New Zealand Maori also fought against racism and for the welfare of their people, but in a different way. By comparison with Indians and African Americans, they spoke less of freedom and liberty but more of justice and fairness. Maori incorporated those ideas into their heritage and used them as instruments against exploitation and discrimination. In the process, Maori and their ways became New Zealand symbols of the "We Principle," an ideal of reciprocity that was an important reality in its own right.

Leading examples were two spiritual leaders in Taranaki who worked together in the Parihaha for many years, and later moved apart. They were Te Whiti o Rongomai and Tohu Kakahi. Te Whiti had a quiet manner, and much *mana* among Europeans. Tohu was a large man with a "deep grating" voice; Europeans felt threatened by him. Together they became leaders of their people. Older histories describe their strategy as passive resistance. More accurately, it was active nonviolent resistance.

They joined a tradition that advocated nonviolent resistance in many parts of the United States and the British Empire. Among the first to put it in writing was Henry David Thoreau, who developed an idea of "civil disobedience" in America as a way of resisting slavery and the Mexican War. An English biographer showed Thoreau's pamphlet to Mahatma Gandhi, and from Gandhi it found its way to Martin Luther King Jr.

In New Zealand Te Whiti and Tohu were very much in this tradition and autonomously invented their own version of nonviolent resistance. Their strategy had mixed results. It failed to stop the taking of Maori lands, but it succeeded in other ways. Te Whiti and Tohu both understood the immense political advantage of having right on their side and putting their oppressors clearly in the wrong. They did not end oppression but created a framework within which oppression could not flourish and in the end would die. At the same time, these leaders helped to revive the spirit of Maori culture. They struggled against processes of cultural decay and worked to preserve Maori spiritual values and Maori faith in themselves. In this they succeeded brilliantly. Te Whiti and Tohu kept their culture alive in a period of loss and danger and linked it to the pursuit of justice.

Racism and the Maori Struggle for Justice: Apirana Ngata, 1890–1943

New Zealand did not have the equivalent of Jim Crow in its fullest sense. Segregation of Maori and Pakeha did not exist in law. Intermarriage was always lawful and often occurred between Pakeha and Maori. Nothing in New Zealand's history compared with American miscegenation laws that made intermarriage a crime in many states. New Zealand had nothing like the elaborate structures of racial segregation that were enacted and enforced against African Americans in the South, Asians on the Pacific coast, and American Indians in the Dakotas. From the late nineteenth century, all of these American systems were as sweeping as Jim Crow laws in the South.[16]

Racism in New Zealand took other forms. It existed more as a matter of custom than law, but in some places the customary effect was much the same. An example was the South Auckland town of Pukekohe, which confined Maori to a neighborhood called "the reservation" and excluded them from pubs, cinemas, and swimming baths. All of this was firmly established in the early twentieth century and persisted as late as the 1950s. Historian James Belich described Pukekohe as "the capital of New Zealand racism." It was not unique. Racism in New Zealand could be as ugly as anywhere else.[17]

Many people fought against it, and most were Maori. At the turn of the twentieth century, a new generation of leaders called themselves

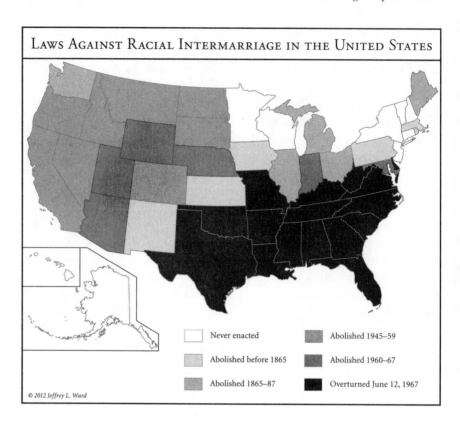

LAWS AGAINST RACIAL INTERMARRIAGE IN THE UNITED STATES

☐ Never enacted	▨ Abolished 1945–59
▨ Abolished before 1865	▨ Abolished 1960–67
▨ Abolished 1865–87	■ Overturned June 12, 1967

© 2012 Jeffrey L. Ward

the Young Maori Party. Among them was Apirana Ngata, the first
Maori to graduate from a New Zealand college, at Canterbury in 1894.
He served in Parliament from 1905 to 1943 and formed alliances with
Pakeha leaders such as Gordon Coates. Ngata worked tirelessly to protect Maori land, support Maori agriculture, raise money for schools,
strengthen tribal government, preserve Maori culture, and nourish
support for Maori arts. He encouraged the teaching of Maori language
and at the same time established programs where young Maori could
improve their English. The object was to strengthen Maori identity
and to improve relations with Pakeha. Belich described Ngata's
strategy as "brilliantly subversive cooperation." He sought to build a
spirit of reciprocity that combined traditional Maori ethics with
Pakeha ideas of fairness and justice.[18]

   After the era of extreme racism, relations between Maori and
Pakeha slowly (very slowly) began to improve. In two world wars, the
military service of Maori troops did much to diminish racist prejudice
among Pakeha. Maori fought with honor in small groups at Gallipoli
and in the large Pioneer Battalion on the Western Front from 1916.

Racism also existed in New Zealand, ca. 1890–1945, and Maori strove against it. A great leader was Sir Apirana Ngata, who worked tirelessly for Maori culture, land, and pride. Here he leads a Haka at Waitangi on the centennial of the treaty in 1940.

Even more in the public eye was the Maori Battalion in the Second World War. Maori champions in sport also had an impact—as did Tom Ellison, a Ngai Tahu athlete who was chosen captain of New Zealand's first national rugby team in 1902.

Prejudice and discrimination persisted in New Zealand. The taking of Maori lands continued well into the twentieth century. Ngata and others tried to stop it. The Maori Land Council was organized in 1900 and slowed the loss of land. But the Native Land Act of 1909 allowed Maori land to be sold freely, and losses accelerated yet again. Racism was often a mask for economic gain in New Zealand during the early twentieth century, as in the United States and through much of the world.

The Revolution Against Racism: The Second World War as a Pivotal Moment

A turning point in both countries came with the Second World War, and a great awakening to the terrible crimes that Fascist regimes committed in the name of race. During the war, Raphael Lemkin, a legal scholar at Duke University, coined the word *genocide* to describe the deliberate destruction of an entire race of human beings. Fascist movements in many forms, including Japanese militarism, are thought to have killed between forty million and fifty million people between 1922 and 1945. All of this awakened the conscience of the world to the evil of racism.[19] Many Americans shared that discovery, slowly at first but with growing momentum. A major factor was the long struggle against Communist regimes that were responsible for the deaths of 80 million people—twice the toll of Fascism. Their victims were conceived as class enemies and killed in new forms of genocide. Americans fought these murderous regimes in the cause of liberty and freedom. This longer struggle, from 1946 to 1989, had an effect similar to that of World War II. It caused Americans to ask if ideas of liberty and freedom were for export only.[20]

The result was a series of countervailing movements that began to accelerate very rapidly in the 1950s. On the one side were many Americans of every creed and color and region who demanded the birthrights of all citizens—in the name of freedom. On the other side were many Americans, often white and southern but of every class and region, who resisted these ideas and demanded the right to live as they had done, secure in their own accustomed ways—in the name of liberty.[21]

One of America's great poets, Langston Hughes, wrote about this great collision between liberty and freedom:

> There are words like *Freedom*
> Sweet and wonderful to say.
> On my heart-strings freedom sings
> All day everyday.
> There are words like *Liberty*
> That almost make me cry.
> If you had known what I knew
> You would know why.[22]

Race prejudice remained very strong in some parts of the United States after the Second World War. Even President Harry Truman shared the racial prejudices of his time and place, and often expressed them in his early life. But after 1945 his attitudes changed. Part of it was about politics. Truman needed the votes of African Americans. Another part was about the Cold War. Soviet propaganda made very effective use of Jim Crow. But mostly it was a genuine change of heart, of a sort that many Americans experienced after World War II.

In 1947, Harry Truman gave a speech at the Lincoln Memorial. He wrote to his sister, "Momma won't like what I say because I wind up quoting old Abe. But I believe what I say and I'm hopeful we may implement it."[23] Truman also created a Civil Rights Committee, which in 1947 issued a major document called *To Secure These Rights.*

A pivot point in the history of racism was World War II, when the world at last awakened to its evils. Under heavy pressure from Afro-American leaders, Franklin Roosevelt issued an executive order banning racial discrimination in war industries. The result was a revolution in economic opportunity, for those welders in New Britain, Connecticut, 1943, and millions of others.

It proposed a sweeping program of reform: desegregation in the armed forces, a Civil Rights Division in the Department of Justice, a U.S. Commission on Civil Rights, tough federal laws against lynching, an end to poll taxes, and new statutes that restored voting rights to African Americans and other minorities.[24]

While Republicans and conservative Democrats controlled Congress, no legislation was possible. Truman took action by executive order. As early as December 1947, he authorized the Justice Department to support a major civil rights case against restrictive covenants in real estate. The result was a Supreme Court decision, in *Shelly v. Kraemer,* that restrictive covenants were unconstitutional. Other cases followed: *Henderson v. U.S.* (1950), a Supreme Court decision against Jim Crow in railroad dining cars. In 1952, Truman's Justice Department filed the most important briefs in the case of *Brown v. Board of Education,* on Jim Crow in education, and *Bolling v. Sharpe,* on segregation in the District of Columbia.[25]

In 1948, as Truman introduced military conscription for the Cold War, he faced a major challenge from Philip Randolph, who organized a Committee Against Jim Crow in Military Service. Randolph met with the president on March 28, 1948, and threatened demonstrations against the draft unless segregation ended in the armed forces. On July 26, 1948, Truman issued an executive order calling for racial integration of the armed forces. By 1950, the air force was the first of the services to abolish the color line. The army

The Long Struggle Against Racial Segregation in the United States, 1950–2000

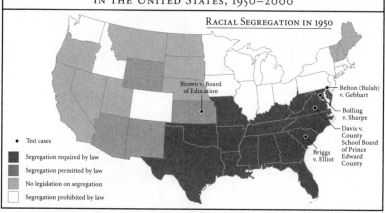

RACIAL SEGREGATION IN 1950

Brown v. Board of Education

Belton (Bulah) v. Gebhart

Bolling v. Sharpe

Davis v. County School Board of Prince Edward County

Briggs v. Elliot

- Test cases
- Segregation required by law
- Segregation permitted by law
- No legislation on segregation
- Segregation prohibited by law

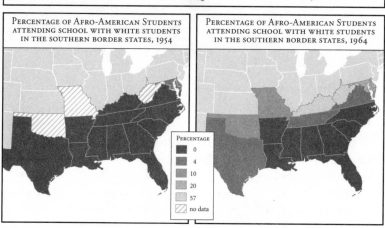

PERCENTAGE OF AFRO-AMERICAN STUDENTS ATTENDING SCHOOL WITH WHITE STUDENTS IN THE SOUTHERN BORDER STATES, 1954

PERCENTAGE OF AFRO-AMERICAN STUDENTS ATTENDING SCHOOL WITH WHITE STUDENTS IN THE SOUTHERN BORDER STATES, 1964

PERCENTAGE
- 0
- 4
- 10
- 20
- 57
- no data

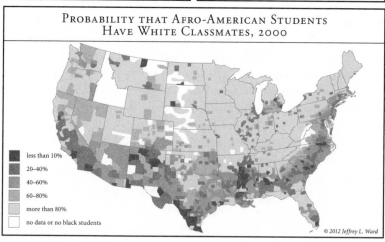

Probability that Afro-American Students Have White Classmates, 2000

- less than 10%
- 20–40%
- 40–60%
- 60–80%
- more than 80%
- no data or no black students

© 2012 Jeffrey L. Ward

followed quickly, and found in the Korean War that integrated combat units were more effective than segregated units. The navy moved slowly, but Truman succeeded in integrating the American armed forces with high success.

President Dwight Eisenhower was less supportive of civil rights, but when segregationists defied the courts, he sent federal troops to Arkansas in support of integration, and a Democratic Congress in 1957 passed a Civil Rights Act, the first since Reconstruction. The Civil Rights Commission and the Civil Rights Division of the Justice Department intervened actively in the cause of freedom.[26] On the right, Senator Strom Thurmond tried to stop the Civil Rights Act of 1957 by a personal filibuster that lasted more than twenty-four hours, the longest on record. He failed, in part because many Americans had begun to join grassroots movements for freedom that spread rapidly through the country.

Riding for Freedom in America

The civil rights movement had thousands of leaders. Throughout the country, men and women came forward with high courage, often at risk to their lives. When they were beaten, or killed, others replaced them in growing numbers.

Among these many leaders, one man was preeminent. In the few years that were given to him, Martin Luther King Jr. stamped his image on this great cause. Others were more important as organizers, but he became the spiritual leader of the civil rights movement and a symbol of its values. He also shaped its tactics in a way that made a difference.[27]

Many stories might be told about Martin Luther King Jr. One of them centers on a moment of contingency. When black leaders in Montgomery, Alabama, organized a bus boycott to protest racism, they searched for a leader who could unite their community. King was a new minister had just come to town. He hadn't been in Montgomery long enough to make enemies and happened to be in the right place at the right time.

He was also the right man. Another story might be told about long preparation and large goals. It is about his Christian upbringing, his early experience of injustice in the South, the example of his father, and a long intellectual journey. He rejected Marxist materialism, its exploitation of individual people, and its rejection of liberty and freedom. "To deprive man of freedom," he wrote, "is to relegate him to the status of the thing." He read

In 1954, the U.S. Supreme Court's ruling against school segregation inspired many Afro-Americans. Among them was Rosa Parks, who in 1955 challenged Jim Crow on a bus in Montgomery, Alabama. Thousands rallied to her support, in a great victory against racism. She credited the Court's decision as an important part of her motivation.

Nietzsche, Bentham, Mill, Hobbes, and Rousseau. None of them spoke to his condition.[28]

Then he met Dr. Mordecai Johnson, president of Howard University, who was just back from India and talked about the work of Gandhi. King recalled the "electrifying" moment when he discovered Gandhi's idea of *satyagraha* (truth and love as force), as a way of linking the teachings of Jesus to the task of fighting for the rights of the dispossessed. That revelation led King to a new idea of freedom, and a new way of reaching it.[29]

On December 2, 1955, Martin Luther King was working in his Montgomery parsonage when the telephone rang. He was asked to make a speech on the bus boycott at the big Holt Street Baptist Church.[30] The African American citizens of Montgomery turned out, and filled the streets for five blocks around the church. Martin Luther King had twenty minutes to gather his ideas, and no time to put them on paper. He wrote later that it was "the most decisive speech of my life."

It was a long speech, rich in the rhetorical cadences of black preaching, and addressed to the nation and the world. Martin Luther King told the story of Rosa Parks. "There comes a time," he said, "when people get tired of being trampled over by the iron feet of oppression. There comes a time, my friends, when people get tired of being plunged across the abyss of humiliation. . . . There comes a time when people get tired."

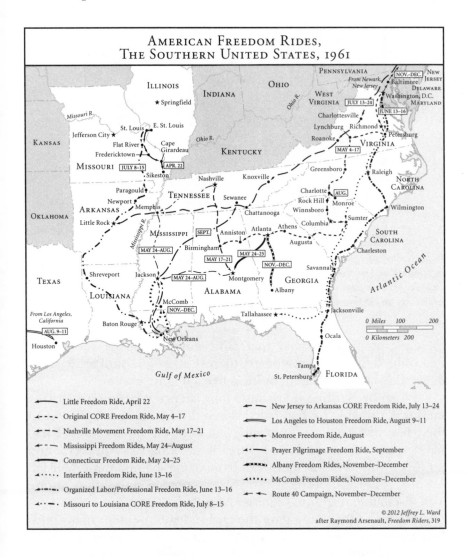

AMERICAN FREEDOM RIDES,
THE SOUTHERN UNITED STATES, 1961

- ▬▬ Little Freedom Ride, April 22
- ◀- - - Original CORE Freedom Ride, May 4–17
- ◀- - Nashville Movement Freedom Ride, May 17–21
- ◀- - Mississippi Freedom Rides, May 24–August
- ▬▬ Connecticut Freedom Ride, May 24–25
- ◀····· Interfaith Freedom Ride, June 13–16
- ◀-·-·- Organized Labor/Professional Freedom Ride, June 13–16
- ◀·-·- Missouri to Louisiana CORE Freedom Ride, July 8–15
- ◀- - New Jersey to Arkansas CORE Freedom Ride, July 13–24
- ◀═══ Los Angeles to Houston Freedom Ride, August 9–11
- ◀◀◀ Monroe Freedom Ride, August
- ◀·── Prayer Pilgrimage Freedom Ride, September
- ◀▪▪▪▪ Albany Freedom Rides, November–December
- ◀▪▪▪▪ McComb Freedom Rides, November–December
- ◀- ◀- Route 40 Campaign, November–December

© 2012 Jeffrey L. Ward
after Raymond Arsenault, *Freedom Riders*, 319

He talked about the boycott as part of a larger cause. "We, the disinherited of this land," he said, "we who have been oppressed so long, are tired of going through the long night of captivity. And now we are reaching out for the daybreak of freedom." He spoke of freedom and justice and love. Most of all he talked about the importance of doing the right thing in the right way. "Let us be Christian in all of our actions."

There was an air of optimism and certainty in his message. "We are not wrong!" he said. "We are not wrong in what we are doing. If we are wrong, the Supreme Court of this nation is wrong. If we are wrong, the Constitution of the United States is wrong. If we are wrong, God almighty is wrong. If we are wrong, Jesus of Nazareth was

*In the summer of 1961, hundreds of "freedom riders" boarded buses to protest persistent seg-
regation in the American South. Most were young black students. Some were met with savage
violence, but their freedom rides awakened the nation and also John and Robert Kennedy who
reluctantly led the federal government to the support of civil rights.*

merely a utopian dreamer that came down to earth. And we are
determined here in Montgomery to work and fight until justice runs
down like water, and righteousness like a mighty stream."[31]

When he finished there was a long silence. Martin Luther King
sat down, thinking he had failed. Then thousands of people rose to
their feet and began to applaud, and kept on applauding. "I had
never seen such enthusiasm for freedom," King remembered, "and
yet this enthusiasm was tempered by amazing self-discipline." He led
his new congregation in a spirit that combined unyielding resolve
with discipline, restraint, dignity, and calm.[32]

Martin Luther King gave the civil rights movement many gifts.
One was his gift of serious thought, which gave meaning to his cause.
Another was nonviolence, and the rule of Christian love and "beloved
community" that sought to bring whites and black together. A third
was a depth of caring for others, the old Christian *caritas*, which Martin Luther King communicated by actions more than words. A young
civil rights worker, John Lewis, remembered a moment on the march
to Selma, Alabama: "I had been hurt, had received a concussion, and
we were walking along in the rain, and he took off a brown cap from
his head and told me, 'John, you need to wear this cap, you've been
hurt.' It was a small thing, but it meant so much to me."[33]

Most important was Martin Luther King's vision of freedom.
Always he appealed to principles of freedom. He made the word itself
into an icon. In some images, a "freedom march" was led by a young

The Montgomery bus boycott gave America a new leader in Martin Luther King Jr.. He led the civil rights movement toward nonviolence and inspired the world with his dream of freedom from racism. Always the American movement was cast in terms of freedom. New Zealand movements against racism gave more attention to fairness and justice. Here King and his son remove a cross that was burned in front of his home.

African American woman, dressed with dignity, holding a simple sign that bore a single word: "Freedom." In other signs it was "Freedom Now." But always it was freedom as the ancient idea of belonging, a principle that brought free people together in love and understanding.

Martin Luther King sometimes talked of equality too. He embraced the old American ideas of equal rights, equality of esteem, equal protection, and equality of opportunity. His notion of equality was a positive idea of leveling the playing field. But mainly he talked of freedom. In his greatest speech, "I Have a Dream," the dream was freedom. His heavy stress on freedom differed from other groups in the civil rights movement, such as the Congress of Racial Equality. Martin Luther King understood a deep truth about America, as many of his critics did not. Equality divides Americans; freedom unites them.[34]

Martin Luther King's contribution was also to give these ideas an image that spread round the world. Articulate and telegenic, he himself became a symbol of the civil fights movement. The media centered its coverage on him.[35]

The more Martin Luther King was admired in the world, the more he was hated by racists in the South. While decent people looked the other way, southern racists made assassination and terror into instruments of power. Among the most savage were a band of Ku Klux Klansmen in Natchez, Mississippi, who gloried in the name of the Cottonmouth Moccasin Gang. In 1966, they resolved to kill a black man (any black man) with one purpose in mind: to draw King onto their ground so that they could assassinate him. In cold blood they murdered an elderly black caretaker named Ben Chester White who happened to be in the wrong place. The Cottonmouth Moccasin Gang failed in their larger object, but others in the South kept trying. In 1968, Martin Luther King was caught in another trap and murdered in Memphis, Tennessee, where he had gone to support a strike of garbage collectors.[36]

The death of Martin Luther King was only the beginning of his career as a symbol of freedom. People everywhere rallied to his cause. Every American state made a holiday of Martin Luther King's birthday (Arizona after long delay), and Congress made it a national holiday as well. His image became an icon of freedom for all the world. It inspired other movements, and enlarged the meaning of freedom into an idea of Christian love for all humanity, even for oppressors.[37]

Marching for Justice in New Zealand

While Afro-Americans were striving against racism in the United States, a parallel struggle was mounted by New Zealand Maori. After the Second World War, Maori who moved to Auckland found themselves victims of racial discrimination in housing. A new national organization called the Maori Women's Welfare League was formed in 1951. Its president was Whina Cooper. One of her first projects was to survey Maori housing and land in Auckland. She was constantly in the news and raised awareness of discrimination and racism through the country. She also appealed for justice, much as Martin Luther King for freedom.

Maori were facing new threats in the 1950s and '60s. Even then land was still being taken from them. A Town and Country Planning Act in 1953 extended zoning regulations to Maori lands. A Rating

Act in 1967 required compulsory sale of Maori land for any unpaid taxes, and the Maori Affairs Amendment Act authorized the seizure of Maori lands that were not used in ways Pakeha regarded as productive. From 1965 to 1975, another 1.5 million acres were taken from Maori.[38] These events inspired a newly invigorated movement in 1968, and a group called the Maori Organisation on Human Rights. It demanded recovery of lands and assets under the Treaty of Waitangi, and a cultural program for the revival of Maori language.

The critical moment came in 1975. Another new association, focusing on land rights, came together in Panmure at the home of Joseph Cooper, son of Whina Cooper. The purpose was not only to raise consciousness of wrongs but also to seek remedies. Most members were described as "young urban radicals" in Auckland, but they asked Whina Cooper, who had just turned eighty that year, to be their leader. She suggested that they call their group Te Roopu Ote Matakite, "those with foresight," and their purpose should be "to help the blind," who "haven't the perception to see the future."[39]

Together they planned a great Maori Land March from Cape Reinga on the northern tip of the North Island to the Parliament buildings in Wellington, by a route that would take them about seven hundred miles. It was conceived as a Maori *hokoi*, a nonviolent march to call attention to the loss of Maori land from the mid-nineteenth century, even to the present. It was designed to link young activists and radicals with entire Maori communities as it marched from one marae to another. An important object was to demonstrate Maori unity and resolve. It was meant to be a demand not only for the land itself but also fairness and justice.

It was done on a very large scale. An attempt was made to engage the entire Maori population of many ages and both genders. Whina Cooper employed many symbols and rituals of deep meaning to Maori. The marchers carried traditional Maori land stakes, and they composed a special song of unity. Whina Cooper had her son draw up a petition called a "memorial of rights." It combined a memory of tradition with a history of loss and made connections to the Treaty of Waitangi, which some were calling the Magna Carta of New Zealand. The memorial was signed by two hundred chiefs at marae along the way. For Pakeha politicians in Wellington there was also a Petition of Grievances, which summarized 150 years of anger and frustration over land losses. It was signed by sixty thousand people.

The march began on September 14, 1975. It was led by Whina Cooper herself, eighty years old and very arthritic, walking painfully with a cane in one hand and holding the hand of a small Maori girl

*In 1975, Maori mounted a major cam-
paign to protect their land from further
seizures. Their leader was Whina Cooper,
who led a great land march from the top of
North Island to Parliament in Wellington.
She awakened many New Zealanders to the
existence of racism in their country*

in the other—a living symbol of enormous power, deeply moving to
Maori and Pakeha alike. Something near to thirty thousand or forty
thousand Maori joined the march along the way. Many Pakeha
watched with respect and admiration. Some offered food and drink.
A few acted otherwise. The head of the Auckland Harbor Bridge
Authority refused to allow the marchers to pass, but Whina Cooper
talked with him, and he became a supporter of the march. A few infuriated Pakeha demonstrated against the march and scattered
sharp shells in the streets of Wellington. They were a small minority.

The marchers moved quickly, with Whina Cooper riding much
of the distance, but also walking every day. Many young Maori
marched the entire way, seven hundred miles in thirty days, faster
than the standard pace of New Zealand infantry on long route
marches. On Monday, October 13, 1975, they entered Wellington
exactly on schedule. In falling rain, Whina Cooper led five thousand
Maori marchers, who completely filled the four-lane highway into
the capital. They entered Parliament grounds singing a song of unity
and were received by Labour Prime Minister Bill Rowling.

Afterward, Maori were not of one mind about their next step.
One group of young marchers camped on the Parliament grounds
for two months, much against Whina Cooper's advice. Some radicals

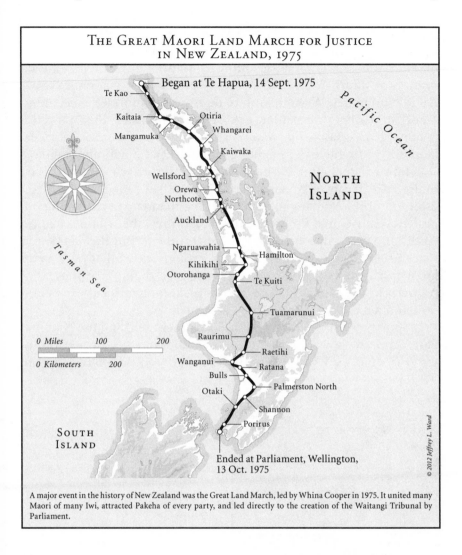

THE GREAT MAORI LAND MARCH FOR JUSTICE IN NEW ZEALAND, 1975

Began at Te Hapua, 14 Sept. 1975

Te Kao

Pacific Ocean

Kaitaia — Otiria

Mangamuka — Whangarei

Kaiwaka

Wellsford

Orewa

Northcote

Auckland

NORTH ISLAND

Ngaruawahia — Hamilton

Kihikihi

Otorohanga — Te Kuiti

Tasman Sea

Tuamarunui

0 Miles   100   200

0 Kilometers   200

Raurimu

Raetihi

Wanganui

Ratana

Bulls

Otaki

Palmerston North

Shannon

Porirus

SOUTH ISLAND

Ended at Parliament, Wellington, 13 Oct. 1975

© 2012 Jeffrey L. Ward

A major event in the history of New Zealand was the Great Land March, led by Whina Cooper in 1975. It united many Maori of many Iwi, attracted Pakeha of every party, and led directly to the creation of the Waitangi Tribunal by Parliament.

turned against her for not being more militant, much as other radicals in the American civil rights movement were unhappy about Martin Luther King. But in New Zealand one of her critics, Eva Rickard, said, "The Maori land march would not have come about if it hadn't been for that old lady. She had the mana and the charisma."[40]

Righting Wrongs in New Zealand: The Waitangi Tribunal

The Great Land March put heavy pressure on a failing Labour government. It also created an opportunity for Matiu Rata, minister of Maori affairs and another extraordinary leader. Born at Te Hapua in the far north, Rata had been a Maori seaman, trade unionist, and Labour Party leader. He combined an engaging and conciliatory manner with a complete devotion to Maori rights. In 1974, Rata drafted a Maori Act, which reversed part of the National Party's hated land policy. Without fanfare he returned more Crown land to Maori in a single term than any previous minister. Rata played a major role in establishing Maori as an official language of New Zealand and took the lead in making Waitangi Day a national holiday.

Immediately after Whina Cooper's land march in 1975, Rata drafted the Treaty of Waitangi Act. This new law called for the establishment of the Waitangi Tribunal, with a mandate to investigate injustices that violated the treaty. It was said that "the tribunal had no teeth" and was only advisory to the government. But Rata answered that the "grievances were sufficiently strongly based that no government worth its salt would be able to ignore them once they were properly investigated." Matiu Rata was reckoning on a culture of fairness and a feeling for justice in New Zealand.[41]

Shortly afterward the Labour government fell, and the National Party came to power, led by Robert Muldoon, who showed no interest in Maori grievances. In 1978, he ordered the police and the

Matiu Rata, minister of Maori Affairs, used the momentum of the land march to draft a new Treaty of Waitangi Act. It created the Waitangi Tribunal, with far-reaching changes for New Zealand.

army to remove the Ngati Whatua from their ancestral lands on Bastion Point by force and launched early morning raids against groups of Pacific Islanders. Muldoon also allowed South Africa's apartheid rugby team to tour New Zealand, after Maori players had been refused entry into that racist nation. This controversy exploded into angry violence. Tom Brooking remembers it as "the greatest civil unrest in New Zealand since the wars of the 1860s."[42]

Through all of this strife the Maori Tribunal got little attention. But in 1980 it got a leader. Edward Taihakurei Durie became chief judge of the Maori Land Court and chair of the Waitangi Tribunal, the first Maori to hold those offices. A careful craftsman of the law, he moved with great deliberation. The Waitangi Tribunal acted in two major cases. One was the development of a Motunui synthetic fuels plant of high priority to Muldoon. Its sewage would have pumped polluting wastes into the fishing grounds of the Ti Ati Awa of Taranaki. The Waitangi Tribunal found for the Maori fishermen, won the support of Maori and environmental groups, and stopped the pollution.

Then the tribunal acted boldly in an even more prominent case, about contested lands on Bastion Point. It recommended a settlement of NZ$3 million to the Ngati Whatua, a halt to development in luxury housing, and preservation of the land as a park under the control of the Maori Iwi whose land it was. Philippa Mein Smith writes that the Waitangi Tribunal was "brought to life" by this case, which "transformed the status of a Constitutional instrument under the 1975 Treaty of Waitangi Act, and Maoridom was abuzz."[43]

Another major expansion came in 1985, after the Labour Party returned to power. Its minister of justice, Geoffrey Palmer, enlarged the jurisdiction of the Waitangi Tribunal to review injustices as early in 1840 and to make recommendations for redress. This it did with great energy. Hundreds of claims were submitted, and large numbers of scholars were employed in a great labor of historical research that turned out to be more complex than anyone imagined. One solution was forbidden. No land could be returned to Maori from Pakeha families who had held it in some cases for generations. But courts and governments found other forms of compensation in Crown lands, franchises, and cash payments. In other acts, the Waitangi Tribunal ruled in 1986 that the Maori language was *taonga*, a "prized possession" protected under Article II of the treaty. The New Zealand government recognized Maori as an official language and launched a large program in its support.

Waitangi Tribunal Reports

As at July 2011

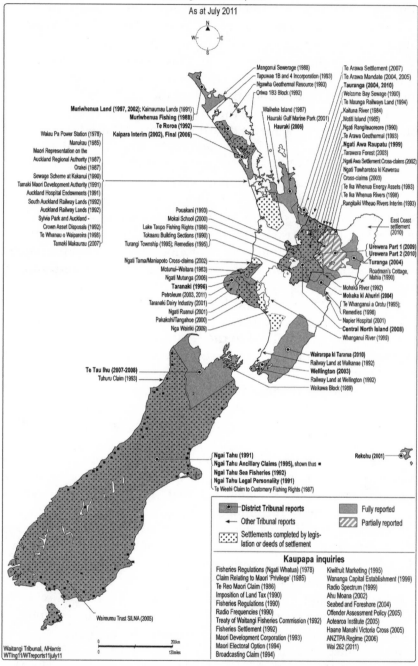

Mangonui Sewerage (1988)
Tapuwae 1B and 4 Incorporation (1993)
Ngawha Geothermal Resource (1993)
Oriwa 1B3 Block (1992)

Te Arawa Settlement (2007)
Te Arawa Mandate (2004, 2005)
Tauranga (2004, 2010)
Welcome Bay Sewage (1990)
Te Maunga Railways Land (1994)
Kaituna River (1984)
Motiti Island (1985)
Ngati Rangiteaoreore (1990)
Te Arawa Geothermal (1993)
Ngati Awa Raupatu (1999)
Tarawera Forest (2003)
Ngati Awa Settlement Cross-claims (2002)
Ngati Tuwharetoa ki Kawerau
Cross-claims (2003)
Te Ika Whenua Energy Assets (1993)
Te Ika Whenua Rivers (1998)
Rangitaiki Wheao Rivers Interim (1993)

Waiheke Island (1987)
Hauraki Gulf Marine Park (2001)
Hauraki (2006)

Muriwhenua Land (1997, 2002); Kaimaumau Lands (1991)
Muriwhenua Fishing (1988)
Te Roroa (1992)
Kaipara Interim (2002), Final (2006)

Waiau Pa Power Station (1978)
Manukau (1985)
Maori Representation on the
Auckland Regional Authority (1987)
Orakei (1987)
Sewage Scheme at Kakanui (1990)
Tamaki Maori Development Authority (1991)
Auckland Hospital Endowments (1991)
South Auckland Railway Lands (1992)
Auckland Railway Lands (1992)
Sylvia Park and Auckland -
Crown Asset Disposals (1992)
Te Whanau o Waipareira (1998)
Tamaki Makaurau (2007)

East Coast
settlement
(2010)

Urewera Part 1 (2009)
Urewera Part 2 (2010)
Turanga (2004)

Pouakani (1993)
Mokai School (2000)
Lake Taupo Fishing Rights (1986)
Tokaanu Building Sections (1990)
Turangi Township (1995); Remedies (1995)

Roadman's Cottage,
Mahia (1990)

Mohaka River (1992)
Mohaka ki Ahuriri (2004)
Te Whanganui a Orotu (1995);
Remedies (1998)
Napier Hospital (2001)
Central North Island (2008)
Whanganui River (1999)

Ngati Tama/Maniapoto Cross-claims (2002)
Motunui–Waitara (1983)
Ngati Mutunga (2006)
Taranaki (1996)
Petroleum (2003, 2011)
Taranaki Dairy Industry (2001)
Ngati Ruanui (2001)
Pakakohi/Tangahoe (2000)
Nga Wairiki (2009)

Te Tau Ihu (2007-2008)
Tuhuru Claim (1993)

Wairarapa ki Tararua (2010)
Railway Land at Waikanae (1992)
Wellington (2003)
Railway Land at Wellington (1992)
Waikawa Block (1989)

Rekohu (2001)

Ngai Tahu (1991)
Ngai Tahu Ancillary Claims (1995), shown thus ■
Ngai Tahu Sea Fisheries (1992)
Ngai Tahu Legal Personality (1991)
Te Weehi Claim to Customary Fishing Rights (1987)

Waimumu Trust SILNA (2005)

- ● - District Tribunal reports
- ← - Other Tribunal reports
- Settlements completed by legis-
lation or deeds of settlement

Fully reported
Partially reported

Kaupapa inquiries

Fisheries Regulations (Ngati Whatua) (1978)
Claim Relating to Maori 'Privilege' (1985)
Te Reo Maori Claim (1986)
Imposition of Land Tax (1990)
Fisheries Regulations (1990)
Radio Frequencies (1990)
Treaty of Waitangi Fisheries Commission (1992)
Fisheries Settlement (1992)
Maori Development Corporation (1993)
Maori Electoral Option (1994)
Broadcasting Claim (1994)

Kiwifruit Marketing (1995)
Wananga Capital Establishment (1999)
Radio Spectrum (1999)
Ahu Moana (2002)
Seabed and Foreshore (2004)
Offender Assessment Policy (2005)
Aotearoa Institute (2005)
Haane Manahi Victoria Cross (2005)
ANZTPA Regime (2006)
Wai 262 (2011)

Waitangi Tribunal, *NHarris*
WTIng11/WTreports11july11

0   200km
0   120miles

The Waitangi Tribunal began with limited powers of inquiry into treaty violations. Its jurisdiction was enlarged by its chairman, Edward Taihakurie Durie, and again by Geoffrey Palmer in 1986. This map in 2011 summarizes the many actions that flowed from its findings.

Yet another surprising expansion came when the National Party returned to power. Its minister of justice, Douglas Graham, strongly supported major recommendations from the tribunal. One group of cases called Sealord was about the fisheries, which had been guaranteed to Maori by the Waitangi Treaty. Sweeping settlements in 1992 gave many tribes a large share of the fishing industry. Another group of claims sought redress for confiscation of lands in the North Island. These settlements included the grant of Crown lands, a large cash payment, and a formal apology by Queen Elizabeth II. A third settlement was with the Ngai Tahu, the tribe that claimed most of the South Island. A complex solution was worked out. More than twenty-five settlements followed by 2010, with a total value of a billion New Zealand dollars.[44]

In 2010, a conservative National government was in power and proposed a major change in the Waitangi Tribunal. Prime Minister John Key gave a speech on Waitangi Day that combined the customary rhetoric of New Zealand with a new message from his conservative party. He began by celebrating New Zealand's traditions and said that "we share a respect for the rule of law, for property rights, and for a basic sense of fairness in which Jack is as good as his neighbour." He noted that all governments and most parties had supported the Waitangi Tribunal. But when Key came to office in 2008, sixty claims were before the tribunal. They were being settled at a rate of 1.6 claims a year. At that rate, he estimated that claims presently before the tribunal would not be settled until 2048. The prime minister said, "We share a desire to complete this redress process," and pledged that they would try to do so by concluding "just and durable treaty settlements by 2014."[45]

Other New Zealand leaders were growing weary of the Waitangi Tribunal. Even Edward Durie remarked on the growing complexity of proceedings. He complained that Maori tribes were no longer at the center of the process and that proceedings were increasingly dominated by lawyers on all sides. Others were concerned about rising legal costs.

The Waitangi Tribunal has been constantly criticized for going too far, or not far enough. But its work has had a major impact. Paul Temm calls the tribunal "the conscience of the nation." It has given new depth of meaning to New Zealand's founding principles of fairness and justice. As New Zealanders think about what might follow the Waitangi Tribunal, those same principles are in active discussion once again. If the tribunal is abolished, it is likely that some other institutional process will follow it.[46]

Righting Wrongs in the United States:
The Indian Claims Commission

In the United States during the twentieth century, there was growing recognition that wrongs had been done to the American Indians by broken treaties, stolen lands, corrupted leaders, cruel wars, and trails of tears. The results were several movements for reform. The Dawes Severalty Act, which had divided tribal lands among individual holders, was a disaster for American Indians and led to very large losses of land. The "Indian New Deal" and the Indian Reorganization Act of 1934 sought another remedy by supporting rights of self-government modeled on traditional ideas of political rights, liberty, freedom, and tribal democracy. It combined that effort with programs for education and economic development.[47] The experience of the Second World War inspired another reform movement for Indians, as it had done for Afro-Americans. In 1946, the United States Indian Claims Commission was created to settle claims for lost Indian lands under 370 tribal treaties made by the federal government. It converted land claims to monetary equivalents and made some progress, but was terminated in 1978 with its work unfinished.[48] Much litigation followed, with mixed results.

Another American attempt at justice was an attempt to settle disputes under the Indian Trust, which has been administered by the federal government. The Indian Trust holds about fifty-six million acres of land for millions of individual owners and many tribes—an immense tangle of "fractionated titles and holders." The trust was mismanaged for many years after it was created by the Dawes Severalty Act, but huge quantities of records have been carefully preserved in caves under Kansas City. In 1996, many plaintiffs sued the Interior Department, claiming that they had been cheated out of $48 billion. Federal courts agreed on everything except the magnitude of losses. The Obama administration proposed a settlement of $3.4 billion, which was accepted by the plaintiffs and the courts. If Congress approves (which may or may not happen), each claimant will get $1,000 plus a sum based on the size of the holding. A new system of consolidated accounts and improved accounting will be created, and an Educational Trust Fund will be established for Indian children. It is a serious and genuine attempt at justice, but most Indians have no trust accounts and will get nothing, and for those who do, in the words of a federal employee, it "won't likely change much of anything—it won't raise Indians out of poverty." Nothing in the history of the United States has come close to the Waitangi Tribunal and its comprehensive quest for fairness and justice. America, for better and for worse, took a different road.[49]

Righting Wrongs for Afro-Americans: Freedom, Liberty, and Affirmative Action

In the United States, leaders on the left proposed something like a tribunal and "reparations for slavery" in joint payments to Afro-Americans. It was much discussed but went nowhere. The idea of reparations to descendants who were many generations removed from slavery was rejected by most Americans.

Another suggestion came from Martin Luther King, who proposed a "program by the government of special compensatory measures" that might help African Americans to overcome by their own efforts the burden of poverty and discrimination. Part of King's plan was compensation and reparation, which failed again.[50]

But another part succeeded. It centered on the expansion of opportunity for individual Americans who had been denied it in the past. This became a policy and a program when President John F. Kennedy issued Executive Order 10925. It ordered every agency in the federal government, when awarding contracts, to undertake "affirmative action to ensure that applicants are employed, and that employees are treated during employment, without regard to their race, creed, color, or national origin."[51]

Four years later Lyndon Johnson issued an additional set of executive orders requiring federal contractors as well as contracting agencies to take "affirmative action in hiring without regard to race, religion, [or] national origin," and later added gender as well. Johnson took up the theme in a commencement address at Howard University. He said, "In far too many ways, American Negroes have been another nation, deprived of freedom, crippled by hatred, the doors of opportunity closed to hope." He added, "We seek not just freedom but opportunity. We seek not just equity but human ability, not just equality as a right and a theory but equality as a fact and equality as a result. To this end, equal opportunity is essential but not enough."[52]

This idea led to affirmative action in another form, quotas for groups who had suffered from discrimination in the past. It also led to proposals for special preferences. This was called "reverse discrimination" and began to be introduced in college admissions and the award of government contracts. Court cases were mixed in their results. The supreme court in the case of *Grutter v. Bollinger* (2003) ruled by a margin of one vote that an admissions policy that considered race as one of many factors without a fixed quota or weight was constitutional. But most cases went the other way. In 2006, the people of Michigan passed an amendment to the state constitution, in effect overruling the U.S. Supreme Court and banning affirmative action in the form of preferential treatment. Affirmative action in the form of quotas or preferential treatment on the basis of race or gender is widely regarded as fundamentally at odds with the values and traditions of liberty, freedom, and individual rights. But other forms of affirmative action are widely and successfully practiced in American colleges and universities today.[53]

Playing the Game in America: Indian Casinos and Tribal Trusts

American Indians also discovered another weapon. They sought a new measure of justice in an entrepreneurial equivalent of *lex talionis*. More than three hundred Indian reservations availed themselves of treaty rights to open gambling casinos. They have used them to empty paleface pockets, sometimes with high success. The growth of Indian casinos was a small part of a national mania for gambling that overspread the United States in the late twentieth century. It took many forms: the casino-cities of Las Vegas and Atlantic City, state lotteries, games of chance on mass media, and the transformation of the stock market and business corporations into high-stakes gambling operations.

American Indians became part of all this. After many generations of poverty and degradation, they found a way to turn a national vice into an instrument of social justice. One of the most successful operations was Foxwoods Casino, wholly owned by the Pequot Tribe in eastern Connecticut. We have seen it in operation. A large high-speed boat collects customers on Long Island and takes them to Connecticut. Once we were on the water and saw the casino boat go past at terrific speed, crowded with happy gamblers on their way to the gaming tables. In the afternoon we saw them returning, a quiet boatload of dejected losers.

By 2006, approximately 220 of 562 federally recognized Indian tribes operated 400 gaming establishments in the United States. Some have been highly profitable. Others have been less successful, or their success has come at a heavy cost, including linkages to organized crime. The tribal casinos of Indians in the United States center on an idea of justice through entrepreneurial liberty—a difficult concept, but one with deep historical roots in America.[54]

Other American tribes have gone a different way. Among the wealthiest are the Southern Utes in Colorado, who own large reserves of natural gas. The tribe has used its wealth to support economic development, especially in renewable energy, which they have connected to their oldest cultural traditions. Executive Director Bruce Valdez, declared, "The environment, Mother Earth, is very sacred to tribal people." They have linked ancient beliefs to a modern economy in a very successful way. Here is an alternative to the casino model, for at least some Indian nations. It has been used with great success.[55]

Playing the Game in New Zealand: Maori Corporations and Entrepreneurial Opportunity

In the late twentieth century, Maori also became entrepreneurial with growing effect. The major players were not individuals but *iwi*, or tribes. An example was the Ngai Tahu, which included most Maori on the South Island, with eighteen marae on both coasts, and approximately eighteen thousand members. Its leader was Sir Tipene O'Regan, one of the great figures in the history of New Zealand. He was widely recognized as "the most effective and prominent tribal leader in New Zealand during the 1980s and 1990s."[56]

We met him on our travels, and he spoke to us of his mixed ancestry, which he puckishly estimated as one-third Irish and one-third Maori. He was a canny politician, and at the same time a wise and faithful steward of his people, devoted to their welfare, and very careful about means. The collective affairs of the Ngai Tahu were in the hands of a council of eighteen people (Te Runanga o Ngai Tahu). As a tribal leader Tipene O'Regan reported to them.

They divided the economic affairs of the Ngai Tahu into two corporations, which in the language of American capitalism were wholly owned subsidiaries of the tribe. One of them was the Ngai Tahu Holding Corporation, which held its collective assets in land, fisheries, and tourism. The other was the Ngai Tahu Development Corporation, which was responsible for funding social, cultural, and educational programs. The money flowed from the holding company to the development corporation—a great deal of money in the 1990s. Much of it came from trading in surplus Crown lands, to which the Ngai Tahu were given right of first purchase. One very valuable block included railway marshaling yards that had been Crown land in the center of downtown Dunedin.

Tipene O'Regan and his business managers traveled widely around the Pacific Rim to raise money in Auckland, Dunedin, Hong

Sir Tipene O'Regan, a leader of the Ngal Tahu, organized a sustained campaign for justice to his people. He revolutionized the material conditions of Maori on the South Island.

Kong, Singapore, and Japan. He told us that at first they were turned away by Pakeha bankers in New Zealand and gained vital support from an elderly Japanese financier of Ainu descent, who had a fellow feeling for Maori in New Zealand and gave them more help at the pivotal moment than all the Pakeha bankers in New Zealand put together.

The corporations of the Ngai Tahu began to flourish and gave proof that the affairs of the iwi were well managed, and the bankers of Auckland and Dunedin began to show interest. "Their claw marks are halfway up our door," said Tipene O'Regan in 1995. From about 1985, the gross assets of the Ngai Tahu increased very rapidly. The Ngai Tahu became very active in the courts. O'Regan estimated in 1995 that 58 percent of their operating budget was spent on litigation. It paid off handsomely. In 1996, Parliament passed the Runanga o Ngai Tahu Act, which gave the tribe a large share of the fisheries, the return of leasehold land in the high country, and other assets worth NZ$170 million. Profits were invested in further growth, and also in the welfare of all members of the tribe, especially its youth. Large sums were spent on education. Tipene O'Regan yielded the role of chief executive to Tahu Potiki, and his public role to his daughter Hana, and then it passed to others in the tribe. It is a remarkable story and has fundamentally changed the condition of the Ngai Tahu.

Many New Zealand iwi have not been as successful. Some lacked the opportunities that came to the Ngai Tahu on the South Island. Others distributed assets that came their way to individual members, with consequences similar to those that often followed from similar actions among American Indians. But the Nagi Tahu have found a way forward, using instruments of free enterprise and institutions of collective belonging to achieve fairness, equity, and justice for an entire people. The story of the Ngai Tahu is an example of what some New Zealanders have achieved by engaging the deepest values of two cultures, Pakeha and Maori together.

Major settlements were made with large tribes. In 1995, the National government came to terms with the Tainui, who got a formal apology for land-taking and a cash settlement of NZ$187 million. But many smaller Maori tribes received little, and individual Maori who lived in the cities, or in remote rural areas, got less than nothing. Unemployment rates among Maori in some districts approached 80 percent. Uneven progress raised new issues of fairness, and the work goes on.

Race and Rights in Settler Societies: International Comparisons

A large literature exists on the comparative condition of indigenous people in settler societies. Much of it centers on English-speaking nations: Australia, Canada, New Zealand, South Africa, and the United States. It concludes that great wrongs were done to indigenous people everywhere. The land was taken everywhere. Racism was widespread. But most of this scholarship also finds that New Zealand, for all its troubles, did a little better than other settler societies in general, and the United States in particular.

American historians share this judgment. A leading example was C. Vann Woodward, one of the most humane and highly respected scholars of his generation. He had a deep interest in the condition of ethnic minorities, and also in comparative history. On comparisons between New Zealand and the United States, Woodward said in his gentle way to a gathering of American colleagues at Dunedin, "I fear it will not be to our advantage."[57]

Some of the most thoughtful work on this subject was done by Robin Winks, an American historian who took a graduate degree at Victoria University in Wellington, married a New Zealander, and devoted his career to the comparative history of English-speaking settler societies. From a lifetime of research, he summarized his findings in one sentence: "The harshest race-relations developed in

Australia, the least harsh in New Zealand, and . . . the experience with white-Indian contact in the United States fell more towards the Australian side, and in Canada more towards the New Zealand side of the scale."[58]

New Zealand historians have been divided on this question. In 1971, Keith Sinclair generally agreed with the international consensus.[59] In 2001, James Belich came to a more complex conclusion. He wrote, "The enduring myth of exceptionally benign Maori-Pakeha relations, of New Zealand as a paradise of racial harmony, is an easy target for historians. New Zealand race relations in the twentieth century *were* better than those of South Africa or the United States, but better is not great." He rightly noted the stubborn persistence of "massive problems": "opportunities denied, power diminished, protests ignored, and persistent prejudice and discrimination until the 1960s." Even so, James Belich concluded that "there is a stubborn kernel of truth in the myth of relatively good Maori-Pakeha relations."[60]

Since 2001, other New Zealand historians have come to a different conclusion. Some have rejected all positive judgments on Pakeha-Maori relations in New Zealand as "unsubtle and shameless nationalism" and a "search for good imperialism."[61] A more nuanced judgment comes from Richard Hill, who concludes that New Zealand's record was "not fundamentally different from any other ex-colony," except that "it possesses a single founding document of powerful symbolism," but that was a major exception.[62]

In recent years other scholars throughout the world have studied this comparative question in close detail. Legal historian Stuart Banner carefully examined the condition of indigenous people in particular parts of New Zealand, Australia, Canada, and the United States, with close attention to detailed comparisons of land-taking and the law. Everywhere he found that huge amounts of land were taken by force or fraud. He also documented major differences in early colonial laws and treaties, which at first were "peripheral to on-the-ground outcomes" but later came "to matter a great deal" and "continue to shape our lives."

Banner concluded that New Zealand's record was stronger in material terms than that of any other settler nation he studied, because of its early commitments to principles of equity and justice. The worst record was in Australia, where the country was declared *terra nullius* at the start, with no treaties or legal rights for Aborigines. In the United States and Canada he discovered patterns that were very mixed, and in an interesting way. Early California law held that

Indian land was *terra nullius,* and Banner found that very little has ever been done to put things right. On the other hand, in the state of Washington, by the actions of one man, Indians received treaty rights at an early date, which later led to major compensation.[63]

In short, Stuart Banner found by careful study and meticulous research that early acts and choices in settler societies made a major difference in what happened later. He also found that New Zealanders have been distinctive in their early attention to justice, fairness, and equity. The values of both British and Maori leaders made it so when they came together in 1840 and agreed to the Treaty of Waitangi. American Indians have had no such document, but through many generations they shared a tradition of liberty and freedom that is strong in their own culture today.

In both countries, individual acts and choices made long ago still have a very long reach. The moral is that it may be the same for us and our posterity. Our acts and choices might also make a difference for the future history of fairness and freedom. We should think carefully before we act, for our descendants may be dealing with our choices for many years to come. And we have no better way to think of their future than by studying our past. Here the experiences of the United States and New Zealand can be instructive, all the more so when we study these two great nations together.

LIB-LABS AND PROGRESSIVES

Two Movements for Social Reform

> New Zealand's distinction lies in her practical application of the principles of civic and economic justice.
>
> —Frank Parsons on Progressive reform in New Zealand, 1904

> There will be no greater burden in our generation than to organize the forces of liberty in our time, in order to make conquest of a new freedom for America.
>
> —Woodrow Wilson on Progressive reform in America, 1912

L ATE IN THE NINETEENTH CENTURY, a movement for social reform spread through many Western nations. It began in the 1870s, reached its climax in the years between 1890 and 1916, and ended in the carnage of the First World War. Historians in the United States call it the Progressive movement. Some think of it as uniquely American. Others study it as an international event, which certainly it was. The global patterns are only beginning to be understood.[1]

Some of these reform impulses were everywhere the same. They rose from a new consciousness of society as a system and a new depth of moral concern about modern problems. Leaders also shared a new faith in social progress through collective action, and new ways of planning toward that end.

In Britain, it began with Joseph Chamberlain's Birmingham Movement for municipal reform (1873) and Samuel Barnett's Toynbee Hall in London (1884), a model for settlement houses throughout the world. From these small beginnings, the reform impulse moved rapidly across the broad spectrum of British politics. Its many varieties embraced the democratic socialism of the Fabian Society on the left, the New Liberalism of David Lloyd George in the center, and the Tory Democracy of Lord Randolph Churchill to the right.

In Germany, reform impulses also took many forms, ranging from the "Social Democracy" of Eduard Bernstein to the authoritarian "Social Monarchy" of Kaiser Wilhelm II. In France the movement gave rise to the new republicanism of Léon Bourgeois and the *Solidaristes*. It also inspired the radicalism of the *Syndicalistes* and the *Parti Ouvrier*. In between was the liberalism of Georges Clemenceau. The leaders of these many causes were in touch with one another throughout the world. They thought of themselves as part of a global process, which truly they were.[2]

Two of the most important Progressive movements developed in New Zealand and the United States. American Progressivism was big, sprawling, pluralist, creative, fiercely combative, and often at war with itself. It stimulated new forms of social thought called pragmatism and instrumentalism. It was ambitious in its purposes and very mixed in its results. New Zealand's Progressive movement was on a smaller scale but large-spirited and highly inventive. Its structure was unique, and so also were its astonishing results. By the measure of other movements mentioned above, it was restrained in tone and manner but remarkably successful in realizing major goals. A comparison of these two reform movements reveals many things about Progressivism in general, national variants in particular, and the role of values in our acts and choices.[3]

Progressive Reform in North America and the South Pacific

In the United States and New Zealand, the roots of Progressive reform may be found in economic and political conditions of the late nineteenth century. In material terms, both countries were more fortunate than most other nations in the world. Good years brought full employment, and even a scarcity of labor. Even in bad years unemployment was low by comparison with Britain and western Europe.[4] Levels of personal income were much above European standards. Housing was cheap, food was abundant, and levels of nutrition were high. At the beginning of the twentieth century, native-born New Zealanders and Americans of European ancestry tended to be about two inches taller than Britons and Europeans of similar stock, and it was much the same for Americans of African and Asian origin. Rates of mortality were lower, especially in the northern United States and southern New Zealand. In the city of Dunedin, it was said that one of the few underemployed workers was the town's gravedigger, a lugubrious Scot named Barr who complained that "folk wudna dee" in the healthy hills of high Otago. These comparative advantages attracted many immigrants to the United States and New Zealand.[5]

But both countries also had major social and economic problems in the late nineteenth century. Their abundant material resources were not distributed equitably. In the United States, wealth was highly concentrated in a few hands. Slums had expanded in cities, and rural poverty was even more widespread. Material disparities were not as great in New Zealand, but similar inequities existed there as well.[6]

These problems were deepened by economic downturns, which happened frequently in both countries. The United States and New Zealand were dependent on world markets for their leading exports: cotton and grain in North America, wool and wheat in the South Pacific (soon to be chilled meat and dairy products). Commodity prices were low and falling in the late nineteenth century. They were also highly unstable.

Both countries suffered severely from the volatility of unregulated markets, but in different ways. The United States experienced a major panic and depression every twenty years with remarkable regularity: 1819, 1837, 1857, 1873, 1893. After each of these downturns, the buoyant American economy revived and began to grow again. This recurrent pattern persuaded some Americans that their open society could grow its way out of trouble, which it had often done before. Even in hard times most of them remained believers in free markets and minimal government. Others observed that social problems persisted in good times as well as bad, and believed that government could make a constructive difference. But this was the opinion of a minority in the United States.[7]

New Zealand's economy was more fragile than that of the United States. Downturns in export markets were more frequent and more protracted. The worst was a long and brutal depression from the 1870s to the early 1890s. Prices for farm products fell sharply, debt surged to high levels, and immigration ceased. Conditions were so miserable that some New Zealanders appealed to the president of the United States for aid in emigrating to America. Others petitioned Australian governments for the price of a passage across the Tasman Sea.[8]

Governing coalitions of wealthy landholders in New Zealand formed and fell apart under the weight of this disaster. Power passed through a shifting set of evanescent alliances that were collectively called the Continuous Ministry. Several leaders tried to do something about widespread suffering, but they were blocked by conservatives in the House of Representatives and the Legislative Council. With creative exceptions, such as John Ballance's "village settlements scheme," systems of relief failed. Conditions went rapidly from bad to worse in a period long remembered by New Zealanders as the "Black Eighties."[9]

New Zealand's Lib-Lab Coalition

The suffering caused by the Black Eighties concentrated minds on the need for reform. The problem was, what sort of reform? That was the question posed by reform candidates in New Zealand's general election of 1890, an event that turned the course of the nation's history. In a time of great suffering, leaders of two political parties joined together and wrought nothing less than a revolution at the polls. Centrist candidates from the Liberal Party won many seats and joined with six independent Labour candidates to form a working majority in Parliament. The result was called the "Lib-Lab" coalition, originally a nickname for the Liberal and Labour Federation, a centrist movement that opposed a full-fledged Labour Party on the left and conservative groups on the right.[10] Historians have recognized the Lib-Labs as the first true party government in New Zealand's history, and the first freely elected Progressive regime in any nation. Once in power, its popularity increased—so much so that the Lib-Lab coalition governed New Zealand for an entire generation, from 1891 to 1912.[11]

New Zealand's Progressive Quintet

The success of the Lib-Lab movement was due in large part to its leaders. They were remarkable men, very mixed in origins and purposes but united by a vision of fairness and social justice for New Zealand. Together they constructed one of the most effective reform coalitions in modern history, and their work was studied throughout the world in the Progressive Era.

The most passionate among them was Jock McKenzie (1839–1901), minister of lands and agriculture in the new Lib-Lab government. We have met him before, a shaggy Scottish giant of a man who stood six feet four inches tall and weighed 250 pounds. His native tongue was Gaelic, and sometimes he returned to it in the heat of parliamentary debate. As a child in Scotland he had witnessed the cruelty of the Highland Clearances. The horror of that injustice stayed with him all his life. He settled on a small farm in northern Otago, and land reform became a sacred cause to him and his many supporters—small farmers like himself. On their behalf, he fought large estate-holders, absentee landlords, dummy purchasers, reckless speculators, and Maori leaders who claimed communal ownership over the land.[12]

McKenzie's slogan was "Millions of hands want acres, and millions of acres want hands." Rarely did he speak on any other subject. He had little interest in urban reform or industrial problems, detested labor unions, and opposed women's suffrage. But he kept faith with his allies and worked to hold the Lib-Lab coalition together. They in turn strongly supported his program of land reform.[13]

A very different leader was William Pember Reeves (1857–1932), a major figure in the Lib-Lab coalition and its first minister of labor. Reeves made a most unlikely reformer. He was a striking figure, tall, slim, and elegant, with fine-boned English features and a clean-cut lantern jaw. Pember Reeves dressed in fashionable gray Prince Albert coats and Edwardian trousers of impeccable cut, and stood out among his colleagues in their rumpled black suits like a sleek gray mockingbird among a flock of crows.[14]

Jock McKenzie as a child in Scotland had witnessed the cruelty and injustice of the Highland Clearances, which turned many families off the land. In New Zealand his passion was land reform and aid to small farmers and landless laborers.

William Pember Reeves was a gentleman progressive who became a Democratic socialist, with a son named Fabian. He worked for industrial reform and social justice.

Reeves was born into the elite of Canterbury, schooled at Christ College, trained as a lawyer, and successful as editor of the city's major newspaper, which his family owned. He was a man of many talents. An able journalist and a brilliant writer, Reeves became one of New Zealand's leading poets and historians. Several of his books are classics of New Zealand literature, still in print and widely read. He was also a famous cricketer and a formidable rugby player for his province, despite his slender build.[15] In 1884 he entered Parliament and discovered yet another talent as an eloquent speaker and skilled debater. Sir Julius Vogel called him the "cleverest young man in the colony." Sir Robert Stout said to him, "Young fellow, if you have as good a stomach as you've got a head, you'll be premier of New Zealand in a dozen years."[16]

Reeves would never become premier—partly because of his temperament, mainly because his politics were too radical. But after 1890, he held three portfolios in the Lib-Lab government as minister of labor, justice, and education. This remarkable young man who had been born to so many advantages came to sympathize deeply with others who had few or none. He began his career as "the workingman's friend" and moved steadily to the left, driven by a deep concern for fairness, social justice, and industrial reform, which came less from experience than from study and reflection. He began to call himself a socialist and published radical tracts, under pseudonyms at the demand of his appalled board of directors. By 1895, he was so devoted to the cause of democratic socialism that he and his wife, Magdalen (Maud) Robison, named their son Fabian. His peers among New Zealand's possessing families bitterly attacked Reeves as a traitor to his class. Undeterred, he continued as a leader of the Lib-Lab coalition until 1896, when he was appointed New Zealand's high commissioner in London. There he became a tireless promoter of Progressive ideas, a close friend of British socialists, and head of the London School of Economics.

A third reformer was Joseph Ward (1856–1930), minister of posts and telegraphs, and later of railways and public health. He had been born in Australia, the son of impoverished Irish Catholic immigrants. As a small child he moved to the town of Bluff in southern New Zealand, where he grew up in the desperate poverty of a broken home, received only a few years of formal schooling, and was fired from his first job for impudence to his employer. Ward became a successful businessman in the town of Bluff, made a fortune in commerce, went bankrupt in a spectacular way, and then made a larger fortune.

Joseph Ward was a self-made capitalist entrepreneur in Southland, who wanted government to be more efficient and businesslike. He thought of the state as a very active supporter of business enterprise.

At the age of twenty-five, Ward was elected mayor of Bluff and began a lifelong career as a political reformer even as he continued in private business. He was appalled by the inefficiency of government, and he threw his energy into the task of making it more businesslike. Always he thought of the state as a supporter of capitalist enterprise, in an active and interventionist role.

A major political asset was his wife, Theresa Dorothea De Smidt, daughter of a political rival in Bluff. They were an attractive couple and made a great splash in society. She was tall, graceful, bright, and very beautiful. He was dark, handsome, lively, and gregarious, an impassioned Progressive reformer who looked the part of an opulent businessman with a big burnished gold watch chain gleaming from his vest. Joe Ward always remembered his humble origins, supported the reforms of his colleagues, and contributed his political gifts to the task of holding the Lib-Lab coalition together. Later he would become its prime minister.[17]

A fourth reformer of a very different stripe was Richard Seddon, the most visible member of the Lib-Lab coalition and its minister of mines and public works. Seddon was what Americans call a populist, an outspoken tribune of the people, and he cultivated the common touch with high success. But his origins were not

Richard John Seddon was a two-fisted populist who flourished among the miners of Westland. His politics began with an idea of fair play among mates and steadily expanded to embrace larger ideas of social justice.

what his rhetoric implied. He had been born into a middle-class English family. His father was the head of an English grammar school in Ecclesfield, Lancashire, where Seddon grew up in a spacious stone house surrounded by servants and the trappings of Victorian respectability.[18]

His family tried to make Seddon into a classical scholar, but he hated Latin and his schoolmasters judged him to be "not a clever boy." He was in fact very clever, but not in a classical way. His own stern father expelled him from school, and he became an apprentice to an iron founder. Seddon worked hard at his job until he came down with smallpox and nearly died. When he recovered, he returned to work and discovered that he had been fired. The experience of that unfairness changed his life. He emigrated to Australia, then moved again to New Zealand during Westland's mining boom of 1866. There things began to go better for him. He held a Board of Trade certificate as a skilled mechanical engineer, did well in the mine fields, prospered as a storekeeper, and went into politics. A big, burly man, Seddon made his reputation as a boxer. "I've often found my fists useful," he said, "but I've never been a bully." He cultivated a rough-hewn manner, carefully nourished a rhetoric of lost *h*'s and working-class idioms, and perfected a political style that was often populist but never democratic. Seddon's nickname of "King Dick" was a comment on his autocratic ways.[19]

Some historians remember Seddon as an unprincipled office seeker. He was always more than that. He was driven by ambition but also by the values that arose from his own experience of cruelty and injustice. The slogan that came to be associated with him was "Fair and square."[20]

Seddon's idea of fairness was a dynamic principle, and it expanded in the course of his career. He began with fairness among his mates, an idea that was tightly constrained by class, race, and gender. At first he was hostile to women's suffrage, Asian immigration, and the upper classes. One might understand Seddon's political career as the Progressive enlargement of that narrow circle. An important political and moral influence was his wife, Louisa, who managed his constituency with skill and made their large and lively household in Wellington almost another branch of the government.

Gradually Seddon became a supporter of votes for women, liberal divorce laws, and hospitals for women. He formed close associations with Asian immigrants, so much so that he was accused by his rivals of being in league with Chinese businessmen. He became interested in Maori affairs and brought Maori leaders into high government positions—James Carroll as minister of native affairs, and the Maori king as a member of both the Legislative and Executive Council.[21] Seddon took up social welfare legislation for the elderly poor in the Pensions Act of 1898. Once again, a major influence was Louisa, who helped him to find a larger purpose and a more generous spirit. That process of political growth is not merely the biography of King Dick Seddon. It is also the history of his nation in Seddon's generation.[22]

Within the Lib-Lab coalition, however, McKenzie, Reeves, Ward, and Seddon had very different purposes. Their individual strengths, ironically, threatened to weaken the common cause, and sometimes did so in moments of ill feeling. Reeves once wrote in exasperation of Seddon, "His head made one think of iron wedges, stone axes, and things meant to split and fracture."[23] These four stallions of the Lib-Lab coalition were restless in the traces of party government, but they were able to pull together because a fifth reform leader held the reins. His name was appropriately John Ballance (1839–93), the first and greatest premier of the Lib-Lab government. He was less eminent than his colorful colleagues but vital to their success.[24]

Ballance was Irish by birth, one of Ireland's quiet men, raised on a farm in Antrim and trained as an ironmonger in Birmingham. In 1866, he moved to New Zealand, and by 1867 he was the proprietor of the highly successful *Wanginui Herald.* In 1875, he was elected

John Ballance was the leader of this reform menagerie. A decent, quiet man, and a canny politician, he was highly respected by his colleagues for his integrity and judgment.

to Parliament. Ballance was a decent, gentle man, with broad sympa-
thies that came from his Quaker mother and Evangelical father,
though he himself, like so many lapsed Quakers, became a freethinker. He sympathized very strongly with Maori and was defeated
for reelection to Parliament in 1881 after he made an outspoken
defense of Te Whiti.

Ballance stuck to his principles, worked hard at the retail business of politics, and never lost another election. As the nation got to
know him, he was much loved for his qualities of character and
respected for his judgment and wisdom. Reeves remembered him as
"a kind, courteous, and considerate chief, always ready to listen . . .
absolutely the most unassuming and unpretentious of all the political leaders."[25] Ballance supported many reforms, but in a manner
that rarely appears among reformers. Historian Peter Coleman
writes that "he conveyed a reassuring sense of political restraint and
responsibility, especially to middle-class voters who held the balance
of power."[26]

New Zealand's very different Progressive leaders were able to
work together in part because of other things they shared. Historian

John Ballance's cabinet, 1892. Back row, from left, Cadman, Carroll, McKenzie, Reeves;
seated, Seddon, Ballance, Buckley, Ward.

John Stenhouse has stressed the importance of their Christian faith. Seddon was a broad-church Anglican, McKenzie a Presbyterian, and Ward a liberal Catholic. Reeves, a freethinker, was the exception. There were always tensions and stresses, especially between Reeves and Seddon, but also a spiritual bond among these men, and it made a difference. Of major importance in the Lib-Lab coalition were their able, active, and highly political wives: Ellen Ballance, Ann McKenzie, Maud Reeves, Louisa Seddon, and Theresa Ward. Most of them played major roles not only in their husbands' careers but in the public life of New Zealand.[27]

Progressive Achievements in New Zealand: The Structure of Politics

When the Lib-Lab leaders came to power, one of their first tasks was political reform. Like Progressives in other English-speaking nations, they believed that a sovereign remedy for the ills of democratic government was more democracy. When they came to power, New Zealand had a bicameral Parliament. The Lib-Labs controlled only the House of Representatives, which was elected by the people. The Legislative Council was appointed for life, and its members strongly opposed reform. The outgoing conservative leader, Sir Harry Atkinson, had packed the Council with seven midnight appointments, who did all in their considerable power to block Progressive measures.

A hard struggle followed. The reformers took their case to the country and won popular support, but the Council remained obdurate, and two royal governors refused to intervene. In desperation, the reformers appealed to the Colonial Office and to the Privy Council in Britain. Imperial authorities strongly supported the cause of democracy in New Zealand and ordered the royal governor to act in its support—an unfamiliar face of imperialism. Terms of service on the Council were reduced from life tenure to a fixed term of seven years. More important, the lower house gained authority to appoint as many new councilors as it pleased.

Ballance used these new powers with wisdom and restraint. He did not pack the Council with reformers, as Atkinson had packed it with conservatives. But the possibility of such a thing broke the power of the Legislative Council, much as the House of Lords would be broken by British Progressives. This reform was large in consequences. It converted the government of New Zealand to a full-fledged unicameral democracy. The Council continued to exist, but only in a vestigial way, and was finally abolished in 1950.

Ballance met strong opposition, but he succeeded in cutting the ground out from under strident and uncompromising opponents. His political style made a difference—a combination of resolve with restraint that won moderate Conservatives to the cause of reform. At the same time, Ballance brought the Lib-Lab ministry a reputation for fairness—a major asset in New Zealand. That combination was extraordinarily effective.

Another political reform greatly strengthened the Lib-Lab movement in a different way. It gave women the vote in 1893, and made New Zealand the first nation in the world to do so. Many Lib-Lab leaders were not happy, thinking that women would vote for Conservative candidates. But once again John Ballance held his coalition together by a combination of quiet strength and steady purpose. To everyone's surprise, New Zealand women supported the new reforms. The Lib-Labs in turn took up other issues that were strongly favored by women—temperance most of all.

Progressive Achievements in New Zealand:
Social and Economic Reform

A major group of Progressive measures centered on Jock McKenzie's program for land reform. Most of his ideas sprang from a single purpose, which was to help small-farming families get land of their own, and keep it. McKenzie's program had many parts. It began with the Land and Income Tax Assessment Act (1891), which imposed a tax on big tracts of unimproved land, a graduated tax on large cultivated estates, a stiff surcharge on absentee owners, and an income tax.

Other means to the same end were the Lands for Settlements Acts (1892), which, as we have seen, created a fund for buying large estates and dividing them into smallholdings. Another part of that law gave the government power to buy land by "compulsory purchase" at a "fair price." It also created "leases in perpetuity" for 999 years at very low rent and allowed families without capital to acquire a farm on terms as favorable as freehold. The Advances to Settlers Act (1894) authorized loans to small farmers at low interest for the improvement of stock and lands. The money was raised overseas. The Lands Improvement and Native Lands Acquisition Act (1894) was intended to break up communal holdings (mostly Maori) into individual farms (mainly Pakeha), a measure that was deeply resented by Maori and rightly condemned by historians.

At the same time, a Ministry of Agriculture was founded in 1892 (with McKenzie as head). It was followed by the Dairy Industry Acts in 1892, 1894, and 1898 and a Slaughtering and Inspection Act in 1900. McKenzie's land laws gave sweeping powers to the government to seize lands from unwilling sellers and break them into small holdings. The powers were used with restraint but to great effect. Altogether Jock McKenzie's land reforms had a major impact on New Zealand.[28]

Yet another of McKenzie's programs was about conservation, or, as we would say, the environment. Here again New Zealanders were very active at an early date. Among the results were the country's first national parks, at Tongariro in 1894 and Egmont in 1900, and a Scenery Preservation Act in 1903. McKenzie was also instrumental in the first full legislation of the Queen's Chain, which guaranteed fair and open access for all New Zealanders to a strip of land, equal in width to one surveyor's chain (then sixty-six feet; now twenty-two meters), along the coasts, larger lakes, and rivers of the nation. By that law, to this day, the land cannot be sold or leased to private owners and is open to all. Even with changes and exceptions the Queen's Chain remains an important expression of ecological fairness and natural justice.[29]

A third part of the Lib-Lab program centered on William Pember Reeves's ideas for industrial reform. With his leadership, Parliament in 1891 passed the first of fourteen Factory Acts, which were called "the fullest labor code in the world." Other Factory Acts in 1894 set standards for health and safety, regulated the employment of women, outlawed child labor, and required government inspection of any place where two or more people worked. A Shop Assistants Act established a maximum fifty-two-hour week for women and youths under eighteen. A maximum forty-eight-hour week for factory labor followed in 1900.[30]

The capstone of Reeves's program was the Industrial Conciliation and Arbitration Act (1894), the first compulsory arbitration law in the world, widely regarded as a model in other nations. It allowed any group of fifteen or more workers to declare themselves a union and engage in collective bargaining. If disputes could not be resolved, the new law required owners and workers to submit their differences to compulsory settlement by a judge of New Zealand's Supreme Court. Judicial decisions enlarged this process. Under the arbitration act, for example, judges began to require minimum wages at a level that would allow a worker to "maintain a wife and three children in a fair and reasonable standard of comfort."[31]

Yet another reform impulse came from Richard Seddon. His motives were very mixed. Always he thought about the next election and his working majority in Parliament. He said of the voters in his inimitable way, "You should always keep something up your sleeve for next year. Keep the bastards on a string and then they'll keep you in Office."[32] But for all his electoral cynicism, Seddon had a deep and genuine interest in distributive justice, an idea that lay near the heart of his reforms. In 1898, his ministry passed an Old Age Pensions Act that gave small pensions to poor people of advanced age who were respectable, sober, and faithful to their families and had stayed out of jail. In 1905, the Workers Dwelling Act authorized the state to build housing and rent it to workers at low rates. A later measure in 1907 was the Plunket system of health care for women and children.

Another set of Lib-Lab reforms was led by Joe Ward. His purpose was to enlarge the role of government in the economy. As postmaster general he was responsible not only for the mail but for telegraph, telephone, and cable communications. Ward moved quickly to lower the price of toll calls. He introduced penny postage, made efficient service more broadly available at lower cost, and greatly expanded the volume of service. Later he became minister of railroads, which were already state-owned. Ward was the legislative leader of the Bank of New Zealand Guarantee Act, (1894) which gave the government effective control of the bank, with powers to appoint its president and, more importantly, its auditor. The State Coal Mines Act (1901) authorized the government to nationalize coal mining, which it did. The State Fire Insurance Act (1903) put the state in the insurance business, competing with private enterprise to bring a higher standard of service to the people of New Zealand. None of these measures rose primarily from a socialist ideology. The Bank Act was a desperate measure, drafted and passed in one frantic evening. Its purpose was to rescue the country's banking system after private businessmen had brought it to the brink of ruin in 1894. Ward always remained a strong believer in capitalism and mixed enterprise. His object was to make the system more rational, more efficient, more productive, and, most of all, more fair.

For two decades, the Lib-Lab coalition succeeded remarkably in sustaining its reform impulse. After 1893, when Ballance died and Seddon and Ward became premiers, the pace of reform slowed but never ceased. At the same time, economic conditions rapidly improved in New Zealand in the early and mid-1890s. The Lib-Labs were given credit for the return of prosperity. Some historians have been skeptics, but the reforms were a powerful stimulus for a troubled economy. In a world depression of the early 1890s, New Zealand began to improve before other nations. As global conditions brightened after 1896, its reformers rode a rising tide of prosperity.

The Lib-Labs remained in power for twenty-one years. So great was their success that Conservatives could stand against them only by taking up Progressive ideas. A Conservative alliance against the Lib-Labs took the name of the Reform Party, and a successful self-made farmer, William Massey, led the Conservatives to victory in 1912. Once they were in power, New Zealand returned to labor strife and violence. Labor unions became more militant, and the new government used force against them. General strikes in 1912 were fought by conservative volunteers called "Massey's Cossacks." The

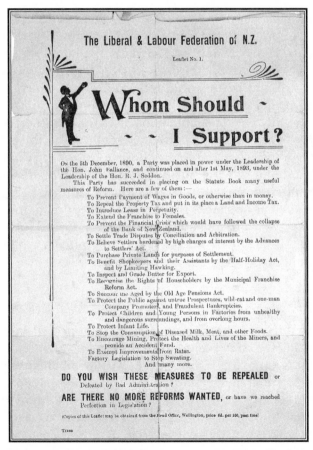

The many achievements of the Lib-Lab Coalition were summarized in this electioneering handbill.

start of the First World War saved the Conservative government, which remained in power under Massey and later Gordon Coates for sixteen years, until finally it fell in another economic crisis as deep as the Black Eighties. The troubles that followed the fall of the Progressive government have further enhanced its reputation, but it is still bitterly attacked from the extreme right and far left.

Throughout the Progressive Era, forward-looking reformers in many countries looked to New Zealand as a model. European and American leaders journeyed halfway around the world to study its institutions. Among them were British Fabians Beatrice and Sidney Webb, and French writers André Siegfried and Albert Métin. They were drawn by the substance and spirit of the New Zealand way, which Métin called "socialism without doctrines." Many observed that New Zealand's reform movement had greatly diminished corruption in public life. It was also given credit for moderating differences of rank and class, which remained strong in Europe.

Many American Progressives were deeply interested in the Lib-Lab reforms. Henry Demarest Lloyd wrote that New Zealand was "the political brain of the modern world." Josiah Strong declared that "New Zealand is the social laboratory from which the world should learn much." Southern Populist Tom Watson urged that America should "New Zealandize itself." Western Progressive William Smythe announced that he was going to "fight to build up California on New Zealand lines." Boston reformer Frank Parsons proclaimed that it was "the birthplace of the twentieth century" in its development of mixed enterprise, its modern systems of social welfare, and what he called the "mutualism" of mankind. The example of New Zealand had a major impact on Progressive thinking in America, but the main lines of Progressive reform would develop on other lines there.[33]

Origins of American Progressivism

A very different Progressive movement appeared in American politics during the early twentieth century. It had great success at the polls. From 1900 to 1916, in fact, Progressive candidates won four out of five presidential elections. After 1912, they gained control of Congress and were strong in state governments. Many measures were enacted. On balance, however, the American record of success and failure was very mixed—more so than in New Zealand.

The Progressive movement in America was so large and diverse that it is difficult to single out a few leading figures who might be

American progressives founded many different reform movements, often with high success. Jane Addams worked in Chicago for the welfare of the urban poor, with strong support from wives of wealthy business leaders in that city. Her achievements were widely imitated.

compared with the Lib-Lab coalition. Much of the American reform movement operated outside the usual boundaries of politics. It included journalists Frederic Howe, Henry Demarest Lloyd, and Albert Shaw; social workers Jane Addams and Robert Woods; jurist Louis Brandeis; scholars Richard Ely and Charles Beard; writer Upton Sinclair; and architects and designers Frederick Law Olmsted and Frank Lloyd Wright. It also had many leaders in state and local politics, such as Samuel "Golden Rule" Jones in Toledo, Hazen Pingree in Detroit, and Tom Johnson in Cleveland.

These American Progressives were more diverse than New Zealand's reformers. Even as most shared similar Progressive impulses, they came from different ethnic groups and brought different regions, religions, and ideologies to the cause of social reform. Many did not know each other, except through their works. The complexity of American institutions kept them apart and turned them in different directions.

If one thinks of Progressivism as a national political movement, the three most important figures were Theodore Roosevelt, Woodrow Wilson, and Robert La Follette. They had much in common. All were of the same generation, born only three years apart. All entered politics with strong conservative connections and were converted to the cause of reform by events and experiences. In midcareer, they came to call themselves Progressives and supported many of the same measures. But they came from different parts of the country, went to different schools, joined different political parties, and developed different ways of thinking about the world. They did not get on well together, and the story of their troubled relations is central to the history of Progressivism as a severely fragmented national movement in the United States. In that regard, their careers make a striking contrast with those of Progressive leaders in New Zealand.

The first—and last—great Progressive leader in national politics was Robert La Follette (1855–1925). He was a rough-hewn western man, born in a two-room log cabin, raised on a frontier farm in Wisconsin, and educated at the University of Wisconsin. La Follette became a leading trial lawyer in his state, closely tied to conservative Republicans. By his own account, a turning point came in 1891 when the state leader of the Republican Party, a saturnine character named Philetus Sawyer, offered him a bribe to influence a judge. La Follette broke with the bosses and launched a reform movement within the Republican Party. To the people of Wisconsin he became "Fighting Bob," who pounded the podium against corruption until his fists began to bleed. The Republican bosses tried to stop him by bribery, and then by force. La Follette defeated them by moving a party convention to the gymnasium at the University of Wisconsin and recruiting campus athletes to keep order. After a fierce struggle and many defeats he was elected governor from 1900 to 1906.

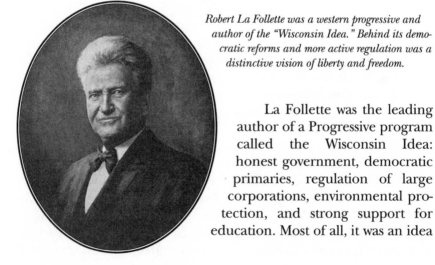

Robert La Follette was a western progressive and author of the "Wisconsin Idea." Behind its democratic reforms and more active regulation was a distinctive vision of liberty and freedom.

La Follette was the leading author of a Progressive program called the Wisconsin Idea: honest government, democratic primaries, regulation of large corporations, environmental protection, and strong support for education. Most of all, it was an idea of a free society. La Follette declared, "Free men of every generation must combat renewed efforts of organized force and greed to destroy liberty." He entered the U.S. Senate in 1906 and founded a new national Progressive Party in 1912. He hated war, voted against American entry in the First World War, and was vilified by the Republican Party. Still, he was reelected to the Senate by 70 percent of the vote. In 1924, the Progressive Party nominated him for president of the United States, and he received six million votes (20 percent of the electorate). He remained in the Senate until his death in 1925.

Among La Follette's many enemies was Theodore Roosevelt (1858–1919), a patrician Progressive born to privilege in New York and bred to a unique tradition that combined an attitude of noblesse oblige with enormous energy in the cause of right. Quoting Virgil he

Theodore Roosevelt's progressive vision was called the New Nationalism. He accepted the existence of large-scale corporations and other institutions and sought to regulate and reform them to serve the common good.

said, "I wish to preach, not the doctrine of ignoble ease, but the doctrine of the strenuous life."[34]

An early photograph shows Theodore Roosevelt as a small child watching a funeral procession for Abraham Lincoln. He grew up during the Civil War, and that event had a great impact on him. All his life he was fascinated by war. He was also inspired by the northern cause of liberty and union, and became a staunch American nationalist. When later he raised his hand to take the oath as president, Roosevelt wore a ring that held a lock of Lincoln's hair.[35]

Roosevelt received a secular education at Harvard, tried careers in law and business, found them boring, went into politics, and won a seat in the New York legislature in 1882. Two years later he suffered a shattering blow when his wife and mother died on the same day, February 14, 1884. Roosevelt sank into a deep depression, retreated to a ranch in the Dakotas, and lived in seclusion for two years. At last he recovered from his grief, returned to New York, remarried, and threw himself into Republican politics. He was appointed civil service commissioner in Washington, where he closely observed the corruption that pervaded even the highest levels of American politics in the Gilded Era. Roosevelt wrote in disgust, "When they call the roll in the Senate, the senators do not know whether to answer 'present' or 'guilty.' " In New York City he became president of the Board of Police Commissioners and discovered the linkage of politics, business, and crime that dominated municipal governments in many American cities.

He went back to Washington in 1897 as assistant secretary of the navy, played a role in bringing on Spanish-American War, recruited his own regiment of Rough Riders, and emerged from a skirmish in Cuba as the hero of San Juan Hill. Largely on the strength of his war record he was elected governor of New York. Once again the corrupt alliance of business and politics in Albany deeply offended his patrician values, and he shocked the leaders of the Republican Party by becoming an enthusiastic reformer. To be rid of him, party bosses kicked him upstairs—as William McKinley's vice president. Then McKinley was assassinated in 1901, and Mark Hanna cried in horror, "That damned cowboy is president of the United States!" As others have observed, it was not the cowboy but his Progressive horse that appalled the Republican bosses.

The new president was forty-two years old. The result was an enormous release of energy in the cause of reform. He declared that "aggressive fighting for the right is the noblest sport the world affords." In that spirit he attacked the "malefactors of great wealth," tried to tame the trusts, expanded the regulatory role of the federal government, and protected the environment. After he left office, he developed these reform ideas into an expansive ideology that he called the New Nationalism. It sought a renewal of the nation, not by breaking up large private corporations but by regulating them in the public interest. Roosevelt also supported Progressive political reforms, such as direct primary elections (which he always won), initiative, referendum, and recall. When Republican leaders refused to follow him, he joined the Progressive Party and became its presidential candidate.

When Roosevelt split the Republican Party, the victor was Woodrow Wilson (1856–1924). Wilson was the son and grandson of Presbyterian ministers, born in Virginia and raised in Georgia, South Carolina, and North Carolina. The Civil War was an important part of his youth, but in a way that differed from Roosevelt's experience. Wilson was a witness to the horror and cruelty of war, the pain of crushing defeat, and the agony of Reconstruction. He was also touched by the Confederate idea of a sacred cause and shared a southern gentleman's idea of liberty as individual autonomy and

Woodrow Wilson was called his progressive vision the New Freedom. It was a southern vision of individual autonomy and a smaller scale of organization in American life.

personal independence. Less happily, he also shared the racial attitudes of his native region.

Wilson was raised in a deeply religious household and educated
in a tradition of Christian humanism at Princeton. He tried his
hand at practicing law in Atlanta, did badly at it, and went to graduate school at Johns Hopkins University, where he earned a doc-
torate in history and politics. He joined the faculty at Princeton,
flourished as a scholar and teacher, and in 1902 became its president. In eight years he turned a sleepy college into a great university
that still bears the imprint of his values. In 1910, New Jersey's corrupt Democratic leaders put him up for governor, thinking that
they could manage him. Once in office, he broke with their machine,
and in ten months enacted a sweeping reform program. In 1912 he
was elected president, and he led another Progressive reform movement
in Washington.

Progressive Achievements in America

The American Progressives enacted many of their measures.
At the top of their agenda was political reform. Progressives
wished to make the polity more responsive to the people. In particular, they were much concerned about the corruption of power
by party bosses and machines, and the corruption of wealth by
great corporations and special interests. Endemic corruption of
both kinds was (and remains) the greatest failure of American
institutions. The Progressives, more than any other reformers in
the long history of the republic, made a determined effort to
deal with it. They succeeded in enacting many reforms, mostly
on the state level: primary elections, secret ballot, initiative, referendum, recall, and, in national politics, the direct election of
U.S. senators.

Also urgently important to American Progressives was economic
reform. They worried about the concentration of wealth and power
in large trusts and corporations. They won passage of the Clayton
Antitrust Act (1914), the Federal Reserve Banking System (1913),
and the Federal Trade Commission (1914). Reformers also tried
to make the distribution of wealth more even. They were responsible for the introduction of progressive income taxation. After massive resistance by conservative courts, they enacted a constitutional
amendment in 1913 that allowed income taxes. The Tariff Act of
1913 and the Revenue Act of 1916 created a system of graduated
taxes on incomes and estates. Progressives also imposed corporate

taxes on capital and profits. The object was not to make the rich poorer, but the poor richer. It was also to create equity in fiscal policy.

Progressives also enacted regulatory statutes that were intended to protect workers and consumers. Leading examples on the federal level were the Pure Food and Drug Act (1906) and the Meat Inspection Act (1906). Many states added more extensive regulatory statutes in every sector of the economy.

An important area of reform was the conservation of natural resources. Here the United States led the world with the invention of a new artifact, the national park. The first in the world was Yosemite National Park, opened during the presidency of Republican Ulysses S. Grant four years after the Civil War. The second was Yellowstone National Park in 1872. Twenty-five others followed in the period from 1890 to 1916. Other Progressive conservation measures included the Reclamation Act in 1902 and the Antiquities Act in 1906, which protected scenic and historic lands as "national monuments." In 1916, reformers founded the National Park Service to administer a large national system. Today nearly all countries in the world have national parks on a Progressive model that was invented in the United States.

Yet another area of Progressive reform was public education. The "common school" developed earlier and more broadly in the United States than in any other Western nation. In some New England states, children had on the average twelve years of schooling as early as 1820. The country led the world in higher education, with the founding of thousands of colleges, though higher learning in universities lagged until the twentieth century. America also led the way with free public libraries. Their open stacks, organized by subject on the Dewey Decimal or Library of Congress system, were open to everyone without charge. American libraries were designed to promote freedom of individual access and choice. In that way they were very different from the closed-stack libraries of European nations.[36]

In the 1920s, the era of Progressive reform came to an end in the United States, as it did throughout the world. The record of success and failure was very mixed and different from New Zealand's. In American politics, Progressives had succeeded in changing the institutional rules. They enacted primary elections, secret ballots, the right of referendum, the power of recall, direct election of U. S. senators, and women's suffrage. These structural reforms had a major impact. In that part of their agenda, they had great success.

But in functional terms, they failed to achieve their larger purposes. Party bosses and political machines remained firmly in power.

After all the Progressive reforms were in place, corruption was if any-thing worse than before. The increasing complexity of politics under the new reforms became an opportunity for the men they were meant to control. Corruption continued to bridge the gap between capitalism and democracy. After the election of 1920, the appalling misconduct of the Harding administration reached deep into Con-gress, the executive branch, the federal courts, and the White House itself. During the 1920s, peculation became more of a problem on every level of government. In Maryland's beautiful old State House at Annapolis during the 1930s, a lobbyist remarked that he was not surprised to find that money made a difference, but he was amazed to discover how much could be done with a five-dollar bill. The problem was at once petty and profound.[37]

The story was the same with other reforms. Roosevelt, Wilson, and La Follette all wished to control the large trusts that destroyed competition in many sectors of the American economy. They broke some of the more extreme monopolies but failed to curb the con-centration of economic power. Many sectors of the economy were still dominated by a few corporations that were able to control mar-kets and fix prices, sometimes in collusion with the very government agencies that were supposed to be regulating them. The most egre-gious price-fixing happened through "fair trade statutes" that were modeled on Progressive legislation, but with an opposite intent. Despite a generation of reform, by the 1920s American financial institutions were riddled with the incompetence, corruption, and malfeasance that led to the crisis of 1929.

Another major goal of Progressives had been to do some-thing about inequalities of wealth. They succeeded in enacting systems of graduated taxation, but these reforms had little impact on the distribution of wealth and income. By 1929, wealth-inequality reached the highest levels in American history. Poverty also increased, with extreme suffering among desperately poor families in the rural South and the urban North.

In labor policy, American Progressives were less successful than their New Zealand colleagues. Nine northern states enacted com-pulsory arbitration, but other states did little, and Congress nearly nothing. Strife between capital and labor grew worse in the United States during the Progressive Era. Industrial violence rose to high levels in the period from 1890 to 1935.

In regard to conservation, Progressives had created national parks, national forests, and wilderness reserves. They had protected public and private lands throughout the country—a remarkable achievement that has been imitated by every other country in the world. In the 1920s, however, with a few exceptions, national parks stopped growing, public lands were exploited for private profit, and pollution of the environment increased. A new pattern appeared after 1916. Acreage in preservation increased under Democratic administrations and stagnated or actually declined under Republicans.[38]

It was the same again in social legislation. One of the most radical Progressive experiments was Prohibition, enacted by the votes of northern reformers and southern fundamentalists in 1917, with strong support from women's organizations. It was in some ways the most sweeping experiment in social engineering that Progressives undertook. It required a constitutional amendment, and its enactment was an extraordinary achievement in social politics. In operation, Prohibition succeeded in reducing the consumption of alcohol, but it caused a rapid growth in organized crime and corrupted public agencies charged with its enforcement. The social cost was so high that it was abandoned by those who had sponsored it. The "noble experiment" was, on the whole, an ignominious failure, and it was repealed by another generation of reformers in 1933.[39]

John Dewey's movement for Progressive education and Wisconsin's model of a university in the service of the people also succeeded in one way and failed in another. Both were widely adopted throughout the nation, but in the twenties the reforms began to go wrong. Dewey himself was appalled by the use that school administrators and "curriculum specialists" made of his work to destroy rigorous learning in classrooms. In the 1920s, he turned against his own disciples, with good reason. Progressive education was another noble experiment that went wrong. In almost every aspect of the American Progressive movement, sweeping reforms were successfully enacted, yet the reformers failed to realize their larger goals. The outcome was very different from that in New Zealand. The question is why.

Closed Fist and Open Hand:
Reform Coalitions and Political Institutions

A clue might be found by a comparative study of acts and choices in Progressive reform movements. New Zealand's reformers, for all their tensions and conflicts, were usually able to work together. They were very different in their purposes, but they made common cause, and the Lib-Lab coalition held together for twenty-one years.

In the United States, the three top Progressive leaders in national politics were at each other's throats. Now and again they worked together, as when La Follette and Wilson joined forces on an act to improve working conditions in the maritime industry, and to enact the Adamson Act, which imposed an eight-hour day on interstate railroads and placed limits on child labor. But these were the exceptions. They began as rivals and became enemies. Relations among them were increasingly marked by extreme personal animosity. Wilson disliked Roosevelt as a violent, irresponsible, bellicose bully, a self-indulgent chauvinist who was often out of control, and an untrustworthy ally who was most dangerous to his friends. Roosevelt despised Wilson as a "damned Presbyterian hypocrite." La Follette detested them both.

Their hostility also grew from a conflict of principles. These three men tried to solve the nation's problems in fundamentally different ways. Roosevelt's New Nationalism, Wilson's New Freedom, and La Follette's Wisconsin Idea had different goals. On the fundamental question of the trusts, Wilson wished to break up large ones into smaller units. Roosevelt wanted to regulate large trusts for the public good, rather then break them up. La Follette thought in terms of a more active role for government and worked to replace private ownership with public control in some parts of the American economy. The three men spent as much time battling each other as they did fighting the trusts.

Their mutual dislike was further reinforced by the structure of American politics, which amplified their differences. The federal system, with its complex checks and balances, was meant to institutionalize conflict, which it did all too well. New Zealand's parliamentary system rewarded cooperative effort and required the construction of coalitions.

Another factor was the regional and cultural complexity of American society. Among different regions and states there was a wide disparity in attitudes and acts. By and large the South lagged far behind. The northeastern and midwestern states produced their own reform agendas. National reform leaders brought their own regional identities and values to American politics.

Still another problem was the existence of plural elites. The American Progressive movement was not only divided between leaders such as Roosevelt and Wilson and La Follette but fragmented into many different parts. Separate groups led efforts on particular issues. Progressive education had leaders distinct from the leaders of conservation, Prohibition, and women's suffrage. Social and cultural reformers were generally separate from political. Some corporate leaders favored economic reforms for their particular purposes but opposed social measures. Labor leaders went their own way.

Whatever the cause, the consequences were clear. Wilson, Roosevelt, and La Follette achieved many things, but they were unable to make common cause. American reform was a dynamic but disorderly set of rival movements. It was distracted by constant quarreling among rival leaders. The free and open competition of ideas was a great strength; the fragmentation of reform was a grievous flaw.

Wilson once said to the young Franklin Roosevelt, "Roosevelt, we Progressives never beat the conservatives because they, wanting to disturb nothing, and maintaining a purely defensive position, have the cohesiveness and resistance of a closed fist; but we, being determined to make progress and each knowing best how it should be done and being therefore utterly unable, any of us, to support any others of us, have about as much striking power as you'd expect from the fingers of an open hand, each pointing in a slightly different direction."[40]

Conservative Responses in New Zealand and the United States

As Wilson observed, another critical factor in the career of any reform movement is the response of its opponents. Here again, New Zealand and the United States went different ways. One important part of the difference rose from the manner in which Progressive reformers dealt with conservative opponents. Equally important was the response of conservatives themselves.

In New Zealand, through many generations, conservative leaders have often been remarkably forward-looking in their social policies. This pattern was set before the Progressive Era. A leading example was Sir Harry Atkinson (1831–92), a blunt, honest country squire who became a leader of the Continuous Ministry and served three times as premier from 1876 to 1891. Atkinson shared the visceral conservatism of a small oligarchy who controlled New Zealand's government and did not approve of the Lib-Lab leaders who came to power in 1891. But he was a decent, moderate, enlightened man, and for his own conservative reasons made his peace with many reform measures at a remarkably early date. As early as 1882 he favored a system of national insurance. As he grew older he became more open to other reforms, including women's suffrage, broader suffrage for men, proportional representation, and even the income tax.

Another example was Robert Stout, twice premier of New Zealand, in 1877–79 and 1884–87. Stout was a Scottish immigrant and a successful barrister, deeply conservative on many questions, and in his early years strongly opposed to state intervention in economic and social questions. But he became increasingly sympathetic to rights for women, penal reform, and land reform. When the Lib-Lab reformers came to power, Stout responded in a constructive and even sympathetic way. His biographer, D. A. Hamer, writes that Stout "did much to forge a reconciliation of labour and middle-class liberal interests in Dunedin on a common platform of labour reform."[41]

After the Lib-Lab regime, William Massey's conservative Reform Party held power into the 1920s and accepted many Progressive measures. One of its leading members was Dunedin's William Downie Stewart, the third political generation of a remarkable Dunedin family. His manuscript autobiography is one of the great unpublished works in New Zealand history. Stewart wrote that "the reform party under Mr. Massey, although it was descended from the old continuous or Conservative party, was really an alternative Liberal or social reform party." He and his father did more than any others to introduce compulsory arbitration.[42]

Massey's successor as prime minister was Francis Bell, a descendant of the old Wakefield-Bell connection, and one of many prime ministers from the old landholding elite of Napier. Bell was conservative on many social and cultural questions, but he strongly favored the subdivision of great estates and supported other reform measures. "We are not only the protectors of property," he said, "but we are also the protectors [of people in] distress."[43]

Running like a bright thread through the fabric of all of these conservative governments was a sense of fairness and an idea of comity in the nation. Stewart wrote of his father that he celebrated "qualities of caution, fairmindedness, and capacity to see both sides of every question." The same attitudes were shared by Massey and Coates, and later by National Party leaders. A similar spirit appeared two generations later in Robert Muldoon, who also greatly expanded social welfare programs. To read Muldoon's four autobiographies is to find an exceptionally strong sense of kinship with Progressive reformers such as Seddon, whose life he studied with close attention.

In general, New Zealand had remarkably little in the way of the hard-right, hard-core conservatism that was stronger in Britain, the United States, and Canada. Even conservatives as staunch as the Pharazyn brothers in Wairarapa and the sheep owners of Canterbury supported women's suffrage and other Progressive measures. A major factor was the epic failure of minimal welfare programs in the long depression of the 1880s. Even conservatives were persuaded by that experience that something should be done.[44]

All this was unlike what happened in the United States. Since the collapse of the Federalist Party in 1816 and the Whig Party in 1854, and the transformation of the Republicans from the party of Abraham Lincoln and Theodore Roosevelt to the party of Strom Thurmond and Richard Nixon, conservative leaders in America had stridently opposed Progressive reforms and were deeply hostile to reform leaders. There were important exceptions. Some leaders of large corporations and oligopolies favored some regulatory measures, often as a way of beating down their competition. But conservative leaders in the United States made a concerted effort to disrupt Progressive programs, destroy the reputation of Progressive leaders, and turn the substance of reforms against their spirit.[45]

Reform in America during the twentieth century faced entrenched, rigid, and deeply ideological partisan opposition from the right that had no equal in New Zealand. An example was the intense and bitter hostility of Republican "stand-patters" to Theodore Roosevelt. Even more partisan in the next generation was the conservatism of Henry Cabot Lodge at the end of his career. In his early years Cabot Lodge had supported Civil Service Reform, the Sherman Antitrust Act, and the Food and Drug Act. But as he grew older he became a narrow and vindictive partisan who did all in his considerable power to block the reforms of Woodrow Wilson.[46]

Another major obstacle to reform in America was conservative American judges. From 1888 to 1930, three conservative chief justices—Melville Fuller and Edward Douglass White and William Howard Taft—led the Supreme Court in striking down or crippling many reforms, always in the name of liberty: *United States v. E. C. Knight Co.* (1895) which gravely weakened the Sherman Antitrust Act; the *Income Tax Cases* (1895) which declared progressive income taxes unconstitutional; *In re Debs* (1895), which allowed injunctions against union organizing; *Smyth v. Ames* (1898), which struck down the regulation of railroad rates; *Lochner v. New York* (1905), which declared that maximum-hours laws violated freedom of contract; *Hammer v. Dagenhart* (1919) and *Bailey v. Drexel Furniture Co.* (1922), which found restraints on child labor to be unconstitutional.

These attitudes were widely shared among America's possessing classes. Theodore Roosevelt wrote, "The great bulk of my wealthy and educated friends regard me as a dangerous crank." La Follette was feared as a dangerous radical. Wilson was despised as a pious academic fool. Conservative foes of Roosevelt, Wilson, and La Follette felt that their own material interests were deeply threatened by reform.

Political Traditions

A major contrast between these two nations rose from the political traditions within which they operated. New Zealand Progressives began with a strong tradition of intervention by the state to promote social justice. Leaders of every major party and many political persuasions accepted the legitimacy of strong intervention by the central government.

William Pember Reeves wrote of New Zealand in 1898, "There was nothing novel there in the notion of extending the functions of the state in the hope of benefiting the community or the less fortunate classes of it. Already, in 1890, the state was the largest landowner and receiver of rents, and the largest employer of labour. It owned nearly all the railways, and all the telegraphs, and was establishing a state system of telephones. It entirely controlled and supported the hospitals and lunatic asylums, which it managed humanely and well. It also, by means of local boards and institutions, controlled the whole charitable aid of the country. . . . It was the largest trustee, managed the largest life insurance business, and educated more than nine-tenths of the children. Nearly all the sales and leases of land went through its transfer offices."

Reeves continued, "It will thus be seen that the large number of interesting experiments sanctioned by the New Zealand Parliament after 1890, though they involved new departures, involved no startling changes of principle. The constitution was democratic; it was simply made more democratic. The functions of the state were wide; they were made yet wider. The uncommon feature of the eight years, 1890–98, was not so much the nature as the number and degree of the changes effected and the trials made by the Liberal-Labour fusion."[47]

All of Reeves's remarks accurately described New Zealand in 1890, but few of them applied to the national government of the United States, or even to its state and local governments. There were some exceptions. The federal government was the largest landowner in the United States, but mostly of arid western lands that were thought to be of little productive value. It received very little in the way of rents and employed few workers. American state and local governments did educate most schoolchildren, though less than the 90 percent in New Zealand. In general, the United States had no tradition of "extending the functions of the state" on anything approaching the scale of operations in New Zealand, where Progressive leaders inherited a strong tradition of public intervention in economic and social problems.

In 1890, the "functions of the state" were shrinking in America, as the courts and legislatures turned increasingly toward laissez-faire. The level of activity by government was very low, and falling lower. The federal government did not own the railroads or the telegraph or the national telephone networks, which were in private hands. It played a very small role in charitable relief, and states and local governments did less than the churches and other voluntary organizations. It played no role whatever in insurance, which was a vast private enterprise of competing companies. It did not conduct land transactions except for the initial purchase of western lands.

American Progressives struggled against a tradition that limited government in the nineteenth century to a minimal role of regulator and order keeper. Further, the federal system compounded the problem by imposing a complex set of checks and balances on local, state, and national governments. America's Progressive leaders were not only restricted by this tradition but divided by it as well. They argued fiercely among themselves on questions that found New Zealanders more nearly united. Even so, American Progressives pushed against these limits, but it was heavy work, and the results were less satisfactory.

Labor Movements in Open Systems: The Paradox of Militancy and Violence

One of the deepest contrasts between the United States and New Zealand in the Progressive Era appears in the history of their labor movements. Before 1935, approximately 60 percent of New Zealand's workforce outside agriculture belonged to a union. The comparable figure in the United States in 1935 for "non-agricultural employment" was 13 percent.[48]

New Zealand's labor movement was one of the strongest in the world and also one of the least violent. The worst outbreak of labor violence was in the mining town of Waihi in 1912, when strike-breakers attacked a union hall. A gunshot rang out, and a constable fell wounded. The outraged police fell upon a miner named Fred Evans, who was thought to have fired the shot, and gave him such a beating that Evans later died of blows to the head. This, according to historian Raymond Richards, was "the sole death in the history of industrial strife in New Zealand."[49]

In the United States that entire pattern ran in reverse. Throughout most of American history, unions organized only a small minority of the workforce. The only exception was the period from 1936 to

1945. After the Wagner Act and other measures created a more friendly climate for labor organization, unions expanded rapidly. By 1945, they organized nearly 36 percent of American workers outside of agriculture. This was their high-water mark.[50]

Most studies find that the American labor movement was much weaker than that in New Zealand in quantitative terms, and yet it was very violent throughout its history, from the first eighteenth-century "strikes" of seamen and maritime workers to the urban mobs of the 1830s, the Molly Maguires of the 1860s, the bloody violence of both capital and labor in the General Strike of 1877, the Homestead Massacre in 1892, the IWW violence in the West, the Memorial Day Massacre in 1937, the Harlan County Wars in Kentucky, the violence in "Bloody Williamson" County in Illinois, and much more.

These differences between the two nations were deeply rooted in their culture and history. In New Zealand, capital and labor shared the same culture and ethnicity. They thought of themselves as one people. In America, labor violence was compounded by racial hatred, ethnic jealousy, and religious strife, and deepened in the South and West by ingrained folk traditions of regional violence. Kentucky's "Bloody Harlan" County was violent in ways that had existed in the American backcountry for two centuries, and the British borderlands for a thousand years before. All this makes a dramatic contrast between the two nations.

Another great question is to understand why workers in New Zealand, Australia, Britain, and western Europe formed strong socialist movements and "mass-based parties of the Left," while workers in the United States did not. To this classic problem, many solutions have been suggested: (1) the divisive effect of ethnicity, region, and race on class consciousness and labor movements in America; (2) the impact of individualism on American workers; (3) higher rates of mobility and internal migration in the United States; (4) American abundance and higher standards of living—the idea that socialism foundered on "shoals of roast beef and apple pie"; (5) America's middle-class majority; (6) the strength of opposition; and (7) the violence of repression in the United States.

Another approach to this problem is put forward by Erik Olssen and Jeremy Brecher, in a close comparison of American workers in the brass factories of Connecticut and New Zealand workers in the railway shops of Otago. Mainly it is a tale of two factories, the Hillside Railway Workshops in Dunedin and the Scovill Manufacturing Company in Waterbury. In the American case, Olssen and Brecher found evidence of fierce competition in a large market, which put a premium

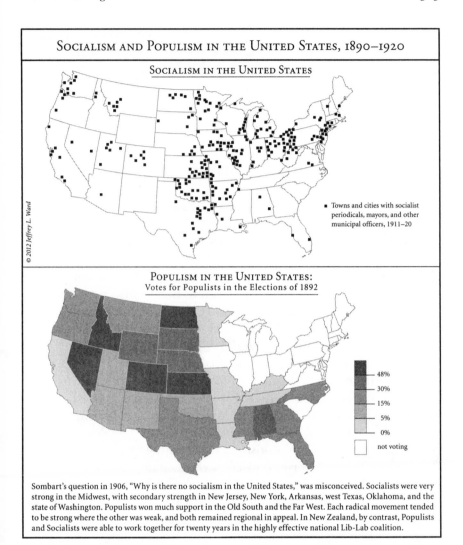

SOCIALISM AND POPULISM IN THE UNITED STATES, 1890–1920

SOCIALISM IN THE UNITED STATES

■ Towns and cities with socialist periodicals, mayors, and other municipal officers, 1911–20

© 2012 Jeffrey L. Ward

POPULISM IN THE UNITED STATES:
Votes for Populists in the Elections of 1892

48%
30%
15%
5%
0%
not voting

Sombart's question in 1906, "Why is there no socialism in the United States," was misconceived. Socialists were very strong in the Midwest, with secondary strength in New Jersey, New York, Arkansas, west Texas, Oklahoma, and the state of Washington. Populists won much support in the Old South and the Far West. Each radical movement tended to be strong where the other was weak, and both remained regional in appeal. In New Zealand, by contrast, Populists and Socialists were able to work together for twenty years in the highly effective national Lib-Lab coalition.

on productivity gains. Corporations moved rapidly toward labor-saving devices and a reduction of labor costs. Layoffs were widely and increasingly used. "In the United States," the historians write, "they transformed the old factory system and destroyed shop culture; in New Zealand, by contrast, shop culture survived and enabled skilled men to preserve key elements of the old factory system."

Olssen and Brecher observe that in New Zealand "under the old system the skilled men planned the work to be done and decided who would do it; they hunted up their own tools, borrowed them if necessary, or even made them; they drove their planes and lathes at the speed they deemed appropriate; and left their tools where they last used them when they finished a job." What emerged from their research was a complex comparative history of two different economies and two distinct sets of social values that developed as historical processes in New Zealand and the United States.[51]

The Balance Sheet

These two Progressive movements shared some of the same strengths. Both movements brought a new seriousness and breadth to politics and social reform in their nations. They encouraged people to think in terms of social systems, and of instrumental reform and weaknesses.

They also shared some of the same weaknesses. Reforms in both America and New Zealand tended to be for whites only. In New Zealand, with the exception of Ballance, the Lib-Lab coalition showed little interest in Maori. McKenzie, even as he was driven by his sense of injustice against the cruelty of the Highland Clearances of his native Scotland, promoted Maori clearances that were at least as cruel in New Zealand, all in the cause of Progressive reform.

American Progressives by and large showed little interest in the condition of blacks and Indians. This was especially the case with Woodrow Wilson and southern Progressives. California reformers were strongly hostile to Asians, and Minnesota and Wisconsin Progressives were not supporters of Indian rights. There were token efforts in both countries. Theodore Roosevelt invited Booker T. Washington to dine at the White House, and even that small gesture caused an uproar. Seddon performed token acts of a similar nature for Maori. But these were the exceptions. Both New Zealand and American Progressives shared a common weakness that derived not from Progressivism itself but from the intense racial feeling of their age.

In other ways the two national movements were different in their strengths and weaknesses. New Zealand led the world in four areas of social legislation: gender rights, land reform, social insurance, and compulsory arbitration. Here it built upon its values of fairness and equity. In at least three areas the United States led the world: schools, public libraries, and national parks. Where the Progressive movement in America worked to expand liberty and freedom, it won; where it found itself in conflict with these ideas, it lost. One might imagine another sort of reform program that combined those strengths. But this would await another season.

PART III

OPEN SOCIETIES IN
WORLD AFFAIRS

FOREIGN AFFAIRS, EXTERNAL RELATIONS

Two Ways of Thinking About the World

> Americans are our brothers, of the same speech and of the same blood, but they are of another nation. They have different aims, different objects, different hopes, and other aspirations.
>
> —Francis Bell in the New Zealand Parliament, 1917

IN MATTERS OF DIPLOMACY, the people of New Zealand and the United States might be described as distant friends. Many international questions find them on the same side, but they think differently about what Americans speak of as foreign affairs and New Zealanders have sometimes called external relations.[1]

Here again two kindred nations are divided by a common heritage. Long ago, English-speaking people developed distinctive ways of thinking about others in the world. In 1993, Malcolm McKinnon began a major study of New Zealand's diplomacy by quoting an eminent Victorian on that subject. In 1855, Charles Dickens observed that his countrymen "had a notion that it was a sort of divine visitation upon a foreigner that he was not an Englishman, and that all kinds of calamities happened to his country because it did things that England did not, and did not do things that England did."[2]

That Anglo-Saxon attitude was transplanted to North America and the South Pacific. Through many generations, it was reinforced by Puritan and evangelical habits of moralizing in Manichaean terms of black and white, right and wrong, good and evil—especially evil. To English-speaking Protestants, the world has always appeared to be the Devil's playground. The practical problem is what to do about it. Should one strive against evil in the world, or seek to live apart from it? Most nations do not have that luxury of choice, but in New Zealand and the United States this ancient Donatist dilemma has shaped much thinking about the world.[3]

Similarities: The Rule of Regional Hegemony in America

From the start, British emigrants to North America and New Zealand responded to the problem of evil by trying to move away from it. On ships bound for seventeenth-century Massachusetts and nineteenth-century Otago, departure sermons were preached from the same biblical text: "Come out from among them, and be ye separate, saith the Lord, and touch not the unclean thing; and I will receive you."[4]

Once transplanted to another environment, that separatist impulse took a new form. In North America and the South Pacific, English-speaking immigrants sought to keep evildoers at a distance. They did not want colonies of other nations anywhere nearby. In North America, British settlers and soldiers moved quickly to take over foreign posts—peacefully where possible, forcibly when necessary. They seized neighboring Dutch colonies (1664), annexed Swedish settlements (by 1700), captured French possessions in Acadia (1710–55), and conquered the St. Lawrence Valley (1759–60).

After independence, the new United States pursued a similar policy by other means. As national wealth increased, purchase became the method of choice. American leaders bought Louisiana from France (1803), East Florida from Spain (1819), the Gadsden Purchase from Mexico (1853), Alaska from Russia (1867), and great tracts of lands from Indians. When offers of purchase failed, Americans did not hesitate to use force. They took West Florida from Spain (1810), annexed Texas by an unconstitutional resolution (1844), and seized the vast lands of California, Utah, New Mexico, and Arizona from the Mexican Republic in 1848 as spoils of war. The United States also moved quickly to stop European powers from planting colonies in the Western Hemisphere. In 1823, President James Monroe and Secretary of State John Quincy Adams laid down a rule that the American hemisphere was off-limits to European powers. Most presidents endorsed the Monroe Doctrine, and many supported it by armed force.[5] In 1865, the Lincoln administration moved federal troops to the southern border and prepared for war with France if necessary to bring down the Mexican empire of Napoleon III. In

1898, the McKinley presidency dismantled the remains of Spain's American empire by war.[6]

During World War II and the Cold War, seven presidents expanded the Monroe Doctrine to exclude "foreign ideologies," such as Fascism and Communism, from the American hemisphere. Franklin Roosevelt suppressed a Fascist Vichy regime in Martinique by mobilizing an airborne division. He threatened war with the Vargas regime in Brazil for refusing to admit American airbases in the struggle against Nazi submarines in the Atlantic. The United States also demanded the subordination of the Brazilian economy to Henry Wallace's Board of Economic Warfare and dispatched more than two thousand officials to Brazil as "ambassadors of good will." The foreign secretary of that country warned that if any more ambassadors of good will arrived, "Brazil would be obliged to declare war on the United States."[7]

This policy of regional hegemony continued during the Cold War, when the United States intervened many times in Central America and Caribbean nations. In 1954, on orders from President Eisenhower, the Central Intelligence Agency brought down the left-leaning government of Jacobo Arbenz in Guatemala. In 1962, John Kennedy ended the expansion of Soviet armed forces in Cuba, at the risk of nuclear war. Lyndon Johnson, Ronald Reagan, and George H. W. Bush sent troops into the Dominican Republic, Nicaragua, Grenada, and Panama to suppress what they perceived to be alien regimes and foreign ideologies. Richard Nixon used covert means to bring down a socialist government in Chile.[8]

After the end of the Cold War, the United States liberalized its hemispheric policy, promoted free trade in NAFTA (North American Free Trade Agreement) and CAFTA (Central America Free Trade Agreement), and supported democracy and the rule of law throughout its region. Today many Americans believe that the Monroe Doctrine no longer applies, but the rule of regional hegemony persists in more subtle forms.[9]

New Zealand's Regional Hegemony in the South Pacific

New Zealand did much the same thing in its own neighborhood. Sir Julius Vogel often asserted that his country was destined to take up "a commanding position in regard to the Pacific Islands." Premier Harry Atkinson insisted in 1884 that "the Anglo-Saxon race must predominate in these seas." Many other leaders shared that attitude.[10]

When New Zealand was still an infant colony, it began to annex nearby territories. As early as 1840, Governor William Hobson claimed sovereignty over French settlers at Akaroa, American sealers on Stewart Island, and German missionaries in the Chatham Islands. A generation later in 1887, New Zealand annexed the Kermadec Islands, six hundred miles north of Auckland. It added the Cook Islands and Niue Island in 1901 and the Tokelau Islands in 1925. New Zealand leaders urged British annexation of Fiji (1874), the creation of a British protectorate for Tonga (1900), and Australian acquisition of Papua New Guinea. They strongly opposed French sovereignty in the New Hebrides and helped create a condominium there.[11]

This hegemonic policy continued through the twentieth century. When the First World War began, New Zealand troops quickly seized Western Samoa from Germany on August 29, 1914. During World War II, New Zealanders joined Americans and Australians in the arduous task of expelling Japanese forces from the South Pacific. Through the Cold War, New Zealand governments were highly sensitive to any sort of Soviet presence in their region. Rumors of Russian warships in the Tasman Sea caused a spasm of concern in 1976, similar to earlier "Russian scares" in the nineteenth century. When the New Hebrides Islands became the independent nation of Vanuatu in 1980, New Zealand worked closely with the United States and Australia to bring down a Marxist government and to keep the Soviet Union, Libya, and Cuba at a distance.[12]

New Zealand and the United States were quick to establish a broad area of hegemony in their respective regions. This photograph shows New Zealand troops in the process of seizing western Samoa from Germany immediately after the World War I began in 1914.

New Zealand also enforced an idea of regional order on native peoples in the South Pacific. Civil unrest brought swift intervention. During the 1920s, New Zealand troops suppressed insurrections in Samoa at the same time that United States Marines embarked on similar missions in the Caribbean and Central America. In 1961, a New Zealand warship was sent to keep the peace in the Ocean Islands. From 1977 to 1978, New Zealand's national police dealt with domestic disorders in the Cook Islands. During the 1980s and 1990s, a "Ready Reaction Force" was formed for use throughout the Pacific Islands. Early in the twenty-first century, New Zealand supported a multinational Regional Assistance Mission, which intervened to maintain self-government and the rule of law in the Solomon Islands.[13]

For more than a century, regional hegemony was a continuing theme in New Zealand's history. Indigenous people in the South Pacific responded much as Latin America reacted to the Monroe Doctrine. In Western Samoa, for example, New Zealand's autocratic administrator General Sir George Spafford Richardson enforced a policy that he called "Samoa mo Samoa," Samoa for Samoans. What he meant was Western Samoa for New Zealand, and other powers keep out. Native leaders responded by organizing the Samoa Mau movement and turned the same slogan against New Zealanders, whom they saw as an unwelcome imperial power.[14] Samoa finally gained self-government in 1959 and independence in 1962. But as Malcolm McKinnon observed, "Independence meant to New Zealand something different from its meaning in Africa and Asia. . . . Future governors of the country were expected to be both well-disposed towards New Zealand and also in full control of their country."[15]

In general, the United States and New Zealand established regional hegemonies at a very early date. In every generation some Americans and New Zealanders tried to moderate or change this course. But the habit of regional hegemony persisted in both nations through many generations. It is more subtle today, but very much alive.[16]

Global Policies: America's Great Rule of Unilateralism

Beyond the regional level, Americans and New Zealanders went different ways. The United States for many generations preferred unilateral action in pursuit of liberty and freedom. New Zealand favored association with others in multilateral efforts to promote fairness and justice in the world. Differences in size partly explained these choices, but other factors were important. Leaders in both countries were driven by different calculations of material interest and by two distinct sets of ethical principles.

The American idea of unilateralism appeared long before the War of Independence. It was strong in New England as early as the first generation of settlement, when leaders of the Massachusetts Bay Colony cut the cross of St. George out of their English flag, framed their own laws, minted their own money, levied their own taxes, admitted and expelled immigrants as they pleased, banished anyone who displeased them, conducted their own foreign relations, made war as if they were a sovereign power, and in general kept the rest of the world at bay, especially King Charles I and Archbishop William Laud. Imperial authorities tried to crack down, with little success. A spirit of autonomy grew stronger with these events and persisted in New England and other American colonies for five generations before 1763, when more sustained British attempts to assert control led to revolution and independence.[17]

After the War of Independence, that tradition of autonomy and unilateralism gave rise to a policy of noninvolvement in the *political* affairs of other regions. The classic statement was George Washington's Farewell Address (1796). He laid it down as an iron law: "Tis our true policy to steer clear of permanent alliances with any portion of the foreign world. . . . The great rule of conduct for us in regard to foreign relations, is, in extending our commercial relations to have with them as little political connection as possible."[18]

In the early republic, Washington's "great rule of conduct" became a sacred text. On his birthday in 1812, the children of Boston marched through the streets with small copies of the Farewell Address suspended from chains around their necks.[19] Other founders repeated the same advice, often in similar words. Thomas Jefferson's first inaugural address recommended "honest friendship with all nations, entangling alliances with none."[20] Alexander Hamilton wrote, "Permanent alliance, intimate connection with any part of the foreign world is to be avoided," even as he favored international trade and intellectual exchange.[21]

The Constitution of the United States deliberately made treaties very difficult to ratify, by requiring the approval of the president, two-thirds of the Senate, and also a majority of the House of Representatives if appropriations were needed. As a result, many presidents came to share an almost pathological aversion to treaty-making. In both world wars, the United States refused to make formal alliances even with its closest friends. It made a point of entering World War I as an "associated power" rather than a formal ally of Britain and France. In World War II, Franklin Roosevelt refused Winston Churchill's repeated requests for a treaty of alliance, partly to preserve his freedom of action but mainly because he did not trust the judgment of the Senate.[22]

Not until 1947 did this policy change. As the Cold War developed, the Truman administration strongly supported the United Nations, and members of both political parties constructed a web of alliances in Europe and Asia. This effort to maintain collective security throughout the world continued from 1947 to 1975. But after the loss of the Vietnam War in 1975, and the collapse of the Soviet Union in 1989, Washington's "great rule of conduct" and Jefferson's hostility to "entangling alliances" once again gained strength in the United States. Something of that attitude appeared in the refusal of both Democratic and Republican leaders to ratify the Kyoto Treaty on environmental protection. More extreme was the unilateralism of many (not all) conservative Republicans in the presidency of George W. Bush. Many were hostile to transnational institutions for the rule of law in world affairs. Most opposed environmental agreements. Some were hostile to public health conventions.

Equally intense was a new isolationism on the left wing of the Democratic Party. After the trauma of Vietnam, many (again, not all) liberal Democrats turned sharply against American efforts to maintain collective security throughout the world. Some leaders of the Democratic Party opposed deployment of armed forces, even to deal with terrorists who murdered American citizens with impunity, or with pirates who seized American ships on the high seas.

Other Americans in both parties, including centrists such as John McCain and Hillary Clinton, were more actively interventionist and multilateral. But in the twenty-first century, leaders on the Democratic left and Republican right adopted extreme versions of George Washington's "great rule" and Thomas Jefferson's fear of "entangling alliances."[23]

Another Path: New Zealand's Great Rule of Association

An important theme in New Zealand's history is the growth of independence, in the sense of national sovereignty. Malcolm McKinnon observes that most studies of New Zealand's place in the world center on this process, and rightly so. But one might pose another question. Once New Zealanders affirmed or achieved a condition of independence, how did they use it? Here another theme appears, one that coexists with independence in interesting ways.[24]

From the start, New Zealanders independently chose the path of partnership with others. They strongly supported international associations to preserve collective security, to support their material interests, and to promote an idea of justice among nations. In pursuit of these goals, they changed partners several times in the twentieth and twenty-first centuries. They also experimented with unilateralism for a brief period in the 1980s. But their great rule of association remains a national tradition.

In the beginning, this idea took the form of close affiliation with the British Empire, and later with the British Commonwealth, an identity with deep meaning for many generations of New Zealanders. It dominated policy from the earliest years of settlement to the twentieth century. In 1930, Liberal Prime Minister George Forbes told New Zealand's Parliament, "It is only by strengthening the ties which bind us to the rest of the empire that we can hope to realize the general benefits we all hope for."[25] Most of New Zealand's prime ministers felt the same way. Conservatives such as Gordon Coates of Kaipara celebrated the imperial connection, as one might expect.[26] New Zealand's most radical prime minister, Michael Joseph Savage, supported it at a critical moment, even as his own feelings were divided. In 1939, when Britain declared war on Germany, he announced on New Zealand radio, "Where she goes, we go, where she stands, we stand. We are only a small and a young nation, but we are one and all a band of brothers, and we march forward with a union of hearts and wills."[27]

This way of thinking faded in the late twentieth century, when loyalty to the empire was mocked as "colonial cringe."[28] But six generations of New Zealanders did not think that way. To listen to the language of men as disparate as Gordon Coates on the right, George Forbes in the center, and Michael Savage on the left is to learn that all of these strong-minded men combined loyalty to the British Empire with pride in New Zealand's growing sense of nationhood. Most of them deeply believed that an imperial connection was the best way to protect their vital interests, and to promote their values in the world. All of them felt a moral obligation to support the empire but also insisted that its cause must be just.

Colonial cringe had nothing to do with it. New Zealanders did not hesitate to tell British leaders how they should act and what they should do, often in very blunt language. When Prime Minister George Forbes was in London for an imperial conference in 1930, that staunch imperial loyalist was so outspoken in his criticism of British policy that the dominions secretary was finally provoked to say, "Mr. Forbes, we were delighted to meet you, but thank God you are going!"[29]

Men such as George Forbes, Gordon Coates, and Michael Savage (a very diverse trio) supported the imperial connection as an instrument of progress, enlightenment, the rule of law, and concern for others. For them it represented a genuine ideal of peace and moral order in the world. An example was Brigadier James Hargest, DSO and Bar, a veteran of the Gallipoli campaign who went on to serve in the Second World War. In 1936, he urged his fellow members of Parliament that it was "essential we should maintain the strength of our Empire . . . believing that our Empire will never be the aggressor in any international dispute."[30]

New Zealanders also favored imperial association because of their own strategic interests. They believed that their country was too small to stand alone. In the nineteenth century they felt a need for British troops to keep peace at home, and for the Royal Navy to patrol the Pacific. When the empire did not support them, they looked for other partners. In 1870, for example, Britain caused a crisis in imperial relations by withdrawing troops from New Zealand as part of a cost-cutting program throughout the empire. Only a year earlier, Maori warriors had killed settlers in Taranaki, and many Pakeha

New Zealanders combined an idea of imperial association with a pride of nationhood and a strong spirit of independent thought. A leading example in the early twentieth century was Prime Minister George Forbes. To look into his face and to follow his encounters with British leaders is to see that "colonial cringe" had nothing to do with it.

New Zealanders were outraged by Britain's decision. The General Assembly passed resolutions of censure, and angry members threatened to leave the empire. It is interesting that they did not propose independence but another form of association. Several New Zealand leaders suggested that their country should apply for statehood in the American Union. The government actually began trade talks with the United States at that time.[31]

But other factors reinforced the strength of imperial association. As early as the 1860s a majority of all New Zealanders (Pakeha and Maori together) were of British descent. Many maintained strong family ties to relatives in the "mother country." This was very different from the United States, where as early as 1850 everyone was the member of an ethnic minority. The only common element among America's many ethnic groups was their identity with America itself. And cultural values made a difference. Americans linked ideas of liberty and freedom to national independence and no entangling alliances. New Zealanders connected ideas of fairness and justice in the world to their great rule of international association with others.[32]

The First World War as a Pivotal Moment for Both Nations

In the "Great War," as it was called, both New Zealanders and Americans supported the same side, though not in the same way. Americans were very slow to enter the war. At first they perceived it to be a European struggle between old regimes that did not share the principles on which the American republic was founded. Not until 1917, when Russia left the war and Germany recklessly attacked American citizens on the high seas, did Woodrow Wilson lead the United States into the war. He persuaded most Americans that they were supporting Britain and France in a great struggle for liberty, freedom, and democracy.

Wilson's war message to Congress was cast in these terms. He declared, "The right is more precious than peace, and we shall fight for the things which we have always carried nearest our hearts . . . for the rights and liberties of small nations, for a universal dominion of right by such a concert of free peoples as shall bring peace and safety to all nations and make the world itself free."[33] On January 8, 1918, Wilson summarized his specific war aims in the famous Fourteen Points. Nine of them referred to liberty, freedom, and self-determination as moral rights.[34]

New Zealanders understood the purposes of the First World War in other terms. Sir Francis Bell, soon to be minister of external

For many generations, American foreign policy centered on a rule of unilateral action in pursuit of national interest, and the cause of liberty and freedom. In World War I American war aims were symbolized in this Philadelphia celebration of liberty and freedom on Armistice Day, November 11, 1918.

relations, declared that the war was for "the cause of justice." Sometimes he also spoke of "liberty and justice" as a "heritage and birthright." But Bell and others put heavy stress on civilization, decency, fair play, and loyalty to the mother country. Where Americans thought of liberty and freedom for individuals and nations, New Zealanders were thinking more in terms of mutual obligations, justice, and equity.[35]

Once begun, the First World War profoundly changed the international condition of both nations. In 1914, New Zealand was brought into the war as a British colony, without even being consulted. Five years later, it went to the peace conference at Versailles as an independent nation with its own voice in world affairs—a revolution in external relations.

For the United States, the First World War was a turning point in another direction. Since the nineteenth century, the republic had been expanding its role in foreign affairs—first in its own hemisphere and the Pacific. In 1914, it still remained a regional power, with little presence in European affairs. By the end of the Great War, the United States briefly became the strongest power in the world. In November 1918, its military strength was approaching that of Britain and France combined. Its economy was much the strongest in the world. As the nations gathered for the peace conference at Versailles, many people throughout the world expected the United States to take the lead in a global effort to prevent a world war from happening again.[36]

Versailles and the League of Nations: Opposite Policies, 1919–39

At Versailles, President Woodrow Wilson chaired the commission to draft a covenant for a League of Nations. Much of the document came from his pen. He struggled painfully with difficult problems of "self-determination," but public opinion in Europe rallied to him, despite the entrenched hostility of European leaders. When he was done in 1919, most Americans also supported the treaty and the league, as did three-quarters of state legislatures and simple majorities in both houses of Congress.[37]

But the Constitution required ratification by two-thirds of the Senate. Even before the Versailles Treaty arrived in that chamber, it was opposed by a "round-robin" of thirty-nine Republican senators, enough to defeat the treaty by seven votes. Their spokesman was Henry Cabot Lodge, a creative statesman in his youth who became

Woodrow Wilson's purposes in World War I appeared in his Fourteen Points, which were about liberty, freedom, self-determination, open covenants, and the rule of law. At Versailles in 1919 he found himself in deep conflict with European leaders such as Georges Clemenceau.

an increasingly narrow and vindictive partisan, consumed by personal jealousy of President Wilson. Lodge himself had actually proposed a League of Nations that was very similar to what was agreed, but reversed himself when Wilson put it forward.[38]

The president, for his part, was so infuriated by Republican "Irreconcilables" that he alienated moderate "Reservationists" as well. Wilson was exhausted by the duties of his office and in failing health. He turned away from the Senate, took his case to the country, and a great struggle followed. Wilson's internationalism was strongly supported in the South, and also by liberals and moderates throughout the country. It was opposed by conservatives, by voters of German, Irish, and Italian descent, and by midwesterners and New Englanders who wanted no part of entangling alliances or world governments. In the end everybody lost. Under heavy strain, Wilson suffered a crippling stroke and his campaign collapsed. The United States never signed the Treaty of Versailles, never joined the League of Nations, and remained technically at war with Germany, Austria, and Hungary for many years.[39]

Wilson's successor, Republican President Warren Harding, ran for office on what appeared to be a solemn promise to join the League of Nations. After the election of 1920, he broke his word and turned against the league. The United States refused even to join international health programs, and leaders in the State Department did not bother to answer their mail from league officials. As late as 1935, the small band of Irreconcilables in the Senate kept the United States out of the World Court, though once again a majority of Americans wished to join. In this long-running American controversy, both sides claimed to be defenders of liberty and freedom. Internationalists insisted that freedom at home was linked to freedom throughout the world. "Isolationists," as they came to be called, talked of freedom in one nation, at the same time that Stalinists in the Soviet Union were speaking of "socialism in one country."[40]

Once again, New Zealand went the opposite way during the 1920s and 1930s. New Zealand politicians on the left and right were initially not enthusiastic about the league. Harry Holland (1868–1933), Australian-born immigrant editor of the radical *Maoriland Worker*, attacked the league as a capitalist cabal, and the New Zealand Labour Party also opposed it for a time. Conservative Nationalist backbenchers insisted that their loyalty was to the empire, not the league. But a moderate majority of New Zealanders were in the middle on this question, and they came to favor the league. New Zealand joined it as an independent nation and soon became a staunch supporter.[41]

A central figure was Sir William Joseph Jordan, "Bill Jordan" to his countrymen. He had emigrated from Britain in 1904 and worked his way up from a penniless day laborer to success as a small businessman. At the same time that Jordan did well as a capitalist, he also became a Christian socialist. Photos show him in a double-breasted business suit with a small trilby hat perched on the top of a very large head. Jordan helped to found the New Zealand Labour Party but was often at odds with its leaders. He supported the First World War when they opposed it, joined the army, and was severely wounded in 1918. After the war Jordan was elected to Parliament by large majorities through the 1920s and became very popular in the country, but leaders of his own party resented his independence and rejected his ideas. When Labour rose to power in 1935, Jordan was denied a cabinet post and sent to London as New Zealand's high commissioner and representative in the League of Nations—a place of exile for fractious leaders.[42]

Jordan embraced his new job with enthusiasm and became a prominent figure in the League of Nations. He thought of it as a way of protecting small nations and as an institution for preserving peace in the world. To those ends, he took the lead in trying to put teeth in

William Joseph Jordan was New Zealand's commissioner in London and representative to the League of Nations. He warned early and often of Fascist aggression, worked for collective security, and urged the rearmament of open societies. New Zealanders supported him in pursuit of international justice. Americans went another way in the name of liberty and independence.

the league, much against the wishes of Britain and other European powers. Jordan spoke powerfully in favor of provisions for military action against aggressors, while British diplomats were observed to be squirming "restlessly in their seats." He succeeded in persuading the league to appoint a commission to study the question, but after a few acrimonious meetings, European and British delegates deliberately blocked the measure by procedural objections.[43]

New Zealanders of different parties and ideologies rallied to Bill Jordan's leadership. His attempts to strengthen the league were endorsed by civil servants such as Carl Berendsen, Labour leaders including Michael Savage and Peter Fraser, and enlightened conservatives such as William Downie Stewart. Malcolm McKinnon writes, "Generally Labour New Zealand was as far removed as right-wing New Zealand from the isolationist and secessionist nationalism found in Ireland, South Africa, Canada, and had little of the left-isolationist nationalism found in Australia."[44]

Within the league, New Zealand became a world leader for collective security in the 1930s, so much so that people began to speak of it as "small power rampant," a common phrase of the period. The United States by contrast was a "large power dormant." American leaders of both parties gravely weakened the league. New Zealanders to the left and right worked tirelessly to make it stronger.

Fascism: Collective Security vs. Isolationism

For open societies, the central problem of foreign policy in the 1930s was the rise of Fascism in Europe and militarism in Asia. Many people in both New Zealand and the United States were shocked by these events, but they responded in different ways. New Zealand leaders redoubled their efforts to strengthen collective security. That purpose appeared in the foreign policy of New Zealand's First Labour Government through the late 1930s. Its leaders spoke of a "moral foreign policy" and supported Bill Jordan's efforts to resist Fascist aggression and to strengthen the League of Nations by reform of its covenant.[45]

In 1935, Fascist Italy attacked Ethiopia. The world powers temporized, vacillated, or looked the other way. In top secret meetings, leaders in Britain and France even proposed to join Italy in the partition of Ethiopia. The government of New Zealand was outraged by that idea and strongly opposed it. After the war, it refused to recognize Mussolini's regime in Ethiopia.[46]

New Zealand also took the lead in opposing Fascist intervention in Spain. When Mussolini and Hitler sent military aid to Franco, Bill

Jordan demanded that the League of Nations should compel a "withdrawal of foreign combatants forthwith." His speeches were a sustained attempt to awaken the conscience of the Western nations. "The people are our concern," he demanded. "What is the Council definitely going to do?

In 1937, Japan attacked China. Once again New Zealand took a leading role, and Jordan was the most articulate supporter of collective security in the league. He demanded sanctions, military action against Japan, and aid for China, with strong backing in New Zealand not only from the left but also from a strong strain of Churchillian liberal conservatism on the right. Centrist leaders shared a concern for the rule of international law and an intense antipathy to dictators of every persuasion. There were some exceptions in New Zealand. A few "deeply insular" voices were heard from the back benches, but they did not determine policy or set the tone of debate.[47]

Jordan warned again and again that Fascist aggression threatened the peace of the entire world. "The earth is being menaced," he told the league. No great power supported him in the mid-1930s. Britain and France recognized Franco's regime when it appeared to be winning, just as they had recognized the Italian conquest of Ethiopia. Stalin made a pact with Hitler and joined him in devouring eastern Europe. New Zealand steadfastly refused to acknowledge the legitimacy of Fascist aggression, even as many conservative British leaders did so.

Through all of this, the United States remained aloof. Some of the loudest voices in American foreign policy during the late 1920s and early 1930s came from isolationists on the left and right. To the left was Senator Hiram Johnson of California, an old Progressive who complained that the principle of collective security would require Americans to be "riot police in every nation's back yard." He denounced the Treaty of Versailles, attacked the League of Nations, opposed the World Court, resisted military preparedness, and did his best to stop Lend-Lease. In 1945, he cast the only negative vote in the Senate against the charter of the United Nations. By that date his influence was gone, but before the war Hiram Johnson was a power in the land.[48]

To the right was William Borah, a Republican from Idaho. He was the image of a six-term senator, with a leonine head, craggy features, a snow-white mane, and a gift for oratory that resembled biblical prophecy. It was observed that few leaders could equal "his ability to arouse the country on a public question."[49] He was deeply conservative on foreign affairs. A native son of the Middle West, Borah had never left the United States and was reflexively hostile to people

Revisionist scholars have challenged the accuracy of terms such as "isolationist" and "irreconcilable," but they fit Senator William Borah. He angrily opposed the Versailles Treaty, the League of Nations, and the World Court. Through his long service in the Senate he fought Wilson and Franklin Roosevelt and had a major impact on opinion in the Congress.

unlike himself. As chairman of the Foreign Relations Committee, he became "the most powerful voice on foreign affairs in the country." Borah was called the "Great Opposer," the most irreconcilable of all Irreconcilables on the Versailles Treaty, the League of Nations, and the World Court. As dictators of the right and left attacked their neighbors, Borah rejected collective security in every form and urged unilateral disarmament. Hiram Johnson called him "our spearless leader."[50] Some historians have challenged the accuracy of the label "isolationist" for these men, but it accurately described Hiram Johnson and William Borah. The politics of the Senate and a long tradition of noninvolvement gave them great power.[51]

Their enemy was Franklin Roosevelt, who had a very different worldview. He had learned to speak French and German as a child, lived much of his youth abroad, and became a strong internationalist. For his secretary of state he chose Cordell Hull, a Wilsonian idealist who hated Fascism, aggression, and appeasement. But Roosevelt was careful not to get ahead of American opinion, and isolationists continued to shape the debate over foreign policy.

Two Rearmament Programs

In 1938, Bill Jordan reported to his government that the League of Nations had failed to keep the peace or deter aggression in Europe and Asia. New Zealand embarked on a new policy of collective security, primarily within the British Commonwealth. The Labour government, which had long opposed military spending, now began to rearm. It founded an active Air Department in 1937 and increased appropriations for planes and pilots. At the same time, it built a modern naval dockyard at Devonport near Auckland, acquired large warships, and expanded its Territorial Army. Defensive measures were undertaken in close association with Britain and the British Commonwealth. A strategic center for the Pacific was Singapore. New Zealand contributed more than a million pounds to its development— a large sum for a small nation in an economic depression.[52]

The United States also began to rearm, but with reluctance. After a decade of neglect in the 1920s, the country was militarily very weak. Its aging warships were obsolete, and its air forces nearly nonexistent. When Calvin Coolidge was told that the Army Air Corps did not have enough first-line aircraft even for its handful of pilots to fly, he made a joke of it: "Why can't we just buy one airplane and have all the pilots take turns." American politicians to the left and right shared that hostility to military spending.[53] Here again the great exception was Franklin Roosevelt. As early as 1933, he was quick to recognize the strategic importance of airpower and seapower for America's security. In 1934, he used New Deal funds to build the new aircraft carriers *Yorktown* and *Enterprise* and new classes of modern cruisers and destroyers. These were the ships that would win the pivotal Battle of Midway in 1942 and the hard-fought Solomons campaigns. They were there only because Roosevelt had acted decisively eight years earlier, when Congress and the country were strongly opposed to rearmament.[54]

Roosevelt also began the expansion of military aviation. He launched major construction programs in 1937 and 1938, not primarily of the planes themselves but of big plants and massive equipment necessary for their mass production—a providential act of foresight. Word reached him that Fascist Germany was building an atomic weapon that could give it world supremacy. Ironically Roosevelt had to obtain some of the funds for development of nuclear weapons as deterrents from the Carnegie Endowment for International Peace.[55]

In Washington and Wellington, rearmament had fundamentally different goals during the late 1930s. New Zealand's program was meant to be a contribution to collective security within the Commonwealth. America was preparing to fight alone if need be. Roosevelt's two-ocean navy and his huge programs for aircraft construction of long-distance bombers were designed to defeat Fascist enemies without an ally if necessary.

The Second World War, 1935–39: Allies of Two Kinds

New Zealand and the United States entered the Second World War in ways that differed from their involvement in the First. As we have seen, in 1914, New Zealand had been brought into the war by British leaders without even token consultation. In 1939, it made its own decision and issued a separate declaration of war, which was delivered to Germany not through Great Britain but by way of the American embassy in Berlin. This time in New Zealand cities there was no jingoism or joyous "mafficking," as it was called after the militant celebrations of Mafeking Night in the Boer War. New Zealand went to war in 1939 with deep foreboding, remembering the bitter cost of the last one, and knowing well what the next was likely to be.[56]

But most New Zealanders agreed that Fascist aggression had to be stopped. They had no doubt that the cause of Britain, France, and Poland was their own. When conservative leader Gordon Coates of Kaipara strongly supported the Labour government on the war, he observed that "what he liked to call British traditions of honesty and fair play were threatened by Hitler on the rampage." Other New Zealanders spoke of freedom and democracy, but the strongest themes were collective security, world justice, humanity, and cooperation with others in "defence of civilization."[57]

In America, opinion on the war was at first very different. Most people in the United States detested German Fascists and Japanese militarists. Even Colonel Robert McCormick's conservative and isolationist *Chicago Tribune* despised Adolf Hitler almost as much as it reviled Franklin Roosevelt. But as late as 1941 many Americans did not believe that Hitler's attack on Poland or Japanese aggression in China were cause for the United States to enter the war. Once again, the great rule of noninvolvement prevailed. President Roosevelt was careful to respect prevailing opinion that was stronger in Congress than in the country.[58]

Then came Pearl Harbor, and even isolationists called for war. Colonel McCormick's *Chicago Tribune* demanded a fight to the finish against Japan—not for Roosevelt's large-minded ideas of liberty and the rule of law but for the rule of retaliation, *lex talionis*. Pearl Harbor united a divided country—against Japan. Even after Pearl Harbor Americans were not ready to fight Germany, until Hitler settled the question by declaring war on the United States. Only then did the nation join together against the Axis powers.[59]

When the Pacific war began, other strains were growing within the British Commonwealth. New Zealand had vigorously supported a policy of collective security in the Pacific. At heavy cost it helped pay for the great base at Singapore, with the understanding that Britain's "main fleet" would use it to keep the peace in the region. But in the dark days of 1940, British leaders warned New Zealand and Australia that the Royal Navy would be unable to "send a fleet to the Far East."[60]

Pearl Harbor was followed by a series of shattering defeats for the Allies in the Pacific. In six months, three Western empires fell to surprise attacks by smaller Japanese forces. The worst military disaster was in Malaya, where a Japanese army of 30,000 men defeated more than 130,000 British, Indian, and Australian troops. The quickest collapse was that of the Dutch East Indies, which fell in two weeks. The most painful defeat for the United States was in the Philippines, where American and Filipino forces kept fighting for five months but were forced to surrender in May 1942. Encouraged by these victories, Japanese leaders launched another round of aggression. They invaded New Guinea, attacked Australia from the air, and moved deeper into the South Pacific.[61]

In 1942, as Japanese forces were advancing rapidly, most of New Zealand's trained troops were in the Middle East, and the country was nearly defenseless. Britain was unable to offer help. These events brought a revolution in New Zealand's external relations—but within its traditional frame. Once again New Zealanders formed close connections with others in yet another system of collective security, this time with the United States and Australia. New Zealand historian Keith Sinclair remembered the desperate days in early 1942, when old men and youths such as himself stood guard on the North Island with obsolete weapons, some from the Anglo-Maori Wars. Sinclair recalled the dangerous moment when he saw "a grey ship slipping down the Hauraki Gulf, then two, then ten." To his amazement, "it was not the Japanese who invaded New Zealand" but twenty thousand United States Marines.[62]

When they arrived, sixty thousand battle-hardened New Zealanders were fighting the Germans in Africa and Europe. In an hour of grave danger, New Zealand made the extraordinary decision to maintain its major military strength on the other side of the world. Not many nations would have done such a thing. Even as Japanese forces moved rapidly south, New Zealand's leaders made the same strategic choices as did their allies in Britain and the United States— that both Germany and Japan must be defeated, but that Germany was the most dangerous foe and the first priority. That decision is still debated in New Zealand, though it turned out to be the right choice for the conduct of the war. New Zealand troops played a vital and arguably a decisive role in the two pivotal battles at El Alamein in North Africa, which together were the turning point in campaigns against the Axis in Africa and the Mediterranean. The decision to keep them there was a testament to New Zealand's faith in collective security. It rested on a clear perception that the national interest lay in the strength of its international associations.[63]

After the fact, several scholars in New Zealand have remembered this period as a time of "dual dependency" on Britain and the United States. That phrase is not correct. New Zealand's policy during the war was not to be dependent on any nation but to join the grand coalition as an independent partner, always on its own terms. As the war went on, Churchill and Roosevelt held Prime Minister Peter Fraser in high regard, for his courage, resolve, integrity, and autonomous judgment.[64] With his leadership, New Zealand operated as a partner in the grand coalition,. As late as 1941, New Zealand maintained only a single diplomatic mission in London. During the war, permanent legations were established in the United States, Canada, Australia, and the Soviet Union. A separate Department of External Affairs was created in 1943.[65]

After the collapse of the League of Nations, and the failure of Britain to protect its dominions in the Pacific, Prime Minister Fraser's task was to construct another broad system of collective security— which he did, and very rapidly.[66] In 1944, Fraser signed New Zealand's first bilateral treaty with Australia. This was the Canberra Pact, in which the two Pacific powers agreed that military bases in the region could not be a basis for territorial claims, and that no changes of sovereignty could be taken without their mutual agreement. U.S. Secretary of State Cordell Hull found his nation excluded by a South Pacific analogue to the Monroe Doctrine, and he responded with an explosion of righteous wrath, with no apparent effect on his allies. The Canberra Pact also framed a system of trusteeship of Pacific islands and proposed a regional commission, which seriously displeased leaders in Washington and London. This was hardly an expression of dual dependency.[67]

The United Nations: Two Ideas of International Organization

As the war approached its end, New Zealand historian Chris Trotter observed that "scores of young and idealistic people argued, wrote, planned, and dreamed about a new society. One source of inspiration was the newly formed United Nations." Many young

Americans shared that hope, but Yanks and Kiwis had different plans for this infant organization.[68]

In 1945, Prime Minister Fraser led a delegation of New Zealanders to San Francisco and took an active role in the creation of the United Nations. They built a coalition of small nations and tried to change the new organization in the same way that their predecessors had sought to reform the covenant of the League of Nations. New Zealand's diplomatic representatives sought stronger commitments for collective security against aggression and tighter guarantees of territorial integrity. One of them, Carl Berendsen, complained that the great powers "made no pledges, no guarantees, and no undertakings."[69]

New Zealand's delegation also proposed a larger role for the General Assembly and opposed a veto in the hands of the United States, Britain, France, China, and the Soviet Union as "unfair and indefensible," in Fraser's words.[70] The Americans wanted more power for themselves and other large nations, as a way of serving their national interest and also as an expression of their traditional ideas of a free society. Vetoes had long been built into American constitutions as a way of protecting liberty and freedom from tyranny of the majority. Fraser and his fellow New Zealanders deeply disagreed. He wrote, "It is very bad if one nation can hold up the advancement of mankind." Fraser was defeated, and the great powers got their vetoes. But New Zealand's delegates kept working toward their goals for many years. In time the United Nations developed partly on the lines that Fraser and the others had envisioned at San Francisco—a forum for the protection of small nations, and an active protector of collective security through peacekeeping forces. The United Nations is a compromise between different ideas that were held by the United States and New Zealand in San Francisco. The result is a solution that satisfies nobody and is indispensable to all.[71]

Once again, as in the League of Nations, New Zealand became a world leader in what might be called "small-power diplomacy." In that role, it broadened its range of association with other powers. New Zealand's diplomatic posts continued to multiply rapidly, from one in 1940 to five in 1945, eight in 1960, forty-four in 1991, fifty-six in 2006.[72] During that same period, the United States also greatly increased its engagement in the world. Throughout the critical years after World War II, leaders in New Zealand and the United States combined the pursuit of national interest with a principled approach to foreign policy, but their interests and principles were not the same.

The Cold War

Then came another global conflict, unlike any other in world history. It rose in response to aggressive Communist movements around the world, led by a Stalinist dictatorship in the Soviet Union. That country had been severely weakened by the Second World War. In 1945, its economy was shattered, its cities destroyed, its farms ruined, and more than twenty million people had been killed. After the war, when the Western democracies rapidly demobilized, Joseph Stalin maintained a large army and actually expanded his forces in uniform, with huge numbers of internal security troops. Stalin saw an opportunity to stabilize his regime by conquest of neighboring states. The West watched in horror as fourteen nations were liberated from Fascist tyranny in eastern Europe, only to fall under Communist tyranny from 1944 to 1948. In China, another Communist tyranny defeated a corrupt Nationalist regime. Chairman Mao proved to be more destructive of human life than even Stalin or Hitler had been.[73]

These regimes dominated their populations by terror and violence on a scale that the world had never seen. During the Second World War from 1937 to 1945, Fascist regimes killed between forty million and fifty million people, many in cold blood and in scenes of unimaginable savagery. But these atrocities of the Fascist right were exceeded by the crimes of the Communist left. A careful study by French scholars, many from the left, concluded that Communist regimes were directly responsible for the deaths of between eighty million and one hundred million human beings in the years from 1920 to 1989. Most were their own citizens, and many were killed with extreme cruelty by Communist executioners. As with German Fascism and Japanese militarism, the world was slow to discover the magnitude of these crimes. Their scale defied belief and was generally denied by supporters in open societies, even when quantitative evidence emerged after 1989.[74]

The people of the United States, much against their inclination, felt themselves compelled to take the lead against Communist aggression, which was perceived to be a direct threat to liberty and freedom. The result, in the early years of that struggle, was a strong bipartisan consensus for anti-Communism, with little dissent until the war in Vietnam. Other nations were more divided. In Britain and western Europe, many on the left detested capitalism, disliked the United States, and sympathized with the social purposes of Communism. The problem of the Cold War was compounded by these divisions, by the enormous size of Communist military forces, and by nuclear weapons.

In America, several small circles of leaders, both Democrats and Republicans, guided the United States through these difficult years. They have been called the "wise men," which arguably they were, and "the American establishment," which they were not. That unitary English phrase does not fit the pluralism of American elites. One group of Harry Truman's wise men came out of the U.S. Army and West Point: George Marshall, Omar Bradley, Matthew Ridgeway, and many others who inherited a stoic tradition of honor, duty, integrity, and service to the country. Others were dour Scotch-Irish Presbyterians, schooled at Princeton: George Kennan in Democratic administrations; the Dulles brothers among Republicans. A third group were New Yorkers and New Englanders who went from Yale to Wall Street and then into public service (Averill Harriman, Robert Lovett). A fourth group consisted of Harry Truman's poker-playing, bourbon-drinking backcountry buddies from Missouri, Kentucky, and the southern highlands: Charles Ross, Fred Vinson, Clinton Anderson, Tom Clark—rough diamonds but highly skilled in the art of democratic politics. These plural American elites were open to talent. They recruited the sons and grandsons of Irish Catholic immigrants such as John J. McCloy and James Forrestal; Jewish Americans such as David Lilienthal and Benjamin Cohen; and Afro-Americans Ralph Bunche and Thurgood Marshall.

Harry Truman found the wisdom to bring these very different men together at the center of his administration. Even in their diversity, they shared a deep devotion to liberty, freedom, and a republic of laws. Many believed that Communist systems were fundamentally unsound and would inevitably fail. Most agreed that the path of wisdom was to contain specific acts of Communist aggression by sufficient force but to avoid a major war that could become a nuclear apocalypse. While they waited for Communist regimes to collapse under the weight of their crimes and follies, they also sought to build open systems in other nations through programs such as the Marshall Plan.[75]

This was something new in American history—a prolonged struggle without the promise of quick victory. It was also a struggle that the United States could not win by itself. For the first time in its history its leaders began to construct a vast web of alliances around the world: NATO, SEATO, CENTO, and many more. These American commitments were carefully hedged. For example, in negotiations that led to the formation of NATO, European leaders asked for a fixed commitment to support any nation that was attacked. American leaders, still mindful of Washington's "great rule," agreed only that each nation must "take such actions as it deems necessary, including the use of armed force." When the NATO Treaty was being signed at Washington in 1949, Dean Acheson was amused to hear the Marine Band play George Gershwin's song "It Ain't Necessarily So."[76]

In New Zealand, early opinion on the Cold War was more divided than in America but less so than in Europe. Some New Zealanders on the right were strongly anti-Communist. Others on the left were anti-capitalist and sympathetic to the Soviet Union. Among the latter were D. P. Costello, a Russian-speaking intelligence officer during World War II and later New Zealand's chargé d'affaires in Moscow. Costello believed that the "principal responsibility" for the Cold War "lies not with the Russians but fairly and squarely on the present US administration." Other New Zealanders who sympathized with Communism were Jock Barnes of the Watersiders Union and civil servant W. B. Sutch, who headed the New Zealand delegation in the United Nations and ran the Department of Industries and Commerce in Wellington.[77]

With these exceptions, most New Zealanders supported the centrist policy of containment from 1946 to 1965. A steady voice at the center was Carl Berendsen, secretary of internal affairs, head of the Prime Minister's Department, secretary of the war cabinet, and minister in Washington from 1943 to 1952. Berendsen got on well with Americans, but he wrote to his friend Alister McIntosh, "There is much in the American policy and attitude to which I take exception. . . . I do not share their belief that political democracy is synonymous with free enterprise capitalism." He thought that an obsession with liberty and freedom set the United States apart from "other people, like ourselves who, foolish democrats though we may be, are attempting some middle way."[78]

Even so, Berendsen firmly believed that Communist regimes were fundamentally in the wrong, and that "no right-thinking person could possibly hesitate for a moment in approving the line that the Americans are taking. . . . [W]e cannot go on sacrificing millions of people to the totalitarian way of life. . . . [I]t would be morally wrong to do so." Berendsen concluded, "The only thing I do see in black and white is the necessity of establishing an effective system of collective security."[79] Berendsen held much the same strong view of Communism in the 1950s as he did of Fascism in the 1930s. Malcolm McKinnon writes, "Berendsen's thinking provides one of the connections between 1930s anti-Fascist collective security and 1950s anti-Communist collective security."[80]

Both New Zealand and the United States
were fortunate to have their "wise men"
after World War II. These were statesmen
of long experience and mature judgment.
In New Zealand a strong and steady leader
was Carl Berendsen. His values were different from those of American leaders, but
they made common cause on major issues of
foreign policy.

Other leaders lent their weight to this policy. Like the United
States, New Zealand also had a group of "wise men" who reinforced
the center in New Zealand politics during the Cold War. Besides
Berendsen, they included the civil servant Alister McIntosh. Working
with them were National Party leaders such as "Gentleman Jack"
Marshall and Christian Nationalist Keith Holyoake and socialists
Arnold Nordmeyer and Walter Nash (a lay reader in the Anglican
Church). These men steered their parties toward the center and
built a broad base of consensus around an idea of collective security
in the early years of the Cold War.[81]

The Korean Crisis and the ANZUS Alliance

In 1950, the Cold War became a hard struggle for both New
Zealand and the United States. The policy of containment came
under heavy strain. A major test occurred in that year when Communist North Korea attempted to conquer its southern neighbor, in a
war of aggression. Now it is known that the attack was approved in
the Soviet Union and China, in part because of a careless statement
by American Secretary of State Dean Acheson that Korea was outside
the American "defense perimeter." On June 25, 1950, the North
Korean army moved across the 38th parallel, confident that American troops would not oppose them.[82]

Another of New Zealand's wise men was civil servant Alister McIntosh, who helped to guide his country, its allies, and the world through a difficult and dangerous era.

To the shock of Communist leaders, Truman resolved to fight. He intervened in Korea with strong support from both political parties, and the United Nations rallied to his leadership after Soviet diplomats had walked out. The burden of the war fell heavily on South Korea itself and the English-speaking nations, who had rapidly demobilized after 1945 and were wholly unprepared for war in 1950. The new South Korean army lacked the resources to stand against the masses of North Korean invaders. The only American forces in reach were garrison troops in Japan who lacked training and equipment. New Zealand's army was unable to put even a brigade of troops into the field, and its first-line fighter aircraft were in long-term storage.[83]

But the populations of both nations supported intervention in Korea, and their governments acted with courage and resolve. The United States once again mobilized on a large scale. Altogether six million Americans served in uniform during the Korean War, more than in the First World War. Leaders in Washington prepared to fight two major wars at the same time against Communist aggression—one in eastern Asia, the other in western Europe. American leaders also made clear a determination to use nuclear weapons against the Soviet Union, if necessary to stop acts of aggression.

In New Zealand a newly elected Conservative government headed by Canterbury businessman Sidney Holland dispatched warships to Korea and announced that ground forces would follow. Holland timed his public announcement to precede statements by Britain and Australia. Recruiting offices in New Zealand were swamped with volunteers. New Zealanders rallied to that cause, and their troops served in Korea until 1954. In a quiet Auckland neighborhood and other towns, one finds memorials to New Zealanders who served in what has been called a "forgotten war" and helped to keep a larger peace in a very violent world.

New Zealand's contribution was small in material terms but large in moral impact. Its representatives helped to construct a diplomatic position in support of collective security, and its leaders spoke eloquently of international justice and the rule of law. The purposes of the United States were cast more in terms of a struggle for liberty and freedom against a Communist aggressor.

In 1951, when the Korean War was approaching its climax, representatives of the United States, Australia, and New Zealand created yet another mutual defense pact called ANZUS. Here again the United States hedged its commitment. In case of attack on any nation, American diplomats could offer only a vague promise that their country would "meet the common danger in accordance with its constitutional processes." The Australians and New Zealanders were not happy with that formulation, but the agreement worked for a generation.

The Agony of Vietnam

Then came Vietnam. Communist leaders in North Vietnam, after defeating France at Dien Bien Phu, attempted to unite their divided nation by force. The policy of containment was severely tested. The United States, Australia, and New Zealand recognized an obligation under the SEATO Pact to support the Saigon regime in South Vietnam, even though it was deeply corrupt and disliked by its own people. The administration of Lyndon Johnson committed five hundred thousand U.S. troops. The New Zealand government of Prime Minister Keith Holyoake reluctantly joined the Americans and Australians in the war.[84]

The armed forces of the SEATO allies won every major battle and lost the war. The military challenge was compounded by the size of the country (three times larger than Korea), by safe havens that could not be attacked, by the difficulty of fighting a land war on the

Asian mainland, and by massive support for North Vietnam from China and the Soviet Union. A decisive factor was domestic opposition to the war, which rapidly increased in the United States, New Zealand, and most Western nations after the Tet Offensive in 1968.[85]

Questions of right and wrong in Vietnam were blurred by corruption and tyranny in South Vietnam, by the errors of American leaders, and by crimes such as the massacre at My Lai on March 16, 1968, when undisciplined American troops under an incompetent officer murdered at least 450 unarmed South Vietnamese civilians, mostly women, children, and the elderly. In America, the war was fought mainly by working-class conscripts, while children of the middle class escaped service through student deferments. Alienation and anomie spread through the American armed forces, which in the later years of the Vietnam War suffered an unprecedented collapse of discipline and morale.

These problems began in the presidency of John Kennedy, increased rapidly during the administration of Lyndon Johnson, and grew much worse in the years of Richard Nixon. The Nixon administration had little respect for the rule of law in foreign or domestic affairs. It violated the rights of neutral nations such as Cambodia and Laos without restraint. The peace movement gathered momentum after the bombing of Cambodia in 1969 and the invasion of Cambodia by American troops in 1970. At home, high officials repeatedly violated the rights of American citizens and authorized crimes by agents of the federal government. Consumed by deep fears, President Nixon himself systematically abused the powers of his office and alarmed many members of his own party. By the measure of criminal indictments and convictions, the Nixon administration was the most corrupt and tyrannical in American history. It ended in the Watergate crisis, with the resignation of the president on the eve of his impeachment. The disaster of the Nixon presidency brought the American Republic to the lowest ebb in its long history.[86]

Anti-Nuclear Diplomacy:
The Rupture Between New Zealand and the United States

As these domestic difficulties increased, the Cold War alliance began to come apart. New Zealanders grew increasingly unhappy with American foreign policy. Prime Minister Norman Kirk made a point of not visiting the United States during the Nixon years, except to address the United Nations.[87] The Carter administration angered

New Zealanders in another way. It raised the ethical tone in Washington, but Prime Minister Robert Muldoon complained about President Carter's "habits of making far-reaching decisions without consultation, and then expecting his friends and allies to back him up."[88]

A growing source of conflict was the question of nuclear weapons, an issue of deep concern in New Zealand, in part because three nuclear powers did much of their testing in the South Pacific. The United States had exploded atomic and hydrogen bombs on the islands of Eniwetok and Bikini in 1952 and 1954. France also conducted its major tests in the South Pacific after Algeria won its independence in 1962. British Prime Minister Anthony Eden attempted to test nuclear weapons on islands that belonged to New Zealand without even bothering to notify New Zealanders. The result was an explosion of anger throughout the antipodes.[89]

The antinuclear campaign has been interpreted as an expression of a new intensity of independence in foreign relations, with a particular concern about the Pacific environment, which was being polluted by the nuclear tests of France, Britain, and the United States. But something else was going on here.[90] The peace movement gathered new strength in the early 1980s, when the Reagan administration changed the foreign policy of the United States. It abandoned the doctrine of containment and began to speak of the destruction of the "Evil Empire" in the Soviet Union. Military spending increased, and the Reagan administration deployed a new generation of forward-placed Pershing missiles, which were designed to destroy "command and control" in a way that Soviet leaders perceived as a "first strike" capability. International tensions increased sharply, and the antinuclear movement surged throughout the Western world. It gathered strength in the United States, where university towns adopted their own foreign policy. The city of Cambridge, Massachusetts, unilaterally declared itself a nuclear-free zone, much to the fury of the city of Washington.

New Zealanders began to oppose visits by nuclear-powered warships of the United States Navy unless the American government accepted liability for any accident. To the disappointment of the antinuclear movement, the United States willingly agreed to do so. Antinuclear leaders changed their position and insisted that visits by all nuclear-powered, nuclear-armed, and "nuclear-capable" ships were unacceptable. Labour Prime Minister David Lange sought a compromise: ships with nuclear powered engines would be allowed in New Zealand, but not those with nuclear weapons. Elements within the

Labour Party were more radical than its leaders, and in 1982 and 1983 the party voted to end alliances with nuclear nations.[91]

The trouble came to a head in 1985, when the U.S. Navy proposed a routine "goodwill" visit to New Zealand by the aging destroyer USS *Buchanan*. In 1979, *Buchanan* had been welcomed there. Everyone knew that she was not equipped with nuclear weapons, but the U.S. Navy (like others) refused to make public statements about the armament of individual ships or aircraft. The radical wing of the Labour Party, led by Helen Clark and Margaret Wilson, seized that issue as a way of shattering the ANZUS alliance and driving their party and the nation to the left. After a large demonstration in Auckland, Prime Minister Lange yielded. The Labour government refused to admit USS *Buchanan* to New Zealand ports on the entirely fraudulent ground that she was "nuclear-capable" and might possibly be carrying nuclear weapons.[92]

The United States was caught by surprise. President Ronald Reagan and Defense Secretary Caspar Weinberger believed that the Cold War was approaching its climax, and that American efforts to destroy the Evil Empire of Communism were undercut by peace movements in Western nations. Their responses were as passionate as the attacks upon them. Only in New Zealand did the peace movement gain control of a national government. When its ruling Labour Party continued to exclude American warships from New Zealand ports, the United States announced that New Zealand's actions had breached the terms of the ANZUS treaty. It terminated military relations, stopped exchanges of intelligence, ordered New Zealand officers to leave the United States, and reduced diplomatic relations to low-level contacts. The Reagan administration virtually broke relations with New Zealand.[93]

Australia, Japan, and other Pacific nations supported the American position, but New Zealand's Labour Government was unrepentant. It enacted its antinuclear policy into law and banned all nuclear-armed or nuclear-powered ships. New Zealand's antinuclear policy symbolized a diplomatic revolution. In the 1980s, New Zealand had developed a new unilateral approach to international affairs.

Lange's Labour government did not only break fundamentally with the United States under Reagan. It also moved farther apart from Britain under Margaret Thatcher. New Zealand troops were withdrawn from Cyprus and Singapore after a presence of thirty years. For many decades, big New Zealand warships had been built in British yards, as sister ships of vessels in the Royal Navy. In 1988–89,

New Zealand decided to purchase two new ANZAC-class frigates of Australian construction and signed an option for two more—a heavy loss to Britain's shrinking shipbuilding industry.

Part of this policy arose from a deeply felt objection in New Zealand to the habitual bullying of small nations by big powers. People who believe deeply in fairness and justice do not take kindly to bullies of any persuasion. Even moderate and conservative leaders were outraged by the actions of the Reagan administration, and not thrilled by Margaret Thatcher. Sir John Marshall, who had long been supportive of the American alliance, observed that the United States adopted "a high-handed and uncompromising attitude, which has antagonized many New Zealanders who were in other respects pro-American."[94]

On the other side, Mr. Reagan and Mrs. Thatcher believed that New Zealand leaders had betrayed the cause of liberty and freedom, disrupted a system of alliances that was vital to world peace, and attempted to destroy the American policy of containing of Communist aggression through nuclear deterrence. They complained that New Zealand's freedom was protected through military alliances and that Labour leaders were happy to enjoy the benefits of peace but unwilling to pay the cost. Prime Minister David Lange was perceived as weak, duplicitous, and vacillating.

The nuclear issue was itself urgently important to both sides. It was deepened by another conflict between two sets of ethical principles. America's militant and uncompromising defense of liberty and freedom in the world clashed fundamentally with New Zealand's ideals of equity and justice in international affairs and its antipathy to bullies even of a friendly persuasion. By the late 1980s, New Zealand's formal alliance with the United States had gone the way of its special relationship with Britain. In 1986, New Zealanders were asked what nations posed a "military threat" to their country. To the amazement of many Americans, one in six mentioned the United States.[95]

The antinuclear movement entered a more dangerous phase when secret agents of the French government entered New Zealand with orders to disable the Greenpeace ship *Rainbow Warrior*, which was about to sail from Auckland on a voyage of protest against French nuclear tests in Muroroa. On the night of July 10, 1985, these agents attacked their target in Auckland harbor. Everything went wrong with the French operation. The ship was not disabled but destroyed by two bombs. A Portuguese photographer died in the blast. New Zealand police caught the French agents red-handed, and with clear evidence of their guilt. Altogether it was the most extreme violation of national sovereignty in New Zealand's history. In the scandal that followed, the French minister of defense was forced to resign, and the head of the covert intelligence agency in Paris lost his job. The French government demanded the return of its agents and threatened trading sanctions. The government of New Zealand allowed the French agents to plead guilty to a lesser charge of manslaughter and gave them a reduced sentence to ten years in a New Zealand prison.[96]

New Zealand had nowhere to turn but the United Nations. The secretary general negotiated a typical settlement, whereby France agreed to pay $US7 million in compensation and promised not to block the import of New Zealand butter and meat into the European Economic Community. The agents were to be turned over to the French and were required to serve three years in a French military prison on Hao Atoll. This was done, but once in French hands they were immediately released, in complete defiance of the UN and New Zealand, and they returned to their country as national heroes.[97]

By 1990, New Zealanders were so militantly antinuclear that they found themselves in a bizarre new conflict, this time with Great Britain. Queen Elizabeth II planned a visit for the 150th anniversary of the Waitangi Treaty, aboard her royal yacht *Britannia*, officially a commissioned ship in the Royal Navy. New Zealand law required of every naval vessel of any nation a formal guarantee that the ship was not carrying a nuclear weapon. The Royal Navy had the same policy as the U.S. Navy and refused to confirm or deny the presence or absence of nuclear weapons aboard the Queen's yacht. Prime Minister Lange refused entry, and *Britannia* steered clear of New Zealand waters.[98]

With each of these events, antinuclear politics became so popular in New Zealand that members of the conservative National Party joined the cause. In 1995, the ruling National government sent a warship to the French test site, freighted with a heavy cargo of National Party leaders in the unlikely role of antinuclear demonstrators, as Labour Party leaders had done before them. But these politics came at a cost. New Zealand found itself without allies. The rupture of intelligence links with former friends had allowed the Greenpeace incident to happen in the first place. The United States and Britain did nothing to support New Zealand against France.

Diplomacy in a New Age: Retrospect and Prospect

After the Cold War with the Soviet Union ended in 1989, a new era began in world affairs. It was marked by new forms of danger and insecurity. The first result was an explosion of regional conflicts that the Cold War had kept in check. Once again, New Zealand began to move toward a new system of collective security. In 1991, Foreign Minister Don McKinnon declared, "It's patently obvious that the interests of small countries like New Zealand lie in the direction of collective security. So yes, we are rejoining the western camp, but on our own terms."[99]

Those terms were an important part of a new world order. In the United States, the administration of President Bill Clinton did not seek to dictate policy to its allies. Decisions were made by consultation and negotiation, with more room for the autonomy of individual states. The United States learned to live with New Zealand's antinuclear posturing. Working relations were restored.

Once again, when crises developed, the English-speaking nations came together, not so much because of formal alliances but because of a mutuality of interest in the world. New Zealand supported the American intervention in Grenada in October 1983, though also expressing concern for the Commonwealth. It also supported the American invasion of Panama and the British defense of the Falklands. Mrs. Thatcher called New Zealand's response "absolutely magnificent."[100]

New Zealand also sent troops to Somalia, and into the Gulf War, and stood together with the United States in the struggle against terrorism. In 1998, Islamic terrorists attacked American embassies in Tanzania and Kenya. More than five thousand people were killed or wounded, most of them innocent Africans. The United States responded with a unilateral strike against terrorist facilities in Sudan and Pakistan. In the immediate aftermath, most nations in the world remained silent, and only five states stood together. Among them were the United States, Great Britain, Australia, and New Zealand. Once again, the fulcrum of world order was the relationship that bound English-speaking nations to one another.[101]

Distant Friends in a New Millennium

At the dawn of the twenty-first century, the United States and New Zealand were governed by leaders with profoundly different values. President George W. Bush was a born-again Christian, oil-patch entrepreneur, sometime fighter pilot in the Texas Air National Guard, and arguably the most conservative chief executive in American history. Labour Prime Minister Helen Clark was a secular academician, veteran peace marcher, and left-wing social democrat. No love was lost between them. Even so, the United States and New Zealand remained distant friends in war and diplomacy. In the twenty-first century, troops of both nations soldiered together in Iraq and Afghanistan. Diplomats and intelligence officers of both nations worked together to disrupt terrorist networks.

American foreign policy was driven by two great purposes: to promote its national interest, and to serve the cause of liberty and freedom in the world. New Zealand has steered its policy by another constellation of guiding stars. Its conduct of external relations is guided by powerful values and purposes: national interest and regional hegemony, independence and collective security, a strong antipathy to bullies of all persuasions, and a continuing attachment to ideas of justice, equity, and fairness in the world.[102]

GREAT CRASH AND LONG SLUMP

Responses to a World Depression

> You say you are waiting for a fair deal for the producers. We all are, and some of us wonder if we are living in a madhouse. Some have goods to burn and cannot find purchasers; while others are practically starving because they have no money to buy. . . . Social Justice must be the guiding principle, and economic organization must adapt itself to social needs.
>
> —Prime Minister Michael Savage, 1933

> I prefer and I am sure you prefer that broader definition of liberty under which we are moving forward to greater freedom, to greater security for the average man than he has ever known before in the history of America.
>
> —President Franklin Roosevelt, 1934

NEW ZEALAND AND THE UNITED STATES had much experience of hard times in the twentieth century. On our travels, we met elderly New Zealanders who keenly remembered the suffering of the "Long Slump" in the 1920s and 1930s. Americans of the same age also recall the shock of the "Great Crash" in 1929, and the agony of the Depression that followed.[1]

This disaster was a world event—the collapse of a global economy that was integrated in its markets but fragmented in their control and deeply divided in values and purposes.[2] Many people perceived the Great Depression as a failure of open societies, capitalism, and democracy. More than a few turned away from those ideals. Closed systems multiplied rapidly around the world. In 1933, twenty-five free governments existed on the continent of Europe. By 1941, only two survived.[3]

A few nations with strong democratic traditions moved in the opposite direction. They struggled to make their opening societies more open, more fair, and more free. Two leading examples were New Zealand and the United States. When their economies failed, both countries returned to the first principles on which they had been founded. New Zealanders thought mainly of rebuilding their institutions on a basis of what Premier Michael Savage called their "guiding principle of social justice." Most New Zealanders agreed, even as they differed on the meaning of that idea. Americans left and right searched for what President Franklin Roosevelt called a "broader definition of liberty" and "greater freedom," but they understood those ideas in very different ways.

New Zealand's Long Slump

The Great Depression did not begin on Wall Street, as many Americans (and anti-Americans) fervently believe. Its origins are to be found in Europe as a direct result of the First World War, which killed ten million young men in the prime of their productive lives and wrecked the economies of Russia, Germany, Austria, Italy, France, and Great Britain.[4]

New Zealand was one of the first countries outside Europe to be severely affected. Its economy had flourished during the war. When the troops came home, employment was at first strong and the price of real estate surged.[5] But things began to go wrong as early as 1919. Part of the trouble was the movement of commodity prices for leading exports. Markets for New Zealand butter, meat, and wool had always been volatile. After the Armistice in 1918, the government of the United States virtually gave away huge stocks of surplus food and commodities that had accumulated during the war. The market value of food exports fell sharply from 1919 to 1922, and again from 1924 to 1926, and once more from 1929 to 1931. Through the 1920s, the export-driven economy of New Zealand suffered from chronic instability. The secular trend was a long decline, punctuated by short and unsustained recoveries.[6]

Those problems were compounded by New Zealand's heavy dependence on the British economy. In the decade after the First World War, four-fifths of New Zealand's primary exports went to the

United Kingdom, which was in a prolonged decline during the 1920s. England suffered a general strike in 1926. Scotland struggled through one of the worst downturns in its history. The result was contraction and further instability in New Zealand's primary markets.[7]

Debt was another problem. By the end of the 1920s, on a per capita basis, New Zealand had run up the largest national debt in the world. In some years, nearly 40 percent of its public spending went for interest payments on the national debt, much of it to foreign creditors.[8]

These problems reverberated through the domestic economy. As early as 1922, New Zealand was in recession. In 1925, political leaders were speaking of a "slight depression," and again by 1927 of a full-scale "economic depression."[9] The economy revived in 1928–29; then felt the full force of the world depression from 1929 to 1934. New Zealand suffered severely from its effects. The value of exports and imports fell nearly by half in the five years after 1928. National income dropped from £150 million to £90 million, a reduction of 40 percent. Poverty increased sharply. In a country that produced a vast abundance of food for export, people had trouble feeding their families. In 1932, crowds of desperate women in Dunedin, Auckland, ChristChurch, and Wellington attacked grocery stores in search of food for their children, in scenes repeated through the world. Other crowds of unemployed men marched for jobs in the same cities and sometimes were attacked by mounted police.[10]

In one way, New Zealanders did better than most major economies. Historians reckon that rates of unemployment peaked at 12 to 15 percent, compared with 20 to 25 percent in the United Kingdom, 25 to 30 percent in the United States and Australia, and 40 to 45 percent in Germany. Everywhere, minorities were hardest hit. When unemployment was officially 12 percent in New Zealand, it was 40 percent among Maori males. In the United States, nobody has been able to measure unemployment among American Indians, African Americans, and recent immigrants in those terrible years.[11] And in every country, actual numbers of people without work were larger than the official statistics. But economic historian G. R. Hawke observes that relative differences among nations are "not really in doubt." A careful study by the League of Nations confirmed that judgment. Its index of industrial employment (1929 = 100) fell to 83.1 in New Zealand and 62.5 in the United States, during the worst years.[12]

In 1932, hunger and unemployment drove many New Zealanders and Americans into the streets. This demonstration on Cuba Street in Wellington was dispersed by mounted police. Observe the dress of the demonstrators—dark suits, white shirts, conservative neckties, and snap brim hats.

New Zealand's Conservative Man at the Center, 1925–35: Coates of Kaipara

These patterns derived largely from choices that leaders made in both countries. Through much of the Long Slump, New Zealand was governed by conservative coalitions in an unstable party system. The man at the center was Gordon Coates of Kaipara. An extraordinary character, he was a rough-hewn, big-shouldered, good-natured gentleman farmer from Northland. In the First World War Coates joined the army and became a national hero, the very model of a New Zealand leader. He was much respected and loved by men who served with him for his courage and devotion to their welfare. His countrymen knew him to be a decent and honorable man, always as good as his word. After the war, even his political opponents held Gordon Coates in high esteem, and in 1925 he was said to be the most popular man in Parliament. During the next decade, Coates served as prime minister (1925–28), opposition leader (1928–31), minister of public works (1931–33), and minister of finance (1933–35) in a coalition government. More than any other leader, he shaped New Zealand's response to the challenges between the Long Slump from 1925 to 1935.[13]

Gordon Coates was a moderate conservative who shaped economic policy in New Zealand from 1925 to 1935. He tried many experiments with some success but failed to stop the nation's slide into the depth of the Great Depression. In the 1920s he was said to be the most popular man in New Zealand. By 1935 the country had turned against him.

In 1928, visiting Oxford scholar Margery Perham sat in a parliamentary gallery and observed him in action. At that time, the rival United Party was briefly in power, and Coates was a leader of the loyal opposition. Perham wrote, "A great broad-shouldered man, with a suggestion of swagger, came into the House, a youngish, vigorous, red bull of a man. He helped the ministers out, encouraged them, decided a point of order over the Chairman's head, wandered about the House, sitting down now on the Labour leader's sofa, now actually going across to sit with one of the Government. This was Gordon Coates."[14]

Coates was a party man, yet never strongly partisan. He belonged to the conservative Reform Party, but he was not doctrinaire in his conservatism. With his good friend William Downie Stewart and other New Zealand conservatives, he "inherited the tradition of activism" in government. Coates himself was pragmatic, flexible, and experimental in his policy choices.[15]

When unemployment began to rise during the 1920s, Coates met with men who were out of work and arranged for an expansion of public works. As prime minister in 1926–27 he authorized additional jobs on railroads, highways, and other public projects. Always he tried to avoid useless make-work, partly because he believed that real work needed to be done and partly because he thought that men needed to take pride in what they did.[16] Coates's favorite program was a "small farms plan" to help New Zealand families return to the land. He made a major effort to promote agricultural employment, with some success. Farm wages dropped by half from 1929 to 1933, but the number of paid farm workers in New Zealand actually increased from 83,000 in 1928–29 to 92,700 in 1933–34. In the countryside, he kept men working.[17]

Other politicians shared Coates's purposes. As the Long Slump grew into the Great Depression from 1929 to 1935, the coalition government was run by three leaders: Coates himself, his friend Downie Stewart of the conservative Reform Party, and their rival George Forbes of the liberal United Party. All of these men sympathized with the suffering around them and recognized a collective responsibility for relieving it. At the same time, they strongly opposed the dole and rejected deficit spending as unworkable for New Zealand and regarded it as unwise for any nation. Those imperatives limited choices but did not stop them from acting.

In the private sector, many of New Zealand's business leaders shared that centrist way of thinking. By comparison with American corporations, they were slow to put people out of work. Individual employers in New Zealand made special efforts to protect the jobs of family heads, sometimes at considerable cost. Also very different from America were the attitudes of organized labor. In 1931, New Zealand's Arbitration Court cut wages by 10 percent; union leaders accepted that decision as fair and necessary to keep people working. This collective web of individual decisions in New Zealand rationed work and reduced wages to keep as many people employed as possible. Much of it centered on ideas of fairness and social justice that were stronger in New Zealand than in the United States. It also had another effect. The New Zealand system of rationed work slowed the pace of decline and speeded recovery for the economy as a whole. The American system of layoffs was functional in the short term for the economics of individual corporations but dysfunctional for the economy as a whole. In short, the horizon of economic decision-making tended to be broader in New Zealand than in the United States.[18]

Coates also pushed through Parliament a law that protected people against the loss of homes, farms, and businesses when they were unable to meet mortgage payments. The same statute helped

New Zealanders to refinance mortgages at lower interest rates. In addition, Coates enacted a system of family allowances: two shillings a week to poor families for every child over the first two. It was a pathetically small sum, but urgently important to families who could qualify, with total earnings of less than four pounds a week.[19]

As the depression deepened after 1932, Coates was minister of finance and George Forbes was prime minister in a coalition government. These men began to worry about the possibility of a complete collapse of the economy and ordered the army to make contingency plans for feeding the entire nation if necessary.[20] Coates also introduced important structural reforms. When he came into office, six banks were dominant. Only one had its headquarters in the country. New Zealanders had little control over their financial institutions. To deal with this problem, Gordon Coates and Downie Stewart founded a new institution: the Reserve Bank of New Zealand, with responsibility to promote the "economic welfare of the dominion." It had broad powers to control monetary policy and authority to regulate the flow of financial credit. The Reserve Bank remains one of New Zealand's most important economic institutions, and another of Coates's many enduring legacies.[21]

In 1933, Coates also made another monetary experiment with less success. He devalued the New Zealand pound by 20 percent, in hope of making exports more competitive. By the standards of the time it was a bold and courageous act of leadership, but it failed in its purpose when other countries lowered their export prices. The major effect of devaluation was to raise the cost of imports, and the measure became intensely unpopular. Even Coates's close friend Downie Stewart opposed it and resigned from office on principle.[22]

Coates kept trying. He attempted other structural reforms within the framework of New Zealand's institutions and set an example of concerned conservative leadership. But in the early 1930s nothing seemed to work. Conservatives attacked him as a "socialist interventionist." Radicals condemned him as a heartless defender of capitalism. A Labour handbill showed a photograph of men harnessed to a chain harrow, doing work that was usually performed by draft animals. Looking on was an image of King Dick Seddon, saying, "This! In God's Own Country!"[23]

Opponents spread a rumor that when a delegation of unemployed workers complained they had nothing to eat, Coates replied, "You can eat grass." It was false, but he had failed to end the depression, and voters held him responsible. By 1935, the most admired leader in New Zealand had become "the most hated man in the country," in the words of one historian.[24]

This New Zealand image of men harnessed like horses to chain harrows was used by the Labour Party in its campaign against Gordon Coates and his policies. It had a great impact on the country.

The Great Crash in the United States

While that drama was playing out in New Zealand, another story was unfolding on the other side of the globe. The United States was one of the last nations to be caught in the Long Slump, but when at last it happened the American economy did not merely decline. It came down with a mighty crash that shook the world to its economic foundations.[25]

In the 1920s, while other nations struggled and suffered, the United States had grown more prosperous. Its economy moved quickly through a sharp recession in 1920–21 and then began to grow at a rapid rate. In North America, the entire decade was remembered as the "Roaring Twenties." The frontier was still open, and the volume of new land-takings in the 1920s was the highest in American history. Cities were growing and factories were booming. Personal income rose 26 percent from 1921 to 1929. Official unemployment fell to 1.8 percent in 1926. So strong was the flow of revenue into the national treasury that federal taxes were cut three times. Even so, the national debt shrank from $24 billion to $16 billion.[26]

By the mid-twenties, the American economy seemed stronger than ever. Financial markets boomed, and the value of common stocks quadrupled from 1921 to 1929. But the circle of investment in the stock market remained very small. Fewer than 2.5 percent of Americans owned stocks in 1929; less than 1.1 percent had brokerage accounts. The major players were large investors who bought stocks on margin with borrowed money, often in the form of "call loans" at interest of 10 or even 20 percent from brokers or business corporations, which were themselves among the biggest plungers in the market. Corporate executives were learning to think about themselves in new ways. A model was Alfred Sloan, who wrote in his autobiography that his job as head of General Motors was not to make cars; it was to make money.[27]

These corporate "money men" borrowed capital from banks, which in turn were borrowers of federal funds at 3.5 percent. The result was a saturnalia of borrowing and a giant pyramid of debt. Many investors made money, and the market jumped over the moon. Corporate leaders expressed optimism about the future, and economists celebrated free markets as engines of eternal growth. Conservative Republicans issued ringing declarations of faith. They won office with promises of low taxes and no interference with capitalism.[28]

Times were good for many Americans in the Roaring Twenties, but not for all of them. In 1928, the distribution of wealth and income reached the highest levels of inequality in the country's history, to that point. Farmers (then one-fourth of American workers) were hit hard by falling commodity prices in the southern and western states. New England's factory towns were in trouble. Consumption lagged behind production, inventories grew dangerously, and business failures rose in 1927 and 1928. Unemployment began to climb, still at low levels but more than doubling from 1.8 percent in 1926 to 4.2 percent in 1928. Another sign of trouble appeared in Florida, where a real estate bubble had been fueled by fraud and corruption. Prices surged dangerously, then suddenly collapsed.[29]

The governors of the Federal Reserve System raised discount rates three times to 5 percent in the spring of 1929, hoping to discourage speculation with borrowed money. Industrial production began to fall, but the stock market kept rising. In August 1929, the Fed drove the discount rate to 6 percent, and stock prices at last came down a little in September. Many rejoiced in what appeared to be a much-needed correction.

Then came the reckoning. As stock prices began to fall, lenders called in their loans. Margin calls multiplied, and speculators were compelled to sell into a falling market. On Wednesday, October 23, 1929, the market crashed, and panic seized the country. That "Black Wednesday" was followed by a Blacker Thursday and, on October 29, 1929, by the Blackest Tuesday in American history. By November, stocks had lost one-third of their value, and the big pyramid of debt began to collapse under its own weight.[30]

Crash! After a long period of prosperity in the 1920s, the American economy began to falter, and in 1929 the stock market suddenly collapsed in a great crash that shook the world economy to its foundations. Economists have tried to separate the crash from the depression, but they were closely linked.

The nation's banks were deeply involved, and the crash became a full-blown financial crisis. The American banking system had long been unstable. Even in the prosperity of the 1920s, about 500 banks failed every year. In 1929, 659 banks went under, a number that did not seem greatly alarming. But then in 1930 the Bank of United States closed its doors, after suffering heavy losses in the stock market. It was owned by Jewish entrepreneurs who served immigrants in lower Manhattan. Anti-Semitic "white shoe" bankers contemptuously called it the "Pants Pressers Bank" and showed no interest in supporting it. The Fed did nothing helpful, and strong financial institutions watched complacently as weaker ones went under. It was a fatal mistake. The fall of the "Pants Pressers Bank" brought down others, and the dominos began to drop across the country: from 659 bank failures in 1929 to 1,352 in 1930 and 2,294 in 1931.[31]

In earlier financial crises, leaders had emerged within the banking community to restore stability. During the Panic of 1907, J. P. Morgan had intervened decisively and added liquidity in a shaken system. Others followed his example. The result in 1907 was remembered as the "rich man's panic," a sharp but very short downturn without a prolonged depression or persistent high levels of unemployment.[32] When another sharp recession followed World War I, central banker Benjamin Strong and the Federal Reserve Bank of

New York did something similar with great success. But Morgan died in 1913 and Strong in 1928. This time financial leadership was weaker in the private sector, and the problems were much larger.[33]

Public leaders did no better. After the crash of 1929, the governors of the Federal Reserve System followed the economic orthodoxy of their day. They acquiesced in a catastrophic contraction of credit and allowed the money supply (M2) to shrink from $47 billion to $32 billion in 1933.[34] Historians are still trying to understand their thinking. One purpose was to protect American gold reserves, by far the largest in the world. An obsession with gold became a major part of the problem. Repeated research has demonstrated beyond doubt that economies most tightly shackled to gold had the slowest and weakest recoveries.[35] Altogether, the response of central bankers in 1929–31 was an epic failure of leadership. Even conservative Treasury Secretary Ogden Mills later said that "for a great central banking system to stand by with a 70 percent gold reserve without taking active steps in such a situation was almost inconceivable and almost unforgivable."[36]

Private bankers compounded the problem. They deeply feared concentration of regulatory control in Washington, seeing it as a threat to free enterprise in general and to their wealth and power in particular. Through the years they had already succeeded in decentralizing decision-making in the Fed, beyond the intent of its founders. Their actions rose from altruism as well as self-interest. Most believed that a free market would repair itself more quickly if governments got out of the way. That laissez-faire remedy was tried through four years. It turned a major decline into an epic disaster.

America's Conservative Men at the Center:
Hoover and Mellon, 1929–33

In this catastrophe the central figures were President Herbert Hoover and Secretary of the Treasury Andrew Mellon. Hoover was upright, honorable, thoughtful, and highly intelligent—a man of strong intellect and sterling character. He was one of the most able men to serve as president, and one of the least successful. Raised to Quaker values, Hoover was trained as a mining engineer. He made a fortune in private business by the age of forty and distinguished himself in philanthropy. During the Great War he ran a large program for the relief of civilians in Belgium and northern France, and after the Armistice he led a larger effort to feed starving millions in Europe during the winter of 1918–19, with much success. Everyone admired

President Herbert Hoover's well-meaning but ill-conceived policies deepened the depression. He signed the Smoot-Hawley Tariff Act, which hugely increased trade barriers. Major trouble flowed from fiscal and monetary decisions and the design of economic policy. More damage was done by congressional Democrats, who were recklessly partisan and obstructionist.

him. Franklin Roosevelt, then assistant secretary of the navy, declared that Hoover was "certainly a wonder and I wish we could make him President of the United States. There could not be a better one."[37]

Many people perceived Hoover as a man of the political right. He thought of himself as a man of the social center. In 1922, he wrote a small book called *American Individualism*, which equally condemned "laissez-faire" on the right and "state socialism" on the left. Hoover thought of American individualism as a middle way—an ideal of creative service to others in a society where power was broadly distributed.[38]

A major factor in Hoover's thinking was the Constitution. He did not believe that the federal government possessed the constitutional authority to intervene actively in the economy. Always he was deeply hostile to a strong state and fearful of an active bureaucracy. Herbert Hoover devoted his life to the relief of suffering, primarily through voluntary associations. He believed that coercive national programs sapped the energy and initiative of a free people.[39]

As the Depression grew worse in the United States, Hoover encouraged state and local governments to create public works programs. He reluctantly favored some federal assistance to business through the Reconstruction Finance Corporation. But in general, Hoover thought of the economy as the realm of private enterprise, and he pledged no "dictation or interference by government in business." His thinking was very similar to that of many presidents before him. In American depressions that began in 1819, 1837, 1857, and 1873, James Monroe, Martin Van Buren, James Buchanan, and Ulysses Grant did very little and were not expected to intervene. In 1893–94, Grover Cleveland took "a hard line against aid to the unfortunate.[40]

Hoover began by doing much more than his predecessors. At first he thought that the problem was a minor recession and acted very quickly. He invited top business leaders to the White House and urged them to keep up wages, increase investment, and spend more for maintenance projects, and some did so. Hoover also advised the states to organize construction projects, asked Congress to spend $150 million for public works, advised the Federal Farm Board to support farm prices by buying crops, persuaded the Federal Reserve to lower discount rates and increase the money supply, and urged a small tax cut. On May 1, 1930, he told the country that "we have passed the worst." Later that year he proclaimed that "the depression is over."[41]

But it had barely begun. As the country sank deeper into the abyss, Hoover concluded from the failure of his early efforts that federal intervention could make things worse by undercutting individual effort and threatening the solvency of the government. He favored rigid adherence to conservative monetary policy, kept the United States on the gold standard, and presided over a severe contraction in the money supply—33 percent—which did grave injury to the economy.[42]

The same thing happened in fiscal policy. To protect the solvency of the government as revenues declined, Congress and state legislatures reduced spending. Public debt of the federal government shrank from 1929 to 1931, and federal taxation increased. Hoover's Federal Farm Board turned away from price supports and sold its stockpile of crops into a falling market, with catastrophic results for American farmers. He opposed national relief programs. When Congress passed the Emergency Relief and Construction Act, Hoover refused to spend most of the money. The federal government under Hoover's leadership made things worse.[43]

Other errors were made in tariff and trade policy. Many public and private leaders in the United States, as in other nations, responded to the collapse of the world economy by demanding new tariffs for the protection of domestic industry. The Smoot-Hawley Tariff Act (1930) raised tariffs to the highest levels in American history, nearly 50 percent ad valorem. A thousand economists warned Hoover that it was an act of consummate folly, but Congress pushed ahead with the new tariff. Hoover refused to veto it and bore a large part of responsibility for what followed. The leading economy in the world set a bad example. Tariff rates doubled in Australia, Britain, and France and trebled in Germany. The result was yet another severe contraction of international trade at the worst possible time.[44]

One of Hoover's deepest errors was to fear and distrust the citizens of his own nation. As the Depression grew worse, veterans asked for the loans on bonus certificates that Congress had already approved in 1924. Congress agreed, and authorized the money in 1930. Hoover vetoed it as fiscally unsound. Congress passed it over his veto. In 1931, about seventeen thousand veterans came to Washington, demonstrating in support of the bonus, and some refused to go home. Hoover agreed to give them just enough money to go away and ordered that those who remained be removed. General Douglas MacArthur acted against Hoover's orders, and did it with tanks, bayonets, and gas. The country was shocked and deeply divided by the scenes that followed. After the election of 1932 a visitor to Washington found that armed regulars were posted throughout the city on the president's orders.[45]

More conservative than Herbert Hoover was his secretary of the treasury, Andrew Mellon. Hoover described him as a "liquidationist" and wrote that Mellon's policy in the Great Depression was to "liquidate labor, liquidate stocks, liquidate farmers, liquidate real estate." Mellon believed that the Great Crash was not a bad thing. He wrote that "it will purge the rottenness out of the system. High costs of living and high living will come down. People will work harder, and lead a moral life. Values will be adjusted, and enterprising people will pick up the wrecks from less competent people."[46] Mellon applied this policy during the Depression by "weeding out" weak banks, cutting off credit, and refusing loans when they were most needed. He refused to put more money in circulation and reduced the federal budget.[47]

Mellon and Hoover were not alone in these mistakes. Leadership in Congress also failed in both political parties. Democrats gained control of both houses in 1930. Many were as conservative as the Republicans. In 1931–32, they were also as virulent and obstructive in their partisanship as congressional Republicans would be in the Clinton and Obama administrations. Even modest proposals for reform were reflexively attacked. In 1932, New York Governor Franklin Roosevelt observed that "there is no room in this country for two reactionary parties." But that's what it had in 1931.[48]

The errors of public officials in both parties were compounded by decisions of private businessmen. Some acted on the policy that Hoover attributed to Mellon: "liquidate labor." One result was to

Another failed leader was Treasury Secretary Andrew Mellon.

institutionalize the layoff, as American workers began to call it, more so than in other eras and much more so than in other countries such as New Zealand. A leading example was Henry Ford. He responded ruthlessly to the Great Depression and laid off two-thirds of his workers. Ford also refused to cooperate with others in the rescue of Michigan's largest banks and brought them to ruin.[49] Individual decisions by corporate leaders as ruthless as Ford helped to turn an economic downturn into a disaster. Policies that seemed rational and even constructive for a particular corporation were wildly irrational and deeply destructive for a national economy. In 1933, when the United States still had the largest national product in the world, it also had one of the highest rates of unemployment among developed nations.[50]

The Great Depression in the United States was great because the failure of leadership was so general. It was public and private, liberal and conservative, Democratic and Republican, presidential and congressional; it included Federal Reserve bankers and corporate leaders. Some of it rose from rigid orthodoxies of the right and left.

The Crisis in America

As conditions grew worse, American society became more deeply divided. Many with wealth and power seemed utterly unable to empathize with the poor and weak. In New York City, unemployed men fought for scraps of garbage to feed their hungry families, while others lived in opulence and blamed the victims for what went wrong. Class divisions were reinforced by ethnic prejudice, religious bigotry, and extreme racism. The result was the collapse not merely of an economy but of a comity. America was becoming many nations, and they lived increasingly apart.

The cruelest suffering came in the winters. During the winter of 1931–32, food riots broke out in Minneapolis. Hundreds of people attacked grocery stores, smashed doors and windows, and took food for their families. One infuriated storeowner drew a gun and threatened to shoot the rioters; they broke his arm and returned to their purpose. Similar scenes occurred in many cities. The next winter of 1932–33 brought more violence throughout the United States, and it took many forms. Farmers used force to stop foreclosures and tax-seizures. Labor violence increased among field hands in California's Imperial Valley, cannery workers on the Pacific coast, longshoremen in San Francisco, miners in Appalachia, and teamsters in Minnesota. It spread among factory workers in the South, the Midwest, and New England.[51]

As the economy sank into the depths of the Great Depression, political leaders became increasingly the objects of ridicule, resentment, and even hatred. Impeachment proceedings began against Treasury Secretary Andrew Mellon. Hoover ended them by appointing Mellon ambassador to Great Britain and increased his own unpopularity. As his campaign train toured the nation in 1932, the president found himself so disliked that a public appearance in Detroit threatened to ignite an insurrection.[52]

Similar scenes were happening in other countries, and the result was a general crisis of open societies and democratic government throughout the world. After the First World War many nations had moved hopefully in the direction of self-determination and representative institutions. Now they were losing faith in democracy. Fascism and Communism spread rapidly. One nation after another was taken over by brutal dictators of the left and right.[53]

Even in the English-speaking world, where traditions of self-government had the deepest roots, people turned against democratic institutions. In New Zealand and the United States, some people to the left expressed admiration for totalitarian leaders to the left and right. On the right, Americans as diverse as Father Charles Coughlin, Huey Long, Joseph Kennedy, and Charles Lindbergh all spoke positively of European Fascism. Lindbergh made three visits to Germany and reported that Hitler's government had "a sense of decency and values which in many ways is far ahead of our own." Nazi leaders were so pleased that they awarded Lindbergh one of their highest decorations, the Order of the Golden Eagle. His wife, Anne Morrow, warned her husband that it was a golden albatross that they had put around his neck.[54]

In both the United States and New Zealand, people on the right feared that a Communist revolution might break out from below. Those on the left worried about Fascist repression and a military coup. New Zealand's Labour leaders remembered the Territorials and "specials" who mustered as "Massey's Cossacks" in 1913. American radicals and liberals shared a similar suspicion of army officers who had suppressed the bonus march with a heavy hand. In both countries the fears were without foundation. The great majority of military officers in America and New Zealand supported their constitutional governments, but they also were deeply uncertain of its prospects in a dangerous world.[55]

A Pivotal Moment: The Election of Franklin Roosevelt

Then, in the depth of the Great Depression, two extraordinary leaders suddenly rose to power in North America and the South Pacific. In 1932, Franklin Delano Roosevelt was elected president of the United States. In 1935, Michael Joseph Savage was chosen prime minister of New Zealand. These two men shared important qualities in common. Each had a strong character, a restless spirit, broad vision, deep Christian faith, and a sense of kinship with others less fortunate than themselves. But they were profoundly different in social origins, political purposes, economic policies, and cultural values.

Roosevelt was a patrician reformer—born to wealth, raised to privilege, and educated by private tutors, top schools, and grand tours. In his early years he learned to speak German and French and acquired the easy grace of a gentleman who was absolutely confident of his place in the world. So narrow was the social circle of his early life that he married his fifth cousin, Eleanor Roosevelt.[56]

A turning point came in the summer of 1921, when Roosevelt fell ill and was severely crippled by a disease that his doctors diagnosed as polio. In his affliction he found an inner strength that transformed him. Eleanor said that the experience made him a more serious man. He also became increasingly a man of hidden depths and high complexities: "the most complicated human being I ever knew," wrote Frances Perkins, his secretary of labor and the first woman to serve in a cabinet.[57]

At least three American political traditions came together in Franklin Roosevelt's thought. His Hudson Valley ancestors had been great landholders and patrician Democrats since the early republic, when some of them supported Thomas Jefferson and his vision of minimal government. This tradition combined a Jeffersonian idea of liberty with a strong sense of privilege and civic responsibility.

Another part of his thinking came from more distant forebears, who were three-quarters New England Yankee. He returned to New England for his schooling at Groton, where his gifted teacher and lifelong friend Endicott Peabody gave him an idea of Christian stewardship, and also the inner strength of his Puritan ancestors.[58]

A third ingredient, often forgotten, was his involvement in the commercial world of New York City. For a time, Franklin Roosevelt went into private business. In 1921, he was vice president in the New York office of the Fidelity and Deposit Company. Roosevelt described himself as a "hard boiled insurance man." He believed deeply in the strength of the capitalist system and supported the idea of free enterprise all his life, even as he became a strong critic of prevailing business ethics.[59]

Each of these elements was grounded in an idea of liberty and freedom. All of them together shaped Roosevelt's career as a Progressive Democrat in the New York Senate (1910–13), assistant secretary of the navy in Woodrow Wilson's administration (1913–21), reform governor of New York (1929–33), and president of the United States (1933–45).

Throughout his career, Franklin Roosevelt described his politics as "a little left of center." The operative word was "center." His ideal was a free and open society, democratic in its politics, capitalist in its economy, and individuated in its social system. His purpose was to preserve that system in an hour of peril, and also to reform it. His instruments were an active government, a strong presidency, and a united Democratic Party.[60]

Conservatives raged against him as a dangerous radical and a traitor to his class. Radicals reviled him as the running dog of reactionary capitalism. Academic scholars complained that he rejected their ideologies (which was true) and that he was incoherent, inconsistent, and shallow (entirely false). None of those critics understood this extraordinary man, in large part because of the way that he operated. He was a skillful professional politician, highly practiced in the arts of deception, and he did not explicitly define his purposes except in the most general terms.

Roosevelt was sometimes accused of being unprincipled, but in fact he had very strong principles. Once he was asked about his philosophy. "Philosophy?" he replied. "I am a Christian and a democrat—that's all."[61] It has been said that the only original contribution of Americans to philosophy is pragmatism. Roosevelt was a pragmatist in both the philosophical and popular senses of that word. He judged the moral value of actions by their uses and results. At the same time, he was very flexible and experimental. Here was a key to his thoughts and acts. At Oglethorpe University in 1932 he said, "The country needs, and unless I mistake its temper, the country demands bold, persistent experimentation." He continued, "It is common sense to take a method and try it. If it fails, admit it frankly and try another. But above all, try something."[62] For Roosevelt, flexibility was a fixed principle, and it operated within a frame of large moral purposes. In 1932, he tried to explain that combination. "Have you ever stopped to consider," he asked a friend, "that there is a difference between ideals and methods of obtaining them?"[63]

A Pivotal Moment in New Zealand: The Election of Michael Savage

In New Zealand, Michael Savage (1872–1940) made a striking contrast to Franklin Roosevelt. Of Irish Catholic ancestry, he was born in Australia and raised in a slab hut on a hardscrabble farm in the province of Victoria, where his parents struggled to support seven children. Savage was the youngest child, and his early years were heavy with misfortune. He watched helplessly as his mother died of appendicitis, his sister bled to death in childbirth, one of his brothers died of pneumonia, and another was lost to typhoid fever. Physicians were unable to save them and may have killed at least one. Always Savage remembered the poverty of his origins, the agony of unemployment, the failure of medical care, and the grinding misery of his early life.[64]

After a few years in a small school that his father had helped to build, Savage went to work at the age of thirteen as a shopkeeper's apprentice. He did well until his employer failed during the hard times of 1893. More than 25 percent of men were out of work that year in Victoria. Unable to find another job, he moved to Melbourne and found that half the men there were also unemployed.[65]

Savage took up the life of a homeless "bushman" or "swagman," wandering through the Australian outback without steady work or a home of his own. He lived rough, slept in a hollow tree, and survived on rabbits that he caught in the outback. His biographer Barry Gustafson writes, "The bushmen were physically, mentally, and emotionally strong and independent. . . . They distrusted authority, deferred to no one as their better, believed in the inherent dignity, worth, and basic equality of all men, and valued mateship above all else."[66]

In 1893, Savage found work as a station hand in New South Wales, began to involve himself in union organizing, and was promptly fired. He moved back to Victoria, worked as a miner and mechanic, earned a license as a mining engineer, and slowly began to get ahead. But always he identified with the laborers and miners who had been his mates, and he tried to organize them into a radical labor movement and democratic socialist party. Just as he was beginning to do well, the mines shut down again in 1906, and the volatile Australian economy failed once more. Friends told him that prospects were brighter in New Zealand, and that its government was more enlightened. In 1907, Savage crossed the Tasman Sea with a single shilling in his pocket and started over, working as a flax-cutter in the growing season and a brewery hand in the winter. Within a year he was elected president of the Brewery Workers Union and became a central figure in the fledgling New Zealand Labour Party, always speaking for the dispossessed.[67]

Savage was outwardly a man of great simplicity, but, as with Roosevelt, there were deep complexities in his thought. His principles combined ideas of democratic politics and socialist economics with a deep Christian faith. In New Zealand he came to be known for

In 1935 a leader emerged in New Zealand. Michael Savage was a Christian socialist of humble origins, a highly skilled politician, and in the judgment of Karl Berendsen, was New Zealand's most able prime minister in that era.

his charitable works on relief committees and hospital boards. His biographer writes that "Savage was generous not only with public funds. People constantly appeared at the door of his house seeking clothes, food and money." One day he gave away all of his own suits except the one on his back. On another occasion, a man came to the door and asked for food to feed his family. Savage went to the kitchen, took the Sunday roast out of the oven, and gave it away. His household made do with Saturday leftovers.[68]

Savage carried that spirit of Christian *caritas* into politics. He said, "My efforts are aimed at establishing the Kingdom of God upon Earth." In 1919, he was elected to Parliament for Auckland West, and he held that seat for the rest of his life. He was a brilliant political strategist, and led his party to a landslide victory and became New Zealand's first Labour prime minister in 1935.

A man who knew him well was Carl Berendsen, an able civil servant who became permanent head of the Prime Minister's Department and worked for many of New Zealand's national leaders. Berendsen observed that Savage was the most able leader who ever served as prime minister. More than that, Berendsen remembered him as "a transparently good man, the nearest to a true Christian" that he had ever met in politics.[69] Others were not happy with him. On the far left his former friend and future rival Jack Lee wrote that Savage "can be inspired but can never inspire."[70] That judgment was far off the mark. In his gentle way, Mickey Savage inspired many New Zealanders in his time.[71]

Election Night, 1935. Radical change came to New Zealand with the election of its first Labour government in 1935. It turned the country toward a socialist program that was profoundly different from the American New Deal.

Red Feds and New Dealers

On coming to power in 1935, Savage's first act was to choose a cabinet. He drew them mainly from the senior ranks of the Labour movement. The average age of his cabinet was fifty-seven; none was under fifty. All but two had been manual laborers. Most had been leaders of the New Zealand Federation of Labour, popularly known as Red Feds. Before 1912, their principles were very similar to those of American radical socialists Daniel De Leon and William "Big Bill" Haywood, who led the Industrial Workers of the World (better known as the IWW or the Wobblies) in the United States in 1906–8. So close were the two groups in early years that the Red Feds painted Wobbly slogans on their union hall and adopted IWW constitutional documents word for word.[72]

In both the United States and New Zealand, leading Wobblies and Red Feds went to prison during the First World War for resisting conscription and opposing the government. After the peace, their paths diverged. In the United States, Wobblies chose the path of revolutionary violence and were driven to the far fringe of American life. In New Zealand, Red Feds chose political action, gained control of the Labour Party, and moved toward the center of power. In 1935, no fewer than seven of Savage's twelve cabinet ministers were former Red Feds. Among them was Peter Fraser, who would follow Savage as

Labour ministers in 1935 were very unlike leading New Dealers in 1933. The Labour leaders tended to be older. All but two had worked as manual laborers. Many had been members of the Federation of Labour, which had ties to the American IWW, though never as violent.

New Zealand's very able prime minister during World War II. He had been imprisoned for sedition in World War I. Others included Bob Semple, Paddy Webb, Tim Armstrong, and Bill Parry. In American terms it was as if men such as De Leon and Haywood and other early Wobbly leaders had gained control of the government of the United States in 1933. Other leaders of different backgrounds also joined these new reform movements. Among them were women such as Elizabeth McCombs in New Zealand and Frances Perkins in the United States. They were among the first women to rise to positions of power in either country.[73]

American New Dealers were very different from New Zealand's Red Feds. Many were very young. Most were of the middle class. They tended to be lawyers, college professors, and civil servants. The great majority were liberal Democrats, a little left of center like their president, with small minorities from the far left and the conservative right. They represented a broad range of ethnic and religious groups and many reform traditions. Within the inner circle around Roosevelt were Harold Ickes, an old La Follette Progressive reformer; Henry Wallace, an agrarian reformer from Iowa; Felix Frankfurter, a Jewish intellectual reformer, born in Vienna and schooled at Harvard; Raymond Moley, an academic reformer and professor of political science at Columbia; Rexford Tugwell, a silk-stocking patrician reformer from New York; the aforementioned Frances Perkins, an old-stock Yankee who became a labor reformer; and Cordell Hull, a southern liberal reformer in the Wilsonian tradition.[74]

Both the New Deal and the First Labour Government brought women into high office. Elizabeth McCombs, shown here, became a major figure in Parliament. Frances Perkins was FDR's Secretary of Labor through four terms and also a very close advisor to the president.

Franklin Roosevelt presided happily over this reform menagerie with a style of leadership that was at once pragmatic and principled, open and devious, intensely altruistic and not always scrupulous as to means. Something similar was happening not only in Washington but also in state capitals and city halls. A number of state legislatures enacted their own New Deals, and some were very inventive. Every branch of government was involved in this national movement. Private foundations, commissions, universities, labor unions, and voluntary associations also played a role. Franklin Roosevelt himself added something more, and it made all the difference. This patrician leader exercised an unexpected gift for reaching the American people.[75]

The First New Deal, March 9–June 16, 1933: A Revolution in Governance

Roosevelt took office in a moment of great danger. During Hoover's four disastrous years in office, industrial production fell by 50 percent, and unemployment rose to a record high—officially over 25 percent of the workforce, actually higher. The money supply (M2), national product (real GNP), and price levels (wholesale and retail) all contracted by more than 33 percent—their steepest recorded drops in American history. On Wall Street, Dow Jones stocks lost 89 percent of their value. From 1930 to 1933, 5,504 banks shut their doors. By March 4, 1933, Roosevelt's inauguration day, governors in almost every state had ordered a "banking holiday" to protect the rest. On that morning, most banks in the country were closed. The flow of money and credit virtually ceased. Before the president took office, the financial system had collapsed.[76]

The new president began by acting decisively to revive the financial system—and with unprecedented speed. On March 5, he called an emergency session of Congress. On March 6, he proclaimed a four-day national banking holiday. On March 9, Congress supported him, and Roosevelt started a process for reopening the banks as soon they were determined to be sound.

The first and most vital step was to restore hope and confidence throughout the republic. To that end, Roosevelt faced a major problem of communication. Most of the nation's newspapers were owned by Republicans and conservative Democrats. They were not happy about his election. Roosevelt needed to take his case directly to the people. At ten o'clock in the evening, Eastern Time (seven o'clock on the West Coast) he spoke to the nation by radio. It was not a

Franklin Roosevelt and Herbert Hoover made a dramatic study in contrasts. Roosevelt overflowed with optimism. He was eager to pursue a very active and experimental program of mixed enterprise. Above all he expressed great trust and confidence in the American people, and they reciprocated

speech, but more like a conversation. The subject was banking. The tone was informal, intimate, relaxed, and very effective. The new medium of national radio carried the president's words into American living rooms, where millions of American families gathered around their radio sets. The voice itself was mellow, calm, and confident. The president spoke with a patrician accent that his gifted political advisor Louis Howe had taught him to use without a hint of condescension. It wasn't the way that most Americans talked, but it had an air of calming authenticity, and on the evening of March 12, 1933, it calmed the nation in a critical moment. The next morning, the banks reopened. Money, credit, and confidence revived, and America's capitalist institutions began to function again. It was a triumph for Franklin Roosevelt, for presidential leadership, and for his method of direct communication with the people. Harry Butcher of CBS called it a "fireside chat," and the phrase caught on. Many fireside chats followed, first with the nation, then the world. A fireside chat on May 27, 1941, was thought to have reached 85 million listeners throughout many English-speaking nations.[77]

The president employed other ways to reach the people. He encouraged them to write him directly; 450,000 did so in his first week, and many more through his career. Many got a reply. Roosevelt expanded his staff in the White House mailroom from one person under Hoover to seventy people who helped to answer the flow of letters.[78]

With most newspaper owners against him, Roosevelt found other ways to be in touch with the American people. His fireside chats were informal radio conversations that reached millions of Americans in their living rooms and won many to the president.

He also used presidential press conferences on a new scale and in a new way. The first of them was on March 8, 1933, when 125 reporters were invited into the White House. New rules were established. His predecessors had required written questions, submitted in advance. Here again Roosevelt created a more open process. Spontaneous questions were encouraged. Answers were either "on the record," "off the record," or "for background." Reporters were expected to play by the rules, and most of them did so. Roosevelt treated journalists with respect—making them partners in controlling the news, mostly on his terms. All of these methods of communication expanded the power and authority of the presidency and created a new style of democratic leadership that is now part of most open societies.[79]

Roosevelt's Hundred Days

The first three months of the New Deal set a standard by which every subsequent administration would judge itself in American history. In that short period, President Roosevelt and congressional Democrats enacted an extraordinary array of reform measures, which together displayed the complex character of the New Deal.[80]

Congress began by agreeing to the president's request for an Emergency Banking Act, and did it in an extraordinary way. The bill was introduced and passed on the first day of the session, by unanimous vote in the House with only seven dissenters in the Senate. It expanded the open-market operations of the Federal Reserve and gave the president sweeping powers over currency, credit, foreign exchange, and banking regulation. Almost everybody agreed in its major purpose, which was to get the nation's system of privately owned banks back on their feet and to provide liquidity for the economy. The object was to revive private enterprise by public action. This was the central mission of the New Deal.[81]

Almost every week brought another major act. On March 20, the Economy Act balanced the federal budget by reducing salaries of government employees, cutting pensions, and streamlining government agencies to save money. Roosevelt's first New Deal took bold action without an increase in federal spending—which increased its legitimacy but slowed the recovery.[82] On March 22, another popular measure was the Beer-Wine Act, which ended national prohibition, imposed a federal tax on liquor, and recognized the power of the states to regulate the sale of alcohol. An enabling constitutional amendment followed quickly.

On March 31, the Civilian Conservation Corps Reforestation Relief Act put unemployed young people to work in temporary employment on much-needed public projects. Franklin Roosevelt understood something that other leaders did not, from his time to our own: in hard times, the political key to recovery in a free economy is employment, and public effort must prime the private pumps. Instantly he attacked that problem, and passed a major piece of legislation within a month of taking office. The president mobilized four federal agencies and ordered them to cooperate on the Civilian Conservation Corps. Agriculture, Interior, Labor, and the War Department all pitched in. He recruited some of the most able officers in the army and ordered them to help organize this civil project. George Marshall and Omar Bradley taught others about efficiency and integrity. At the same time, these upright soldiers learned how to lead large numbers of free people in a common effort.[83]

Unlike other American stimulus projects before and after, the CCC had an immediate and dramatic impact. This was not trickle-down economics but a surge from the bottom up. It reached Americans who were most in need of a helping hand—and in large numbers. Approximately 250,000 young men between eighteen and twenty-five were put to work on useful economic projects, such as the building of roads and bridges across the country. They repaired an American environment that had been ravaged by unrestrained exploitation. They stopped soil erosion, planted trees, built flood-control systems.

In his first hundred days Roosevelt immediately tackled the problem of unemployment. His Civilian Conservation Corps offered work to two million Americans. This and other measures cut unemployment in half, but the problem persisted and even increased after 1937.

By 1941, two million Americans had been employed in useful labor for thirty dollars a month; it was an experience that many of them remembered with pride. Their work improved the country. It also helped restore a sense of dignity and an ethic of work.[84]

On April 19, Roosevelt took the United States off the gold standard and broke the "golden fetters" that had shackled the American economy to a dysfunctional monetary system. A period of deflation (often more destructive than moderate inflation) came to an end. Prices and wages began to rise.[85] On May 12, the Federal Emergency Relief Act pumped funds into state and local welfare programs on a large scale. That same day, an Agricultural Adjustment Act established parity prices for farmers who reduced their crops. On May 18, the Tennessee Valley Authority created a public corporation to build dams and power plants. The object was to promote private development by public means in a deeply depressed region of the southern highlands.

In late May and early June, another series of laws sought to reduce fraud and corruption in financial markets. The Federal Securities Act on May 27 regulated the issue of new stocks and bonds, with strict requirements of disclosure. On June 16, the last day of the session, four major laws were passed. The Glass-Steagall Banking Act expanded the Federal Reserve, insured private bank deposits, and required deposit banks to stay out of the stock market. A Farm Credit

Act aided in refinancing farm mortgages at low rates over long periods, so that families could keep their private property. The Emergency Railroad Transportation Act regulated railroad holding companies, simplified rate-making, and expanded regulatory supervision to strengthen railroad corporations. The National Industrial Recovery Act created a system of "fair trade codes" in major industries and founded a National Labor Board to enforce collective bargaining. Title II of the act established the Public Works Administration, authorized billions for public projects, and attempted to revive business by self regulation and fair competition. Along the way other measures cracked down on fraudulent bankruptcy and levied taxes on dividends and excess profits.

The Fundamental Achievement of the First New Deal

Roosevelt's most important achievement was not any one of these New Deal programs in particular, or even all of them together. After a disaster in which business leaders, private corporations, and free markets had failed miserably, many people were ready to try something else. Roosevelt seized that opportunity. He succeeded in changing the fundamental attitudes of Americans toward the role of the national government in their lives. This change allowed the New Deal to revolutionize the relationship between the government and the nation itself and to strengthen a system of free enterprise.[86]

Other scholars have recently observed that the New Deal was also a turning point in another way, one that partisans of the left and right both deeply resented. In the words of three leading economic historians, the effect of its reforms was to promote "the extrication of government from control by political parties." Major economic questions had been increasingly politicized in a partisan way since the early republic. An example was trade policy. For many years it had oscillated between low-tariff Democrats and high-tariff Republicans, in a cycle that was driven largely by partisan imperatives. In 1934, New Deal Democrats introduced something new. The Reciprocal Trade Agreements Act gave the president authority to negotiate tariff agreements that did not require specific congressional approval. Gradually Congress moved other processes of economic regulation outside the arena of party debate and into the hands of nonpartisan institutions. Other examples included the regulation of monetary policy, financial markets, banking practices, and health and safety rules. Congress retained its powers of oversight and legislation, but it delegated the management of the economy to nonpartisan agencies. Michael Bordo observes that "with the New Deal . . . social programs began to exist independently of political involvement and party affiliation," a dramatic change from the history of Civil War–era pensions, for example. Conservative Republicans opposed all of these changes and reversed some of them in the years to come when they regained power. But economic realities in America and conditions in the world reinforced this tendency for many years.[87]

At first sight the New Deal has seemed a very mixed bag. Critics from the left and the right have complained endlessly of incoherence. But in fact the New Deal had a highly coherent purpose. Its object was to use public measures to promote private enterprise in most sectors of the economy. Its primary goal was not to create systems of welfare dependence but to help people help themselves. Wherever possible it supported similar actions by state and local governments, all the more so because Roosevelt was worried about opposition from a conservative Supreme Court. And it tried to do these things in ways that Americans of every region, class, and ethnicity could support. Its distinct character is very clear when compared with the reforms adopted by New Zealand's First Labour Government.

New Zealand's First Labour Government

In New Zealand, Michael Savage was elected on December 3, 1935, and sworn in as prime minister on December 6, 1935. The transition period, which spanned four difficult months in the United States, took three days in New Zealand. Savage was a strong leader, but he was very careful to govern through collective decisions by cabinet and Parliament. Like Roosevelt in the United States, he also faced the problem of reaching the people directly. He did it in a new spirit that most New Zealanders approved.

Savage got on well with reporters, but, like Roosevelt, he distrusted newspaper owners and editors, who were strongly conservative. Also like Roosevelt, he sought a way to reach a broad public directly and found a solution in radio, but he did so differently. Savage made some use of fireside chats, but mainly he did something else. In 1936, New Zealand became the first nation in the world to broadcast parliamentary debates by radio throughout the country. Savage declared, "Parliament under our democratic constitution is the mainspring of governmental power. . . . We cannot bring the people into Parliament, but through the medium of radio broadcasting we can bring Parliament to the people, so that at their own firesides they may listen to the most important discussion of questions vitally affecting their own lives."

Some leaders predicted that the public would be bored, but the broadcasts were a great success for the Labour government. Voters throughout the nation followed the debates with close attention. Savage made himself minister of broadcasting, nationalized the broadcasting system, and used it fairly to broadcast daily news. He was deeply interested in television as early as the mid-1930s and was one of the first to recognize its political possibilities.[88]

Savage's Sweeping Reforms

On his first day in office, Savage suspended the customary ritual of wearing top hats and morning coats. He instantly convened a cabinet meeting, rolled up his sleeves, and got down to work. The Labour government began with the task of relieving distress throughout the nation. It did so as boldly and effectively as Roosevelt, but in a very different way.

The first measure had no counterpart in the New Deal. Savage and his colleagues agreed that the national government would pay all unemployed workers an immediate "Christmas bonus" equal to one week's pay, without restrictions of race or gender. The cabinet also suspended foreclosures on mortgages and rents for some housing. It raised pay on public works projects, pegged welfare payments for Maori to the same level that Pakeha received, increased the number of nurses, hired more teachers, and expanded secondary schools.

These and other emergency measures were designed to relieve suffering and poverty by immediate action and by direct payments to those who needed them. They put people to work, and they were also meant to establish a principle of fairness, equity, and social justice throughout the country. In both substance and spirit these acts had no true counterpart in the American New Deal. A sweeping legislative program followed close behind. Savage believed that the government should intervene to protect the poorest workers in New Zealand—especially unskilled laborers and farmers. "Our mission," he said, "is to give some real security to those who are producing in abundance and living in poverty."[89]

The Finance Act of 1936 ordered the restoration of cuts in salaries and wages since the start of the slump. The Factories Amendment Act, the Shops and Offices Amendment Act, and the Agricultural Workers Act, all enacted in 1936, limited hours and fixed the minimum wage at two pounds a week. The Industrial Conciliation and Arbitration Amendment Act, also of 1936, restored compulsory arbitration, expanded the powers of the arbitration court, and set a new standard of equity for a man's wage—it must be sufficient to support a wife and three children. Parliament also ordered compulsory union membership, which trebled in three years, from 80,000 to more than 249,000 by 1938.[90]

In foreign trade, where the New Deal was moving toward lower tariffs and free trade, New Zealand's Labour government went the opposite way and became more actively interventionist. In 1938, import licenses were used to control the balance of trade and to encourage domestic industry.

A similar interventionist approach was taken in domestic markets. The Primary Products Marketing Act fixed prices for butter and cheese above depressed market levels and supported them with government guarantees. Savage also promised and delivered direct-price supports for dairy products in 1936, and later for eggs, honey, apples, pears, and other farm products. This was different from the more market-centered approach in the American New Deal, which used parity payments to farmers as a way of keeping surplus crops off the market.

Where Franklin Roosevelt spoke of a larger definition of liberty and freedom, the argument for the Labour program in New Zealand was made in terms of fairness and social justice. Labour leaders in New Zealand thought and spoke in terms of a "fair price" or "just price" in relation to the costs of production and a decent cost of living, which took precedence over a market price. In the same spirit, the New Zealand Fair Rents Act in 1936 fixed housing costs by another standard of fairness and forbade increases unless approved by a judge.

Historian Keith Sinclair commented, "Whether a socially 'just' price would prove to be the same as an average market price remained to be seen."[91] To close the gap between the "just price" and "market price" of real estate, the New Zealand government began to build and rent houses on a large scale. In short, it went into the business of house construction, with designs and dimensions set in cabinet meetings, once again working from earlier Progressive Era measures.[92]

With the leadership of Savage, the First Labour Government launched a massive program of nationalization in many sectors of the economy. It built on trends that had been established in New Zealand by earlier reform governments. Savage declared, "We intend to begin where Richard John Seddon and his colleagues left off." In 1935, much of New Zealand's economy—railroads, insurance, and postal savings—was already owned and operated by the government. A conservative government led by Coates had nationalized private mortgage corporations to help farmers. There was a strong pattern of continuity in New Zealand's program of nationalization, and a deep difference from the American New Deal.[93]

Under the Labour governments of Savage and Fraser, public ownership expanded rapidly. The Reserve Bank Amendment Act of 1936 gave the government sweeping powers of control over the Bank of New Zealand. During the next decade many industries were nationalized: iron and steel in 1937, coal mines in 1942, airlines in 1944, and the Bank of New Zealand in 1945. This policy continued to 1949, when Labour fell from power. It gave New Zealand one of the most socialized economies in the free world.[94]

In one important way the New Zealand system was different from other socialized regimes such as Sweden and similar to the New Deal. Savage centered his purposes on the welfare of individuals in New Zealand rather than the equalization of classes. Many of his reforms were designed to support an ideal of individual autonomy and individual empowerment. In that respect, they were like American reforms in their ends but different in their means. New Zealand's Mortgagors and Lessees Rehabilitation Act and the State Advances Corporation Act were sweeping measures designed to keep farmers on the land and families in their own homes, much like several New Deal measures, but in New Zealand the instruments were public institutions, owned by the state. Private savings were protected in the Post Office Savings Bank, in a manner much like the American program of Federal Deposit Insurance. The difference was that American banks remained privately owned and New Zealand's major bank was nationalized.

The reform program of New Zealand's Labour government also went farther than the American New Deal in other areas. It guaranteed a free education for everyone to the age of nineteen and created a national library system open to every person. These reforms were not part of the American New Deal. A major factor was the federal structure of the American system, which had made state and local governments responsible for education.

Overall, the reform measures in both countries shared similar goals but pursued them in different ways. New Zealand's Labour government tried to create a national system of social justice with heavy use of collective ownership. The American New Deal worked mainly within a system of private ownership and free enterprise.

Two Programs of Social Security

Most American historians distinguish between two New Deals. The second New Deal followed Franklin Roosevelt's Annual Message to Congress in January of 1935. Its central theme was "greater freedom" through "greater security for the average man." In the year that followed, Congress and the president enacted many new laws, of which the most important was the Social Security Act. New Zealand's Labour government did something similar as it prepared for a general election in 1938. It enacted a Social Security Bill that has been called "probably the most important single piece of legislation in New Zealand's history."[95]

The social problems that called these statutes into being were similar—the same cruel combination of chronic unemployment, forced retirement, and destitution in old age. The names of the legislative programs were identical, but their provisions were very different.[96]

The Social Security Act in the United States has been called by critics a chaotic mix of many approaches to welfare. In fact it had a very strong central purpose. Though furiously denounced from the right and the left, its object was to use the power and resources of the national government to help Americans to prepare for their own needs after retirement, and to model a public program on systems of private insurance.[97]

In company with many other Americans from his Puritan ancestors to our own time, Roosevelt did not like welfare programs in the form of alms for the poor. "The Federal Government must and shall quit this business of relief," he said. "I am not willing that the vitality of our people be further sapped by the giving of cash. . . . We must preserve not only the bodies of the unemployed from destitution, but also their self-respect, their self-reliance."[98]

His administration worked with Congress and others to design a different set of welfare programs: opportunities for useful and meaningful employment; a program of unemployment insurance (with federal money and state agencies); and a public system of old-age insurance. To fund these programs, most wage-earning Americans were required to contribute to a trust fund through a tax on their earnings. The cost was to be borne jointly by the workers themselves and by their employers. The result was a system of social security that was more comprehensive than anything before in American history but not universal. From the start American Social Security did not assist those who most needed help. People who had no taxable wages were excluded at the outset, as also were most farm laborers and domestic workers. Even for those who were part of the system, payments always fell far below the cost of living. They were intended as supplements to personal savings and private income.[99]

The size of benefits (at first $10 to $85 a month) varied with the amount of money that workers paid into the system. They were supported by special taxes that were highly regressive. People with the lowest wages paid the largest proportion of their income. The primary object of Social Security in the United States was to help Americans provide for their old age in periods of unemployment and to strengthen a system of private enterprise. To avoid trouble from a conservative Supreme Court, only the old-age benefits were a uniform national program. Another program of unemployment insurance was put primarily in the hands of the states, with material assistance from the federal government.

By comparison with other nations, Social Security was a conservative system. W. E. Leuchtenburg wrote, "In no other welfare system in the world did the state shirk all responsibility for old age indigency and insist that funds be taken out of current earnings of workers."[100] Even so, the most astonishing fact about Social Security was not that it passed in so conservative a form but rather that it passed at all in so conservative a nation. Right-wing Republicans and southern Democrats did all in their power to destroy it. Passage of the act was followed by litigation, and the Supreme Court sustained its constitutionality by a single vote.[101]

The special character of this American system is more clear when it is compared with programs in other countries. New Zealand's Social Security Act of 1938 had a different purpose. Its primary object was to guarantee a living income for everyone in New Zealand. Benefits were authorized for every form of poverty that its authors could imagine. An additional emergency benefit plan was added for anyone who might have been left out. Most benefits were subject to a means test. The size of payments was determined by need, not by the level of contributions paid to the system. The taxes that paid for New Zealand's measures were progressive rather than regressive. In short, New Zealanders designed a social security system primarily on a basis of fairness. The American system was devised to create a measure of security that might stabilize a system of free enterprise.

The two social security laws also covered different risks. In America Roosevelt had hoped to include provisions for medical care, public health, maternity and child care, and special programs for disabled children. These parts of his program were defeated by intense lobbying, much of it from the American Medical Association, the leading trade organization of physicians, who feared for their income and independence. Their lobbyists went to work on Capitol Hill with high success. President Roosevelt removed health care from Social Security in fear of losing the entire program.

New Zealand went a different way. In 1938, it created a national health system that provided free medical services, subsidized hospital costs, and made health care available to all. The medical profession in New Zealand strongly opposed the new system and threatened a strike. Savage threatened to import doctors to operate the new program, and the physicians gave way. But the New Zealand Health System was a compromise between the Labour government and the medical and dental profession—a mix of public subsidies and private payments for medical and dental care. In the United States, no compromises were possible on this issue. A national health system was stopped in its tracks.[102]

The difference between these reform programs was partly a function of different purposes. It was also the consequence of different systems of governance. In America's pluralist federal and congressional system, many groups had a say in the design of programs, and many agencies had a role in their operation. The New Deal was a series of compromises. In New Zealand's centralized parliamentary system, its Social Security Act was written by six men. The National Health Plan was largely driven by the will of one man, Michael James Savage. These processes made a major difference in the results.

Opponents of Reform: Two Conservative Traditions

Another important factor, often neglected by historians of reform, was the response of conservatives. Here again we find a major difference between New Zealand and the United States. The New Deal was fiercely opposed by infuriated conservatives who attacked it as radical, socialist, even Communist and Fascist. In Washington, Felix Frankfurter's home in Georgetown was called "the little Red House which dictated to the big White House." Conservative Democrats such as Al Smith were as outspoken against the New Deal as were members of the Republican Party.

The United States has many conservative elites, and they were hostile to the New Deal and Franklin Roosevelt for many reasons. Conservative southern Democrats opposed their own president on many major pieces of New Deal legislation as dangerous to the South's traditional folkways and a threat to its system of race relations. Conservative Republicans saw the New Deal as hostile to capitalism and private property. Physicians were among the most inveterate enemies of the New Deal and especially feared a national health plan. Lawyers and judges believed that much of the New Deal was unconstitutional, a menace to the rule of law, and hostile to the legal profession. The threat of intervention by a conservative Supreme Court limited many New Deal measures.

Many of these conservative groups organized the American Liberty League. They tried to defeat Roosevelt and the New Deal in the congressional elections of 1934, and again in the presidential race of 1936. The president skillfully made the Liberty League itself into a campaign issue. He called its leaders "economic royalists," compared them to the bumbling tyrant George III, and identified the New Deal with liberty, freedom, and the American Revolution. His conservative opponents were crushed at the polls. In 1936, Franklin Roosevelt won 523 electoral votes. His conservative opponent won 8 electoral votes. Even after that experience, American conservatives were more hostile to the New Deal.[103]

In New Zealand, conservatives responded differently to social reform. Some were very outspoken against the Labour government in the 1930s. Editors and cartoonists used some of the same rhetoric that was heard in the United States. Conservative leaders of the National Party opposed social security. Sidney Holland declared that social security was not "applied Christianity" but "applied lunacy." He promised that the National Party would "put an end to this sort of thing when we get into power."[104]

But many conservatives in New Zealand, such as William Downie Stewart, were more moderate and constructive, as they had been in the Progressive Era. In Parliament during the 1930s, some supported many reform measures and attempted to refine and improve them. This was a major difference between the two nations through the nineteenth and twentieth centuries.

Two Experiences of Reform

In summary, the American New Deal and New Zealand's First Labour Government shared much in common, but their principles and policies were very different. In most cases Roosevelt's New Deal used public instruments to support free enterprise and private ownership of production. It expanded the role of government as stimulator, regulator, and sponsor of large projects beyond the reach of private capital. It rejected the ideas of laissez-faire policy that had failed disastrously in the Great Depression. But always its primary goal was a larger idea of individual freedom for Americans.[105]

The primary purpose of New Zealand's First Labour Government was to promote social justice. To that end, its leaders were democratic socialists. Their policy was to expand public ownership of the means of production, by nationalizing many institutions and industries.

*A major difference between New Zealand
and the United States in hard times was
the response of leading conservatives. An
example in Dunedin was William Downie
Stewart, who responded to the Great Depression with reasoned moderation, sympathy
for the suffering poor, constructive compromise, and a willingness to act for the common good. Conservatives in America went
the other way in the 1930s, and again in
the early twenty-first century.*

A comparative approach indicates that widely shared interpretations of the New Deal fundamentally misconceived. The first error is
that they had no consistent ideology. Precisely the same mistake has
been made about New Zealand's First Labour Government. To study
these movements in a comparative perspective is to discover that
Roosevelt's New Deal and Savage's First Labour Government had
very clear values and purposes, which were profoundly different
from one another.[106]

Yet another error is the mistaken idea that the American New
Deal represented a triumph of "big government" and a very large
expansion of government employment and public expenditures. A
comparative perspective is enlightening in that respect. In 1939, 25
percent of New Zealand's workers worked for national or local governments. The comparable proportion in the United States, circa
1940, was 8 percent—of workers in federal, state and local governments combined.[107] Tax payments in the United States increased by
45 percent from 1932 to 1940. In New Zealand they went up by 91
percent from 1929 to 1938.[108]

Contrary to common belief, the growth of government purchases of goods and services did not accelerate during the New Deal. The trend line rose at a constant rate from 1870 to 1970, with the exception of sharp surges during the two world wars. The New Deal represented no break in that linear process and no acceleration of government spending. The trends were very different in New Zealand. Here is yet another indicator of different purposes and means in the two reform movements. The New Deal was less active in the expansion of government and more active in promoting free enterprise and individual autonomy. New Zealand moved in a different direction. The differences between these reform movements rose from ethical choices that were deeply rooted in cultures and institutions.[109]

From a comparison of these two reform movements, a question comes to mind. Might a third way be found? Could it combine liberty and freedom with fairness and justice in an optimal way? In 1940, that was a problem for the future. In the twenty-first century, it is a question for our time.

MILITARY TRADITIONS

Ways of War in Open Societies

> She never draws the sword except for civilisation and
> for fair play.
>
> > —Representative John Bollard, explaining why
> > New Zealand should aid Britain in the Boer War

> We, too, born to freedom, and believing in freedom,
> are willing to fight to maintain freedom.
>
> > —President Franklin Roosevelt, explaining why
> > America should aid Britain in World War II

I N MOST MAJOR WARS of the twentieth century, New Zealand
and the United States were allies. During the First World War,
Dinks and Doughboys found themselves fighting on the same
side. In World War II, Yanks and Kiwis served in the same campaigns.
Through the long struggles in Korea and Vietnam, New Zealanders
and Americans soldiered on the same fields. In the early twenty-first
century, men and women of both nations were on the same teams in
Haiti, Bosnia, Kuwait, Somalia, and Afghanistan.[1]

This long association did not derive from an identity of values,
or a unity of culture. It was not sustained by ties of kinship, or supported by a mutuality of material interest. Leaders in both nations
were keenly aware of their differences, especially when they worked
together. In intervals of peace they disagreed profoundly on many
questions: the League of Nations in the 1920s, collective security
during the 1930s, the design of the United Nations in the 1940s,
nuclear policy from 1949 to 1989, the Middle East in 1990s, and
the Iraq war in the twenty-first century.[2]

But when the big wars began, the people of New Zealand and the United States sooner or later found themselves on the same side, fighting mortal enemies to open societies. Many such enemies launched deadly attacks on open systems: monarchists and aristocrats in old regimes of middle Europe in 1914–18, Fascists of many nations in 1939–45, Asian militarists in 1941, Communists in the Cold War, and Islamic terrorists in the twenty-first century. This long trend in the military history of New Zealand and the United States has been remarkably durable for nearly a hundred years. It is full of clues to the character of both nations. More important, it can help us to understand the ways of war in open societies—a subject dangerously misunderstood by friends and enemies alike.

In 1917, for example, Germany's General Erich Ludendorff was informed that the United States was about to enter the First World War. "The Americans are just bluffing," he told a young officer, and added, "I have no fear of American troops, for a nation that has no military education whatsoever is not proficient at war." A year later, the citizen armies of open societies in the British Commonwealth, France, and the United States had broken Germany's war machine, and General Ludendorff was a fugitive in Switzerland, so bewildered by what had happened he became a pacifist.[3]

Many leaders of closed systems have shared General Ludendorff's contempt for open societies in general, and anglophone nations in particular. Before 1939, English-speaking people never maintained large standing armies in time of peace. They rarely fortified borders or cities in a serious way, for their security lay in command of the sea. Since the seventeenth century, their laws firmly established civilian control over military services. Their top leaders were rarely trained for war, and their people were hostile to martial discipline. In the modern era, these nations rarely required compulsory military training in time of peace, with the exception of New Zealand in the period between 1904 and 1909. As early as the mid-seventeenth century, English-speaking countries recognized the right of "conscientious objection" to military service, unlike many nations. All this evidence persuaded Ludendorff that open societies "had no military education whatsoever" and were "not proficient at war."

He was tragically mistaken, in large part because he did not understand the history of open societies, with disastrous results for the peace of the world. The United States and New Zealand had much military experience. They fought wars in every generation: sixteen generations of warfare in America (1607–2010); six generations in

New Zealand (1845–2010). Both nations developed military traditions that were so distant from Ludendorff's experience that he could not think of them as military at all.

The American Experience of War, 1607–2010

An important key to understanding American ways of war is the long history of fighting between European settlers and Native Americans. As we have seen, in the first permanent settlement at Jamestown, combat began on the very first night, April 26, 1607. The same thing happened in New England on December 8, 1620, when the *Mayflower* Pilgrims landed on Cape Cod's First Encounter Beach.[4]

The many wars that followed between English-speaking colonists and Indians were among the most cruel and bloody in American history. In Virginia's Indian War of 1622–24, a majority of English settlers died, and many Native Americans. During King Philip's War in 1675–76, as many as 10 percent of New England's entire European population perished. Nobody has been able to count the cost for the Indians.[5] American ways of war began to develop in those conflicts. They were horrific struggles. Both sides fought desperately for lands and homes. Defeat for settlers and Indians alike brought suffering worse than death. There were no mutually accepted rules of engagement, except the brutal rule that the winner takes all.

These early American conflicts were linked to six major European wars from 1689 to 1774. All of them spread to the New World and were fought by Indians, settlers, and European professionals. Every colonial generation, without exception, had direct experience of these wars.[6] From 1774 to 1865, another sequence of major wars established the United States as an independent nation and a continental power. The longest was the Revolutionary War (1775–83). In New England towns where we can make a count, more than 90 percent of men of military age served in combat. By 1783, half the women of Marblehead and Charlestown were widows. The most costly was the American Civil War (1861–65), with six hundred thousand military deaths and many civilian casualties, especially among African Americans in the South.[7]

Then came another long wave of global conflicts that marked the emergence of the United States as a world power. Only three of these wars were formally declared: the Spanish-American War in 1898, the First World War in 1917, and World War II in 1941. In addition, American armed forces also fought more than two hundred undeclared wars from 1789 to 1935 alone. That number did not include Indian wars; the U.S. Army's list of casualties in Indian wars from 1865 to 1890 fills a large volume in small print. Since 1945, American troops have also served in many undeclared small wars and four very large ones. At the date of this writing in 2010, American armed forces are on the ground in more than 140 nations throughout the world. Altogether, the armed forces of the United States have been fighting somewhere in the world almost every year since the republic began.[8]

Two American Military Traditions

This long experience shaped ways of war in the United States in several ways. After 1789, most of America's little wars were fought by small volunteer forces of regulars under professional officers. These men made war a career, even a calling. They thought of fighting as a continuous activity in a violent world where there is always soldiering to be done. They lived and died by a soldier's code of courage, duty, and honor. In the United States, regular officers were also trained to believe that they were honor-bound to serve the republic, respect the Constitution, and support the rule of law. Most have upheld those principles with high integrity.[9]

They came in disproportionate numbers from American cultures with warrior ethics of different kinds. Some from the South inherited a Cavalier ethic that had been transplanted from England in the seventeenth century: Light Horse Harry Lee, J.E.B. Stuart, and the gallant John Pelham. Others of New England stock kept the relentless creed of the Puritan tradition and Cromwell's implacable New Model Army: among them Ulysses Grant and William Sherman. More than a few were raised in the old Stoic tradition of the republic, from George Washington to George Marshall. Many inherited a different warrior ethic from Irish, Welsh, and North British Borderers and became hard-drivers in many American wars—a progeny of Morgans, Waynes, Jacksons, MacArthurs, Pattons, and Sheridans. Others were American Indians who fought the United States and later led its armed forces in world wars: the Cherokee carrier admiral Jocko Clark, to name but one example. Several African warrior traditions passed from Mali, Ghana, and Angola to African Americans in military service today. More than a few American leaders were German Americans, raised to an ethic of discipline and order: Pershing, Nimitz, Eisenhower, Arnold, Spaatz, Eaker. And there were the soldier-intellectuals: from Henry "Old Brains" Halleck to David

Petraeus. All these warriors together were the Regulars who shared a professional code and practiced many ways of war.[10]

In America, another and profoundly different martial tradition emerged among citizen-soldiers who did most of the fighting in the big wars. These amateurs regarded themselves not as warriors but as civilians. They tended to think of war in instrumental terms, as a hard job that had to be done from time to time. Their object was to go about it in a practical-minded way, finish it quickly, and return to the ordinary business of life. Many officers in America's citizen-armies were not professional soldiers. In the nineteenth century they were often elected by the men they tried to lead (command was out of the question). Discipline was not strict, and training was not rigorous. Performance was uneven, to say the least, but some civilians in uniform were among the most successful generals in American history: Nathanael Greene, Henry Knox, and most officers in the War of Independence. In the Civil War they included college professor Joshua Chamberlain, railroad man Grenville Dodge, brilliant backcountry

Americans were heirs to many different ways of war. J.E.B. Stuart of Virginia was a soldier in the Cavalier tradition that reached back to Prince Rupert and the Royalist cause in the English Civil Wars. He was the master of bold cavalry actions that were designed to seize the initiative and control the tempo of war. A striking contrast was William Tecumseh Sherman, who inherited another way of war from his New England Puritan ancestors. His object was to use massive force in an implacable campaign to destroy the means of resistance and the will to resist.

fighter Nathan Bedford Forrest, and millions more in the First and Second World Wars.

Ethics of War in Open Systems

American ways of war were shaped by many elements that characterize open societies. Free people are used to making their own choices. Before they embark on a war, most want to know if it is necessary, and some ask if it is just. These questions were about how and why the war began, and the not-so-simple issue of who fired the first shot. The most effective war leaders in American history have been sensitive to the importance of these ethical issues. In the American Revolution, Samuel Adams advised Augustine Washington to "put your enemy in the wrong and keep him there, a good rule in war as in politics." Abraham Lincoln was careful to do the same thing in the Civil War, as did Woodrow Wilson in World War I and Franklin Roosevelt in World War II.[11]

From time to time, a few American leaders went to war in another way. A leading example was the decision of Jefferson Davis and other Confederate leaders to fire the first shot at Fort Sumter, in the hope of drawing Virginia to the Confederacy. They succeeded in that particular purpose but gave Abraham Lincoln a great moral advantage, and he made the most of it. Another example was George W. Bush's preemptive war on Iraq. Both Jefferson Davis and George Bush forfeited much of the moral high ground in the way they went to war. They alienated friends throughout the world and gratified their enemies.[12]

After these conflicts began, American ethics have also tended to shape their course and conduct. In the twentieth century, open societies rarely initiated major aggressive wars, despite frequent allegations to the contrary. As a rule, open societies were attacked first, and their enemies seized the initiative. Early campaigns in America's major wars were often defeats or outright disasters: the New York campaign in 1776; Bull Run in 1861–62; the first six months of the Pacific War in 1941–42; the Battle of the Atlantic in 1942; the agony of the 24th Division in Korea during the summer of 1950; and surprise attacks on the World Trade Center by Islamic terrorists in 2001.

After the shock of these disasters, open systems tended to rally. Often they responded more creatively than closed societies. With effective leadership (not always the case), they were able to engage the energy of free people in the war effort. They exploited the initiative of autonomous people who manage their own affairs, drew on the material resources of a mixed economy, and tapped the moral strength of open cultures. Closed systems have other military advantages, which are most evident in the early stages of a war, but their strengths tend to be wasting assets as the struggle goes on.

The resources of open societies tend to increase as they mobilize for war. Sooner or later they gain control of the tempo of events, and the initiative passes into their hands. These pivotal moments happened in the American War of Independence during the winter of 1776–77; in the Union cause during the Civil War by 1863; in World War I during the summer of 1918; in World War II during the summer and fall of 1942; in the Korean War when General Matthew Ridgway replaced Douglas MacArthur. This pattern is strong when open societies are united in support of a war, or nearly so. But the course of events was different in the War of 1812, the Mexican War, and the Vietnam War, when Americans were deeply divided.

As major conflicts move toward a conclusion, American ways of war tend to be distinctive in their goals. The purposes are usually the same: to end the war as quickly as possible, and to remove the cause of conflict. But means to that end have been variable. In some wars Americans sought nothing less than complete defeat of the enemy regime—never the destruction of a people or a nation, but the dissolution of a hostile regime and a rapid return to peace. One way that Americans have tried to achieve that goal has been by demanding the unconditional surrender of the aggressor, as Grant did in the Civil War, Pershing tried to do in World War I, and Franklin Roosevelt did in World War II, much to the disapproval of European leaders. But since 1775 only these three wars were fought for unconditional surrender. Most other conflicts were limited wars. Their object was not to remove or destroy an opposing regime but to change its behavior. In quantitative terms, limited conflict has always been the most common American way of war.[13]

In changing circumstances, Americans have also invented other ways of war. One of them appeared after the development of nuclear weapons, which threatened total destruction of both sides, and even the extinction of life on the planet. The result was a new strategy of long struggle, centered on the containment of an aggressive enemy until the opposing regime collapses internally—as happened in the Cold War.

Yet another way of war grew from a technology that allows the controlled use of very precise weapons to strike directly at the heart or head of a hostile group. In these many conflicts, American leaders have continuously reinvented traditional ways of war in new combinations.

Not all wars followed this general pattern of flexible and, one might say, pragmatic warfare, but most conflicts have done so through sixteen generations.

New Zealand Ways of War, 1840–1914

New Zealanders of both British and Polynesian descent also inherited strong military traditions. Maori were and are a militant people with an elaborate warrior ethic. British colonists in the nineteenth century also introduced military traditions that had deep roots in their cultural past. Many prominent leaders of British colonization of New Zealand were veterans of the Napoleonic Wars. All early governors were military or naval officers who lived by ideals of honor, courage, and duty.

In the mid-nineteenth century, these proud and bellicose people went to war. A series of small collisions grew into major conflicts that British settlers called the Maori Wars, and Maori called *te riri pakeha*, the "White Men's Battles." The fighting reached its climax in two periods, from 1845 to 1847 and again from 1860 to 1872, with smaller conflicts earlier and later.[14]

Maori won many battles but lost the wars, and yet their warrior spirit has survived. On the Pakeha side, the fighting was done by British Regulars, Maori allies, and also by New Zealand settlers. The experience of these conflicts in the nineteenth century shaped male New Zealanders' sense of themselves in the twentieth century. An abiding memory of those events reinforced the military heritage of Maori and Pakeha alike.[15]

These New Zealand Native Wars were unlike America's Indian wars in some respects. There was much hard fighting with atrocities on both sides, but nothing to match the sustained savagery of native wars in the United States. British and Maori ways of war were more elaborately rule-bound. One side did not normally seek the total destruction of the enemy. The object was usually to establish a new form of coexistence. A leading example is the career of Te Kooti, a brilliant Maori guerrilla fighter, sometimes very brutal, both to Pakeha and also to Maori where *utu* was involved. This great warrior was often defeated but never destroyed. Finally, he was allowed sanctuary in the King Country, where he became a religious leader, renounced fighting, and helped to end the Native Wars.[16] All of this helped to shape the military heritage of New Zealand. The result was a tradition of warfare that was elaborately regulated by law and custom, both Maori and Pakeha. Another was a tendency for wars to be limited in

New Zealanders also inherited many different military traditions. One of them was the Maori way of war. These formidable warriors combined close collective effort with acts of individual daring and courage. They were quick to adopt new technology, and they also kept a strict ethical code that greatly impressed their opponents.

their purposes—much more so than in the history of the United States. New Zealanders on both sides did not think of total victory or unconditional surrender. They went to war for specific goals.

Within that frame, warfare was a continuing part of New Zealand's culture and history. Both Pakeha and Maori took pride in their military heritage. In the twentieth century, young New Zealand males in each culture became heirs to both traditions. Today they devote most of their lives to peaceful pursuits, but they were (and are) raised on heroic tales of courage and service. At an early age, young men were taught to think of themselves as the stewards and guardians of this highly articulated tradition.[17]

Historically, both Maori and Pakeha were quick to volunteer for military service throughout the British Empire when opportunities appeared—again, mostly in small wars with limited goals. When British forces were having trouble in the Sudan, Ngati Haua leader Hote Tamehana offered to lead two hundred Maori warriors to help pacify that part of Africa.[18] Pakeha New Zealanders offered their services to the United States during the Spanish-American War. More than

Another New Zealand way of war was that of highly disciplined British regulars. A third way was that of New Zealand's undisciplined citizen soldiers, especially its mounted infantry, who earned high respect for combining the mobility of cavalry with the strength of infantry.

seventeen thousand volunteered for service in the Boer War of 1899–1901, a greater proportion than in Britain itself, or any other colony. They established a reputation for courage and loyalty to one another. The official British history of the Boer War observed that New Zealand's mounted infantry were "by general consent regarded as, on average, the best mounted troops in South Africa." These small imperial wars reinforced New Zealand's military tradition. Jock Phillips writes, "The Boer War served to entrench military prowess as a central element of the white New Zealand male identity."[19]

So strong was this tradition that in 1902 Parliament passed a law requiring military instruction in every New Zealand school. In 1909, it went farther and enacted compulsory military service. Every able-bodied boy in New Zealand was compelled to serve as a military cadet from the age of twelve and to join a Territorial Battalion at eighteen.[20] When this system of compulsory military service was created, no nation on earth was hostile to New Zealand, and yet so pervasive was its military tradition that compulsory service was enacted with only three dissenting votes in Parliament. Its primary purpose was not material interest or military defense but the promotion of martial values in the coming generation.[21] Not all New Zealanders approved of this tradition. Recent revisionist scholarship has turned up (and celebrated) many exceptions among conscientious objectors, peace societies, anti-militarist leagues, libertarians, and women's organizations. But those groups themselves testified to the strength of the military tradition that they opposed.[22]

Formative Experiences: New Zealand in the First World War

The First World War was a pivotal moment in New Zealand's history. More than any other event in the twentieth century, it encouraged New Zealanders to think of themselves as a nation and also reinforced their military traditions. When the war began in 1914, they volunteered with high enthusiasm. A reporter asked George Bernard Shaw, "Do you not think that New Zealand's action in sending troops to the Great War showed the strength of our attachment?" Shaw answered, "You went into it out of pure devilment! You need not have sent those troops unless you had liked. You could have joined the Germans if you liked."[23]

More than 40 percent of New Zealand's male population of military age served overseas in World War I. British officers complained that they were undisciplined, "turbulent," and "always ready for trouble," but enemies and allies alike judged New Zealanders to be among the best infantry in the war.[24] For that reputation, they paid a heavy price. At Gallipoli in 1915–16, 12,256 New Zealanders came ashore; all but 900 were killed or wounded. The memory of Gallipoli remains strong in New Zealand, but many more casualties happened on the Western Front, where its infantry suffered losses four times greater than in the Dardanelles. Altogether, New Zealand troops who went overseas in World War I suffered 59,483 casualties, of which 18,166 were killed. In proportion to population, this was a higher rate of loss than in any other combatant nation in the First World War.[25]

World War I had a major impact on New Zealand's military tradition. The nation suffered heavy losses on the western front and at Gallipoli, as in this photograph of wounded men at Anzac Cove on April 7, 1915. The legacy was not a memory of useless slaughter but of courage, heroism, and sacrifice in a noble cause.

The cultural impact of the Great War on New Zealand was very powerful, but not in the way that we might automatically assume from antiwar literature written in its aftermath. Gallipoli and the Western Front were remembered by New Zealanders in the 1920s not for useless slaughter but for courage and sacrifice in a noble cause. New Zealand's military tradition was made stronger, not weaker, by the First World War.[26] Its strength appeared in 1922 when Britain came to the brink of war with Turkey. More than fourteen thousand New Zealanders swarmed to recruiting stations. Young men who had missed the last "show" were eager for a war of their own. Some old soldiers, like fire horses, were ready to go at the first alarm.[27]

This attitude continued through the twentieth century. Jock Phillips remembers, "It was one of my first articles of faith, a certainty of early boyhood—one day I would fight in a war. My father's generation had the Second World War; my grandfather's the First World War, and further back were other wars—the Boer War, the New Zealand wars, wars against Napoleon, crusades against the Arabs. Every 20 years, it seemed, there was a war in which a new generation of young men could prove their manhood. We would eventually get our war, and we would of course, 'do well.' That was another article of faith, that New Zealanders were 'good at war.' Once again, we would prove ourselves the finest of the Empire's sons." The lessons of the First World War in New Zealand were about the nobility of military service, the importance of courage, and the meaning of sacrifice.[28]

The United States in the First World War

World War I was also important in the military experience of the United States, but the lessons drawn from it were not primarily about courage and sacrifice. They were about the instrumental effect of massive mobilization and about total concentration on the task at hand as a way of gaining quick and certain victory.

The United States kept out of the war for three years. In 1914, many Americans, including President Woodrow Wilson from his childhood, vividly remembered the Civil War and knew the horrific cost of modern war, as Europeans did not. Americans at first were dubious about both sides and wanted no part of a European slaughter. But they were appalled by growing evidence of German atrocities in France and Belgium (recently confirmed by new research).[29] Many were outraged by German submarine attacks on neutral American shipping and astonished by a German attempt to provoke war between Mexico and the United States. After tsarist Russia withdrew from the war, the Allies increasingly appeared to represent the cause of liberty and freedom. In 1917, the full weight of the German army shifted to the Western Front, and the tide of battle turned against Britain and France. To Woodrow Wilson and many other Americans, the prospect of German victory was perceived as dangerous to American interests and principles. On April 6, 1917, the United States entered the war.

Once committed, Americans acted in their customary way: they mobilized resources with extraordinary concentration on the task at hand. Within a year, American armed forces expanded from fewer than 180,000 men to more than five million. The navy was greatly increased, and a huge armada of ships was built in record time to carry American troops to European battlefields three thousand miles away. [30]

The next step was to seek quick and decisive victory over the German army. This part of the job proved to be more difficult than Americans had imagined. Very few American troops entered combat in 1917. Training and deployment took time—and time was of the essence. In the spring of 1918, Germany mounted the largest offensive in the war. Exhausted French and British armies were driven back once again to the river Marne near Paris, and German troops came close to victory.

Then at last American troops began to pour into France. At Étaples, in April 1918, a war-weary English nurse named Vera Brittain was walking to her crowded hospital when a large column of troops marched past, "swinging rapidly" toward the Front. She had seen many marching columns go by, but these men looked different to her experienced eye, with "an unusual quality of bold vigour in their swift stride."

"They looked larger than ordinary men," she wrote. "Their tall straight figures were in vivid contrast to the under-sized armies of pale recruits to which we had grown accustomed. At first I thought their spruce, clean uniforms were those of officers, yet obviously they could not be officers, for there were too many of them; they seemed, as it were, Tommies in heaven. Had yet another regiment been conjured out of our depleted Dominions? I wondered, watching them move with such rhythm, such dignity, such serene consciousness of self-respect. But I knew the colonial troops so well, and these were different; they were assured where the Australians were aggressive, self-possessed where the New Zealanders were turbulent." Then the other nurses cried, "Look! Look! Here are the Americans!"[31]

More than half a million American troops reached France by the spring of 1918, a million by midsummer, two million by the early fall, and millions more were on their way—more than combined strength of French and British armies on the Western Front. They attacked into the teeth of the German offensive at Cantigny, at Belleau Wood, and again at Château-Thierry where the Front was closest to Paris. Some American units fought beside the French army on the Aisne and Marne. Others went into action alongside the British, Canadians, Australians, and New Zealanders. In September, the Western Allies mounted their own offensive, and the German army was defeated all along the Front. In October, the Allies drove seventy kilometers—forty-five miles—to Sedan and cut German rail connections to the Rhine.

The cost was heavy. In only a few months, the U. S. Army and Marine Corps lost 300,000 killed and wounded. France alone lost another million men in the last half-year of the war. Britain and the Dominions suffered heavily as well. But this time the results were dramatic and decisive. The German army, which had almost won six months earlier, suddenly found itself on the edge of disaster. Its defeated generals urgently sought an armistice to prevent complete catastrophe.

American commanders strongly opposed an armistice. General John Pershing demanded unconditional surrender, in the tradition of Ulysses Grant, but French and British leaders did not agree.

The American experience of World War I was very different: late entry, massive mobilization, brief hard-fought combat with heavy losses, and quick victory. All this reinforced an instrumental American way of war.

Pershing was appalled. "What an enormous difference a few more days would have made," he wrote. "What I dread is that Germany doesn't know that she was licked. Had they given us another week, we'd have taught them." Many Americans believed that Pershing was correct, but unconditional surrender was not the way of war among European elites.[32]

The American experience of World War I was not one of long struggle and stalemate but of sudden intervention and sweeping victory. It reinforced the national tradition of an instrumental approach to major wars, with complete mobilization, maximum effort, and massive blows at the heart of the enemy. In the years that followed, the dismal consequences of the Armistice further confirmed the policy of unconditional surrender in American thinking.

After the Armistice, the United States disbanded its army and returned as rapidly as possible to what President Warren Harding called "normalcy." New Zealand did the same. By 1923, the U.S. Army shrank from six million to 133,000 men; New Zealand's regular army contracted in roughly the same proportion. A dramatic reduction in naval armament was achieved in the Washington Conference of 1921–22, where the five leading maritime powers agreed to reduce their fleets, with the largest cuts coming in the American and British navies. But even as the English-speaking people dismantled their armed forces, their military traditions were stronger than ever and had been invigorated by the memory of the First World War.

New Zealand and the United States in the Second World War

In the 1930s, the world moved inexorably toward war yet again, and the English-speaking nations were in their customary state of unpreparedness. As late as 1938, the U. S. Army had 185,000 men, and New Zealand's army consisted of 510 regulars. The Belgian army was larger than the number of soldiers on active duty in all the English-speaking nations combined. The open societies awakened very slowly to the painful fact that closed systems and totalitarian tyrannies were a fundamental threat.[33]

When the next European war began in 1939, New Zealand once again was very quick to join it. There were no extravagant celebrations, only a grim feeling that this war had to be fought and could not be lost. Within a few months the "first echelon" of New Zealand's expeditionary force had been dispatched to the other side of the world.[34]

From 1939 to 1941, Americans were divided by the war. Most sym-pathized with the Allied nations, but many did not. Some Irish Catho-lics were hostile to Britain. More than a few German and Italian immigrants were sympathetic to their native lands. In the Midwest and New England, Roosevelt-hating Republicans detested "That Man in the White House" and demanded that the nation think of "America first."[35]

Not until the Japanese attacked Pearl Harbor on December 7, 1941, and Roosevelt manipulated Hitler into declaring war on the United States did the nation come together. Then it rallied as never before, with only one negative vote in Congress. It stood united in the belief that Fascist Germany and militarist Japan had become fun-damental threats to American freedom. With remarkably little dis-sent, Americans mobilized the full productive resources of their nation and supported the goals of the war. Nearly all agreed on the strategy of seeking total defeat of Fascist regimes by massive blows at the heart of their power. American war aims were nothing less than that—and also nothing more.

There would be no talk of an armistice this time, and no nego-tiated peace. Roosevelt followed the tradition of Ulysses S. Grant and John J. Pershing and demanded the unconditional surrender of the Nazi regime, a position that he forced on his disapproving comrade-in-arms Winston Churchill after Pearl Harbor. Most Americans agreed with their president. The object was not merely to defeat Fas-cist Germany and militarist Japan but to destroy Fascism and milita-rism themselves. The United States worked closely with its allies, but Roosevelt, as we have seen, refused to make a formal alliance with Britain and prepared to fight alone if necessary.[36]

Everything hinged on mobilization. Among the English-speaking nations, New Zealand mobilized more fully than any other, as it had done in the First World War. Once again it suffered heavy combat losses. New Zealand sent 135,000 men and women overseas and lost 27,300 killed and wounded, about 1 in 175 of its population. By com-parison other Commonwealth nations lost 1 in 372, and the United States 1 in 775.[37]

The English-speaking countries mobilized their resources on a larger scale than other nations. Despite much talk in the 1930s about the superior strength and efficiency of totalitarian nations, the his-tory of the Second World War showed that open societies were more successful in concentrating their strength on the task at hand.

The method varied from one country to another. New Zealand conscripted women into war work. They were "manpowered" into factories and fields, forbidden to strike, and fined if they failed to

In World War II most combatant nations mobilized on a massive scale but in different ways. Most nations including New Zealand conscripted civilian labor, male and female, as with these women who worked at repairing street car tracks. The United States was unique in not conscripting labor during the war. Workers found jobs through a free market, which proved more effective and productive.

work. Civil consumption of scarce resources was severely rationed; in 1942, American servicemen in Wellington and Auckland were amazed by the economic controls.

The United States converted its economy to war-work on a larger scale than any other nation but maintained its tradition of free labor. There was no conscription of civilian workers in America. The population strongly supported the war effort, and free institutions proved more efficient than state controls, which were much more extensive in New Zealand. The Roosevelt administration chose a flexible policy of mixed enterprise, which was far superior to command economies of the left and right, and also more productive than systems founded on rigid, doctrinaire neoclassical free-market ideologies.

Strategy, Operations, and Tactics in World War II

Every combatant nation had its own way of waging war. In 1945, for example, Soviet Marshal Grigori Zhukov explained to General Dwight Eisenhower the Red Army's tactical doctrine for clearing a mine field. "When we come to a mine field," Zhukov explained, "our infantry attacks exactly as if it were not there. The losses we get from personnel mines we consider only equal to those we would have gotten from machine guns and artillery, if the Germans had chosen to defend that particular area with strong bodies of troops." Eisenhower commented, "I had a vivid picture of what would happen to any American or British commander if he pursued such tactics, and I had an even more vivid picture of what the men in any one of our divisions would have to say about the matter, had we attempted to make such a practice part of our tactical doctrine." The Soviet Army was known for its highly successful system of "deep battle," but also for "human wave" tactics such as the one General Zhukov used even in mine fields, which made Russian combat losses by far the highest in the world.[38]

The German *Wehrmacht* invented other tactics. In attack, their motto was "*Klotzen, nicht Kleckern,*" which might be loosely translated as "Shatter 'em, don't spatter 'em."[39] A German offensive often began with a human wave of advancing infantry. American troops described with amazement the advance of masses of glassy-eyed German foot soldiers, walking slowly across open ground. When the German infantry opened a breach by weight of numbers, armored units exploited it with heavy concentration of force. The final stage was rapid envelopment of the surrounded enemy in a *Kesselschlacht,* or "cauldron of destruction." German forces also made defensive tactics into a high art, fighting stubbornly in what they called a graduated defense, or defense in echelon. They used terrain with great skill and added interlocking fields of fire. Violent counterattacks were a German specialty.

Japanese armed forces had large ambitions and aggressive purposes, but small numbers and scarce resources. They made maximum use of stealth as strategic and tactical doctrines: surprise attacks, complex feints, subtle ruses, infiltration on many levels, and at critical moments the shock of the screaming *banzai* charge or later the *kamikaze* attack. On defense in fixed positions, Japanese troops were the most stubborn fighters in the world. Many Western armies spoke of resisting to the last man; only the Japanese actually did it. Even when hugely outmatched and defeated, they refused to surrender and fought to the death. Sacrificial acts were thought to make the most use of limited resources—and limited them still farther.

The tactical doctrines of these three dictatorships—Soviet, German, and Japanese—shared common elements that were typical of closed societies. They were extravagant of human life and took a very heavy toll of their own people. Hitler, Stalin, and Japanese militarists also had to commit a major part of their resources to the control of their own dominions. A large proportion of the many millions of deaths in Germany, the Soviet Union, and the Japanese Empire were inflicted by tyrannical regimes on subject populations, often their own. In various ways, closed systems also made deliberate use of brutality, terror, and atrocity as instruments of discipline and weapons of war. At the start of the Second World War, these methods were effective against open societies that were ill-prepared to resist. They took the world by surprise, and the dictatorships won battle after battle in the first years of the war.

The Western democracies were unable to use those tactics. Free populations were not willing to be sent like sheep to the slaughter. The English-speaking nations were compelled to find other ways of fighting. The United States and New Zealand did so in different ways. In the United States, the problem was compounded by America's strategic practice of closing with the enemy and destroying his armed forces and his will to resist by a massive *coup de main*. This had been the strategy in the Civil War and the First World War. Most top American leaders adopted it in World War II.

The problem was how to make it work without heavy loss of life. The American people demanded that their generals be bold in strategy and tactics but also prudent with the lives of their men—a difficult combination. To that end, the United States Army adopted tactical doctrines that made deliberate use of material abundance to minimize its own losses and maximize the cost to the enemy. In the 1920s and 1930s, while Germans were inventing the blitzkrieg, American officers perfected what they called the holding attack. It was highly aggressive, but in a controlled way. The attacking force was divided into two or three parts. The first group pinned down the enemy from the front with heavy fire. The second group probed for a vulnerable point in the flank or rear and attacked while the volume of fire increased. A third unit was held in reserve, ready to exploit any opening. General George Patton summarized the idea in his inimitable prose: "Hold him by the nose, and kick him in the ass."[40]

In the Second World War, the holding attack was combined with massive application of material force. Tactical doctrine in the United States Army was marked by very close integration of infantry, armor, artillery, and air—more so than in any other army. At Fort Sill, Oklahoma, artillery doctrine was highly developed before the war to achieve quick response, careful fire control, and TOT (time on target) barrages, in which the massed fire by many batteries of medium and heavy artillery could be ordered on short notice to fall without warning on a particular point at a single moment with shattering force. In 1942, Rommel wrote that the hardened veterans of his Afrika Korps were "astounded by the flexibility and accuracy of the

American artillery." It grew more effective as the war went on. U.S. forces were first to use newly invented VT (or proximity) fuses that caused lethal air bursts that were devastating against infantry.

American tactical doctrine also used air support on an unprecedented scale. New methods of communication were perfected by General Elwood Quesada. New weapons such as napalm, armor-piercing rockets, anti-personnel bombs, and AZON bombs (the first smart bombs, in use by 1944) were rapidly developed and deployed. They took a horrific toll on enemy forces. Closed societies were much less innovative, despite their talk of "wonder weapons."

American tactical doctrine was also marked by a high degree of flexibility. Even in 1942, when the Afrika Korps gave the U.S. Army a heavy defeat at Kasserine Pass, German commanders observed that American troops had "far better and more plentiful equipment and their tactically more flexible command." Rommel noted that "the tactical conduct of the enemy's defense had been first class. They had recovered very quickly after the first shock and had soon succeeded in damming up our advance by grouping their reserves to defend the passes and other suitable points." What was "astonishing," Rommel continued, "was the speed with which the Americans adapted themselves to modern warfare. In this they were assisted by their extraordinary sense for the practical and material, and by their complete lack of regard for tradition and worthless theories."[41]

German Colonel Hans von Luck had the same impression. In 1942, the American Army was very green and far less battle-wise than the British veterans of the excellent 8th Army, but Luck noted that "in one respect they seemed to have the edge over their British allies: they were extraordinarily flexible; they adapted immediately to a changed situation and fought with great doggedness." He added, "We discovered later, in Italy, and I personally in the battles in France in 1944, how quickly the Americans were able to evaluate their experience and through flexible and unconventional conduct of a battle, convert it to results."[42]

This flexibility required communications, transportation, intelligence, and other supporting services, all of which were highly developed in the U.S. Army. It mobilized the expertise of its citizen-soldiers. It developed excellent communications by field radios and field telephones, and it recruited an entire battalion of telephone company executives and scientists, who gave the army the first direct-dial long-distance telephone system in the world, so that any unit could call another directly. It hired John D. Hertz, founder of the rental car industry, to design a new branch of service called the

Transportation Corps. His contribution was to find solutions to logistical problems in modern war.[43]

The flexibility of the American armed forces was also a strength in many combat situations. Americans did better in open, fluid campaigns where individual initiative had an impact—as in the Normandy breakout; quick response in the Battle of the Bulge; the combat engineers at Amblève; improvised defenses on the Elsenborn Ridge; rapid exploitation at the Remagen bridge; and the secret drive of American airborne troops across the North German coast in 1945. It was the same in naval operations such as destroyer engagements in the South Pacific, carrier actions in the Central Pacific, double-teaming of the 3rd and 5th Fleets, new methods of replenishment at sea, and aggressive submarine campaigns in the North Pacific after 1943. In the air war, the same operational flexibility appeared in the tactics of the American Volunteer Group in China before Pearl Harbor; the development of skip-bombing in the Bismarck Sea; the hunt for Admiral Yamamoto; the reduction of Pantelleria; the Hump supply line over the Himalayas; the Big Weeks during the air war over Germany; and the final fuel and transportation campaigns that wrecked the German economy in the last year of the war. America's allies were not comfortable with this unconventional way of making war. British leaders Bernard Montgomery and Alan Brooke believed that American commanders lacked a professional knowledge of military doctrine. They never understood that Americans had another way of thinking about "professional," "knowledge," "military," and "doctrine" itself.

British ways of war, in which New Zealanders were trained, were very different from those of American forces. On the strategic level the primary British method was the indirect approach. Like their American opposite numbers, strategists in the British Commonwealth were deeply concerned with minimizing losses. But unlike Americans, with their abundant material resources, the British found a solution that was a product of scarcity. It consisted in a strategy of slowly weakening a stronger opponent by repeated strikes at targets of opportunity on the periphery.

This approach made the best of use of maritime strength and military weakness. It had been Britain's dominant strategy for two centuries. British leaders used it against the much larger armies of France in the eighteenth century and with great effect against Napoleon in the early nineteenth century. The great exception was the Western Front in World War I. The heavy cost in human life persuaded British leaders never to repeat the same error. In World War

II they made war against Germany in a series of blows on the periphery, using Britain's traditional command of the sea, with combined services striking hard, holding territory where possible, or withdrawing to strike again.

New Zealand troops were used in this way through most of the war. They fought in the Middle East, Greece, Crete, Africa, Italy, and Yugoslavia. These campaigns were proposed by Churchill and British commanders. They were carefully monitored by Prime Minister Peter Fraser, by the War Cabinet, and by the entire New Zealand Parliament in secret session, which kept very close watch on the Expeditionary Force.[44]

Scarcity was even more of a factor for New Zealand. It had dug deep into its resources, to send into the Mediterranean and African theaters a remarkably full and balanced force of exceptionally high quality, with its own supporting services. If the Expeditionary Force were lost, it could not be replaced. Fraser kept a close eye on casualty lists. Military commanders were under strict instructions to keep losses at a minimum. They needed no urging. Tactical and operational choices were shaped accordingly.

The troops were led with great care, but also with boldness, and were committed to desperate adventures in Greece and Crete and Africa, where they fought with courage. Still, their commanders always tried to keep open a line of retreat, and in the disasters of 1941 they managed to get most of them away to fight again. When the battle on Crete went awry, Fraser intervened to overrule decisions by British General Archibald Wavell and secured the evacuation of four thousand men who would otherwise have been lost.[45]

In combat, New Zealanders tended to be highly aggressive, but in ways that limited casualties. One method was a distinctive use of mobility, which played a major role in their tactics, with sudden advances by sea or land, swift retreat in the face of superior force, and then another advance. Another was a tactical doctrine long used by British forces from Clive and Wellington to Montgomery and Slim: advancing into a strong defensive position, then drawing the enemy upon them. This was done repeatedly in North Africa. A third method was to make use of surprise attacks at night with the bayonet, a weapon rarely employed in combat by American armies in World War II. "We almost always attacked at night," Major-General Sir Harold Kippenberger wrote. Americans almost always attacked in daylight, when their material resources could be deployed for maximum advantage.[46] New Zealanders were also proficient in infiltration and improvisation, as at Cavendish Road in the Cassino campaign, where they managed to create a tank track through mountainous terrain that was thought to be impassable. A British officer who served beside them observed that New Zealand troops were exceptionally "self-reliant and able to act independently . . . natural improvisers, and improvisation is fifty per cent of infantry fighting."[47]

The New Zealanders, like the British Army, were not so successful at integration of arms. Colonel Hans von Luck observed that "as almost always with the British they carried out their tank attacks without accompanying infantry." Communications in the field were a chronic deficiency, with grave consequences in many campaigns from Crete to Arnhem. But the infantry was superb.[48]

Military Leadership in World War II

A related difference between Americans and New Zealanders appeared in regard to military leadership. America's top commanders in World War II had remarkably little personal experience of war. Dwight Eisenhower and Omar Bradley had never been under fire; during the First World War they were kept in the United States as trainers of troops. Mark Clark had one day of combat experience in World War I. Henry "Hap" Arnold, later commanding general of the Army Air Forces, arrived at the Front on Armistice Day and saw no combat at all.

It was the same in the navy. Ernest King and Chester Nimitz were staff officers in World War I. Raymond Spruance was an electrical officer at the New York Navy Yard. Marc Mitscher commanded airfields on Long Island and in Miami. Admiral William "Bull" Halsey commanded a destroyer but saw no action. There were major exceptions in every service—MacArthur, Marshall, Patton, and Leahy. And there were many exceptions in one service: marine officers had considerable combat experience in police actions throughout the world. But overall, no nation had ever entrusted so much military power to leaders with so little direct experience of combat as did the United States in the Second World War.

Most American commanders in the war had been trained as military administrators, and to a particular style of highly layered administration. At every level, officers had autonomy in the execution of their orders and were judged by their results. American officers at field grade and higher were able military administrators, but they were not very close to their men. They expected a large measure of autonomy from senior officers, and extended it to others, but were merciless with anyone who failed to get results. Officers who didn't measure up were summarily fired.

New Zealand's forces were small, and its commanders had considerable experience of war. Nearly all field grade and general officers had been in heavy combat during the First World War. Most had been decorated for valor. Several had won the Victoria Cross. The model New Zealand leader was the commander of the Expeditionary Force, Bernard Freyberg, a handsome man with an athletic physique and a polished manner. He had been born in Britain and raised in New Zealand and was training to be a dentist when war broke out in 1914. On his way to Europe he stopped in Mexico and was said to have soldiered with Pancho Villa. By 1915, he was in the Aegean, where he became a friend of Rupert Brooke and the soldier poets, and his feats of courage became legend. At Gallipoli, he swam the Dardanelles in the night with flares to mislead the Turks. In Flanders, he led his men in the capture of Beaucourt. He emerged from the war with the Victoria Cross, three DSOs, and twenty-seven wounds. It was a miracle that he survived.

In 1939, Freyberg was almost the inevitable choice to command the Expeditionary Force. He was at first distrusted by many New Zealanders. Some on the left remembered that he had served with Massey's Cossacks in suppressing the strikes of 1913. Others on the right were not sure of an officer who confessed to enjoying Jane Austen novels. More than a few New Zealanders were suspicious of his British origins. But he proved himself in two wars. "Though a Briton

New Zealand's military commanders developed a highly successful style of leadership in World War II. An example was General Bernard Freyburg. He led from the front, cultivated informal relations with his troops, and adopted a policy of strict fairness without distinction of rank.

by birth," wrote one veteran, "he thought and acted as a New Zealander throughout the war."[49]

New Zealanders liked Freyberg's style of leadership. Even as a corps commander he led from the front. In Greece it was said that he had "nine staff cars shot from under him." In Crete he went riding from one hot spot to another on the back of a motorcycle with an officer who had been a professional stunt rider. In Africa he was nearly killed in a firefight. Often Freyberg was in the thick of the action.[50]

New Zealanders also liked the way he ran his division, with a group he called "the cabinet." A British officer observed, "The cabinet consisted of Freyberg and the senior brigadiers, and when an operation was being prepared plans would be fully, and even outspokenly, debated. Freyberg would listen carefully to everyone in turn, then sum up and make the final decision. These cabinet meetings constantly mystified British and American generals who had no experience of such a democratic approach to waging war . . . but it was in practice brilliantly successful. The New Zealand division was in the best sense a great amateur combination—a gifted civilian body that had learned the craft of war the hard way, and now excelled at it."[51]

Freyberg was known for his loyalty and fairness to all who served with him, even to a fault. He was criticized for his extreme reluctance to remove subordinates, but his men loved him for the way that he looked after them. "We admired and obeyed him because he believed in us," one of them wrote. "We knew he always insisted that we be supplied with the best rations available and that all our facilities should be the best that could be got." In Freyberg's New Zealand Army, loyalty flowed in both directions.[52]

On the battlefield Freyburg was highly aggressive, but in a paradoxically cautious way. He was very careful with the lives of his men. Whenever orders from British commanders placed his division at needless risk, he replied, "Well, I'll just have to let my government know about that one."[53] At the same time his tactics were built on the tradition of New Zealand's highly mobile mounted infantry. Freyberg favored night attacks, and rapid movements by motorized infantry using "the speed of their vehicles to the full in attack to gain surprise." Often he and his division were committed to desperate missions. He had a genius for fighting hard, then extricating his men from what looked to be certain destruction. This happened in Greece, and again in Crete, and once more in North Africa. Three times the Germans almost trapped Freyberg's troops. Three times they inflicted substantial losses on the enemy and lived to fight again. They were such a thorn in Rommel's side that the German commander ordered a special effort to destroy them. Once in North Africa three Axis armored divisions surrounded the New Zealand Division and attacked: 15th Panzer to the west, 21st Panzer to the east, and the Italian Ariete division to the south. Rommel wrote, "The fighting between my forces and the New Zealanders grew to an extraordinary pitch of violence, and my headquarters was soon ringed by burning vehicles." The New Zealanders lost 1,600 men to Rommel, and many more to the Royal Air Force, which kept bombing them by mistake. In the night that followed, Freyberg found a weak point in the German lines and ordered a wild bayonet charge in the moonlight. In fierce fighting Freyberg himself was severely wounded, but the New Zealanders escaped to fight again. Three of Rommel's best divisions were "so worn down that they also were forced to retreat to the west." It was a brilliant feat of combat leadership and infantry fighting.[54]

After the war several academic writers were severely critical of Freyberg's leadership, but German commanders who fought him had a very different opinion. Rommel and Mellenthin wrote of Freyburg with respect and even a tone of affection as an "indomitable commander" and regarded his New Zealand Division as "among the elite of the British army." Rommel added, "I should have been very much happier if it [the New Zealand Division] had been safely tucked away in our prison camps instead of still facing us."[55]

Under Freyberg, the New Zealand Division had many able combat commanders. One of them was Howard Kippenberger, a barrister and first-class soldier who had been severely wounded as a private in the First World War. He was very attentive to his men and led them from the front until he lost both feet in a German minefield at Cassino. New Zealanders thought he was "our best man . . . irreplaceable."[56] Another was Lieutenant Colonel Humphrey Dyer, a high-school headmaster who commanded the Maori Battalion, and defended them against higher authority with such loyalty that he was relieved of command and sent home. Yet a third was Colonel Tiwi Love, who succeeded Dyer; his men called him "the Bull." These three New Zealanders were all individuals, and yet they shared a common tradition of leadership. They were combat officers who led from the front, brave beyond imagining, loyal to a fault, decent and fair-minded, close to their men and very careful of their lives.

When Americans and New Zealanders met, they were surprised by differences in their systems of command. American leaders were

Another outstanding officer was Lt. Col. Howard Kippenberger, left, who literally wrote the book on leadership of New Zealand infantry in World War II. He was also a keen observer of practices in other armies.

no less brave and loyal, but in World War II they operated differently. Once, Kippenberger was quartered with an American regimental commander and was amazed by the distance of senior officers from the men under their command. "It was plain that none of them had been forward or were at all in touch with their men," he wrote. The American commander of the 143rd Infantry told Kippenberger that "his divisional commander never came forward as far as regimental headquarters, that he never went farther himself than to his battalion headquarters." Kippenberger concluded, "All this revealed a very different system of command."[57]

Kippenberger quoted an epigram that was popular in his army: "Always think two [echelons] down." He observed that American officers thought one echelon down. The American system allowed for greater flexibility and autonomy on each level. The New Zealand system created more integration and more cohesion. It bound units together in a way that marked another contrast with American ways of war.[58]

Unit Cohesion and Individual Initiative in World War II

The greatest strength of the New Zealand Army was its infantry, which allies and enemies alike judged to be "among the finest infantry soldiers in the world." Their greatest admirers may have been the

Germans who fought them. Allies agreed. A British officer, Fred Majdalany, who fought beside the 2nd New Zealand Division at Cassino, remembered its quiet strength and "almost arrogant conviction of invincibility." He observed that a New Zealand infantryman was "a man proud of his toughness but seldom flaunted it." Some writers have challenged these mythologizing judgments, arguing that "the New Zealander, once in uniform exhibited, as an individual the same human failings and strengths as any other man," which is true enough. New Zealanders did not have some sort of natural genius for soldiering. If the infantry was as good as its reputation, it was matter of training, morale, leadership, culture, and values.[59]

John MacLeod, an officer in the New Zealand Army and a close student of this subject, has published a corrective to the more extreme statements of national pride, but he also noted that "the relatively informal and to some extent egalitarian life style of New Zealanders brought about a unique operational style. New Zealanders concentrated more on the individual and small-group skills and relationships" This made all the difference in the infantry.[60]

New Zealand troops in every branch of service were trained as infantry and were expected to serve in that role. At Crete, two New Zealand regiments of field artillery fought ferociously as foot soldiers and called themselves "infantillery." Even New Zealand's 1st Petrol Company served as infantry with such distinction that an entire volume of New Zealand's official history is devoted to their service.[61]

All this had deep roots in the mounted infantry of the Boer War, and the New Zealand infantry that served in Gallipoli and France. To be an "infanteer" in New Zealand was to claim high honor. The nation took pride in the achievements of its foot soldiers. New Zealand writer Dan Davin found himself in England when the war began and went to a British recruiting office. He recorded the conversation.

> I see you are a New Zealander
> Yes.
> So you play rugby football
> Yes.
> You'll want to join the infantry then?
> Yes.[62]

In the United States Army, many infantry units distinguished themselves in the Second World War, but the infantry itself was not a corps d'elite as in New Zealand. The American Army carefully tested its eleven million men and assigned them according to ability. The brightest went into code-breaking work. The Army Air Force also received people with high scores, as did the Engineers and the Signal Corps. Then came artillery and armor. America's citizen-soldiers excelled at making war with machines: flying machines, armored machines, code machines. Men unqualified for these jobs were sent into the infantry.

Some infantry units did well in the war. The Army ground forces included many excellent infantry outfits, large and small. Regular units, such as the 1st, 2nd, and 3rd infantry divisions, the 25th Infantry, and the Philippine Scouts performed with distinction. So did some National Guard divisions. The 29th Infantry Division led the first wave at Omaha Beach and the breakout at St.-Lo. One of its Virginia regiments was descended from the Stonewall Brigade in the Civil War. A Baltimore regiment traced its origins from Smallwood's Maryland Regiment, which saved Washington's army on Long Island in 1776. The 30th Division was a proud North Carolina outfit with a long pedigree. It stopped an entire German Panzer army at Mortain, a critical battle in 1944. The 45th National Guard Division was one of the best in the army. Several draftee divisions were also first class. The six marine divisions were mostly seagoing infantry, and they earned a reputation for excellence among foe and friend alike, even the United States Army. The 82nd and 101st Airborne infantry divisions were superb light infantry. The Tenth Mountain Division was a specialized infantry division that distinguished itself. But allies and opponents believed that the U.S. Army was strongest in its other branches. As we've seen, German commanders had high respect for American artillery, air, and armor; they were not so much impressed by its infantry. These were the same Germans who held New Zealand infantry in high esteem.

Why the difference in reputation between American and New Zealand infantry? A conventional answer for many years has been small-unit cohesion and replacement systems. That answer has been broadened by the work of Civil War historian James McPherson, who stresses not one factor but three: unit cohesion, unit pride, and a just cause. New Zealand infantry had all three. It had exceptional cohesion, reinforced by the structure of New Zealand's society. It was observed of New Zealand's 2nd Division, which saw heavy action in Greece, Crete, Africa, and Italy, that "it was a microcosm of New Zealand serving overseas, a family affair with a potent clannish spirit. A man would rather remain a sergeant in a New Zealand battalion than be commissioned into an English regiment."[63]

This cohesion created strong bonds. An officer in the British Army observed, "The New Zealand infantry also had great unit pride. It thought of itself as a corps d'elite, forced always to excel. If a man did well it would for a certainty get back to his home town or village. If he did badly it would get back too." These bonds were especially strong in the Maori Battalion.[64]

Officers and noncoms did not wear insignia of rank. "Nobody put up stripes in our outfit, that was for base blodgers," one man remembered. He wrote that noncoms wore "the things that counted, the red triangle patch of an infantry brigade and the white on black New Zealand flash."[65] Professional soldiers were amazed by the lack of military protocol. One senior British officer complained to General Freyburg that New Zealand troops failed to salute him. Freyburg is said to have replied, "Ah yes, but if you wave to them, they'll wave back."[66]

What European officers called good order and discipline, New Zealanders derided as "swank" and American GIs called "Mickey Mouse" and "chickenshit." The two nations were similar that way, New Zealanders more so. Even officers expressed a casual and good-humored contempt for the rituals of military order, and woe to a commander who stood on ceremony. Officers

New Zealanders took great pride in their superb service of the Maori battalion in World War II. Its reputation had a major impact on attitudes toward race and culture after World War II.

received little deference to their rank; they had to earn the esteem of their men. Many did so and were remembered with high respect. Too many were killed or wounded before their men got to know them and were replaced by others. Some of the best officers rose from the ranks with battlefield commissions, a practice that became increasingly common.

Freyberg strictly enforced rules of fairness among officers and men, in a way that happened in no other army. In Italy he made a point of ordering that in hotels and rest areas all New Zealanders should have equal access to the same facilities without regard to rank. Once again, an idea of fairness was linked to a spirit of belonging and a sense of cohesion. This was one of the greatest strengths of New Zealand's infantry, and a source of its legendary status.

Why Men Fought in World War II

In the nineteenth century, French Colonel Ardant du Picq made a study of courage and fear on the battlefield by interviewing veterans of the Algerian and Crimean wars. He concluded that fear was universal and even constant in battle, but that men stand and fight because of the greater fear of what would happen if they turned and ran, and that these other fears must be instilled by officers and discipline.[67]

Colonel du Picq's inquiries were interrupted when he himself was killed in the Franco-Prussian War. Other scholars followed in his footsteps, among them the American journalist S.L.A. Marshall. Like du Picq, Marshall searched for what might be called universal laws of courage and fear. He agreed with du Picq that "fear is general among men," even constant and universal, but took a more democratic approach to the problem. Instead of arguing that officers and discipline made all the difference, the American investigators believed that men fight mainly from fear of letting down their comrades.[68]

After the Second World War these ideas were developed by a team of American sociologists led by Samuel Stouffer, who reiterated Marshall's judgments and added that soldiers were consumed by fear, fought for buddies, and were not motivated by large purposes and principles. This idea hardened into an academic orthodoxy among sociologists (not historians) and was widely repeated by journalists and novelists. More recent research supports these findings in two respects: most rational people experience fear in war, and men in combat fight for their comrades. But this model is mistaken in other ways. Studies of other American wars, including the Iraq War, the Civil War, and the War of Independence, all report evidence that soldiers in those three wars fought in different ways—for "comrades and a cause," in the words of James McPherson.[69]

Further, comparative study also yields evidence that fear and courage are not constant in war but highly variable. New Zealand officers read Marshall's work and testified that it did not match their experience. They were astonished by his assertions that "fear is general among men in combat," so much so that 75 percent of infantrymen never fired their weapons in action, and that "these men were consumed not merely by fear but also by terror, but did not wish to appear cowards to their comrades."

"Not so," replied Colonel Humphrey Dyer, commander of the Maori Battalion, "no seasoned infantryman would agree with it." Dyer thought that Marshall's generalizations applied only to "immature and nervous soldiers, and that after several actions, a well-trained soldier becomes a seasoned fighter who takes pride in his trade."[70] Many New Zealand veterans of prolonged combat in the Second World War rejected Marshall's statements. Colonel Leonard Thornton surveyed veterans on this question and found that Dyer's opinion was "supported unanimously by all respondents." They agreed that all men have "a certain amount of fear before an attack," but that all but a few "succeed in concealing and overcoming it," and felt "a kind of exhilaration once the attack is under way." They agreed that among New Zealand infantry once an attack was under way a flow of adrenaline "generally carried soldiers through." New Zealanders spoke of what they called "combat fever" or "battle fever," an "extreme excitement which causes the adrenalin to flow." One New Zealander wrote, "In the desert we were all the subject of this."[71]

General Kippenberger was surprised to discover from his own observations of both armies how American troops behaved: "If the men felt afraid, they made no effort to conceal their feelings." This seemed to him very different from his own countrymen. New Zealand officers set an example of courage under fire. A soldier wrote that Freyberg "helped us enormously by his personal bravery."[72] Another factor was the strong support that New Zealand infantrymen gave each another. A veteran remembered that "almost everything we undertook was carried out as a group operation, so we were not given to thinking in personally heroic terms." Noel Gardiner wrote, "Morale means having faith in yourself and your companions. This as a division we never lacked. We had as much confidence as any soldiers who ever confronted an enemy. The more we trained, the greater was our morale."[73] New Zealanders and Americans both found the courage to fight, but in different ways. The differences were rooted in different cultures and cultural values.

Heroes and Heroism in Two Nations

Every nation is revealed in its choice of heroes. In the wars of the twentieth century, very different hero-figures emerged in New Zealand and the United States. New Zealand's greatest hero in World War II was Captain Charles Upham, the only soldier in that vast conflict to win the Victoria Cross twice for acts of valor and endurance that surpass belief.[74]

Upham was a New Zealander to his core. Much of the nation's history entered into his upbringing. His mother traced her descent to the "first four" immigrant ships of the Canterbury pilgrims. His father was a prosperous barrister in Christchurch. As a child, Upham was "reared in the English manner" in a big house on Gloucester Street with maids, nannies, gardeners, and the best preparatory schools. He was small for his age and slightly built, with ice-blue eyes and fine-boned features, but there was an air to him that set him apart, even as a child. One of his first tests came on his arrival at Christ's College, Christchurch. As a "new boy" he saw three school bullies brutally hazing a small fat lad who was unable to defend himself. "Leave him alone, you pigs," Upham shouted, and instantly charged the bullies. They were amazed and gave way.[75]

Upham continued his schooling at what is now Lincoln University and decided to become a farmer. He worked as what New Zealanders call a musterer, or shepherd, in the back blocks of Canterbury. There he lived in the open, slept rough, and grew into a man of "wiry strength, of great physical endurance," with "complete indifference to personal comfort."[76]

In 1939, Upham went to war, not because his friends did so but "out of conviction that the Nazis had to be stopped."[77] He enlisted as a private, and rose through the ranks to become captain and company commander. Always he thought of his men as his mates and lived close to them. Jock Phillips writes that he "called his men by their Christian names, he swore at them, he even got drunk with them," and "was noted for his extreme almost obsessive modesty and his insistence on transferring credit from himself to his men."[78]

Upham always led from the front. At Crete he stayed with his men even after he was wounded twice and came down with jaundice, dysentery, and pneumonia. He was known not only for his valor but

New Zealand's Captain Charles Hazlitt Upham was the only combat soldier in any army to win the Victoria Cross twice. Photograph ca. 1941.

for his kindness, even to animals who were also the victims of war. At one desperate moment in the long retreat in Crete, he went back over the rugged hills to set free some mules that had been tethered without water or forage.

In Africa, at the bloody infantry fight on Ruweisat Ridge, Upham's company suffered heavy losses from a German 88 assault gun. He led his company against the German gun, destroyed it, and killed or wounded its entire crew. In combat he fought with a blood-lust that sometimes appalled his men, but after the fight they were astonished to find him moving among the German wounded. One remembered that "Charles was bending over the wounded men, one after another, and was giving them a long draught from his own water-bottle. The Germans drank gratefully."

Upham was never a parade-ground soldier. He could not remember the proper commands at drill, or get his uniform quite right, and he became a legend for showing up to receive the Victoria Cross wearing a mismatched pair of yellow socks. He is remembered for many things: two Victoria Crosses and his mismatched yellow socks, his bloodlust in battle and chivalry to his enemy, his courage as a child, and his "modesty of a natural gentleman." He represented a New Zealand ideal of manhood: a hard but gentle man, and fair.

Even today, the story of Charles Upham is still told to young New Zealanders, as he had been taught about other New Zealanders before him. Among his models was the Maori leader Taratoa, who drew up a code of conduct for his fighters, and carried a calabash of cold water to a wounded British soldier in the same spirit. When Upham was a boy at Christ's College in Christchurch, he and his classmates were taught to honor Taratoa's spirit and to learn from Maori. Upham also followed the example of New Zealand's Pakeha heroes in the Boer War. Sergeant William Mahood, Sergeant Major William James Hardham, and Lieutenant John Hughes all distinguished themselves in similar ways.[79] New Zealand's greatest hero in the Boer War was Captain Maddocks, "an unassuming mild-mannered, courteous gentleman, who possesses the courage of half-dozen men." He was remembered as a "colonial officer who knew all of his men, fraternized with them," and treated them with respect. In World War II, General Freyburg and Brigadier George Herbert Clifton were kindred figures. All were remembered for unimaginable feats of physical courage, and for the decency with which they treated others.[80]

American heroes in both world wars were very diverse, but the most celebrated of them made a contrast with New Zealand's Captain Upham, not so much in their actions as in the way that their country remembered them. The most prominent American warriors were portrayed as heroic loners, often far beyond the fact. In the First World War, for example, the leading hero was Sergeant Alvin Cullom York.[81] In World War II, another leading American hero was a navy flier named Butch O'Hare, who was recommended for two Medals of Honor—as rare as two Victoria Crosses. He won the first of them for defending his aircraft carrier USS *Lexington* in a desperate fight. It happened late in the afternoon on February 20, 1942, when a formation of eight Japanese bombers suddenly appeared over the ship. Only two American fighters were able to intercept. One was flown by O'Hare, the other by his wingman, Duff Dufilho. The Japanese thought they had a clear approach to the carrier and did not notice two small Grumman aircraft above them. At the last minute, O'Hare's wingman discovered that his guns would not fire, but stayed in formation. O'Hare, whose guns did fire, swooped down on the Japanese force, hitting two bombers on the right side. He rolled and turned back into the Japanese planes, now in range of heavy American antiaircraft fire. He flew through the flak and hit two more Japanese bombers on his second pass. A third pass knocked out two more Japanese planes. He dispersed what remained of the Japanese formation just as his ammunition ran out. On board the *Lexington,* the crew watched in fascination, forgetting their own danger. "Which one of our boys is that?" one said. "He is alone, outnumbered, and he is winning the fight."[82]

When Butch O'Hare returned to the carrier, he was recommended for America's highest combat decoration. He didn't want it. His squadron leader remembered that "Butch begged me for a whole evening not to recommend him." But he was mentioned in dispatches as "chiefly responsible for the destruction of six enemy planes, and ordered home to meet President Roosevelt and accept the Medal of Honor.[83] The navy sent him around the country to win support for the war effort. He was handsome, modest, likeable, and more than a little vulnerable, and Americans took him to their hearts. Butch hated the role of hero that he was asked to play and wanted desperately to be back in the sky. It was against navy regulations to send Medal of Honor winners into combat again, but O'Hare pulled strings and returned to the fleet, where he worked at developing new tactics for night fighters. It was dangerous, lonely work. On the night of November 26, 1943, he disappeared. He might have been shot down by a Japanese bomber, or possibly by friendly fire. However it happened, he died alone in a dark sky. Today, his memorial is Chicago's O'Hare International Airport. When one is traveling alone among thousands of solitary travelers, it is a good place to remember Butch O'Hare.

Other American heroes were not loners. Many winners of the Medal of Honor were men who hurled themselves on an enemy grenade to save the lives of comrades by a selfless act of sacrifice. Their country honored their sacrifice, but it celebrated Sergeant York and Butch O'Hare and Audie Murphy. In the highest ranks, the two favorite commanders in the media were George Patton and Douglas MacArthur, both also perceived as heroic loners. The contrast with New Zealand is striking. The difference was more a matter of image than of reality, but images count for much in memories of the past and expectations for the future.

Conclusion: Open Societies Revisited

In 1942, the Afrika Korps captured a famous character in the war, New Zealand's Brigadier G. H. Clifton. He was taken to the German commander, General Erwin Rommel, who found the New Zealander to be "a brave man and very likeable," but the German officer could not understand why Clifton had come halfway around the world to fight a German army in the middle of an African desert. "Why are you New Zealanders fighting?" Rommel asked. "This is a European war, not yours. Are you here for the sport?"

Clifton was amazed by the question. Later he wrote, "Realizing that he really meant this . . . I held up my hands with the fingers closed and said, The British Commonwealth fights together. If you attack England, you attack Australia and New Zealand too." Rommel was as baffled by that answer as Clifton had been by the question. He made no comment, except to wish his prisoner the best of luck. Immediately after the interview, Brigadier Clifton politely excused himself and escaped from a lavatory window (much to Rommel's amusement), made his way back to his unit, and went on to other adventures in the war.[84]

The same questions that Rommel put to his New Zealand captive were also asked of Americans who were fighting far from home. Their answers tended to be similar in spirit but very different in substance from those of Brigadier Clifton. Somebody asked Sergeant York why he kept fighting in France. He said, "Liberty and freedom are so very precious that you do not fight to win them once and stop." Americans and New Zealanders both explained their acts by appeals to principle, but even on a battlefield those principles were not the same.

WORLD CRISIS

Restructuring in Open Systems

> American liberty and how to preserve it . . . economic freedom and how to restore it.
>
> > —Clark S. Judge and the White House Writers Group on Reaganomics in the United States, circa 1986
>
> Perestroika, albeit of a particular New Zealand flavour.
>
> > —Martin Holland and Jonathan Boston on Rogernomics in New Zealand, 1990

T HE LATE YEARS of the twentieth century were yet another time of troubles for New Zealand, the United States, and most nations in the world. After a long period of growth and prosperity, the global economy slipped into a steep decline, circa 1968. This was not merely an economic contraction. It was also a social crisis. Political systems failed in many countries. Violence and crime increased in most societies. The consumption of drugs and drink surged. Young people lost faith in established institutions, and elders lost patience with the young. Family disintegration rose to unprecedented levels. The intellectual mood was marked by a corrosion of doubt and despair.[1]

These troubles were most disruptive in closed societies and command economies. Many Marxist dictatorships totally collapsed, or disintegrated in chaotic events such as China's Cultural Revolution, or were radically transformed by new movements such as *glasnost* and *perestroika* in the former Soviet Union. Open societies also came under heavy strain, but they tended to be more resilient. Most of them experienced reform rather than revolution. Two comparative examples are the United States and New Zealand.

The Crisis in America

In the United States, the economic decline began during the winter of 1968–69. It started as a "policy recession," deliberately induced by the governors of the Federal Reserve System. They were much worried about inflation, which had risen from 1 percent in 1950 to 5 percent in the mid-1960s. These well-meaning men believed that prices were rising because the American economy was "overheated," and since 1966 they had tried to cool it without much success. The Fed raised interest rates to the highest levels in half a century. A long expansion in the money supply (M1) was brought to an end. The economy slipped into a shallow recession in 1967, but prices kept rising, and the dynamic American economy soon began to boom again.[2]

The chairman of the Federal Reserve Board, a cheerful and decent man named William McChesney Martin, famously remarked that his role was "to take away the punch bowl just when the party gets going." In 1968, when the economy began to gather strength again, Chairman Martin and his colleagues tightened credit, raised interest rates, and curbed the money supply. At their urging, Congress added a much-hated surcharge of 10 percent on income taxes.[3] These measures brought America's long boom of the 1960s to a sudden halt. The "policy recession" began at last, but its consequences were not as the Fed had intended. Unemployment increased and the economy stagnated, but inflation stubbornly persisted. Economists were baffled by this phenomenon, which Paul Samuelson may have been the first to call "stagflation" in 1973. The Fed shifted nervously from brakes to accelerators and back to brakes again, but nothing seemed to work.[4]

Then came an historical event that economists had not predicted, or even imagined. In 1973, an international cartel of oil producers called OPEC (Organization of the Petroleum Exporting Countries) restricted supplies of petroleum and drove the price of benchmark crude from $3 to $12 a barrel. They had been trying to raise prices for years but had been stopped by abundant supplies of cheap American oil. By 1973, those reserves were much depleted, and OPEC had its way. The American reaction, in the words of John M. Blair, "approached pure panic."[5] While Americans struggled to deal with soaring prices, OPEC struck again. In 1978–80, another oil shock sent prices surging to $40 a barrel. The economic impact was severe, all the more so because other commodity prices were rising rapidly at the same time. The result was the worst peacetime inflation in American history. In its wake came a sharp fall in real income, high rates of unemployment, and shattering social disorder. The price shocks of 1973–74 and 1978–81, and their attendant troubles, correlated closely with surges of drugs, drink, and crime.[6]

The economic crisis of the 1970s did not rise from an overheated American economy, as the Federal Reserve Board mistakenly concluded. It was not caused primarily by American fiscal policy during the Vietnam War, as economists still erroneously believe. The troubles had a deeper root. This was a world crisis, created by massive acceleration in population growth, rising standards of living, and increases in aggregate demand. The consequences included deep imbalances in prices and wages, disparities in public income and expenditures, and growing inequality in the distribution of wealth.[7]

American Responses: Nixon and Intervention

President Richard Nixon was a conservative Republican who had long raged against "big government" and the economic policies of John Maynard Keynes. As the conditions grew worse, he amazed the nation by announcing a sudden conversion. "Now I am a Keynesian," he told an astonished interviewer. Nixon imposed wage and price controls to slow inflation and used many Keynesian devices to stimulate economic growth. He also tried to freeze wages and prices, against the advice of neoclassical economists. One advisor later remembered, "I warned him, citing Heraclitus, that you can't step in the same river twice." Nixon answered, "You can if it's frozen."[8] But the troubles continued to grow. Nixon's price and wage controls came under attack from unions and corporations and were abandoned. Stagnation persisted, inflation continued its upward climb, and economic policy was in extreme disarray.[9]

Restructuring from the Left: Jimmy Carter and Deregulation

During the mid-1970s, a new spirit of public policy began to stir in Washington. A straw in the wind was a meeting of leading American economists, called by President Gerald Ford in 1975. "There was full professional agreement on only one remedy," John Kenneth

Galbraith remembered, "that government regulations should be reviewed to remove any obvious impediments to market competition." Galbraith's younger colleagues were moving rapidly toward neoclassical economics. They believed that free markets were better regulators than public authorities. The rallying cry was "deregulation."[10]

After the election of 1976, President Jimmy Carter's liberal Democratic administration was drawn to this approach. In 1978, his administration introduced a complex plan to reduce federal regulation of routes and prices in the airline industry while preserving service to small communities. Deregulation followed in the trucking industry, railroads, and savings and loan associations. The price of natural gas was permitted to move more freely in response to market conditions, which stimulated large increases of supply, and lowered prices in turn. Banks and other business corporations were given more latitude in borrowing and lending.[11]

Deregulation appeared to help, but it proved to be painfully difficult. Reform did not come easily to America's intricate federal system, with its many entrenched interest groups and complex checks and balances. Nevertheless, the Carter administration made a strong beginning. It is interesting that this new trend toward deregulation, market-centered reforms, and smaller government came from a liberal Democratic president. Its major goal was to improve the condition of ordinary Americans. But Jimmy Carter's team did not succeed in shaping the social character of these new reforms. After 1980, they passed into other hands and took on a different purpose.

Restructuring as deregulation in the United States began in a major way during the presidency of Jimmy Carter. On October 24, 1978, he signed the airline deregulation bill into law. This first wave of progressive deregulation was designed to serve the welfare of most Americans.

Restructuring from the Right: Reaganomics

In 1981, Ronald Reagan became president. His conservative administration moved away from the liberal character of the Carter years and embraced the complex purposes of its own constituency.[12] Reagan's supporters included business leaders and affluent families who wanted lower taxes (especially on capital gains), stronger protections for private wealth, deep cuts in welfare programs, and less economic regulation. At the same time, Reagan drew support from fundamentalist Protestants and conservative Catholics who demanded more social regulation of abortion, sexual behavior, and public morals. A third constituency of military veterans were appalled by America's weakness in foreign affairs and dismayed by the degradation of its armed forces after Vietnam. They insisted on a forward foreign policy and a revival of military strength.[13]

The policies of the Reagan administration reflected this mix. In general, it favored less regulation of the economy and more regulation of personal lives on issues such as abortion and sexuality. Most of all it sought to cut taxes, which was increasingly the central and defining issue of the Republican Party. Reagan's first major act was to slash income taxes by 25 percent, without making equal reductions

After 1981, restructuring took on a different character. Here Ronald Reagan signs the Tax Reform Act of 1986. Its major beneficiaries were larger corporations and people of wealth. The result was rapid growth of inequality in income and wealth.

in public spending. Republicans succeeded in shrinking support for education, housing, transportation systems, environmental protection, urban development, and the arts and humanities. But they were unable to control spending for costly entitlement programs such as Social Security, Medicare, and Medicaid, and they greatly increased government spending on military defense.[14]

The inevitable consequence of tax-slashing and continued spending was an enormous federal deficit. Overall, the Republican Reagan administration added more to the national debt than all previous American presidents combined. Republicans in Congress and the executive branch discovered that they could use the deficit to stop spending on the social programs they disliked. They also changed the distribution of taxation, reducing income taxes in the top bracket from 70 percent to 50 percent, and then to 28 percent, but increasing total taxes on the lower middle class. Republicans in the Reagan years drove down levies on large estates and corporate profits and raised regressive Social Security taxes, excise taxes, and sales taxes in the states. The middle class and working poor paid a larger proportion of their income for taxes than did the very rich.[15]

The result was an increase in economic inequality. During the eight years of the Reagan administration (1981–89), the proportion of total income received by the top 20 percent of American households rose from 41 to 45 percent, while the share of the bottom 20 percent actually fell from 5.3 to 4.6 percent. By 1989, the richest 5 percent of American families received more income than the bottom 50 percent combined. This new trend began circa 1969, gained momentum in the Reagan years, and continued for the next twenty years, to the early twenty-first century. In America it followed forty years of growing equality, from 1929 to 1969. Nowhere in the world was that trend reversed more dramatically than in the United States.[16]

Restructuring from the Center: George H. W. Bush and Bill Clinton

After Ronald Reagan left office in 1989, his successors George H. W. Bush and Bill Clinton joined in a heroic effort to deal with his deficit. Both men and their allies in Congress balanced the federal budget and reduced the national debt. They did it by controlling expenditures and raising some taxes—acts of high courage in American politics. Both presidents were severely punished at the polls by millions of American voters who demanded the benefits of an active government but did not wish to pay for it. In 1992, George H. W. Bush was denied a second term in large measure because he raised taxes. Two years later, the Clinton administration suffered heavy midterm losses in the elections of 1994, for the same cause.

Restructuring continued in the Clinton administration (1993–2001) and came increasingly from the political center. Vice President Al Gore led a program for "reinventing government," which succeeded in shrinking the federal government by three hundred thousand employees and increasing efficiency in some departments.[17] Public regulation of private enterprise was further reduced. More than three hundred trade agreements removed restraints on international commerce. Antitrust regulation diminished, with a few spectacular exceptions. Major industries became concentrated in manufacturing, entertainment, and communications. Computer software was dominated by one large business corporation, which was allowed to acquire a virtual monopoly in important sectors of its industry. The aerospace industry was dominated by three large corporations that then became two. The Telecommunications Act of 1996 eliminated ownership restrictions in the communication industry. A brief period of cutthroat competition soon led to greater concentration.[18]

The American banking system had traditionally had been more decentralized than the financial institutions of most developed countries. Now it rapidly became concentrated. Banks and financial corporations were given an increasingly free hand. Part of Roosevelt's very wise Glass-Steagall Act was repealed, a disastrous error by Bill Clinton and Republican allies in Congress. Deposit banks were allowed to play the markets with the life savings of depositors, which they did with reckless abandon.[19]

Corporate managers were given free rein over labor policies, which were increasingly driven by the pursuit of profitability through "downsizing" and "outsourcing." American workers were laid off by the millions. Able and faithful employees with long service were discharged without warning. Those who kept their jobs lived in fear of losing them. Job insecurity increased very rapidly.[20]

At the same time, centrist Clinton Democrats and conservative Republicans joined together to make major cuts in welfare programs. The largest change came with the Personal Responsibility and Work Opportunity Reconciliation Act of 1996, introduced by conservative Representative Clay Shaw Jr. and signed by liberal President Clinton. This complex statute ended welfare as an entitlement program. It replaced "Aid to Families with Dependent Children" (a New Deal measure) with "Temporary Assistance for Needy Families." New laws limited benefits to five years, required recipients to begin working within two years, reduced benefits for unmarried parents under the age of eighteen, ended benefits for immigrants, and gave the states more latitude in their own programs. Overall, from 1997 to 2000, welfare rolls shrank by 53 percent.[21]

A net result of all these policies was a further growth of inequality during the Clinton administration.[22] For America's most prosperous families, the 1990s were the best of times. Deregulation and tax cutting brought them more income with less effort than ever before. Returns to capital investment were the highest in American history. Stock values inflated rapidly. But while the rich flourished and the upper middle class did well, the lower middle class fell farther behind, and the working poor suffered severely. Americans who lived on their wages were forced to work longer hours and hold several jobs merely to stay even. In general, the wealth and income of the top 20 percent increased greatly through the Bush and Clinton presidencies. The income share of the bottom 80 percent of the American population declined.[23]

In the era of Ronald Reagan, George H. W. Bush, and Bill Clinton, a deregulated America became more free but less fair. With a few honorable exceptions across party lines—liberal Ted Kennedy, centrist Jim Webb, and conservative Jack Kemp—top political leaders in both major parties did very little to promote fairness or social justice in American life.[24]

Restructuring from the Far Right: George W. Bush

After the election of 2000, one of the first acts of this very conservative Republican administration was to make deep cuts in income taxes, without concomitant reductions in federal spending. Then, on September 11, 2001, Islamic terrorists mounted a surprise attack on the World Trade Center in New York and the Pentagon in Washington at heavy cost in human life. The Bush administration mounted a massive anti-terror campaign, which Americans of all parties strongly supported. It also started a preemptive war against Iraq, which divided the country. And it fought both of these wars without paying for them. Federal deficits soared from 2001 to 2009, to levels even above those of the Reagan administration.

At the same time, the Bush administration allowed the financial industry an increasingly free hand. In great waves of mergers and acquisitions, assets of productive and profitable corporations were looted and destroyed. Major security markets lost their primary function—the mobilization of capital—and became corrupt casinos in which gambling games were rigged by insiders for their own gain.

The result was instability, fraud, and corruption. Continuing financial deregulation allowed increasing instability, which ended in the Great Crash of 2007–08, the worst since 1929, and a painfully slow recovery thereafter.

The Economic Crisis in New Zealand

While these trends were developing in the United States, another process of restructuring was happening in New Zealand. The boom of the 1960s lasted five years longer in the South Pacific than in North America but ended more abruptly. In 1973–74, the New Zealand economy slipped into a steep decline. The cause was commonly attributed to a conjunction of two events. In 1973, Britain entered the European Common Market, ended special trading relations with the Commonwealth, and imposed tariffs on New Zealand goods. As late as 1952, the mother country had taken 65 percent of New Zealand's exports and supplied 55 percent of its imports. This trading connection had slowly declined through the 1960s, and after 1973 it came nearly to an end.[25]

Another blow came in 1973–74, when the oil shock hit New Zealand harder even than the United States. New Zealanders responded with a strong collective effort. People were asked to pitch in together and "do their bit" by not using their cars one day a week. Many did so. The government sought to develop alternative sources of energy. But these measures were slow to take effect. The surging price of energy spread inflation through New Zealand.[26]

That combination of soaring prices and shrinking exports did major damage to an economy that was dependent on foreign trade. In 1974–75, New Zealand's national product per capita leveled off and began to fall. At a time when the American economy was growing more slowly, New Zealand experienced actual contraction. In constant dollars, national product per capita declined six years running during the 1970s.[27]

First Responses in New Zealand:
Muldoon and Intervention from the Right

The first response to economic crisis in New Zealand was similar to early reactions in the United States. Prime Minister Robert Muldoon was an aggressive leader—strong-willed, self-taught, and so self-absorbed that he published his autobiography four times. He was a conservative populist who thought of himself as a protector of

Prime Minister Robert Muldoon's policies caused a major crisis in New Zealand. The economy was already weakened by changes in foreign trade and by world inflation. Muldoon's reckless spending threatened national bankruptcy and economic collapse.

the "ordinary bloke." He also believed deeply in New Zealand's welfare state and cherished its tradition of a tightly managed economy.[28]

As economic conditions worsened, Muldoon responded by expanding government intervention. When the price of lamb fell sharply, the government imposed "subsidized minimum prices." When the cost of oil rose, Muldoon introduced price controls and launched a "Think Big" program to develop alternative sources of energy by public enterprise, at high expense. He increased spending for public welfare, promising every elderly couple a free pension equal to 80 percent of the median wage, funded from general revenues.[29]

Muldoon's largesse made him popular with an army of voters. Pensioners strongly supported his program, but its cost was greater than the nation could bear. By the estimates of Muldoon's own government, public debt soared from $1 billion to $11 billion, an enormous sum at that time. Other hidden obligations, uncovered by Muldoon's successors, carried the national debt to $20 billion.

While Muldoon enacted his public programs, the national economy of New Zealand slipped deeper into decline. Trade imbalances increased. Unemployment rose sharply. Inflation accelerated. The worse conditions grew, the more active Muldoon became. When the general price level rose sharply after the second oil shock in 1982, he ordered a general freeze on wages, prices, rents, dividends, directors' fees, interest, and exchange rates and kept it in place for twenty months. When the New Zealand dollar threatened to fall, he supported it at ruinous cost.

Business leaders who had backed Muldoon became increasingly concerned. Politicians in his own National Party grew unhappy with his leadership. The tide of opinion began to turn against him. In

1984, National lost a vote in Parliament on nuclear policy, and Muldoon made a rare tactical error. He called a "snap" election in the expectation that the country would support him. The result was a disaster for his party. Dissident National leaders broke away to form a separate New Zealand Party and drew 12 percent of the vote. That division allowed a Labour government to win the election with a plurality of popular votes and a strong majority in Parliament.[30]

On the day after the election, the Bank of New Zealand announced that the nation's currency reserves were nearly exhausted, and it closed the foreign exchange market. The country was on the edge of default. Labour blamed Muldoon's "Think Big" policies and his lavish spending. Muldoon blamed Labour for destroying confidence in New Zealand's monetary system. The transition that followed was a critical moment for New Zealand.[31]

Roger Douglas and Restructuring from the Left

The incoming Labour government was led by Prime Minister David Lange, not a strong or steady leader.[32] On economic questions, the dominant figure was Finance Minister Roger Douglas, who urged a revolutionary restructuring of the economy, more radical and sweeping than any reform program in New Zealand's history. Many members of his party did not agree, but Douglas had his way. With his leadership, one of the most tightly controlled economies in the free world moved rapidly toward deregulation and privatization.[33]

In the fall of 1984, Douglas removed public controls on the international flow of private capital. For the first time in many years,

Economic restructuring in New Zealand was led by Roger Douglas and the new Labour government after 1984. To the dismay of many in his own party, Douglas enacted a sweeping program of privatization and deregulation. Here again as in the United States, restructuring began on the left and moved to the right.

New Zealand companies were allowed to borrow freely abroad, and foreign companies were given more latitude in New Zealand. Controls on foreign exchange were lifted. New Zealanders were permitted to deal freely in overseas currencies. Import quotas and license-systems were abrogated. Tariffs were reduced, and price controls were abolished.[34]

Another part of the reform program was monetary. In March 1985, the Labour government decided to float the New Zealand dollar and began to regulate it in a new way—not by pegging the exchange rate at a fixed level, as Muldoon had tried to do, but by manipulating interest rates. Here was a form of regulation that operated within the market, not against it.[35]

In 1987, the government passed the State-Owned Enterprises Act and opened the way for privatizing New Zealand's many public assets. A large part of the national economy had long been run by state monopolies. Many of these public companies were sold (in whole or part) to private investors, who were often foreign corporations. New Zealand Telecom went to Ameritech–Bell Atlantic. The Bank of New Zealand was acquired by National Australia Bank. New Zealand Rail was bought by the Wisconsin Central consortium. New Zealand's State Insurance System was sold to Norwich Union Insurance. The proceeds of these sales were used to pay down New Zealand's national debt. Other enterprises remained public but were ordered "to operate as a successful business." They were required to be "as profitable and efficient as comparable businesses not owned by the Crown" but also were instructed to be good employers and to exhibit "a sense of social responsibility by having regard to the interests of the community in which it operates." This was privatization with a social conscience—something that did not appear in American restructuring.[36]

For New Zealand it was a painful transformation. Rates of economic growth fell again after 1984. Unemployment rose to 12 percent, as high as in the worst years of the 1930s. At the same time, inflation accelerated in the first years. The program of Roger Douglas was strongly opposed by labor unions and leaders on the far left, and by others who felt that control of the economy was passing into the hands of foreign capitalists who cared nothing for New Zealand. But then the economy turned up, and the reform impulse found more support in the nation. A general election in 1987 gave Labour an increased majority and a mandate for further reform.[37]

The impact of Rogernomics was different from that of Reaganomics in the United States and Margaret Thatcher's reforms in the United

Kingdom. Even as the Labour government introduced sweeping free-market reforms, it sought to maintain a principle of social equity as well as economic efficiency. The results appeared in quantitative evidence. Public spending on income support, superannuation (social security), and pensions all increased after the enactment of Roger Douglas's program.[38]

This program of restructuring in New Zealand combined two major elements. One centered on privatization, deregulation, and market-based reform. The other engaged an active commitment to fairness and social justice. These purposes appeared explicitly in Roger Douglas's dual concern for "security and fairness" in his design for the reform of superannuation plans. They were also evident in his policy of a "halfway house" for state-owned enterprises, called SOEs in New Zealand. And it appeared in his two goals of "care and responsibility" in welfare programs. Douglas always insisted that "the social goals of the first Labour Government [in 1935] are the same social goals of the Labour Party and Labour Government today [in 1987]."[39]

In that pattern one observes the distinctive character of economic restructuring in New Zealand during its formative stage in the Fourth Labour Government, from 1984 to 1990. Martin Holland and Jonathan Boston described the result as "perestroika, albeit of a particular New Zealand flavour."[40] Roger Douglas was not alone in his concern for "fairness." As we have seen, all major parties committed themselves to that idea, but they differed on its meaning. Some of the deepest differences were not between the parties but within them. Labour leaders to the left favored an idea of fairness as equality. Others thought more in terms of fair opportunity and equity in individual rights and responsibilities.

Among Labour leaders, the issue of fairness came to a head in an argument over taxation. In 1987, Roger Douglas proposed to reform New Zealand's steeply graduated income tax. The top income tax rate had been 66 percent even on moderate incomes. It was reduced to 32 percent. A consumption tax of 10 percent (later 12.5) was levied on goods and services. Douglas also tried to replace a tax on business income with a levy on business assets, to encourage productivity.[41]

Prime Minister David Lange strongly disagreed with Roger Douglas on taxation. They tried to compromise, but the Labour Party was so deeply divided that Lange and Douglas could no longer find common ground.[42] In 1988, Lange forced Douglas to resign as minister of finance. Many MPs supported the policies of Douglas, and Prime Minister Lange resigned. His replacement as prime minister was Geoffrey Palmer, a centrist who tried to hold the party together. A general election followed, and the Labour government fell from power in 1990.[43]

The Third Stage: Restructuring from the Right

The incoming National Party and its prime minister, Jim Bolger, continued the reform movement, but in a different spirit. Its driver was Finance Minister Ruth Richardson. She always insisted that fairness was one of her primary goals. "The only sustainable welfare state," she said, "is one that is fair and affordable."[44]

It soon became clear that Richardson's idea of fairness was very different from that of Labour leaders who preceded her. In the midst of a sharp recession, the National government reduced income support for the poor. It abolished family benefits in 1991 and introduced user fees for the national health system in 1992. New Zealand's superannuation scheme had to be cut back, as its cost was insupportable. The question was how to do it. National leaders favored an income test, which they thought fair. Others deeply disagreed. This approach was later changed by multiparty agreement to an increase in the minimum age for a pension from sixty to sixty-five, which many thought more equitable.[45]

This second wave of restructuring from the right in the 1990s had very different consequences than the efforts of Roger Douglas and the Fourth Labour Government in the 1980s. Jim Bolger's National Party passed a new Employment Contracts Act in 1991 that made union membership voluntary and allowed the negotiation of individual employment contracts, a heavy blow to New Zealand's labor movement, which had been among the strongest in the world. The National Party also attempted to privatize health and medical services. It introduced major changes in the control of health care and replaced elected area health boards with appointed Regional Health Authorities, which could enter into contracts with private insurance companies for local communities.[46]

This more conservative approach to restructuring was deeply unpopular. In 1993, National nearly fell from power. Ruth Richardson was removed from her post as minister of finance and resigned from Parliament to pursue a business career. Her party shifted toward the center. Even as the National Party's program differed from that of the Labour government, it was forced to accept the principle of the welfare state and many of its institutions. Conservative National leaders continued to make many cost-cutting changes in New Zealand's system of health care, but they were careful to preserve the system itself—a very different policy from that of conservatives in the United States. National leaders modified the system of accident compensation but kept the system largely intact. They privatized housing assistance by shifting to vouchers, which could be spent in public or private accommodation, but they kept the program in being.

Both New Zealand and the United States extended free-market principles and mechanisms in many areas. Both shifted control from the public to the private sector. But they did so by different means and to different ends. Even as New Zealand and the United States moved through a similar sequence of stages, they went about the business of reform and restructuring with radically dissimilar purposes. New Zealand preserved its traditional concern for social justice. In the broad realm of social and economic policy, some leaders of both the National and Labour parties shared an idea of fairness that was not much evident in the United States during this period.

Constitutional Restructuring in the United States: Nixon's Crimes and Their Aftermath

In the midst of these many economic reforms, the United States and New Zealand also experienced another process of political restructuring in their systems of government. Americans underwent a severe test of their constitutional system during the presidency of Richard Nixon (1969–74).[47] His presidential administration stretched the prerogatives of executive power far beyond the law, farther than any president had ever done. "When the President does it," Richard Nixon told television journalist David Frost after his resignation, "that means that it is not illegal."[48]

The idea that the president and his administration were above the law appeared in many forms during the Nixon years. One of them was a radical expansion of "executive privilege," which claimed presidential immunity from judicial proceedings and legislative oversight. Another was the doctrine of "presidential impoundment," which Nixon used to nullify laws that displeased him. A third was the claim that the president had the right to infringe the rights of individuals whenever he or his lieutenants believed that national security was threatened in some undefined way. A fourth asserted the right and power of the president to make war on other nations without the authorization of Congress. A fifth was the doctrine that the president and not the judiciary was the final arbiter of the Constitution.[49]

These constitutional doctrines were not entirely of Richard Nixon's making. The imperial presidency, as Arthur Schlesinger Jr. called it, had been in the making since Theodore Roosevelt and Woodrow Wilson. It had gathered momentum in the administrations of John Kennedy and Lyndon Johnson, who both behaved as if the common constraints of public law and private morality did not apply to them. But Nixon went farther than any president who had preceded him. He began to act in ways that directly violated the American Constitution.[50]

Nixon also extended the prerogatives of the imperial presidency to all the president's men. The result was a series of high crimes and misdemeanors of unprecedented magnitude in American history. President Nixon and Secretary of State Henry Kissinger made war on Cambodia and Laos in 1970, without approval of Congress or warrant under international law. This policy succeeded only in spreading the disaster of Vietnam through all the sovereign states of Indochina. Crimes against individual Americans were explicitly authorized by Nixon himself. Many more were committed by Attorney General John Mitchell and dozens of presidential aides. Some of these actions were reported by the press, but Americans were caught up in their own problems and increasingly alienated from politics in general. Many looked the other way.[51]

All American presidencies, without exception, have suffered cases of misconduct, but the presidents themselves were typically the victims, rather than the perpetrators of these acts. Here again, the Nixon administration was something new. Historian C. Vann Woodward wrote, "Heretofore, no president has been proved to be the chief coordinator of the crimes and misdemeanors charged against his administration in his office."[52]

As the president's men grew more corrupt in their acts, public scandals began to multiply. Many were exposed by journalists and editors at the *Washington Post* and investigated by Democratic Senator Sam Ervin of North Carolina, Republican Senator Howard Baker of Tennessee, and independent prosecutor Archibald Cox, of Wayland, Massachusetts.[53]

In 1973, Nixon's vice president, Spiro Agnew, was forced from office after a career of bribery led to conviction in a criminal case. In 1974, evidence of criminal acts by President Nixon himself persuaded men in his own party to turn against him, and the Judiciary Committee of the House of Representatives voted to recommend articles of impeachment by a large bipartisan majority. In the face of trial and conviction, Nixon resigned from office. A pardon by his successor, Gerald Ford, blocked criminal proceedings, but the former president was driven from office in deep disgrace. He was later disbarred and forbidden to practice law. Four of Nixon's cabinet officers were found guilty in criminal trials, and many White House officials went to prison.[54]

These troubles led to constitutional reforms and to an expansion of civil liberties in the United States. A series of new laws were passed to prevent Nixon's corruption from happening again. The War Powers Act (1973) restricted the president's powers to commit U.S. troops abroad for long periods without congressional authorization. The National Emergencies Act (1976) gave Congress the responsibility of review over presidential use of emergency powers. Other measures forbade American officials to use assassination against citizens of other nations and prohibited American corporations from bribing officials of other governments. The Congressional Budget and Impoundment Control Act (1974) gave Congress the means to override impoundments. Federal courts also declared presidential impoundment to be unconstitutional. The Supreme Court restricted electronic surveillance of private citizens without warrant. Congressional investigations forced the Defense Department to end counterintelligence activities against civilians within the United States. The Foreign Intelligence Surveillance Act (1978) put narrow limits on surveillance of individuals by all federal agencies.[55]

New rights for all Americans were added by federal legislation. An expanded Freedom of Information Act (passed over President Ford's veto in 1974) enlarged the rights of individual citizens. The Privacy Act of 1974 recognized a constitutional right to privacy that appeared nowhere in the Constitution.[56] The crimes and follies of the Nixon presidency led to a long period of constitutional reform and political restructuring. The primary purpose of nearly all new measures was to strengthen democratic processes, to protect the rule of law, and to enlarge the liberty and freedom of individual Americans.

Constitutional Restructuring in New Zealand:
The Muldoon Era and Its Consequences

Ten years after the Watergate affair, New Zealand also experienced its own constitutional crisis. It was many years in the making and came suddenly to a head on July 16, 1984, during a moment of transition after a national election. Prime Minister Robert Muldoon and his National Party had been voted out of office, but power did not change hands until after the return of the election writs, a formal process that normally took several weeks.[57]

In that transitional period, the country found itself in a major financial crisis. The treasury was nearly bankrupt. The New Zealand dollar was plummeting, and urgent steps were necessary to prevent a collapse of the foreign exchange market and foreign trade. The two parties blamed each other. The incoming prime-minister-designate, David Lange, held Muldoon's heavy spending responsible, and wished to devalue the New Zealand dollar. The outgoing prime minister believed that the Labour Party had undermined confidence in the national currency, and wanted to support it as he had been doing for many years.[58]

So deep was the animosity between these leaders that Muldoon was unwilling to cooperate with the incoming prime minister in any way and refused even to meet with him. Muldoon was increasingly alone in his defiance, abandoned by his own party, and dismissed as its leader. In a brief but very painful moment, the nation found itself without a functioning government. Nothing could be done until the election writs were returned.[59]

That crisis flowed in large part from the character of Muldoon, who had governed New Zealand for nine years (1975–84) in an arbitrary way. He bullied friends and enemies alike, and his high-handed methods of governing were as troubling to his own party as to the opposition. Muldoon went for long periods without calling Parliament into session and then convened it when the opposition Labor Party was about to have its periodic party conferences.[60]

Muldoon was no Nixon. Most of his actions were within the law, though some were thought to go beyond it. A case in point was a controversy over Muldoon's attempt to build the Clyde Dam in Otago. A judicial body called the Planning Tribunal refused to grant the necessary water rights for its construction. Muldoon and his friends went forward anyway and passed a special statute in defiance of the court.[61]

Many people believed that Muldoon's action was unconstitutional. He strongly disagreed. The question was difficult to settle, because New Zealand's constitution was not a single fundamental document. It embodied English enactments of great antiquity, a few fragments of New Zealand's Constitution Act of 1852, the British Statute of Westminster in 1931, and a web of traditions, customs, and statutes. Some elements were obscure, others were obsolete, and more than a few were contradictory.[62]

During the 1970s, New Zealanders began to study the structure of their government with a more critical eye. Their leader was Geoffrey Palmer, a professor of law at Victoria University in Wellington and also at the University of Iowa in the United States. In 1979, he published a careful analysis and scathing critique of New Zealand's constitution and government called *Unbridled Power.* But nothing was done. New Zealanders preferred to muddle through with the system that they knew.[63]

Five years later, the succession crisis of 1984 persuaded many people that something had to be done. The result was a movement for a written constitution. Here again, Palmer took the lead. Even as he pursued a full-time or double-time academic career, he held a seat in Parliament and became a leader in the Labour Party. In 1984, he was chosen deputy prime minister in the Fourth Labour Government. Two years later he took the lead in drafting a new constitution for New Zealand.

It was a very short document, barely four pages long. Palmer himself observed that "much of the working of our system of government cannot be discerned from it." Mainly it codified New Zealand's unwritten constitution with a distant royal sovereign, a unicameral Parliament, responsible ministers, and an independent judiciary. At the same time, it established clear rules for transitions. Most important, it repealed the Constitution Act of 1852,

New Zealand also restructured its political and constitutional institutions. Here the prime mover was Geoffrey Palmer, who took the lead in drafting a new Constitution (1986), New Zealand's first bill of rights (1990), and a proposal for proportional representation that was adopted in 1993.

the Statute of Westminster of 1931, and the New Zealand Constitution Amendments of 1947. For the first time, it firmly established New Zealand's complete legislative independence from Great Britain.[64]

There were major differences between this document and the fundamental law of the United States. New Zealand's Constitution was an act of Parliament, not a higher law that was ratified by the people. One part of it, a section that required triennial elections, was "entrenched," which meant that it could only be changed by three-quarters of the Parliament or by a popular referendum. But the idea of "entrenchment" was not itself entrenched, and could be changed merely by a majority in Parliament—a fundamental difference from amendments to the United States Constitution, which require approval by two-thirds of both houses of Congress and ratitication by three-quarters of all the states. Another striking difference was the incompleteness of the document. The larger part of New Zealand's system remained unwritten. Even so, the Constitution put the country on a new foundation. It firmly established the independence of the nation, the legitimacy of its institutions, and the existence of fundamental written law.[65]

Five years later, after the resignation of David Lange in 1989 and the split within the Labour government, Geoffrey Palmer became prime minister of New Zealand and served until just before the election of 1990, when Labour lost its majority. Palmer was an improbable politician—quiet, intelligent, and thoughtful, with the manner of a scholar. Some in the press complained that he was not good copy. In fact he was one of the most creative and successful reform leaders in the history of New Zealand.[66]

In 1990, Palmer played yet another major role in the history of his country by drafting New Zealand's first Bill of Rights. The people of his nation had long enjoyed many rights and liberties as part of the English common law tradition. Not much was written about a New Zealander's rights in a rounded or definitive way. As a consequence, New Zealand's record in civil liberties was very mixed. Radicals and dissenters had no written constitutional protections. The New Zealand police did not consistently respect free speech, freedom of religion, rights of assembly, and other civil rights that are regarded as fundamental in the United States and have long been guaranteed by the American Bill of Rights. A case in point during the 1930s was the behavior of New Zealand police toward three nurses who wished to serve on the Republican side during the Spanish Civil War. The nurses were interrogated at length and treated roughly by police who did not like their politics. Similar cases arose in regard to striking workers, conscientious objectors in both world wars, and protesters in many public causes.[67]

These problems came to a head in New Zealand during the 1970s and 1980s, when protest movements began to occur more frequently over the war in Vietnam, apartheid in South Africa, Maori rights, environmental issues, and other questions. Some of these protests took the form of large and disorderly street demonstrations. The New Zealand police, like their colleagues in the United States, did not at first know how to deal with them. Many individual policemen in both nations were conservative in politics and not sympathetic to the demonstrators. The result was violence from all sides, some of it committed by the guardians of order. The police were rough with civil rights demonstrators during the South African rugby tours and even rougher against Maori protests.[68]

These conflicts led to increasing concern about individual rights. Here again the leader was Geoffrey Palmer. As minister of justice in the Labour government, he submitted a white paper on the problem and drafted a Bill of Rights for New Zealand. After five years of debate, Parliament enacted it in 1990.[69]

In substantive terms, the American and New Zealand Bills of Rights share many provisions in common. Both guarantee freedom of religion, freedom of expression, freedom of assembly, habeas corpus, a right to counsel, presumption of innocence, and speedy trial in the presence of one's accusers. Both restrict searches and seizures, forbid cruel punishments, and include protections against arbitrary arrest, double jeopardy, and self-incrimination. They prohibit what are called "ex post facto" laws in the U.S. Constitution and "retroactive penalties" in New Zealand. Most important, both documents end with a caveat that the enumeration of some rights is not meant to deny the existence of others. They affirm an idea of expanding rights as a living tradition.[70]

In other ways the two Bills of Rights are very different. American rights are in some respects more extensive. New Zealand has no guarantee of trial by jury, and no provision for the separation of church and state, as in the American First Amendment. It does not recognize a right to keep and bear arms (much cherished by many Americans) and does not require warrants for searches and seizures. Lacking a federal system, it has no reservation of rights to states or local governments.[71]

But in other respects, New Zealand's rights are more sweeping than in the United States. They guarantee the right of freedom of movement, a right not to be subjected to medical experiments, and a right to refuse medical treatment. The cultural rights of minorities are guaranteed in a way that does not figure in American law. Freedom from discrimination is defined more broadly and more clearly than in the American Thirteenth, Fourteenth, and Fifteenth Amendments, which were enacted after the Civil War.[72]

In these differences, one discovers the importance of time and the historical moment. The American Bill of Rights preserves seventeenth- and eighteenth-century ideas of political and legal rights. In particular it protects specific rights that were actually violated by British imperial officials in the years before the American Revolution. New Zealand's document incorporates ideas of human rights that developed in the nineteenth and twentieth centuries.

There are also other substantive contrasts. The American Bill of Rights has always been primarily a charter of individual liberties. Two centuries of judicial interpretation have expanded them by enlarging existing rights (cruel and unusual punishment), adding entirely new ones (the right of privacy), and requiring state and local governments to respect the provisions of the federal Bill of Rights. Mainly the Bill of Rights protects individuals against institutions, and especially against the arbitrary power of government. In that way, the American tradition of liberty and freedom is one of the most exalted in the world, and still very radical by comparison with other English-speaking nations.

The New Zealand Bill of Rights does some of that, and something else. One article refers explicitly to fairness. Another guarantees that "every person has the right to the observance of the principles of natural justice." Geoffrey Palmer observes that "unless otherwise stated, natural justice and fairness are used interchangeably." Under the Bill of Rights, these ideas are a fundamental part of New Zealand's public law.[73] The idea of "natural justice" as "fairness" is foreign to the American constitutional tradition. Many American judges and lawyers would not know what to make of it.

New Zealanders seem more comfortable with the idea of natural justice. Geoffrey Palmer was thinking of it mainly as a procedural idea when he wrote, "The rules of natural justice are defined today as including the requirement of an unbiased tribunal, the hearing of both sides of the case, and open courts with the possibility of press." But it is also invoked as a substantive idea. Mainly it comes down to an idea of institutional fairness, which is different from the tradition of rights in the United States. New Zealanders, in short, have joined an idea of fairness to a conception of rights, in ways that go far beyond American constitutional law.

On the other hand, American ideas of liberty, freedom, and individual rights are in many ways stronger than in New Zealand. The U.S. Bill of Rights is also part of the Constitution. Acts of Congress and state legislatures that are understood to violate it are often declared unconstitutional by the courts and become null and void. New Zealand's Bill of Rights is a parliamentary statute and is not "entrenched." It does not constrain Parliament from legislating as it pleases by majority vote.

Yet another difference appears in the cultural status of these two documents. The Bill of Rights does not loom large in the consciousness of New Zealanders. We spoke about it with highly intelligent, widely read people who were deeply engaged in their responsibilities as citizens. None could remember when it was passed, or what it included, or if it had been invoked in *any* prominent proceeding. One distinguished scholar told me, "It really doesn't matter to us."

That attitude is very different from the status of the Bill of Rights in the United States. American citizens are keenly aware that they have rights, including many that appear in neither the Constitution nor the Bill of Rights. In this attitude they are constitutionally correct, for Madison's Bill of Rights explicitly guarantees an American right to other rights that are not enumerated. Since the 1930s, when the Bill of Rights was rediscovered in the United States, most Americans have believed that this great document is fundamentally and urgently important to their way of life.

Political Restructuring in Two Nations

In the late twentieth century, leaders in New Zealand and the United States also attempted to reform their political institutions in other ways. The crises of the 1970s created a mood of anger and frustration with political processes. Both countries shared a similar sense of institutional dysfunction, but dealt with it in different ways.

In the 1980s, many New Zealanders were unhappy with both of their major political parties. Some were also displeased by the fate of other parties that tried to challenge them. During the election of 1978, for example, the Social Credit Party won 16 percent of the popular vote but received only one seat out of ninety-seven in Parliament. In 1981, its share of the electorate grew to 21 percent, and its seats in Parliament increased from one to two. The New Zealand First Party was treated even more unfairly. It won 12 percent of the vote in 1984 and received no seats at all. The Labour Party in 1978 and 1981 won more popular votes than National but fewer seats in Parliament. The National Party in 1993 won only 35 percent of the popular vote but gained a majority in Parliament. A team of political scientists in Wellington observed that the results of these elections gravely weakened the idea that New Zealand's system of representation was "fair" and "just."[74]

Prime Minister Muldoon showed no interest in electoral reform, but his calamitous career was thought to be a strong argument in its favor. After he fell from power, a Royal Commission on the Electoral System was appointed in 1985. Once again, the central figure was Geoffrey Palmer. The commission did its work quickly and delivered a report in 1986. It began by defining a set of criteria for democratic systems. The first criterion was "fairness between political parties." By "fairness" in this instance it had in mind an idea of proportionality: "The number of seats gained by a political party should be proportional to the number of voters who support that party."

After some research and much debate, the commission recommended a new system that was inspired by European models of proportional representation. Every elector was given two votes: one for a local candidate, the other for a nationwide party. Parties that won at least 5 percent of the vote were assigned seats in proportion to their share of the electorate. Separate representation for Maori was retained, in proportion to the number of Maori voters who chose to register on Maori rolls.[75]

This proposal was called the Mixed Member Proportional Electoral System, or MMP for short. It was strongly resisted. Many older voters were accustomed to the status quo, which was called First Past the Post (FPP), or winner-take-all, which is the way that most Americans normally expect elections to happen. Others objected to the complexity of the new system. More than a few supporters of both major parties feared that the leading parties, Labour and National, would be fatally weakened. Some predicted that ministers in power would find it very difficult to govern. But most New Zealanders supported the idea. They had become profoundly uncomfortable with the winner-take-all system, which seemed very unfair to them. Since 1951, every government in power had had the support of less than half of the electorate.[76]

In 1993, the new system of proportional representation was approved by a nationwide referendum. It began to have a major impact even before an election took place. Groups broke away from both major parties, and new parties began to multiply. The first general election under MMP was held in 1996. National received 34 percent

Open Societies in World Affairs

of the vote and 37 percent of seats in Parliament. Labour won 28 percent of the electorate and 31 percent of Parliament. Five smaller parties gained 38 percent of the vote and 33 percent of the seats. By that test of fairness, proportional representation was thought to be a success.

But as a system of government, the outcome was more doubtful. The National Party put together a governing coalition with the New Zealand First Party, but it was very fragile, and had only 50.9 percent of Parliament. The coalition came apart in 1999, when Prime Minister Jennie Shipley fired Deputy Prime Minister Winston Peters, the head of the New Zealand First Party. The government fell and was followed by a coalition of Labour and two other parties that was even more brittle. The next prime minister, Helen Clark, had more success in building coalitions, remarkably so. But the new system continued to create major difficulties for governance.[77]

Critics of the new system worried about these problems. Some noted that New Zealand had adopted proportional representation at the same time that other nations such as Italy abandoned it for a winner-take-all system after a long period of instability. But whatever the practical weaknesses of proportional representation, its ethical imperatives remained very strong in New Zealand. Winner-take-all is perceived to be fundamentally unfair as a democratic process.

Electoral reforms were also proposed in the United States in the same period. Through the past two centuries, many American writers (mostly lawyers and university professors) have suggested various systems of proportional representation for the United States. Among the first to do so was Timothy Ford, a Yankee lawyer in Charleston, South Carolina, during the 1780s who had an idea later called "concurrent majority" to protect an oligarchy of Low Country planters against the more populous yeoman farmers of the upcountry. Ford's ideas were used by his law student John C. Calhoun as a way of protecting slaveholders from a growing anti-slavery majority in national politics. He found little support for this reform, even in his own state. The doctrine of "concurrent majority" was regarded by most Americans (even most South Carolinians in the nineteenth century) as brilliant but unsound. Many thought it was a political heresy, fundamentally hostile to democracy, which Americans define as majority rule.

In the 1990s, suggestions remarkably similar to Calhoun's idea of a concurrent majority were ironically put forward by Lani Guinier, a radical feminist and black activist. She proposed something comparable to Calhoun's plan as a way of giving more power to Afro-Americans, by reserving seats for them in proportion to their population. Scarcely anyone noticed outside of academe until Lani Guinier was nominated by President Bill Clinton to a high position in the Justice Department.[78] When Americans became aware of her ideas, there was a storm of disapproval in Congress and throughout the nation. By 1991, most Americans rejected a system in which blocks of seats were specially reserved for people of any race, gender, or class as profoundly anti-democratic, unfree, and unjust. Their idea of democracy was a representation of individuals, not races, classes, genders, or any other groups. Guinier insisted that her plan for proportional representation of black people in Congress was a matter of "fundamental fairness." The media began to mock her as "the Quota Queen." President Clinton, after promising strong support to his own nominee, quickly reversed himself and withdrew her nomination. The controversy deepened American opposition to any system of quotas or proportional representation.[79]

The Guinier Affair happened in the United States at the same time that New Zealand was enacting its new system of proportional representation. The two nations moved in opposite directions. Americans are as uncomfortable with ideas of proportional representation as New Zealanders have been with the idea of winner-take-all.

At the same time, many in the United States share a sense of growing frustration with their electoral system. Nevertheless, American politics were also transformed in the 1980s and 1990s, but by a process of restructuring without reform. The United States developed a system of representation in which Congress increasingly responded not to the will of the majority but to the growing pressure of wealthy contributors and highly organized interest groups. The leading cause was the growing cost of winning election to high office. Meaningful reform of an increasingly corrupt electoral process had some success but was defeated by conservative opposition in Congress and the Supreme Court.

The problem was compounded by a failure of political journalism in the United States. Both print and television media turned increasingly to tabloid journalism and edge journalism, diminishing the flow of information and deepening the national mood of alienation from politics. In 1996, a survey of attitudes toward American institutions found that confidence was very high in religious organizations, colleges, universities, charities, and health organizations. It was also positive toward the military, cultural organizations, and small business. At the very bottom were the mass media, large business corporations, political parties, and government. Of all American institutions confidence was lowest in the Congress. Only 3 percent of Americans expressed high confidence in Congress; 4 percent in political parties; 5 percent in business corporations; and 6 percent in the media.[80]

The electoral consequences appeared in voter behavior. New Zealanders have among the highest levels of electoral participation in the world. Americans have the doubtful distinction of some of the lowest levels of voting in any Western nation.

In New Zealand, turnout in general elections by eligible voters has fluctuated in the range of 80 to 95 percent through most of the twentieth century. It fell sharply in the troubled years of the 1970s but revived in the 1980s and rose after proportional representation was introduced in 1993. There are many exceptions. In 1990, proportions of nonvoting in Maori districts was 41 percent, compared with 16 percent in other districts. Many young New Zealanders also stay away from the polls: 29 percent of voters in the age group eighteen to twenty-four don't vote, compared with 7 percent of those aged fifty-five to sixty-four. Renters and tenants vote less frequently than homeowners. Still, in the country at large, most New Zealanders vote in general elections.

In the United States, voting trends are very different. During the nineteenth century, turnout was high and stable. Approximately 70 or 80 percent of adult white males voted in most presidential elections from 1840 to 1896. Turnout began to fall in the election of 1900 and kept on falling through most of the twentieth century. In the presidential election of 1996, 49 percent of Americans of voting age cast ballots, and that number did not much rise in the twenty-first century. Participation is lower in local elections, primaries, and congressional contests.

Comparative study helps to explain why some people vote and others do not. There are many theories. The rational choice model asserts that people decide to vote on the basis of their own sense of personal and material stakes in the outcome. A competition model hypothesizes that voting is high where there is a serious difference and a strong choice. The structural model holds that impediments to participation, such as registration procedures and residence requirements, all have made a major difference. A civic responsibility model holds that people vote from a sense of civic duty and moral obligation.

An interesting test has been made in New Zealand. Did participation rise in closely contested seats and fall in safe seats? In 1990, this factor was found to have some importance, but only in a very small way: nonvoting in seats where national candidates were thought to be safe was only 17.2 percent. Competition was not the major factor. New Zealanders vote even in noncompetitive elections as an act of civic responsibility. Americans do not.[81]

Health and Welfare Programs in Two Societies: Accident Compensation

Other striking contrasts between New Zealand and the United States appear in social welfare and insurance programs. We discovered one of them when a friend suffered an injury in an athletic event. To our amazement, she was compensated by the government. New Zealand's Accident Compensation Act is a system of no-fault compensation and rehabilitation for all New Zealanders. It was proposed in 1967, enacted in 1972 by the ruling National Party, and expanded in 1973 by a Labour government to cover all accidents, no matter how or why they happened. The program is run by a public agency called the Accident Compensation Corporation and funded by taxes on employers and employees according to the danger in their work, from a low of 0.2 percent for teachers to a high of 8 percent for professional rugby players. The cost of injury in automobile accidents is covered by a share of revenue from gas taxes and registration fees. In the period from 1994 to 1999, the program paid out approximately NZ$1.4 billion on 1.4 million claims. About one-third were work-related. Roughly 6 percent were motor vehicle accidents. More than 10 percent were sporting injuries.[82]

The program has the support of most political parties, though they have disagreed on its details and many changes have been made. In 1999, a conservative government allowed employers to buy private accident insurance. A Labour-Alliance coalition in 2000 returned all coverage to the public program, with a commitment that it must outperform private companies in costs, coverage, service, and efficiency—which it has done.

As part of this program, the right to sue for damages was limited. Lawyers have tried to find an opening for litigation. New Zealand courts have allowed them to sue for "mental trauma," which is roughly comparable to American "pain and suffering," and also to seek "exemplary damages," which are somewhat like "punitive damages" in the United States. Mental trauma was covered under a law of 1982 but removed in 1992, and the number of suits has grown rapidly in cases of medical malpractice and workplace injuries. But New

Zealand courts have held down the awards to small sums in most cases, much smaller than awards for libel and defamation.[83]

All of this makes a dramatic contrast with American practices. In the United States accidents are also compensated, but in a different way—mainly by private insurance, and sometimes by protracted tort litigation. The American system yields large payments to a few accident claimants. In 1987, for example, a railroad tank car filled with a dangerous chemical caught fire in New Orleans, and a cloud of vapor passed over a nearby neighborhood. Residents were evacuated in time, and nobody was killed or seriously injured, but a small army of lawyers appeared, and the neighbors brought suit against five transportation companies, not for physical injuries (there were none) but for punitive damages. Ten years later, after much extravagant legal maneuvering, a jury awarded eight thousand plaintiffs the sum of $3.5 billion for "mental anguish." Lawyers stood to gain one-third of that amount. As these words were written, the judgment was appealed and the case was still before the courts.[84]

Another case in the United States was brought by tort lawyers for a woman who spilled a cup of hot coffee on herself in a fast-food restaurant. She sued the restaurant and won a judgment of $2.7 million, later reduced to $640,000. Some of the largest settlements were class action suits against tobacco companies. In one Texas case alone the tobacco companies agreed to a settlement of $17.3 billion. The biggest gainers were the tort lawyers themselves, who received $3.3 billion.[85] American tort litigation brings large settlements to a few people (and larger settlements to their lawyers), but most victims of accidents in the United States get nothing.[86]

New Zealanders are appalled by the American system of tort law. Americans in turn are astonished by New Zealand's system of public accident compensation. They believe that if people are paid for having accidents, they will have more of them. New Zealanders reply that their system is rarely abused. Whatever the truth may be, it is clear that the American and New Zealand systems were grounded in different ethical principles. The American system rests on an idea of individual freedom. The New Zealand system is based on an idea of fairness.

Conclusion

Both nations restructured many institutions during the late twentieth century. In economics, constitutional law, politics, health, and social welfare, Americans of both parties embraced a radical extension of an ideology of liberty, freedom, and especially free enterprise. A system that was already one of the most libertarian in the world became still more libertarian.

New Zealanders also worked to make their institutions more open and free, but they balanced the new reforms with a tradition of fairness and natural justice that had been strongly rooted in that nation's history and values. In the twenty-first century, restructuring has continued in New Zealand under a conservative National government that came to power in 2008. Prime Minister John Key was a banker and foreign exchange trader for Merrill Lynch, and a centrist-conservative who often speaks of both fairness and freedom on public questions. His government has taken the idea of fairness in new directions. An example is Minister of Justice Simon Power, who gave a speech on crime and justice and centered his thoughts on fairness. Power said, "Fairness is one of those things that people often say plays a big part in the New Zealand psyche. All crime is unfair. . . . An overwhelming 92 percent of New Zealanders said they wanted a fair go for victims." To that end he laid out a policy of increased penalties for criminal acts, more surveillance, more weapons for police, privatization of prisons, and a Victim Compensation Scheme funded by levies on criminals, which "puts victims' rights first."[87]

Strongly opposed to the National Party is a rising star of the Labour Party. He is David Clark, a Presbyterian minister and warden of Selwyn College, who was nominated for a Labour seat from Dunedin North. Like leaders of the National Party, he also appealed to fairness, but in a different way. In a statement on Labour values and the New Zealand Dream he wrote, "These values are rooted in the fact that New Zealanders have an underlying sense of fairness. It's what makes New Zealanders tick. We love to see everyone have a fair go." Clark opposed a National policy that reduced taxes on the rich and imposed a consumption tax that fell "disproportionately on the poor." He called it "National's reverse Robin Hood policy: taking from the poor to give to the rich" and wrote, "All of this insults and undermines the fundamental sense of fairness that New Zealanders share."[88]

Altogether, the main finding in this history of restructuring might be summarized in a sentence. New Zealand added liberty and freedom to fairness and justice; the United States added liberty and freedom to freedom and liberty.

CONCLUSION

Learning to Be Free and Fair

A nation that seeks to be fair, but not free,
Has never been either, nor ever can be.

A nation that strives to be free, but not fair,
Will always be neither, for they make a pair.

—found on the road to Alcaroa

W HAT HAVE WE LEARNED in this inquiry? We began with a question about New Zealand and the United States, two countries that are comparable in many ways. Both belong to a community of English-speaking nations that James Belich calls the "Angloworld," and James Bennett the "Anglosphere."[1] Both are "settler societies" or "new world societies," which grew from the interplay of European colonists and indigenous populations. Most important for this work, both are open societies.

The idea of an open society was invented by Henri Bergson in 1935 and developed by Karl Popper during the Second World War. In more than half a century, their work has inspired a large literature. These men thought of the open society as an epistemic and ontological idea. Popper observed that the primary purpose of an open system is to enable individual people to think for themselves and to make the meaningful choices in their lives.[2]

We have studied open societies in another way, as functioning historical systems that began to emerge in the Western world during the early modern era. They were similar in many ways, but not the same. As a matter of empirical fact, they tend to have democratic polities, mixed-enterprise economies, pluralist cultures, an abiding concern for human rights, and a deep respect for the rule of law.

Within that common frame they have developed in many different forms, in part because they were founded on differently prioritized values. Americans think of an open society as a free society, centered primarily on the values of liberty and freedom that are deeply rooted in American history.[3]

New Zealanders are more mindful of fairness, justice, and equity, which have long been an important part of their experience.[4] Other cultures are much concerned with equality in its many meanings: equality before the law, equality of social status, equality of material condition, equality of opportunity, and equality of esteem.[5]

These principles (and others) vary broadly among open societies, and within them. That is why the encompassing idea of an open society is increasingly useful and even indispensable to an understanding of their history of the modern world. As a framing tool, it helps us to think about the similarities of open systems while we also study their differences.

Toward a History of Open Societies in the Modern World

After the democratic revolutions of the eighteenth century, open societies began to multiply throughout the world. That powerful trend was sustained for many generations, but sometimes it ran in reverse. The largest reversal occurred during the depression decade of the 1930s. In 1932, twenty-five open societies existed in continental Europe. By 1942, only two remained: Sweden and Switzerland. The rest were destroyed by Fascist and Communist enemies. A major turning point followed during World War II. In the pivotal years 1942–45, Fascist systems were defeated by a very mixed alliance of open societies and closed Communist systems. A period of mixed tendencies occurred in the early and middle years of the Cold War, when closed Communist regimes multiplied in the world, and open societies also grew more numerous.

Then a new trend appeared, circa 1975. It was marked by rapid and continuing growth of open societies throughout the world. That tendency has been studied in annual surveys by Freedom House, a centrist-liberal organization. Every year it has used a consistent set of empirical indicators to measure the strength of democratic processes, political rights, civil liberties, and respect for free expression.

These tests have been applied to most sovereign nations in the world (194 countries in 2011). The results show that the number of open societies increased every year from 1975 to the early twenty-first century, and closed systems tended on balance to become more open.[6]

That long trend began to lose momentum circa 2002. The number of open societies in the world suddenly ceased rising, and fluctuated for a few years. In 2005, their numbers began to fall, and kept falling every year from 2006 to 2011. Part of the cause was the economic collapse of 2007–8, but the annual surveys showed that this period of decline in open societies began before the crash. Other factors, political and social, were clearly involved. In the early twenty-first century, the strongest open systems, the United States and the European Union, were faltering in many ways, while closed societies such as China appeared to be doing better.[7]

All of these patterns appeared in the evidence gathered each year by Freedom House. Another annual survey of a different design was sponsored by the libertarian-conservative Heritage Foundation, with the support of Dow Jones & Co. and the *Wall Street Journal.* From 1995 to 2011, it assessed 179 national economies on ten tests of economic freedom: minimal regulation of business, no tariffs, low taxes, low public spending, few restrictions on investment, low inflation, no price controls, openness to competition, unlimited property rights, little political corruption, and "labor freedom," which it defined in a unique way as no restrictions on layoffs or firings of workers. This survey found that "economic freedom" according to that conservative definition increased from 1996 to 2008, declined briefly from 2008 to 2010, and then turned sharply upward again in 2011.[8]

These two annual surveys by Freedom House and the Heritage Foundation studied different things. Taken together they suggest a complex double tendency. Liberal-democratic open societies declined during the early twenty-first century. At the same time, libertarian-conservative free economies increased. A new sort of society developed around the world. It was increasingly a closed system in its hostility to democracy, tolerance, cultural pluralism, human rights, civil liberties, and the rule of law. But it also supported a free economy in terms of property rights, free markets, and autonomy for business corporations, as long as they did not challenge the established regime. One example of such a system existed in Bahrain, circa 2010, which ranked near the bottom of Freedom House measures of democracy, free expression, and human rights but close to the top on the Heritage Foundation's scale of economic freedom. Another example is China, which is not an open society in regard to political democracy and human rights. But it continues to move toward economic freedom, as defined by the conservative Heritage Foundation. That tendency was happening in other systems—a new combination of a closed society and a free economy. The pattern in China in particular appears to some observers as a more successful model for emulation than the United States or the European Community. To anyone who cares about open societies, these trends are troubling.[9]

But not all empirical signs point in the same direction. Since 2010, other trends and events are more positive. In a period of severe material stress, closed systems around the world have faced strong challenges from their own oppressed people in Tunisia, Egypt, Libya, Syria, Côte d'Ivoire, Sudan, Myanmar, and China. And even while some open systems have been struggling in the United States and the European Community, others have gained strength and stability in Brazil, Chile, Australia, Canada, and New Zealand. Taken together, this evidence of mixed tendencies suggests that we are living in an historic moment when the fate of open systems is hanging very much in the balance. At such a juncture, our choices and actions in the early twenty-first century could make a major difference. One way to inform our thinking is to study conditions not only in our own country, but around the world.

Some of the most instructive examples appear when we compare counter-tendencies within different open systems. The United States and New Zealand make two dramatic studies in contrast. In 2010, for example, public debt as a proportion of gross domestic product was 65 percent in the United States and 11 percent in New Zealand. Annual public deficits in national accounts by the same measure were 11 percent in the United States and 3 percent in New Zealand. In 2010, American unemployment rates were near 9 percent and slow to improve; in New Zealand they were below 6 percent and improving more rapidly. In terms of inequality, the United States achieved the highest level of income concentration of any developed nation. New Zealand had among the lowest, though inequalities were rising there as well. In surveys of political corruption, New Zealand achieved one of the best records of 188 nations and in 2008–9 rose to first place for honesty in government; the United States was well down the list, and falling. Similar contrasts appear in trends and measures of political partisanship, legislative stalemate, judicial dysfunction, infrastructure decay, home foreclosures, family stress, drug consumption, and social violence.[10]

It should be emphasized that these contrasts have not been constant through time. In the late 1970s, 1980s, and 1990s, New Zealand did worse than the United States. The important point is not that one open society is categorically and continuously superior to another, but that they have tended to function differently, with varying results. The problem is to understand how and why. The opportunity is to learn from one another.

Learning from Other Open Systems: New Zealand and the United States

That is what this inquiry has been about. What might Americans and New Zealanders learn from their comparative histories? One approach would be to analyze these two systems in material terms. Another is to examine the values on which these open societies are organized. That is the primary approach here.

We might take a lead from Alexis de Tocqueville, who observed that values such as liberty and freedom exist as *habitudes du coeur*, "habits of the heart."[11] They might be studied as vernacular ideas, from the Latin *vernaculus*, "native-born," "customary," or "ordinary."[12] In the early modern era, linguists used the word *vernacular* to describe the common speech of any group.[13] Similar methods might be applied to a culture's common stock of ideas, which historians have recently studied with increasing success. A leading example, and a seminal work of major importance, is Stuart Schwartz's *All Can Be Saved*, a history of religious tolerance as a vernacular idea in the Portuguese and Spanish colonial empires. In *Champlain's Dream* (2008) I tried to do something similar for vernacular ideas of humanity in Québeçois, Acadien, and Métis cultures in America during the early seventeenth century. And *Albion's Seed* (1989) and *Liberty and Freedom* (2005) did the same thing for vernacular ideas of liberty and freedom in Britain and anglophone American colonies and the United States during the seventeenth and eighteenth centuries.[14]

In that same spirit, this inquiry has studied vernacular ideas of fairness and "natural justice" in New Zealand, in juxtaposition to ideas of liberty and freedom in the United States. Most English-speaking people throughout the world share these ideals. New Zealanders are consciously a free people, yet few of them have anything like the American obsession with living free. Americans often speak of fairness. Many try to be fair, and most wish to be treated fairly, but they have nothing to compare with New Zealanders' highly developed vernacular ideas of fairness as the organizing principle of their open society.

The ideal of a free society is America's North Star, the great Polaris by which political navigators have steered their courses through four centuries. The ethics of fairness and natural justice are New Zealand's Southern Cross, a constellation of fundamental values that have been at the center of public discourse for many generations.[15]

Important opportunities arise from the histories of these societies. Americans and New Zealanders have accumulated much experience of those vernacular ideas. These moral abstractions are fundamental to our happiness and instrumental in our modern societies. They have inspired many specific virtues in the lives that people actually live. At the same time, they have given rise to more than a few abuses and vices. These problems have rarely been studied as such. What follows is a short list of practical virtues and vices of liberty, freedom, and fairness—conceived not as hypothetical problems or conceptual possibilities but as historical patterns of actual conduct. They are virtues and vices that actually exist in the world and can be studied by methods of historical inquiry.

The Virtues of Liberty in America

Let us begin with some of the many virtues of liberty, in the sense of rights of individual independence.[16] At its best, this great idea encourages the *virtue of individual responsibility.* Insofar as we are truly able to live in a condition of liberty, we are given powers of choice that enable us to become agents in our own lives. This in turn gives us a measure of moral autonomy in our lives and invites us to assume responsibility for our acts. Individual responsibility is an instrumental virtue. It helps us to live virtuously in many other ways.

In that process, liberty also encourages the *virtues of individual striving, creativity, and achievement.* These principles inspire us to make a difference in the world, and they increase our power to do so. Genuinely free societies are marked by a spirit of individual striving and by the release of individual energy, which is an instrument of great good and happiness in the world.

The idea of liberty, when truly understood, also invites and even requires us (in the sense of an ethical obligation) to respect the liberty of others, just as we would wish our rights to be respected by them. This is the *virtue of respect for the liberties of other individuals.* All of these virtues flow from the idea of liberty as the rights of autonomy.

A *Vice of Liberty as* Laisser Asservir: *Liberty to Take Away the Liberty of Others*

The most exalted virtues in the world can also give rise to practical vices in particular ways. Vernacular values of liberty as autonomy are a case in point. One very cruel vice has often occurred in American history. It is the habit of some people to claim that their own endowment of liberty as autonomy gives them a right and power to diminish or destroy the liberties of others.[17]

Among the earliest American examples were people in New England's Puritan colonies who demanded religious liberty for themselves and used it to destroy the religious liberty of others. Other examples were liberty-loving people in all American colonies, and especially in the southern states from the seventeenth to the nineteenth century, who insisted that they possessed the liberty to keep slaves. In the United States they created a unique system of slavery that was justified in terms of the liberty of the master. This vice of liberty grew more vicious when it was combined with the idea of race slavery and justified the enslavement of other people solely because of their racial and ethnic origins. The result was a linkage of a master's liberty and a slave's subjection to the idea of race.

That way of thought changed the meaning of liberty itself. It became an idea of liberty as *laisser asservir,* an inalienable right of one person to enslave another. The logic of this idea carried its believers to libertarian ideas of maximal protection for private property, to complete autonomy for the individual slave owner, and to minimal government except where its powers were needed to enforce slavery. Long after Emancipation and the end of de jure slavery in 1865, echoes of these ideas remain very strong in other forms.

Before 1865, the more that southerners tried to defend slavery, the greater was their distance from the ways of an open society. Their attempts to reconcile slavery with liberty could not survive close criticism, as many southerners knew well. In the nineteenth century, the southern idea of liberty as the power to enslave another was increasingly incompatible with a free press, free speech, and open discussion. Southerners tried to stifle dissent by brute force and to shut down the flow of ideas from the North. In 1856, the *Richmond Examiner* raged against "Our Enemies, the Isms." The result was a Great Repression, which Clement Eaton compared to the descent of a "cotton curtain" around the South. By 1860, the southern states were increasingly becoming a closed society that seemed as threatening to northerners as slavery itself.[18]

The Civil War and the abolition of race slavery were not the end for this vice of liberty as *laisser asservir*. It continued for many years in various forms of quasi-slavery and exploitation, which were also justified in terms of liberty-as-autonomy for the exploiter. Quasi-slavery, and even slavery outright, still exists in the United States today, in sweatshop labor, agricultural quasi-bondage, domestic servitude, coercive prostitution, and other forms of exploitation that continue in America and many countries throughout the world.

Liberty as Anarchy: The Vice of Liberty Against Law

Another vice of liberty appeared early in the history of the American Revolution. In the summer of 1775, John Adams was on the road in Massachusetts and met "a common horse jockey" who was "always in the Law, and had been sued in many Actions, at almost every Court." The jockey said, "Oh! Mr. Adams what great Things have you and your colleagues done for us! We can never be grateful enough to you. There are no Courts of Justice now in this Province, and I hope there will never be another!"

Adams was shocked, even stunned. He wrote in his diary, "Is this the Object for which I have been contending? said I to myself, for I rode along without any Answer to this Wretch. Are these the Sentiments of such People? And how many of them are there in this Country? . . . If the Power of the Country should get into such hands, and there is a great Danger that it will, to what Purpose have we sacrificed our Time, health and every Thing else? Surely we must guard against this Spirit and these Principles, or we shall repent of all our Conduct." But then he thought again, and wrote more hopefully that "the good Sense and Integrity of the Majority of the Body of the People, came in to my thoughts for my relief, and the last resource was after all in a good Providence."[19]

This is the vice of liberty as anarchy. It is rooted in the mistaken idea that one person is at liberty to violate laws that exist to protect the liberty of all people. Examples are motorists who run through red lights and stop signs when they find it convenient to do so, and yet are outraged when someone runs a red light on them. Similar patterns appeared on a larger scale in the United States during the early twenty-first century when private citizens and public officials behaved as if the laws of the republic did not apply to them and they were at liberty to break those laws whenever it pleased them to do so.

The Vice of Demanding Liberty's Benefits and Rejecting Its Burdens

From a very early date to our own time, other Americans have demanded the benefit of liberty and have denied any responsibility to bear its burdens or pay its costs in a modern society. These people want roads and bridges that allow them to speed freely on their libertarian way but resist the idea that they should pay taxes to support them. They complain about the ignorance of the young but refuse to agree that they should support schools. They demand complete security for their own property but resent courts and laws and government.

Many American libertarians are consumed by an obsessive hatred of taxation. In the spring of 2008, when federal income tax returns came due, they organized hundreds of "tea parties" to protest the payment of taxes, even though rates of taxation in America are lower than they have been for many years, and also lower than in most other developed societies throughout the world.

They claimed to embody the spirit of the American Revolution, which they remember inaccurately as a tax revolt. The American revolutionaries of 1776 objected not to taxation but to taxation without representation. After 1789, they taxed themselves more heavily than Parliament had ever proposed to do. Americans of that generation understood that taxes were fundamental to a free republic. In the twenty-first century, a great many people in the United States reject that idea. Politicians pander to their selfishness. Demagogues relentlessly encourage intense hostility to taxes and foster an attitude of alienation from government.

To demand the benefits of a free society and yet to refuse to bear its burdens or to pay its expenses is not merely selfishness and hypocrisy. It is profoundly destructive to society itself. Taxation is not only the price of civilization, as Oliver Wendell Holmes observed. It is also the price of liberty and freedom. To oppose all new taxes in the name of liberty is to threaten the destruction of liberty itself. This has been happening in the United States during the twenty-first century.

The Virtues of Freedom in America

The practical virtues and vices of freedom are different from those of liberty, just as the words themselves differ in their origin and meaning. Liberty is about the rights and responsibilities of independence and autonomy. Freedom is about the rights and responsibilities of belonging to a community of other free people. An example is the right to vote, or the right to participate freely in a community, which is what Martin Luther King was talking about when he and others demanded "Freedom, Now" in the movement for civil rights.

This idea of freedom as the right of belonging inspires many practical virtues. One of them is the *virtue of civic engagement*, which is fundamental to an open society. It matters not whether our political principles are of the left, right, or center. The idea of freedom encourages and even requires us (again, in that sense of ethical obligation) to assume a civic role in our society. In the operation of that principle, it also invites us to do so in a way that respects the civic role of others.

In yet another dimension of our being, the idea of freedom as a right of belonging to a community of other free people applies not only within our own time but across many generations. It asks us to remember that we are not the first or last generation to walk upon this earth. When understood in those terms, the idea of freedom is a right of belonging to a community that exists through time, and even beyond our own time. This entails *the virtue of stewardship*. The responsibilities of mutual belonging make us stewards of the land, and of our society, for others who will come after us, and they in turn for their posterity.

These are some of the practical virtues of freedom. There are many more. Other people might compile a different list. In various ways, they are a set of moral obligations—even moral imperatives—that are borne by those of us who believe in liberty and freedom, and are privileged to possess them in our lives, as members of open or opening systems.

Vices of Freedom: Sundown Towns

The idea of freedom as rights of belonging also has given rise to many practical vices. One of them is to claim a license for one's self-governing community to persecute others unlike ourselves. Among the worst and most widespread examples were the thousands of American towns in the twentieth century that excluded Americans who were of other ethnic or religious groups, and denied rights of belonging to others who lived or worked there, while demanding it for themselves.

A common practice was to forbid African Americans to remain in a community after sundown. Those who refused to obey were forcibly expelled. Sometimes they were beaten or killed.[20] These communities were called "sundown towns," and the most astonishing fact is that there were so many of them in the United States. Historians knew of their existence but thought that they were rare, until James Loewen studied the subject in detail and was amazed to discover that sundown towns existed in every part of the country, *except* the Deep South. The state of Illinois, for example, in 1970 had 671 towns with more than a thousand inhabitants. Of that number, Loewen estimated that as many as 475 towns (71 percent) were sundown towns. They were entirely white, and many actively excluded African Americans.[21]

These towns multiplied in the United States during the late nineteenth century, and continued to do so in much of the twentieth century. They included towns of many sorts and sizes. Not until the 1960s did they begin to disappear. Sundown towns excluded African Americans in different ways. Many did so by enacting by local ordinances, which took different forms. Some forbade African Americans to buy, rent, or hold property. Others explicitly forbade them to remain after dark. On rare occasions when these ordinances were challenged in court, they were usually found to be unlawful or unconstitutional or both. But local governments ignored the courts, and communities continued to enact sundown laws. They did so by processes that were democratic but unconstitutional, unlawful, and often criminal in the formal judgment of American courts. The people who did these things exercised their freedom in a way that denied it to others. This is a vice of freedom as the right of belonging. It has happened often in American history.

Another Vice of Freedom: The Demand for Civic Rights Without Civic Responsibility

Another common vice takes many familiar forms in the United States. One of them appears in people who demand the privileges of citizenship but can't be bothered with its responsibilities. The United States today has one of the lowest rates of voting participation in any well-established open society. When Americans are asked why they do not vote, they respond with many justifications. Some say that no candidates are worthy of their support, or that all political parties are equally fraudulent, or that all governments are corrupt, or that political promises are lies, or that they can't tell who is for what, or that the process is too complex. All of these claims are false. American nonvoters complain that they are uninformed but make no effort to inform themselves. They condemn corruption in politics but act in ways that make it more corrupt. They demand responsibility from others and take no responsibility for themselves. In all of these ways, this vice of freedom is profoundly destructive of a free and open society. And yet many of us do it, as I have done it, with many a self-serving explanation and no valid excuse.

The Virtues of Fairness in New Zealand

Vernacular ideas of fairness in New Zealand also entail many practical virtues in daily lives. As we have found, fairness operates as both a procedural and a substantive idea. In its substantive meaning, the idea of fairness entails the *virtue of not taking undue advantage of others*. It operates as a restraint on power in all its forms. It asks no more—and no less—from ourselves than we would ask of others. In substantive terms, fairness means fair shares, which are not necessarily equal shares. It is the idea of an outcome that is proportionate to what one deserves.

That idea in turn inspires *the virtue of reciprocity*, which in its ethical meaning is akin to the Golden Rule. Fairness is about doing unto others as we would have them do unto us. It also means that we can ask no more of others than we would have them ask of us. In its procedural meanings, the idea of fairness means *the practical virtue of playing by the rules*. It is about settling differences by mutually accepted processes that are thought to be honest and impartial. More than that, fairness is about *the practical virtue of fair play*, which means something more than playing by the rules. It is about acting in a spirit that aspires to right conduct, straight dealing, honest talk, and impartial judgment. Most of all, fair play is an attitude, as well as an act. In all of these ways, substantive and procedural, the idea of fairness is about the *practical virtue of decency* in the ways that we treat others and expect to be treated.

Vices of Fairness in New Zealand: The Tall Poppy Syndrome

The ethical idea of fairness, with all its many virtues, has sometimes been corrupted into a set of attendant vices. One such vice has been so widely perceived in New Zealand that it has its own name in common speech. New Zealanders call it "the Tall Poppy Syndrome." It might be defined as envy or resentment of a person who is conspicuously successful, exceptionally gifted, or unusually creative.

More than that, it sometimes became a more general attitude of outright hostility to any sort of excellence, distinction, or high achievement—especially achievement that requires mental effort, sustained industry, or applied intelligence. All this is linked to a mistaken idea of fairness as a broad and even-handed distribution of mediocrity. The possession of extraordinary gifts is perceived as unfair by others who lack them. Those who not only possess them but insist on exercising them have sometimes been punished for it.[22]

New Zealand lexicographers believe that *tall poppy* is an Australian expression, which appears in the *Australian National Dictionary* with examples as early as 1902. It is also widely used in New Zealand, where it has given rise to a proper noun, an adjective, and even a verb. Successful people are called "poppies," and when abused for their success they are said to be "poppied" by envious others. In 1991, a Wellington newspaper reported that successful businessmen "are being 'tall-poppied' by other New Zealanders."[23]

We were told by many people in New Zealand that the Tall Poppy Syndrome is not as strong as it used to be, and that it never applied to all forms of achievement. One New Zealander observes that "there's no such thing as a tall poppy playing rugby."[24] Nearly all New Zealanders take pride in the music of Dame Kiri Te Kanawa and in the mountaineering of Sir Edmund Hillary, who were rarely tall-poppied.[25]

But other bright and creative New Zealanders have been treated with cruelty by compatriots who appear to feel that there is something fundamentally unfair about better brains or creative gifts, and still more so about a determination to use them. This attitude is linked to a bizarre and destructive corruption of fairness, in which talented young people are perceived as tall poppies and are severely persecuted. Perhaps the most deleterious work of the Tall Poppy Syndrome is done in schoolyards and classrooms among the young. In any society, nothing is more destructive than the persecution of children because they exercise gifts that others lack.[26] It discourages not only excellence itself but the striving for excellence. Taken to an extreme, the great good that is fairness can become an evil, and even a sin—one of the Seven Deadly Sins, which is the sin of envy.

Vices of Fairness: "Turnabout Is Fair Play"

Another vice of fairness rises from the idea that one ill turn deserves another. Among schoolyard bullies, the argument is made that it is only fair for big children to abuse little ones, because the bigger children were themselves abused when very small. This form of *lex talionis*, the rule of retaliation, tends to become unfair in several ways at once. It is common, even normal, for retaliation to fall on an innocent third party who was not responsible for the original act of unfairness. Many examples abound in the history of vengeance. Another form of unfairness occurs when an eye for an eye becomes two eyes for an eye, and the original act of unfairness is continuously compounded. In *The Life and Uncommon Adventures of Captain Dudley Bradstreet* (1755), a character framed a phrase for this attitude: "Turnabout is fair play."

Vices of Fairness: "Done by Lunch"

Another vice sometimes appears in a society where fairness and justice are thought to guarantee everyone a steady job and fixed wage without regard to merit or achievement. One result is that there is no reward for industry or penalty for sloth. Another is that some lazy people ride on other people's backs. In the mid-twentieth century this pattern was observed repeatedly in New Zealand by visitors from other countries.

Evidence appears in survey research and interviews of emigrants from the United Kingdom who settled in New Zealand in the period from 1946 to 1975. They were amazed by attitudes toward work that they found in their new country. Megan Hutching did the interviews. She writes, "Many recall being told to slow down because they were working too hard." One immigrant said to her, "English people were used to working harder," and in New Zealand "my day's work was done by lunchtime." Another commented on the "slower pace of life." A third remembered that New Zealanders worked very slowly at their regular jobs, then hurried home and toiled at a terrific rate in their "leisure" hours.[27]

Others from abroad made similar observations. American servicemen in World War II were astonished by work habits of New Zealand "wharfies," stevedores who worked in Wellington harbor. In the summer of 1942, United States Marines were frantically preparing for their assault on Guadalcanal in the Solomon Islands and were combat-loading their supplies and gear in transports and cargo ships. Lieutenant Colonel Merrill B. Twining, the division operations officer, remembered that even in this moment of high urgency the Wellington wharfies worked very slowly, and often not at all. Twining wrote in his memoir that the wharfies were "a likeable, manly group," but "there was a constant series of strikes, or work stoppages, as they called them. None were serious or of long duration, but in total they had the effect of slowing unloading operations to a snail's pace. 'Raining' and 'they hadn't got their mackintoshes' were favorite reasons for ceasing operations. The ships furnished refreshments to the night shift. They enjoyed the way we made our coffee. Then came the night I was notified, 'They're off the job again. They want tea instead of coffee.' We had none. More time lost. The highest daily record was fourteen strikes in twenty-four hours."[28]

These accounts are not much in evidence during the early years of the country's history or in our own time. They happened mostly in a middle period of New Zealand's history from the late nineteenth through the mid-twentieth century. The question is why. One part of the answer was a corruption of an ethic of fairness. It appeared in the idea that to be required or even expected to work hard for others or for everybody or even for oneself is very unfair. The root of it was a desire to share the benefits of a fair society without fully sharing its burdens or responsibilities.

Open societies that center on liberty and freedom function differently in that respect. By comparison, many studies show that Americans work very hard at their jobs, harder than most people, too hard for their health and happiness. They work longer hours, take shorter vacations, and often do it by choice—most of all when they are working for themselves. A British visitor who stayed with us was appalled by what he called the American obsession with work. "Why is everyone so driven?" he asked.

Not everyone is driven in America. One finds idleness in protected jobs, and in some (not many) possessors of tenure in universities, and among idle members of what Thomas Jefferson called America's tinsel aristocracy. But even within American groups who do not have to labor for a living, one finds that most people are hard workers and constant strivers.

The key difference may not be an ethic of work itself, as Max Weber believed, but rather an ethic of striving. Why do people strive? For materialists it is about the size of the rewards. Americans strive hard in a system of free enterprise, because they have material incentives for striving. But they also have moral incentives. Surveys also show that for all the complaints of critics, most Americans like much of their work and find personal reward in it. They believe that striving will make their lives better, and help others as well. Not all Americans think this way, but many do.

Attitudes were different in New Zealand during the mid-twentieth century, where visitors observed that striving was "not on." People who tended to strive hard to get ahead were not admired. It ran against the grain. Another part of it may have been a feeling that demands to bear the burdens of fair society are themselves unfair. The virtues of fairness can turn into vices when they are not balanced by other values.

Remedies: Fairness Tempered by Liberty and Freedom

Since 1984, New Zealanders have made a concerted effort to add more liberty and freedom to their deep concern for fairness. This was the purpose of the many reforms by both Labour and National governments. Economic restructuring was a movement toward privatization, free markets, and free enterprise, which revolutionized the New Zealand economy. But at the same time, most reformers in New Zealand also cherished their heritage of fairness.

The New Zealand Constitution and its first Bill of Rights expanded ideas of individual liberty. New Zealanders also enlarged their ideas of freedom in many important ways. The movement for Maori rights borrowed from the American civil rights movement and was very creative in its own acts. The three waves of New Zealand's feminists expanded the rights of women. At the same time, New Zealanders worked to preserve traditions of fairness and even to enlarge them. One example is proportional representation in Parliament, which was thought to be more fair than the "first past the post" system. Another is New Zealand's Accident Compensation Commission, which is thought to be more fair than the American tort system. In short, New Zealanders have been trying to create a better balance among liberty, freedom, and fairness by enlarging these ideas.

Remedies: Liberty and Freedom Tempered by Fairness

Americans restructured their institutions in a different spirit. With much urging from libertarian conservatives and neoclassical economists, the great republic shifted away from freedom as a right of belonging in a free society and toward an idea of liberty as an individual's right to be left alone by government and to have more complete control of property.

This tendency developed rapidly in the administrations of Ronald Reagan and the senior George Bush. It appeared in some of the New Democratic politics of Bill Clinton, who attempted to combine free-market economics with a social conscience. It continued in more extreme forms during the administration of the younger George Bush.

But while this was happening in Washington, popular currents began to flow in a different direction. In the summer of 1998, for example, a reporter for the *Wall Street Journal* interviewed John Mariotti, a prosperous business consultant in Knoxville, Tennessee. Mr. Mariotti had done well for himself. He was sitting on the back porch of his affluent home with a view of a lake, and a Mercedes in his driveway. But the reporter found Mr. Mariotti in a pensive mood, reflecting on the "unfairness of life." What outraged Mariotti was that other Americans had more than he did, and deserved it less. The reporter found that "amid the economic boom, many of the 'Haves' envy the 'Have Mores.'" The reporter talked to Barry Dichter, a partner in a "white shoe" law firm. By comparison with most people, Mr. Dichter had a princely income. But he was unhappy that others had bigger incomes without earning them. "There are a lot of lucky lightning strikes going on," he said.[29]

In San Francisco, psychoanalyst Mark Levy had done very well by most measures. Then he read that a young founder of Yahoo! had made a billion dollars, and it ruined Dr. Levy's day. "Here I am about to go to work on a holiday," Dr. Levy complained, "and I'm reading about a guy who is 31 and a billionaire. I don't know these kids. Maybe they're not so happy. But it's hard to stomach this kind of discrepancy. . . . Where is the justice in this?" Here was a very American conception of unfairness as an idea of relative deprivation of exceptional advantages.[30]

It was also the dawning of a consciousness among people (even those who had done very well) that the American system is gloriously free (and we cherish our liberty and freedom more than ever), but it is not very fair. There was also a growing idea that the politics of both parties, in the era of Bush and Clinton and Bush again, and Obama too, had made an unfair system even less fair than it had been before.

The American system has greatly expanded its ideas of liberty and freedom, and it has succeeded remarkably in mediating between competing ideas of what it means to be free. But we have not done well with fairness. A few political leaders have appealed to this idea of fairness, with mixed results. From time to time fairness has become very prominent in American public life, as it did in Lincoln's presidency, and those of Theodore Roosevelt and Woodrow Wilson. Another such moment was the era of Franklin Roosevelt, when much was made of an idea of fairness in the New Deal. A third was the presidency of Harry Truman, which converted the New Deal into the Fair Deal. But after the departure of Truman, fairness faded rapidly in American public life. Comparatively little was heard of it in a public way from the mid-1960s to the early 1990s.

And yet American attitudes are changing yet again. Even in partisan exchanges, both sides speak not merely of fairness but of fundamental fairness, which elevates the idea into a moral principle that is a foundation of social ethics. That idea has been growing in the twenty-first century.

And something else has been changing in the material condition of the United States. After four centuries, Americans are also running against the limits. The old feeling of boundlessness is not so strong. Studies find that many Americans who work for large corporations have either lost their jobs in the recent past or fear that they might lose them in the near future. This is increasingly the case with highly paid workers in top jobs, such as senior executives in corporations and partners in law firms. There is also a very widespread feeling that jobs can be lost without regard to merit or achievements. More Americans are awakening to the discovery that their economic system may be free, but it is deeply unfair in substantive and procedural ways.

Some Americans have accepted unfairness in a fatalistic way, while they are prepared to fight to the death for their freedom and liberty. We return to John Kennedy's famous pronouncement, "Life is unfair." One might ask, must the cosmic unfairness of our condition be compounded by our own acts? This great question is expanding every day in the press, in the media, and throughout American life. As it does so, Americans have much to learn from New Zealanders about their ideas of fairness, and about their experience of combining it with liberty and freedom.

Learning to Be Fair and Free

In actual operation, freedom and liberty and fairness can be mutually reinforcing. Each of these ideas has the power to reinforce the other's virtues and correct its vices. In regard to liberty and freedom, something has gone profoundly right in America. These great ideas are spreading rapidly around the world, and changing as they grow. Many nations in the past generation have invented for themselves fundamental laws that enlarge and protect freedom and liberty in various ways. Democracy also has been spreading around the world. Models of free enterprise and mixed enterprise have been multiplying in every nation, never twice the same way.

At the same time, something else has also gone profoundly right in New Zealand. Ideas of fairness are highly developed here—perhaps more so than anywhere else in the world, though Australians, Canadians, and Britons may disagree. This not to argue that life in New

Zealand is always fair, or that Americans are always free. But the idea of fairness, like liberty and freedom, is itself an artifact of high importance. Many generations of New Zealanders have tried to make that idea work. On the subject of fairness, no nation in the world has more to teach than New Zealand; and no country has more to learn than the United States.

It is interesting how children in New Zealand are taught about fairness. One of the most effective teachers was Sir Edmund Hillary. He and his Nepalese companion, Tenzing, were the first people who are known to have reached the summit of Mount Everest. For that achievement, and still more for the spirit in which it was done, Hillary and Tenzing became heroes throughout the world. New Zealanders also admire these men in another way, for their integrity, character, decency, and fairness.

In 1987, New Zealand's Parliament founded the Hillary Commission, with Sir Edmund as its namesake. Its explicit purpose was to "promote fair play and good sporting behavior while discouraging a win-at-all costs attitude among children." It concerned itself not only with conduct on the playing field but more broadly with the extension of fair play to social relations in general. The Hillary Commission and its successors sponsored a "Fairplay Programme" and "Don't Get Ugly" campaigns in 95 percent of New Zealand's schools. In its first ten years it reached 120,000 teachers. More than a million students studied fairness, and learned about it.[31]

‚ Our own learning process started in Auckland, with a welcoming ceremony at a Maori marae. In these meeting places, the wooden rafters are often painted with haunting designs in great swirls of line and color. Their complex geometry expresses the play of opposites— male and female, earth and sky, dark and light—which are fundamental to Polynesian thought. Something similar has happened in Western thinking, with its founding ideas of community and individual, opportunity and security, liberty and justice, freedom and fairness. But these pairs are not opposites. "Fair" and "free" are two ideas that are useful as ways of reinforcing each other. After titanic struggles against many forms of tyranny and cruelty, the world today is slowly learning to be free and fair. In New Zealand and the United States, many generations have been learning from the experience of those who came before them. So might we.

APPENDIX

Fairness in Other Disciplines

THIS BOOK IS THE FIRST TO BE PUBLISHED on the history of fairness. It will not be the last, in large part because of the progress of knowledge in other fields. During the late twentieth century, fairness became a problem of growing importance in many learned disciplines. The result has been an outpouring of research and analysis. The purpose of this appendix is to explore that expanding literature in its relevance to the history of fairness. At the same time, it suggests several ways in which historical inquiry might contribute to the progress of knowledge in some of the following fields.

A. Linguistics: Fairness as a Problem of Language
B. Moral Philosophy: Fairness as a Problem of Ethics
C. Behavioral Sciences: Is Fairness an Animal Instinct?
D. Genetics and Evolution: The Uses of Reciprocal Altruism?
E. Brain Research: A Neuroscience of Fair Play?
F. Social and Cultural Sciences: Fairness in Cross-Cultural Research
G. Economics: Fairness and Free Markets
H. Mathematics and Folk Rituals of Fairness: The Problem of Fair Division

A. Linguistics: Fairness as a Problem of Language

"What are we saying when we say that something is fair?" Thus experimental economist Bart Wilson frames one of many linguistic questions about *fair* and *fairness*.[1] Wilson draws on the work of Anna Wierzbicka, an historical linguist at Australian National University. In 2006 she published an important essay, "Being FAIR: Another Key Anglo Value and Its Cultural Underpinnings." Wilson himself and other scholars have joined in a creative discussion of her pathbreaking work.[2]

Wierzbicka takes up the etymology of the words *fair* and *fairness*. She finds that they are "distinctly Anglo in origin" and "have no equivalents in other European languages (let alone non-European ones)." Our research confirms one major part of her conclusion but suggests a correction. Cognates for *fair* and *fairness* are not unique to early English. They have also turned up in old Frisian, Danish, Norwegian, and Icelandic, and long existed in those languages with meanings similar to English. It would be more accurate to say that these words have long been distinctive to a family of North European languages.[3]

Wierzbicka is correct in concluding that *fair* and *fairness* had no cognates or exact equivalents in most major modern languages before the mid-twentieth century, and that translation of these words from English is very difficult. She also notes that after 1945, *fair* and *fairness* were introduced as English borrowings into German, Dutch, colloquial French, Polish, Slovenian, and many other languages. In the twenty-first century *fair* and *fairness* are on their way to becoming universal in major languages throughout the world.[4]

This finding has opened a second linguistic question. Can vernacular ideas of *fair* and *fairness* be understood only by speakers of English? Linguistic bloggers on Wierzbicka's work have expressed impassioned opinions on many sides of this question. Some inquirers believe that understanding is not so narrowly constrained, but can be communicated (sometimes with difficulty) to speakers of another language.[5]

Many languages have contributed unique or distinctive words to the common linguistic stock of humankind. If we study the transmission of ideas that these words represent, we find clear evidence in this historical process that speakers of a given language can understand the meaning of words that come to them from other cultures. But in these linguistic transactions, we also observe that it is more difficult to explain or discuss terms such as *fair* or *fairness* in languages that do not have those elaborately embedded words, without very cumbersome processes of translation that often yield inaccurate results.

In much the same way, it is not easy to understand *Schadenfreude* in any language other than German, or *panache* in any language other than French, or *fairness* in any language other than English and its Norse cousins without using the original words as meaning units. The consequence is that all of these words have been introduced into other languages. English speakers have borrowed *Schadenfreude* and *panache*, much as German speakers after 1945 adopted *die Fairness* and French soccer fans cry *"pas le fair-play"* when something unfair is done to one of their players. In this linguistic borrowing we find evidence that words such as *fair* and *fairness* are understood across linguistic lines. We also find proof of the utility of the original word. Here historical inquiry can contribute to a solution of linguistic problems.[6]

The great anglophone family of *fairness* words has been changed, enlarged, reinvented, and put to many different uses by English-speaking and non-English-speaking people in the course of a very long history. This opens a third linguistic problem about the substantive meaning of *fair* and *fairness* as it changed through time and varied from one culture to another.

Wierzbicka offers a thoughtful model of historical change in the vernacular meaning of *fairness* among English speakers. She believes that the meaning of *fairness* in old English was very different from what it is today—that *fair* was used as a "general word of commendation," that our ethical meaning appeared in the eighteenth century as "an artifact of modern Anglo culture," and that "the familiar twentieth-century sense of *unfair* (as for example, in *unfair competition*) emerged and spread widely only in the nineteenth century."[7]

Here again, research for this book yielded findings that confirmed Wierzbicka's model in some ways and contradicted it in others. In Old Norse and Anglo-Saxon uses, *fagr* was indeed often used as "a general word of commendation." But linguists have found that specific ethical meanings coexisted with this one at an early date. For example, Mark Liberman studied uses of *fair* and *fairness* in sources such as LION. He discovered that something very similar to our range of modern ethical meaning for *fair* was well established as early as the fifteenth century. Liberman gathered examples from the poetry of John Skelton (1460–1529):

> Play fayre play, madame, and loke ye play clene
> Or ells with gret shame your game wylbe sene.

And from the verse of Robert Henryson (1430–1499?):

> Whether call ye this fair play, or nocht
> To set your maister in sa fell effray.

Other examples appeared in early ballads of Robin Hood (1100–1470)

> Arise, arise, proud fellow,
> And thou shalt have faire play

Liberman also finds many passages in Shakespeare's poetry and plays where *fair* and *fairness* had a broad range of moral meanings. Clearly the ethical uses that some writers have judged to be a response to modernity were common and customary in English usage at an earlier date.[8] Wierzbicka also suggests that procedural meanings of *fairness* and *fair* are the key to modern usage. But a growing range of examples indicates that these words had both substantive and procedural applications in early medieval England.

Historical evidence also suggests that uses of *fair* and *fairness* did change in other ways during the late eighteenth and early nineteenth centuries. These words became more nearly universal in their range of reference, more systemic in their meaning, and yet more varied in their applications. They became more elaborately substantive and procedural in many particular ways. In the twentieth century *fair* and *fairness* increasingly developed a broad and very complex range of highly technical meanings that are specific to particular modern disciplines, professions, and fields of endeavor. In that evidence we find confirmation of Wierzbicka's hypothesis that *fair* and *fairness* have become more useful in modern social systems and more widely used in cultures of growing complexity.[9]

And yet even as *fair* and *fairness* changed in these complex ways, they also preserved a core of vernacular meaning that emerged as early as the fifteenth century, and in some respects a millennium earlier. We have a striking paradox here. *Fair* and *fairness* are very old words with long-established ethical meanings. But they have also been continuously renewed through at least seven centuries and are increasingly useful in modern open societies. The pattern of linguistic change in these meanings was not revolutionary or evolutionary but involutionary. It changed, by becoming more elaborately the same. In that process, *fairness* has become increasingly useful in the modern world for several reasons. Its double meaning as a substantive and procedural term is helpful in many ways. So also is what Wierzbicka calls its relational meaning, which makes it increasingly relevant to problems of pluralist cultures and individuated societies. *Fairness* and *fair* also have become increasingly useful as a meta-ethic. Its range and flexibility allow it to mediate among different ethics, and to promote their coexistence without diminishing their distinct meaning. In that way it can also mediate between different ideas of right and wrong in pluralist societies and can help to integrate them into a complex modern culture while at the same respecting their integrity.

Another closely related linguistic problem centers on the meaning of *fair* and *fairness* in their relation to other ethical terms. Wierzbicka, Wilson, and I took different disciplinary approaches to this question, and all of us came to similar conclusions. We found that *fairness*, *justice*, and *equity* have fundamentally different core meanings in English usage. All refer to ideas of right conduct. In my understanding (Wierzbicka, Wilson, and others disagree in detail), *justice* refers to an idea of law (*ius*); *equity* to principles of even or equal treatment in some respect (*aequitas*); and *fairness* to not taking undue advantage of others in rivalries, conflicts, or competitions (*faegernyss*, before AD 1000).

Patterns of actual use are complex. In English usage, words such as *justice*, *equity* and *fairness* tend to overlap, and in other languages they sometimes coincide, but meaning-patterns in English have distinctly different centers.[10] It is interesting that meanings of *fair* and *fairness* did not emerge from a single text or treatise. They developed historically within a very broad vernacular process where all of us were more creative than any one of us.

B. Moral Philosophy: Fairness as a Problem of Ethics

Philosophers have written at length about liberty, freedom, equality, justice, and equity. But they showed remarkably little interest in the study of fairness until the work of John Bordley Rawls. He was a philosopher in the American grain and a believing Christian, born and raised in a big Maryland family with deep roots in that border state between the North and South, where cousins and neighbors, blue and gray, found ways to coexist. They did so while maintaining very deep differences, by preserving an indispensable sense of fairness in their dealings with one another.

Perhaps that capsule history may explain why John Bordley Rawls devoted himself to major problems of moral philosophy, and how he chose to deal with a problem of justice that had engaged many philosophers before him. He was not happy with the utilitarian ethics of Jeremy Bentham, who argued for the greatest good for the greatest number, as if everyone were an interchangeable part, and he did not accept the ethics of Karl Marx, who submerged individuals into masses and classes. These were very un-Maryland ways of thinking.

In place of Utilitarianism and Marxism, John Rawls invented another theory of justice that was more in the tradition of Locke, Hume, and Kant but went beyond it as ethical problems in the new world of America reached far beyond old Europe. In 1971, he published *A Theory of Justice*, which moved the entire field in a new direction. Rawls began with the idea of the "inviolability" of each individual person, which "even the welfare of society as a whole cannot override." On that basis he argued passionately for an idea of moral philosophy as justice to individuals, in two ways. The first was the "principle of greatest equal liberty" in which "each person is to have an equal right to the most extensive basic liberty compatible with a similar liberty for others." The second was "the principle of (fair) equality of opportunity [*sic*]." Rawls called these two ideas fairness. It was an apposition that was useful to his inquiries but different from most vernacular meanings of *fairness* and *fair*.[11]

Rawls was deeply interested in the problem of distributive justice, as it is called in his field. He believed that "while the distribution of wealth and income need not be equal, it must be to everyone's advantage." To that end he devised a thought-experiment in which people would come together and operate behind a "veil of ignorance" as to their own interests. All individuals in that "original position" would be asked to choose an idea of fairness in distributive justice without regard to their own condition. Rawls felt confident that they would agree to his idea of "fair distribution," which would not seek equal shares for everyone but would maximize the size of the minimal share. This he called a "maximin" principle of fairness.

The work of John Rawls has many strengths. It addressed central problems of moral philosophy in a serious and thoughtful manner. It did so in a highly original way, on the basis of a mastery of major work in his field. The first edition of *A Theory of Justice* was a dense philosophical treatise that sold more than two hundred thousand copies and has been translated into more than twenty languages. During the late twentieth century it moved to the center of moral philosophy and had a major impact on other fields.

Colleagues celebrated and criticized it in equal measure. Robert Nozick and other conservative libertarians criticized Rawls from the right, and argued that justice as fairness should give more attention to liberty, freedom, and individual rights of rich and middling people, as well as to the welfare of the poorest people.[12] Egalitarian critics from the left complained that Rawls had given too much attention to liberty and too little to equality.[13] A third critique was the communitarian approach of Amitai Etzioni and his vision of a fair society as a "three-legged stool," which sought to combine the private and public purposes of right and left, with a unifying idea of community.[14] Another triadic approach was Peter Corning's idea of fair society that combined equality (for basic needs), equity (for rewards to merit), and reciprocity.[15]

Other moral philosophers such as Charles Taylor, Michael Sandel, and Alasdair MacIntyre challenged the assumption in Rawls's "veil of ignorance" that people could or should make major ethical choices without regard to their own values and interests. These colleagues argued that justice and fairness should respect the variety of cultural beliefs, the integrity of many different sets of moralities, and the diversity of interests in modern communities.[16]

Sustained critiques of Rawls also came from Marxists who insisted that his theory of justice did not understand the material basis of injustice in capitalist systems. Feminists urged more attention to issues of justice in private as well as public transactions. Economists objected to the maximin idea and asserted the absolute priority of untrammeled liberty and freedom in free markets, which they regarded as fundamental to any system of social ethics. Another school of political theorists called Straussians wanted more attention to fundamental ideas of absolute natural rights.[17]

Yet another line of criticism was more empirical. Experimental economists designed several games to test ethical choices by individual players. One game was played by forty-four groups of students in three universities. Each individual player was put in John Rawls's "original position" and asked to choose from among different models of distributive justice. One option was Rawls's maximin model, which he had hoped that all would approve. It was rejected unanimously by all forty-four groups. Other studies found that most respondents also rejected the idea of distributive justice as equal shares. They did so not because their material interests were opposed to these ideas but because the players genuinely believed that equal shares were unfair. They also did not agree that distributive justice could be left to a free market. Most of these players thought that unitary solutions were incomplete. They tended to favor complex solutions that mediated among different ideas of fairness.[18]

To study vernacular ideas of what is fair in New Zealand and the United States is to find that people do not understand fairness or justice as a single unitary idea. They think of it as something more complex: procedural and substantive. They tend to define it in different substantive ways but are more apt to share procedural thinking. Fairness was usually thought to require honesty, candor, and openness. It was also sometimes understood as an ethic that can be used to reconcile competing ideas of right and wrong, in ways that contending parties could accept as legitimate, without determining a particular outcome.[19]

John Rawls himself became increasingly aware of this complexity, and progressively more comfortable with it, border-state Marylander that he was. His theory of justice as fairness might be understood not as a fixed position but as a dynamic process. In later works, he moved closer to vernacular ideas of fairness and tended to embrace their diversity. The refinement of philosophical thinking on fairness and the progress of historical research have thus moved on converging lines. Some moral philosophers as individuals still dream of finding the true idea of justice and fairness that works always and everywhere. But moral philosophers as a group have embraced many ideas of justice in an open-ended way. There is truth and wisdom in that larger process.[20]

C. Behavioral Sciences: Is Fairness an Animal Instinct?

Through the twentieth century, students of animal behavior began to explore the subject of fairness in another way. They closely observed the conduct of monkeys, chimpanzees, apes, dogs, birds, insects, vampire bats, and other species. In one set of experiments, Frans de Waal found that capuchin monkeys rejected inequitable rewards with a display of anger and were "not profit-maximizing," in his phrase. Many of these inquiries concluded that animals had an innate sense of "inequity aversion," as de Waal called it.[21]

Similar results were reported from experiments on dogs by a team of Austrian scientists and from studies of chimpanzees by Richard Wrangham. Journalists covered these findings and proclaimed that "monkeys have a sense of fairness" and "dogs seem to know what's fair." Some writers concluded from this research that an idea of "fairness" was an instinct among animals of many species.[22]

Other scientists in the same field have pointed to problems in this research. Experimenters had no difficulty in demonstrating that animals of many species are unhappy about receiving smaller shares, but no animal in their experiments appears to have objected to a larger one. Their responses do not demonstrate the existence of abstract ideas of equity, or justice, or fairness. Those principles operate on another level of altruism that does not appear in this research.[23]

Waal agrees that his monkeys "did not seem to follow a fairness *norm*" and never gave away food "to equalize distribution." But he hypothesized that other species may have taken the next step. He writes, "For apes, on the other hand, we cannot rule out a fairness norm." And chimpanzee mothers have been observed to break a stick in half and give pieces equally to their offspring.[24]

Other scientists have reviewed these experiments and challenged some of those inferences. Evolutionary biologist Marc Bekoff questioned the conclusion in some of these studies that animals were giving evidence of moral altruism and "inequity aversion." But he also suggested a mediating possibility. Bekoff writes that in most cases animals "are responding negatively to being treated less well" but are also "picking up on what being treated less well means, and that's really important."[25]

D. Genetics and Evolution: The Uses of Reciprocal Altruism?

A related approach was taken by Robert Trivers, who developed a model of "reciprocal altruism" in animal species. His idea of altruism differs from that of moral philosophers who understand it as a selfless concern for others.[26] The prevailing model of reciprocal altruism in animals is commonly understood as behavior that seeks gain from cooperative effort. Since Peter Kropotkin's research as early as 1900 on cooperation among animals, scientists have found many instances of reciprocal altruism in this sense, and in a vast variety of animal species. Some of the most dramatic examples appear in marine mammals such as porpoises who swim for long periods beneath others of the same species who are ill or in peril, supporting them near the surface so that they can continue to breathe. Many terrestrial animals adopt orphans or strays of their own or other species in the same spirit.[27]

Birds, mammals, and other creatures often sound warnings when predators approach—an action that makes others more safe but causes individuals who give warning calls to become more vulnerable. Animals also instinctively feed one another—a familiar pattern among parents and children of many species. A much discussed example is that of vampire bats, who regurgitate fresh blood and give it to adults in the same group.[28]

Some varieties of carnivorous and predatory animals do not prey on others who are very young, or on animals of a different gender, or on creatures that are protected in various special ways. This behavior has been observed among animal families, groups of various sizes, and entire species.[29]

Insect groups also have highly developed patterns of cooperative behavior, as E. O. Wilson has found in his work on ants. But he and others have pointed out that cooperation is not the same as altruism, reciprocal or otherwise. One could, for example, observe on slaveholding plantations in the antebellum American South instances of masters and slaves who cooperated in various ways. But that sort of cooperation was a coerced and exploitative relationship. It has very little to do with principles of fairness, or equity, or justice, nor was it truly reciprocal or altruistic in any ethical sense. The same distinction would apply to selfless behavior in ants.

Among primates there are clearly instances of forms of truly reciprocal altruism that appear to be grounded in something like equity, justice, or even fairness. An example would be troops of baboons, monkeys or chimpanzees that take turns grooming one another in evenhanded ways. Other individual animals in examples cited above have been observed to sacrifice themselves for the survival of their group. Some have interpreted these actions as genetically driven for the purpose of preserving a species or its genes. This has given rise to a large literature, notably Richard Dawkins's classic work, *The Selfish Gene*. Other scholars such as Stephen Jay Gould have challenged his interpretation and argued that genes are not active drivers but "passive recorders" of evolution.[30]

An historian wonders if a balance might be found among rival interpretations in this field of inquiry. One might conclude that something like reciprocal altruism is clearly evident in many animals, that its consequences are in some ways functional for the survival of a species, and that these patterns of cooperation and reciprocity are in some cases similar to acts of altruism among humans. But these behavioral forms of reciprocal altruism are not the same as perceptions of fairness, equity, or justice, which rise to perceptions of disinterested abstraction that operate on another plane. Recent research by Michael Tomasello at the Max Planck Institute for Evolutionary Anthropology finds evidence that two-year-old human children are naturally and uniquely cooperative, with what appears to be a combination of innate and learned behavior. As they mature in groups, they respond to expectations that encourage or discourage cooperation in various forms. In that process we learn to model or guide our actions on abstract ideas of fairness, equity, justice, freedom, and liberty, and sometimes on opposite abstractions. Tomasello finds that human children differ from other species in that respect, and also from one another.[31]

Other scientists such as Martin Nowak have developed evolutionary models for many species that center not on competition but cooperation. He argues that cooperation is fundamental to the evolution of complexity, and that selfless behavior in forms such as reciprocity, generosity, and kindness are fundamental to cooperative effort. Nowak does not discuss fairness, but he might have done so. Ideas of fair play might be understood as a cooperative way to promote competition and vice versa: a competitive way to promote cooperation. One might take the inquiry to another level by hypothesizing that it is not competition or cooperation alone that is the key here but their dynamic interaction. This may help us to understand why ideas of fairness become more important as systems grow more complex.[32]

E. Brain Research: A Neuroscience of Fair Play?

Other inquiries are advancing very rapidly today in the new field of neuroscience. Researchers have discovered the existence of neural networks in the human brain that appear to have some connection to selfish and selfless thinking. A network called the mesolimbic reward pathway has been linked to the pursuit of material gain, and also to responses to food and sex. Other parts of the brain in the subgenual cortex and the adjacent septal region have connections to selfless actions, charitable giving, and social affiliation. These descriptive patterns have been replicated in many studies.[33]

Other neuroscientists have begun to think in terms of a system of moral reasoning in general, and even an ethic of fairness in particular, which may be deeply rooted in the structure of the human brain and operative in its neural processes. A leader in this work is Donald Pfaff, a neurobiologist and author of *The Neuroscience of Fair Play: Why We (Usually) Follow the Golden Rule*. Pfaff draws a strong conclusion from his own inquiries into the human brain. He writes: "I believe that we are wired to behave in an ethical manner toward others, and they toward us. But with all the life-supporting functions that the brain handles from one millisecond to the next, only a few are likely to be capable of sparking an ethical response. These must be circuits crucial to our survival." He thinks that this cerebral process happens not in a particular part of the brain but in the entire operation of its complex circuitry.[34]

Another neuroscientist, Joshua Greene, has reported evidence that some particular regions of the brain become active when one is making ethical choices.[35] One such area has been described as "the cleft behind the center of the forehead," which appears to be involved in feelings of empathy for others. Another is a part of the brain in back of the ear, "which is involved in gathering information about others." A third and fourth are the posterior cingulate and the precuneus, which are linked to strong emotions. This work is more serious and substantive than it appears in summaries for nonscientists. We should not dismiss it out of hand.[36]

Several neuroscientists have gone yet another way and suggested the existence of a "moral instinct," or even a "moral faculty," which may be part of the human brain.[37] Intellectual historians have heard some of these ideas before. They remember physiological models of moral faculties in pseudosciences such as phrenology that were in vogue during the nineteenth century. One might wonder about the empirical strength of imputed connections that would link the structure and function of the brain to substantive patterns of thought or belief, especially in a determinist way. But this work is still in its infancy, and it is advancing rapidly. It should be received with respect. The portals in our own brains should remain open to these possibilities.

F. The Social Sciences: Fairness in Cross-Cultural Studies

If ideas of fairness and fair-minded acts are instinctive in origin, behavioral in nature, genetic in drivers, and deeply embedded in the structure of our brains, one might expect to find them widely distributed and similar in form and function. This question has been tested by another empirical method of cross-cultural research on ethics in general and fairness in particular among human populations. Many studies have been completed. Most of them yield results that are broadly similar in two ways.[38]

First, they find that most cultures and societies have what we have called vernacular ideas of right conduct such as fairness, justice, equity, or other forms of altruism. These values have been found in most human groups. Second, these values themselves vary widely from one culture to another, and the pattern of variance is complex in substance and detail. One study of four developed Pacific nations finds that people in China and South Korea value distributive justice very highly but are less concerned about interactive justice. In the United States and Japan it is the other way around. People in these various societies assign different priorities to substantive and procedural fairness.[39]

Other cross-cultural studies by region in Canada and the United States have found that most people value some degree of fairness as distributive justice. But frequencies and intensities of concern for fairness, equity, and justice have varied broadly from one region to another. One study found that the highest intensity of concern for distributive justice appeared in the province of Manitoba, which in the 1980s elected socialist leaders. The lowest intensity of concern for distributive justice was in the state of Florida, which gave strong support to conservative leaders.[40]

Other studies of individual human subjects have found that the quality and intensity of "inequity aversion" in general, and "fairness" in particular, are highly variable from one group to another and are culturally constructed in some degree. These research projects, unlike others on chimpanzees, monkeys, and dogs, strongly suggest that ideas of fairness in human societies are actively studied, modeled, abstracted, taught, learned, and deliberately chosen, at least in some degree.

Partly in response to behavioral and genetic models of fairness, a large team of social scientists led by Joseph Henrich designed an experiment to measure the strength of ideas of fairness in different types of societies. They developed a variant of the game called Dictator, a familiar tool of teaching and research in economics and social sciences. Their purpose was to measure the strength of fairness, operationally defined as "inequity-aversion," hostility to selfishness, and propensity to share with others.

Henrich's team studied responses of 2,100 people who lived in fifteen societies throughout the world. The societies were chosen to represent different stages of social development. They included populations of hunter-gatherers, marine foragers, horticulturalists, pastoralists, farmers, wage-workers, and others who lived in highly developed commercial and industrial economies.[41]

The study found that ideas of fairness and sharing among families and small groups existed in many groups. But qualitative forms and quantitative intensities varied from one group to another in a patterned way. As social units became larger and more complex in their economic systems of production and exchange, and stronger in religious beliefs, their members tended to become increasingly willing to share with strangers and to treat others fairly.[42]

From this evidence the researchers concluded that fairness was not hardwired into the human condition in a behavioral or genetic or neural way but had developed in a process of cultural and social evolution, driven by the evolutionary change of social systems themselves. Henrich observed, "You can't get the effects we're seeing from genes. These are things you learn as a consequence of growing up in a particular place."[43]

Historical inquiries yield confirming evidence in some respects. The history of the words *fair* and *fairness* as ethical terms also find a pattern of change from what one scholar has called "tribal brotherhood to universal otherhood," much as Henrich and his team concluded. But these inquiries have yielded different patterns of timing, sequence, and cause. Some intellectual and religious historians date early evidence of that movement from the spread of Christianity, or from other universal religions that began to appear as early as the fifth century before the Christian era. Other work finds a second movement with the growth of humanism, the Enlightenment, and evangelical religion in the modern era.[44]

Brandon Keim summarizes an anthropological literature on this subject in another way. He writes, "Kindness towards strangers is a baffling human trait, given that strangers appear to have been treated with suspicion and violence for most of human history." But then, as Keim puts it, "something changed." Small family-based groups formed hunter-gatherer tribes. With the advent of agriculture, tribes gave way to city-states, and then to nation-states. Some anthropologists say all this was only possible because people were willing to treat total strangers in a manner once reserved for kin.[45]

G. Economics and Political Economy: A Problem of Fairness and Free Markets

Another important literature on fairness and justice has developed in economics, and it has changed remarkably through time. In the mid-nineteenth century, questions of justice (more than fairness) were at the center of what was then called political economy. But in the twentieth century, many economists (not all) lost interest in these issues, especially in the United States. Josh Hendrickson, an American academic economist, explains why he went that way. He observes that noneconomists are "often concerned with what is fair," particularly in regard to record profits for large corporations, and record prices for their customers. But he adds, "As an economist I do not care and neither should you. . . . [B]usinesses exist because they want to make a profit. Now I know that you may be thinking it is not fair that Exxon is making a record-high profit when American consumers are suffering from high prices at the pump. But who decides what is fair? . . . How do we define "fair" in terms of economics? . . . Economists do not believe in fairness because what is fair is not a science. . . . [R]eporters and politicians tend to focus their attention on fairness in order to appeal to those who fear they are being treated unfairly. Meanwhile economists recognize this effort as pointless."[46]

In the late twentieth century other American economists went different ways. Some of them revived the idea of political economy with a strong ethical content. One group centered their work on a single moral imperative, which was the principle of freedom. Some condemned the principle of fairness as fundamentally hostile to freedom. A leader was Milton Friedman. On the Fourth of July 1977, he published an essay titled "Fair versus Free," with particular attention to Fair Trade Laws and to the Fairness Doctrine, by which a liberal Federal Communications Commission in 1949 required broadcasting companies that covered controversial questions to provide "reasonable opportunities for contrasting views." Friedman argued against the Fairness Doctrine in the following propositions:

— There is no objective standard of "fairness."
— "Fairness" is strictly in the eye of the beholder.
— If speech must be fair, then it cannot also be free; someone must decide what is fair.
— It would have to be controlled by a government bureau.
— [Therefore,] when "fairness" replaces "freedom," all our liberties are in danger.[47]

Friedman misrepresented the Fairness Doctrine, which did not require that "speech must be fair," but rather that some speakers with different opinions should have a reasonable opportunity to be heard. During the Reagan administration, the Fairness Doctrine was abolished in 1987 by a conservative FCC.[48]

In the late twentieth century, Milton Friedman's views spread widely among libertarian conservatives and free-market economists. Recent empirical research finds that students majoring in economics in American universities tend to be more hostile to ideas of fairness than students with other majors; further, the more economics they study, the more hostile they become to fairness.[49]

More recently, other economists have taken more positive approaches to fairness. Some of this new work has been done within the framework of market-centered neoclassical economics. A large body of research has been done in the flourishing subfield of experimental economics. It seeks to establish prevailing ideas of fairness through game theory and survey research. These studies yield strong evidence that people bring to their economic transactions a set of normative values about fairness. Further, those projects find that these values can be observed empirically. They make a difference in the structure and function of markets.

One team found by survey research that perceptions of unfairness in the acts of marketers created inefficiencies in the operation of markets themselves. As markets were perceived to be more unfair, they grew less efficient, in part because people withdrew from what they believed to be rigged games. A leader in this research is Daniel Kahneman, a psychologist who won the Nobel Prize in Economics for applying the insights of one discipline to the progress of another.[50]

Other research has studied this problem in another way, by carefully observing the choices of individuals in surrogate markets that were developed as a form of very serious gaming. This method of inquiry produced very much the same result. Individual people made choices not always as profit-maximizing actors but sometimes on the basis of ideas of fairness. When they met instances of what they perceived to be gross unfairness, they withdrew from market transactions, or changed them, or punished unfair marketers in ways that made economic systems function less efficiently, or even kept them from operating at all.[51]

In short, fairness as a vernacular idea can be observed empirically and historically. It can also be observed to make a difference in the way that economic systems function. In short, unfairness sometimes may serve the interests of some people, but fairness serves us all. It is demonstrably so by materialist measures and rigorous empirical tests, to all but the most devoted believers in *Homo economicus* and the law of fang and claw.[52]

Another question of fairness in economics centers on the specific substantive issue of very high pay for top executives in large American corporations, which surged to unprecedented levels in the United States during the late twentieth century. The author remembers coming out a meeting of a nonprofit board in Boston with a group of CEOs in the 1990s. They were themselves very highly paid, but in the elevator the conversation turned to reports of much higher returns for other CEOS that had been reported that morning. They expressed high moral outrage.

Scholars and scientists in several disciplines have asked if the question of fairness in executive compensation might be studied empirically. In 2009, one interesting answer came from Professor Venkat Venkatasubramanian, a scientist trained as a chemical engineer. He began with empirical data. In American corporations, the ratio of total compensation for CEOs to that of an "average employee" rose from a range of 25–40:1 in the 1970s to 344:1 in the decade after 2001. By another measure, of CEO pay as a multiple of the minimum wage, the American ratio in the United States rose from about 50:1 in 1965 to 866:1 in 2007, while ratios remained about 20–40:1 in Europe and 10–15:1 in Japan.[53]

Professor Venkatasubramanian observed that the tools of his science might help to develop an empirical test of fairness. He used the pattern of lognormal distribution in mathematics, and the principle of maximum entropy in information science and physics, as a measure of fairness in the distribution of returns in a free-market economic system at equilibrium. These tools provide a measure of disorder, or aberration in the function of a physical system. When applied to the distribution of compensation in European economies and East Asian economies such as Korea and Japan, the patterns were lognormal throughout other national economies and were so in the United States to about 1970. Thereafter, American distribution continued to be lognormal for the bottom 95 percent of income recipients, but the patterns increasingly became severely distorted for top percentiles, and very severely so for CEOs of large corporations.[54]

This happened at the same time when other studies yielded evidence of what might politely be called dysfunction in behavior of corporate boards and compensation committees. Further, many studies also found that magnitudes of CEO compensation did not correlate in positive ways with measures of performance. Similar patterns appeared in compensation of top figures in American financial institutions, universities, law firms, lobbying firms, and political contributions.[55] In a word, from about 1970 to 2010, the American system grew grossly unfair in patterns of high executive compensation, both by the very different qualitative tests of John Rawls and Robert Nozick, and also by these quantitative measures.[56] It did so in both procedural and substantive patterns, which were closely linked.

This recent research also shows a strong connection between values of fairness and the operation of free markets. The more free a market becomes, the more important are perceptions of fairness to its function. These findings may also apply to other institutions in a free and open society. In these ways problems of fairness are growing more prominent in economics, even as some economists have chosen to move in the opposite direction.

H. Mathematics, Managerial Studies and Folk Rituals of Fairness:
    The Problem of Fair Division

Inquiries on the subject of fairness also appear in the literature of mathematics and symbolic logic. Some of this work centers on what has been called the "cake-cutting problem." Most Americans are familiar with a family folk ritual for dividing a cake fairly between two children: one cuts the cake; the other gets first choice. Several scholars have tried to expand this idea into a model of "fair division" among three or more people. Large families in the United States have been quick to find a very simple solution that works: the one who cuts the cake gets the last choice.

Academic writers were not satisfied with that solution. They tried to frame a mathematical model that would work for any number of people. They could do it easily enough for two people. But for as few as three people, a mathematical model of a cake-cutting solution became highly complex. When four people were involved, the mathematical model collapsed under the weight of its complexity.[57]

Others have been inspired by the cake-cutting solution to build models of fair division in divorce settlements, diplomatic disputes, and economic distribution. A few have worked on a principle of fair division for objects more complex than a simple cake. British scholars started with the cutting of a raisin cake when some people want cake and others want raisins. This problem has given rise to a new idea of fairness as "envy-free" distribution, which is popular among libertarians, but less so among egalitarians.[58]

The result is another interesting literature, with important by-products for historical knowledge. In the process of testing various models of fair division, several scholars have done research on the importance of fairness in different cultures. One study concludes that "universally across cultures, people value fairness highly and emotionally." But they also find that some cultures value fairness more highly than others. The highest values appear in cultures that have a language of fairness, a history of that idea, and deeply rooted folkways such as the custom of cake-cutting itself, in which one child divides and the other gets first choice.[59]

In our contemporary world, the mathematics of fair division and the accumulated wisdom of historical experience are increasingly useful and even necessary to the strength of open societies. Our inherited folk rituals of fairness such as the traditional ritual of cake-cutting are more relevant than ever to the problems of our time.[60]

NOTES

Preface

Epigraph: Henry Demarest Lloyd to George Jones, Sept. 14, 1899, Lloyd Papers, State Historical Society of Wisconsin, quoted in Peter J. Coleman, *Progressivism and the World of Reform: New Zealand and the Origins of the American Welfare State* (Lawrence, KS, 1987), 50.

1. For a census of protected kauri trees in Coromandel at Waiomu Kauri Grove, Waiau Kauri Grove, and fifteen other reserves, see http://www.thecoromandel.com.

2. For many years, New Zealand schoolchildren memorized its elevation at 3,764 meters—until 1991, when 10.4 meters of rock tumbled off the top. That event was received as a national calamity. Mount Cook–Aroaki is still New Zealand's most beloved mountain.

3. We cherish a set of excellent histories by Philip Ross May, *The West Coast Gold Rushes* (Christchurch, 1962), a major work; *Hokitika: Goldfields Capital* (Christchurch, 1964), with one of the best dust jackets I've seen; and a collection of essays, *Miners and Militants: Politics in Westland* (Christchurch, 1975).

4. An image of this scene, photographed by Craig Potton, appears on the jacket of this book.

5. On Captain Cook, of whom more later, a monument of New Zealand historiography is John Beaglehole's edition of Cook's *Journals*, published by the Hakluyt Society in four volumes with large portfolios of charts, and a first-class biography. For subsequent scholarship the best guides are two excellent books by John Robson, *Captain Cook's World* (Auckland and Seattle, 2000) and *The Captain Cook Encyclopedia* (Auckland, London, and Honolulu, 2004).

6. Ralph Markby, *Snow Business: Sixty Years of Skiing in New Zealand* (Dunedin, 2008).

7. This passage appears in Samuel Butler's *A First Year in Canterbury Settlement* (London, 1863) and was repeated in *Erehwon* ("nowhere" spelled backwards).

8. We are advised that "punting in Oxbridge garb is more a tourist-related activity than a general pattern among the locals."

9. *New Zealand Herald*, Feb. 24, 2011.

10. Peter Tremewan, *French Akaroa: An Attempt to Colonise Southern New Zealand* (Christchurch, 1990); idem, "The Nanto-Bordelaise Company," in *Rural Canterbury: Celebrating Its History*, ed. Garth Cant and Russell Kirkpatrick (Wellington, 2001), 25.

11. "Ship's bell, circa 1450," Museum of New Zealand Te Papa Tongarewa, online collections, http://collections.tepapa.govt.nz.

12. These places are in a subregion of Northland called the Kauri Coast. Most of the trees are gone, but many survive near Dargaville and Kaeo in the Waipoua Forest (the largest), Puketi Forest (the most informative), Omahaita Forest, and Trounson Kauri Park. Pouto Peninsula is another fascinating place of ancient petrified kauri trees and fossilized leaves. All have Web sites.

13. The Chapel of the Runholders is also called the Church of the Good Shepherd, and now has its own Web site. Its altar window can now be seen online. When we were there the waters of the lake were not bright and clear as in the digital image, but milky white with the mountain runoff, and very striking in another way.

14. In the 1920s, the American writer Zane Grey loved to go fishing for silver trout in the streams that flow into Lake Taupo. See his *Tales of an Angler's Eldorado, New Zealand* (new ed., Lyon, MS, 2000); it draws on three of his earlier celebrations of freshwater and saltwater fishing in New Zealand: *Angler's Eldorado* (New York, 1926); *Swordfish and Tuna* (New York, 1927); and *Tales of Freshwater Fishing* (New York, 1928). All have become classics of fishing literature.

15. John Stenhouse, "Religion and Society," in *The New Oxford History of New Zealand*, ed. Giselle Byrnes (South Melbourne, 2009), 323–56; idem and B. Knowles, eds., *The Future of Christianity* (Adelaide, 2004); Peter Donovan, ed., *Religions of New Zealanders* (Palmerston North, 1990).

16. On the problem of national identity, see Byrnes, *New Oxford History of New Zealand*, 1–19; Giselle Byrnes and Catharine Coleborne, "The Utility and Futility of 'The Nation' in Histories of Aotearoa New Zealand," *New Zealand Journal of History* 45 (2011): 1–14.

17. Desmond Stone, ed., *Verdict on New Zealand* (Wellington, 1959).
18. Albert Métin, *Socialism Without Doctrine*, tr. Russell Ward (Sydney, 1977); André Siegfried, *Democracy in New Zealand*, tr. E.V. Burns, intro. William Downie Stewart (London, 1914); Henry Demarest Lloyd, *A Country Without Strikes*, intro. William Pember Reeves (New York, 1902); idem, *Newest England: Notes of a Democratic Traveller in New Zealand, with Some Australian Comparisons* (New York, 1900).
19. One of the most lively accounts is Margery Perham, *Pacific Prelude: A Journey to Samoa and Australasia, 1929* (London, 1988).
20. See below, chap. 12.
21. Butler, *First Year in Canterbury Settlement*, chap. 4; cf. similar impressions of Jane King, *New Zealand Handbook* (Chico, CA, 1996), 18.
22. *Wellington Dominion*, April 16, 1934, quoted in George Bernard Shaw, *What I Said in New Zealand* (Wellington, 1934), 29.
23. Philip Ziegler, *Diana Cooper* (London, 1981), 244–45.
24. Beatrice Webb, Diary, Aug. 24, 1898, in *The Webbs in New Zealand, 1898*, ed. D. A. Hamer (Victoria, BC, 1959, 1974), 54–55, 61; Sidney Webb, as quoted in Siegfried, *Democracy in New Zealand*, 75; the Webbs' Stalinist principles appear in *Soviet Communism: A New Civilization* (London, 1935) and *The Truth About Soviet Russia* (London, 1942).
25. Karl Popper, *Unended Quest: An Intellectual Autobiography* (La Salle and London, 1974; rev. ed., 1976, 1982), 111–12.
26. David P. Ausubel, *The Fern and the Tiki: An American View of New Zealand National Character, Social Attitudes and Race Relations* (New York, 1960), 12–13.
27. Popper, *Unended Quest*, 111–12.
28. Anthony Trollope, *Australia and New Zealand* (Melbourne, 1873), 632.
29. Melbourne *Age*, June 18, 1977, quoted in *Heinemann Dictionary of New Zealand Quotations*, ed. Harry Orsman and Jan Moore (Auckland, 1988), A7, 2.
30. Ethnic surveys of the United States by the Census Bureau found that the proportion of the American people who reported having British ancestry (in whole or part) was 41 percent in 1921–24, and 21 percent in 1970–71. More recent surveys found 22 percent "English" in 1979, and a more dubious count of 14 percent English, British, Scottish, and Scotch-Irish in 2005. The only larger ethnic group in 2005 was German. *SAUS* (2008) table 51; (1997) table 57; (1981) table 42; (1976) table 40; U.S. Bureau of the Census, *Current Population Reports*, series P-20. In recent surveys another 20 million identify their ancestry as "American" and refuse to be more specific, sometimes with expressions of high hostility to census takers and the government: "You're already taxing my kids. Do you want to tax my ancestors too!" A large proportion of these self-described "Americans" come from the southern Highlands, and many are probably of British ancestry.
31. This transformation in the period mainly of the early twentieth century (ca. 1914–59) is the theme of Keith Sinclair's classic *History of New Zealand* (Auckland and Harmondsworth, 1959; rev. ed., 1969; rev. and enlarged ed., 1980; 3rd rev. ed., 1988; 4th rev. ed., 1991; 5th rev. ed. with additional material by Raewyn Dalziel, 2000). For recent scholarship of high quality, see Damon Salesa, "New Zealand's Pacific," in Byrnes, *New Oxford History of New Zealand*, 149–72 and Judith A. Bennett's excellent *Natives and Exotics: World War II and Environment in the South Pacific* (Honolulu, 2009).
32. Jock Phillips and Terry Hearn, *Settlers: New Zealand Immigrants from England, Ireland and Scotland, 1800–1945* (Auckland, 2008), 26; *New Zealand Official Yearbook* (2006), table 6.05 (citizenship approvals, 2004–5).
33. A new interpretation appears in James Belich's brilliant *History of the New Zealanders*, in which the history of New Zealand becomes a sequence of "progressive colonisation" (1840s–1880s), "recolonisation" (1880s–1920s), and "decolonisation" (mainly 1973–85). Cf. James Belich, *Making People: A History of the New Zealanders from Polynesian Settlement to the End of the Nineteenth Century* (Auckland, 1996); and idem, *Paradise Reforged: A History of the New Zealanders from the 1880s to the Year 2000* (Auckland, 2001).

34. Leslie Lipson, *The Problem of Equality: New Zealand's Adventures in Democracy* (Chicago, 1948), review by D. R. Larson, *Journal of Politics* 10 (1948): 841–42.

35. For a thoughtful discussion by an Australian historian, see Geoffrey Blainey, *The Tyranny of Distance* (Melbourne, 1966, 1968; rev. ed., South Melbourne, 1982; 21st century ed., Sydney, 2001); cf. Francis Cairncross, *The Death of Distance: How the Communications Revolution Is Changing Our Lives* (Boston, 2001).

36. The more one studies the history of New Zealand, the more one finds of interaction with other places from an early date. Maori often visited New South Wales before 1840. New Zealand had communications by telegraph and cable as early as the 1860s, and active cultural exchange with other nations through the nineteenth and early twentieth centuries. Jeanine Graham remembers the range of published international materials that were available to her as a ten-year-old child in the Reading Room of the Inangahua County Council. The same memory appears in Pauline O'Regan, *Aunts and Windmills* (Wellington, 1991), 42.

37. W. B. Sutch, *The Quest for Security in New Zealand, 1840–1966* (Wellington, 1966); Leslie Lipson, *The Politics of Equality: New Zealand's Adventures in Democracy* (Chicago, 1948); David P. Ausubel, *The Fern and the Tiki: An American View of New Zealand National Character, Social Attitudes and Race Relations* (New York, 1960).

38. H. G. Wells, *The Future of America: A Search After Realities* (New York, 1906), 21.

39. Karl Popper, *The Open Society and Its Enemies* (2 vols., London, 1945; 1st U.S. ed., Princeton, NJ, 1950; rev. ed., 1962), 1:7–17, 169–201. Popper's "key point" appears in idem, *The Lesson of This Century: With Two Talks on Freedom and the Democratic State; Karl Popper Interviewed by Giancarlo Bosetti* (London and New York, 1997), 71.

The model of open and closed societies first appeared in Henri Bergson, *Two Sources of Morality and Religion* (London and New York, 1935). Popper also acknowledged similarities between his idea of the open society and Graham Wallas's idea of a "great society" and Walter Lippmann's *The Good Society* (New York, 1937). Open societies in *Fairness and Freedom* are understood not as a philosopher's ideal type but as empirical and historical phenomena that actually exist in the world, take many forms, and have changed through time. This inquiry goes beyond Popper in that way, but not against him.

For assessments of Popper's work, see Ian Jarvie and Sandra Pralong, eds., *Popper's Open Society After Fifty Years: The Continuing Relevance of Karl Popper* (London and New York, 1999). A discussion of his work in epistemology appears as the anonymous essay "Karl Popper," in the online *Stanford Encyclopedia of Philosophy*, first published Nov. 13, 1997; substantive revision Feb. 9, 2009.

For Popper himself, see his memoir, *Unended Quest*. On Popper's career in New Zealand, where he taught at the University of Canterbury from 1937 to 1946, see the essay by Peter Munz in *Dictionary of New Zealand Biography* online, http://www.teara.govt.nz/en/biographies.

Introduction

1. *Cockie* is short for *cockatoo*, a nineteenth-century slang term for small entrepreneurs. New Zealand's "cow-cockie vote" calls to mind America's "country-western culture," which in the years from 1828 to 2008 produced at least ten backcountry presidents from Andrew Jackson to George W. Bush—more than from any other ethnic or regional group in the United States.

2. See *Liberty and Freedom* for a vernacular and visual history of liberty and freedom in daily discourse, and an analysis of more than five hundred vernacular ideas of liberty and freedom through American history.

3. *Wellington Dominion*, Aug. 17, 1994.

4. Barry Gustafson, *His Way: A Biography of Robert Muldoon* (Auckland, 2000), 237–89.

5. Brian Easton, ed., *The Making of Rogernomics* (Auckland, 1989); Michael Bassett, *Working with David* (Auckland, 2008); Roger Douglas and Louise Callan, *Toward Prosperity* (Auckland, 1987).

6. Roger Douglas, *Unfinished Business* (Auckland, 1993), 150.
7. Since we used these materials in 1995, a systematic survey has been completed by Matthew Gibbons, in "Election Programmes in New Zealand Politics, 1911–1996" (unpublished Ph.D. thesis, University of Waikato, 2000). Gibbons has also compiled *An Annotated Bibliography of New Zealand Election Programmes Since 1905* (Waikato, 2003), available online. Much of the material in the bibliography is from the Political Ephemera Collection in the University of Waikato Library's New Zealand Collection, supplemented by the holdings of other major libraries throughout New Zealand. It does not include many manifestos and policy papers.
8. Jim Bolger and Ruth Richardson, *Economic and Social Initiative—December 1990* (Wellington, 1990), 11. To the right of Jim Bolger were other conservatives who argued that it was fair for everyone to be able to keep the fruits of his labor, and his parents' and grandparents' labor, without confiscation by the government. We did not find this idea in the form of political manifestos, but heard it in conversation with conservative acquaintances.
9. *Fair Shares: Labour Party Budget, 1994* (Wellington, 1994).
10. *Fair Go for Youth*, Labour Party Direction Paper, 1992. See also Elizabeth Tennet on this document in New Zealand Parliament, Aug. 19, 1992, New Zealand Hansard Archive.
11. Jim Anderton, *Fairness and Balance for New Zealand: New Labour Party Economic Standard*, July 24, 1989.
12. Ibid.; thanks to Jeanine Graham and Jock Phillips on Jim Anderton.
13. *Making Choices; Social Justice for Our Times* (n.p., 1993), Political Ephemera, New Zealand Collection, Waikato University Library; *Voices for Justice: Church, Law and State in New Zealand* (Palmerston North, 1994).
14. "Social Justice Initiative" (Jan. 1993); "Social Justice Statement" (1994?), 31, Political Ephemera, New Zealand Collection, Waikato University Library; Jeanine Graham to the author, Feb. 5, 2010.
15. Maxine Barrett, "Standard and Foundation for Social Policy," *Toward a Fair and Justice Society* (Wellington, 1988), vol. 3, pt. 1. The Royal Commission received submissions from many people not in academe; the academicians framed the published report around the work of Harvard Professor John Rawls. Cf. Rawls, *A Theory of Justice* (Cambridge, MA, 1971; rev. ed., 1999); idem, "Justice as Fairness: Political Not Metaphysical," *Philosophy and Public Affairs* 14 (1985): 223–52; idem, *Justice as Fairness: A Restatement*, ed. Erin Kelly (Cambridge, MA, 2001).
16. *New Zealand First, Manifesto, 1993* (n.p., 1993); *New Zealand First, the Leadership, the Vision, the Policies, and the Kiwi Spirit* (n.p., 1996); http://www.nzfirst.org.nz/policies.html. For critiques, see Martin Hames, *Winston First: The Unauthorized Account of Winston Peters' Career* (Auckland, 1995).
17. *Mana* 9 (Winter 1995): 85.
18. Annette Sykes, "Cyclone and 'Sedition,' " *Mana* 9 (Winter 1995): 20–21, 85.
19. National Council of Women, *A Matter of Fairness: Employment Equity* (n.p., 1990). "Equal pay for equal work" had already become mandatory for public employment. See Melanie Nolan, *Breadwinning: New Zealand Women and the State* (Christchurch, 2000), 230–66.
20. New Zealand Business Roundtable, *In Pursuit of Fairness: A Critique of the Employment Equity Bill* (n.p., 1990).
21. *Greenlink: Newsletter of the Green Party* 3 (Feb. 1990): 2.
22. Raymond Mehlhopt, *New Zealand NEO Party Manifesto* (n.p., n.d.).
23. "Free and fair trial" appears in the New Zealand Bill of Rights and in the proceedings of the New Zealand Human Rights Commission. It is also prominent in nations that were part of the second British Empire: India and Pakistan, Bangladesh, Kenya and Nigeria, South Africa, Australia, and New Zealand.

24. New Zealand Fair Trading Act, 1986, Public Act 121; see http://www.legislation. govt.nz/act/public/1986/0121. This law has been actively enforced. In 2002, Michael Helsby Knight was found guilty of thirty-three breaches of the New Zealand Fair Trading Act for deceptive and unfair claims about cosmetics and other products. Two years later, he received heavy fines for repeated acts of unfairness in travel deals. Officials who enforced the Fair Trading Act described Mr. Knight as "no stranger" to their proceedings. He was severely punished for unfair and deceptive practices that are unhappily routine in the United States. See *ENZ Business and Commerce News*, Aug. 10, 2004; see also http://www.nzherald.co.nz/business/news/article. cfm?c_id=3&objectid=3583383.

25. Hillary Commission for Sport, Fitness and Leisure, *Firestone Fairplay Manual* (1997); idem, Final Results and Financial Statements, New Zealand Parliamentary Papers, 1/8/7/4 (2002) E.32; both available online at http://www.hillarysport.org.nz.

26. "New Zealand Sails Off with the Cup," *New York Times*, May 15, 1995; Alan Sefton, *Sir Peter Blake* (Auckland, 2004; Dobbs Ferry, NY, 2005), 335–59.

27. The *English Dialect Dictionary* is a more helpful source than the *Oxford English Dictionary*.

28. The phrase appears in Google Ngrams of "American English," probably for books of antipodean origin or references published in the United States.

29. Elizabeth Orsman and Harry Orsman, *The New Zealand Dictionary* (Auckland, 1994, 1995), 34, s.v. "buck." It does not appear in Google Ngrams for American or English books.

30. Ibid., 264, s.v. "spin." It does not appear in any American or English books analyzed by Google Ngrams.

31. Ibid., 38, s.v. "burl." It does not appear in American or English books analyzed by Google Ngrams.

32. *Wellington Dominion*, Oct. 27, 1992; H. W. Orsman, ed., *The Dictionary of New Zealand English: A Dictionary of New Zealandisms on Historical Principles* (Auckland and Oxford, 1997), 251, s.v. "fair suck of the sav" This expression did not appear in any American or English books analyzed by Google Ngrams.

33. Orsman and Orsman, *New Zealand Dictionary*, 75, s.v. "dinkum." All lexicographers agree that it is an Australian and New Zealand word. The New Zealand expressions *straight dinkum* and *square dinkum* do not appear in British or American books.

34. Alexander Aitken recalled that the Second Battalion of the Rifle Brigade was called "Square Dinks," and others were called the "Diamond Dinks," after the shape of their patches; *Gallipoli to the Somme* (Oxford, 1963), 46.

35. H. W. Williams, *Dictionary of the Maori Language* (1844, 1917; Wellington, 1971), 416, s.v. "tika"; Orsman and Orsman, *New Zealand Dictionary*, 319, s.v. "tika"; H. M. Ngata, *English-Maori Dictionary* (Wellington, 1993), 144.

36. Louis S. Leland Jr., *A Personal Kiwi-Yankee Dictionary* (1980, Dunedin, 1994), 21, s.v. "best."

37. All of these examples are from Orsman and Orsman, *New Zealand Dictionary*, 319, s.v. "Yankee."

38. Google NGrams finds zero use of these New Zealand expressions for unfairness in British or American books.

39. Orsman and Orsman, *New Zealand Dictionary*, 274, s.v. "stumer"; 743, s.v. "slinter/slenter"; 743, s.v. "swiftie"; 184–85, s.v. "crookie," "crook."

40. For an excellent and very helpful essay on *fair* and *fairness* by a distinguished cultural and historical linguist, see Anna Wierzbicka, "Being FAIR: Another Key Anglo Value and Its Cultural Underpinnings," in *English: Meaning and Culture* (New York and Oxford, 2006), 141–70. See also Bart Wilson, "Fair's Fair," http://www.theatlantic.com/business/ print/2009/01/fairs-fair/112; Bart J. Wilson, "Contra Private Fairness," May 2008, http:// www.chapman.edu/images/userimges/jcunning/Page_11731/ ContraPrivateFairness05–2008.pdf; James Surowiecki, "Is the Idea of Fairness Universal?" Jan. 26, 2009, http://www.newyorker.com/online/blogs/jamessurowiecki/2009/01/is; and Mark Liberman, "No Word for Fair?" Jan. 28, 2009, http://languagelog.ldc.upenn. edu/nll/?p=1080.

41. *Oxford English Dictionary*, s.v. "fair" and "fairness." Cognates for the English *fairness* include *fagr* in Icelandic and Old Norse, *retferdighet* in modern Norwegian, and *retfaerighed* in modern Danish. See Geír Tòmasson Zoëga, *A Concise Dictionary of Old Icelandic* (Toronto, 2004), s.v. "fagr." For Frisian, see Karl von Richthofen, *Altfriesisches Wörterbuch* (Gottingen, 1840); idem, *Friesische Rechtsquellen* (Berlin, 1840). On this point I agree and disagree with Anna Wierzbicka. She believes that *fair* and *unfair* "have no equivalents in other European languages (let alone non-European ones) and are thoroughly untranslatable" ("Being FAIR," 141). This is broadly true, but with the exception of Danish, Norwegian, Frisian, and Icelandic. Also I'd suggest that the words can be translated into other languages, but without a single exactly equivalent word. I believe that people of all languages are capable of understanding the meaning of *fair* and *fairness*, even if they have no single word for it.

42. *OED*, s.v. "justice," "equity."

43. *Webster's New World Dictionary, 2nd College Edition*, ed. David B. Guralnik (New York and Cleveland, 1970), s.v. "fair"; *OED*, s.v. "fair."

44. Ancient cognates for *fair* included *fagar* in Old English and *fagr* in Old Norse.

45. W. J. Sedgefield, *Selections from the Old English Bede, with Text and Vocabulary, on an Early West Saxon Basis, and a Skeleton Outline of Old English Accidence* (Manchester, London, and Bombay, 1917), 77; and in the attached vocabulary list, s.v. the noun "faeger" and the adverbial form "faegere." Also Joseph Bosworth and T. Northcote Tollen, *An Anglo-Saxon Dictionary, Based on Manuscript Collections* (Oxford, 1882, 1898), s.v. "faeger," ff.

46. Not to be confused with this word is another noun *fair*, for a show or market or carnival, from the Latin *feria, feriae, feriarum*, festival or holiday—an entirely different word, with another derivation and meaning.

47. Liberman, "No Word for Fair?"

48. *OED*, s.v. "fairness," 1.a,b,c.

49. For *fair* and *fairness* in Shakespeare, see *King John* V.i.67. For *fair and square* in Francis Bacon in 1604 and Oliver Cromwell in 1649, see *OED*, s.v. "fair and square."

50. Herein lies one of the most difficult issues about fairness. How can we distinguish between ordinary circumstances where fairness means that all people should be treated alike, and extraordinary circumstances where fairness means different treatment? This problem often recurs in cases over affirmative action in the United States. No court has been able to frame a satisfactory general rule, in part because of ideological differences on the bench.

51. Procrustes was a memorable character in Greek mythology, a son of Poseidon called Polypaemon or Damastes, and nicknamed Procrustes, "the Stretcher." He was a bandit chief in rural Attica who invited unwary travelers to sleep in an iron bed. If they were longer than the bed, Procrustes cut off their heads or feet to make them fit; if too short he racked them instead. Procrustes himself was dealt with by his noble stepbrother Theseus, who racked him on his own bed and removed his head according to some accounts. In classical thought, and modern conservatism, the iron bed of Procrustes became a vivid image of rigid equality. The story was told by Diodorus Siculus, *Historical Library* 4.59; Pausanias, *Guide to Greece* 1.38.5; and Plutarch, *Lives*, Theseus 2.

52. Jesse Byock, *Viking Age Iceland* (London, 2001), 171–84; the best way to study the origin of fairness in a brutal world is in the Norse sagas themselves, especially *Njal's Saga*, trans. and ed. Magnus Magnusson and Hermann Palsson (London, 1960, 1980), 21–22, 40, 108–11, 137–39, 144–45, 153, 163, 241, 248–55; *Egil's Saga*, trans. and ed. Hermann Palsson and Paul Edwards (London, 1976, 1980), 136–39; *Hrafnkel's Saga and Other Icelandic Stories*, trans. and ed. Hermann Palsson (London, 1971, 1980), 42–60.

53. Matthew 25:40; John 4:19–21; Luke 10:27.

54. The vernacular history of humanity, expanding in the world, is a central theme in David Hackett Fischer, *Champlain's Dream* (New York and Toronto, 2008); as the expansion of vernacular ideas of liberty and freedom is central to *Albion's Seed* (New York and Oxford, 1989) and *Liberty and Freedom* (New York and Oxford, 2005); and the present inquiry is about the expansion of vernacular ideas of fairness in the world. One purpose of all these projects is to study the history of ideas in a new key. Another purpose is to move toward a reunion of history and moral philosophy, while history also becomes more empirical and more logical in its epistemic frame.

55. For data on frequency, see Google Labs, Books Ngram Viewer, http://ngrams.googlelabs. com, s.v. "fairness" and "natural justice." Similar patterns and inflection-points appear for the corpus of "English," "British English," and "American English," in the full span 1500–2000, smoothing of 3. Here again on the history of *fairness*, I agree and disagree with Wierzbicka ("Being FAIR," 141–67). The ethical meanings of *fairness* first appeared earlier than she believes to be the case. But I agree on the very important point that ethical use of *fairness* greatly expanded circa 1800.

56. Fred W. Friendly, *The Good Guys, the Bad Guys, and the First Amendment* (New York, 1976) is the classic work on the fairness doctrine. Quotations in this paragraph are from Carrie Menkow-Meadow and Michael Wheeler, eds., *What's Fair: Ethics for Negotiators* (Cambridge, 2004), 57; Philip J. Clements and Philip W. Wisler, *The Standard and Poor's Guide to Fairness Opinions: A User's Guide for Fiduciaries* (New York, 2005); *Merriam-Webster's Dictionary of Law* (Cleveland, 1996), s.v. "fundamental fairness"; *Approaching a Formal Definition of Fairness in Electronic Commerce: Proceedings of the 18th IEEE Symposium on Reliable Distributed Systems* (Washington, 1999), 354. Other technical uses of fairness can be found in projects directed by Arien Mack, editor of *Social Research*, director of the Social Research Conference series, and sponsor of many Fairness Conferences and also of a Web site called Fairness.com.

57. An excellent discussion of fairness, the best I have found in print, is George Klosko, *The Principle of Fairness and Political Obligation* (Savage, MD, 1992; rev. ed., 2004). It is similar to this formulation on many points, but different on others.

58. On different meanings of *fairness*, *justice*, and *equity* I broadly agree with Wierzbicka ("Being FAIR," 144–51), and would add understandings of substantive difference in vernacular meanings as above, with evidence in both origins and vernacular applications of these words.

59. Thanks to Professor Laurent Dubois of Duke University for his advice on French usage.

60. Thucydides, *The Peloponnesian War* (written ca. 423–411 BC), quotes an exchange between the envoys of Athens and the commissioners of Melos. The Athenians tried to bully the smaller city-state, and the Melians replied that their alliance should be *ta eikota kai dikala*, both "equitable and just [lawful]" (5.90). A British scholar loosely translates *eikota* as "fair play," but the Melians were thinking in terms of equity. Cf. Rex Warner's translation of *The Peloponnesian War* (Penguin ed., Baltimore, 1954), 360.

61. Mark Liberman ("No Word for Fair?") has calculated the frequency of the word *fair* in common use, as measured by its occurrence in six large datasets of written texts and conversational transcripts (each called a "corpus" by linguists). All produce similar results: *Fair* occurs once in every 10,000 to 15,000 words. This means that English speakers hear or read the word *fair* with great frequency. Frequencies in Global English, British English, and American English are about the same.

62. David Malouf, "The LaFontaine-Baldwin Lecture," University of Toronto, March 12, 2004, http://www.icc-icc.ca/en/assets/pdf/lectures/DavidMalouf_Lecture.pdf; see also David Malouf, "Made in England: Australia's British Inheritance," *Quarterly Essay* 12 (2003): 1–66.

63. Adrian Walsh, Gerard O'Brien, and Babette Smith are quoted by Stephen Matchett in "Fair-Go Ethos Key to Stormy Date," *Australian*, May 1, 2010, http://www.the australian. com/au/new/opinion/fair-go-ethos. . . .

64. Fischer, *Le Rêve de Champlain* (Montreal and Paris, 2011),16–17. 603–5.

65. Seymour Martin Lipset, *Continental Divide: The Values and Institutions of the United States and Canada* (London and New York, 1990, 1991), 8–54 passim; idem, *American Exceptionalism: A Double-Edged Sword* (New York, 1996), 88–108.

66. Much information is on the Web site of the Canada Revenue Agency at http://www.cra-arc.gc.ca. The queen's speech appeared in many Canadian and British newspapers on July 6, 2010. This account draws from "Queen Trumpets Canadian Freedom, Fairness and Sacrifices in Afghanistan," http://www.thetelegram.com/News/Canada—World/2010-07-06.

67. Marian L. Tupy, "Forget Freedom. The UK Poll Is All About Fairness," May 3, 2010, http://www.cato-at-liberty.org/forget-freedom-the-uk-poll-is-all-about-fairness/; Andrew McFarlane, "Five Meanings of Fair—Which Is the Fairest of Them All?" *BBC News Magazine*, Oct. 7, 2010; http://www.bbc.co.uk/news/magazine-11492207; John Kay, "How the British Prefer to Register Displeasure," *Financial Times*, Oct. 26, 2010. Churchill's phrase, or something like it, was used by John Donne as early as 1611, by Lord Byron, by many British writers in the twentieth century, and often by Churchill himself as early as 1899. See Richard Langworth, *Churchill by Himself: The Definitive Collection of Quotations* (London and New York, 2008, 2011), 589–93.

68. *Atlanta Journal Constitution*, Aug. 9, 2010; "Australian Slang 'Fair Dinkum' Gets Airline Passenger into Trouble," *Fox News*, Aug. 10, 2010, http://www.foxnews.com/story/0,2933,292920,00.html; "Nick Bryant's Australia: Fair Dinkum," http://www.bbc.co.uk/blogs/thereporters/nickbryant/2007/11/fair_dinkum.html; Michael Quinion, "Fair Dinkum," http://www.worldwidewords.org/qa/qa-fai3.htm.

69. Bruce Burgoyne, ed., *Enemy Views* (Bowie, MD, 1996), 131; Washington to Samuel Blachley Webb, Jan. 8, 1777, *Papers* 8:16; Farewell Address, 1796, Avalon Project, http://avalon.law.yale.edu/18th_century/washing.asp.

70. Abraham Lincoln, Special Message to Congress, July 4, 1861; Lincoln to Simon Cameron, Aug. 10, 1861; Address at Cooper Union, Feb. 27, 1860; Speech to 166th Ohio Regiment, Aug. 22, 1864; Roy Basler, ed., *The Collected Works of Abraham Lincoln* (New Brunswick, NJ, 1953), 3:522–50, 4:438, 4:480, 7:512.

71. Theodore Roosevelt, Address at the New York State Fair, Syracuse, Sept. 7, 1903.

72. Theodore Roosevelt, *The New Nationalism* (1910), ed. William E. Leuchtenburg (Englewood Cliffs, NJ, 1961), 26, 30; "We Stand at Armageddon," 1912.

73. Woodrow Wilson, First Inaugural Address, March 4, 1913.

74. "The words most often on his lips to describe what he regarded as the good democratic society were 'free,' 'fair,' and 'decent.' " Frances Perkins, *The Roosevelt I Knew* (New York, 1946), 5.

75. Harry Truman, Message to Congress, Sept. 6, 1945, Samuel Rosenman, Oral History Interview, Truman Library, 57–61.

76. William Safire, "Is Life Unfair?" *New York Times*, July 19, 1999.

77. Ibid.

78. *New York Times*, June 10, 1997, business section, D28 in the New England edition.

79. Hiawatha Bray, "Unfair Is Fine," *Boston Globe*, Nov. 4, 1999, C1.

80. Orr Kelly, *Never Fight Fair! Navy SEALs' Stories of Combat and Adventure* (Novato, CA, 1995), 1; Eric Greitens, *The Heart and the Fist: The Education of a Humanitarian, the Making of a Navy SEAL* (New York, 2011), 189.

81. Mark Lilla, "The Historic Election: Four Views," *New York Review of Books* 17 (Dec. 9, 2010): 58.

82. *Renewing America's Promise: The 2008 Democratic National Platform*, approved Aug. 25, 2008. This document invokes *fair* 23 times, *fairness* 4 times (an interesting difference of proportion from New Zealand texts), *unfair* 2 times, and *fairly* 2 times. Exemplary phrases are "candor, accountability and fairness," p. 6; "fairness and opportunity for all," p. 8; "fair, neutral and democratic," and "smart and right and fair and good," p. 8.

83. Cliff Mason, "The Obama Plan: What Is Fair?" Feb. 20, 2009, http://www.cnbc.com.

84. Google Ngrams, s.v. "fairness," "freedom," and "free," in American English, 1900–2000.

85. This is the subject of another book, Fischer, *Liberty and Freedom*. Suffice to say that most political movements and public debates in the United States centered on different understandings of these ideas. See Fischer, *Albion's Seed*, 199, 410, 595, 777.

86. Google Ngrams, s.v. "liberty," "freedom," "free," "fairness," and "natural justice." Broadly similar trends appear in the following corpora: "English," "British English," "1 million English."

Settler Societies

1. Tony Garnier, quoted in R.C.J. Stone, *Logan Campbell's Auckland* (Auckland, 2007), 231.
2. C. R. Knight, *The Selwyn Churches of Auckland* (Wellington, 1972), 7–8, 19, 43–45.
3. The term *settler society* is widely used by historians throughout the world, but rarely in the United States. It describes the origins of the following nations:

     America (23 nations): USA, Canada, Mexico, Guatemala, Belize, Honduras, Nicaragua, Costa Rica, Panama, Colombia, Venezuela, Guyana, Suriname, French Guiana, Brazil, Paraguay, Bolivia, Uruguay, Argentina, Chile, Peru, Ecuador, Colombia.

     Caribbean (26): Anguilla, Antigua and Barbuda, Aruba, Bahamas, Barbados, Bonaire, Cayman Islands, Cuba, Curaçao, Dominica, Dominican Republic, Guadeloupe, Grenada, Haiti, Isla de Margarita, Jamaica, Martinique, Montserrat, Netherlands Antilles, St. Kitts and Nevis, St. Lucia, St. Vincent and the Grenadines, Trinidad and Tobago, Turks and Caicos, Virgin Islands, British Virgin Islands.

     Atlantic Ocean (9): St. Helena, St. Pierre and Miquelon, São Tomé and Principe, Bermuda, Cape Verde, Gibraltar, Iceland, Falklands, Greenland.

     Pacific Ocean (20): Australia, New Zealand, American Samoa, Cook Islands, Galápagos, New Caledonia, Fiji, Vanuatu, Wallis and Futuna, Tuvalu, Solomon Islands, Nauru, New Caledonia, French Polynesia, Kiribati, Micronesia, Marshalls, Palau, Marianas, Guam.

     Indian Ocean (6): Comoros, Mayotte, Seychelles, Mauritius, Reunion, Maldives.

     Former Soviet Union (7): Russia (Siberia), Azerbaijan, Armenia, Kazakhstan, Turkmenistan, Uzbekistan, Kyrgyzstan.

     Middle East (1): Israel.

     Africa (5): Liberia, Sierra Leone, South Africa, Zimbabwe, Kenya.

     East Asia (2): Macau, Hong Kong.

     Many other nations, not included in this list, grew from cultural migrations before the tenth century. They include nearly all the nations in Europe, and most countries in East Asia and Africa.

4. David Hackett Fischer, *Albion's Seed* (New York and Oxford, 1989) 784.
5. "Maverick," *New England Historic and Genealogical Register* 69 (1915): 146–59; Clifford Shipton, *Roger Conant* (Cambridge, MA, 1945); Charles Francis Adams, *Three Episodes of Massachusetts History* (Boston and New York, 1892), 1:328–35; these paragraphs expand on Fischer, Albion's Seed, 785.
6. John Josselyn, *Two Voyages in New England* (Hanover, 1988), 12; Edward Johnson, *Wonder-Working Providence* (1654; facsimile ed., Delmar, NY, 1974), 64; Mitford Mathews, *Dictionary of Americanisms* (Chicago, 1951), 1036.
7. Peter Cleave, "Old New Zealand, New Zealand," *Illusions*, Oct. 24, 1995, 24. For an excellent and well-balanced history of these early settlers, see Trevor Bentley, *Pakeha Maori* (Auckland, 1999). The stories of Catherine Hagerty and Charlotte Badger appear on p. 37.
8. Frederick Maning (1811?–83) published *History of the War in the North of New Zealand Against the Chief Heke* (Auckland, 1862) and *Old New Zealand: A Tale of the Good Old Times by a Pakeha Maori* (Auckland, 1863) and drafted a third, unpublished work called *Young New Zealand*, of the same vintage as Stephen Douglas's *Young America*.

     For Maning's biography, see David Colquhoun, "Frederick Edward Maning," *Dictionary of New Zealand Biography* 1:265–66, which draws upon the author's "Pakeha Maori: The Early Life and Times of Frederick Edward Maning" (MA thesis, Auckland University, 1984). Also very helpful are the introduction and bibliography by Alex Calder to his edition of Maning's *Old New Zealand and Other Writings* (Leicester, London, and New York, 2001). On Maning's settlement, see J. Lee, *Hokianga* (Auckland, 1987); one of the best commentaries is by Peter Gibbons in the *Oxford History of New Zealand Literature in English*, ed. Terry Sturm (Auckland, 1998), 31–112.

9. Maning, *Old New Zealand*, 1–2.

10. Keith Sinclair, *History of New Zealand* (Auckland and Harmondsworth, 1959; 5th rev. ed. with additional material by Raewyn Dalziel, 2000), 46.

11. David Quinn, ed., *The Voyages and Colonising Enterprises of Sir Humphrey Gilbert* (2 vols., London, 1940); Karen Kupperman, *Roanoke: The Abandoned Colony*, 2nd ed. (New York, 2007); Henry O. Thayer, *The Sagadahoc Colony* (Portland, ME, 1892); Peter H. Morrison, "Architecture of the Popham Colony, 1607–1608" (M.A. thesis, University of Maine, 2007), www.library.umaine.edu/theses/pdf/MorrisonPH2002.pdf.

12. William Bradford, *Of Plymouth Plantation, 1620–1647*, ed. Samuel Eliot Morison (New York, 1952), 75–76, 208, 304, 340–42.

13. Ibid., 76; merchants to Moscovy drew up similar documents for the duration of their voyages.

14. Ibid., 75–76, 151.

15. Richard Wolfe, *Hell-hole of the Pacific* (Auckland, 2005), 49–54, 71–85, 187–93; an excellent and carefully balanced history. Also helpful for the environment is R. Cassell, J. Lee, et al., *The Enduring Land: The Story of the Bay of Islands Maritime and Historic Park*, published by the park staff (Russell, 1989); an older work of enduring value is M. M. King, *Port in the North* (Russell, 1948).

16. *Sydney Gazette*, Aug. 18, Oct. 16, 1838.

17. For a fascinating look at another early New Zealand settlement, see Judith Binney, ed., *Te Kerikeri, 1770–1850: The Meeting Pool* (Wellington, 2007). Early settlements in the South Islands by Australian and American sealers and traders had a different tone. See Erik Olssen, *A History of Otago* (Dunedin, 1984, 1987), 6–19; Charles and Neil Begg, *The World of John Boultbee: Including an Account of Sealing in Australia and New Zealand* (Christchurch, 1979); and C.W.S. Moore, *Northern Approaches* (Dunedin, 1958). For early settlements in North America, the best work is still Charles Herbert Levermore, *Forerunners and Competitors of the Pilgrims and Puritans* (2 vols., Brooklyn, 1912). This subject has been neglected in recent years, and offers many opportunities to scholars.

18. For the founder effect in genetics, see William B. Provine, "Ernst Mayr," *Genetics* 167 (July 1, 2004): 1041–64.

19. For a more extended discussion, see Fischer, *Albion's Seed*, 13–205; the definitive work is Robert Anderson's massive and meticulous *The Great Migration Begins* (3 vols., Boston, 1995) and *The Great Migration: Immigrants to New England, 1634–1635* (Boston, 2000), a monument of scholarship. Other volumes are in progress.

20. Francis J. Bremer, *John Winthrop: America's Forgotten Founding Father* (Oxford, 2003), 118–23, 125–70; John Winthrop, "Litle Speeche" on Liberty, 1645, in *The Journal of John Winthrop, 1630–1649*, ed. Richard S. Dunn, James Savage, and Laetitia Savage (Cambridge, MA, 1996), 584–89; idem, "A Modell of Christian Charity," in *Winthrop Papers, 1498–1654* (6 vols., Boston, 1929–92), 2:282–95.

21. Roger Williams, *The Bloody Tenent of Persecution* (London, 1644); idem, *The Bloody Tenent Yet More Bloody* (London, 1652).

22. Ibid.; John Winthrop, "Speech to the General Court," July 3, 1645, John Cotton, *An Exposition upon the 13th Chapter of Revelation* (London, 1656), 71–73; Francis Higginson, "New England's Plantation" (London, 1630), excerpts in Sanford H. Cobb, The Rise of Religious Liberty in America (1902 New York, 1968), 161; Nathaniel Ward, *The Simple Cobler of Aggawam in America* (1645; London, 1647), para. 4.

23. John Cotton, *Treatise of the Covenant of Grace* (London, 1652, 1659), a sermon preached in Boston, ca. 1635; John Winthrop to Sir Simonds D'Ewes, July 21, 1634, *Winthrop Papers* 2:172.

24. Fischer, *Albion's Seed*, 207–418.

25. Warren M. Billings, *Sir William Berkeley and the Forging of Colonial Virginia* (Baton Rouge, 2004), 107.

26. Journals of the House of Burgesses, 1619–58/59, 74, quoted in Edmund Morgan, *American Slavery–American Freedom* (New York, 1975), 146.

27. Leonard Labaree, *Conservatism in Early American History* (New York, 1948), 7; Grace L. Chickering, "Founders of an Oligarchy: The Virginia Council, 1692–1722," in *Power and Status: Officeholding in Colonial America*, ed. Bruce C. Daniels (Middletown, CT, 1986), 255–77.
28. Wilcomb E. Washburn, *The Governor and the Rebel* (Chapel Hill, NC, 1957; New York, 1972), 50, 55.
29. Edmund Burke, "Speech on Conciliation with the Colonies, 20 March 1775," in *Speeches and Letters on American Affairs* (London, 1908), 94.
30. Fischer, *Albion's Seed*, 419–603.
31. For the vast literature on William Penn, and more than forty biographies, see Fischer, *Albion's Seed*, 456n. There is no good modern edition of Penn's many published writings. An excellent distillation in one volume is Frederick Tolles and E. Gordon Alderfer, *The Witness of William Penn* (New York, 1957). Penn's manuscripts are published in Mary Dunn and Richard Dunn, eds., *The Papers of William Penn* (5 vols., Philadelphia, 1981–86).
32. Luke 6:31.
33. Jean R. Soderlund, *Quakers and Slavery: A Divided Spirit* (Princeton, NJ, 1988).
34. David Hackett Fischer, "Isaac Norris and the State House Bell," in *Liberty and Freedom*, 50–60.
35. Fischer, *Albion's Seed*, 605–782.
36. Patrick Henry, "Speech in Virginia Convention," March 20, 1775, in William Wirt Henry, *Life, Correspondence and Speeches* (3 vols., New York, 1891), 1:262; David Hackett Fischer, "Rattlesnakes, Hornets, & Alligators: Backcountry Visions of Liberty as Individual Autonomy," in *Liberty and Freedom*, 75–84.
37. Other regions had interesting cultures, but none were more than one hundred thousand people in 1790.
38. W. J. Gardner, "A Colonial Economy," in W. H. Oliver and B. R. Williams, eds., *The Oxford History of New Zealand* (Wellington and Oxford, 1981), 57–86, at 59.
39. Philip Temple, *A Sort of Conscience: The Wakefields* (Auckland, 2002), an excellent, accurate, balanced, and comprehensive work; a helpful compendium is M.F.L. Prichard, *The Collected Works of Edward Gibbon Wakefield* (Auckland, 1969); quotations from C. E. Carrington, *John Robert Godley of Canterbury* (Christchurch, 1950), 49.
40. Temple, *A Sort of Conscience*, 8–32.
41. Ibid., 54–111. Sensational trial reports were published in several editions: *The Trial in Full of Ewd Gibbon Wakefield and Others for the Abduction of Miss Turner* (London, 1827); *An Accurate Report of the Trial of Mr. Edwards Gibbon Wakefield . . .* (Liverpool, 1827).
42. Temple, "This Black Place," in *Sort of Conscience*, 114–25; on Elizabeth Fry's role, ibid., 117; Edward Gibbon Wakefield, *Facts Relating to the Punishment of Death in the Metropolis* (London, 1831). Wakefield's work had an impact on Charles Dickens, *Sketches by Boz* (London, 1836).
43. Edward Gibbon Wakefield, *Facts Relating to the Punishment of Death in the Metropolis* (1831), in M. F. Lloyd Prichard, ed., *The Collected Works of Edward Gibbon Wakefield* (Auckland, 1969), 228, 250, 251, passim.
44. On cruelty and unfairness in the treatment of prostitutes and chimney sweeps, see Edward Gibbon Wakefield, *England and America: A Comparison of the Social and Political State of Both Nations* (2 vols., London, 1833), 1:73–74.
45. Edward Gibbon Wakefield, *Swing Unmasked* (London, 1831); Rollo Arnold, *The Farthest Promised Land* (Wellington, 1981), 21; Eric Hobsbawm and George Rudé, *Captain Swing* (Harmondsworth, 1973).
46. Wakefield, *England and America* 1:iv, 45; 2:316.
47. The seminal work was Edward Gibbon Wakefield, *A Letter from Sydney* (London, 1829), which contains most of the major elements in his thinking, along with his "Cure and Prevention of Pauperism, by Means of Systematic Colonisation," published in the *Spectator* in April 1830.

48. The theory of sufficient price was developed more fully in Edward Gibbon Wakefield and John Ward, *The British Colonization of New Zealand* (London, 1837) and Wakefield's *A View of the Art of Colonisation* (London, 1849).

49. Temple, *A Sort of Conscience*, 534–41.

50. Edward Gibbon Wakefield, *A Statement of the Objects of the New Zealand Association* (n.p., 1837); Patricia Burns, *Fatal Success: A History of the New Zealand Company* (Auckland, 1989), 44; Temple, "The Ingenious Projector," in *A Sort of Conscience*, 188–208; Carrington, *John Robert Godley*, 58.

51. Other historians disagree, but see William Wakefield, "Tory Diary," May 21, 1839, typescript, Hocken Library, Dunedin.

52. Diana Beaglehole, "Political Leadership in Wellington: 1839–1853," in *The Making of Wellington, 1800–1914*, ed. David Hamer and Roberta Nicholls (Wellington, 1990) 165–94.

53. Brad Patterson, " 'A Queer Cantankerous Lot': The Human Factor in the Conduct of the New Zealand Company's Wellington Surveys," in Hamer and Nicholls, *Making of Wellington*, 65–74.

54. Roberta Nicholls, "Elite Society in Victorian and Edwardian Wellington," in Hamer and Nicholls, *Making of Wellington*, 195–225.

55. Ibid., 210–11; on landtaking, David Hamer, "Wellington on the Urban Frontier," in Hamer and Nicholls, *Making of Wellington*, 227–54.

56. Francis King, "Why Did They Come Here? From the Weald to Wellington," in *Something of Interest: Proceedings of the 1994 Conference Held by the New Zealand Society of Genealogists*, ed. Vivien M. Parker (Hamilton, 1994), 143–52; this essay draws on the author's thesis, "From the Weald to Wellington, a Study of Six Pauper Families Who Emigrated from Staplehurst in Kent to Port Nicholson in Wellington in April 1840" (University of Kent at Canterbury, 1991).

57. Wellington's rates of offenses for violence and drunkenness were much above the national average to 1867, and tended to converge thereafter. For evidence and judgment, see Miles Fairburn and Stephen Haslett, "Did Wellington Province from the 1850s to 1930 Have a Distinctive Social Pattern?" in Hamer and Nicholls, *Making of Wellington*, 255–83.

58. Margaret Alington, "Life After Death," in Hamer and Nicholls, *Making of Wellington*, 129–50; Hamer, "Wellington on the Urban Frontier," 239.

59. Fairburn and Haslett, "Did Wellington . . . Have a Distinctive Social Pattern?" 274–76; Hamer, "Wellington on the Urban Frontier," 243.

60. *Plymouth Journal*, Nov. 5, 1840, as quoted in Raewyn Dalziel, "Emigration and Kinship: Migrants to New Plymouth, 1840–1843," *New Zealand Journal of History* 25 (1991): 112–28, 116, a model work. J. Rutherford and W. H. Skinner, eds., *The Establishment of the New Plymouth Settlement in New Zealand, 1841–1843* (New Plymouth, 1940, 1969) is a helpful collection of primary materials including instructions, journals, diaries, logs, and passenger lists. Jock Phillips and Terry Hearn, *Settlers: New Zealand Immigrants from England, Ireland, and Scotland, 1800–1945* (Auckland, 2008), 32, 76, follows the continuing connections between New Zealand and English villages such as Holston and Helsworthy.

61. A. B. Scanlan, *Egmont: The Story of a Mountain* (Wellington, 1961), 13–17.

62. Raewyn Dalziel, "Popular Protest in Early New Zealand," *New Zealand Journal of History* 20 (1986): 3–26, 25.

63. William Fox, *The Six Colonies of New Zealand* (London, 1851), 36.

64. *Letters from New Plymouth* (London, 1843).

65. For a reconstruction of the Taranaki Mob, see Frances Porter, *Born to New Zealand: A Biography of Jane Maria Atkinson* (Wellington, 1989), vi–vii, 2–10; see also Judith Bassett, *Sir Harry Atkinson* (Auckland, 1975); and Guy H. Scholefield, ed., *The Richmond-Atkinson Papers* (2 vols., Wellington, 1960), 1:5–9, 18–28.

66. Scholefield, *Richmond-Atkinson Papers* 1:18–28, a generous collection of correspondence within this group. See, in particular, for decisions to emigrate, C. Hursthouse Jr. to C. W. Richmond, n.d. [ca. Oct. 1850], 1:62–64.

67. Charles Hursthouse, *An Account of the Settlement of New Plymouth, in New Zealand* (London, 1849), 3, 32. Much material on relations with Maori appears in Scholefield, *Richmond-Atkinson Papers*; see, in particular, J. C. Richmond to Maria Richmond, April 15, 1851, and C. W. Richmond to T. Richmond, Aug. 27, 1855, 1:90–92, 176–77.

68. On the Oxford Movement, the three classic works are John Henry Newman, *Apologia pro Vita Sua* (Oxford, 1864); H. P. Liddon, *Life of E. B. Pusey* (4 vols., London, 1893–97), with correspondence among the leaders; and R. W. Church, *The Oxford Movement: Twelve Years, 1833–1845* (Oxford, 1891). More recent work in a very large literature includes Owen Chadwick, ed., *The Mind of the Oxford Movement* (Oxford, 1960); E. R. Fairweather, ed., *The Oxford Movement* (New York, 1964); C. Dawson, *The Spirit of the Oxford Movement* (Oxford, 1933); and C. Brad Faught, *The Oxford Movement: A Thematic History of the Tractarians and Their Times* (University Park, PA, 2003).

69. For Keble's life and works, John Taylor Coleridge, *Memoir* (Oxford, 1869); Walter Lock, *John Keble* (London, 1905; Ann Arbor, 2005); and Georgina Battiscombe, *John Keble: A Study in Limitations* (New York, 1964); and for primary material, John H. Newman, *Correspondence of John Henry Newman with John Keble and Others* (London, 1917). His most widely read work was *The Christian Year* (1827), which probably sold half a million copies in the nineteenth century.

70. Carrington, *John Robert Godley*, 13; Charlotte Godley, *Letters from Early New Zealand by Charlotte Godley, 1850–1853*, ed. John R. Godley (1936; Christchurch, 1951); John Kilbracken, "The Godleys of Killegar," Steven Grainger, "Who Was Godley?" and Jean Garner, "The First 'First Lady,' Charlotte Godley, 1821–1907," in *Remembering Godley: A Portrait of Canterbury's Founder*, ed. Mark Stocker (Christchurch, 2001), 12–18, 19–26, 56–77.

71. Edmund Bohan, "Godley, Fitzgerald and the Ideals of Pilgrim Canterbury," in Stocker, *Remembering Godley*, 38–55.

72. John Robert Godley, *Letters from America* (London, 1844); Carrington, *John Robert Godley*, 13.

73. Carrington, *John Robert*, 47; John R. Godley, *A Selection from the Writings and Speeches of John Robert Godley*, ed. J. R. Fitzgerald (Christchurch, 1863).

74. James Hight, *The Origin and Inception of the Canterbury Settlement* (Wellington, 1938); L. C. Webb, "The Canterbury Association and its Settlement," in *A History of Canterbury*, ed. James Hight and C. R. Straubel (3 vols., Christchurch, 1957), 1:135–233.

75. E. G. Wakefield to J. R. Godley, June 22, 1850, quoted in Hight and Straubel, *History of Canterbury* 1:169–70.

76. Charlotte Macdonald, *A Woman of Good Character: Single Women as Immigrant Settlers in Nineteenth-Century New Zealand* (Wellington, 1990), 43–45; K. A. Pickens, "The Origins of the Population of Nineteenth Century Canterbury," *New Zealand Geographer* 33 (1977): 69–75. This essay draws on the author's dissertation, "Canterbury, 1851–1881: Demography and Mobility, A Comparative Study" (Washington University, St. Louis, 1976).

77. C. Godley, *Letters from Early New Zealand*; Colin Amodeo, *The Summer Ships, being an account of the first six ships sent out from England by the Canterbury Association in 1850–1851* (Christchurch, 2000), a meticulous account with passenger lists and much detail; see also idem, *The Mosquito Fleet of Canterbury: An Impression of the Years 1830–1870* (Christchurch, 2005), 61–78, with much detail on Port Victoria (later Lyttelton Harbor) and on the maritime history of Canterbury.

78. Gerald Hensley, "John Robert Godley," *Dictionary of New Zealand Biography* 1:151–52.

79. Garner, "First 'First Lady,' Charlotte Godley," 56–77; C. Godley, *Letters from Early New Zealand*, 112–13, 179, 182, passim.

80. Edmund Bohan, "Godley, FitzGerald and the Ideals of Pilgrim Canterbury," 38–58; idem, *"Blest Madman": FitzGerald of Canterbury* (Auckland, 1998); W. David McIntyre, "James Edward Fitzgerald, 1818–1896," *Dictionary of New Zealand Biography* 1:126–28.

81. Bohan, "Godley, FitzGerald and the Ideals of Pilgrim Canterbury," 43.

82. Stocker, *Remembering Godley*, 78–112.

83. By the census of 1858 the population of Otago was Scottish, 66 percent; English and Welsh, 26 percent; Irish, 4 percent; everyone else, 4 percent. By 1870, the proportion of immigrants from the United Kingdom who were of Scottish origin was 51.5 percent. Data from death registers yield similar results. In 1870, comparable numbers for Southland were 61.4 percent from Scotland. No other region in New Zealand reached 21 percent Scottish. Phillips and Hearn, *Settlers*, 32, 54–56, 149, 173–74. Two classic works of high quality are very helpful: T. M. Hocken, *Contributions to the Early History of New Zealand* (London, 1898), with primary documents and valuable appendices; [James Barr], *The Old Identities; Being Sketches and Reminiscences During the First Decade of the Province of Otago* (Dunedin, 1879). The leading histories of the province are A. H. McLintock, *The History of Otago: The Origins and Growth of a Wakefield Class Settlement* (Dunedin, 1949; Christchurch, 1975), chaps. 4, 5, 6; and Olssen, *History of Otago*, 31–49.
84. Tom Brooking, " 'Out of Midlothian': Scots Migration to New Zealand, 1840–1914," in *The Tartan and the Gold: Papers Presented at the New Zealand Society of Genealogists' Conference* (Dunedin, 1989), 1–21. This work derives in part from research by Val Maxwell on immigrants to Otago, 1848–60, and by J. Morris on assisted immigrants to New Zealand, 1871–79; and R. H. Campbell and J.B.A. Dow, *Sourcebook of Scottish Economic and Social History*. Similar results were obtained from quantitative study of death registers by Phillips and Hearn, *Settlers*, 173–74. The best work on Scottish emigration is Tom Brooking and Jennie Coleman, eds., *The Heather and the Fern: Scottish Migration and New Zealand Settlement* (Dunedin, 2003). Burns, *Letters of Rev. T. Burns*, n.p., n.d., ca. 1848.
85. *Otago Journal* 8 (1852): 128.
86. *Otago Journal* 5 (Nov. 1849): 74ff.
87. Hugh Trevor-Roper, "The Invention of Tradition: The Highland Tradition of a Scotland," in *The Invention of Tradition*, ed. Eric Hobsbawm and Terence Ranger (Cambridge, 1992), is an Englishman's attempt at Scottish history, and very far it is from the facts in North Britain.
88. Phillips and Hearn, *Settlers*, 167–70; Tom Brooking, "Sharing Out the Haggis: The Special Scottish Contribution to New Zealand History," in *The Heather and the Fern*, ed. Tom Brooking and Jennie Coleman (Dunedin, 2003), 49–65.
89. Thomas Burns to James MacAndrew, April 14, 1844, ms. Hocken Library, University of Otago, Dunedin.
90. Thomas Burns, *Early Otago and Genesis of Dunedin: Letters of Rev. T. Burns . . . 1848–1865* (Dunedin, 1916). This work had a history of its own; it is a cache of letters discovered in England, 1916; one part of them for the years 1852–57 was lost when a German submarine torpedoed the ship *Arabic* off the coast of Ireland. Also helpful are letters in the Hocken Library; Ernest N. Merrington, *A Great Coloniser: The Rev. Dr. Thomas Burns, Pioneer Minister of Otago and Nephew of the Poet* (Dunedin, 1929), 50–63; Tom Brooking, *And Captains of Their Souls: Cargill and the Otago Colonists* (Dunedin, 1984); and W. Downie Stewart, ed., *The Journal of George Hepburn on His Voyage from Scotland to Otago in 1850* (Dunedin, 1934).
91. *Early Otago, and Genesis of Dunedin: Letters of Rev. T. Burns*, n.p., copy in the Hocken Library, Dunedin; *New Zealand Journal*, July 3, 1847. Burns's early letters and Cargill's shipboard speech explicitly discussed the New England model. See their "Scheme of the Scottish Settlement of Otago," *Otago Journal* 1 (1848): 1; Cargill to the Secretary of the Dunedin Association, Sept. 23, 1848, ibid., 56.
92. John Thomson to Thomas Thomson of Dalkeith, Oct. 18, 1848, *Otago Journal* 4 (1849): 59–60.
93. McLintock, *History of Otago*, 274–82; Olssen, *History of Otago*, 34, 43.
94. Dorothy Page, "Finding Our Lost Foremothers: Women's Lives in Nineteenth Century Otago," in *The Tartan and the Gold*, 242–57.
95. Tom Brooking's paper "Piping a Rough Equality" captures the strong egalitarian theme in Dunedin, but that idea operated within narrow bounds. It survived for many years in the politics of the city, even to our own time.

96. For uncovenanted settlements, see Fischer, *Albion's Seed*, 183.
97. Fox, *Six Colonies*, 40; Russell Stone, "Auckland's Political Opposition in the Crown Colony Period, 1841–1853," in *Provincial Perspectives: Essays in Honour of W. J. Gardner*, ed. Len Richardson and W. David McIntyre (Canterbury, 1980), 15–35.
98. John Logan Campbell, *Poenamo* (1881; Auckland, 1973), 22–81 passim; Webster is called by his Maori name, Wepiha; also R.C.J. Stone, *Young Logan Campbell* (Auckland, 1982), 48–65; L. W. Melvin, "The Strange Case of William Webster," *Historical Review* 16 (1968): 14–21; Patricia Adams, "William Webster," *Dictionary of New Zealand Biography* 1:578–59.
99. Fox, *Six Colonies*, 41; H. B. Morton, *Recollections of Early New Zealand* (n.p., 1925), quoted in R.C.J. Stone, *Makers of Fortune: A Colonial Business Community and Its Fall* (Auckland, 1973), 5.
100. John Logan Campbell to his father, Aug. 9, 1841, quoted in Stone, *Makers of Fortune*, 5.
101. This great man has had a great biographer in R.C.J. Stone: *Young Logan Campbell* (Auckland, 1982); *The Father and His Gift: John Logan Campbell's Later Years* (Auckland, 1987); *Makers of Fortune: A Colonial Business Community and Its Fall* (Dunedin, 1973); and *John Logan Campbell's Auckland: Tales from the Early Years* (Auckland, 2007), a collection of wonderful stories, handsomely published by the Auckland University Press. This body of scholarship is truly extraordinary for the depth of its research, the excellence of its analysis, and the grace of its prose. It is also leavened by a happy sense of humor! Campbell himself wrote *Poenamo* (1881), a memoir that is a classic of New Zealand literature.
102. Campbell, *Poenamo*, 13–15, chap. 2.
103. Stone, *Young Logan Campbell*, 35–107; Campbell, *Poenamo*, 21–81.
104. Campbell, *Poenamo*, 231.
105. The count of committees and boards is from R.C.J. Stone, "John Logan Campbell," *Dictionary of New Zealand Biography* 1:68.
106. William Swainson, *New Zealand and Its Colonization* (London, 1859); G. P. Barton, "Sir William Martin," *Dictionary of New Zealand Biography* 1:277–79.
107. C. R. Knight, *The Selwyn Churches of Auckland* (Wellington, 1972), 7–8.
108. Her memoir was published posthumously as Mary Ann Martin, *Our Maoris* (London, 1884).
109. R.C.J. Stone, "Redcoat and Bluejacket," in *Logan Campbell's Auckland*, 132–51.
110. Stone, "The Tree on One Tree Hill," and "How Rugby Came Ashore and Found Its Way to Eden Park," in *Logan Campbell's Auckland*, 52–62, 201–14.
111. R.C.J. Stone, *From Tamaki-Makau-Rau to Auckland* (Auckland, 2001), 284–95.
112. Stone, *The Father and His Gift*, 126–27.
113. *Nelson Examiner*, May 28, 1842.

Two British Empires

Epigraphs: J. R. Seeley, *The Expansion of England* (Boston, 1883), 85; James Morris, *Pax Britannica* (New York, 1968), 516.
1. Peter Marshall, "The First and Second British Empires: A Question of Demarcation," *History* 49 (1964): 13–23; Seeley, *Expansion of England*; Vincent T. Harlow, *The Founding of the Second British Empire, 1763–1793* (2 vols., London, 1952, 1964); and various essays in William Roger Louis et al., *The Oxford History of the British Empire* (5 vols., Oxford, 1998–99), esp. P. J. Marshall, "The First British Empire," and C. A. Bayly, "The Second British Empire," 5:43–53, 54–72.
2. Arthur Berriedale Keith, *Constitutional History of the First British Empire* (Oxford, 1930); John P. Halstead, *The Second British Empire: Trade, Philanthropy, and Good Government, 1820–1890* (Westport, CT, 1983); Frederick Madden and David Fieldhouse, eds., *Select Documents on the Constitutional History of the British Empire and Commonwealth* (Westport, CT, 1985–87); Louis et al., *Oxford History of the British Empire*.
3. J. H. Elliott, *Empires of the Atlantic World: Britain and Spain in America, 1492–1830* (New Haven, CT, 2007).

4. The Lords of Trade might be thought of as a transitional institution, which began to assert effective control over the American colonies; see Winfred T. Root, "Lords of Trade and Plantations, 1675–1696," *American Historical Review* 23 (Oct. 1917): 20–41. A strong case has recently been made for the mid-1670s as the pivot point, rather than the 1680s or 1690s. See Stephen S. Webb, *1676: The End of American Independence* (New York, 1984).

5. Andros awaits his biographer. The most useful study, and a generous collection of primary materials, is W. H. Whitmore, *The Andros Tracts . . . with Notes and a Memoir of Sir Edmund Andros* (3 vols., Boston, 1868; New York, 1968). Quotations are from 1:ix, xxxiv. Andros's commission and arbitrary powers appear in Francis N. Thorpe, ed., *Federal and State Constitutions, Colonial Charters, and Other Organic Laws* (7 vols., Washington, 1909) 3:1863–67.

6. David S. Lovejoy, *The Glorious Revolution in America* (New York, 1972).

7. The best secondary account is still Lovejoy's *Glorious Revolution in America*, but the title is a misnomer, for these were truly American Revolutions. For primary materials, see Charles M. Andrews, ed., *Narratives of the Insurrections, 1675–1690* (1915, 1943; New York, 1967); Michael G. Hall et al., eds., *The Glorious Revolution in America: Documents on the Colonial Crisis of 1689* (Chapel Hill, NC, 1964); and Robert Earle Moody and Richard Clive Simmons, eds., *The Glorious Revolution in Massachusetts: Selected Documents, 1689–1692* (Boston, 1988).

8. No rounded full-scale study of Nicholson has been put into print. Many years ago, an unpublished biography was in the collections of the Johns Hopkins University. Among the best scholarship is that of Bruce McCully, "From the North Riding to Morocco: The Early Years of Governor Francis Nicholson, 1655–1685," *William and Mary Quarterly*, 3rd ser. 19 (1962): 534–56; McCully also did a brief but well-documented and empathetic sketch for the *Dictionary of Canadian Biography*, available online. A recent sketch is Kevin Hardwick, "Nicholson, Sir Francis," in the British *Dictionary of National Biography*, available online to subscribers.

9. The classic analysis is still Edmund Burke, *Speeches and Letters on American Affairs* (1908; London, 1956).

10. His writings were collected in Beilby Porteus, ed., *The Works of Archbishop Secker, with his Life* (6 vols., London, 1811).

11. Norman Sykes, *From Sheldon to Secker: Aspects of English Church History, 1660–1768* (Cambridge, Eng., 1959), 216–18.

12. Bernhard Knollenberg, *Origin of the American Revolution, 1759–1766* (New York, 1961), 85.

13. Seeley, *Expansion of England* (Boston, 1883), 69.

14. Paul Knaplund, *James Stephen and the British Colonial System, 1813–1847* (Madison, WI, 1953); also important are his recollections, *Memoirs of James Stephen, Written by Himself for the Use of His Children*, ed. Merle M. Bevington (London, 1954).

15. Sir James Stephen, Minute dated March 15, 1839, C.O. 209/4/326–31, in W. David MacIntyre and W. J. Gardner eds., *Speeches and Documents on New Zealand History* (Oxford, 1971), 8–10.

16. Ibid.

17. Ibid.

18. Paul Moon, *Hobson, Governor of New Zealand, 1840–1842* (Auckland, 1998) is the best full-length biography; G. H. Scholefield, *Captain William Hobson* (London, 1934) is still very helpful on Hobson's early career. Kenneth A. Simpson, "William Hobson," *Dictionary of New Zealand Biography* 1:196–98, is an excellent short biography.

19. Claudia Orange, *The Treaty of Waitangi* (Auckland, 1987).

20. On Hobson's health, see Moon, *Hobson*, 116–53.

21. H. W. Williams, *A Dictionary of the Maori Language* (1844, 1917; Wellington, 1971), s.v. "wai," "tangi"; Moon, *Hobson*, 75–115.

22. Quoted in Keith Sinclair, *History of New Zealand* (Auckland and Harmondsworth, 1959; 5th rev. ed. with additional material by Raewyn Dalziel, 2000), 71.

23. For a more extended discussion and sources, see chap. 3 below.

24. Moon, *Hobson*, 182–87; Hobson's instructions and replies are in *British Parliamentary Papers: Colonies: New Zealand* (Shannon, Ireland, 1967–70), 17:22–26, 595; 28:146–67, 469, 609.

25. Moon, *Hobson*, 276–81.

26. Paul Moon, *FitzRoy: Governor in Crisis, 1843–1845* (Auckland, 2000); H.E.L. Mellersh, *FitzRoy of the Beagle* (New York, 1968); Richard Lee Marks, *Three Men of the Beagle* (New York, 1991).

27. Moon, *FitzRoy*, 153–86; Ian Wards, "Robert FitzRoy," *Dictionary of New Zealand Biography* 1:132; idem, *The Shadow of the Land* (Wellington, 1968).

28. J. Adams, "Governor FitzRoy's Debentures and Their Role in His Recall," *New Zealand Journal of History* 20 (1986): 44–63; Sinclair, *History of New Zealand*, 75.

29. Moon, *FitzRoy*, 254–77; James Belich, "The Governors and the Maori, 1840–1872," in *Oxford Illustrated History of New Zealand*, ed. Keith Sinclair (Oxford, 1998), 77; I. Wards, *The Shadow of the Land: A Study of British Policy and Racial Conflict in New Zealand, 1832–1852* (Wellington, 1968).

30. G. P. Barton, "William Martin," *Dictionary of New Zealand Biography* 1:277–79; G. Lennard, *Sir William Martin* (Christchurch, 1951).

31. H. W. Tucker, *Memoir of the Life and Episcopate of George Augustus Selwyn, D.D.* (London, 1900); John H. Evans, *Churchman Militant: George Augustus Selwyn, Bishop of New Zealand and Lichfield* (London, 1964); Warren E. Limbrick, ed., *Bishop Selwyn in New Zealand, 1841–1867* (Palmerston North, 1983), and unobtainable on the antiquarian book market; idem, "George Augustus Selwyn," *Dictionary of New Zealand Biography* 1:387–89, with the old sailor quoted on 388; George Augustus Selwyn, Visitation Journals, 5 vols. in ms., Hocken Library, Dunedin.

32. Limbrick, "Selwyn."

33. George Augustus Selwyn, *New Zealand, Part 1: Letters from the Bishop to the SPG* (London, 1844), 20.

34. Selwyn, *Journals*, Feb. 3, 1844; a chronology of Selwyn's journeys in New Zealand is in Evans, *Churchman Militant*, 255–258, and of his Melanesian journeys in ibid., 259–60.

35. Selwyn, *Journals* 5:63.

36. Charlotte Mary Yonge, Christabel Rose Coleridge, and Arthur Innes, et al., eds. *Monthly Packet: Half-Yearly Volume*, new ser. 12 (July–Dec. 1896): 672.

37. Patricia Burns, *Te Rauparaha: A New Perspective* (Wellington, 1980), 2.

38. Speech of 1882, quoted in James Rutherford, *Sir George Grey, K.C.B., 1812–1898: A Study in Colonial Government* (London, 1961), 5.

39. Rutherford, *Sir George Grey*, 6, quoting James Milne, *The Romance of a Pro-Consul* (London, 1899), 29.

40. Ibid., 12–13.

41. His associates included the Irish gentleman J. P. FitzGerald; Dr. and Mrs. P. Wilson in Mt. Plymouth, whose home was "one place where he could relax and abandon all artificiality"; Dr. Sinclair, colonial secretary, botanist, and a businessman who advised Grey; and young Apollo Dillon, "a rare friendship, unspoilt by any suggestion of patronage or subservience." Also there were Swainson, Col. Winyard, McLean, Bell, Mantell, Cooper, Knight, Shepherd, and Domett. Many were military officers such as Captain Maxwell, Sir Everard Home, Captain Sotheby, Colonel Hulme, and Colonel McCleverty. See Rutherford, *Sir George Grey*, 279–80.

42. Rutherford, *Sir George Grey*, 283.

43. George Grey, *Nga Mahi a Nga Tupuna* (1854), later translated as *Polynesian Myths* (1855), preface.

44. Rutherford, *Sir George Grey*, 234, quoting Milne, *Romance*, 117.

45. Rutherford, *Sir George Grey*, 234.

46. Tim Shadbolt, speech at the Booksellers' Conference, Rotorua, May 5, 1985, in Harry Orsman and Jan Moore, eds., *The Heinemann Dictionary of New Zealand Quotations* (Auckland, 1988), 583.

47. Edgar Watson Howe, *Travel Letters from New Zealand, Australia and Africa* (Topeka, KS, 1913), 83.

Indians and Maori

Epigraphs: Virginia Irving Armstrong, ed., *I Have Spoken: American History Through the Voices of the Indians* (Chicago, 1971), 116; Judith Binney, *Redemption Songs: A Life of Te Kooti Arikirangi Te Turuki* (Auckland, 1995), 474.

1. The use of *Pakeha* was recorded as early as 1815. Its origin is much debated by lexicographers. The word appears to be related to other Maori terms for whiteness, such as *pakeho* for limestone or white clay.

   Many scholars believe that *Pakeha* derives from *pakepakeha* or *pakehakeha*, which meant strange spirits with white skins. This idea was put forward in the nineteenth century by Anglican Archdeacon H. L. Williams in the *Journal of the Polynesian Society* 2 (1893) and has found its way into the historical literature. Other scholars observe that Maori had other nouns for fairies or supernatural beings, malign or friendly, such as *patupaiarehe, paiarehe, patuparehe,* or *parehe.*

   The *Oxford Dictionary of New Zealand English* concludes that the term is of "uncertain origin," but "the association with *pakepakeha* var. *pukehakeha,* 'imaginary pale-skinned beings,' is the least unlikely of those suggested." Careful discussions appear in Sidney J. Baker, "Origins of the Words Pakeha and Maori," *Journal of the Polynesian Society* 54 (1945): 223–31; and H. W. Orsman, ed., *The Dictionary of New Zealand English: A Dictionary of New Zealandisms on Historical Principles* (Auckland and Oxford, 1997), s.v. "Pakeha."

2. On the history and customs of the *marae,* there is a wonderful book by Anne Salmond, *Hui: A Study of Maori Ceremonial Gatherings* (Wellington, 1975).

3. For expressions in print, see Monty Soutar, "Maori War Effort Overseas in the Second World War," in *The Oxford Companion to New Zealand Military History,* ed. Ian McGibbon (Auckland, 2000), 309–11; W. Gardiner, *Te Mua o te Ahi: The Story of the Maori Battalion* (Auckland, 1992); and the official history, J. F. Cody, *28 (Maori) Battalion* (Wellington, 1956).

4. The history of the *haka* is a wonderful subject. It is today a living art form in New Zealand, cherished by Maori and Pakeha alike. Many newly invented *haka* can be found online.

5. Keri Hulme's *The Bone People* (London, 1985) was published to international acclaim, and won Britain's Booker Prize in the year of its publication.

6. Other works include Michael King, *Te Ao Hurihuri: Aspects of Maoritanga* (Auckland, 1992), the first anthology of works by Maori authors on Maori issues; *Nga Iwi o te Motu: One Thousand Years of Maori History* (1997) had a long reach. King's *Te Puea* (1977), *Whina* (1983), and *Apirana Ngata* (1988) were studies of major Maori leaders; and *Tomorrow Comes the Song: A Life of Peter Fraser* (with Michael Bassett, 2000), *Frank Sargeson: A Life* (1995), and *Wrestling with the Angel: A Life of Janet Frame* (2000) examined leading Pakeha figures in politics and literature. Other monographs discuss Maori tattoos, Maori portraiture, and a Maori *marae.*

7. James Belich, *Making Peoples: A History of the New Zealanders, from Polynesian Settlement to the End of the Nineteenth Century* (Auckland, 1996) and *Paradise Reforged: A History of the New Zealanders, from the 1880s to the Year 2000* (Auckland, 2001). This has been followed by an even larger work, *Replenishing the Earth: The Settler Revolution and the Rise of the Anglo-World, 1783–1939* (Oxford, 2009).

8. Anne Salmond, *Two Worlds: First Meetings Between Maori and Europeans, 1642–1772* (Auckland, 1991), 13, 517; *Between Two Worlds: Early Exchanges Between Maori and Europeans, 1773–1815* (Auckland, 1997); *The Trial of the Cannibal Dog: Captain Cook in the South Seas* (Auckland, London, and New Haven, 2003); *Aphrodite's Island: The European Discovery of Tahiti* (Auckland, 2009; Berkeley, 2010); *Hui: A Study of Maori Ceremonial Gatherings* (Wellington, 1975); *Eruera: The Teachings of a Maori Elder; Eruera Stirling as told to Anne Salmond* (Auckland and Oxford, 1980).

A pathbreaking work of comparative history is Kerry R. Howe, *Race Relations in Australia and New Zealand: A Comparative Survey, 1770s–1970s* (Auckland, 1977). For responses to this excellent work, see Malcolm Wood, "Oh Islands in the Sun," on the Web site of Massey University, Te Kunenga Ki Purehuroa, http://www.massey.ac.nz/massey/about-massey/news.

9. See Joe S. Sando, or Paa Peh of the Jemez Pueblo, *Pueblo Profiles: Cultural Identity Through Centuries of Change* (Santa Fe, 1995). He published many books on the history and culture of his people and became director of the Institute for Pueblo Research, Albuquerque, New Mexico.

10. Joe S. Sando, "My Visit with the Maoris," *Te Maori* 1 (1970?): 29–31, 46.

11. Joe Sando, "Teach Indian Students to Succeed," ibid., 27–31. See Alice Storey et al., "Radiocarbon and DNA Evidence for a Pre-Columbian Introduction of Polynesian Chickens to Chile," *Publications of the National Academy of Sciences* 104, no. 25 (June 2007): 10335–39.

12. "Reflections from Two Worlds," *Te Maori* 1 (1969?) 42; see also. Sando, *Pueblo Profiles*.

13. *New Zealand Official Yearbook* (2002), 5, 112–13, 125–27, table 6.1, table 6.6, figure 6.4; *Statistical Abstract of the United States* (2003), table 12.

14. Ibid. for population and census definition of Pacific Islanders, and for estimates of overlap, see *New Zealand Official Yearbook* (2002), 134–35.

15. Ibid.

16. *Statistics New Zealand* (1994); *New Zealand Official Yearbook* (2006), sections 5.1–5.4. On the demographic history of Maori, see Ian Pool, *Te Iwi Maori: A New Zealand Population Past, Present & Projected* (Auckland, 1991), 29–58, 75–103. For American Indian population north of the Rio Grande ca. 1492, long-standing estimates of 1 million, and anthropologist Henry Dobyns's estimate of 18 million, are thought to be too low and too high by most scholars. Cherokee demographer Russell Thornton estimates a population of 7 million north of Mexico in 1492, in *American Indian Holocaust and Survival: A Population History Since 1492* (Norman, OK, 1987). Geographer William Denevan reckons 3.79 million. William Douglas Ubelaker works carefully from estimates for individual tribes to a total estimate of 1.85 million in "North American Indian Population Size, A.D. 1500 to 1985," *American Journal of Physical Anthropology* 77 (1988): 289–94.

17. Brenda K. Manuelito, "Intermarriage with Non-Indians," in *Encyclopedia of North American Indians*, ed. Frederick E. Hoxie (Boston, 1996), 295–297; J. Harré, *Maori and Pakeha: A Study of Mixed Marriages in New Zealand* (New York, 1966); idem, "Maori-Pakeha Intermarriage," in *The Maori People in the 1960s*, ed. E. Schwimmer (Auckland, 1972), 118–31.

18. "Population by Selected Ancestry Group, 1990," *Statistical Abstract of the United States* (1997), table 56; Russell Thornton, "Population: Precontact to the Present," in Hoxie, *Encyclopedia of North American Indians*, 501.

19. Sando, "My Visit with the Maoris," 29.

20. Mario Pei, *The Story of Language* (1949; New York, 1960); David S. Rood, "Siouan," in *The Languages of Native America: Historical and Comparative Assessment*, ed. Lyle Campbell and Marianne Mithun (Austin, 1979), 243–44.

21. Ibid.

22. J. C. Beaglehole, ed. *The Journals of Captain James Cook on His Voyage of Discovery*, vol. 1 (Cambridge, Eng., 1955), 566–67; Salmond, *Trial of the Cannibal Dog*, 38–39, 116, passim.

23. Some scholars believe that Aotearoa was the Maori name for the North Island, where the great majority lived. Others think that it referred to all of New Zealand. Both meanings appear in the earliest recorded usages, ca. 1855–57. The official name of the country is now Aotearoa New Zealand. For a discussion, see Orsman, *Dictionary of New Zealand English*, s.v. "Aotearoa." They also called North Island *Ahi no Maui*, Maui's Fire, and the South Island *Te Wai Pounamu*, Greenstone Waters; Salmond, *Trial of the Cannibal Dog*, 110–11, 114, 146–50. For Polynesian navigation by clouds, see David Lewis, *We, the Navigators: The Ancient Art of Landfinding in the Pacific* (1927; 2nd ed., Honolulu, 1994), 216–23.

24. When asked what we should call all of them together, they said that "Indian" was as good as any, and better than most, if used with honor and respect.

25. "Original Tribal Names of Native North American People," www.native-languages.org/original.htm.

26. H. W. Williams, *A Dictionary of the Maori Language* (1844, 1917; Wellington, 1971), s.v. "ngai, ngati"; Angela Ballara, *Iwi: The Dynamics of Maori Tribal Organisation from c. 1769 to c. 1945* (Wellington, 1998), 111–58.

27. Among many excellent modern works on these Polynesian migrations are David Lewis, *We, the Navigators: The Ancient Art of Landfinding in the Pacific* (1972; 2nd ed., Honolulu, 1994), a brilliant reconstruction of Polynesian noninstrumental methods of celestial navigation, and other ancient ways of navigating by the study of subsurface phosphorescence, with the aid of Polynesian seaman Tevake and a Melanesian, Hipour; on complex simulations and tests of journeys an excellent contribution is Geoffrey Irwin, *Prehistoric Exploration and Colonisation of the Pacific* (1992; Cambridge, Eng., 1994). Atholl Anderson, "Slow Boats from China: Issues in the Prehistory of Indo-Pacific Seafaring," *Modern Quaternary Research in Southeast Asia* 16 (2000): 13–50, is heuristically useful.

28. Ranginui Walker, *Ka Whawhai Tonu Matou: Struggle Without End* (Auckland and London, 1990), 38. The author is of the Whakatohea Iwi in Opotiki. He took this verse from field research by a New Zealand scholar of mixed Maori-Irish descent and two names: Te Rangihiroa/Sir Peter Buck, *The Coming of the Maori* (Wellington, 1948), 40. For the controversy over these questions see below, note TK.

29. George Grey, *Poems, Traditions, and Chants of the Maori: Ko nga Moteatea, me nga Hakirara o nga Maori* (Wellington, 1851); idem, *Polynesian Mythology and Ancient Traditional History of the New Zealand Race* (n.p., 1855); James Rutherford, *Sir George Grey, K.C.B., 1812–1898: A Study in Colonial Government* (London, 1961), 277–78; Keith Sinclair, "Sir George Grey," *Dictionary of New Zealand Biography* 1:161; for all this as a family project by Maori and Greys alike, see Edmund Bohan's excellent *To Be a Hero: A Biography of Sir George Grey, 1812–1898* (Auckland, 1998), 97.

30. S. Percy Smith, *Hawaiki—The Whence of the Maori* (Christchurch, 1898); idem, *The Lore of the Whare-wananga* (New Plymouth, 1913, 1915).

31. Rosalind P. Murray-McIntosh, Brian J. Scrimshaw, P. J. Hatfield, and David Penny, "Testing Migration Patterns and Estimating Founding Population Size in Polynesia by Using Human mtDNA Sequences," *Proceedings of the National Academy of Sciences* 95, no. 15 (1998): 9047–52; also David Penny, Rosalind Murray-McIntosh, and G. L. Harrison, "Estimating the Number of Females in the Founding Population of New Zealand: Analysis of mtDNA Variation, *Journal of the Polynesian Society* 111 (2002): 207–21. Other studies of Y-chromosome haplotypes find evidence that Maori were among the most genetically homogeneous populations on record. See P. A. Underhill, G. Passarino, A. A. Lin, S. Marzuki, P. J. Oefner, L. L. Cavalli-Sforza, and G. K. Chambers, "Maori Origins, Y-Chromosome Haplotypes and Implication for Human History in the Pacific," *Human Mutation* 17 (2001): 271–80.

32. For a survey of archaeological research, see Atholl Anderson, "Origins and Society of Pre-European South Polynesia," in *The New Oxford History of New Zealand*, ed. Giselle Byrnes (South Melbourne, 2009), 21–46; for the use of linguistic materials to study Maori origins, see Douglas G. Sutton, *The Origins of the First New Zealanders* (Auckland, 1994), 96–135; and for ecology and climatology, ibid., 136–208, and Alexander T. Wilson, "Isotope Evidence from Past Climatic and Environmental Change," in *Climate and History*, ed. Robert I. Rotberg and Theodore K. Rabb (Princeton, NJ, 1981), 251–58. Archaeologist Atholl Anderson ("Origins," 23) argues to the contrary that the canoe legends contain "serious deficiencies" (true enough of Percy Smith's versions). But he goes too far when he asserts that "only an archaeological approach is currently possible." Murray-McIntosh and her colleagues conclude ("Testing Migration Patterns," 9047) that their mtDNA results are "consistent with a general understanding of Maori oral history as well as the results of recent canoe voyages recreating early transoceanic voyages." She is correct. Hard empirical evidence is converging here from many disciplines in support of Maori canoe legends as the history of events that actually happened.

33. Wilson, "Isotope Evidence"; also David Hackett Fischer, "Climate and History: Priorities for Research," ibid., 241–50.

34. The conference was organized by the D'Arcy McNickle Center at the Newberry Library in Chicago. Many tribal leaders were present, from the Apache in the Southwest to the Wampanoag in the Northeast. It was one of a series of gatherings that followed throughout the country. See Frederick Hoxie et al., *The Impact of Indian History on the Teaching of United States History* (2 vols., Chicago, 1985).

35. Alfonso Ortiz, *The Tewa World: Space, Time, Being, and Becoming in a Pueblo Society* (Chicago, 1969); cf. E. James Dixon, *Quest for the Origins of the First Americans* (Albuquerque, 1993).

36. For journeys by boat or "land bridge," see Dixon, *Quest for the Origins of the First Americans*; Brian Fagan, *The Great Journey: The Peopling of Ancient America* (New York, 1987); and also Carole A. S. Mandryk, "Invented Traditions and the Ultimate American Origin Myth: In the Beginning . . . There Was an Ice-Free Corridor," in *The Settlement of the American Continents: A Multidisciplinary Approach to Human Biogeography*, ed. C. Michael Barton, Geoffrey A. Clark, David R. Yesner, and Georges A. Pearson (Tucson, 2004), 113–20.

37. For many years historians dated the origins of American Indians to approximately 11,500 years ago, on the basis of sites found in 1932 near Clovis, New Mexico. Other sites have been dated to 12,500 years BP (before the present) at Monte Verde in central Chile, and to 14,290 BP in Oregon's Paisley Caves. See Anthony T. Boldurian and John L. Cotter, *Clovis Revisited* (Philadelphia, 1999); Tom D. Dillehay, *Monte Verde: A Late Pleistocene Settlement in Chile* (2 vols., Washington, 1989, 1996); John Noble Wilford, "Evidence Supports Earlier Date for People in North America," *New York Times*, April 4, 2004.

38. Tom D. Dillehay and David J. Meltzer, *The First Americans: Search and Research* (Boca Raton, FL, 1991); Donald K. Grayson, *Americans Before Columbus: Ice Age Origins* (Pittsburgh, 1988).

39. Edward Durie, "The Law and the Land," in *Te Whenua, te Iwi: The Land and the People*, ed. Jock Phillips (Wellington, 1987), 17; for a thoughtful discussion, see John Patterson, *People of the Land: A Pacific Philosophy* (Palmerston North, 2000), 13–24.

40. Shepard Krech III, *The Ecological Indian: Myth and History* (New York, 1999), 211–13; idem, ed., *Indians, Animals, and the Fur Trade: A Critique of 'Keepers of the Game'* (Athens, GA, 1981).

41. Krech, *Ecological Indian*, 211–29; Douglas Hurt, *Indian Agriculture in America: Prehistory to the Present* (Lawrence, KS, 1987), Brian Donahue, *The Great Meadow* (New Haven, CT, 2004), 24–53; Peter Thomas, "Contrastive Subsistence Strategies and Land Use as Factors for Understanding Indian-White Relations in New England," *Ethnohistory* 23 (1976): 1–18.

42. David Hackett Fischer, *Champlain's Dream* (New York and Toronto, 2008), 523.

43. Atholl Anderson, "A Fragile Plenty: Pre-European Maori and the New Zealand Environment," in *Environmental Histories of New Zealand*, ed. Eric Pawson and Tom Brooking (Melbourne, 2002), 35–41; Tom Brooking, *The History of New Zealand* (Westport, CT, 2004), 14–16; Belich, *Making Peoples*, 37–58, 67–75.

44. Belich, *Making Peoples*, 37–58, 67–75, is excellent on this subject. On nutrition, see Pool, *Te Iwi Maori*, 40–42.

45. Orsman, *Dictionary of New Zealand English*; Williams, *Dictionary of the Maori Language*, s.v. "hapu" and "whanau." The English *whanauistic* means "relating to the communal nature of the whanau."

46. Ballara, *Iwi*, 160–64, 217–18, 332–36.

47. John Patterson, *Exploring Maori Values* (Palmerston North, 1992); Roy W. Perrett and John Patterson, "Virtue Ethics and Maori Ethics," *Philosophy East and West* 41 (1991): 185–202; C. Barlow, *Tikanga Whakaaro: Key Concepts in Maori Culture* (Auckland and New York, 1991); for Maori sayings, H. M. Ngata, *English-Maori Dictionary* (Wellington, 1993) 380, 512.

48. For a primary account, see "Observations by George Percy, Master," 1607, in *Purchas His Pilgrims* 4:1685–90; rpt. in Lyon Gardiner Tyler, ed., *Narratives of Early Virginia, 1606–1625* (New York, 1907), 10.

49. The leading primary source is William Bradford, *Of Plymouth Plantation*, ed. S. E. Morison, (New York, 1952), 69–70.

50. The best primary source is Robert Juet, *Juet's Journal; The Voyage of the Half Moon*, intro. John T. Cunningham, ed. Robert M. Lunny (Newark, NJ, 1959), 35–36, 14–15, 30, passim.

51. Helen Rountree, *Pocahontas's People: The Powhatan Indians Through Four Centuries* (Norman, OK, 1990); Jenny Hale Pulsipher, *Subjects unto the Same King* (Philadelphia, 2005); on Pontiac, Richard White, *The Middle Ground* (Cambridge, Eng., 1991); Colin G. Calloway, *The Scratch of a Pen: 1763 and the Transformation of North America* (Oxford, 2006); on Tecumseh and Tenskawatawa, Gregory Dowd, *A Spirited Resistance: The North American Indian Struggle for Unity, 1745–1815* (Baltimore, 1992); Vine Deloria, *Behind the Trail of Broken Treaties: An Indian Declaration of Independence* (New York, 1974).

52. Paul Havemann, "Euro-American Law of Nations and Indigenous Peoples," in *Indigenous Peoples' Rights in Australia, Canada, and New Zealand*, ed. Paul Havemann (Oxford and Auckland, 1999), 14.

53. For the primary sources and commentary, see Grahame Anderson's very handsome book *The Merchant of the Zeehaen: Isaac Gilsemans and the Voyages of Abel Tasman* (Wellington, 2001), 88–98, which I was delighted to find in our wonderful Port in a Storm Bookstore, Mount Desert Island, Maine. Salmond, *Between Two Worlds*, 75–84.

54. Salmond, *Two Worlds*, 147–67; for New France and communications in first encounters, see Fischer, *Champlain's Dream*, 124–34, and again 157, and once more 176–82.

55. Michael King, "Tangata Whenua Respond," in King, *The Penguin History of New Zealand* (Auckland, 2003), 179–80.

56. J. R. Elder, ed., *The Letters and Journals of Samuel Marsden* (1832); Henry Williams, *The Early Journals of Henry Williams, 1826–1840*, ed. Lawrence M. Rogers (Christchurch, 1961); Allan K. Davidson and Peter J. Lineham, eds., *Transplanted Christianity* (1987); Judith Binney, *The Legacy of Guilt: A Life of Thomas Kendall* (Auckland, 1968; Wellington, 2005).

57. Belich, *Making Peoples*, 136.

58. For a very thoughtful and important work by a philosopher and student of Maori thought, see John Patterson, *Exploring Maori Values* (Palmerston North, 1992).

59. Quoted in Claudia Orange, *The Story of a Treaty* (Wellington, 1989), 9.

60. For a survey of these voyages, see Samuel Eliot Morison, *The European Discovery of America: The Northern Voyages* (New York and Oxford, 1971), 89, 339–463, 497–544, and *The Southern Voyages* (New York and Oxford, 1974); Lawrence A. Clayton et al., *The De Soto Chronicles* (2 vols., Tuscaloosa, AL, 1993), 2:143–45; James McDermott, *Martin Frobisher, Elizabethan Privateer* (New Haven, CT, 2001), 180–81; Ramsay Cook, ed., *The Voyages of Jacques Cartier* (Toronto, 1993), xxxviii–xxxix; Fischer, *Champlain's Dream*.

61. For discussion, see my book *Champlain's Dream*.

62. Erik Olssen, "Mr. Wakefield and New Zealand as an Experiment in Post-Enlightenment Experimental Practice," *New Zealand Journal of History* 31 (1997): 197–218.

63. Erik Olssen, unpublished manuscript on the timing of first encounters. For the importance of the Enlightenment in Captain James Cook's first encounters in New Zealand and the South Seas, see Salmond, *Trial of the Cannibal Dog*, xix–xxi.

64. For Champlain, the Montagnais, the woman of Panounias, Anadabijou, and Bessabes, see Fischer, *Champlain's Dream*, 129–34, 178–87, passim, and H. P. Biggar, ed., *Works of Samuel de Champlain* (6 vols., Toronto, 1922–35) 1:101–11, 294–96.

65. For Cook, Tupaia, and the Maori chiefs, see Salmond, *Trial of the Cannibal Dog*, 123, 124, 135; Salmond, *Two Worlds*; J. C. Beaglehole, ed., *The Endeavour Journal of Joseph Banks, 1768–1771* (2 vols., Sydney, 1962) 1:417–19, 439–46.

66. Alice Nichols, *Bleeding Kansas* (New York, 1954), 19.

67. Grant Foreman, *Indian Removal: The Emigration of the Five Civilized Tribes of Indians* (1932; 11th ed., Norman, OK, 1989); David G. Fitzgerald and Duane H. King, *The Cherokee Trail of Tears* (Portland, OR, 2005); Thurman Wilkins, *Cherokee Tragedy: The Ridge Family and the Decimation of a People* (Norman, OK, 1988); Arrell Morgan, *The Chickasaws* (Norman, OK, 1971); Arthur H. De Rosier Jr., *The Removal of the Choctaw Indians* (Knoxville, TN, 1970); Michael D. Green, *The Politics of Indian Removal: Creek Government and Society in Crisis* (Lincoln, NE, 1982); Anthony F. C. Wallace, *The Long, Bitter Trail: Andrew Jackson and the Indians* (New York, 1993).

68. In 2007, a poll found that 73 percent of Maori thought of Waitangi Day as "significant" and "meaningful" for them; only 36 of Pakeha New Zealanders did so. But this was from the United Future NZ Party, which had an ax to grind against the event. "Waitangi Day Poll," www.scoop.co.nz/stories/PA0702/S00084.htm, Feb. 7, 2007.

69. On Waitangi Day in 2010, Prime Minister John Key was attacked by two men, who were arrested and sentenced to hundreds of hours of community service.

70. Specially helpful in a large literature are James Belich, *The New Zealand Wars and the Victorian Interpretation of Racial Conflict* (Auckland, 1986); Belich, *Making Peoples*, 156–64; R. D. Crosby, *The Musket Wars: A History of Inter-Iwi Conflict* (Auckland, 1999); and Angela Ballara, *Taua: "Musket Wars," "Land Wars" or Tikanga?* (Auckland, 2003). Primary materials include Henry Williams, *The Early Journals of Henry Williams, 1826–1840*, ed. Lawrence M. Rogers (Christchurch, 1961); John Liddiard Nicholas, *Narrative of a Voyage to New Zealand* (2 vols., 1817; n.p., 2010); Robert McNab, *Historical Records of New Zealand* (2 vols., 1908–14; n.p., 2010).

71. E. Ramsden, *Busby of Waitangi, H.M.'s Resident at New Zealand, 1833–1840* (Wellington, 1942); idem, "James Busby: The Prophet of Australian Viticulture," *Journal and Proceedings of the Royal Australian Historical Society* 26 (1940): 361–86; Claudia Orange, "James Busby," *Dictionary of New Zealand Biography* 1:61–62. Papers and an engaging portrait in his early years are in the Turnbull Library, Wellington, and available on http://www.nzhistory.net.

72. Paul Moon, *Hobson, Governor of New Zealand, 1840–1842* (Auckland, 1998), 58–115, now the best work on Hobson in New Zealand; G. H. Scholefield, *Captain William Hobson* (London, 1934), is still very useful, especially on Hobson's earlier career in the Royal Navy; also Kenneth Simpson, "William Hobson," *Dictionary of New Zealand Biography* 1:196–99.

73. Many eyewitness accounts survive. The best is William Colenso, *The Authentic and Genuine History of the Signing of the Treaty of Waitangi* (1890; Christchurch, 1971), http://waitangi.com/colenso/colhis1.html.

74. Midshipman Henry Wandesforde Comber, "Journey of the Herald, 1838–1842," February 5, 1840, ms., University of Canterbury Library Collections, http://www.canterbury.ac.nz/voyages/herald/waitangi_jnl.shtml.

75. Colenso, *Waitangi*, 3.

76. Claudia Orange in *The Treaty of Waitangi* (1987; Wellington, 1990); idem, *The Story of a Treaty* (Wellington, 1989). The English and Maori texts differed in some material ways. Ross and Walker suggest that translator Henry Williams may have modified the Maori text to mislead the chiefs. It is true that *mana* would have made it more clear, and was used by them in the Declaration of Independence of 1835. The phrase in Article II, *te tino rangatiritanga*, came closer to "sovereignty." See Ruth Ross, "Te Tiriti o Waitangi: Texts and Translations," *New Zealand Journal of History* 6 (1972): 129–57; Walker, *Ka Whawhai Tonu Matou: Struggle Without End*, 90–93, 289–90.

77. Walker, *Ka Whawhai Tonu Matou*, 94, 95–97; Moon, *Hobson*, 101–10.

78. Hugh Kawharu, ed., *Waitangi: Maori and Pakeha Perspectives of the Treaty of Waitangi* (Auckland, 1989), pt. 1; Ross, "Te Tiriti o Waintangi"; Orange, *Treaty of Waitangi*, 40–44; Belich, *Making Peoples*, 193–203.

79. Walker, *Ka Whawhai Tonu Matou*, 105; Moon, *Hobson*, 103–13.

80. In Jock Phillips, ed., *Settler and Migrant Peoples of New Zealand* (Auckland, 2006), 14.

81. Walker, *Ka Whawhai Tonu Matou*, 106–10; with an excellent map of the land blocks from Harry C. Evison, *Ngai Tahu Land Rights and the Crown Pastoral Lease Lands in the South Island of New Zealand* (Christchurch, 1987), 8.

82. On land purchases, see Rutherford, *Sir George Grey*, 163–87; on land disposal, ibid., 188–203; on Grey's policy toward Maori, ibid., 204–33; very helpful is the work of James Belich, *Making Peoples: A History of New Zealanders* (Auckland and London, 1996), 190–203, passim.

83. Brian Gilling, "Raupatu: The Punitive Confiscation of Maori Land in the 1860s," in *Raupatu: The Confiscation of Maori Land*, ed. Richard Boast and Richard S. Hill (Wellington, 2009), 13–30; Brooking, *History of New Zealand*, 59–60, 80–82.

84. Ray Fargher, *The Best Man Who Ever Served the Crown? A Life of Donald McLean* (Wellington, 2007), 144–46, 269; Tony Ballantyne, "The State, Politics, and Power," in Byrnes, *New Oxford History of New Zealand*, 115–16; Belich, *Making Peoples*, 265–67.

85. W. K. Jackson and G. A. Wood, "The New Zealand Parliament and Maori Representation," *Historical Studies* 11 (1964): 383–96; M.P.K. Sorrenson, "A History of Maori Representation in Parliament," in *"Towards a Better Democracy": Report of the Royal Commission on the Electoral System* (Wellington, 1986), appendix B; N. Atkinson, *Adventures in Democracy: A History of the Vote in New Zealand* (Dunedin, 2003).

86. For general works of high quality on American Indian wars, see Robert Utley and Wilcomb Washburn, *Indian Wars* (Boston, 1977); Gregory Dowd, *A Spirited Resistance: The North American Indian Struggle for Unity, 1745–1815* (Baltimore, 1992). For Maori wars and warfare, see James Cowan, *The New Zealand Wars: A History of the Maori Campaigns and the Pioneering Period* (2 vols., Wellington, 1922–23); James Belich, *The New Zealand Wars and the Victorian Interpretation of Racial Conflict* (Auckland, 1986); Ian McGibbon, *Oxford Companion to New Zealand Military History* (Auckland, 2000), s.v. "New Zealand Wars," "Maori Traditional Warfare."

87. S. M. Barrett, *Geronimo's Story of His Life* (New York, 1907); Angie Debo, *Geronimo: The Man, His Time, His Place* (Norman, OK, 1976).

88. Ruth Allan, *Nelson: A History of Early Settlement* (Wellington, 1965).

89. Dorothy Urlich Cloher, *Hongi Hika, Warrior Chief* (Auckland, 2003).

90. "History of the War in the North . . . Told by an Old Chief of the Nag Puhi Tribe," in Frederick Maning, *Old New Zealand* (1887; Auckland, 1973), 215.

91. Rutherford, *Sir George Grey*, 78; F. E. Maning, *History of the War in the North of New Zealand Against the Chief Heke* (Auckland, 1862); T. Lindsay Buick, *New Zealand's First War; or, The Rebellion of Hone Heke* (Wellington, 1926); R. Burrows, *Extracts from a Diary Kept . . . during Heke's War in the North in 1845* (Auckland, 1886).

92. Rutherford, *Sir George Grey*, 79.

93. Ibid., 9, 79.

94. James Alexander, *Bush Fighting*, (London, 1873), 178–79; Cowan, *New Zealand Wars* 2:16–17, 30–31, 72, 76, 504.

95. Alexander, *Bush Fighting*, 14–19, 156–58, 172–74, 225–27, passim.

96. Ngahuia Dixon, "Taratoa, Henare Wiremu," *Dictionary of New Zealand Biography* 1:430.

97. Debo, *Geronimo*; Stephen Ambrose, *Crazy Horse and Custer* (New York, 2003); Robert M. Utley, *The Lance and the Shield: Sitting Bull and His Times* (New York, 1993).

98. Richard G. Hardorff, *The Oglala Lakota Crazy Horse: A Preliminary Genealogical Study and an Annotated Listing of Primary Sources* (New York, 1985); Mari Sandoz, *Crazy Horse, the Strange Man of the Oglalas* (New York, 1945); Armstrong, *I Have Spoken*, 101, 103, 116.

99. According to Edward Sylvester Ellis, a Comanche war chief, Toch-a-way, introduced himself to Sheridan and said, "Me Toch-a-way, me good Indian." Sheridan was heard to reply, "The only good Indians I ever saw were dead." Emily Morison Beck et al., *John Bartlett, Familiar Quotations* (1882; 14th ed., Boston, 1968), s.v. "Philip Henry Sheridan."

100. James Alexander, *Incidents of the Maori War* (London, 1863), vi, 33–34; Alexander, *Bush Fighting*, 9, 174, 179.

101. Alexander, *Incidents of the Maori War*, 124.

102. Pool, *Te Iwi Maori*, 59–131; *New Zealand Official Yearbook* (2002), 112; George Rawick, *The American Slave: A Composite Autobiography* (Westport, CT, 1972–79).

103. Anthony F. C. Wallace, *The Death and Rebirth of the Seneca: The History and Culture of the Great Iroquois Nation, Their Destruction and Demoralization, and Their Cultural Revival at the Hands of the Indian Visionary, Handsome Lake* (New York, 1970), 111, 115, 149–50; R. David Edmunds, *The Shawnee Prophet* (Lincoln, NE, 1983).

104. Wallace, *Death and Rebirth*, 228–26; Vernon Kinietz and Erminie Wheeler-Voegelin, eds., *Shawnese Traditions* (Ann Arbor, MI, 1939).

105. Wallace, *Death and Rebirth*, 239–318; A. C. Parker, *The Code of Handsome Lake, the Seneca Prophet* (1913; Osweken, ON, 1967, 1990), 20–138.

106. Dowd, *Spirited Resistance*.

107. Theda Perdue, "Native American Revitalization Movements in the Early Nineteenth Century," in *New Worlds? The Comparative History of New Zealand and the United States*, ed. Jock Phillips (Wellington, 1989), 59–76, 71; idem, "The Sequoyah Syllabary and Cultural Revitalization" in *Perspectives on the Southeast: Linguistics, Archaeology, and Ethnohistory*, ed. Patricia B. Kwachka (Athens, GA, 1994), 116–26.

108. Christopher Miller, *Prophetic Worlds: Indians and Whites on the Columbia Plateau* (New Brunswick, NJ, 1985); Michael Hittman, *Wovoka and the Ghost Dance: A Sourcebook* (Carson City, NV, 1990).

109. George Fronval and Daniel Dubois, *Indian Signals and Sign Language* (1978; New York, 1994), 63.

110. Armstrong, *I Have Spoken*, 66.

111. Chief Joseph, "An Indian's Views of Indian Affairs," with an introduction by William H. Hare, *North American Review* 178 (April 1879) 412–33, at 433.

112. U.S. Congress, Senate Committee on Labor and Public Welfare, Special Subcommittee on Indian Education, Dec. 1–15, 1969, pt. 1, 221–22; Armstrong, *I Have Spoken*, 157.

113. Fischer, *Liberty and Freedom*, 386–87.

114. Ian Wards, *Shadow of the Land* (Wellington, 1968), 39.

115. Maning, *Old New Zealand*, 206–7.

116. Alister Matheson, "Matiu Parakatone Tahu," *Dictionary of New Zealand Biography* 1:414–15.

117. G. E. Gorst, *The Maori King* (1864, 1959; Auckland, 2001); L. S. Rickard, *Tamihana the Kingmaker* (Wellington, 1963); Alan Ward, "Toa and Tumuaki: Contrasting Leadership in the Early King Movements," *Te Maori* 1 (1969): 47–59.

118. Evelyn Stokes, "Wiremu Tamihana Tarapipipi," *Dictionary of New Zealand Biography* 1:515–18A.

Frontier and Bush

Epigraphs: Walt Whitman, "Song of the Open Road," in *Leaves of Grass* (1891–92), Justin Kaplan, ed., *Whitman, Poetry and Prose* (Library of America ed., New York, 1982), 297–307; W. H. Oliver, "Counter-revolution," in *The Penguin Book of New Zealand Verse*, ed. Ian Wedde and Harvey McQueen (Auckland, 1985), 331–32.

1. It is now called Otari Wilton's Bush, with the increasing attention to Maori names, a happy trend. But in this case it should surely remain Wilton's Bush, as it would not be there if it were not for Job Wilton. His prevoyance deserves to be remembered.

    Now the bush is growing again in Karori, on a square mile that has been set apart as the Karori Wildlife Sanctuary, behind a high-technology stainless steel fence and deep underground barriers to keep invasive predators at bay. These "ecological islands" are multiplying in many regions of New Zealand. Karori Wildlife Sanctuary (also called Zealandia by its promoters) has its own Web site, as do ecological islands in general.

2. For the history of Karori and the Wellington suburbs, see Chris Cochran, "Styles of Sham and Genuine Simplicity: Timber Buildings in Wellington to 1880," in *The Making of Wellington, 1800–1914*, ed. David Hamer and Roberta Nicholls (Wellington, 1990), 108; Beryl Smedley, *Homewood and Its Families* (Wellington, 1980) 18–20.

3. Rollo Arnold, *The Farthest Promised Land: English Villagers, New Zealand Immigrants of the 1870s* (Wellington, 1981); *New Zealand's Burning: The Settlers' World in the Mid 1880s* (Wellington, 1994); "The 'Revolt of the Field' in Kent," *Past & Present* 64 (1974) 71–95; "Dynamics and Quality of Trans-Tasman Migration, 1885–1910," *Australian Economic History Review* 26 (1986): 1–20; "The Village and the Globe," *ANZHES Journal* 5 (1976): 1–13; *Settler Kaponga, 1881–1914: A Frontier Fragment of the Western World* (Wellington, 1997).

4. Frederick Jackson Turner, "The Significance of the Frontier in American History," *Annual Report of the American Historical Association for the Year 1893*, 199–227 (quotation on 199); Ray Allen Billington, *Frederick Jackson Turner: Historian, Scholar, Teacher* (New York, 1973), 124–29.

5. Turner, "Significance of the Frontier in American History," 221–23. For Turner's debt to Loria, see ibid., 207, and Lee Benson, *Turner and Beard: American Historical Writing Reconsidered* (New York, 1960), 21–23.

6. Walter Prescott Webb, *The Great Frontier* (Austin, TX, 1952); Walker D. Wyman and Clifton B. Kroeber, eds., *The Frontier in Perspective* (Madison, WI, 1957); Peter J. Coleman, "The New Zealand Frontier and the Turner Thesis," *Pacific Historical Review* 27 (1958): 221–37; Walter Nugent, "Comparing Wests and Frontiers," in *The Oxford History of the American West*, ed. Clyde Milner et al. (New York, 1994, 1996), 803–33.

7. Donald Denoon, *Settler Capitalism: The Dynamics of Dependent Development in the Southern Hemisphere* (Oxford, 1983), a major work.

8. For leading exemplars of the "new western history" in the United States, see Patricia Nelson Limerick, *The Legacy of Conquest: The Unbroken Past of the American West* (New York, 1987); Richard White, *"It's Your Misfortune and None of My Own": A New History of the American West* (Norman, OK, 1991); and Charles Wilkinson et al., "Paradise Revised," in *Atlas of the New West*, ed. William E. Riebsame et al. (Boulder, CO, 1997), and other essays in that very handsome book.

9. A key word is *contingency*. Scholars began to use it in different ways, but always as a way of getting beyond determinist models. Stephen Jay Gould, working from the Burgess Shale fossils, remodeled the history of evolution as an open process, punctuated by accidents of various kinds, and called that idea contingency. He titled his book *Wonderful Life* (New York, 1989), after the Jimmy Stewart movie. James McPherson in *Battle Cry of Freedom* (New York, 1988) revised the history of the Civil War around four turning points when it might have ended one way or another, and called that model contingency. I wrote a history of the outbreak of the American War of Independence, around a model of people making choices and choices making a difference in the world, and I called it contingency (*Paul Revere's Ride*). Here are three different contingency models, centered on accidents, turning points, and choices. For further discussion and other models, see David Hackett Fischer and James Kelly, *Bound Away: Virginia and the Westward Movement* (Charlottesville, 2000).

10. John C. Weaver, *The Great Land Rush and the Making of the Modern World, 1650–1900* (Montreal, 2003, 2006), 3–7, 348-60, passim.

11. Ellsworth Huntington, *Civilization and Climate* (1915; New Haven, CT, 1945); O.H.K. Spate, "Toynbee and Huntington: A Study in Determinism," *Geographical Journal* 118 (1952): 406–24, with discussion, 424–28.

12. These comparative estimates are in U.S. gallons, converted from New Zealand data from cubic meters. They are for consumption rather than withdrawals. The most recent data in *Statistical Abstract of the United States* (2008), table 357, is for 1995; *New Zealand Official Yearbook* (2002), 367–68; (2006) 357, undated, but ca. 2000; see also Vivian Pullar and Marian McLeod, *Facts New Zealand* (Wellington, 1993), 16, 162.

13. Karl Wittfogel, *Oriental Despotism: A Comparative Study of Total Power* (New Haven, 1957); Karl Butzer, *Early Hydraulic Civilization in Egypt: A Study in Cultural Ecology* (Chicago, 1976); Robert Raikes, *Water, Weather and Prehistory* (London, 1967).

14. *Statistical Abstract of the United States* (2006), table 1298, 825–26. Data are for 2006.

15. Ibid., table 351; *New Zealand Official Yearbook* (2006), 303, 311.
16. *Statistical Abstract of the United States* (1997), table 367; *New Zealand Official Yearbook* (1998), table 1.1
17. *Historical Statistics of the United States* (1975), series J8–15.
18. Malcolm McKinnon, *Historical Atlas of New Zealand* (Auckland, 1997), 144; Arnold, *New Zealand's Burning*, 15–21, 115–29, 250–84.
19. John Higham, *From Boundlessness to Consolidation* (Ann Arbor, 1969), 5–20.
20. David Hackett Fischer, *Albion's Seed: Four British Folkways in America*, 567; James T. Lemon and Gary B. Nash, "The Distribution of Wealth in Eighteenth-Century America," *Journal of Social History* 2 (1968): 1–24.
21. For New Zealand, see Tom Brooking, "Use It or Lose It: Unravelling the Land Debate in Late Nineteenth-Century New Zealand," *New Zealand Journal of History* 30 (1996): 142; for America, see Fischer, *Albion's Seed*.
22. Richard L. Bushman, *From Puritan to Yankee: Character and the Social Order in Connecticut, 1690–1765* (Cambridge, MA, 1967), 54–72; Kenneth A. Lockridge, *A New England Town: The First Hundred Years* (New York, 1970), 139–64.
23. Fischer, *Albion's Seed*, 747–53.
24. John Mackey, *The Making of a State Education System* (London, 1967), 122.
25. Jim McAloon, *Nelson: A Regional History* (Nelson, 1997), 10–71; Ruth M. Allan, *Nelson: A History of Early Settlement* (Wellington, 1965), 238–52.
26. Jeanine Graham, *Frederick Weld* (Auckland and Oxford, 1983), 6–39.
27. Monro to Stafford, Oct. 20, 1857, Stafford Papers, as quoted in Alister McIntosh, *Marlborough: A Provincial History* (Blenheim, 1940), 194–95.
28. David Armstrong, "John Perry Robinson," *Dictionary of New Zealand Biography* 1:369–70.
29. G. R. Hawke, *The Making of New Zealand: An Economic History* (Cambridge, Eng., 1985); Frederick Lloyd Whitfield Wood, *This New Zealand* (Hamilton, 1946), 34.
30. David Hackett Fischer, *The Great Wave: Price Revolutions and the Rhythm of History* (New York and Oxford, 1996), 139, 291–300.
31. These 444 owners included 40 absentees, 37 banks and other corporations, 79 family companies, and 266 individuals. Tom Brooking, *Lands for the People? The Highland Clearances and the Colonisation of New Zealand: A Biography of John McKenzie* (Dunedin, 1996), 75. The source of these data is "Return of 5,000 Acre Blocks and Upwards Showing Absentee Owners, Banks, and Individual owners," *Appendices to the Journals of the New Zealand House of Representatives*, 1890, H-22a. For estates in probate, see Margaret Galt, "Wealth and Income in New Zealand c. 1870 to c. 1939" (diss., Victoria University, 1985), 24, table 3.3.
32. Conversations with Tom Brooking.
33. L.G.D. Acland, *The Early Canterbury Runs* (1930, 1940, 1946; 3rd ed. with glossary of station words, 1951; 4th ed., Christchurch, 1951), a classic work, mostly on North Canterbury; also Robert Pinney, *Early South Canterbury Runs* (Wellington, 1971) and *Early Northern Otago Runs* (Auckland, 1981); Peter Holland and Ray Hargreaves, "Tussock into Wool," in *Rural Canterbury: Celebrating Its History*, ed. Garth Cant and Russell Kirkpatrick (Wellington, 2001), 41–59; Jim McAloon, *No Idle Rich: The Wealthy in Canterbury and Otago, 1840–1914* (Dunedin, 2002), 29–54.
34. W. J. Gardner, *A Pastoral Kingdom Divided: Cheviot, 1889–94* (Wellington, 1992); D. Cresswell, *The Story of Cheviot* (Cheviot, 1951); Brooking, *Lands for the People?* 75–77.
35. On the growth of inequality and wealth concentration, see Jeffrey G. Williamson and Peter H. Lindert, *American Inequality: A Macroeconomic History* (New York, 1964), 33–63; on the persistence of opportunity, see Merle Curti et al., *The Making of an American Community: A Case Study of Democracy in a Frontier County* (Stanford, CA, 1959).
36. Gardner, *Cheviot*, 80; Hawke, *Making of New Zealand*, 93.
37. Gardner, *Cheviot*, 205.
38. Brooking, *Lands for the People?* 245.
39. Gardner, *Cheviot*, 211.

40. Brooking, *Lands for the People?* 245–56.
41. Unpublished tabulations by Tom Brooking, University of Otago. Numbers do not add to 100 percent; the remainder of holdings were in the hands of managers. In available data for the United States, owners include full owners and partners. Tenants include lessees and shareworkers. Primary data for 1950 include a mixed category for part owner, part lessee. Estimates for 1880 include the entire population; those for 1900, 1910, and 1930 refer to white population only.
42. Galt, "Wealth and Income in New Zealand, c.1870 to c. 1939," 24, table 3.3.
43. Tom Brooking, " 'Busting Up' the Greatest Estate of All: Liberal Maori Land Policy, 1891–1911," *New Zealand Journal of History* 26 (1992): 78–98; Tom Brooking, *The History of New Zealand* (Westport, CT, 2004), 80–81.
44. For maps of Maori land losses, see Allan Ward, *National Overview* (3 vols., Wellington, 1997), 1:xviii–xxii.
45. Brooking, *History of New Zealand*, 81.
46. James Belich, *Paradise Reforged: A History of the New Zealanders, from the 1880s to the Year 2000* (Auckland, 2001), 200–201; Brooking, " 'Busting Up' the Greatest Estate of All."
47. Seddon's relationship with Maori is a major theme in Tom Brooking's forthcoming biography of Seddon. For Coates and Maori, see Michael Bassett, *Coates of Kaipara* (Auckland, 1995), 26, 73, 132.
48. Richard Langworth, a leading student of Churchill's life and thought, writes that this quotation is "unattributed" and "cannot be found in the memoirs of his colleagues." But Langworth concludes that it is "a likely remark, for he certainly had these thoughts from time to time in World War II." See Richard Langworth, *Churchill by Himself: The Definitive Collection of Quotations* (London and New York, 2008, 2011), 124, s.v. "Characteristics of Americans." I would add that it is true not only to the life and language and thought of Churchill but also to the character and conduct and history of his American cousins.

Federalists and Centralists

Epigraphs: Thomas Jefferson, First Inaugural Address, March 4, 1801, in *The Life and Selected Writings of Thomas Jefferson*, ed. Adrienne Koch and William Peden (New York, 1944), 322; Harry Atkinson, in *New Zealand Parliamentary Debates*, Sept. 19, 1876, 22 (1876): 376–79; W. David McIntyre and W. J. Gardner, eds., *Speeches and Documents on New Zealand History* (Oxford, 1971), 111.

1. Julia Gatley, ed., *Long Live the Modern: New Zealand's New Architecture, 1904–1984* (Auckland, 2008); http://www.parliament.nz/em-NZ/AboutParl/HstBldgs/Buildings/Beehive.
2. The Beehive is attributed to British architect Basil Spence, who visited New Zealand in 1965. The building was completed in 1982. It reminded us of other works of British architecture, such as James Sterling's History Faculty at Cambridge and his annex for Queen's College in Oxford.
3. William C. Allen, *History of the United States Capitol: A Chronicle of Design, Construction, and Politics* (Washington, 2001) and Glenn Brown, ed., *History of the United States Capitol* (Washington, 1998), are official histories.
4. Arend Lijphart, "The Demise of the Last Westminster System?" *Electoral Studies* 6 (1987): 97–114; idem, *Democracies: Patterns of Majoritarian and Consensus Government in Twenty-One Countries* (New Haven, CT, 1984); Elizabeth McLeay, *The Cabinet and Political Power in New Zealand* (Auckland, 1995), 7; Woodrow Wilson, *Congressional Government* (Baltimore, MD, 1885).
5. For a discussion of the many American ideas of liberty and freedom in the United States, see David Hackett Fischer, *Liberty and Freedom* (New York and Oxford, 2005).
6. Michael Kammen, *Deputyes & Libertyes: The Origins of Representative Government in Colonial America* (New York, 1969, 1972), 12–51, with a collection of primary sources; Gordon Griffiths, *Representative Government in Western Europe in the Sixteenth Century* (Oxford, 1968); Gordon Griffiths, Lesley Simpson, and Woodrow Borah, "Representative Institutions in the Spanish Empire in the Sixteenth Century," *The Americas* 12 (1955–56): 223–57.

7. David Hackett Fischer, *Albion's Seed: Four British Folkways in America* (New York and Oxford, 1989), 196, 405, 590, 772, 815; Bernard Bailyn, *The Origins of American Politics* (New York, 1970), chaps. 1, 2.

8. William Holdsworth, "The Conventions of the Eighteenth Century Constitution," *Iowa Law Review* 17 (1931–32): 161–80; the classic American statement is [John Adams,] *Thoughts on Government: Applicable to the Present State of the American Colonies. In a Letter from a Gentleman to His Friend* (Philadelphia, 1776).

9. William Fox, *The Six Colonies of New Zealand* (London, 1851; facsimile ed., Dunedin, Hocken Library Facsimile no. 12, 1971), 26–29, 112, 137–43.

10. W. P. Morrell, *The Provincial System in New Zealand, 1852–1876* (1932; 2nd rev. ed., Christchurch, 1964), 23; Fox, *Six Colonies of New Zealand*, 27.

11. J. Rutherford and W. H. Skinner eds., *The Establishment of the New Plymouth Settlement in New Zealand, 1841–1843* (1940; 2nd ed., New Plymouth, 1969), 176–82.

12. Erik Olssen, *A History of Otago* (Dunedin, 1984), 39, 40.

13. Diana Beaglehole, "Political Leadership in Wellington: 1839–1853," in *The Making of Wellington, 1800–1914*, ed. David Hamer and Roberta Nicholls (Wellington, 1990), 170.

14. L. C. Webb, "The Canterbury Association and Its Settlement," in *A History of Canterbury*, ed. James Hight and C. R. Straubel (Christchurch, 1957), 173ff.

15. R.C.J. Stone, *Young Logan Campbell* (Auckland and Oxford, 1982), 94–96, 202–6.

16. Jim McAloon, *Nelson: A Regional History* (Whatamango Bay, 1997), 14–42, 45–47, 62–63.

17. Morrell, *Provincial System in New Zealand*, 48–90. This is an excellent work, still the best on its subject. Stocks of the first edition were destroyed in the London Blitz. Also of high quality is A. H. McLintock, *Crown Colony Government in New Zealand* (Wellington, 1958), 259–410.

18. Morrell, *Provincial System in New Zealand*, 48–71, 84–95; McLintock, *Crown Colony Government in New Zealand*, 344–73.

19. Mary Patterson Clarke, *Parliamentary Privilege in the American Colonies* (New Haven, CT, 1943); John F. Burns, *Controversies Between Royal Governors and Their Assemblies in the Northern American Colonies* (Boston, 1923); Jack P. Greene, *The Quest for Power: The Lower Houses of Assembly in the Southern Royal Colonies* (Chapel Hill, NC, 1963), 171–222; Leonard W. Labaree, *Royal Government in America* (New Haven, 1930), 172–311.

20. "An Act for the Better Securing the Dependency of His Majesty's Dominions in America upon the Crown and Parliament of Great Britain," March 18, 1766, 6 George III c. 12, *The Statutes at Large*, ed. Danby Pickering, 27:19–20. Historians conventionally call it the Declaratory Act. It was modeled on a similar law for Ireland and passed "without a division" by the House of Commons on the same day that the Stamp Act was repealed. For context and discussion, see Edmund S. Morgan and Helen Morgan, *The Stamp Act Crisis: Prologue to Revolution* (Chapel Hill, NC, 1953), 268–91 passim.

21. Still the most comprehensive history of British imperial attempts to rule America in the pivotal years from 1759 to 1766 is Bernhard Knollenberg, *Origin of the American Revolution* (New York, 1960, 1961).

22. W. David McIntyre, "Imperialism and Nationalism," in *The Oxford History of New Zealand*, ed. Geoffrey Rice, 2nd ed. (Auckland and Oxford, 1992), 337.

23. W. David McIntyre and W. J. Gardner, *Speeches and Documents on New Zealand History* (Oxford, 1971), documents 28, 31, 32, 41, 127, 128; Mai Chen and Sir Geoffrey Palmer, *Public Law in New Zealand* (Oxford, 1993, 1994), 152–85.

24. Peter Gibbons, "The Climate of Opinion," in Rice, *Oxford History of New Zealand*, 335.

25. James Belich, *Paradise Reforged: A History of the New Zealanders, from the 1880s to the Year 2000* (Auckland, 2001), 431–35.

26. Ibid., 444; G. R. Hawke, *The Making of New Zealand: An Economic History* (Cambridge, Eng., 1985), 221.

27. Belich, *Paradise Reforged*, 431, 433–34.

28. John Fiske, *The Critical Period of American History, 1783–1789* (New York, 1888); Merrill Jensen, *The New Nation* (New York, 1950).

29. Richard Beeman, *Plain, Honest Men* (New York, 2009); Jack Rakove, *Original Meanings: Politics and Ideas in the Making of the Constitution* (New York, 1996); Calvin Jillson, *Constitution Making: Conflict and Consensus in the Federal Convention of 1787* (New York, 2003); for two centuries of revisionist writing, see Charles Beard, *Economic Interpretation of the Constitution of the United States* (New York, 1913) and Woody Holton, *Unruly Americans and the Origins of the Constitution* (New York, 2007).

30. John Adams, *Thoughts on Government* (Philadelphia, 1776); idem, *Defence of the Constitutions of Government of the United States of America* (London, 1787–88).

31. Hamilton, speech in the Federal Convention, 1787, *Federalist Papers*, Reports on Credit and Manufactures, in Richard B. Morris ed., *Alexander Hamilton* (New York, 1957), 119–32, 133–48, 232–55, 263–74.

32. Jefferson to Samuel Kercheval, July 12, 1816, and to John Taylor of Caroline, May 28, 1816, in *Life and Selected Writings*, ed. Adrienne Koch and William Peden (New York, 1944), 668–76.

33. James Madison, *Federalist* 10 and 51; Marvin Meyers, *The Mind of the Founders: Sources of the Political Thought of James Madison*, 2nd ed. (Hanover, NH, 1973), 66–85, 129–33, 179–90.

34. David Hackett Fischer, *Washington's Crossing* (New York and Oxford, 2004); Samuel Morison, "Young Man Washington," in Morison, *By Land and by Sea* (New York, 1966), 161–80.

35. Paul W. Conner, *Poor Richard's Politicks: Benjamin Franklin and His New American Order* (New York, 1965), 111–20.

36. Alison L. LaCroix, *The Ideological Origins of American Federalism* (Cambridge, 2010) is a thoughtful study of American federalism as an idea, and also a survey of a large literature on that subject.

37. James McPherson, *Battle Cry of Freedom*, 202–853 (New York, 1988) and *Ordeal by Fire* (New York, 1982, 1992, 2009).

38. James Madison, *Federalist* 51, in Alexander Hamilton, James Madison, and John Jay, *The Federalist*, ed. Jacob Cooke (Cleveland, 1961), 351, 361.

39. Hamilton, Madison, and Jay, *Federalist*, esp. 1, 9 (Hamilton), 2 (Jay), and 10, 14, 51 (Madison); Jefferson, First Inaugural Address, March 4, 1801, in *The Life and Selected Writings of Thomas Jefferson*, ed. Adrienne Koch and William Peden (New York, 1944), 321–24.

40. For surveys of New Zealand's Critical Period from different perspectives, see Morrell, "The Abolition of the Provinces," in *Provincial System in New Zealand*, 243–85; Keith Sinclair and Raewyn Dalziel, *A History of New Zealand*, rev. ed. (Auckland, 2000), 157–78; Philippa Mein Smith, *A Concise History of New Zealand* (Cambridge, Eng., 2005), 84–86; and Tony Ballantyne, "The State, Politics and Power, 1769–1893," in *The New Oxford History of New Zealand*, ed. Giselle Byrnes (South Melbourne, 2009), 99–124.

41. This follows an excellent biography, Edmund Bohan's *Edward Stafford: New Zealand's First Statesman* (Christchurch, 1994). Quotations are from 244, 99.

42. Judith Bassett, *Sir Harry Atkinson* (Auckland, 1975).

43. Henry Sewall, *The Journal of Henry Sewall, 1853–1857*, ed. W. David McIntyre (2 vols., Christchurch, 1980); Edmund Bohan, *Blest Madman: FitzGerald of Canterbury* (Christchurch, 1998); W. David McIntyre, "James Edward FitzGerald," *Dictionary of New Zealand Biography* 1:391–93.

44. Raewyn Dalziel, *Julius Vogel: Business Politician* (Auckland, 1986); Erik Olssen and Marcia Stenson, *A Century of Change: New Zealand, 1800–1900* (Auckland, 1989, 1994), 254.

45. Anthony Trollope, *Australia and New Zealand* (2 vols., London, 1873); Raewyn Dalziel, "The Southern Islands: New Zealand and Polynesia," in *The Oxford History of the British Empire: The Nineteenth Century*, ed. Andrew Porter (Oxford, 1999), 584.

46. Morrell, *Provincial System of New Zealand*, 271.

47. Dalziel, *Julius Vogel*, 170, 174.

48. Morrell, *Provincial System of New Zealand*, 256.

49. Harry Atkinson, in *New Zealand Parliamentary Debates*, Sept. 19, 1876, 22 (1876) 376–79; W. David McIntyre and W. J. Gardner, eds., *Speeches and Documents on New Zealand History* (Oxford, 1971), 111.

50. Bohan, *Edward Stafford*, 349.

51. Morrell, *Provincial System of New Zealand*, 276.

52. For an excellent discussion, see Ballantyne, "The State, Politics, and Power, 1769–1893."

53. Philip J. Lampi et al., *A New Nation Votes*, a Web site sponsored by Tufts University and the American Antiquarian Society, http://elections.lib.tufts.edu/aas_portal/index.xq.

54. *Statistical Abstract of the United States* (2003), tables 334, 468, 506. Among federal agencies employing law enforcement officers with powers of arrest are the Coast Guard, the Customs Service, the Federal Bureau of Investigation, the Immigration and Naturalization Service, the Secret Service, the Internal Revenue Service, the Postal Inspection Service, the National Park Service, the Drug Enforcement Agency, the Capitol Police, the Forest Service, the Fish and Wildlife Service, and the U.S. Marshals Service.

55. Richard S. Hill, *The Colonial Frontier Tamed: New Zealand Policing in Transition, 1867–1886* (Wellington, 1989), 284, 366.

56. John O'Donovan, "Address to the New Zealand Police Force," 1920, quoted in ibid., 367.

57. Richard S. Hill, *The Iron Hand in a Velvet Glove: The Modernisation of Policing in New Zealand, 1886–1917* (Wellington and Palmerston North, 1995).

58. Ibid., 163–240; Richard S. Hill, *A Policeman's Paradise? Policing a Stable Society, 1918–1945* (Wellington and Palmerston North, 1999), 1–37.

59. Hill, *Policeman's Paradise?* 46–47.

60. *Statistical Abstract of the United States* (2008), 325, 448, 509; *New Zealand Official Yearbook* (2008), fig. 10.03, 214–16.

61. *Statistical Abstract of the United States* (1997), table 313; *New Zealand Official Yearbook* (1998), table 10.2; (2006), table 10.03.

62. For further discussion, see Fischer, *Albion's Seed*. For a massive compilation of data, which confirms the magnitude and persistence of regional differences, see Randolph Roth, *American Homicide* (Cambridge, MA, 2009), 3–8, with data online in the Historical Violence Database, http://cjrc.osu.edu/researchprojects/hvd. Roth is mistaken in writing, "No matter where Americans live, their risk of being murdered is higher than it is in any other first-world democracy" (3). This is not the case when one compares New England with European nations. He also understates patterns of regional persistence in differential rates. But overall he has made a major contribution.

63. *Statistical Abstract of the United States* (2008), tables 299, 306.

64. This survey was reported by Joe Hallinan for Newhouse News Service and published under various titles by many American newspapers. See, e.g., *Mobile Register*, July 30, 1993, available online at http://www.trosch.org/tro/mpr-7g30.htm.

65. For the United States, in sixty-five years from 1930 to 1995, the U.S. Bureau of Prisons recorded 4,332 executions under federal and state laws. Sources are *Historical Statistics of the United States* (1975), series H1155–1167; *Statistical Abstract of the United States* (1997), table 362; with corrections and additions through 2006 from *Statistical Abstract of the United States* (2008), table 343.

66. Numbers have been increasing in both countries: in New Zealand to 7.420 on Dec. 29, 2005; and in the United States to 1,525,924 in 2005. *Statistical Abstract of the United States* Relative proportions have remained approximately the same. Cf. *New Zealand Official Yearbook* (2000), 247; (2006) 212; *Statistical Abstract of the United States* (1997), table 354; (2008), table 337.

67. *World Prison Brief*, International Centre for Prison Studies, School of Law, King's College, London, 2009.

68. Ruth M. Allan, *Nelson: A History of Early Settlement* (Wellington, 1965), 173, 348, 394.

69. Nelson Eucation Act of 1856, *Ordinances of . . . the Province of Nelson* (Nelson, 1864).

70. The relative strength of education in New Zealand's provinces appears in these data, ca. 1867–68:

71. Mackey, *Making of a State Education System*, 135.

72. *Parliamentary Debates*, Aug. 18, 1869, 6 (1866): 526.

73. Peter J. Lineham, "Charles Christopher Bowen," *Dictionary of New Zealand Biography* 1:33–34; George Ranald Macdonald, "Sir Charles Christopher Bowen, KCMG," in *An Encyclopaedia of New Zealand*, ed. A. H. McClintock (Wellington, 1966), s.v. "Bowen."
74. Lineham, "Bowen."
75. Elizabeth Gordon, *Finding Our Own Voice* (Canterbury, 2008), 40.
76. James William Fulbright, speech in the U.S. Senate, *Congressional Record*, March 27, 1964.

Immigrants, Voluntary and Assisted
  Epigraphs: Hector St. John Crèvecoeur, *Letters from an American Farmer* (1787), motto on frontispiece of the work; Alfred Simmons, *Old England and New Zealand . . . Extracts from the Author's Diary of his Voyage to New Zealand, in Company with 500 Emigrants* (London, 1879), epigraph on the first page of the work after the introduction, 13.
1. Fischer, *Albion's Seed: Four British Folkways in America* (New York and Oxford, 1989), 783–812, passim; Stephan Thernstrom, ed., *Harvard Encyclopedia of American Ethnic Groups* (Cambridge, MA, 1980), 476–508, passim, increasingly dated but still the leading work on its subject; David Reimers, *Still the Golden Door: The Third World Comes to America* (New York, 1985).
  For New Zealand, a major contribution is Jock Phillips and Terry Hearn, *Settlers: New Zealand Immigrants from England, Ireland and Scotland, 1800–1945* (Auckland, 2008); works of general interest on particular ethnic streams include Tom Brooking and Jennie Coleman, eds., *The Heather and the Fern: Scottish Migration and New Zealand Settlement* (Dunedin, 2003); Donald Akenson, *Half the World from Home: Perspectives on the Irish in New Zealand* (Wellington, 1990); Lyndon Fraser, ed., *A Distant Shore: Irish Migration and New Zealand Settlement* (Dunedin, 2000); Manying Ip, ed., *Unfolding History, Evolving Identity: The Chinese in New Zealand* (Auckland, 2003); Rollo Arnold, "Some Australasian Aspects of New Zealand Life," *New Zealand Journal of History* 4 (1970): 54–76.
2. For a pioneering comparative study, see Donald Akenson, "Immigration and Ethnicity," in *New Worlds? The Comparative History of New Zealand and the United States*, ed. Jock Phillips (Wellington, 1989), 28–58.
3. Immigration statistics are uncertain at best. The problem is compounded by the fact that so much immigration has been outside the law, or against it. Official counts have always been far below the actual flow. Impressionistic estimates have sometimes erred in the opposite direction.
  For the area that is now the United States, total immigration from 1607 to 1790 was long estimated at less than 1 million people. New evidence shows that the number may have been closer to 2 million. They included 400,000 immigrants from Africa, 150,000 from Germany before 1790, 400,000 from Scotland and Ireland, and 500,000 from England and Wales, plus many other groups. For evidence and sources, see Philip D. Curtin, *Atlantic Slave Trade* (Madison, WI, 1969) and subsequent revisions; Fischer, *Albion's Seed*, 16, 226, 420, 608–9, 787.

Province	Population	Total Revenue	Education Spending	Students in Public Schools	Students in Private Schools
Auckland	48,321	£196,667	£3,000	1,406	3,258
Wellington	21,950	166,444	2,714	970	1,793
Nelson	23,814	170,634	5,680	1,668	650
Canterbury	53,866	562,807	6,751	2,178	2,297
Otago	48,577	503,755	11,698	3,298	1,546

Note: Students for 1867 except Auckland public schools, which are for 1868. Source: John Mackey, *The Making of a State Education System* (London, 1967), 135.

After the achievement of independence (1776–83) immigration greatly increased to a total of between 45 million and 55 million from 1790 to 1980. Cf. the undercount by Richard Easterlin, "Immigration: Social Characteristics," in Thernstrom, *Harvard Encyclopedia of American Ethnic Groups*, 476, and the discussions in *New Zealand Official Yearbook* (2000), 103–5.

Total gross immigration, much of it illegal, greatly increased in the United States by approximately 15 million, 1980–99. The largest annual flows in American history may have added another 15 million from 2000 to 2010. Of those totals, the number of illegal immigrants in the country has been estimated to be at least 10 million people (*New York Times*, August 4, 2010). The sum of these numbers yields a total gross immigration to what is now the United States of approximately 90 million people from 1607 to 2010, perhaps as many as 100 million.

In New Zealand migration reached very low levels in the 1970s and 1980s, with net outmigration in 1975 and 1987–88. In the early twenty-first century net long-term immigration reached record levels ca. 2003. See *New Zealand Official Yearbook* (2006), 96–98.

4. Rates of emigration, especially return-migration, were very different in the two nations. In the nineteenth century, statisticians observed that every great flow of population creates a strong counterflow. Some thought they had discovered a constant law of migration. In actuality, they had found an historical variable. In America, return-migration was small until the late nineteenth century. Then it became very large among a few immigrant groups: 48 percent of Greeks, 55 percent of Italians (1899–1924). But overall, it remained low.

New Zealand was another story. Return-migration was always larger than in the United States. In difficult periods it exceeded immigration—as during the black decade of 1880s, the Great Depression of 1929–35, World War II (1939–45), and the difficult years of the 1970s and 1980s. Even in good times, many people left New Zealand for Britain and the United States in earlier periods. They went mainly to Australia in the late twentieth century, often in search of opportunities that could only be found in larger economies. Some New Zealanders feared a "brain drain." Others believed that the balance flowed the other way. Prime Minister Sir Robert Muldoon observed that New Zealanders who moved to Australia raised the IQs of both nations. On balance, there was probably little net brain drain in either direction, but a continuing circulation of energy and effort.

5. See David Hackett Fischer, *The Great Wave: Price Revolutions and the Rhythm of History* (New York and Oxford, 1996), 9, 158, 273–77, 318n, 415–19.

6. For a discussion of waves and cycles, see ibid., 9, 158, 273–77, 318n., 414–17. The journals called *Cycles, Kyklos, Futures,* and *Technological Forecasting and Social Change* publish many essays on cycles and waves.

7. For immigration statistics in the United States, see *Historical Statistics of the United States* (1975), 97–130, and *Statistical Abstract of the United States* (2000), tables 4–5. For New Zealand, see *New Zealand Official Yearbook* (2006), 96–98, 102–21.

8. For a thoughtful discussion of "gold and immigration," see Jim McAloon, "The New Zealand Economy, 1792–1914," in *The New Oxford History of New Zealand*, ed. Giselle Byrnes (South Melbourne, 2009), 206–12.

9. A key to this very interesting period of population movement throughout the world, and a major work of modern historiography, is Jan Romein, *The Watershed of Two Eras* (Middleton, CT, 1978).

10. *Statistical Abstract of the United States* (2008), tables 4–5, 46; *New Zealand Official Yearbook* (2006), 96–98.

11. Ian K. Steele, *The English Atlantic, 1675–1740: An Exploration of Communications and Community* (New York, 1986); Bernard Bailyn, *The Peopling of British North America: An Introduction* (New York, 1986); idem, *Voyagers to the West: A Passage in the Peopling of America on the Eve of the Revolution* (New York, 1986).

12. On the broad international spread of Calvinism, unknown to most American historians, see a pathbreaking work by Menna Prestwich, ed., *International Calvinism, 1541–1715* (Oxford, 1986); on Apollos Rivoire, see Fischer, *Paul Revere's Ride*, 6.

13. Willi Paul Adams, *The German Americans: An Ethnic Experience* (Indianapolis, 1993); Willard Whitaker and Gary Horlacher, *Broad Bay Pioneers* (Rockport, ME, 1998); James G. Leyburn, *The Scotch Irish: A Social History* (Chapel Hill, NC, 1962).

14. Fischer, *Albion's Seed*, 3–205; Charles M. Andrews, *The Colonial Period of American History* (4 vols., New Haven, CT, 1934–38), vol. 1, chap. 18; David Cressy, *Coming Over: Migration and Communication Between England and New England in the Seventeenth Century* (Cambridge, Eng., 1987); Jacob Marcus, *The Colonial American Jew* (3 vols., New York, 1970).

15. For indentured servants, see David Galenson, *White Servitude in Colonial America* (Cambridge, Eng., 1984); Wesley Frank Craven, *White, Red, and Black: The Seventeenth-Century Virginian* (Charlottesville, VA, 1971), 5; Russell Menard, "Immigration to the Chesapeake Colonies in the Seventeenth Century," *Maryland Historical Magazine* 68 (1973): 323–29; Fischer, *Albion's Seed*, 226–32.

16. Edmund Morgan, *American Slavery, American Freedom* (New York, 1975).

17. Roger Ekirch, *Bound for America: The Transportation of British Convicts to the Colonies, 1718–1775* (Oxford, 1987, 1990).

18. David Hackett Fischer and James Kelly, *Bound Away: Virginia and the Westward Movement* (Charlottesville, VA, 2000); Peter Clark and David Souden, eds., *Migration and Society in Early Modern England* (London, 1987).

19. Sally Schwartz, *A Mixed Multitude* (New York, 1987), 81–119.

20. Marion T. Bennett, *American Immigration Policies* (Washington, 1963).

21. The major decision was *City of New York v. Miln* (1837), 36 U.S. 102; later reversed in *Edwards v. California* (1941), 314 U.S. 160.

22. For the major Catholic populations, see Oscar Handlin, *Boston's Immigrants* (1941; rev. ed. Cambridge, MA, 1959); Alexander DeConde, *Half Bitter, Half Sweet: An Excursion into Italian-American History* (New York, 1971); Robert Rumilly, *Histoire des Franco-Américains* (Montreal, 1958); and William I. Thomas and Florian Znaniecki, eds., *The Polish Peasant in Europe and America* (2 vols., Boston, 1918–20), great classics all. For religious pluralities by county in 1950, 1970, and 2000, see various editions of Edwin S. Gaustad, *Historical Atlas of Religion in America* (New York, 1962, 1976) and *New Historical Atlas of Religion in America* (Oxford and New York, 2000), all with foldout maps.

23. David Ward, *Cities and Immigrants: A Geography of Change in Nineteenth-Century America* (New York, 1971); Raymond Gastil, *Cultural Regions of the United States* (Seattle, 1975): Wilbur Zelinsky, *The Cultural Geography of the United States* (Englewood Cliffs, NJ, 1973; rev ed., 1992).

24. Jesse T. Carpenter, *The South as a Conscious Minority, 1789–1861* (New York, 1930).

25. Paul W. Conner, *Poor Richard's Politicks: Benjamin Franklin and His New American Order* (New York, 1965), 84–87, 143, 241.

26. James Morton Smith, *Freedom's Fetters* (Ithaca, NY, 1956).

27. John Higham, *Strangers in the Land: Patterns of American Nativism* (New Brunswick, 1988); Tyler Anbinder, *Nativism and Slavery: The Northern Know Nothings and the Politics of the 1850s* (Oxford, 1992); John R. Mulkern, *The Know-Nothing Party in Massachusetts: The Rise and Fall of a People's Movement* (Boston, 1990); Steven Taylor, "Progressive Nativism: The Know-Nothing Party in Massachusetts," *Historical Journal of Massachusetts* 28 (2000): 167–85.

28. *Henderson v. Mayor of NY*, 82 U.S. 259 (1875).

29. Vincent Cannato, *American Passage: The History of Ellis Island* (New York, 2009).

30. Robert A. Divine, *American Immigration Policy, 1924–1952* (New York, 1957, 1972).

31. Jerome Edwards, *Pat McCarran: Political Boss of Nevada* (Reno, NV, 1982).

32. *Historical Statistics of the United States* (1975), 105–20.

33. Lawrence Fuchs, *The American Kaleidoscope: Race, Ethnicity, and the Civic Culture* (Middletown, CT, 1990).

34. Erik Olssen and Marcia Stenson, *A Century of Change: New Zealand, 1800–1900* (Auckland, 1989, 1994), 233.

35. Phillips and Hearn, *Settlers*, 32–33; Jock Phillips et al., eds., *Settler and Migrant Peoples of New Zealand* (Auckland, 2006), 23–27. Edward Gibbon Wakefield's plan of assisted migration appears in his *Proposal for Colonizing Australasia* (1829).

36. Phillips and Hearn, *Settlers*, 32–33; Phillips et al., *Settler and Migrant Peoples of New Zealand*, 23–27.

37. The full story is not known, as some of the provincial records have disappeared. The best general study is Phillips and Hearn, *Settlers*, 34–41.

38. Ibid., 41–45.

39. Rollo Arnold, *The Farthest Promised Land: English Villages, New Zealand Immigrants of the 1870s* (Wellington, 1981), 36–62, 79–100; Olssen and Stenson, *Century of Change*, 235–37; Phillips and Hearn, *Settlers*, 43.

40. Phillips et al., *Settler and Migrant Peoples of New Zealand*, 30.

41. Phillips and Hearn, *Settlers*, 45.

42. Ibid., 47–50; Val Wood, *War Brides: They Followed Their Hearts to New Zealand* (Auckland, 1991); Katie Pickles, "Pink Cheeked and Surplus: Single British Women's Inter-war Migration to New Zealand," in *Shifting Centres: Women and Migration in New Zealand History*, ed. Lyndon Fraser and Katie Pickles (Dunedin, 2000), 63–80.

43. Megan Hutching, *Long Journey for Sevenpence: An Oral History of Assisted Immigration to New Zealand from the United Kingdom, 1947–1975* (Wellington, 1999), 9–11.

44. Ruth Alexander, *The Royal New Zealand Fencibles, 1847–1852* (Auckland, 1997); Ian Ward, "Fencibles," in *The Oxford Companion to New Zealand Military History*, ed. Ian McGibbon (Auckland, 2000), 164–65.

45. Phillips and Hearn, *Settlers*, 40–41.

46. James Belich, "War," in *The Future of the Past: Themes in New Zealand History*, ed. Colin Davis and Peter Lineham (Palmerston North, 1991), 122.

47. Phillips and Hearn, *Settlers*, 38, 47, 57, 60–61, 79, 87–89, 111, 122, 131.

48. Ann Beaglehole, "Immigration Regulation," in Phillips et al., *Settler and Migrant Peoples of New Zealand*, 52–55.

49. Ibid., 56–59.

50. *New Zealand Official Yearbook* (2006), table 5.16.

51. Ibid., 97, 104–6.

52. Phillips and Hearn, *Settlers*, 30–50; J. B. Condliffe, *New Zealand in the Making: A Study of Social and Economic Development* (1930; London, 1959); Keith Sinclair, *History of New Zealand* (Auckland and Harmondsworth, 1959; 5th rev. ed. with additional material by Raewyn Dalziel, 2000), 98, 101–5, 107, 167–68; W. P. Morrell, and D. Hall, *A History of New Zealand Life* (Christchurch, 1962); Olssen and Stenson, *Century of Change*, 237; W. D. Borrie, *Immigration to New Zealand, 1854–1938* (Canberra, 1991); K. W. Thomson and A. D. Trlin, eds., *Immigrants in New Zealand* (Palmerston North, 1970).

53. Arnold, *Farthest Promised Land*.

54. Hutching, *Long Journey for Sevenpence*, 54–61.

55. Ibid., 83.

56. V. C. Goodall, *"Flock House": A History of the New Zealand Sheepowners' Acknowledgement of Debt to the British Seamen Fund* (Palmerston North, 1962); Phillips and Hearn, *Settlers*, 49.

57. Kathyrn Peacocke, "William Ranstead," *Dictionary of New Zealand Biography* 1:PGTK; Jim McAloon, "Frederick Riley Cooke," ibid. 1:PGTK. Also W. R. Edge, *Clarion Settlers per "Kumara," "Wakanui," "Tokomaru," "Paparoa," and "Rakaia" in 1900* (Auckland, 1974); Phillips and Hearn, *Settlers*, 47.

58. Rollo Arnold, "The 'Revolt of the Field' in Kent," *Past and Present* 64, no. 1 (1974): 88; J. R. Pole, *The Pursuit of Equality in American History* (Berkeley, CA, 1978; rev. ed., 1993).

59. Alfred Simmons, *Old England and New Zealand* (London, 1879).

60. Ibid.

61. Jock Phillips to the author, Feb. 2, 2010.

62. Henning Bender and Birgit Larsen, eds., *Danish Emigration to New Zealand* (Copenhagen, 1990); James N. Bade, ed., *The German Connection: New Zealand and German-Speaking Europe in the Nineteenth Century* (Oxford, 1993); Andrew Trlin, *Now Respected, Once Despised: Yugoslavs in New Zealand* (Auckland, 1991).

63. Donald Akenson, a leading historian of New Zealand's Irish population, reckons their numbers as follows, as a proportion of total population (exclusive of indigenous Maoris):

Year	Irish Catholics	Irish Protestants
1861	11.0%	2.1%
1871	13.9%	4.7%
1881	14.1%	4.8%
1891	13.9%	4.8%
1901	14.2%	4.5%
1911	13.9%	4.3%
1921	13.4%	4.0%
1936	13.1%	3.9%
1945	13.2%	3.9%
1951	12.9%	3.8%

Source: Akenson, "Immigration and Ethnicity in New Zealand and the USA—The Irish Example," in Phillips, *New Worlds*, 46.

Women's Rights

1. Laurel Ulrich, *Good Wives: Image and Reality in the Lives of Women in Northern New England, 1650–1750* (New York, 1982); Raewyn Dalziel, "The Colonial Helpmeet: Women's Role and the Vote in Nineteenth-Century New Zealand," *New Zealand Journal of History* 11 (1977): 112–23.

2. David Hackett Fischer, *Albion's Seed: Four British Folkways in America* (New York and Oxford, 1989), 286–306; Julia Cherry Spruill, *Women's Life and Work in the Southern Colonies* (1938; New York, 1972), 236–41; *Archives of Maryland* 4:417.

3. Wolfgang Amadeus Mozart, Christoph Friedrich Bretzner, and Gottlieb Staphanie, *Die Entführung aus dem Serail* (Vienna, ca. 1780–81), act II, lines 8–9. The score is online at MozartProject.org and the Web site of the International Music Score Library Project. See also Volkmar Braunbehrens, *Mozart in Vienna, 1781–1791* (New York, 1990), 60–78.

4. Raymond Williams, *Keywords: A Vocabulary of Culture and Society* (New York, 1976); *Oxford English Dictionary*, s.v. "ism," "feminism."

5. Judith Sargent Murray, "On the Equality of the Sexes," *Massachusetts Magazine* 2 (March 1790): 32–35. Her other writings on the condition of women include "Desultory Thoughts upon the Utility of Encouraging a Degree of Self-Complacency, Especially in Female Bosoms," *Gentleman's and Lady's Town and Country Magazine* 1 (1784): 251–53; *The Gleaner* (Boston, 1798). Cf. Mary Wollstonecraft, *A Vindication of the Rights of Woman* (1792; New York, 1967); Mary Beth Norton, *Liberty's Daughters* (Boston, 1980); Ronald Hoffman and Peter J. Albert, eds., *Women in the Age of the American Revolution* (Charlottesville, VA, 1989).

6. Richard H. Chused, *Private Acts in Public Places: A Social History of Divorce in the Formative Era of American Family Law* (Philadelphia, 1994); Martin Schultz, "Divorce in Early America: Origins and Patterns in Three North Central States," *Sociological Quarterly* 25 (1984): 511–26.

7. Linda Kerber, *Women of the Republic* (Chapel Hill, 1980).

8. Mark Van Doren, ed., *Correspondence of Aaron Burr and His Daughter Theodosia* (New York, 1929).

9. Margaret Fuller, "The Great Lawsuit. Man *versus* Men. Woman *versus* Woman." *Dial* 4 (1843): 1–47; idem, *Woman in the Nineteenth Century* (New York, 1845); Ralph Waldo Emerson et al., *Memoirs of Margaret Fuller Ossoli* (2 vols., Boston, 1852).

10. Harold Kirker and James Kirker, *Bulfinch's Boston, 1787–1817* (New York, 1964); Eleanor Pearson DeLorme, "The Swan Commissions," *Winterthur Portfolio* 14 (1979): 361–95; John F. Stegeman and Janet A. Stegeman, *Caty: A Biography of Catharine Littlefield Greene* (Athens, GA, 1985, 2000); Bessie Rowland James, *Anne Royall's U.S.A.* (New Brunswick, NJ, 1972; Cynthia Earman, "An Uncommon Scold: Treasure-Talk Describes Life of Anne Royall," *Library of Congress Information Bulletin*, Jan. 2000, http://www.loc.gov/loc/lcib/0001/royall.html.

11. The idea of domesticity was invented by William Taylor and presented at a conference in Chatham, Massachusetts, 1963. The pathbreaking work is Nancy Cott, *The Bonds of Womanhood: "Woman's Sphere" in New England, 1780–1835* (New Haven, CT, 1977).

12. Sally G. McMillen, *Seneca Falls and the Origins of the Women's Rights Movement* (New York, 2008), 90–98.

13. Ellen Carol DuBois, *Feminism and Suffrage: The Emergence of an Independent Women's Movement in America, 1848–1869* (Ithaca, NY, 1978), 39.

14. Ibid., 48.

15. Elizabeth Cady Stanton, *Eighty Years and More: Reminiscences, 1815–1897* (1898; New York, 1971).

16. John Cowie Reid, *Auckland Star*, May 30, 1964.

17. Dalziel, "The Colonial Helpmeet," 119–20, citing John R. Godley, ed., *Letters from Early New Zealand by Charlotte Godley, 1850–1853* (Christchurch, 1951), 282.

18. Evelyn Hosken, *Life on a Five Pound Note* (Timaru, 1964), 112, quoted in Harry Orsman and Jan Moore, eds., *Heinemann Dictionary of New Zealand Quotations* (Auckland, 1988), 48–49. The same tale is told of other families in New Zealand.

19. Marion Diamond, *Emigration and Empire: The Life of Maria S. Rye* (New York, 1999), 107, 123.

20. Charlotte Macdonald, "Maria Susan Rye," *Dictionary of New Zealand Biography* 1:380–82; idem, *A Woman of Good Character* (Wellington, 1990), 28–36.

21. Charlotte Macdonald, "Caroline Cadette Howard" [Caroline Alpenny], *Dictionary of New Zealand Biography* 1:204.

22. Mary Müller, *An Appeal to the Men of New Zealand* (n.p., 1869).

23. Joan Stevens, ed., *Mary Taylor, Friend of Charlotte Brontë: Letters from New Zealand and Elsewhere* (Auckland, 1972); Charlotte Macdonald, ed., *The Vote, the Pill and the Demon Drink: A History of Feminist Writing in New Zealand, 1869–1993* (Wellington, 1993), 13–31.

24. Polly Plum [Mary Colclough], "What Women Want," "Polly Plum's Opponents," and "Answers to Jellaby Pater," *New Zealand Herald*, July 31, August 14, August 18, 1871, in Macdonald, *Vote, Pill and Demon Drink*, 27–31.

25. Beryl Hughes, "Kate Milligan Edger," Cherry Hankin, "Helen Connon," Dorothy Page, "Caroline Freeman," *Dictionary of New Zealand Biography* 1:125–26, 95–96, 158–59.

26. Hankin, "Connon"; Philippa Mein Smith, *A Concise History of New Zealand* (Cambridge, Eng., 2005), 88.

27. Hughes, "Edger," Hankin, "Connon," Page, "Freeman."

28. Melanie Nolan and Caroline Daley, "International Feminist Perspectives on Suffrage: An Introduction," in *Suffrage and Beyond: International Feminist Perspectives*, ed. Daley and Nolan (New York, 1994), 1.

29. Quoted in Maxine McGrannachan, *A Fair Field and No Favour: The Story of Margaret Home Sievwright. 1844–1905* (Gisborne, 1993), 39.

30. Raewyn Dalziel, "Presenting the Enfranchisement of New Zealand Women Abroad," in Daley and Nolan, *Suffrage and Beyond*, 61; Sandra Coney, *Standing in the Sunshine: A History of New Zealand Women Since They Won the Vote* (Auckland, 1993); Tessa Malcolm, "Kate Sheppard," *Dictionary of New Zealand Biography* 2:459–61.

31. Raewyn Dalziel, "Anna Paterson Stout," *Dictionary of New Zealand Biography* 2:483–84; W. H. Dunn and I.L.M. Richardson, *Sir Robert Stout* (Wellington, 1961); Coney, *Standing in the Sunshine*, 21.

32. Elspeth M. Simpson, "Margaret Home Sievwright," *Dictionary of New Zealand Biography* 2:463–64; Coney, *Standing in the Sunshine*, 21; McGrannachan, *Fair Field and No Favour*.

33. Coney, *Standing in the Sunshine*, 20; Roberta Nicholls, "Amey Daldy," *Dictionary of New Zealand Biography* 2:109–10.

34. William Sievwright, *Free Association of Women Electors* (Wellington, 1893).

35. *New Zealand Parliamentary Debates* 48:202; Dunn and Richardson, *Sir Robert Stout*, 119–20.

36. Nicholls, "Daldy"; Coney, *Standing in the Sunshine*, 20.

37. Julius Vogel, *Anno Domini 2000; or, Woman's Destiny* (London, 1889).

38. Patricia Grimshaw, *Women's Suffrage in New Zealand* (Auckland, 1972), 38.

39. Dalziel, "Presenting the Enfranchisement of New Zealand Women Abroad," 53.

40. Grimshaw, *Women's Suffrage*.

41. Nolan and Daley, "International Feminist Perspectives on Suffrage," 4.

42. Grimshaw, *Women's Suffrage*, 116.

43. Dalziel, "Presenting the Enfranchisement of New Zealand Women Abroad," 62.

44. Ibid., quoting Kate Sheppard, *Woman Suffrage in New Zealand* (n.p., 1907), 15.

45. Raewyn Dalziel, "Women in New Societies," in *New Worlds? The Comparative History of New Zealand and the United States*, ed. Jock Phillips (Wellington, 1989), 9–10, quoting Maud Wood Park, "New Zealand," Women's Rights Coll., vol. 40, Schlesinger Library, Radcliffe College, Cambridge, MA.

46. Dalziel, "Presenting the Enfranchisement of New Zealand Women Abroad," 56.

47. Rebecca J. Mead, *How the Vote Was Won: Woman Suffrage in the Western United States, 1868–1914* (New York, 2004).

48. Jacqueline Van Vorens, *Carrie Chapman Catt: A Public Life* (New York, 1996); Robert Booth Fowler, *Carrie Catt, Feminist Politician* (Boston, 1986).

49. Katherine H. Adams and Michael L. Keene, *Alice Paul and the American Suffrage Campaign* (Urbana, IL, 2007).

50. Anne Firor Scott and Andrew MacKay Scott, *One Half the People: The Fight for Woman Suffrage* (Urbana, IL, 1982); Aileen S. Kraditor, *The Ideas of the Woman Suffrage Movement, 1890–1920* (New York, 1981).

51. Jane Addams, *The Second Twenty Years at Hull House* (New York, 1930), 103; idem, *Peace and Bread in Time of War* (1922; Boston, 1960), 132–51; David Hackett Fischer, *Liberty and Freedom* (New York and Oxford, 2005), 450.

52. Jean Batten, *Alone in the Sky* (Auckland, 1934, 1979); Ian Mackersey, *Jean Batten: The Garbo of the Skies* (New York, 1999); Jean L. Backus, *Letters from Amelia, 1901–1937* (Boston, 1982); Doris Rich, *Amelia Earhart: A Biography* (Washington, 1989); Susan Ware, *Still Missing: Amelia Earhart and the Search for Modern Feminism* (New York, 1993).

53. In American data, the inflection point for the surge in marriage and fertility rates was in 1942–43, and the peak was 1957. See *Historical Statistics of the United States* (1975), series B20, B36–41; Ansley J. Coale and Melvin Zelnik, eds. *New Estimates of Fertility and Population in the United States* (Princeton, NJ, 1963).

54. Jessica Weiss, *To Have and To Hold: Marriage, the Baby Boom, and Social Change* (Chicago, 2000) is an excellent and well-balanced work; Elaine Tyler May, *Homeward Bound: American Families in the Cold War* (New York, 2008) is a dark interpretation, heavily ideological, which links domesticity to the Cold War.

55. Barbara Deckard, *The Women's Movement* (New York, 1979), 332.

56. Sara Evans, *Personal Politics: The Roots of Women's Liberation in the Civil Rights Movement and the New Left* (New York, 1979).

57. Ibid., 214–15.

58. Betty Friedan, *The Feminine Mystique* (New York, 1963); Nancy Cott and Elizabeth Pleck, *A Heritage of Her Own: Toward a New Social History of American Women* (New York, 1979).

59. Bruno Bettelheim, "Individual and Mass Behavior in Extreme Situations," *Journal of Abnormal Psychology* 38 (1943): 432–50; Eugen Kogon, *The Theory and Practice of Hell* (New York, 1946); Olga Lengyel, *Five Chimneys: The Story of Auschwitz* (Chicago, 1947). For other work influenced by this literature, see Stanley Elkins, *Slavery* (Chicago, 1959; 2nd ed., 1968).

60. Judith Hole and Ellen Levine, *Rebirth of Feminism* (New York, 1971), 81.

61. Gerda Lerner, *The Majority Finds Its Past* (Oxford, 1979), 38–39, and "Women's Rights and American Feminism," 48–61; for an academic understanding of the movement centered mainly on equality, see William H. Chafe, *Women and Equality: Changing Patterns in American Culture* (New York, 1977).

62. Margot Roth, "Housewives or Human Beings?" *New Zealand Listener*, Nov. 20, 1959, in Macdonald, *Vote, Pill and Demon Drink*, 6, 138–41.

63. Macdonald, *Vote, Pill and Demon Drink*, 162; Coney, *Standing in the Sunshine*, 142.

64. Sonja Davies, *Bread and Roses* (Auckland, 1984; 2nd ed., Masterton, 1993); idem, *Marching On* (Auckland, 1997); Eva Rickard obituary, *New Zealand Herald*, Dec. 9, 1997; Sue Kedgley biography, Green Party Web site, www.greens.org.nz/people/suekedgley.

65. Melanie Nolan, *Breadwinning: New Zealand Women and the State* (Canterbury, 2000), 230–66.

66. Macdonald, *Vote, Pill and Demon Drink*, 161–205, reproduces the major documents in this campaign.

67. Some scholars have argued that yet another wave of feminism began in this period, but none of the usual indicators of a feminist movement appeared.

68. It is commonly called "third-wave feminism," by people who remember only the "second-wave" new feminism of their youth and all other activity that is dimly remembered as "first-wave feminism." If so, it would be the fifth wave in the United States and fourth in New Zealand, but there is no evidence of a wave of feminism beginning circa 1990. Feminist activity was declining, not increasing, in that period, though other movements for women's rights were strong.

69. World Economic Forum, *Women Leaders and Gender Parity: Global Gender Gap Report* (Geneva, 2008, 2010).

70. Louise Chunn, "Helen, Our Lost Leader," *Guardian*, Nov. 22, 2008.

71. Hillary Rodham Clinton, *Living History* (New York, 2003); Carl Bernstein, *A Woman in Charge* (New York, 2007); Anne Kornblut, *Notes from the Cracked Ceiling* (New York, 2009).

72. Dalziel, "Presenting the Enfranchisement of Women Abroad," 62.

Racist Wrongs

1. George M. Fredrickson, *Racism: A Short History* (Princeton, NJ, 2002) is in many ways an excellent and thoughtful work, but fundamentally misconceived in its attempt to link religious belief and racial prejudice in the early modern era. That relationship was not a two-cell but a four-cell problem. The most murderous racists were pagan.

2. Johann Friedrich Blumenbach, *De generis humani varietate nativa [On the Natural Variety of Humanity]* (Göttingen, 1776), a dissertation at the University of Göttingen in Germany. In later works Blumenbach argued that variation within races was greater than the variance between them, and some individual Africans, Amerindians, and Malay-Polynesians were not inferior to "Caucasians," a term of his invention. See Sara Eigen, "Self, Race, and Species: J. F. Blumenbach's Atlas Experiment," *German Quarterly* 78 (2005): 277–98.

3. Joseph Arthur, Comte de Gobineau, *Essai sur l'inégalité des races humaines* (4 vols., Paris, 1853–55).

4. Jacob-Peter Mayer, Maurice Degros, and Jean-Jacques Chevallier, eds., *Correspondance d'Alexis de Tocqueville et d'Arthur de Gobineau*, in *Alexis de Tocqueville, Oeuvres Complètes*, vol. 9 (Paris, 1959); an English abridgement appears in John Lukacs, ed., *Tocqueville: The European Revolution & Correspondence with Gobineau* (New York, 1959), 176–336.

5. In the United States the translator was Henry Hotze, a Swiss aristocrat who moved to Mobile, Alabama, circa 1850, and worked with an Alabama physician, Dr. Josiah Clark Nott. Together they translated the first volume of Gobineau's work as *The Moral and Intellectual Diversity of Races, with Particular Reference to their Respective Influence in the Civil and Political History of Mankind* (Philadelphia, 1856). For the American impact, see Lonnie A. Burnett, *Henry Hotze, Confederate Propagandist* (Tuscaloosa, AL, 2008); and Robert E. Bonner, "Slavery, Confederate Diplomacy, and the Racialist Mission of Henry Hotze," *Civil War History* 51 (2005): 288–316. In Germany, the translator of Gobineau and founder of the Gobineau Society was Ludwig Schemann, *Versuch über die Ungleichheit der Menschenracen* (Bayreuth, 1897); see also Michael D. Biddiss, *Father of Racist Ideology: Social and Political Thought of Count Gobineau* (New York, 1970); Joachim Fest, *Hitler* (New York, 1975); Richard Evans, *The Coming of the Third Reich* (London, 2003).

6. Historians are not of one mind on the subject. Vann Woodward's *Strange Career of Jim Crow* (Oxford, 1955) argued for a period of "forgotten alternatives" between the end of slavery and the beginning of Jim Crow. Close studies of individual states found that segregation developed earlier in law and custom. See Roger A. Fischer, *The Segregation Struggle in Louisiana, 1862–1877* (Urbana, IL, 1974); Howard N. Rabinowitz, "From Exclusion to Segregation: Southern Race Relations, 1865–1890," *Journal of American History* 63 (1978): 325–50.

7. Rayford W. Logan, *The Betrayal of the American Negro from Rutherford B. Hayes to Woodrow Wilson* (New York, 1997); idem, *The Negro in American Life and Thought: The Nadir, 1877–1901* (New York, 1954).

8. Ian Pool, *Te Iwi Maori: A New Zealand Population Past, Present & Projected* (Auckland, 1991), 59–131; *NZOY* (2002), 112; George Rawick, *The American Slave: A Composite Autobiography* (Westport, CT, 1972–79.)

9. Alfred Simmons, *Old England and New Zealand* (London, 1879), 19.

10. Richard Taylor, *The Past and Present of New Zealand* (London, 1868), 111.

11. Simmons, *Old England and New Zealand*, 106.

12. Quoted in Rucolph Vecoli, "The Lady and the Huddled Masses," in Wilton S. Dillon and Neil G. Kotler, eds., *The Statue of Liberty Revisited* (Washington, 1994), 68.

13. Glenda Elizabeth Gilmore, *Gender and Jim Crow* (Chapel Hill, NC, 1996), xv.

14. Charles M. Payne, *I've Got the Light of Freedom: The Organizing Tradition and the Mississippi Freedom Struggle* (Berkeley, CA, 1995), 1.

15. Gilmore, *Gender and Jim Crow*, xv–xxi.

16. Joel Williamson, *New People: Miscegenation and Mulattoes in the United States* (Baton Rouge, 1995).

17. Angela Ballara, *Proud To Be White? A Survey of Pakeha Prejudice in New Zealand* (Auckland, 1986), 98–103; for racism in Pukekohe, see James Belich, *Paradise Reforged* (Auckland, 2001), 190.

18. Belich, *Paradise Reforged*, 215.

19. Raphael Lemkin, *Axis Rule in Occupied Europe* (Washington, 1944), 19, 79–95; Ryszard Szawlowski, "Raphael Lemkin (1900–1959), the Polish Lawyer Who Created the Concept of 'Genocide,' " *Polish Quarterly of International Affairs* 2 (2005): 98–133.

20. Stéphane Courtois et al., *Le livre noir du communisme: crimes, terreur, répression* (Paris, 1997).

21. James T. Patterson, ed., *Brown v. Board of Education* (Oxford, 2001); Richard Kluger, *Simple Justice: The History of Brown v. Board of Education and Black America's Struggle for Equality* (New York, 1983).

22. Langston Hughes, "Refugee in America," in *Selected Poems of Langston Hughes* (New York, 1981), 290.

23. Alonzo L. Hamby, *Man of the People: A Life of Harry S. Truman* (New York and Oxford, 1995), 433.

24. President's Committee on Civil Rights, *To Secure These Rights* (Washington, 1948); Mary L. Dudziak, *Cold War Civil Rights: Race and the Image of American Democracy* (Princeton, NJ, 2000), 79.

25. Dudziak, *Cold War Civil Rights*, 90, 94.
26. Ira Glasser, *Visions of Liberty: The Bill of Rights for All Americans* (New York, 1991), 221, 223.
27. For general works, David Garrow, *Bearing the Cross: Martin Luther King, Jr., and the Southern Christian Leadership Conference* (New York, 1986); Taylor Branch, *Parting the Waters: America in the King Years, 1954–63* (New York, 1988); some of this section follows David Hackett Fischer, *Liberty and Freedom* (New York and Oxford, 2005), 603–7.
28. Martin Luther King Jr., *Autobiography*, ed. Clayborne Carson (New York, 1998), 20, 23.
29. Ibid., 23.
30. Martin Luther King Jr., *Stride Toward Freedom: The Montgomery Story* (1958; Boston, 1986), 30–55.
31. King, *Autobiography*, 60.
32. King, *Autobiography*, 60–61.
33. John Lewis, interview, Feb. 23, 1999, http://www.time.com/time/community/transcripts/1999/022399lewis.html.
34. Martin Luther King Jr., "I Have a Dream," first published in *Negro History Bulletin* 21 (May 1968): 16–17; rpt. in Martin Luther King Jr., *I Have a Dream: Writings and Speeches That Changed the World*, ed. James M. Washington (New York, 1996), 102–6.
35. The mass media also popularized a simplified history in which King "launched the civil rights movement," much to the resentment of others and to the embarrassment of King himself. Richard Lentz, *Symbols, the News Magazines, and Martin Luther King* (Baton Rouge, 1990).
36. Payne, *I've Got the Light of Freedom*, 397.
37. Branch, *Parting the Waters*; David Garrow, *Protest at Selma* (New Haven, 1978); John J. Ansbro, *Martin Luther King Jr.: The Making of a Mind* (Maryknoll, NY, 1982).
38. Michael King, *Whina: A Biography of Whina Cooper* (Auckland, 1983), 207; T. J. Hearn, *Taupo-Kaingaroa Twentieth Century Overview: Land Alienation and Land Administration* (Wellington, 2004), quoted in Philippa Mein Smith, *A Concise History of New Zealand* (Cambridge, Eng., 2005), 111.
39. King, *Whina*, 206.
40. Quoted in ibid., 228.
41. David Barber, "Obituary: Matiu Rata," *Independent*, July 28, 1997, http://www.independent.co.uk/news/people/obituary-matiu-rata-1253022.html.
42. Tom Brooking, *The History of New Zealand* (Westport, CT, 2004), 148.
43. Smith, *Concise History of New Zealand*, 233.
44. Richard S. Hill, *Maori and the State: Crown-Maori Relations in New Zealand/Aotearoa, 1950–2000* (Wellington, 2009), 221–45; Stuart Banner, *Possessing the Pacific: Land Settlers and Indigenous People from Australia to Alaska* (Cambridge, MA, 2007), 315.
45. "Prime Minister's Waitangi Day Speech," Feb. 26, 2010, http://www.nzherald.co.nz/multiculturalism/news/article.cfm?c_id=58&objectid=10624511.
46. Smith, *Concise History of New Zealand*, 232–36; Paul Temm, *The Waitangi Tribunal: The Conscience of the Nation* (Auckland, 1990).
47. Graham Taylor, *The New Deal and American Indian Tribalism: The Administration of the Indian Reorganization Act, 1934–35* (Lincoln, NE, 1980).
48. Harvey D. Rosenthal, *Their Day in Court: A History of the Indian Claims Commission* (New York, 1990); Alison R. Bernstein, *American Indians and World War II: Toward a New Era in Indian Affairs* (Norman, OK, 1991).
49. Patrick Reis, "Obama Admin Strikes $3.4B Deal in Indian Trust Lawsuit," *New York Times*, Dec. 8, 2009; "*Cobell* Settlement Waits for Congress," *Indian Country Today*, Dec. 24, 2009, http://www.indiancountrytoday.com; Maria Streshinsky, "Triumph and Tragedy in Indian Country," *Atlantic Online*, Dec. 14, 2009, http://www.theatlantic.com.
50. Wilcomb E. Washburn, *Red Man's Land, White Man's Law* (1959; 2nd ed., Norman, OK, 1995), with an historical survey, 25–87; Rosenthal, *Their Day in Court*, vii–viii, 245–62; Robert A. Williams Jr., *Like a Loaded Weapon: The Rehnquist Court, Indian Rights, and the Legal History of Racism in America* (Minneapolis, 2005), 161–97.

51. John F. Kennedy, Executive Order 10925, Establishing the President's Committee on Equal Employment Opportunity, March 6, 1961, http://www.thecre.com/fedlaw/legal6/eo10925.htm.

52. Lyndon B. Johnson, "Commencement Address at Howard University," 1965, Lyndon Baines Johnson Presidential Library and Museum website, http.lbjlib.utexas.edu/was/index.php?pid=60553.

53. Terry Anderson, *The Pursuit of Fairness: A History of Affirmative Action* (New York and Oxford, 2005) is an excellent work, balanced and careful.

54. Steven Andrew Light and Kathryn R. L. Rand, *Indian Gaming and Tribal Sovereignty: The Casino Compromise* (Lawrence, KS, 2005).

55. Andrew Silvers, "Southern Ute Executives Give Lecture on Renewable Resources," *Shorthorn*, Nov. 18, 2009; Kirk Johnson, "A New Test for Business and Biofuel," *New York Times*, Aug. 17, 2009.

56. Brooking, *History of New Zealand*, 198–99.

57. This exchange occurred in public meetings at Otago University in 1995.

58. Robin W. Winks, *The Relevance of Canadian History: U.S. and Imperial Perspectives* (Toronto, 1979; Lanham, MD, 1988), 23. The same judgment was shared by American social scientists such as Seymour Martin Lipset, who agreed entirely with Winks.

59. Keith Sinclair, "Why are Race Relations in New Zealand Better than in South Africa, South Australia, or South Dakota?" *New Zealand Journal of History* 5 (1971): 121–27; K. R. Howe, *Race Relations: Australia and New Zealand: A Comparative Survey, 1770s to 1970s* (Wellington, 1977).

60. Belich, *Paradise Reforged*, 190.

61. Deborah Montgomerie favored comparative approaches as a way of studying "forms of imperial control" and "strategies of native resistance and survival," and did precisely that in "Coming to Terms: Ngai Tahu, Robeson County Indians and the Garden River Band of Ojibwa, 1840–1940" (PhD diss., Duke University, 1993); I am grateful to Prof. John Thompson for an opportunity to read this dissertation in his office. See also Deborah Montgomerie, "Beyond the Search for Good Imperialism: The Challenge of Comparative Ethnohistory," *Koha, Essays in Honour of M.P.K. Sorrenson, New Zealand Journal of History* 31 (1997): 153–68.

62. Richard S. Hill, "Maori and State Policy," in *The New Oxford History of New Zealand*, ed. Giselle Byrnes (South Melbourne, 2009), 513–36, 536.

63. Banner, *Possessing the Pacific*, 315–20.

Lib-Labs and Progressives

Epigraphs: Frank Parsons, *The Story of New Zealand: A History of New Zealand from the Earliest Times to the Present* (Philadelphia, 1904), 691, 715, quoted in Peter J. Coleman, *Progressivism and the World of Reform: New Zealand and the Origins of the American Welfare State* (Lawrence, KS, 1987), 54; Woodrow Wilson, *The New Freedom* (1913; New York, 1916), 3–32, 55–78, 275–94; "Conquest of a New Freedom," speech delivered at the Washington Baseball Park, Indianapolis, Indiana, Oct 3, 1912, in *A Crossroads of Freedom: The 1912 Campaign Speeches of Woodrow Wilson*, ed. John Wells Davidson (New Haven, 1956), 325.

1. James T. Kloppenberg, *Uncertain Victory: Social Democracy and Progressivism in European and American Thought* (New York, 1986); Daniel T. Rodgers, *Atlantic Crossings: Social Politics in a Progressive Age* (Cambridge, 1998); Thomas Bender, *A Nation Among Nations: America's Place in World History* (New York, 2006); and a large literature cited in Kloppenberg, 511–28, Rodgers, 511–12, and Bender, 341–48.

2. Peter Flora and Arnold J. Heidenheimer, eds., *The Development of Welfare States in Europe and America* (New Brunswick, NJ, 1981); Gary Marks, *Unions in Politics: Britain, Germany, and the United States in the Nineteenth and Early Twentieth Centuries* (Princeton, 1989); Stefan Berger, *The British Labour Party and the German Social Democrats, 1900–1931* (Oxford, 1994); Gerhard Ritter, *Social Welfare in Germany and Britain: Origins and Development* (Leamington Spa, 1986).

3. An excellent pioneering work is Peter J. Coleman, *Progressivism and the World of Reform: New Zealand and the Origins of the American Welfare State* (Lawrence, KS, 1987), one of the best comparative and interactive studies of New Zealand and the United States in any period.

4. Tom Brooking, "Economic Transformation," in *The Oxford History of New Zealand*, ed., Geoffrey Rice, 2nd ed. (Auckland and Oxford, 1992), 230.

5. Thomas M. Hocken, *Contributions to the Early History of New Zealand* (London, 1898), 176.

6. This derives from David Hackett Fischer, "Corruption: An American History," unpublished manuscript, which includes a quantitative study of scandalous corruption in the mayoral administrations of twelve American cities from the early nineteenth to the late twentieth century.

7. For structure and conjuncture in world economic conditions, see David Hackett Fischer, *The Great Wave: Price Revolutions and the Rhythm of History* (New York and Oxford, 1996).

8. R. J. Campbell, "The 'Black Eighties'—Unemployment in New Zealand in the 1880s," *Australian Economic History Review* 16 (1977): 67–82; G. R. Hawke, *The Making of New Zealand: An Economic History* (Cambridge, Eng., 1985), 66–84; C.G.F. Simkin, *The Instability of a Dependent Economy: Economic Fluctuations in New Zealand, 1840–1914* (Oxford, 1951.)

9. New Zealand historians are not of one mind about politics in this period. See Raewyn Dalziel, "The 'Continuous Ministry' Revisited," *New Zealand Journal of History* 21 (1987): 46–61; and David Hamer, *The New Zealand Liberals: The Years of Power, 1891–1912* (Auckland, 1988).

10. The phrase was used as a pejorative by others to the left and right. A writer in the *Maoriland Worker*, Oct. 20, 1911, raged against the centrist coalition as "a nauseous mixture of Lib.-Labism and cold tea." For this and other examples, see H. W. Orsman, ed., *The Dictionary of New Zealand English: A Dictionary of New Zealandisms on Historical Principles* (Auckland and Oxford, 1997), s.v. "Lib-Lab." and "Lib.-Labism."

11. Hamer, *New Zealand Liberals.* Dean Burnham's model of "critical elections," which caused fundamental realignments in a political system, works as well for the history of New Zealand as it does for the United States, but the dates and directions were not the same. In the United States, critical elections occurred in 1800, 1828, 1860, 1896, 1912, 1932, 1960, and 1980. In New Zealand, they happened in 1890, 1911, 1935, 1949, 1960, 1984, and 1990. Walter Dean Burnham, *Critical Elections and the Mainsprings of American Politics* (New York, 1970), 1–10, 175–93.

12. Tom Brooking, *Lands for the People? The Highland Clearances and the Colonisation of New Zealand: A Biography of John McKenzie* (Dunedin, 1996), an excellent biography. John "Jock" McKenzie (1839–1901) is often confused with Mackay John Scobie McKenzie (1845–1901), commonly called Scobie McKenzie, an economic liberal, social conservative, and strong enemy of Jock McKenzie's reforms.

13. Ibid.

14. Keith Sinclair, *William Pember Reeves, New Zealand Fabian* (Oxford, 1965), still the best biography.

15. A classic of New Zealand history is *The Long White Cloud Ao Tea Roa* (London, 1898; 3rd ed., rev. and enlarged by the author, London, 1924); another major work is *State Experiments in Australia and New Zealand* (2 vols., London, 1902), still the best on its subject. Two volumes of poetry are *New Zealand and Other Poems* (London, 1898) and *The Passing of the Forest and Other Verse* (London, 1925).

16. Sinclair, *William Pember Reeves*, 69, passim.

17. R. A. Loughnan, *The Remarkable Life Story of Sir Joseph Ward* (Wellington, 1929); Michael Bassett, "In Search of Sir Joseph Ward," *NZHJ* 21 (1987): 112–24.

18. J. Drummond, *The Life and Work of Richard John Seddon, Premier of New Zealand, 1893–1906* (Christchurch, 1906); R. M. Burdon, *King Dick* (Christchurch, 1955); T.E.Y. Seddon, *The Seddons* (Auckland, 1968).

19. Drummond, *Life and Work of Seddon*, 9.

20. J. Lockwood, "Politics and Personality: Seddon and His Electorates," in *Miners and Militants*, ed. P. R. May (Christchurch, 1975), 48–79.

21. Tom Brooking explores this neglected part of Seddon's career in his forthcoming work. It will change our understanding of this extraordinary man in many ways.

22. I am grateful to Tom Brooking for his advice and suggestions.

23. Reeves, *Long White Cloud Ao Tea Roa*, 295.

24. Timothy McIvor, *The Rainmaker: A Biography of John Ballance, Journalist and Politician* (Auckland, 1989), a very informative and deeply interesting biography. A note on political terms: the head of government in New Zealand was usually called premier to 1900, and thereafter officially prime minister.

25. Erik Olssen and Marcia Stenson, *A Century of Change: New Zealand, 1800–1900* (Auckland, 1989, 1994), 396.

26. Coleman, *Progressivism and the World of Reform*, 27.

27. John Stenhouse, "God's Own Silence: Secular Nationalism, Christianity, and the Writing of New Zealand History," *New Zealand Journal of History* 38 (2004): 52–71.

28. Brooking, *Lands for the People?* 163–64.

29. McKenzie's Land Act of 1892 extended the Queen's Chain to the entire coast of New Zealand, lakes more than acres in area, and rivers more than thirty-three feet wide. The subsequent legislative and judicial history is very unclear. Owners of abutting lands frequently deny access and get away with it. Today government documents recognize that about 70 percent of the coast is open. See Tom Brooking, *The History of New Zealand* (Westport, CT, 2004), 82; idem, *Lands for the People?* 110, 179, 311; Allan McMillan, "The Queen's Chain—Another Broken Promise," New Zealand Association of Freshwater Anglers Web site, July 3, 2002, http://www.nzffa.net/index.php?option=com_content&view=article&id=78:the-queens-chain&catid=45:access&Itemid=65; Mark Hickford, "Law of the Foreshore and Seabed," http://www.teara.govt.nz/en/law-of-the-foreshore-and-seabed.

30. Raymond Richards, *Closing the Door to Destitution* (University Park, PA, 1994), 72.

31. Ibid., 73.

32. Coleman, *Progressivism and the World of Reform*, 39; W. B. Sutch, *Poverty and Progress in New Zealand: A Reassessment* (Wellington, 1969), 151.

33. Coleman, *Progressivism and the World of Reform*, 52, 56, 57; Parsons, *Story of New Zealand*.

34. Speech to the Hamilton Club of Chicago, April 10, 1899; an allusion to Virgil's "Ignobilis otii" in the *Georgics* 4.564.

35. William E. Leuchtenburg, *Theodore Roosevelt: The New Nationalism* (Englewood Cliffs, NJ, 1961).

36. Lawrence A. Cremin, *Transformation of the School: Progressivism in American Education, 1876–1957* (New York, 1961).

37. Private conversation with the author.

38. *Historical Statistics of the United States* (1975), "Nature Parks, Monuments and Allied Areas," series H806–28, pp. 396–97.

39. Daniel Okrent, *Last Call: The Rise and Fall of Prohibition* (New York, 2010); Richard Hamm, *Shaping the Eighteenth Amendment* (Chapel Hill, NC, 1995).

40. Rexford Tugwell, "The New Deal: The Progressive Tradition," *Western Political Quarterly* 3 (1950): 395–96.

41. David Hamer, "The Law and the Prophet: a Political Biography of Sir Robert Stout, 1844–1930" (MA thesis, University of Auckland, 1960); idem, "Sir Robert Stout," *New Zealand's Heritage* 50 (1971): 1391–96; idem, "Robert Stout" *Dictionary of New Zealand Biography* 2:484–87.

42. William Downie Stewart, "Three Generations," ms. autobiography, Hocken Library, University of Otago.

43. William Downie Stewart, *The Right Honourable Sir Francis H. D. Bell* (Wellington, 1937).

44. David Thomson, *A World Without Welfare: New Zealand's Colonial Experiment* (Auckland, 1998).

45. On corporate support of regulation, see Gabriel Kolko, *Railroads and Regulation, 1877–1916* (New York, 1970); idem, *The Triumph of Conservatism: A Reinterpretation of American History, 1900–1916* (Glencoe, IL, 1963).

46. John A. Garraty, *Henry Cabot Lodge* (New York, 1953).
47. Reeves, *The Long White Cloud Ao Tea Roa*, 282–83.
48. *Historical Statistics of the United States* (1976), series D951; Richards, *Closing the Door to Destitution*, 73.
49. Richards, *Closing the Door to Destitution*, 72.
50. *Historical Statistics of the United States* (1975), series D951.
51. Erik Olssen with Jeremy Brecher, "New Zealand and United States Labour Movements: The View from the Workshop Floor," in *New Worlds? The Comparative History of New Zealand and the United States*, ed. Jock Phillips (Wellington, 1989), 96–112, esp. 98–99.

Foreign Affairs, External Relations
1. An excellent history, centering on the theme of national independence, is Malcolm McKinnon, *Independence and Foreign Policy* (Auckland, 1993); a helpful review of other approaches, and an interpretation that centers on transnational themes and globalization, is David Capie, "New Zealand and the World: Imperial, International and Global Relations," in *The New Oxford History of New Zealand*, ed. Giselle Byrnes (South Melbourne, 2009), 573–98. A comprehensive survey of the American story is George C., *From Colony to Superpower: U.S. Foreign Relations Since 1776* (New York and Oxford, 2008).
2. Charles Dickens, *Little Dorrit* (London, 1855–57), chap. 25, quoted in McKinnon, *Independence and Foreign Policy*, 9.
3. For the Donatist dilemma in its relation to American history, see Edmund S. Morgan, *Visible Saints: The History of a Puritan Idea* (New York, 1963), 2–4, 113.
4. 2 Corinthians 6:17 (King James version).
5. Leading studies are still Dexter Perkins, *The Monroe Doctrine, 1823–1826* (Cambridge, MA, 1927) and Samuel Flagg Bemis, *John Quincy Adams and the Foundations of American Foreign Policy* (rev. ed., New York, 1973). More recent work includes Ernest R. May, *The Making of the Monroe Doctrine* (Cambridge, MA, 1976), William Earl Weeks, *John Quincy Adams and American Global Empire* (Lexington, KY, 1992), and Norman Saul, *Distant Friends: The United States and Russia, 1763–1867* (Lawrence, KS, 1991).
6. Howard Jones, *Abraham Lincoln and a New Birth of Freedom: The Union and Slavery in the Diplomacy of the Civil War* (Lincoln, NE, 1999); Karl Schmitt, *Mexico and the United States, 1821–1973: Conflict and Coexistence* (New York, 1974); Stephen J. Valone, " 'Weakness Offers Temptation': William H. Seward and the Assertion of the Monroe Doctrine," *Diplomatic History* 19 (1995): 585; Cyrus Veeser, "Inventing Dollar Diplomacy: The Gilded Age Origins of the Roosevelt Corollary to the Monroe Doctrine," *Diplomatic History* 27 (2003): 301–26; Lewis Gould, *The Presidency of Theodore Roosevelt* (Lawrence, KS, 1991).
7. Spruille Braden, *Diplomats and Demagogues: The Memoirs of Spruille Braden* (New York, 1971), 275, quoted in Herring, *From Colony to Superpower*, 543.
8. Richard Immerman, *The CIA in Guatemala: The Foreign Policy of Intervention* (Austin, TX, 1982); Piero Gleijeses, *Shattered Hope: The Guatemalan Revolution and the United States, 1944–1954* (Princeton, NJ, 1991).
9. Lars Schoultz, *Beneath the United States: A History of U.S. Policy Toward Latin America* (Cambridge, MA, 1998).
10. Raewyn Dalziel, *Julius Vogel: Business Politician* (Auckland, 1986), 274.
11. Angus Ross, *New Zealand Aspirations in the Pacific in the Nineteenth Century* (Oxford, 1964).
12. Angus Ross, ed., *New Zealand's Record in the Pacific Islands in the Twentieth Century* (Auckland, 1969); McKinnon, *Independence and Foreign Policy*, 197, 259; Owen Wilkes, "The Great Russian Scare of 1976," *Monthly Review*, Aug. 1978, 7–8; G. Barratt, *Russophobia in New Zealand, 1838–1908* (Palmerston North, 1981).
13. Michael J. Field, *Mau: Samoa's Struggle Against New Zealand Oppression* (Wellington, 1984); Jon Fraenkel, *The Manipulation of Custom: From Uprising to Intervention in the Solomon Islands* (Wellington, 2004).

14. J. W. Davidson, *Samoa mo Samoa* (Melbourne, 1967), 112.

15. McKinnon, *Independence and Foreign Policy*, 254–55.

16. John Craig Hammond, "They Are Very Much Interested in Obtaining an Unlimited Slavery: Rethinking the Expansion of Slavery in the Louisiana Purchase Territories, 1803–1805," *Journal of the Early Republic* 23 (2003): 353–80; John H. Schroeder, *Mr. Polk's War: American Opposition and Dissent, 1846–48* (Madison, WI, 1973); Robert L. Beisner, *Twelve Against Empire: The Anti-Imperialists, 1898–1900)* (New York, 1968); for New Zealand, Davidson, *Samoa mo Samoa*, 163–87.

17. Francis Bremer, "Endecott and the Red Cross: Puritan Iconoclasm in the New World," *Journal of American Studies* 24 (1990): 5–22; idem, *John Winthrop: America's Forgotten Founding Father* (New York, 2003), 235–40, 368–73.

18. Victor Hugo Paltsits, *Washington's Farewell Address* (New York, 1935), still an important work; and Felix Gilbert, *To the Farewell Address: Ideas of Early American Foreign Policy* (Princeton, NJ, 1961).

19. David Hackett Fischer, *The Revolution of American Conservatism* (New York, 1965), 122–23.

20. Thomas Jefferson, First Inaugural Address, March 4, 1801.

21. Gilbert, *To the Farewell Address*, 143.

22. Arthur Link, *Woodrow Wilson: Revolution, War and Peace* (Arlington Heights, IL, 1979); Frederick Calhoun, *Power and Principle: Armed Intervention in Wilsonian Foreign Policy* (Kent, OH, 1986); Warren F. Kimball, *Forged in War: Roosevelt, Churchill, and the Second World War* (New York, 1997).

23. Herring, *From Colony to Superpower*, 398–411; but cf. 482–83.

24. McKinnon, *Independence and Foreign Policy*, 1–13.

25. Forbes in *New Zealand Parliamentary Debates* 225 (1930): 539, quoted and discussed in F.L.W. Wood, *The New Zealand People at War: Political and External Affairs* (Wellington, 1958), 13, a volume in the excellent official history of New Zealand in World War II.

26. Michael Bassett, *Coates of Kaipara* (Auckland, 1995), 71.

27. Savage, radio broadcast, Sept. 5, 1939, transcript in David McIntyre and W. J. Gardner, eds., *Speeches and Documents in New Zealand History* (Oxford, 1971), 365–66; Barry Gustafson, *From the Cradle to the Grave: A Biography of Michael Joseph Savage* (Auckland, 1986), 250–51.

28. "Colonial cringe" is an Australian expression that became popular after 1950.

29. Wood, *New Zealand People at War*, 14.

30. McKinnon, *Independence and Foreign Policy*, 9.

31. W. David McIntyre, "Imperialism and Nationalism," in *The Oxford History of New Zealand*, ed. Geoffrey Rice (Auckland, 1992), 339, citing G. C. Henley, "The Withdrawal of British Troops from New Zealand" (unpub. MA thesis, Canterbury University, 1957).

32. On ethnic composition and the relative size of the Maori and Pakeha populations, see *New Zealand Official Yearbook* (2002), 15–16, 112–13.

33. Woodrow Wilson, Address to Congress, Asking a Declaration of War, April 2, 1917; Thomas J. Knock, *To End All Wars: Woodrow Wilson and the Quest for a New World Order* (New York, 1992).

34. Wilson, Message to Congress, January 8, 1918, *Papers* 40:534–39; David Hackett Fischer, *Liberty and Freedom* (New York and Oxford, 2005), 429, 443.

35. William Downie Stewart, *The Right Honourable Sir Francis H. D. Bell: His Life and Times* (Wellington, 1937), 148, 150.

36. On Woodrow Wilson, academic judgments have been highly polarized. Strongly sympathetic, and informed by deep research, is the scholarship of Arthur Link, summarized in his *Woodrow Wilson: Revolution, War and Peace* (Arlington Heights, IL, 1979). Critical of Wilson are John Blum, *Woodrow Wilson and the Politics of Morality;* Lloyd Ambrosius, *Wilsonian Statecraft: Theory and Practice of Liberal Internationalism During World War I* (Wilmington, DE, 1991); and Margaret MacMillan, *Paris 1919: Six Months That Changed the World* (Random House, 2002). More balanced are John Thompson, *Woodrow Wilson* (London, 2002); Thomas J. Knock, *To End All Wars: Woodrow Wilson and the Quest for a New World Order* (New York, 1992); and John Milton Cooper: *Woodrow Wilson: A Biography* (New York, 2009).

37. Knock, *To End All Wars*, 242–59.
38. John M. Cooper, *Breaking the Heart of the World: Woodrow Wilson and the Fight for the League of Nations* (New York, 2001); Lloyd E. Ambrosius, *Woodrow Wilson and the American Diplomatic Tradition: The Treaty Fight in Perspective* (New York, 1987).
39. Ralph Stone, *The Irreconcilables: The Fight Against the League of Nations* (Lexington, KY, 1970).
40. Eugene P. Trani and David L. Wilson, *The Presidency of Warren G. Harding* (Lawrence, KS, 1977), 142; Warren I. Cohen, *Empire Without Tears* (New York, 1987); cf. Selig Adler, *The Uncertain Giant, 1921–1941* (New York, 1965).
41. P. J. O'Farrell, *Harry Holland, Militant Socialist* (Canberra, 1964); Kathryn Peters, "New Zealand's Attitudes to the Reform of the League of Nations," *New Zealand Journal of History* 6 (1972): 81–97.
42. For a biography of Jordan, see Malcolm Templeton's excellent entry in the *Dictionary of New Zealand Biography* and the sketch in the *Encyclopedia of New Zealand* (1966). An account of Jordan by Carl Berendsen, who worked closely with him, appears in *Mr. Ambassador: Memoirs of Sir Carl Berendsen*, ed. Hugh Templeton (Wellington, 2009), 120–28.
43. B. S. Bennett, *New Zealand's Moral Foreign Policy, 1935–1939: The Promotion of Collective Security Through the League of Nations* (Wellington, 1988); McKinnon, *Independence and Foreign Policy*, 14–18.
44. Michael Bassett and Michael King, *Tomorrow Comes the Song: A Life of Peter Fraser* (Auckland, 2000), 168; McKinnon, *Independence and Foreign Policy*, 14–36.
45. Bennett, *New Zealand's Moral Foreign Policy, 1935–1939*.
46. W. David McIntyre, *New Zealand Prepares for War: Defence Policy, 1919–1939* (Christchurch, 1988), 146.
47. McKinnon, *Independence and Foreign Policy*, 37; McIntyre and Gardner, *Speeches and Documents on New Zealand History*, 361–64.
48. Manfred Jonas, *Isolationism in America, 1935–1941* (Ithaca, NY, 1966) 32–33.
49. William E. Leuchtenburg, "William Edgar Borah," *Dictionary of American Biography*, Supp. 2, 49–53; William E. Borah, *American Problems: A Selection of Speeches and Prophecies*, ed. Horace Green (n.p., 1914).
50. Leuchtenburg, "Borah," 51; Earl S. Pomeroy, *The Pacific Slope* (New York, 1965), 242; Lawrence H. Chamberlain in Thomas Donnelly, ed., *Rocky Mountain Politics* (Albuquerque, 1940), 181.
51. Herring, *From Colony to Superpower*, 1, 482.
52. McIntyre, *New Zealand Prepares for War*.
53. Arthur A. Sloane, *Humor in the White House: The Wit of Five American Presidents* (Jefferson, NC, 2001), 61.
54. Edward J. Marolda, *FDR and the U.S. Navy* (New York, 1998).
55. David M. Kennedy, *Freedom from Fear: The American People in Depression and War, 1929–1945* (New York, 1999), 661.
56. Wood, *New Zealand People at War*, 9–10.
57. Bassett, *Coates of Kaipara*, 252.
58. Hadley Cantril et al., *Public Opinion, 1935–1946* (Princeton, NJ, 1951), an invaluable collection of early opinion polls on public affairs in the United States. Much of its abundant data shows that Roosevelt was closer to main currents of American public opinion than to attitudes in Congress and among other elites. See also Richard Norton Smith, *The Colonel: The Life and Legend of Robert R. McCormick* (Evanston, IL, 2003).
59. Gordon W. Prange, *At Dawn We Slept: The Untold Story of Pearl Harbor* (New York, 1981); Steven Casey, *Cautious Crusade: Franklin D. Roosevelt, American Public Opinion, and the War Against Nazi Germany* (New York, 2001).
60. Dominion Secretary to the Governor General of New Zealand, June 28, 1940, *Documents Relating to New Zealand's Participation in the Second World War, 1939–40* (Wellington, 1949), 1:158–59.
61. Ronald H. Spector, *Eagle Against the Sun: The American War with Japan* (New York, 1985), still the best general work on its subject; also very thoughtful is the work of H. P. Willmott,

especially *The Barrier and the Javelin: Japanese and Allied Pacific Strategies, February to June 1942* (Annapolis, 1983). A major new study, deeply informed and carefully balanced, is Craig L. Symonds, *The Battle of Midway* (New York and Oxford, 2011).

62. Keith Sinclair, *History of New Zealand* (Auckland and Harmondsworth, 1959; 5th rev. ed. with additional material by Raewyn Dalziel, 2000), 283.

63. Wood, *New Zealand People at War.*

64. W. D. McIntyre, "From Dual Dependency to Nuclear Free," in Rice, *Oxford History of New Zealand,* 234–57.

65. Capie, "New Zealand and the World," 586–88.

66. Bassett and King, *Tomorrow Comes the Song.*

67. Malcolm Templeton, *Top Hats Are Not Being Taken: Short History of the NZ Legation in Moscow, 1944–1950* (Wellington, 1989); Robin Kay, ed., *Documents in New Zealand's External Relations,* vol. 1, *The Australia-New Zealand Agreement, 1944* (Wellington, 1972).

68. Chris Trotter, *No Left Turn* (Auckland, 2007), 211. Trotter referred to the offices of the *New Zealand Listener,* the Department of Education, the National Film Unit, and the staff of the Army Education and Welfare Service.

69. Quoted in McKinnon, *Independence and Foreign Policy,* 57; Bassett and King, *Tomorrow Comes the Song,* 289–98; Eugene P. Chase, "Peter Fraser at San Francisco," *Political Science* 11 (1959): 20; documents are in *New Zealand Foreign Policy: Statements and Documents, 1943–57* (Wellington, 1972). Cf. Stephen Schlesinger, *Act of Creation: The Founding of the United Nations* (New York, 2003), an American view of its subject, very different in substance and detail from New Zealand accounts.

70. Capie, "New Zealand and the World," 587; Bassett and King, *Tomorrow Comes the Song,* 289–94.

71. McKinnon, *Independence and Foreign Policy,* 57–62; Bassett and King, *Tomorrow Comes the Song,* 285–341.

72. McKinnon, *Independence and Foreign Policy,* 150; Vivian Pullar and Marian McLeod, *Facts New Zealand* (Wellington, 1993), 41; *New Zealand Official Yearbook* (2006), fig. 4.01.

73. For the origin of the Cold War, see Fischer, *Liberty and Freedom,* 574–618, a centrist interpretation. For revisionist works that hold Harry Truman responsible for the Cold War, see Arnold Offner, *Another Such Victory: President Truman and the Cold War* (Stanford, CA, 2000) and Herring, *From Colony to Superpower,* 595–650; the revisionists are revised with new evidence from Soviet archives in John Lewis Gaddis, *The Cold War: A New History* (New York, 2005).

74. Stéphane Courtois et al., *Le livre noir du communisme* (Paris, 1997), 24, 25, passim; for a critical assessment that confirms these findings, see Martin Malia, "The Lesser Evil?" *Times Literary Supplement,* March 27, 1998.

75. Walter Isaacson and Evan Thomas, *The Wise Men* (New York, 1986); cf. Fischer, *Liberty and Freedom,* 574–84, on several circles of wise men in the Truman administration.

76. Herring, *From Colony to Superpower,* 626.

77. Carl Berendsen to Alister McIntosh, March 30, 1948, in Ian McGibbon, ed., *Undiplomatic Dialogue: Letters Between Carl Berendsen and Alister McIntosh, 1943–1952* (Auckland, 1993), 161.

78. Berendsen to McIntosh, August 19, 1947, ibid., 137–38.

79. Berendsen to McIntosh, Sept. 4, 1947, ibid., 139–40.

80. McKinnon, *Independence and Foreign Policy,* 150; Ann Trotter, "Personality in Foreign Policy: Sir Carl Berendsen in Washington," *New Zealand Journal of History* 20 (1986): 167–80.

81. Mary Logan, *Nordy: Arnold Nordmeyer, a Political Biography* (Wellington, 2008); Barry Gustafson, *Kiwi Keith: A Biography of Keith Holyoake* (Auckland, 2007); John Marshall, *Memoirs* (2 vols., Auckland, 1983, 1989); Trotter, *No Left Turn,* 170–200, 238–39.

82. Kathryn Weathersby, "To Attack or Not to Attack? Stalin, Kim Il Sung, and the Prelude to War," *Cold War International History Project Bulletin* 5 (1995): 1–9; William Stueck, *The Korean War: An International History* (Princeton, NJ, 1995); idem, ed., *The Korean War in World History* (Lexington, KY, 2004); a revisionist account is Bruce Cummings, *The Origins of the Korean War* (2 vols., Princeton, NJ, 1981, 1990).

83. Ian McGibbon, *New Zealand and the Korean War* (2 vols., Wellington, 1991, 1996), an excellent work and a model of official history.

84. Ian McGibbon, "New Zealand's Commitment of Infantry Companies in South Vietnam," 1–13; text at http://www.defence.gov.au/army/AHU/doc/The_Australian_Army. . . . Ian McGibbon is at work on an official history of New Zealand's military involvement in the Vietnam War. An excellent official history is Roberto Rabel, *New Zealand and the Vietnam War: Politics and Diplomacy* (Auckland, 2005).

85. H. R. McMaster, *Dereliction of Duty* (New York, 1988).

86. C. Vann Woodward, ed., *Responses of the Presidents to Charges of Misconduct* (New York, 1974).

87. McKinnon, *Independence and Foreign Policy,* 184.

88. Robert Muldoon, *My Way* (Auckland, 1981), 135.

89. Malcolm Templeton, *Standing Upright Here: New Zealand in the Nuclear Age, 1945–1990* (Wellington, 2006), and reviews by Russell Marshall and Bruce Brown in *New Zealand International Review* (May–June 2007); a definitive work within the frame of foreign policy.

90. For protest movements, see Elsie Locke, *Peace People: A History of Peace Activities in New Zealand* (Christchurch, 1992); Kevin Clements, *Back from the Brink: The Creation of a Nuclear Free New Zealand* (Wellington, 1988); and McKinnon, *Independence and Foreign Policy,* 143.

91. David Lange, *Nuclear Free: The New Zealand Way* (Auckland, 1990); Michael Bassett, *Working with David: Inside the Lange Cabinet* (Auckland, 2008).

92. Stuart McMillan, *Neither Confirm nor Deny: The Nuclear Ships Dispute Between New Zealand and the United States* (Wellington and New York, 1987); McKinnon, *Independence and Foreign Policy,* 280–81; Gerald Hensley, *Final Approaches: A Memoir* (Auckland, 2006), 282–84; Trotter, *No Left Turn,* 292–97.

93. M. C. Pugh, *The ANZUS Crisis: Nuclear Visiting and Deterrence* (Cambridge, Eng., 1990).

94. McKinnon, *Independence and Foreign Policy,* 299.

95. Ibid., 294.

96. Michael King, *Death of the Rainbow Warrior* (Auckland, 1986); Hensley, *Final Approaches,* 283–87.

97. Ibid.

98. Lange, *Nuclear Free;* Dolores E. Janiewski, "Yearning and Spurning: New Zealand's Special Relationships with Britain and the United States," in *America's "Special Relationships,"* ed. John R. Dumbrell and Axel R. Schäfer (New York, 2009), 93–114.

99. McKinnon, *Independence and Foreign Policy,* 296.

100. Ibid., 207.

101. Ibid.

102. George W. Bush, Second Inaugural Address, 2005.

Great Crash and Long Slump

Epigraphs: The Savage epigraph combines two statements. The first is a letter to his niece Eileen Savage Brown, October 29, 1933, quoted in Barry Gustafson, *From the Cradle to the Grave: A Biography of Michael Joseph Savage* (Auckland, 1986), 155; the second is from a speech made in opposition, quoted in Keith Sinclair, *History of New Zealand* (Auckland and Harmondsworth, 1959; 5th rev. ed. with additional material by Raewyn Dalziel, 2000); Russell B. White and David W. Levy, *FDR's Fireside Chats* (New York, 1998), Fireside Chat, September 30, 1934.

1. For the use of *Slump, Big Slump,* and *Long Slump* in New Zealand, perceptions of the Slump's timing, and evidence of personal experience, see the oral history in Tony Simpson, *The Sugarbag Years* (Martinborough and Auckland, 1974, 1976), 10, 18, 22, 50. For the United States, compare Studs Terkel, *Hard Times: An Oral History of the Great Depression* (New York, 1970) and Richard Lowitt and Maurine Beasley, eds., *One Third of a Nation: Lorena Hickok Reports on the Great Depression* (Urbana, IL, 1981).

2. For a global perspective, see Charles P. Kindleberger, *The World in Depression, 1929–1939,* rev. ed. (Berkeley, CA, 1986), 291–98. Kindleberger reviews many explanatory models: Friedman and Schwartz on the American monetary system (doubly reductive); Robbins on the gold standard; Keynes on deflation; Hansen on low rates of secular growth; Svennilson on structural disequilibrium. Kindleberger stresses the failure of global leadership. Britain was unable to lead, the United States was unwilling to do so, and the nations turned to autarchy.

3. David Hackett Fischer, *Liberty and Freedom* (New York and Oxford, 2005), 511; Patricia Clavin, *The Great Depression in Europe, 1929–1939* (London, 2000); Richard J. Evans, *The Coming of the Third Reich* (New York, 2004), xv, 232–46; idem, *The Third Reich in Power* (New York, 2005), 612–88; idem, *The Third Reich at War* (New York, 2009), 321–402.

4. Herbert Hoover began his history of this event by writing, "The primary cause of the Great Depression was the war of 1914–1918." Many world leaders agreed. Among the many national economies in decline before 1929 were Britain, Germany, France, and Sweden in Europe; India and China in Asia; Canada, Brazil, and Bolivia in America; Australia, New Zealand, and Japan in the Pacific. See Herbert Hoover, *The Memoirs of Herbert Hoover,* vol. 3, *The Great Depression* (New York, 1952), 2–4.

5. In mid-1919, only seventeen returning servicemen were reported unemployed; 25 percent had received help from the New Zealand government. M. F. Lloyd Prichard, *An Economic History of New Zealand in 1939* (Auckland, 1970), 267.

6. G. R. Hawke, *The Making of New Zealand: An Economic History* (Cambridge, Eng., 1985), 115, 90–92, 127, 142–43; P. Fearon, *The Origins and Nature of the Great Slump* (London, 1979); I. M. Drummond, *Imperial Economic Policy, 1917–1939* (London, 1974); on "chronic instability," see Michael Bassett, *Coates of Kaipara* (Auckland, 1995), 128.

7. F. Capie, "Australian and New Zealand Competition in the British Market, 1920–39," *Australian Economic History Review* 18 (1978): 46–63.

8. Hawke, *Making of New Zealand,* 143.

9. Bassett, *Coates of Kaipara,* 73, 116, 126.

10. For eyewitness accounts of riots and hunger marches, see Simpson, *Sugarbag Years,* 104–35, 108, 118–20, 123, 125, 133.

11. J. Macrae and Keith Sinclair, "Unemployment in New Zealand During the Depression of the Late 1920s and Early 1930s," *Australian Economic History Review* 15 (1975): 35–44; Hawke, *Making of New Zealand;* 122–43; Tom Brooking, "Economic Transformation," in *The Oxford History of New Zealand,* ed. Geoffrey Rice, 2nd ed. (Auckland and Oxford, 1992), 230–53, citing many unpublished theses and dissertations; R. T. Robertson, "Government Responses to Unemployment in New Zealand, 1929–35," *New Zealand Journal of History* 16 (1982): 21–38; W. B. Sutch, *The Quest for Security in New Zealand, 1840 to 1966* (Wellington, 1966), 126; Sinclair, *History of New Zealand,* 256; Bassett, *Coates of Kaipara,* 71–72, 82, 106–7, 117, 128–30, 137–38, 154, 156–62, 177–80.

12. Many scholars agree that actual numbers of unemployed New Zealanders at the peak in 1933 were much above official statistics. Some writers assert that unemployment was "close to 100,000 workers or about 40 percent of all male workers between the ages of the sixteen and sixty five." But these numbers appear internally inconsistent; the official estimate of 12 percent unemployed in the labor force counted 80,000 registered unemployed. A increase from 80,000 to 100,000 would raise the proportion from 12 to 15 percent, not 40 percent. Cf. Simpson, *Sugarbag Years,* 7; repeated in many other works such as Michael King, *Penguin History of New Zealand* (Auckland, 2003), 347. In the United States, one finds similar estimates that unemployment was twice the official rate. But in both countries the higher numbers are as dubious as the official statistics, and much depends on assumptions and definitions. Where controlled comparisons can be made, relative differences appear between the United States and New Zealand, with the United States having the larger rates of joblessness, circa 1933. Hawke observes that while levels of unemployment remain unclear in many economies, "the broad relativity . . . is not really in doubt" between estimated rates of 12–15 percent in New Zealand, 25–30

percent in the United States and Australia, and 44 percent in Germany. For numbers and discussion, see Hawke, *Making of New Zealand*, 124; Brooking, "Economic Transformation," 251–53; Robertson, "Government Responses to Unemployment in New Zealand."

13. Judgments of Coates have changed remarkably through time. He was a hero after the First World War, reviled after the fall of his government in 1935. For a generation, historians Keith Sinclair and R. M. Burdon were sharply critical. Others such as W. B. Sutch who had worked with him were more positive. Major and very positive revaluations appeared in Bruce Farland's pathbreaking study, *Gordon Coates* (Wellington, 1969); a fresh and lively collection of new materials in *Coates' Tales* (n.p., 1995); and an excellent biography by Michael Bassett, *Coates of Kaipara* (Auckland, 1995), 43–97. Philippa Mein Smith summarized recent reassessments when she wrote in 2005, "Coates has been credited with creating a platform for the growth that materialized under the first Labour government" (*A Concise History of New Zealand* [Cambridge, Eng., 2005], 154).

14. Margery Perham, *Pacific Prelude: A Journey to Samoa and Australasia, 1929* (London, 1988), 157.

15. Hawke, *Making of New Zealand*, 145.

16. Bassett, *Coates of Kaipara*, 101, 106–7, 137, passim.

17. Sinclair, *History of New Zealand*, 254–55.

18. Bassett, *Coates of Kaipara*, 165.

19. Ibid., 178, 193–97.

20. Sinclair, *History of New Zealand*, 257.

21. G. R. Hawke, *Between Governments and Banks: A History of the Reserve Bank of New Zealand* (Wellington, 1973); Bassett, *Coates of Kaipara*, 193–212; Smith, *Concise History of New Zealand*, 153–54.

22. Bassett, *Coates of Kaipara*, 188–200.

23. "This! In God's Own Country," Labour Party handbill, n.d. [ca. 1931–35?], Alexander Turnbull Library, Wellington, reproduced in Simpson, *Sugarbag Years*, 56.

24. Bassett, *Coates of Kaipara*, 230–31; Simpson, *Sugarbag Years*, 100.

25. John Kenneth Galbraith, *The Great Crash, 1929* (Boston, 1954); Ben Bernanke, *Essays on the Great Depression* (Princeton, 2000); Charles P. Kindleberger, *The World in Depression, 1929–1939* rev. ed. (Berkeley, CA, 1986); Barry Eichengreen, *Golden Fetters: The Gold Standard and the Great Depression* (New York, 1992); Milton Friedman and Anna Jacobson Schwartz, *A Monetary History of the United States, 1867–1960* (Princeton, NJ, 1963); Jeremy Atack and Peter Passell, *A New Economic View of American History*, 2nd ed. (New York, 1994), 554–624.

26. *Historical Statistics of the United States* (1975), series F15, Y493–94, D85–86, Y506.

27. Alfred Pritchard Sloan, *My Years with General Motors* (New York, 1964); David R. Farber, *Sloan Rules* (Chicago, 2002), 59.

28. *Historical Statistics of the United States* (1975), V38–40 (mergers), V54–56 (corporate income), V24 (failures).

29. Ibid., D85–86 (unemployment), K503 (corn prices), K555 (cotton prices), K54 (rice prices), Y23–24 (business failures); George Soule, *Prosperity Decade: From War to Depression, 1917–1929* (New York, 1947), 229–51, 275–88.

30. Galbraith, *Great Crash*; David M. Kennedy, *Freedom from Fear: The American People in Depression and War, 1929–1945* (New York, 1999).

31. *Historical Statistics of the United States* (1975), series X, 741.

32. Robert F. Bruner and Sean D. Carr, *The Panic of 1907* (Hoboken, NJ, 2007), 89–139.

33. Priscilla Roberts, "Benjamin Strong, the Federal Reserve, and Limits to Interwar American Nationalism," *Economic Quarterly* 86 (2000): 61–98.

34. *Historical Statistics of the United States* (1975), series X, 414–15; Friedman and Schwartz, *A Monetary History of the United States, 1863–1960* (Princeton, 1963); James D. Hamilton, "Monetary Factors in the Great Depression," *Journal of Monetary Economics* 19 (1987): 145–69; Bernanke, *Essays on the Great Depression*, 152–60.

35. Eichengreen, *Golden Fetters;* Bernanke, *Essays on the Great Depression,* chaps. 1–4, esp. 71–84.
36. Mills quoted in Friedman and Schwartz, *Monetary History,* 385; see also Bernanke, *Essays on the Great Depression,* 41–107; Lawrence H. White, "Did Hayek and Robbins Deepen the Great Depression?" *Journal of Money, Credit and Banking* 40 (2008): 751–68.
37. Arthur Schlesinger Jr., *The Crisis of the Old Order* (Boston, 1956), 1:80–82, a severe indictment of Hoover. More positive are Joan Hoff Wilson, *Herbert Hoover: Forgotten Progressive* (Boston, 1975); Harris Warren, *Herbert Hoover and the Great Depression* (New York, 1959); David Burner, *Herbert Hoover: A Public Life* (New York, 1979); William E. Leuchtenburg, *Herbert Hoover* (New York, 2009); idem, "The Wrong Man at the Wrong Time," *American Heritage* 59, no. 2 (Summer 2009): 26–31, 72.
38. Herbert Hoover, *American Individualism* and *The Challenge to Liberty* (1922, 1934; West Branch, IA, 1989), 31–62.
39. Burner, *Herbert Hoover,* 54, 279; Kennedy, *Freedom from Fear,* 46–48, 104–7; Hoover's altruism appears in his own writings, *American Individualism* and *Memoirs: The Great Depression.*
40. Herbert Hoover, Campaign Speech, October 22, 1928, online at http://www.pinzler.com/ushistory/ruggedsupp.html; on previous presidents, Leuchtenburg, "Wrong Man," 27.
41. Leuchtenburg, "Wrong Man," 26.
42. Eichengreen, *Golden Fetters.* In the twenty-first century one still hears impassioned arguments for the gold standard, but empirical and comparative research by Eichengreen and others has demonstrated beyond doubt that the more closely a national economy was bound to the gold standard in 1920s and 1930s, the deeper its decline and the slower its recovery.
43. *Historical Statistics of the United States* (1975), Y358, Y493; American historians have differed in their judgments. Liberal Democratic historians strongly condemned Hoover, Mellon, and Republican and business leaders. Other historians have been more sympathetic to Hoover and strongly critical of Democrats in Congress. Cf. Kennedy, *Freedom from Fear,* 58.
44. Economists disagree on the costs and benefits of the Smoot-Hawley Tariff Act. Some continue to argue that it had a stimulative effect. But most would agree at a minimum that Smoot-Hawley "bears part of the responsibility for the collapse of trade in the early 1930s." When retaliatory measures are added, it was clearly an economic and a political error of the first magnitude. Compare Douglas A. Irwin, "From Smoot-Hawley to Reciprocal Tariff Arrangements: The Chnging Course of U.S. Trade Policy in the 1930s," in *The Defining Moment,* ed. Michael Bordo, Claudia Goldin, and Eugene N. White (Chicago and London, 1998), 325–52 at 333–37; Barry Eichengreen, "The Political Economy of the Smoot-Hawley Tariff," *Research in Economic History* 12 (1989): 1–43.
45. Raymond Moley, *After Seven Years* (New York, 1939), 27.
46. Hoover, *Memoirs: The Great Depression,* 30.
47. Ibid., 30–31; David Cannadine, *Mellon: An American Life* (New York, 2006), an intelligent, informed, and sympathetic biography of an exceptionally unlikeable man; see also Harvey O'Connor, *Mellon's Millions: The Biography of a Fortune* (New York, 1933); Andrew Mellon, *Taxation: The People's Business* (New York, 1924).
48. Jonathan Alter, *The Defining Moment: FDR's Hundred Days and the Triumph of Hope* (New York, 2006), 98.
49. For Ford and layoffs, Robert Lacey, *Ford: The Men and the Machine* (Boston, 1986); for Ford and the Michigan banks, Susan Estabrook Kennedy, *The Banking Crisis of 1933* (Lexington, KY, 1974).
50. Higher rates of official unemployment were recorded in Germany (30.1 percent in 1932), Norway (33.4 percent in 1933), and the Netherlands (32.7 percent in 1936). B. R. Mitchell, *European Historical Statistics, 1750–1975* (New York, 1980), table C2.
51. Irving Bernstein, *The Turbulent Years: A History of the American Worker, 1933–1941* (Boston, 1970).
52. Schlesinger, *Crisis of the Old Order.*
53. Fischer, *Liberty and Freedom,* 511.

54. Ted Morgan, *FDR: A Biography* (New York, 1985); Thomas Kessner, *The Flight of the Century: Charles Lindbergh and the Rise of American Aviation* (New York, 2010), 228–33.
55. Erik Olssen, *The Red Feds: Revolutionary Industrial Unionism and the New Zealand Federation of Labour, 1908–1914* (Auckland, 1988); Melanie Nolan, ed., *Revolution: The 1913 Great Strike in New Zealand* (Christchurch, 2005). Regular troops in New Zealand in general kept well clear of domestic order keeping. An exception was the use of naval parties in 1913, for which local commanders were severely chastised by the Admiralty in London. In the United States, Douglas MacArthur's use of force against bonus marchers was deeply disapproved by Eisenhower and other officers.
56. Among many biographies of Franklin Roosevelt are Geoffrey C. Ward, *Before the Trumpet: Young Franklin Roosevelt, 1882–1905* (New York, 1985); idem, *A First-Class Temperament: The Emergence of Franklin Roosevelt* (New York, 1989); Kenneth S. Davis, *FDR* (5 vols., New York, 1972–2000).
57. Frances Perkins, *The Roosevelt I Knew* (New York, 1946), 3.
58. Roosevelt himself testified to the importance of his Christian faith and of Peabody's example. The best materials are in ms. in the Roosevelt Library, Hyde Park. Most historians are aware of this relationship, but few have studied it, and fewer academic historians have perceived the importance of Roosevelt's Christian beliefs. For exceptions, see Frank Freidel, *Franklin D. Roosevelt: A Rendezvous with Destiny* (New York, 1990), 8–10; Otis L. Graham Jr. and Meghan Robinson, *Franklin D. Roosevelt, His Life and Times* (New York, 1985), 316. For an extraordinary insight into Peabody's career, see Jeff Egerton, "Reverend Endicott Peabody: Tombstone's Quiet Hero," available online at http://www.authorsden.com.
59. The importance of Roosevelt's experience in the insurance business has been brought out by New Zealand historian Raymond Richards, in *Closing the Door to Destitution* (University Park, PA, 1994), 140.
60. Roosevelt described himself as a little left of center in response to a question from May Craig in a press conference on December 19, 1944. The transcript is online at www.presidency.ucsb.edu/news_conferences.php.
61. Perkins, *The Roosevelt I Knew*, chap. 25.
62. Alter, *Defining Moment*, 92–93; Alter is excellent on this insight, and much else in this first-class book. As he points out, some of the words in this vital statement were from writers Rosenman, Lindley, and Tugwell; the thought was from Roosevelt. See also Samuel Rosenman, *Working with Roosevelt* (New York, 1952), 66; Rexford Tugwell, *The Brains Trust* (New York, 1968), 104.
63. Alter, *Defining Moment*, 102; Chris Wallace, *Character: Profiles in Presidential Courage* (New York, 2004), 174.
64. Gustafson, *From the Cradle to the Grave*.
65. Richards, *Closing the Door to Destitution*, 139.
66. Gustafson, *From the Cradle to the Grave*, 30–31.
67. Ibid., 30.
68. Ibid., 140, 184, 213; Richards, *Closing the Door to Destitution*, 140.
69. Gustafson, *From the Cradle to the Grave*, 191.
70. Ibid., 153; Erik Olssen, *John A. Lee* (Dunedin, 1977), 65; Keith Sinclair, *Walter Nash* (Auckland, 1976), 108.
71. Chris Trotter, *No Left Turn* (Auckland, 2007), 366, passim, is an impassioned view from the left, inspired by Seddon and Savage.
72. Gustafson, *From the Cradle to the Grave*, 67–69, 76, 79, 84–85, 100, 179, 253; Michael Bassett and Michael King, *Tomorrow Comes the Song: A Life of Peter Fraser* (Auckland, 2000), 40–42, 48–49, 53, 56–57. The leading study is Erik Olssen, *The Red Feds: Revolutionary Industrial Unionism and the New Zealand Federation of Labour, 1908–1914* (Auckland, 1988).
73. Bassett and King, *Tomorrow Comes the Song*, 40–57.
74. A large literature exists on New Dealers. Recent studies of high quality include Kirstin Downey, *The Woman Behind the New Deal: The Life of Frances Perkins* (New York, 2009); William J. Barber, *Designs Within Disorder: Franklin D. Roosevelt, the Economists, and the Shaping*

of American Economic Policy, 1933–1945 (Cambridge, Eng., 1996); Jeanne Clarke, *Roosevelt's Warrior: Harold L. Ickes and the New Deal* (Baltimore, MD, 1996); Gail Jarrow, *Robert H. Jackson, New Deal Lawyer* . . . (Honesdale, PA, 2008); and Daniel Scroop, *Mr. Democrat: Jim Farley, the New Deal, and the Making of Modern American Politics* (Ann Arbor, MI, 2006).

75. On Roosevelt's leadership, Warren F. Kimball, *The Juggler: Franklin Roosevelt as Wartime Statesman* (Princeton, NJ, 1991) is more broadly helpful than its title suggests. FDR's manuscripts at Hyde Park hold many clues to his leadership, particularly in the private secretary's file.

76. The best studies are William E. Leuchtenburg, *Franklin D. Roosevelt and the New Deal, 1932–1940* (New York, 1963); David M. Kennedy, *Freedom from Fear: The American People in Depression and War, 1929–1945* (New York, 1999); and the work of Arthur Schlesinger Jr. Historians to the left have published many essays and monographs, which attack these centrist syntheses as celebratory and soft on capitalism. Writers from the far right have published dozens of attacks on the New Deal from the other side, but mostly in the form of polemics. These two groups have yet to produce a sustained work of primary synthesis and serious scholarship. The field still belongs to the centrists, by default.

77. The text with much helpful commentary appears in Russell D. Buhite and David W. Levy, eds., *FDR's Fireside Chats* (Norman, OK, 1991), 11–17; for an excellent discussion, see Kennedy, *Freedom from Fear,* 494.

78. Ira R. T. Smith with Joe Alex Morris, *"Dear Mr. President . . .": The Story of Fifty Years in the White House Mail Room* (New York, 1949), 150–70.

79. Merriman Smith, *Thank You, Mr. President: A White House Notebook* (New York, 1946), 15–29; Betty Houchin Winfield, *FDR and the News Media* (New York, 1990, 1994), 27–43.

80. On the Hundred Days, see Alter, *Defining Moment;* James E. Sargent, *Roosevelt and the Hundred Days: Struggle for the Early New Deal* (New York, 1981); and Anthony J. Badger, *FDR: The First Hundred Days* (New York, 2008).

81. Kennedy, *Banking Crisis of 1933.*

82. Julian E. Zelizer, "The Forgotten Legacy of the New Deal: Fiscal Conservatism and the Roosevelt Administration, 1933–1938," *Presidential Studies Quarterly* 30 (2000): 331–58.

83. Neil M. Maher, *Nature's New Deal: The Civilian Conservation Corps and the Roots of the American Environmental Movement* (New York, 2008).

84. John A. Salmond, *The Civilian Conservation Corps, 1933–1942: A New Deal Case Study* (Durham, NC, 1967).

85. Eichengreen, *Golden Fetters;* Michael Bordo and Barry Eichengreen, "Implications of the Great Depression for the Development of the International Monetary System," in Bordo, Goldin, and White, *Defining Moment,* 403–53.

86. Bordo, Goldin, and White, *Defining Moment,* 2–6.

87. Ibid., 10–12; also Irwin, "From Smoot-Hawley to Reciprocal Trade Agreements."

88. Gustafson, *From the Cradle to the Grave,* 196.

89. Ibid., 184.

90. Rice, *Oxford History of New Zealand,* 356.

91. Sinclair, *History of New Zealand,* 268.

92. Bassett and King, *Tomorrow Comes the Song,* 121, 146–47, 202, 249, 334–35.

93. Gustafson, *From the Cradle to the Grave,* 176–229.

94. Sutch, *Quest for Security in New Zealand,* 176–257; Sinclair, *History of New Zealand,* 268.

95. Gustafson, *From the Cradle to the Grave,* 221.

96. For a comparative study of social security in New Zealand and the United States, see Ray Richards, *Closing the Door to Destitution.*

97. David Hackett Fischer, *Growing Old in America* (New York, 1977), 183–87.

98. Franklin D. Roosevelt, State of the Union Address, 1935.

99. See, e.g., Frances Perkins in *New York Times,* January 27, 1935.

100. Leuchtenburg, *Franklin D. Roosevelt and the New Deal,* 132.

101. *Steward Machine Company v. Davis,* 301 U.S. 548; *Helvering v. Davis,* 301 U.S. 619. In *Railroad Retirement Board v. Alton Railroad Co.* the Supreme Court invalidated the Railroad Retirement Act.

102. J. B. Lovell-Smith, *The New Zealand Doctor and the Welfare State* (Auckland, 1966); Elizabeth Hanson, *The Politics of Social Security* (Auckland, 1988); Tom Brooking, *A History of Dentistry in New Zealand* (Dunedin, 1980).

103. Fischer, *Liberty and Freedom,* 488–94.

104. Gustafson, *From the Cradle to the Grave,* 222.

105. Franklin Roosevelt, Second Inaugural Address, January 20, 1937.

106. Sinclair, *History of New Zealand,* 275.

107. In 1940, the proportion had risen to risen to 9.4 percent employed. See *Historical Statistics of the United States* (1975), D1–5, Y272. There was also a difference in proportions working on different levels. In New Zealand in 1935, 16 percent of all workers were employed by the national government and 8 percent worked for local government. See also Richards, *Closing the Door to Destitution,* 100.

108. Cf. Brooking, "Economic Transformation," 246.

109. U.S. Department of Commerce, Bureau of Economic Analysis, *Long Term Economic Growth, 1860–1970,* pt. 1, chart 1, series A33 (constant 1929 dollars).

Military Traditions

Epigraphs: John Bollard, Parliamentary Debates, September 28, 1899; Franklin Roosevelt, Speech, June 19, 1941.

1. Military history languished in the universities for many years. Today it is reviving, as scholars in many disciplines have discovered new epistomological possibilities. The field is important not only for its own sake but for the study of cutting-edge problems. In New Zealand, Ian McGibbon, ed., *The Oxford Companion to New Zealand Military History* (Auckland, 2000) is a superb overview of its subject. An excellent recent survey of interpretations is Roberto Rabel, "New Zealand's Wars," in *The New Oxford History of New Zealand,* ed. Giselle Byrnes (South Melbourne, 2009), 245–68.

2. See above, pp. xxxx.

3. Quoted in Lamar Cecil, *Wilhelm II,* vol. 2, *Emperor and Exile, 1900–1941* (Chapel Hill, NC, 1996), 243.

4. See above, pp. xxxx.

5. John Smith, *A True Relation of Such Occurrences and Accidents of noate as hath happened in Virginia . . .* (London, 1608); William Bradford, *Of Plymouth Plantation,* ed. Samuel Eliot Morison (New York, 1952), 69. The Pilgrims had seen the Indians at a distance several times before, but this was the first meeting. The place is still called First Encounter Beach. It is on Cape Cod, in the present town of Eastham, Massachusetts. For Virginia's Indian War of 1622, see Helen C. Rountree, *Pocahontas's People* (Norman, OK, 1990), 72. For King Philip's War, see Douglas Edward Leach, *Flintlock and Tomahawk* (New York, 1958); and Jill Lepore, *The Name of War* (New York, 1998).

6. English colonists called them King William's War (1689–97), Queen Anne's War (1702–13), the Yamassee War (1727–28), the War of Jenkins' Ear (1739–42), King George's War (1740–48), and the French and Indian War (1755–63).

7. The War of Independence (1775–83), the "Quasi-War" with France (1797–99), the "Barbary Wars" with North African states (1801–05, 1815), the War of 1812 with Britain (1812–15); the Florida Wars (1818–19, 1835–42), the Mexican War (1846–48).

8. S. M. Harrington et al., *The Small Wars Manual: Fleet Marine Force Reference Publication 12–25* (1935, 1940; Boulder, CO, 2001); Max Boot, *The Savage Wars of Peace: Small Wars and the Rise of American Power* (New York, 2002).

9. The leading historian of civil-military relations in the United States is Richard H. Kohn, beginning with *Eagle and Sword: The Federalists and the Creation of the Military Establishment in America, 1783–1802* (New York, 1975, 1985), and many subsequent works. See also Samuel Huntington, *The Soldier and the State: The Theory and Politics of Civil-Military*

Relations (Cambridge, MA, 1981). For recent scholarship, see Thomas Langston, *Uneasy Balance: Civil-Military Relations in Peacetime America Since 1783* (Baltimore, MD, 2003).

10. Louise Barnett, *Touched by Fire: The Life, Death, and Mythic Afterlife of George Armstrong Custer* (New York, 1996); Evan Connell, *Son of the Morning Star* (San Francisco, 1984).

11. Samuel Adams to Jonathan Augustine Washington, March 21, 1775, in *Writings of Samuel Adams*, ed. H. A. Cushing (4 vols., New York, 1907), 2:282–84. On the American Revolution, see David Hackett Fischer, *Paul Revere's Ride* (New York, 1994), 184–201. For the Civil War, see Kenneth Stampp, *And the War Came: The North and the Secession Crisis, 1860–1861* (New York, 1950), 280–86, and Richard Current, *Lincoln and the First Shot* (Philadelphia and New York, 1963), 182–208. For Roosevelt and World War II, see Gordon Prange, *Pearl Harbor: The Verdict of History* (New York, 1986), David M. Kennedy, *Freedom from Fear: The American People in Depression and War, 1929–1945* (New York, 1999), and Waldo Heinrichs, *Threshold of War: Franklin D. Roosevelt and American Entry into World War II* (New York, 1988).

12. Another example was Polk's entry into the Mexican War, which caused very deep divisions in the United States.

13. Another view appears in Russell Weigley's work on the American way of war. His model is an excellent analysis of the Civil War and World War II, but not most other American wars.

14. James Belich, *The New Zealand Wars and the Victorian Interpretation of Racial Conflict* (Auckland, 1986); James Cowan, *The New Zealand Wars: A History of the Maori Campaigns and the Pioneering Period* (2 vols., Wellington, 1922–23).

15. On the contributions of New Zealand soldiers and Imperial regulars, an historical debate has continued for more than a century. Cf. William Fox, *The War in New Zealand* (London, 1866); James Alexander, *Bush Fighting* (1873; London, 2011). A pathbreaking work of major importance on cultural history and gender roles in relation to military history and much else is Jock Phillips, *A Man's Country? The Image of the Pakeha Male: A History* (Auckland, New York, and London, 1987; rev. ed., 1996).

16. Judith Binney, *Redemption Songs: A Life of Te Kooti Arikirangi Te Turuki* (Auckland, 1995).

17. Phillips, *A Man's Country?* 132–216.

18. Ian McGibbon, ed., *The Oxford Companion to New Zealand Military History* (place, year), s.v. "Pendjeh Crisis," 420.

19. Phillips, *A Man's Country?* 154; D.O.W. Hall, *The New Zealanders in South Africa, 1899–1902* (Wellington, 1949). The leading historian of New Zealand's involvement in the Anglo-Boer wars is Richard Stowers, *The First New Zealand Mounted Rifles in the Anglo-Boer War, 1899–1902* (Hamilton, 2000). Stowers has added an even more comprehensive work in *Rough Riders at War: History of New Zealand in the Anglo-Boer War, 1899–1902* (7th ed., Hamilton, 2011).

20. Phillips, *A Man's Country?* 153.

21. Ibid., 154.

22. Graham Hucker, "'The Great Wave of Enthusiasm': New Zealand Reactions to the First World War in August 1914—A Reassessment," *New Zealand Journal of History* 43 (2009): 59–75.

23. George Bernard Shaw, *What I Said in New Zealand* (Wellington, 1934).

24. Vera Brittain, *Testament of Youth* (1933; London, 1978), 386.

25. J. Studholme, *Some Records of the New Zealand Expeditionary Force* (Wellington, 1928); McGibbon, *Oxford Companion to New Zealand Military History*, s.v. "casualties," 80.

26. Christopher Pugsley, *Gallipoli: The New Zealand Story* (Auckland, 1984), 329. An example is the sad career of Lt. Col. Edmund Bowler, who may have been the first New Zealand officer to land at Gallipoli. He was invalided to England, where he launched a campaign to have New Zealand troops withdrawn from Gallipoli, and after the war tried to reveal what he regarded as the truth of Gallipoli, that it was a needless slaughter. He was silenced and shunned in New Zealand. See Frank Glen, *Bowler of Gallipoli: Witness to the Anzac Legend* (Canberra, 2004).

27. W. David McIntyre, *New Zealand Prepares for War: Defence Policy, 1919–1939* (Canterbury, 1988), 128–31.

28. Phillips, *Man's Country?* 132.

29. For many years, reports of German atrocities in the First World War were mocked as Allied propaganda by journalists and literati. Recent and careful research on the atrocities has found hard evidence that they actually happened on a wide scale and were similar to atrocities committed by German troops in the Second World War.

30. *Historical Statistics of the United States* (1975), series Y856.

31. Brittain, *Testament of Youth*, 386.

32. John J. Pershing, *My Experiences in the World War* (2 vols., New York, 1931); Martin Gilbert, *The First World War: A Complete History* (New York, 1994), 486, 503.

33. For detailed tables of strength in the New Zealand Army, 1938–40, see Laurie Barber and John Tonkin-Covell, *Freyberg: Churchill's Salamander* (Auckland, 1989), 279; for the United States, see *Historical Statistics of the United States* (1975), series Y905.

34. The most important oeuvre is the *Official History of New Zealand in the Second World War*, 49 vols., plus 24 monographic "Episodes and Studies," which have been reissued in 2 volumes (Wellington, 1947–86). The collection of primary materials began during the war with the leadership of E. H. McCormick. The editor-in-chief (1946–57) was Major General H. K. Kippenberger. The result is the largest historical project ever completed in New Zealand, and one of the best of many official histories of World War II. In addition to red, navy blue, and sky blue volumes of military history, a series of green-bound studies is also of high quality, including F.L.W. Wood, *The New Zealand People at War: Political and External Affairs* (1958); *Documents Relating to New Zealand's Participation in the Second World War* (3 vols., 1949); J.V.T. Baker, *War Economy* (1965); and Nancy M. Taylor, *The Home Front* (2 vols., 1986).

35. Robert Dallek, *Franklin D. Roosevelt and American Foreign Policy, 1932–1945, with a New Afterword* (New York, 1995).

36. Hadley Cantril et al., *Public Opinion, 1935–1946* (Princeton, NJ, 1951), a major work of primary and secondary scholarship.

37. *Star-Times*, August 13, 1995.

38. Dwight D. Eisenhower, *Crusade in Europe* (Garden City, NY, 1948), 468.

39. Heinz Guderian, *Panzer Leader*, tr. Constantine Fitzgibbon, introduction by Kenneth Mackesy, foreword by B. H. Liddell Hart (New York, 2001), 255.

40. Carlo D'Este, *Patton: A Genius for War* (New York, 1995), 623; Geoffrey Perret, *There's a War to Be Won: The United States Army in World War II* (New York, 1991), 14.

41. B. H. Liddell Hart, ed., *The Rommel Papers* (1953; new ed., New York, 1988), 407, 522.

42. Hans von Luck, *Panzer Commander: The Memoirs of Colonel Hans von Luck* (New York, 1991), 142.

43. Perret, *There's a War to Be Won*, chap. 17.

44. Michael Bassett and Michael King, *Tomorrow Comes the Song: A Life of Peter Fraser* (Auckland, 2000), 207–28, 243–45.

45. Ibid., 215–16.

46. Howard K. Kippenberger, *Infantry Brigadier* (London, 1949; Oxford and London, 1961), 348.

47. Fred Majdalany, *The Battle of Cassino* (Boston, 1957), 214–16, 111.

48. Luck, *Panzer Commander*, 188.

49. Barber and Tonkin-Covell, *Freyberg*, 264n.

50. Ibid., 5.

51. Majdalany, *Battle of Cassino*, 117.

52. Noel "Wig" Gardiner, *Freyberg's Circus* (Auckland, 1981), 168; also idem, *Bringing Up the Rear: The Sequel to Freyberg's Circus, Further Reminiscences of a Kiwi Soldier* (Auckland, 1953).

53. Barber and Tonkin-Cavell, *Freyburg*, 260.

54. Ibid., 261.

55. *Rommel Papers*, 240; F. W. von Mellenthin, *German Generals of World War II: As I Saw Them* (Norman, OK, 1977), 97.

56. Majdalany, *Battle of Cassino*, 195.
57. Kippenberger, *Infantry Brigadier*, 349–51.
58. Ibid., 349.
59. Majdalany, *Battle of Cassino*, 110–12; John McLeod, *Myth and Reality: the New Zealand Soldier in World War II* (Auckland, 1986), 186–87.
60. Ibid.
61. Antony Beevor, *Crete: The Battle and the Resistance* (London and New York, 1991), 112; Dan Davin, *Crete: Official History of New Zealand in the Second World War* (Wellington, 1953), 384.
62. Gordon McLauchlan, "Star Talker," *New Zealand Listener*, June 16, 1984, 82.
63. McLeod, *Myth and Reality*, 110.
64. Ibid., 111, 168.
65. Phillips, *A Man's Country?* 205.
66. Quoted in David Hapgood and David Richardson, *Monte Cassino* (Cambridge, MA, 1984, 2002), 149.
67. Ardant du Picq, *Battle Studies*, tr. John Greely and Robert Cotton (New York, 1920).
68. S.L.A. Marshall, *Men Against Fire* (New York, 1947); for a critique, see Roger Spiller, "S.L.A. Marshall and the Ratio of Fire," *Journal of the Royal United Services Institute* 133 (December 1988): 63–71.
69. Samuel Stouffer et al., *Studies in Social Psychology in World War II: The American Soldier* (Princeton, NJ, 1949); Leonard Wong et al., *Why They Fight: Combat Motivation in the Iraq War* (Carlisle, PA, 2003); James McPherson, *For Cause and Comrades* (New York, 1997); David Hackett Fischer, *Washington's Crossing* (New York, 2004).
70. Wira Gardiner, *Te Mura o te Ahi: The Story of the Maori Battalion* (Auckland, 1992), 170–71.
71. Ibid., 172, 163.
72. Kippenberger, *Infantry Brigadier*, 351; Gardiner, *Freyberg's Circus*, 168.
73. Gardiner, *Freyberg's Circus*, 168.
74. Kenneth Sandford, *Mark of the Lion: The Story of Capt. Charles Upham, V.C. and Bar* (Auckland and London, 1962), 170.
75. Ibid., 18.
76. Phillips, *A Man's Country?* 200.
77. Sandford, *Mark of the Lion*, 24.
78. Phillips, *A Man's Country?* 205.
79. Ibid., 154.
80. Ibid., 144.
81. Alvin York, *Sergeant York: His Own Life Story and War Diary*, ed. Thomas J. Skeyhill (Garden City, NY, 1928).
82. Steve Ewing and John B. Lundstrom, *Fateful Rendezvous: The Life of Butch O'Hare* (Annapolis, MD, 1997).
83. Ibid., 61.
84. Desmond Young, *Rommel: The Desert Fox* (London, 1951), 126–27; Bayerlein's notes reported an independent eyewitness account by Prof. Horster of Wurzburg University; *Rommel Papers*, 282–83.

World Crisis

Epigraphs: Clark S. Judge and the White House Writers Group, in *El Impacto Reagan*, published by La Fundacion Centro de Estudios Americanos (Buenos Aires, 2006). The second half of this quotation is a paraphrase that preserves all of the original language but modifies the syntax. Martin Holland and Jonathan Boston, eds., *The Fourth Labour Government: Politics and Policy in New Zealand*, 2nd ed. (Oxford, New York, and Melbourne, 1990), 1–9.

1. For the troubles of 1968 as a world crisis, see David Hackett Fischer, *The Great Wave: Price Revolutions and the Rhythm of History* (New York and Oxford, 1996), 203–15; also B. R. Mitchell, *European Historical Statistics, 1750–1975*, 2nd rev. ed. (New York, 1981), 777.

2. Robert Aaron Gordon, *Economic Instability and Growth: The American Record* (New York, 1974) 170; the account that follows is drawn from Fischer, *Great Wave*, 204ff.

3. N. Gregory Mankiw, "How to Avoid Recession? Let the Fed Work," *New York Times*, Dec. 23, 2007; Martin also described his policy as "leaning against the winds of inflation or deflation, whichever way they are blowing." Robert P. Bremner, *Chairman of the Fed: William McChesney Martin Jr. and the Creation of the American Financial System* (New Haven, CT, 2004), 5.

4. The term *stagflation* may have been coined by Iain Macleod, a conservative member of Parliament, in 1965. See *House of Commons Official Report (Hansard)*, Nov. 17, 1965, 165. It was brought into common usage by Paul Samuelson, in *Newsweek*, March 19, 1973; see *The Samuelson Sampler* (New York, 1973), 178–80; Alan S. Blinder, *Economic Policy and the Great Stagflation* (New York, 1979); Fischer, *Great Wave*, 205–6.

5. John M. Blair, *The Control of Oil* (New York, 1976), 264; Daniel Yergin, *The Prize: The Epic Quest for Oil* (New York, 1991); Fischer, *Great Wave*, 208.

6. Fischer, *Great Wave*, 208–15, 206–7, 225–28.

7. Ibid.

8. Herbert Stein, *Presidential Economics*, rev. ed. (New York, 1985), 186; Fischer, *Great Wave*, 208, 358.

9. Nixon's statement to Howard K. Smith, after a broadcast interview, was reported in the *New York Times*, Jan. 7, 1971; his Keynesian policies appear in *Public Papers of the President, Richard M. Nixon, 1971* (Washington, 1972), 8.

10. Stein, *Presidential Economics*, 186.

11. W. Carl Biven, *Jimmy Carter's Economy: Policy in an Age of Limits* (Chapel Hill, NC, 2002); Anthony S. Campagna, *Economic Policy in the Carter Administration* (Westport, CT, 1995); Daniel Horowitz, *Jimmy Carter and the Energy Crisis of the 1970s: A Brief History with Documents* (Boston, 2005); Fischer, *Great Wave*, 210.

12. The most comprehensive biography of Ronald Reagan is Lou Cannon, *Governor Reagan; His Rise to Power* (New York, 2003) and *President Reagan: The Role of a Lifetime* (New York, 1991); published together as *Ronald Reagan: A Life in Politics* (2 vols., New York, 2004).

13. Andrew E. Busch, *Reagan's Victory: The Presidential Election of 1980 and the Rise of the Right* (Lawrence, KS, 2005).

14. W. Elliot Brownlee and Hugh Davis Graham, eds., *The Reagan Presidency: Pragmatic Conservatism and Its Legacies* (Lawrence, KS, 2003).

15. Anthony S. Campagna, *The Economy in the Reagan Years: The Economic Consequences of the Reagan Administrations* (Westport, CT, 1994).

16. *Statistical Abstract of the United States* (1997), table 725, p. 470.

17. Donald Kettl, *Reinventing Government: A Fifth-Year Report Card, a Report of the Brookings Institution's Center for Public Management* (Washington, 1998), vi–vii.

18. Telecommunications Act of 1996, Public Law 104–104, 110 Stat. 56; Robert Crandall, *Competition and Chaos: U.S. Communications Since the 1996 Telecom Act* (Washington, 2005); Dale E. Lehman and Dennis Weisman, *The Telecommunications Act of 1996: The "Costs" of Managed Competition* (Norwell, MA, 1996).

19. *The Clinton Presidency: Historic Economic Growth*, a publication of the Clinton Administration, ca. 2000–2001, http://clinton5.nara.gov/WH/Accomplishments/eightyears-03.html.

20. U.S. Bureau of Labor Statistics, *Worker Displacement*, U.S. Department of Labor USDL 02–483; *Statistical Abstract of the United States* (1997), table 642; (2008), table 595.

21. Personal Responsibility and Work Opportunity Act, enacted August 22, 1996, 110 Stat. 2105; Joe Soss, *Success Stories* (Boston, 2002), 65; James Midgley, "The United States: Welfare, Work and Development," *International Journal of Social Welfare* 10 (2001): 284–93; Frances Fox Piven, *The Breaking of the American Social Compact* (New York, 1998); Sharon Hays, *Flat Broke with Children: Women in the Age of Welfare Reform* (Oxford and New York, 2004); Barbara Ehrenreich, *A Step Back to the Workhouse?* (New York, 2003).

22. For distribution of income, see *Statistical Abstract of the United States* (1997), tables 725–26; (2008), tables 668–676.

23. Ibid.

24. Jim Webb, *A Time to Fight: Reclaiming a Fair and Just America* (New York, 2008), 89–109.

25. Malcolm McKinnon, *Independence and Foreign Policy: New Zealand in the World Since 1935* (Auckland, 1993), 216–21.

26. Ibid., 221–24.

27. Tom Brooking, *Milestones: Turning Points in New Zealand History*, 2nd ed. (Palmerston North, 1999), 186; G. R. Hawke, "Before and After 1967–8," in *The Making of New Zealand: An Economic History* (Cambridge, Eng., 1985) 322–37; F. W. Holmes et al., *New Zealand at the Turning Point* (Wellington, 1976).

28. Barry Gustafson, *His Way: A Biography of Robert Muldoon* (Auckland, 2000), an authorized biography of high professional quality. The autobiographies are Robert D. Muldoon, *The Rise and Fall of a Young Turk* (Wellington, 1974); *Muldoon* (Wellington, 1977); *My Way* (Wellington, 1981); *Number 38* (Auckland, 1986); and see also his *The New Zealand Economy: A Personal View* (Auckland, 1985). Muldoon testified that he was "influenced greatly by John A. Lee," and "also always had a soft spot for Norman Douglas who as a bright young man with a Future in Labour politics, followed Lee into the wilderness" (*Rise and Fall of a Young Turk*, 27).

29. Muldoon, *New Zealand Economy*, 109–18; Hugh Templeton, *All Honourable Men: Inside the Muldoon Cabinet* (Auckland, 1995), 115–27; Gustafson, *His Way*, 263–79.

30. Muldoon, *Number 38*, 162–69; Gustafson, *His Way*, 362–83. On the Labour Party in the election, see Roger Douglas and Louise Callan, *Toward Prosperity* (Auckland, 1987), 162–66; on the breakaway New Zealand Party, cf. Robert Jones, *Memories of Muldoon* (Christchurch, 1997), 150ff; Colin James, *The Quiet Revolution* (Wellington, 1986), 102–10.

31. Muldoon, *Number 38*, 172–74; idem, *New Zealand Economy*; Templeton, *All Honourable Men*, 221; Gustafson, *His Way*, 384–97.

32. Michael Bassett, *Working with David* (n. p., 2008); Chris Trotter, *No Left Turn* (Auckland, 2007), 276–84; David Lange, *David Lange: My Life* (Auckland, 2005); David Barber, ed., *Gliding on the Lino: The Wit of David Lange* (Auckland, 1987).

33. For a biography, see Simon Collins, "Who Is Roger Douglas?" in *Rogernomics: Is There a Better Way?* (Auckland, 1987), 2–17; Roger Douglas, *There's Got to Be a Better Way! A Practical ABC to Solving New Zealand's Major Problems* (Wellington, 1980), 20–23; idem, *Unfinished Business* (Auckland, 1993); Douglas and Callan, *Toward Prosperity*.

34. Jonathan Boston and Martin Holland, eds., *The Fourth Labour Government: Radical Politics in New Zealand* (Auckland, 1987); Brian Easton, ed., *The Making of Rogernomics* (Auckland, 1989); Simon Walker, ed., *Rogernomics: Reshaping New Zealand's Economy* (Wellington, 1989).

35. Brian Easton, "From Run to Float: The Making of the Rogernomics Exchange Rate Policy," in idem, *Making of Rogernomics*, 92–113.

36. Douglas, "SOEs—A Half-way House," in *Unfinished Business*, 172–93.

37. Simon Collins, "Rogernomics: The Economic Aftermath," in Easton, *Making of Rogernomics*, 188–206; see also Walker, *Rogernomics*.

38. Major trends can be followed empirically in the *New Zealand Official Yearbook* (2000) data on unemployment (tables 14.2–14.111), 324–27; prices and inflation (tables 26.1–26.9), 545–58; gross domestic product (tables 17.1–17.6), 385–389; and pensions, benefits, and superannuation (tables 7.1–7.4) 157–61); also the *New Zealand Official Yearbook* (2006) data on unemployment (fig. 14.02, and tables 14.10–14.14), 282–84; prices and inflation (tables 17.01–17.04), 332–37; gross domestic product (tables 17.03–17.11), 338–45; and income support and pensions (tables 7.03–7.04), 130–31.

39. These policy objectives appear in Douglas, *Unfinished Business*, especially the foreword, 1–5; and chapters on "Care and Responsibility" (53–82), "Security and Fairness" (145–71), "SOEs—A Halfway House" (172–93), and "Combating Disadvantage" (194–215). Most chapters in this manifesto laid out a mediating strategy, which was sharply criticized from both the left and the right. His comparison of the first and fourth Labour governments is in Douglas and Callan, *Toward Prosperity*, chap. 20, "Means and Ends" (236).

40. Holland and Boston, *Fourth Labour Government*, 1–9.

41. Douglas, *There's Got to Be a Better Way!* 75–77; for a helpful chronology of Roger Douglas's many complex tax reform and fiscal policy measures, see Walker, *Rogernomics*, appendix, 225–44.

42. Brian Easton, "The Unmaking of Roger Douglas," in idem, *Making of Rogernomics*, 171–88.

43. Francis G. Castles, Rolf Gerritsen, and Jack Vowles, eds., *The Great Experiment: Labour Parties and Public Policy Transformation in Australia and New Zealand* (Auckland, 1996), with thanks to Jack Vowles for a ms. copy of this work. Specially helpful on these issues are the editor's introduction and conclusion, and essays by Brian Easton and Rolf Gerritsen on "Economic Reform: Parallels and Differences"; Jonathan Boston and John Uhr on "Reshaping the Mechanics of Government"; and Jack Vowles and Ian McAllister, "Electoral Foundations and Electoral Consequences: From Convergence to Divergence." On the election, see Jack Vowles and Peter Aimer, *Voters' Vengeance; The 1990 Election in New Zealand and the Fate of the Fourth Labour Government* (Auckland, 1993). A striking trend was a sharp decline in political participation during periods of complex restructuring, a pattern that recurs in democratic systems in moments when one would expect interest to surge. Another example was the American republic, ca. 1786–95 (ibid., 41–60).

44. Ralph G. Lattimore and Paul C. Dalziel, *The New Zealand Macroeconomy: A Briefing on the Reforms* (Auckland, 1996), 90.

45. Jim Bolger, *A View from the Top* (Auckland, 1998).

46. Philippa Mein Smith, *A Concise History of New Zealand* (Cambridge, Eng., 2005), 214–15.

47. The most thorough biography of Nixon is a trilogy by Steven E. Ambrose, *Nixon: The Education of a Politician, 1913–1962* (New York, 1987); *Nixon: The Triumph of a Politician, 1962–1972* (New York, 1989); and *Nixon: Ruin and Recovery, 1973–1990* (New York, 1991). One of the most insightful biographies is Herbert S. Parmet, *Richard Nixon and His America* (Boston, 1990).

48. Richard Nixon, interview with David Frost, May 20, 1977. The original tape was accessible on YouTube at the date of this writing.

49. The most scholarly history of Nixon's administration is Melvin Small, *The Presidency of Richard Nixon* (Lawrence, KS, 1999).

50. Arthur Schlesinger Jr., *The Imperial Presidency* (Boston, 1973); see also Andrew Rudalevige, *The New Imperial Presidency: Reviewing Presidential Power After Watergate* (Ann Arbor, 2005); Donald Wolfensberger, "The Return of the Imperial Presidency?" *Wilson Quarterly* 26 (2002): 26–41.

51. These cases are drawn from David Hackett Fischer, "Scandal and Corruption, an American History," unpub. ms.

52. C. Vann Woodward, ed., *Responses of the Presidents to Charges of Misconduct* (New York, 1974), xvi.

53. The leading journalists on this history were Bob Woodward and Carl Bernstein, *All the President's Men* (New York, 1974); idem, *The Final Days* (New York, 2005); and Theodore H. White, *Breach of Faith: The Fall of Richard Nixon* (New York, 1975). The leading history of this journalism and much more is Michael Schudson, *Watergate in American Memory: How We Remember, Forget, and Reconstruct the Past* (New York, 1992).

54. James Doyle, *Not Above the Law: The Battles of Watergate Prosecutors Cox and Jaworski* (New York, 1977).

55. Keith Olson, *Watergate: The Presidential Scandal That Shook America* (Lawrence, KS, 2003).

56. Athan Theoharis, *A Culture of Secrecy: The Government Versus the People's Right to Know* (Lawrence, KS, 1998); "Your Right to Federal Records: Questions and Answers on the Freedom of Information Act and the Privacy Act," http://www.epic.org/open_gov/rights.html.

57. Sources for this paragraph and the two that follow are Gustafson, *Muldoon*, 384–97; Muldoon, *New Zealand Economy*, 127–35; Douglas and Callan, *Toward Prosperity*, 51–62; Templeton, *All Honourable Men*, 211–22.

58. Gustafson, *Muldoon*, 397–422.

59. Easton, "From Run to Float."

60. Jonathan Boston et al., *New Zealand Under MMP: A New Politics?* (Auckland, 1996), 73.

61. Michael Bagge, "Dams Dividing Democracy: Conflict on the Clutha River," in *Landscape/Community: Perspectives from New Zealand*, ed. Tony Ballantyne and Judith A. Bennett (Dunedin, 2005), 31–41.

62. The major constitutional documents are gathered in W. David McIntyre and W. J. Gardner, eds., *Speeches and Documents on New Zealand History* (Oxford, 1971), especially the 1846 Constitution, 57–63; the Constitution Act (1852), 73–84; and the Adoption of the Statute of Westminster (1947), 284–96.

63. Geoffrey Palmer, *Unbridled Power: An Interpretation of New Zealand's Constitution and Government* (Auckland, 1979).

64. For the Constitution itself and other major document and cases, see Mai Chen and Sir Geoffrey Palmer, *Public Law in New Zealand: Cases, Materials, Commentary and Questions* (Auckland 1993), 172–76.

65. Ibid.

66. Neale McMillan, *Top of the Greasy Pole: New Zealand Prime Ministers of Recent Times* (Dunedin, 1993), 8, 10–11, 66, 68, 76, 80, passim.

67. Susan Skudder and Laurie H. Barber, "The New Zealand Nursing Team at the Spanish Civil War," *New Zealand Medical Journal* 96 (1983): 397–98; Susan Skudder, "Bringing It Home: New Zealand Responses to the Spanish Civil War" (Ph.D. thesis, University of Waikato, 1986), 24. For other instances. see Graeme Dunstall, *A Policeman's Paradise? Policing a Stable Society, 1918–1945*, vol. 4 in *The History of Policing in New Zealand* (Wellington, 1999), 253–69.

68. McKinnon, *Independence and Foreign Policy*, 232–49.

69. Chen and Palmer, *Public Law in New Zealand*, pt. 3, "The New Zealand Bill of Rights Act, 1990," 439–599, includes excerpts from Palmer's white paper, "A Bill of Rights for New Zealand," 1985 (445–49); draft bills; and the New Zealand Bill of Rights Act, 1990 (463–45), with case law and legislative histories.

70. "The New Zealand Bill of Rights Act," 1990, ibid., 463–65.

71. Ibid.

72. Ibid.

73. For many discussions of "natural justice," often explicitly identified with fairness, see Chen and Palmer, *Public Law in New Zealand*, 40–42, 144, 706, 928, 951, 964, 979, 983, 990. Palmer's quotation equating natural justice and fairness appears on 964.

74. Boston et al., *NZ Under MMP*, 8.

75. Other ideas of proportional representation were considered: the SM (supplementary member) system; the STV (single transferrable vote) system. But the Royal Commission on the Electoral System recommended the MMP.

76. Jonathan Boston, discussing systems of representation, wrote, "Fairness may not be everything, but it is an extremely important value—and one which has been in short supply for too long" (*Wellington Dominion*, Aug. 17, 1994).

77. Jonathan Boston et al., "Introduction"; Jack Vowles, "The Impact of the 1999 Campaign"; and Stephen Levine and Nigel S. Roberts, "Voting Behaviour in 1999"; all in *Left Turn: The New Zealand General Election of 1999*, ed. Jonathan Boston et al. (Wellington, 2000), 7–15, 141–60, 161–74.

78. Lani Guinier, *The Tyranny of the Majority: Fundamental Fairness in Representative Democracy* (New York, 1994) collects her writings on the subject.

79. Lani Guinier, *Lift Every Voice: Turning a Civil Rights Setback into a New Vision of Social Justice* (New York, 1998).

80. "Public Confidence Levels in Selected Public and Private Corporations," 1996, *Statistical Abstract of the United States* (1997), table 460; Virginia Hodgkinson, Murray Weitzman, and the Gallup Organization, *Giving and Volunteering in the United States* (Washington, 1996).

81. Vowles and Aimer, *Voters' Vengeance*; J. Vowles, "Gender and Electoral Behaviour in New Zealand: Findings from the Present and the Past," *Political Science* 45 (1993): 122–38; Richard Mulgan, *Politics in New Zealand* (Auckland, 2004), 251.

82. Accident Compensation Corporation, *Annual Report* (Wellington, 2000). These reports are accessible online at http://www.acc.co.nz.
83. J. M. Miller, "Compensation for Mental Trauma Injuries in New Zealand," *Australasian Journal of Disaster and Trauma Studies* (1998), http://www.massey.massey.ac.nz//~trauma.
84. *New York Times*, Sept. 10, 1997.
85. *New York Times*, Sept. 14, 2000.
86. Congressional Budget Office, *The Economics of U.S. Tort Liability: A Primer* (Washington, 2003), x–xi.
87. Simon Power, "Restoring Fairness to the Justice System," National Party Annual Conference, Wellington, August 2, 2008, http://www.national.org.nz/Article.aspx?ArticleID=28311.
88. David Clark, "Killing the New Zealand Dream," August 24, 2010, http://www.davidclark.org.nz/2010/08/killing-the-new-zealand-dream/.

Conclusion

1. James Belich, *Replenishing the Earth: The Settler Revolution and the Rise of the Anglo-World, 1783–1939* (Oxford, Auckland, and New York, 2009); James C. Bennett, *The Anglosphere Challenge: Why the English-Speaking Nations Will Lead the Way in the 21st Century* (Lanham, MD, 2004). For a very different approach, see David Hackett Fischer, *Albion's Seed: Four British Folkways in America* (Oxford and New York, 1989).
2. Karl Popper, *The Open Society and Its Enemies* (2 vols., London, 1945; 1st U.S. ed., Princeton, NJ, 1950; rev. ed., 1962), 1:7–17, 169–201. Popper's "key point" appears in idem, *The Lesson of This Century: With Two Talks on Freedom and the Democratic State; Karl Popper Interviewed by Giancarlo Bosetti* (London and New York, 1997), 71.

   The model of open and closed societies first appeared in Henri Bergson, *Two Sources of Morality and Religion* (London and New York, 1935). Popper also acknowledged similarities between his idea of the open society and Graham Wallas's idea of a "great society" and Walter Lippmann's *The Good Society* (New York, 1937). Open societies in *Fairness and Freedom* are understood not as a philosopher's ideal type but as empirical and historical phenomena that actually exist in the world, take many forms, and have changed through time. This inquiry goes beyond Popper in that way, but not against him.

   For assessments of Popper's work, see Ian Jarvie and Sandra Pralong, eds., *Popper's Open Society After Fifty Years: The Continuing Relevance of Karl Popper* (London and New York, 1999). A discussion of his work in epistemology appears as the anonymous essay "Karl Popper," in the online *Stanford Encyclopedia of Philosophy*, first published Nov. 13, 1997; substantive revision Feb. 9, 2009.

   For Popper himself, see his memoir, *Unended Quest: An Intellectual Autobiography* (La Salle and London, 1974; rev. ed., 1976, 1982). On Popper's career in New Zealand, where he taught at the University of Canterbury from 1937 to 1946, see the essay by Peter Munz in *Dictionary of New Zealand Biography* online, http://www.teara.govt.nz/en/biographies.
3. David Hackett Fischer, *Liberty and Freedom* (New York and Oxford, 1989) surveys many different vernacular ideas of liberty and freedom within the United States and briefly examines variants in China, India, and Poland.
4. Michael Sandel, *Justice: What's The Right Thing to Do?* (New York, 2009); idem, ed., *Justice: A Reader* (New York and Oxford, 2007); Amartya Sen, *The Idea of Justice* (Cambridge, MA, 2009); John Rawls, *A Theory of Justice* (1971; rev. ed., Cambridge, MA, 1999); idem, *Justice as Fairness: A Restatement*, ed. Erin Kelly (Cambridge, MA, 2001); idem, *Political Liberalism* (1993; expanded ed., New York, 2005); idem, *Collected Papers*, ed. Samuel Freeman (Cambridge, MA, 1999).
5. J. R. Pole, *The Pursuit of Equality in American History*, 2nd ed., rev. and enlarged (Berkeley, CA, 1968, 1993); Michael Walzer, *Spheres of Justice: A Defense of Pluralism and Equality* (New York, 1983); Amartya Sen, *Inequality Reexamined* (Cambridge, MA, 1992).
6. Freedom House is a nonpartisan voluntary association based in Washington, D.C. For data, see its reports, Arch Puddington, *Freedom in the World, 2010: Erosion of Freedom*

Intensifies (Washington, 2010) and *Freedom in the World, 2011: The Authoritarian Challenge to Democracy* (Washington, 2011), also available online at http://www.freedomhouse.org.

7.   For discussion, see Puddington, *Freedom in the World, 2011*, 1–10.

8.   Terry Miller and Kim R. Holmes, *2011 Index of Economic Freedom* (Washington, 2011), also available online at http://www.heritage.org.

9.   Freedom House since 1972 has graded countries (194 in 2011) on twenty-five measures of democracy, "political rights and civil liberties." The libertarian-conservative Heritage Foundation of ranks uses measures summarized in the text. The only indicator that the two surveys share is political corruption. Cf. Miller and Holmes, *2011 Index of Economic Freedom.* Much of the data derives from the World Bank, *Doing Business, 2005–2010*, http://doingbusiness.org; World Trade Organization, http://www.wto.org; and *World Bank Development Indicators Online* (Washington, 2010), available online by subscription.

10.   Sources of debt and deficits are OECD data by the Institute of Fiscal Studies in www.guardian.uk/news/datablog/2010/debt-deficit; income and wealth inequality from United Nations Development Program, another series from the Central Intelligence Agency World Factbook; unemployment from New Zealand Department of Labour and U.S. Bureau of Labor Statistics; corruption from the Corruption Perceptions Index (CPI), 2010 (2009 data), http://www.transparency.org.

11.   Alexis de Tocqueville, *De la Démocratie en Amerique* (2 vols., Paris, 1835), ed. J. P. Mayer (Paris, 1961), 1:300; also idem, *Voyages en Sicile et aux États-Unis*, in *Ouevres complètes*, ed. J. P. Mayer (Paris, 1957), 1:179.

12.   The Latin origin is from the noun *verna*, a slave born in the master's house; to the adjective *vernaculus*, of a slave born in the master's house; to a figurative expression, widely used in Roman oratory for anything domestic, native, or indigenous.

13.   John Florio, *A World of Words* (London, 1598); idem, *Queen Anna's New World of Words* (London, 1611); for modern usage, William Labov, *Language in the Inner City: Studies in the Black English Vernacular* (Philadelphia, 1972).

14.   Stuart Schwartz, *All Can Be Saved: Religious Tolerance and Salvation in the Iberian Atlantic World* (New Haven, CT, 2007). Fischer: *Albion's Seed: Four British Folkways in America* (New York and Oxford, 1989) on vernacular ideas of order, power, and freedom; *Liberty and Freedom* (New York and Oxford, 2005) on those great principles as vernacular ideas in the United States, studied in part from visual evidence; and for ideas of humanity, *Champlain's Dream* (New York and Toronto, 2008), 36–37, 147, 207, 521–30, and *Le Rêve de Champlain* (Montreal and Paris, 2011), 16–17, 172, 177, 603, 612.

15.   W. B. Gallie, "Essentially Contested Concepts," *Proceedings of the Aristotelian Society* 56 (1955–56): 167–98; Fischer, *Liberty and Freedom*; Eric Foner, *The Story of American Freedom* (New York, 1998), xviii, passim.

16.   For liberty as rights of autonomy, and freedom as rights of belonging to communities (or societies) of other free people, see Fischer, *Liberty and Freedom*, 1–15.

17.   Solomon Northup, *Twelve Years a Slave: Narrative of Solomon Northup a citizen of New York, Kidnapped in Washington City in 1841, and rescued in 1853, from a Cotton Plantation near the Red River, in Louisiana*, ed. with a preface and an appendix of supporting documents by David Wilson (Auburn, Buffalo, and London, 1853), chap. 19. The editor claims that the text is "a faithful history of Solomon Northup's life as he received it from his lips," but the language appears to have been changed for publication. For a modern edition with much supporting documentation of Bass and Epps from the sources, see Sue Eakin and Joseph Logsdon, eds., *Twelve Years a Slave* (Baton Rouge, 1968). For discussions, see Charles Davis and Henry Louis Gates Jr., eds., *The Slave's Narrative* (Oxford and New York, 1985, 1990), 161–63, 232–37; Marion Wilson Starling, *The Slave Narrative: Its Place in American History* (Washington, 1988), 173. Other documentation appears in *The Liberator*, August 22, 1856.

18.   Clement Eaton, *The Freedom-of-Thought Struggle in the Old South* (Durham, NC, 1940; rev. ed., New York, 1964), 191, 347, 349.

19. John Adams, *Diary and Autobiography*, ed. Lyman H. Butterfield (4 vols., Boston, 1961), 3:326; also available online in the Adams Family Papers: An Electronic Archive, Diary through 1776, sheet 21 of 53, June-August 1775, Mass. Hist. Soc. http://www.masshistory.org/digitaladams/aea/diary/.

20. James Loewen, *Sundown Towns: A Hidden Dimension of American Racism* (New York, 2005) is the leading study, and a major work.

21. Ibid., 71.

22. The Tall Poppy Syndrome takes its name from a passage in Livy's *History of Rome*. The tyrannical Tarquin (Lucius Superbus Tarquinius, the last despotic king of Rome, 534–510 BC) received a message from his son Sextus asking what to do about some "chief men" of high ability. Livy wrote: "The king, as if absorbed in meditation, passed into the garden of his house, followed by his son's envoy. There, walking up and down without a word, he is said to have struck off the heads of the tallest poppies with his stick." Sextus took that gesture as a command and proceeded to "rid himself of the chief men." *Livy*, vol. 1, bk. 1.54, ll. 1–10; tr. B. O. Foster, Loeb ed. (14 vols., London and Cambridge, 1926), l:188–89.

23. H. W. Orsman, ed., *The Dictionary of New Zealand English: A Dictionary of New Zealandisms on Historical Principles* (Auckland and Oxford, 1997), s.v. "poppy," def. 2; *Wellington Evening Post*, Sept. 21, 1991; "Knocking Our Tallest Poppies—Entrepreneurs and the Tall Poppy Syndrome," with a full bibliography, http://wms-soros.mngt.waikato.ac.nz/NR/rdonlyres/. . ./Resource25.pdf.

24. Orsman, *Dictionary of New Zealand English*, s.v. "poppy," def. 2, citing *Dominion Sunday Times* (Wellington), Aug. 23, 1992.

25. Everyone delights in Sir Edmund Hillary's being the first to drive overland to the South Pole in a farm tractor in 1958, a very New Zealand feat.

26. Marino Harker Smith, "New Zealand's Tall Poppy Syndrome and PC Madness," http://www.anewnz.org.nz/vision.asp?id=1855.

27. Megan Hutching, *Long Journey for Sevenpence: Assisted Immigration to New Zealand from the United Kingdom, 1947–1975* (Wellington, 1999), 137, 138, 145, passim.

28. Merrill B. Twining, *No Bended Knee: The Battle for Guadalcanal* (Novato, CA, 1996), 24.

29. *Wall Street Journal*, Aug. 3, 1998.

30. Ibid.

31. Hillary Commission for Sport, Fitness and Leisure, *Firestone Fairplay Manual* (1997); idem, Final Results and Financial Statements, New Zealand Parliamentary Papers, 1/8/7/4 (2002) E.32; both available online at www.hillarysport.org.nz.

Appendix

1. Bart Wilson, "Fair's Fair," http://www.theatlantic.com/business/print/2009/01/fairsfair/112; idem, "Contra Private Fairness," January 31, 2009, *Social Science Research Network*, http://papers.ssrn.com/sol3/papers.cfm?abstract_id=989821.

2. Anna Wierzbicka, "Being FAIR: Another Key Anglo Value and Its Cultural Underpinnings," in *English: Meaning and Culture* (New York and Oxford, 2006), 141–170; Wilson, "Contra Private Fairness."

3. Wierzbicka, "Being FAIR," 141.

4. For evidence, see above, introduction, 15–18.

5. James Surowiecki, "Is the Idea of Fairness Universal?" Jan. 26, 2009, http://www.newyorker.com/online/blogs/jamessurowiecki/2009/01/is; Mark Liberman, "No Word for Fair?" Jan. 28, 2009, http://languagelog.ldc.upenn.edu/nll/?p=1080.

6. Surowiecki, "Is the Idea of Fairness Universal?"

7. Wierzbicka, "Being FAIR," 164–66.

8. Liberman, "No Word for Fair?"

9. See above, introduction, 17–18.

10. Wierzbicka, "Being FAIR," 142–53; see also pp. TK above.

11. John Rawls, *A Theory of Justice* (Cambridge, MA, 1971; rev. ed. 1999), 60, 124 quoted; revisions were published in foreign translations and in idem, *Justice as Fairness: A Restatement*, ed. Erin Kelly (Cambridge, MA, 2001), which also reviews the controversial literature by Rawls and many commentators. See also idem, *Political Liberalism* (New York, 1993; expanded ed. 2005); idem, *Collected Papers*, ed. Samuel Freeman (Cambridge, MA, 1999).

12. Robert Nozick, *Anarchy, State, and Utopia* (New York, 1974).

13. Moral philosophers who give more attention to justice and equality include Amartya Sen, *Inequality Reexamined* (Cambridge, MA, 1992); idem, *The Idea of Justice* (Cambridge, MA, 2009); and Michael Walzer, *Spheres of Justice* (New York, 1983); and G. A. Cohen, *Rescuing Justice and Equality* (Cambridge, MA, 2008).

14. Amitai Etzioni, "The Fair Society," in *Uniting America: Restoring the Vital Center to American Democracy*, ed. Norton Garfinkle and Daniel Yankelovich (New Haven, 2005), 211–23; idem, *The Third Way to a Good Society* (London, 2000); idem, *The New Golden Rule: Morality and Community in a Democratic Society* (New York, 1998); idem, *The Spirit of Community* (New York, 1993).

15. Peter Corning, *The Fair Society: The Science of Human Nature and the Pursuit of Social Justice* (Chicago, 2011). Further discussion appears on Corning's blog, "The Fair Society," June 12, 2011. Critiques of his book from the right, center, and left appear in reviews by Kenneth Minogue in the *Wall Street Journal*, April 27, 2011; Roberto De Vogli in the *Stanford Social Innovation Review*, May 18, 2001, 21; and David Spiro in the *New York Journal of Books*, an online journal.

16. Michael Sandel, *Liberalism and the Limits of Justice* (Cambridge, Eng., 1982); idem, *Justice: What's the Right Thing To Do?* (New York, 2009); idem, *Justice: A Reader* (New York and Oxford, 2007).

17. A Marxist critique is Robert Paul Wolff, *Understanding Rawls: A Reconstruction and Critique of "A Theory of Justice"* (Princeton, 1977). A feminist argument is in Susan Moller Okin, *Justice, Gender, and the Family* (New York, 1989). For criticism from economists, see Kenneth Arrow, "Some Ordinalist-Utilitarian Notes on Rawls's Theory of Justice," *Journal of Philosophy* 70 (1973): 245–63; and John Harsanyi, "Can the Maximin Principle Serve as a Basis for Morality?" *American Political Science Review* 69 (1975): 594–606. An egalitarian critique is Sen, *Inequality Reexamined*; also Cohen, *Rescuing Justice and Equality*.

18. Norman Frohlich, Joe A. Oppenheimer, and Cheryl L. Eavey, "Choices of Principles of Distributive Justice in Experimental Groups," *American Journal of Political Science* 31 (1987): 606–36. see also Jennifer L. Hochschild, *What's Fair? American Beliefs About Distributive Justice* (Cambridge, MA, 1981), 27–45.

19. See above, introduction, 18-19.

20. For later statements, see his *Political Liberalism* and *Justice as Fairness: A Restatement*.

21. S. F. Brosnan and F.B.M. de Waal, "Monkeys Reject Unequal Pay," *Nature* 425 (2003): 297–99; Frans de Waal, *Primates and Philosophers: How Morality Evolved* (Princeton, NJ, 2006); idem, *Good Natured: Origins of Right and Wrong in Humans and Other Animals* (Cambridge, MA, 1996).

22. Richard Wrangham et al., eds., *Chimpanzee Cultures* (Cambridge, MA, 1994); "A Jealous Streak? With Treats, Dogs Seem to Know What's Fair," *New York Times*, Dec. 9, 1008; "Dogs Have Sense of Fairness, Study Finds," *Boston Globe*, Dec. 9, 2008.

23. Cf. Clive D. L. Wynne, *Do Animals Think?* (Princeton, NJ, 2004), 1–83.

24. Frans de Waal, *The Age of Empathy* (New York, 2009), 189–91, passim.

25. Quoted in Alexis Madrigal, "Dog unto Others: Canines Have a sense of Fairness," *Wired Science*, Dec. 8, 2008, http://www.wired.com/wiredscience/2008/12/dogenvy/; see also Marc Bekoff and Jessica Pierce, *Wild Justice: The Moral Lives of Animals* (Chicago, 2009).

26. Robert L. Trivers, "The Evolution of Reciprocal Altruism," *Quarterly Journal of Biology* 46 (1971): 35–57; C. Stevens, "Modeling Reciprocal Altruism," *British Journal for the Philosophy of Science* 47 (1996): 533–51; for altruism in theology and moral philosophy, see Thomas Jay Oord, ed., *The Altruism Reader* (Philadelphia, 2007).

27. Peter Kropotkin, *Mutual Aid: A Factor of Evolution* (London, 1902); Waal, *Good Natured*; D. L. Cheney and R. M. Seyfarth, *How Monkeys See the World* (Chicago, 1990).

28. G. Wilkinson, "Reciprocal Altruism in Bats and Other Mammals," *Ethology and Sociobiology* 8 (1988): 85–100.

29. N. Tinbergen, "On War and Peace in Animals and Man," *Science* 160 (1968): 1411–18.

30. Richard Dawkins, *The Selfish Gene* (New York and Oxford, 1976); idem, *The Selfish Gene, 30th Anniversary Edition* (New York and Oxford, 2006); Alan Grafen and Mark Ridley, eds., *Richard Dawkins: How a Scientist Changed the Way We Think* (New York and Oxford, 2006); Stephen Jay Gould, "Caring Groups and Selfish Genes," in *The Panda's Thumb: More Reflections in Natural History* (Harmondsworth, 1990), 72–78.

31. Michael Tomasello, *Why We Cooperate*, The 2008 Tanner Lectures on Human Values, Stanford University (Cambridge, MA, 2009); for a diversity of inquiries and results on this problem, see Dacher Keltner, Jason Marsh, and Jeremy Adam Smith, eds., *The Compassionate Instinct: The Science of Human Goodness* (New York, 2010); and Dacher Keltner, *Born to Be Good: The Science of a Meaningful Life* (New York, 2009).

32. See Martin A. Nowak with Roger Highfield, *SuperCooperators: Altruism, Evolution, and Why We Need Each Other to Succeed* (New York, 2011).

33. Jorge Moll et al., "Human Fronto-Mesolimbic Networks Guide Decisions About Charitable Donation," *Proceedings of the National Academy of Sciences* 103, no. 42 (Oct. 2006): 15623–28; Dharol Tankersly, quoted in "Activation of Brain Region Predicts Altruism," http://www.sciencedaily.com/releases/2007/01/070121162756.htm; Maarten A. S. Boksem and David De Cremer, "Fairness Concerns Predict Medial Frontal Negativity Amplitude in Ultimatum Bargaining," *Social Neuroscience* 5 (2010): 118–28.

34. Donald W. Pfaff, *The Neuroscience of Fair Play: Why We (Usually) Follow the Golden Rule* ((New York, 2007), 4.

35. Joshua Greene, "From Neural 'Is' to Moral 'Ought': What Are the Moral Implications of Neuroscientific Moral Psychology?" *Neuroscience* 4 (2003): 847–50.

36. Corning, *Fair Society*, 75–76.

37. Antonio Damasio, *Descartes' Error: Emotion, Reason, and the Human Brain* (New York, 1994; rev. ed. 2005); Jean Decety, "A Social Cognitive Neuroscience Model of Human Empathy," in *Social Neuroscience: Integrating Biological and Psychological Explanations of Social Behavior*, ed. E. Harmon-Jones and P. Winkelman (New York, 2007), 246–70.

38. For leading examples, see Tae-Yeol Kim and Kwok Leung, "Forming and Reacting to Overall Fairness: A Cross-Cultural Comparison," *Organizational Behavior and Human Decision Processes* 104 (2007): 83–95; Frohlich, Oppenheimer, and Eavey, "Choices of Principles of Distributive Justice in Experimental Groups"; Rebecca Anderson and Amy Otto, "Perceptions of Fairness in the Justice System: A Cross Cultural Comparison," *Social Behavior and Personality* 31 (2003): 557–64; Masaaki Kotabe, Alan J. Dubinsky, and Chae Un Lim, "Perceptions of Organizational Fairness: A Cross-National Perspective," *International Marketing Review* 9, no. 2 (1992): 41–58.

39. Kim and Leung, "Forming and Reacting to Overall Fairness."

40. Norman Frohlich and Joe A. Oppenheimer, *Choosing Justice: An Experimental Approach to Ethical Theory* (Berkeley, CA, 1992); idem and Cheryl L. Eavey, "Laboratory Results on Rawls's Distributive Justice," *British Journal of Political Science* 17 (1987): 1–21.

41. Joseph Henrich, et al., "Markets, Religion, Community Size, and the Evolution of Fairness and Punishment," *Science* 327, no. 5972 (March 19, 2010): 1480–84.

42. For thoughtful commentary, see Karla Hoff, "Fairness in Modern Society," *Science* 327, no. 5972 (March 19, 2010): 1467–68.

43. Quoted in Brandon Keim, "Evolution of Fairness Driven by Culture, Not Genes," interview with Joe Henrich, http://www.wired.com/wiredscience/2010/03/evolution-of-fairness.

44. Benjamin Nelson, *The Idea of Usury, from Tribal Brotherhood to Universal Otherhood* (Princeton, NJ, 1949); Karl Jaspers, *The Origin and Goal of History* (New Haven, CT, 1953).

45. Keim, "Evolution of Fairness Driven by Culture, Not Genes."

46. Josh Hendrickson, "The Economics of Fairness," *The Everyday Economist*, Feb. 1, 2006, http://everydayecon.wordpress.com/2006/02/01/the-economics-of-fairness/. The author is assistant professor of economics at the University of Mississippi.

47. Milton Friedman, "Fair versus Free," *Newsweek*, July 4, 1977, available online at http://www.fff.org/freedom/0292d.asp. Friedman tried to balance his argument against fairness with a defense of fairness in another form. He added, "Is then the search for 'fairness' all a mistake? Not at all. There is a real role for fairness, but that role is in constructing general rules and adjudicating disputes about the rules, not in determining the outcome of our separate activities. That is the sense in which we speak of a 'fair' game and 'fair' umpire."

   His argument begins as a sweeping condemnation of fairness and becomes something different: an argument for procedural fairness and against substantive fairness. The difficulty here is that procedural and substantive issues cannot be so clearly kept apart, as in the case of the Fairness Doctrine, which Friedman misrepresented as entirely or primarily substantive, when it was designed primarily to require a fair game (all players have access to the field), without determining the substantive outcome of the game.

48. Fred W. Friendly, *The Good Guys, the Bad Guys, and the First Amendment: Free Speech vs. Fairness in Broadcasting* (New York, 1976); for arguments against and for, see Adam Thierer, "Why the Fairness Doctrine Is Anything but Fair," Heritage Foundation Executive Memorandum 368, Oct. 29, 1993, http://www.heritage.org/research/reports/1993/10/em368-why-the-fairness-doctrine-is-anything-but-fair; Steve Rendall, "The Fairness Doctrine: How We Lost It, and Why We Need It Back,", Feb. 12, 2005, http://www.fair.org/index.php?page=2053, rpt. June 11, 2011, http://www.commondreams.org/views05/0212-03.htm.

49. Lauren Gross, "Altruism, fairness and Social Intelligence: Are Economists Different?" undergraduate thesis, Stanford University, June 1, 2005, http://economics.stanford.edu/files/theses/theses_2005/Gross.pdf. It also cites and summarizes many other studies. On the other side, see Stanley and Tran, "Economics Students Need Not Be Greedy."

50. For substantive examples, see Daniel Kahneman, Jack L. Knetsch, and Richard Thaler, "Fairness as a Constraint on Profit Seeking: Entitlements in the Market," *American Economic Review* 76 (1986): 728–41; idem, "Fairness and the Assumptions of Economics," *Journal of Business* 59 (1986): S285–S300.

51. Elizabeth Hoffman et al., "Preferences, Property Rights, and Anonymity in Bargaining Games," *Games and Economic Behavior* 7 (1994): 346–80; idem, "The Impact of Exchange Context on the Activation of Equity in Ultimatum Games," *Experimental Economics* 3 (2000): 5–9; Vernon L. Smith, *Rationality in Economics: Constructivist and Ecological Forms* (Cambridge and New York, 2008); Steven J. Kachelmeier et al., "Fairness in Markets: A Laboratory Investigation," *Journal of Economic Psychology* 12, no. 3 (1991): 447–64, Web text posted by the author in Nov. 2010.

52. Sarah Maxwell, *The Price Is Wrong: Understanding What Makes a Price Seem Fair and the True Cost of Unfair Pricing* (Hoboken, NJ, 2008).

53. Venkat Venkatasubramanian, "What Is Fair Pay for Executives? An Information Theoretic Analysis of Wage Distributions," *Entropy* 11 (2009) 766–81, www.mdpi.com/journal/entropy.

54. Ibid.

55. T. Kato, *CEO Compensation and Firm Performance* (New York, 2003); S. Anderson et al., *Executive Excess* (Washington, 2008).

56. Venkatasubramanian, "What Is Fair Pay for Executives?" 778–79; Rawls, *Justice as Fairness;* Nozick, *Anarchy, State, and Utopia.*

57. S. J. Brams and A. D. Taylor, *Fair Division: From Cake-Cutting to Dispute Resolution* (Cambridge, Eng., 1996); D. Denoon and S. J. Brams, *Fair Division: A New Approach to the Spratly Islands Controversy,* New York University, Starr Center for Applied Economics, Economic Research Report RR96–10, 1996.

58. S. J. Brams and A. D. Taylor, "An Envy-Free Cake Division Protocol," *American Mathematical Monthly* 102 (1995): 9.
59. Karl Sigmund, Ernst Fehr, and Martin Nowak, "The Economics of Fair Play," *Scientific American* 286 (January 2002): 82–87; Joseph Henrich et al., "In Search of Homo Economicus: Behavioral Experiments in 15 Small-Scale Societies," *American Economic Review* 91 (2001): 73–78.
60. For three examples in very different professions, see Carrie Menkel-Meadow and Michael Wheeler, *What's Fair: Ethics for Negotiators* (San Francisco, 2004); Philip J. Clements and Philip W. Wisler, *The Standard & Poor's Guide to Fairness Opinions: A User's Guide for Fiduciaries* (New York, 2005); and from a master of CIA tradecraft, James M. Olson, *Fair Play: The Moral Dilemmas of Spying* (Washington, 2006).

LIST OF MAPS

Page 116 **The Trail of Tears, 1829–1847.** Sources include John Wesley Morris, *Historical Atlas of Oklahoma* (Norman, 1986); Francis Paul Prucha, *Atlas of American Indian Affairs* (1990); "Indian Removal," http://www.newworldencyclopedia.org/entry/image:Trails_of_Tears en.jpg; Museum of the Cherokee Indian, The "Trail of Tears," http://www.cherokeemuseum.org/html/collections_tot.htm; "The Arkansas Trail of Tears," http://www.arkansasheritagetrails.com.

Page 118 **The Signing of the Waitangi Treaty, 1840.** Sources include Claudia Orange, *The Treaty of Waitangi* (Wellington, 1987); idem, *The Story of a Treaty* (Wellington, 1989), 15; compilations by Claudia Orange from manuscript treaty sheets in the New Zealand National Archives, Wellington; Malcolm McKinnon, ed., *New Zealand Historical Atlas* (Auckland, 1977), plate 31.

Page 123 **The Loss of Maori Lands; The North Island.** Sources include Te Ara, the Web Encyclopedia of New Zealand, "Te tango whenua— Maori land alienation," hhttp://www.teara.govt.nz/files/m–19476–enz.gif, accessed 3 May 2011; Garth Cant and Russell Kirkpatrick, *North Canterbury*, 18; Eric Pawson and Tom Brooking, eds., *Environmental Histories of New Zealand*, 47; Malcolm McKinnon ed., *New Zealand Historical Atlas* (Wellington, 1997), plate 31.

Page 124 **The Loss of Indian Lands, 1775–1992.** Sources include Frederick E. Hoxie, ed., *Encyclopedia of North American Indians* (Boston, 1996), 291; *Historical Atlas of the United States* (Washington, National Geographic Society, 1988), 46–47.

Page 160 **Access to Land in the United States: Acquisition of New Territory, 1763–2000.** Sources include "Atlantic Seaboard Watershed," usgs. gov; *Historical Statistics of the United States* (1970), table J1–2; *Statistical Abstract of the United States* (Washington, 2008), table 348.

Page 164 **Access to Land in New Zealand: Bursting the Big Estates, 1890– 1940.** Sources include Malcolm McKinnon, ed., *New Zealand Historical Atlas* (Auckland, 1997), plate 59; "Cheviot Estate; Plan shewing Boundaries of Blocks" (n.p., 1893), Alexander Turnbull Library, Wellington.

Page 185 **A Federal System for the United States: Support and Opposition for the Constitution of 1787–89.** Sources include "Ratification of the Constitution," http://jb–hdnp.org/Sarver/Maps/ratification_constitution. jpg; "Twelve States Fight over Ratification of the Constitution," http:// www.columbia.edu/itc/law/witt/raw_images.gif.

Page 194 **New Zealand's Provincial System: Its Rise and Fall, 1852–1876.** Sources include W. P. Morrell, *The Provincial System in New Zealand* (London, 1932); A. H. McLintock, *Crown Colony Government in New Zealand* (Wellington, 1958); "The Provinces, Separation and Abolition," Malcolm McKinnon, ed., *New Zealand Historical Atlas* (Auckland, 1997), plate 51.

Page 199 **American Regions and Homicide Rates.** Compiled from data in U.S. Federal Bureau of Investigation, *Uniform Crime Reports* (Washington, 1936–1940); idem, *Crime in the United States*, annual (Washington, 2005–2010).

Page 202 **Federalism and the Persistence of Cultural Diversity: Regional Language Patterns in the United States, 1950.** Sources include Hans Kurath, *A Word Geography of the Eastern United States* (Ann Arbor, Mich., 1949); Henry Glassie, *Pattern in the Material Folk Culture of the Eastern United States* (Philadelphia, 1968), 39; David Hackett Fischer, *Albion's Seed: Four British Folkways in America* (Oxford, 1989), 832–34.

Page 249 **Votes for the Women's Suffrage Resolution in the United States, May 21, 1919.** Sources are Mark Carnes and John Garraty, eds., *Mapping America's Past* (New York, 1986), 163.

Page 257 **Votes for the Equal Rights Amendment, 1972–1978.** Sources include Mark Carnes and John Garraty, eds., *Mapping America's Past* (New York, 1986), 222

Page 265 **The Long Struggle Against Race Slavery in the United States, 1775–1865.** Sources include Zilversmit, *The First Emancipation: The Abolition of Slavery in the North* (Chicago, 1967); Ira Berlin and Ronald Hoffman, eds., *Slavery and Freedom in the Age of the American Revolution* (Urbana, Ill., 1986); Sidney Kaplan and Emma Nogrady Kaplan, *The Black Presence in the Era of the American Revolution*, revised edition (Amherst, 1989).

Page 270 **Laws against Racial Intermarriage in the United States.** Sources include Joel Williamson, *New People: Miscegenation and Mulattoes in the United States* (New York, 1980, 1984); and http://filipspagnoli.files. wordpress.com/2009/05/anti–miscegenation–laws–map.jpg.

Page 274 **The Long Struggle against Racial Segregation in the United States, 1950–2000.** Sources include Mark Carnes and John Garraty, eds., *Mapping America's Past* (New York, 1986), 210–11; "Brown v. Board of Education and 1950s Segregation Map," National Park Service, Feb. 2, 2005;

Probability that African American Students Have White Classmates, *New York Times*, April 2, 2000.

Page 277 **American Freedom Rides, the Southern United States, 1961.** The source is Raymond Arsenault, *Freedom Riders* (New York, 2006), 319.

Page 283 **The Great Maori Land March for Justice in New Zealand, 1975.** Sources include Michael King, *Whina: A Biography of Whina Cooper* (Penguin, 1983), 220; Malcolm McKinnon et al., eds., "Te Ropu-Te-Matakite; The 1975 Land March," *New Zealand Historical Atlas* (Wellington, 1997) plate 99.

Page 329 **Socialism and Populism in the United States, 1890–1920.** Sources include Mark Carnes, John A. Garraty, and Patrick Williams, "American Socialism in Its Heyday," in *Mapping America's Past* (New York, 1996), 172; David Shannon, *The Socialist Party in America* (New York, 1955); James Green, *Grass-Roots Socialism: Radical Movements in the Southwest, 1895–1943*; Donald Critchlow, ed., *Socialism in the Heartland: The Midwestern Experience* (South Bend, Ind., 1986).

LIST OF ILLUSTRATIONS

ACKNOWLEDGMENTS

This book has been seventeen years in the making. Many people have helped along the way. Chief among them are colleagues in the United States who have an expertise in the history of liberty and freedom. First on the list is James Kelly. When he was museum director at the Virginia Historical Society, we worked closely together, gathering thoughts and materials for his traveling exhibition and my book, *Liberty and Freedom*, published in 2005. I have drawn on that project, which was made possible by a generous grant from the National Endowment for the Humanities, with strong support from director Bruce Cole. Special thanks go to Charles Bryan, head of the Virginia Historical Society, a first class historian and faithful friend. Also very helpful was Jeffrey Ruggles, who joined in the search for unpublished materials.

Jim and I worked with Eric Foner, James McPherson, and Pauline Maier, who served as advisors to our project, read an early draft of *Liberty and Freedom*, and gave generously of their time and expertise on the subject. Other scholars helped in various ways. My Brandeis colleague Tzvi Abusch shared his deep knowledge of ancient languages in a search for linguistic roots of liberty, freedom, and fairness. My Princeton classmate Charles Fuqua at Williams College shared some Greek and Roman materials. At a critical moment Stuart Schwartz helped solve problems in the study of vernacular ideas, by the example of his book *All Can Be Saved* (2008), and in conversation when our paths crossed in Montreal and San Diego. I've also learned much from Michael Kammen, James Kloppenberg, and Morton Keller.

At Oxford, many colleagues helped in a variety of ways: John Prestwich on medieval history, Keith Thomas on early modern Britain, J. R. Pole on the vernacular history of equality, and John Rowett on liberty, freedom and fairness in the nineteenth and twentieth centuries.

An important event for this inquiry was a conference on history and philosophy sponsored by the Templeton Foundation in Newport, Rhode Island. I presented a paper on fairness and freedom and received much helpful advice, especially from Robert Nozick and Joseph Raz, during the conference and afterward. On another occasion, I met John

Rawls briefly through a mutual friend. His work has had a major impact on mine, as it has for many students of fairness and justice. Through the years I have learned much on history and moral philosophy from Michael Sandel, a lifelong friend and former student who keeps teaching his teacher on this subject.

At Brandeis, Robert Reich invited me to try out my thoughts on fairness in his seminar on social justice. I've also learned much from talks, seminars, and conversations on fairness and freedom with colleagues and students at Brandeis and the College of the Atlantic. John Thompson invited me to discuss major problems in a graduate seminar and a faculty seminar at Duke University. H. V. (Henry Vivian) Nelles asked me to give a seminar on the history of open societies at McMaster University in Hamilton, Ontario. Kenneth Mills gave me an opportunity to test some of my ideas about fairness, freedom, and vernacular cultures at the University of Toronto. Raymond Arsenault invited me to talk at the University of South Florida. Charles Dew invited me to give a talk on liberty and freedom at Williams College, and John Demos asked me to lead a seminar on my work at Yale University. Some of the most extraordinary experiences in my career grew from an invitation lecture on the history of freedom and fairness in six Chinese universities, to very bright and lively students and colleagues, with the support of the Chinese government and the sponsorship of the American State Department.

For this book my deepest debts are in New Zealand, where Raewyn Dalziel invited me to talk at Auckland University about my work on British and American history. On this and subsequent visits to Auckland, we remember the kindness of many colleagues and friends, especially Kay and John Irwin.

Raewyn Dalziel also organized speaking engagements and seminars at four other universities in New Zealand, with the sponsorship of the Fulbright Program. At Otago University, Erik Olssen and Tom Brooking were very generous with their time and made possible an extended visit in Dunedin. In Hamilton, Jeanine Graham and Peter Gibbons invited us to visit for a term at Waikato University, where I taught with Ray Richards, explored New Zealand's military history with Laurie Barber, and tramped the bush with Philip and Sylvia Hart. At the University of Canterbury in Christ Church, the history faculty were hospitable and very helpful, especially Trevor Burnard, then a senior lecturer in history. We also had a happy and productive visit in Wellington, at Victoria University, and the offices of the Historical Branch in the Department of Internal Affairs, where we met Jock Phillips, and Malcolm McKinnon.

After our return to the United States we kept in touch with colleagues. When a draft of the New Zealand book was at last completed in 2010, five colleagues took time from their own work, read the manuscript, and sent critiques in great detail. As an expression of thanks this book is dedicated to Tom Brooking, Raewyn Dalziel, Jeanine Graham, Jock Phillips, and Erik Olssen, for their rigorous criticism and generous support. It is also dedicated to Peter Gibbons, for the many conversations that we had at Waikato. And it is also dedicated to the memory of Rollo Arnold. Whatever merit this book may have comes largely from these colleagues; the errors are all my own. To work with New Zealand historians is a privilege and a pleasure. They set a high standard in their own scholarship. We have much to learn from them.

For this book and others, I have had much wise advice from my extraordinary agents, Scott Moyers and Andrew Wylie. At the Oxford University Press, three very able editors had roles in this project. Sheldon Meyer was a friend and advisor for many years and offered helpful counsel for this book. Peter Ginna was deeply involved on a daily basis when he edited *Liberty and Freedom.* On this book I am grateful to Tim Bent at Oxford University Press, for his very close attention to the substance and detail of the work, and especially for his line editing. India Cooper was once again a peerless copy editor. Joellyn Ausanka was the managing editor and did an excellent job, as always. She brought the pieces together, refined the text, organized the illustrations, caught errors that had eluded everybody else, and presided over a five-ring circus with extraordinary skill, tact, judgment, rigor, and good humor. This is the sixth book that she and I have done together.

The task of gathering the illustrations was done by Mally Anderson, Jeremy Lilly, and especially Keely Latcham, who was a model of efficiency and grace. The maps once again were done by Jeffrey Ward, with his extraordinary gift of cartographic creativity. Here again it was a great pleasure to work with him, as we have done together on four books.

At Brandeis, Dona DeLorenzo and Judy Brown ran the office with high efficiency and grace. Thanks go to Jehuda Reinharz, our excellent president, historian, colleague, and good friend for many years. And thanks also to my colleague Paul Jankowski for his interest and support, and especially for the civility and decency that he brings to the academy. My very bright Brandeis undergraduates were quick to see the interpretative possibilities, and they helped me to explore them. In particular I remember Jeremy Stern, who was full of ideas and suggestions.

In the family, my father, John Henry Fischer, was an unfailing source of counsel on this project as on so many others. He continued in that role for everyone in the family to his death in 2009, and the example of his wisdom and judgment is a continuing presence in all of our lives. Many others in the family helped in various ways. My brother, Miles Fischer, and Kate Fischer were a source of advice on some of the difficult problems. The next generation—Susanna, Erik, Annie, Fred, John, Ann, Will, and Kirsten—offered much encouragement. And the generation after that was a source of inspiration: Althea Turner, Mathew Mueller, Kevin Fischer, Eliza Fischer, Samuel Fischer, and Natalie Fischer.

My greatest debt, always, is to Judith. She was a very active collaborator on this project. She traveled in New Zealand, helped with research, turned up many materials, read the manuscript, suggested many improvements, suggested a design for the jacket, and kept the project moving forward. It wouldn't have happened without Judith.

DHF
Mount Desert Island, Maine,
October 2011

INDEX

Note: Page numbers in *italics* refer to illustrations.